Handbook of Research on Consumer Behavioral Analytics in Metaverse and the Adoption of a Virtual World

Pantea Keikhosrokiani
School of Computer Sciences, Universiti Sains Malaysia, Malaysia

A volume in the Advances in Marketing, Customer Relationship Management, and E-Services (AMCRMES) Book Series

Published in the United States of America by
    IGI Global
    Engineering Science Reference (an imprint of IGI Global)
    701 E. Chocolate Avenue
    Hershey PA, USA 17033
    Tel: 717-533-8845
    Fax: 717-533-8661
    E-mail: cust@igi-global.com
    Web site: http://www.igi-global.com

Library of Congress Cataloging-in-Publication Data

Names: Keikhosrokiani, Pantea, 1982- editor.
Title: Handbook of research on consumer behavioral analytics in metaverse and
  the adoption of a virtual world / edited by Pantea Keikhosrokiani.
Description: Hershey, PA : Engineering Science Reference, [2023] | Includes
  bibliographical references and index. | Summary: "The advent of
  Metaverses will have a profound influence on consumer behaviour, from
  how people make decisions and create brand connections to how they feel
  about their avatar embodiment and their purchase in Metaverse. This book
  aims to investigate the social, behavioral, and psychological factors
  that influence Metaverese adoption. The focus then shifts to concepts,
  theories, and analytical approaches for detecting changes in consumer
  behavior in the Metaverse. It offers multidisciplinary research and
  practice in social, psychological, and behavioral analytics to detect,
  forecast, and categorize consumer behavior shifts in the Metaverse and
  help organizations make better decisions. This book will be an
  interdisciplinary project that engages various disciplines such as
  computer sciences, data sciences, marketing, management, and business
  studies.This book offers a future insight into consumer behavior change
  in Metaverse. Covering topics such as the adoption of virtual reality,
  consumer behavior change in Metaverse, consumer behavioral analysis,
  emotional intelligence, purchase decision making in Metaverse, consumer
  segmentation in Metaverse, this premier reference source is a timely
  resource for students and educators of higher education, researchers,
  academicians, and libraries. In academia, the publication will benefit
  researchers, lecturers, and students by providing them with new insights
  into different fields such as behavioral analytics, digital marketing,
  digital transformation, consumer behavior change, decision making, and
  data science. Furthermore, the book is beneficial for business
  executives, entrepreneurs, data analysts, marketers, advertisers,
  government officials, social media professionals by offering them new
  techniques and methods to consumer behavior change using analytical
  techniques"-- Provided by publisher.
Identifiers: LCCN 2022056247 (print) | LCCN 2022056248 (ebook) | ISBN
  9781668470299 (hardcover) | ISBN 9781668470312 (ebook)
Subjects: LCSH: Consumer behavior. | Consumers--Psychology. |
  Shopping--Technological innovations. | Internet marketing. | Metaverse.
Classification: LCC HF5415.32 .C663 2022 (print) | LCC HF5415.32 (ebook)
  | DDC 658.8/342--dc23/eng/20221130
LC record available at https://lccn.loc.gov/2022056247
LC ebook record available at https://lccn.loc.gov/2022056248

This book is published in the IGI Global book series Advances in Marketing, Customer Relationship Management, and E-Services (AMCRMES) (ISSN: 2327-5502; eISSN: 2327-5529)

British Cataloguing in Publication Data
A Cataloguing in Publication record for this book is available from the British Library.

All work contributed to this book is new, previously-unpublished material. The views expressed in this book are those of the authors, but not necessarily of the publisher.

For electronic access to this publication, please contact: eresources@igi-global.com.

Advances in Marketing, Customer Relationship Management, and E-Services (AMCRMES) Book Series

Eldon Y. Li

National Chengchi University, Taiwan & California Polytechnic State University, USA

ISSN:2327-5502
EISSN:2327-5529

MISSION

Business processes, services, and communications are important factors in the management of good customer relationship, which is the foundation of any well organized business. Technology continues to play a vital role in the organization and automation of business processes for marketing, sales, and customer service. These features aid in the attraction of new clients and maintaining existing relationships.

The Advances in Marketing, Customer Relationship Management, and E-Services (AMCRMES) Book Series addresses success factors for customer relationship management, marketing, and electronic services and its performance outcomes. This collection of reference source covers aspects of consumer behavior and marketing business strategies aiming towards researchers, scholars, and practitioners in the fields of marketing management.

COVERAGE

- Ethical Considerations in E-Marketing
- Mobile CRM
- Text Mining and Marketing
- Customer Retention
- Cases on Electronic Services
- Electronic Services
- Mobile Services
- Telemarketing
- Cases on CRM Implementation
- B2B marketing

IGI Global is currently accepting manuscripts for publication within this series. To submit a proposal for a volume in this series, please contact our Acquisition Editors at Acquisitions@igi-global.com or visit: http://www.igi-global.com/publish/.

Titles in this Series

For a list of additional titles in this series, please visit: www.igi-global.com/book-series

Global Agricultural and Food Marketing in a Global Context Advancing Policy, Management, and Innovation
Aluwani Maiwashe-Tagwi (University of South Africa, South Africa) Ailweli Solomon Mawela (University of South Africa, South Africa) and Phineas Khazamula Chauke (University of South Africa, South Arica)
Business Science Reference • © 2023 • 236pp • H/C (ISBN: 9781668447802) • US $250.00

Global Perspectives on the Strategic Role of Marketing Information Systems
Jose Melchor Medina (Tamaulipas Autonomous University, Mexico) Miguel Sahagun (High Point University, USA) Jorge Alfaro (Universidad Catolica del Norte, Chile) and Fernando Ortiz-Rodriguez (Tamaulipas Autonomous University, Mxico)
Business Science Reference • © 2023 • 320pp • H/C (ISBN: 9781668465912) • US $250.00

Enhancing Customer Engagement Through Location-Based Marketing
Amandeep Singh (Chitkara Business School, Chitkara University, India) Amit Mittal (Chitkara Business School, Chitkara University, India) and Murat Unanoglu (İstanbul Aydin University, Turkey)
Business Science Reference • © 2023 • 300pp • H/C (ISBN: 9781668481776) • US $250.00

Big Data Marketing Strategies for Superior Customer Experience
Jose Ramon Saura (Rey Juan Carlos University, Spain)
Business Science Reference • © 2023 • 305pp • H/C (ISBN: 9781668464540) • US $240.00

Managing Festivals for Destination Marketing and Branding
Sharad Kumar Kulshreshtha (North-Eastern Hill University, India)
Business Science Reference • © 2023 • 300pp • H/C (ISBN: 9781668463567) • US $250.00

Handbook of Research on the Interplay Between Service Quality and Customer Delight
Sarmistha Sarma (Institute of Innovation in Technology and Management, India) and Neha Gupta (IBCS, SOA University (Deemed), India)
Business Science Reference • © 2023 • 438pp • H/C (ISBN: 9781668458532) • US $295.00

Cases on Social Justice in China and Perspectives on Chinese Brands
Youssef Elhaoussine (Beijing Normal University-Hong Kong Baptist University United International College, China) and Lulu Wang (Sinotrend Consulting, China)
Business Science Reference • © 2023 • 276pp • H/C (ISBN: 9781668449554) • US $215.00

701 East Chocolate Avenue, Hershey, PA 17033, USA
Tel: 717-533-8845 x100 • Fax: 717-533-8661
E-Mail: cust@igi-global.com • www.igi-global.com

List of Contributors

Table of Contents

Section 1
Introduction

    David Valle-Cruz, Unidad Académica Profesional Tianguistenco, Mexico & Universidad
        Autónoma del Estado de México, Mexico
    J. Patricia Muñoz-Chávez, Universidad Tecnológica de la Zona Metropolitana del Valle de
        México, Mexico
    Rigoberto García García-Contreras, National School of Higher Education, National
        Autonomous University of Mexico, Mexico

Section 2
Understanding Metaverse and the Virtual World

    Kevin Sheng-Kai Ma, Harvard T.H. Chan School of Public Health, Harvard University, USA

    David Roland Andembubtob, School of Computer Sciences, Universiti Sains Malaysia, Malaysia
    Pantea Keikhosrokiani, School of Computer Sciences, Universiti Sains Malaysia, Malaysia
    Nasuha Lee Abdullah, School of Computer Sciences, Universiti Sains Malaysia, Malaysia

    Ozge Doguc, Medipol University, Turkey

Section 5
Future Directions

Detailed Table of Contents

Section 1
Introduction

The metaverse is not just about gaming. It encompasses a wide range of activities, including socializing, education, entertainment, and commerce. It represents an exciting opportunity for companies, as well as consumers, to interact and engage in new ways. It is important to understand the implications of this emerging trend on consumer behavior. This chapter conducts a systematic literature review using the PRISMA methodology, with the goal of understanding how consumer behavior is shaped in the metaverse. The metaverse will allow businesses to reach new customers who are not geographically close and increase the engagement with their current customers. Despite this, it is not all plain sailing, since all types of innovation involve a process of creative destruction. Sectors affected include marketing, education, and healthcare, as well as social effects related to social interaction factors arising from widespread adoption and issues of trust, privacy, bias, misinformation, law enforcement, and psychological aspects related to addiction and the impact on vulnerable people.

Section 2
Understanding Metaverse and the Virtual World

Extended reality (XR)-facilitated technologies, encompassing augmented reality (AR), virtual reality (VR), and mixed reality (MR), have been actively and increasingly involved in various fields and aspects of healthcare. Practical examples covered in this chapter include XR-facilitated surgical systems, rehabilitation modalities for mental illness, and education modules for clinicians and medical students.

In the surgery field, technologies incorporating AR have been increasingly improving the safety and effectiveness of surgery. In mental health rehabilitation, users of head-mounted displays can enter a virtual relaxation world through predesigned VR scenarios. Moreover, AR- and MR-augmented technologies have been incorporated into knowledge platforms and guide simulator practice systems in medical education. Overall, XR-facilitated technologies have promoted personal self-care and patient-centered care, datafication of hospital information, novel disease treatments across various specialties, surgical workflow, and medical education.

Chapter 3

David Roland Andembubtob, School of Computer Sciences, Universiti Sains Malaysia, Malaysia
Pantea Keikhosrokiani, School of Computer Sciences, Universiti Sains Malaysia, Malaysia
Nasuha Lee Abdullah, School of Computer Sciences, Universiti Sains Malaysia, Malaysia

The advent of metaverse has generated a lot of enthusiasm and opened several opportunities for innovation, revolution, and creative thinking among users, customers, and organisations. The seamless operation of users enabled by the fusion of the physical and digital worlds presents both significant potential and problems for every sector of the actual, imaginable, and even perceived industries. The metaverse is undoubtedly developing as a disruptive future trend that will alter the look of interaction, locations, and organisations, although still in its infancy. For this reason, this chapter aims to provide a concise review on the concept of metaverse, which includes discussions on its types, history, features, and technological perspectives. This chapter can assist the system developers in various industries.

Chapter 4

Ozge Doguc, Medipol University, Turkey

The development of technology has transformed the process of product development and customer relationship building. It shows impressive results in deep learning and AI applications. Companies can see farther and make data-driven decisions by leveraging advanced technology solutions managed by AI. Deep learning can be used to analyze and integrate large databases. Considering deep learning activities, it could be a significant opportunity to meet customers' needs and help companies develop profitable new products. Likewise, virtual worlds bring a new approach to marketing. The concept of the metaverse can be described as a simulated reality. Metaverse can enable the creation of virtual reality worlds by integrating online experiences. This chapter discusses how AI and deep learning affect marketing. In this context, industrial opportunities of AI in various marketing activities, AI, strategic marketing, and understanding consumer behaviors will be focused on, and cases of companies using deep learning applications will be included.

Chapter 5

David Roland Andembubtob, School of Computer Sciences, Universiti Sains Malaysia, Malaysia

Pantea Keikhosrokiani, School of Computer Sciences, Universiti Sains Malaysia, Malaysia

Nasuha Lee Abdullah, School of Computer Sciences, Universiti Sains Malaysia, Malaysia

Due to the unique ability of making knowledge freely available anywhere at a very cheap cost, ICT is recognised as a key instrument for delivering excellent education. The new, linked virtual world ushers in an easy and unrestricted movement of data, cash, ideas, goods, and people. It is projected that the usage of the metaverse in education would upend current learning methodologies since it will increase learning strategies, the use of technology, and the options available to students, educators, and education providers. Nevertheless, there are presently few systematic studies on how scholars used immersive virtual reality for academic purposes that noted the use of both expensive and inexpensive head-mounted displays. Therefore, this chapter aims to examine virtual reality and Eduverse from a historical and technological standpoint. The success of virtual reality in education will primarily depend on how motivated students, as the main consumers, become and their capacity to recognise the key components required to reach a suitable degree of learning through virtual reality.

Section 3
Metaverse, Consumer Behaviour, and Adoption

Chapter 6

Babita Singla, Chitkara University, India

Saurabh Bhattacharya, Chitkara University, India

Nithesh Naik, Manipa University, India

A virtual digital environment is created using the metaverse, which also connects the real world. The existence of information technology allows us to do new tasks or carry out routine tasks more effectively. The extended reality, or "metaverse," allows for new kinds of captivating telepresence but may also make mundane activities easier. These technologies help us in our employment, education, healthcare, consumption, and entertainment more and more, but they also present a number of obstacles. The concerns discussed in this chapter are why and will customers adopt the fully immersive territory for various activities like shopping and purchasing any products including bank products.

Chapter 7

Princi Gupta, JECRC University, India

This chapter outlines the understanding of consumer behavior in the virtual ecosystem and the adoption of immersive technologies in the metaverse among consumers. The metaverse is based on the convergence of technologies that enable multisensory interactions with virtual environments, digital objects, and people such as virtual reality (VR) and augmented reality (AR). This chapter covers the impact of consumer behavior in metaverse followed by the strategies adopted by entrepreneurs to work in metaverse to reach consumers. This chapter outlines the metaverse market size, trends, growth, and forecast. This chapter offers a comprehensive framework that examines the metaverse development under the dimensions of metaverse ecosystem. This chapter further aims at identifying the challenges and issues faced in adoption of immersive technologies in metaverse. The metaverse also poses numerous problems to our customary modes of communication and teamwork. The metaverse is significant for retailers for a number of reasons in addition to remaining on the bleeding edge of technology.

Chapter 8

    Kamaladevi Baskaran, Amity University, Dubai, UAE

The present study critically analyses the online shopping experience of consumers and suggests the firm change the operations to adopt the virtual retail world of metaverse and the contribution of e-commerce towards economic growth. All the sectors, including transportation, education, and infrastructure, as well as employment and government, have potential impact on e-commerce. The obstacles to electronic commerce that influence sellers and shoppers will be diminished due to the transformation to the virtual world of metaverse. As UAE is the place for successful implementation of business innovations, a case study of Souq.com acquired by Amazon has been discussed in this study. This case study focuses on fruitful contribution of e-commerce market towards UAE's economic growth and the elements that drive e-commerce development. The study concludes with the identification of e-commerce factors, which has an impact on online shopping experience of metaverse consumers, and addressing the issues that stimulate economic growth through virtual world of metaverse.

Chapter 9

    David Roland Andembubtob, School of Computer Sciences, Universiti Sains Malaysia, Malaysia
    Pantea Keikhosrokiani, School of Computer Sciences, Universiti Sains Malaysia, Malaysia
    Nasuha Lee Abdullah, School of Computer Sciences, Universiti Sains Malaysia, Malaysia

Metaverse is considered one of the platforms that can be used for teaching and learning in higher education. In order to develop, adopt, and use an innovative application or system, the critical success factors are crucial. Consumer behaviours and adoption are crucial to the development of a proposed system based on the metaverse in order to improve the system's usefulness. Consequently, the goal of this study is to evaluate various theories, models, and previous research related to the innovation adoption in order to draw conclusions about the critical success factors for the adoption of the metaverse in education and consumer intention to use.

Chapter 10

    Rajeshwari Krishnamurthy, Great Lakes Institute of Management, Chennai, India
    Shagun Trivedi, Great Lakes Institute of Management, Chennai, India

Despite its growing popularity, the understanding of user experience in the metaverse is limited. In-depth interviews were conducted in a comparative context between gamers and metaverse users to understand their experience in the medium, and NVivo software was used to analyze the findings with Csikszentmihalyi's flow theory as a framework. While most of the flow antecedents and flow outcomes were intact, the 'skill' aspect of flow seems to be different in metaverse, compared to gaming. Aspects such as ease of use, speed, vividness were felt highly by those familiar with metaverse, whereas the gamers more frequently used the medium and found it stimulating and trustworthy. The study offers rich perspectives for metaverse designers, ad agencies, marketing practitioners, and media personnel.

Section 4
The use of Metaverse in Different Disciplines

Chapter 11
Ibrahim Halil Efendioglu, Gaziantep University, Turkey

Metaverse is a virtual reality world where users can interact with each other, buy and sell things, and fulfil their dreams through virtual reality or augmented reality. This technology allows people to participate in social activities and entertainment like never before, providing a different dimension of participation, socialization, and digital living space. In the development process of technology, social media has changed the habits of use and involvement, and this change has revolutionized many areas, from personal space to commercial applications. This chapter reviews and discusses metaverse concepts and marketing. The study findings show that metaverse offers businesses a new way to reach their target audience. Integrating the metaverse into future marketing strategies will be the way forward and for the brand to exist for a long time because metaverse offers brands of all kinds the chance to seamlessly combine the accessibility and convenience of the digital world with the immersive experiences of the physical world.

Chapter 12
Mohammad Daradkeh, University of Dubai, UAE & Yarmouk University, Jordan

Intelligent libraries have been a hot topic in academia, and scholars have offered many insights into the future development of library intelligence. However, there has been little research on the concept and competency characteristics of intelligent librarians as an important driver of library intelligence, which is viewed as a new profession. Meanwhile, the emergence of metaverse has opened up new ideas and impetus for the development of library intelligence, while demanding the professional competence of intelligent librarians. Based on previous research, this chapter examines the evolution of metaverse, its application in libraries, and its advantages. It also discusses the requirements and training routes for intelligent librarians, as well as the concept of intelligent librarians in the context of metaverse. Intelligent libraries, in effect, create a new need for increased cooperation and collaboration between librarians and users. Each party must be aware of their respective roles, responsibilities, and privileges.

Chapter 13
Saravanan P. Veeramuthu, School of Humanities, Universiti Sains Malaysia, Malaysia
Mohamad Luthfi Abdul Rahman, Universiti Sains Malaysia, Malaysia
Moussa Pourya Asl, School of Humanities, Universiti Sains Malaysia, Malaysia
Manonmani Devi M. A. R. Annamalai, Universiti Perguruan Sulthan Idris, Malaysia

The rapid innovations in computer sciences and the emergence of technologies such as virtual reality (VR), augmented reality (AR), metaverse, and similar cyberspaces have greatly impacted the field of education. The radical changes that IR4.0 has made in the teaching approaches and learning behaviours have posed new challenges for students of literary studies in academia. This chapter aims to examine the learning behaviours and challenges of literature students in Malaysian tertiary education in the context of IR4.0. Specifically, the study explores how digital and virtual world has impacted the teaching and learning of literature in academia and thereby seeks to suggest ways to overcome them. It is concluded that effective instruction of literature courses in IR4.0 era requires a combination of pedagogical approaches, technological tools, and cultural sensitivity as well as an effective convergence of the real and the virtual worlds.

Chapter 14

Md. Ashrafuzzaman, Military Institute of Science and Technology, Bangladesh
Rayesa Haque Rupanti, Military Institute of Science and Technology, Bangladesh
Nawrin Tasnim, Military Institute of Science and Technology, Bangladesh
Tasnuba Tabassum Mourin, Military Institute of Science and Technology, Bangladesh

The Healthcare sector is expected to undergo a disruptive change as a result of metaverse technology, which will open the doors for newer treatment possibilities and greater surgical accuracy while enhancing patient outcomes. Since the healthcare industry is one of those most vulnerable industries to technological change, this chapter reviews the applications of Metaverse in healthcare sector. Metaverse has the potential to revolutionize healthcare by fusing robots with AI, VR, AR, the Internet of Medical Devices, Web 3.0, intelligent clouds, edge computing, and quantum computing. Telepresence, digital twinning, and blockchain are three significant technological advances that are converging in the metaverse. Doctors and specialists are using VR to train other medical professionals as they create new ways to improve patient aftermaths. The metaverse continues to develop with the help of 4IR technologies that provide the means to address some of the most fundamental barriers to equitable access to digital healthcare.

Section 5
Future Directions

Chapter 15

Ali B. Mahmoud, St John's University, USA & London South Bank University, London, UK

The metaverse is a new frontier in consumption. It is a digital place where people can buy and consume anything they want, whenever they want. It is an oasis of freedom and choice, and it has the potential to change the way we live and work. The future of the metaverse is placed where data and technology merge to create an experience that's both unique and engaging. With information overload becoming a weekly reality, it is crucial for businesses to understand how their consumers are engaging with their offerings. This chapter synthesised the current research and practice to answer the following questions: How is the metaverse changing the way we consume and communicate? How is Web 3.0 empowering and transforming the metaverse? What are the threats Web 3.0 is bringing to our privacy on the internet?

Preface

Virtual Reality (VR) creates the illusion that virtual encounters are unmediated and real. This technology was first employed by military and health authorities for training through simulations in 1960, but it is now potentially ripe for evaluating social and psychological metrics and dynamics in academic contexts (Estrada Villalba et al., 2021). There are several definitions and viewpoints on the topic of virtual reality, other "realities", and contemporary emergent technologies. The views depend on "who," "why," "from where," and the context in which it is used. It is common to hear the words "augmented reality," "virtual reality," "mixed reality," and "extended reality" (misleadingly shortened as "XR") when referring to how technology alters or creates reality (Rauschnabel et al., 2022). Although VR is not a new technology, recent advancements in immersive technologies, particularly in terms of visualization and interactivity, have made VR more alluring to scholars.

The two technologies of virtual reality and augmented reality are crucial to the creation and development of the metaverse (Mystakidis, 2022). The metaverse is a virtual environment where the digital avatars and those of others from across the world meet to learn, go to school, work, shop, indulge in hobbies, enjoy social interactions, and so forth. The "Corporeity, Interactivity, and Persistence" of the Metaverse distinguishes it from other teaching tools in a major way (Akour et al., 2022). Although there are various studies on theories and analytical techniques that address consumer behaviour changes in the current world (Ezimmuo & Keikhosrokiani, 2022; Keikhosrokiani, 2019, 2020a, 2020b, 2022a, 2022c; Keikhosrokiani et al., 2011; Keikhosrokiani et al., 2013; Keikhosrokiani et al., 2018; Keikhosrokiani, Mustaffa, Zakaria, & Abdullah, 2019; Keikhosrokiani, Mustaffa, Zakaria, & Baharudin, 2019; Keikhosrokiani & Pourya Asl, 2023; Lateef & Keikhosrokiani, 2022; Xian et al., 2022), tracking consumer behaviour change in Metaverse and the adoption of Metaverse by consumers remain a challenge that need to be discussed.

Figure 1 illustrates metaverse requirements which consists of computing breakthroughs, enabling technologies and consumer behavioural factors. The current wave of computing advances and breakthroughs is being driven by current technologies such as augmented reality, virtual reality, mixed reality, extended realities, 3D worlds, wearable devices, and avatars. The term "Metaverse" refers to three-dimensional virtual, augmented, or mixed reality environments in which consumers may behave, explore, and interact with others differently. There are various enabling technologies in the metaverse such as blockchain (Huynh-The, Gadekallu, et al., 2023), Internet of Things (IoT) (Di Martino et al., 2018; Keikhosrokiani, 2021; Keikhosrokiani & Kamaruddin, 2022), digital twins (Promwongsa et al., 2021), big data (Keikhosrokiani, 2022b; Sun et al., 2022), Extended Reality (XR) (Plechatá et al., 2022), 6G technology (Temesvári et al., 2019), and artificial intelligence (Huynh-The, Pham, et al., 2023; Keikhosrokiani et al., 2023; Keikhosrokiani & Pourya Asl, 2023; Teoh Yi Zhe & Keikhosrokiani, 2021). The Metaverse's scope of applicability will grow with further developments, and it may even be incorporated into every part of people's life. Various factors are involved in consumer behaviour towards using metaverse such as job relevance, perceived usefulness, ease of use, output quality, experience, image, beliefs, implementation, voluntariness, facilitating conditions, compatibility, visibility, affect, innovation, time, persuasion, social system, knowledge, decision, self-efficacy, communication channels, social factors, intrinsic and extrinsic motivation, anxiety, and so forth.

Figure 1. Metaverse requirements

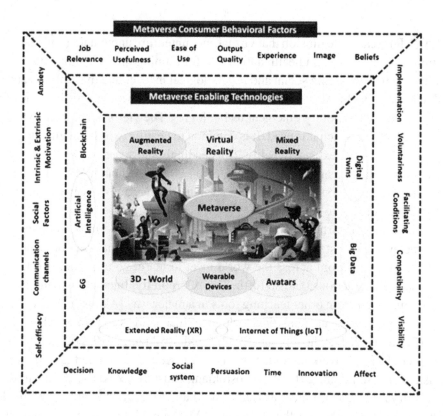

Ambient scene recognition, visual and behavioural analytics may increase brand awareness and hyper-personalization throughout e-commerce operations, as well as consumer retention and acquisition in the virtual retail sector (Kovacova et al., 2022). Although there is already a connection between digital commerce and video games, the Metaverse takes shopping to the next level by offering virtual goods and services, opening new income channels for businesses, and allowing marketers to engage with new generations of customers. The advent of Metaverses will have a profound influence on consumer behaviour—for instance, on how individuals make decisions and create brand connections or how they experience a sense of self and well-being (Akour et al., 2022; Shen et al., 2021; Van et al., 2022). Therefore, it is necessary to investigate Metaverse themes such as customer behaviour in virtual reality (VR), augmented reality (AR), and mixed reality (MR). This book, *Handbook of Research on Consumer Behavioural Analytics in Metaverse and the Adoption of a Virtual World*, aims to investigate the social, behavioural, and psychological factors that influence Metaverse adoption. The focus then shifts to concepts, theories, and analytical approaches for detecting changes in consumer behaviour in the Metaverse. The volume offers multidisciplinary research and practice in social, psychological, and behavioural analytics to detect, forecast, and categorize consumer behaviour shifts in the Metaverse and help organizations make better decisions. This book is an interdisciplinary project that engages various disciplines such as computer sciences, data sciences, marketing, management, and business studies. It offers insights into consumer behaviour change in Metaverse. This authoritative reference source is a great tool for business executives, entrepreneurs, data analysts, marketers, advertisers, government officials, social media professionals, librarians, students and educators of higher education, researchers, and academicians. It covers topics like e-commerce markets, user experience, and immersive technologies.

The book covers topics such as the adoption of virtual reality, consumer behaviour changes in Metaverse, consumer behavioural analysis, purchase decision making in Metaverse, and consumer segmentation in Metaverse. In academia, this publication will benefit researchers, lecturers, and students by providing them with new insights into different fields such as behavioural analysis, digital marketing, digital transformation, consumer behaviour change, decision making, and data science. Moreover, the book will benefit business executives, entrepreneurs, data analysts, marketers, advertisers, government officials, social media professionals by providing them with new techniques and methods in the analytics of consumer behaviour change. The research areas covered in this publication include, but are not limited to behavioural analysis, critical success factors, consumer behaviour, e-commerce markets, extended reality for healthcare, extended reality-augmented technologies, immersive technologies, metaverse, metaverse librarians, metaverse for education, user experience, and virtual ecosystem.

ORGANIZATION OF THE BOOK

The book is organized into five main sections and fifteen chapters. A brief description of each of the chapters is presented as follows:

Section 1: Introduction

In Chapter 1, the PRISMA approach is used to undertake a systematic review with the aim of understanding how consumer behaviour is shaped in the metaverse. The findings of this chapter shows that metaverse will allow businesses to reach new customers who are not geographically close and increase the engagement with their current customers. Despite this, innovation is not without its challenges because it always involves a process of creative destruction. Marketing, education, and healthcare are among the industries that are impacted, as are social effects related to social interaction factors brought on by widespread adoption, as well as problems with trust, privacy, bias, and misinformation. Moreover, the issues with law enforcement and psychological aspects of addiction and the effects on vulnerable people effects on marketing, education, and healthcare industries.

Section 2: Understanding of the Metaverse and the Virtual World

Chapter 2 reviewed extended reality-augmented technologies in healthcare. Extended reality (XR)-facilitated technologies, covering augmented reality (AR), virtual reality (VR), and mixed reality (MR), have been actively and progressively involved in numerous disciplines and elements of healthcare. This chapter's examples in practise include XR- facilitated surgical systems, mental illness rehabilitation techniques, and educational materials for doctors and medical students. In the world of surgery, technologies embracing AR have been enhancing surgical safety and efficacy. Users of head-mounted displays can access predesigned VR scenarios in mental health rehabilitation to enter a virtual relaxation world. Moreover, in the field of medical education, knowledge platforms and simulator practise systems have been integrated with AR- and MR-augmented technologies. Overall, XR-enabled technology has aided in improving surgical workflow, medical education, innovative disease therapies across many specialties, patient-cantered care, and personal self-care.

Chapter 3 aims to provide a concise review on the concept of metaverse which includes discussions on its types, history, features, and technological perspectives. This chapter can assist the system developers in various industries. The Metaverse is undoubtedly developing as a disruptive future trend that will alter the look of interaction, locations, and organisations, although still being in its infancy. Unfortunately, these cutting-edge platforms still haven't overcome their constrained geographic reach, technological limitations, and functional limitations to find widespread adoption outside of their core or primary user communities.

Chapter 4 discusses how AI and deep learning affect marketing. In this context, industrial opportunities of AI in various marketing activities, AI, and strategic marketing, understanding consumer behaviours will be focused on, and cases of companies using deep learning applications will be included. Technology advancements have changed how products are developed and how businesses establish relationships with their clients. In applications involving deep learning and AI, it displays outstanding results. By utilising cutting-edge technological solutions controlled by AI, businesses can see further and make data-driven decisions. Large databases may be analysed and integrated using deep learning. Deep learning operations may present a big chance to address client wants and assist businesses in creating new, lucrative goods. Virtual worlds also provide a fresh method of marketing. One way to think of the metaverse is as a virtual reality. By incorporating internet experiences, Metaverse can enable the building of virtual reality environments.

Chapter 5 examines virtual reality and Eduverse from a historical and technological standpoint. The success of virtual reality in education will primarily depend on how motivated students, as the main consumers, become and their capacity to recognise the key components required to reach a suitable degree of learning through virtual reality. It is projected that the usage of the metaverse in education would upend current learning methodologies since it will increase learning strategies, the use of technology, and the options available to students, educators, and education providers.

Section 3: Metaverse, Consumer Behaviour, and Adoption

Chapter 6 focuses on some concerns related to metaverse adoption such as why and will customers adopt the fully immersive territory for various activities like shopping and purchasing any products including bank products. The study found that Personal Innovativeness (PI) significantly influences people's propensity to use the metaverse. The perceived utility and ease of usage both affect the PI. Several studies contribute to the corpus of knowledge on technology adoption by showing how adoption characteristics like perceived tribality, perceived observability, and perceived compatibility affect the adoption of the Metaverse. User happiness is a crucial factor in determining a user's intention to utilise the metaverse.

Chapter 7 outlines the understanding of consumer behaviour in virtual ecosystem and the adoption of immersive technologies in the Metaverse among consumers. The Metaverse is based on the convergence of technologies that enable multisensory interactions with virtual environments, digital objects, and people such as virtual reality (VR) and augmented reality (AR). This chapter covers the impact of consumer behaviour in metaverse followed by the strategies adopted by entrepreneurs to work in metaverse to reach consumers. This chapter outlines the metaverse market size, trends, growth and forecast. Furthermore, this chapter offers a comprehensive framework that examines the metaverse development under the dimensions of metaverse ecosystem. Moreover, this chapter further aims at identifying the challenges and issues faced in adoption of immersive technologies in metaverse. The Metaverse also poses numerous problems to our customary modes of communication and teamwork. The metaverse is significant for retailers for a number of reasons in addition to remaining on the bleeding edge of technology.

Chapter 8 critically analyses the online shopping experience of consumers, suggest the firm in changing the operations to adopt the virtual retail world of Metaverse and the contribution of e-commerce towards economic growth. E-commerce may be impacted by all industries, including those in the transportation, education, and infrastructure sectors as well as in the employment and government sectors. The transition to the virtual world of Metaverse will reduce the barriers to electronic commerce that affect buyers and sellers. The case study of Souq.com, which was bought by Amazon, has been covered in this research since the UAE is the region where business innovations are successfully implemented. This case study focuses on fruitful contribution of e-commerce market towards UAE's economic growth and the elements that drive e-commerce development. The study concludes with the identification of e-commerce factors which has impact on online shopping experience of Metaverse consumers and addressing the issues that stimulate economic growth through virtual world of Metaverse.

Chapter 9 evaluates various theories, models, and previous research related to the innovation adoption in order to draw conclusions about the critical success factors for the adoption of the metaverse in education and consumer behavioural intention to use. The findings of this chapter revealed that innovativeness, together with perceived usability and simplicity of use, is expressively connected with and influences users' and students' readiness to embrace and utilise metaverse. The acceptance of new technology by a community's culture, the collaboration of co-workers, and the readiness of senior management in enterprises and institutions are other crucial elements that influence consumer behaviour towards the acceptability of the metaverse, particularly in education.

Chapter 10 offers rich perspectives for Metaverse designers, ad agencies, Marketing practitioners and media personnel. An overview of the user experience in the Metaverse has included in this study. The data have been studied using Flow Theory framework, as well as other psychological and behavioural elements. The Metaverse is an innovative media that aims to change how brand marketing is done. For marketing professionals, students, higher education instructors, researchers, academics, IT leaders, and data scientists, this study has enormous ramifications. The factors that need to be emphasised in order to improve user experience in the Metaverse will now be known to Metaverse designers and ad producers.

Section 4: The use of Metaverse in Different Disciplines

Chapter 11 reviews and discusses Metaverse Concepts and Marketing. The study findings show that Metaverse offers businesses a new way to reach their target audience. Integrating the Metaverse into future marketing strategies will be the way forward and for the brand to exist for a long time because Metaverse offers brands of all kinds the chance to seamlessly combine the accessibility and convenience of the digital world with the immersive experiences of the physical world. Metaverse marketing demonstrates its potential for raising awareness for a particular class of goods and services, assisting in the marketing of fresh goods and services, and repositioning existing goods. It is crucial for manufacturers and brands to become familiar with the Metaverse as soon as possible and comprehend its characteristics in order to pave the way for future marketing communication strategies.

Chapter 12 examines the evolution of metaverse, its application in libraries, and its advantages. It also discusses the requirements and training routes for intelligent librarians, as well as the concept of intelligent librarians in the context of metaverse. Intelligent libraries, in effect, create a new need for increased cooperation and collaboration between librarians and users. Each party must be aware of their respective roles, responsibilities, and privileges. Smart individuals play a crucial role in everything from smart communities to smart libraries. The most crucial component of the intelligent library system and the main force behind the growth of intelligent libraries are clever librarians. A new profession focused on intelligent libraries has emerged as a result of the fast development of intelligent technology and changes in the general social environment. Intelligent librarians are public cultural service providers with a feeling of self-motivation.

Chapter 13 aims to examine the learning behaviours and challenges of literature students in Malaysian tertiary education in the context of IR4.0. Specifically, the study explores how digital and virtual world has impacted the teaching and learning of literature in academia and thereby seeks to suggest ways to overcome them. It is concluded that effective instruction of literature courses in IR4.0 era requires a combination of pedagogical approaches, technological tools, and cultural sensitivity as well as an effective convergence of the real and the virtual world.

Chapter 14 reviews the applications of Metaverse in healthcare sector. Metaverse has the potential to revolutionize healthcare by fusing robots with AI, VR, AR, the Internet of Medical Devices, Web 3.0, intelligent clouds, edge computing, and quantum computing. Telepresence, digital twinning, and blockchain are three significant technological advances that are converging in the metaverse. Doctors and specialists are using VR to train other medical professionals as they create new ways to improve patient aftermaths. The metaverse continues to develop with the help of 4IR technologies that provide the means to address some of the most fundamental barriers to equitable access to digital healthcare.

Section 5: Future Directions

Chapter 15 synthesised the current research and practice to answer the following questions: How is the metaverse changing the way we consume and communicate? And how is Web 3.0 empowering and transforming the metaverse? Moreover, what are the threats Web 3.0 is bringing to our privacy on the internet? This chapter has examined the potential for Web 3.0 to revolutionise how we interact with and utilise the Metaverse. This chapter has discussed the technical requirements for Web 3.0, as well as the opportunities, challenges, and potential privacy threats associated with this technology, as well as the reactions of consumers. Evidently, the development of Web 3.0 is set to have a significant impact on the Metaverse, bringing with it both opportunities and obstacles.

Finally, I would like to thank the contributors and reviewers for their high-quality intellectual work to publish this book.

Pantea Keikhosrokiani
School of Computer Sciences, Universiti Sains Malaysia, Malaysia

REFERENCES

Akour, I. A., Al-Maroof, R. S., Alfaisal, R., & Salloum, S. A. (2022). A conceptual framework for determining metaverse adoption in higher institutions of gulf area: An empirical study using hybrid SEM-ANN approach. *Computers and Education: Artificial Intelligence, 3*.

Di Martino, B., Rak, M., Ficco, M., Esposito, A., Maisto, S. A., & Nacchia, S. (2018). Internet of things reference architectures, security and interoperability: A survey. *Internet of Things, 1-2*, 99-112.

Estrada Villalba, É., San Martín Azócar, A. L., & Jacques-García, F. A. (2021). State of the art on immersive virtual reality and its use in developing meaningful empathy. *Computers & Electrical Engineering, 93*, 107272. doi:10.1016/j.compeleceng.2021.107272

Ezimmuo, C. M., & Keikhosrokiani, P. (2022). Predicting Consumer Behavior Change Towards Using Online Shopping in Nigeria: The Impact of the COVID-19 Pandemic. In P. Keikhosrokiani (Ed.), *Handbook of Research on Consumer Behavior Change and Data Analytics in the Socio-Digital Era* (pp. 210–254). IGI Global. doi:10.4018/978-1-6684-4168-8.ch010

Huynh-The, T., Gadekallu, T. R., Wang, W., Yenduri, G., Ranaweera, P., Pham, Q.-V., da Costa, D. B., & Liyanage, M. (2023). Blockchain for the metaverse: A Review. *Future Generation Computer Systems, 143*, 401–419. doi:10.1016/j.future.2023.02.008

Huynh-The, T., Pham, Q.-V., Pham, X.-Q., Nguyen, T. T., Han, Z., & Kim, D.-S. (2023). Artificial intelligence for the metaverse: A survey. *Engineering Applications of Artificial Intelligence, 117*, 105581. doi:10.1016/j.engappai.2022.105581

Keikhosrokiani, P. (2019). *Perspectives in the Development of Mobile Medical Information Systems: Life Cycle, Management, Methodological Approach and Application*. Academic Press.

Keikhosrokiani, P. (2020a). Behavioral intention to use of Mobile Medical Information System (mMIS). In P. Keikhosrokiani (Ed.), *Perspectives in the Development of Mobile Medical Information Systems* (pp. 57–73). Academic Press. doi:10.1016/B978-0-12-817657-3.00004-3

Keikhosrokiani, P. (2020b). Success factors of mobile medical information system (mMIS). In P. Keikhosrokiani (Ed.), *Perspectives in the Development of Mobile Medical Information Systems* (pp. 75–99). Academic Press. doi:10.1016/B978-0-12-817657-3.00005-5

Keikhosrokiani, P. (2021). IoT for Enhanced Decision-Making in Medical Information Systems: A Systematic Review. In G. Marques, A. Kumar Bhoi, I. de la Torre Díez, & B. Garcia-Zapirain (Eds.), *Enhanced Telemedicine and e-Health: Advanced IoT Enabled Soft Computing Framework* (pp. 119–140). Springer International Publishing. doi:10.1007/978-3-030-70111-6_6

Keikhosrokiani, P. (Ed.). (2022a). *Big Data Analytics for Healthcare: Datasets, Techniques, Life Cycles, Management, and Applications*. Elsevier Science. doi:10.1016/C2021-0-00369-2

Keikhosrokiani, P. (2022b). *Big data analytics for healthcare: Datasets, techniques, life Cycles, management, and applications* (1st ed.). Elsevier. doi:10.1016/C2021-0-00369-2

Keikhosrokiani, P. (Ed.). (2022c). *Handbook of Research on Consumer Behavior Change and Data Analytics in the Socio-Digital Era*. IGI Global. doi:10.4018/978-1-6684-4168-8

Keikhosrokiani, P., Naidu, A. B., Iryanti Fadilah, S., Manickam, S., & Li, Z. (2023). Heartbeat sound classification using a hybrid adaptive neuro-fuzzy inferences system (ANFIS) and artificial bee colony. *Digital Health*, *9*. doi:10.1177/20552076221150741 PMID:36655183

Keikhosrokiani, P., & Kamaruddin, N. S. A. B. (2022). IoT-Based In-Hospital-In-Home Heart Disease Remote Monitoring System with Machine Learning Features for Decision Making. In S. Mishra, A. González-Briones, A. K. Bhoi, P. K. Mallick, & J. M. Corchado (Eds.), *Connected e-Health: Integrated IoT and Cloud Computing* (pp. 349–369). Springer International Publishing. doi:10.1007/978-3-030-97929-4_16

Keikhosrokiani, P., Mustaffa, N., Sarwar, M. I., Kianpisheh, A., Damanhoori, F., & Zakaria, N. (2011). A Study towards Proposing GPS-Based Mobile Advertisement Service. Informatics Engineering and Information Science.

Keikhosrokiani, P., Mustaffa, N., Sarwar, M. I., & Zakaria, N. (2013). E-Torch: A Mobile Commerce Location-Based Promotion System. *The International Technology Management Review*, *3*(3), 140–159. doi:10.2991/itmr.2013.3.3.1

Keikhosrokiani, P., Mustaffa, N., & Zakaria, N. (2018). Success factors in developing iHeart as a patient-centric healthcare system: A multi-group analysis. *Telematics and Informatics*, *35*(4), 753–775. doi:10.1016/j.tele.2017.11.006

Keikhosrokiani, P., Mustaffa, N., Zakaria, N., & Abdullah, R. (2019). Assessment of a medical information system: The mediating role of use and user satisfaction on the success of human interaction with the mobile healthcare system (iHeart). *Cognition Technology and Work*. Advance online publication. doi:10.100710111-019-00565-4

Keikhosrokiani, P., Mustaffa, N., Zakaria, N., & Baharudin, A. S. (2019). User Behavioral Intention Toward Using Mobile Healthcare System. In Consumer-Driven Technologies in Healthcare: Breakthroughs in Research and Practice (pp. 429-444). IGI Global. doi:10.4018/978-1-5225-6198-9.ch022

Keikhosrokiani, P., & Pourya Asl, M. (2023). *Handbook of Research on Artificial Intelligence Applications in Literary Works and Social Media*. IGI Global. doi:10.4018/978-1-6684-6242-3

Kovacova, M., Horak, J., & Higgins, M. (2022). Behavioral analytics, immersive technologies, and machine vision algorithms in the Web3-powered Metaverse world. *Linguistic and Philosophical Investigations*, *21*(0), 57–72. doi:10.22381/lpi2120224

Lateef, M., & Keikhosrokiani, P. (2022). Predicting Critical Success Factors of Business Intelligence Implementation for Improving SMEs' Performances: A Case Study of Lagos State, Nigeria. *Journal of the Knowledge Economy*. Advance online publication. doi:10.100713132-022-00961-8

Mystakidis, S. (2022). Metaverse. *Encyclopedia*, *2*(1), 486–497. doi:10.3390/encyclopedia2010031

Plechatá, A., Makransky, G., & Böhm, R. (2022). Can extended reality in the metaverse revolutionise health communication? *NPJ Digital Medicine*, *5*(1), 132. doi:10.103841746-022-00682-x PMID:36056245

Promwongsa, N., Ebrahimzadeh, A., Naboulsi, D., Kianpisheh, S., Belqasmi, F., Glitho, R., Crespi, N., & Alfandi, O. (2021). A Comprehensive Survey of the Tactile Internet: State-of-the-Art and Research Directions. *IEEE Communications Surveys and Tutorials, 23*(1), 472–523. doi:10.1109/COMST.2020.3025995

Rauschnabel, P. A., Felix, R., Hinsch, C., Shahab, H., & Alt, F. (2022). What is XR? Towards a Framework for Augmented and Virtual Reality. *Computers in Human Behavior, 133*, 107289. doi:10.1016/j.chb.2022.107289

Shen, B., Tan, W., Guo, J., Zhao, L., & Qin, P. (2021). How to Promote User Purchase in Metaverse? A Systematic Literature Review on Consumer Behavior Research and Virtual Commerce Application Design. *Applied Sciences (Basel, Switzerland), 11*(23), 11087. doi:10.3390/app112311087

Sun, J., Gan, W., Chen, Z., Li, J., & Yu, P. S. (2022). *Big data meets metaverse: A survey.* arXiv preprint arXiv:2210.16282.

Temesvári, Z. M., Maros, D., & Kádár, P. (2019). Review of Mobile Communication and the 5G in Manufacturing. *Procedia Manufacturing, 32*, 600–612. doi:10.1016/j.promfg.2019.02.259

Teoh Yi Zhe, I., & Keikhosrokiani, P. (2021). Knowledge workers mental workload prediction using optimised ELANFIS. *Applied Intelligence, 51*(4), 2406–2430. doi:10.100710489-020-01928-5

Van, H. T., Si, T. N., Quynh, A. V. T., Kieu, T. N. T., & Vo, T. T. T. (2022). A Conceptual Framework for Determining Metaverse Adoption in Vietnam IT Enterprises. *2022 IEEE/ACIS 7th International Conference on Big Data, Cloud Computing, and Data Science (BCD).* doi: 10.4018/978-1-6684-4168-8.ch00610.4018/978-1-6684-4168-8.ch006

Xian, Z., Keikhosrokiani, P., XinYing, C., & Li, Z. (2022). An RFM Model Using K-Means Clustering to Improve Customer Segmentation and Product Recommendation. In P. Keikhosrokiani (Ed.), *Handbook of Research on Consumer Behavior Change and Data Analytics in the Socio-Digital Era* (pp. 124-145). IGI Global. 10.4018/978-1-6684-4168-8.ch006

Section 1
Introduction

Chapter 1
Towards the Understanding of Consumer Behavior in the Metaverse:
A Systematic Literature Review Using the PRISMA Methodology

David Valle-Cruz
https://orcid.org/0000-0002-5204-8095
Unidad Académica Profesional Tianguistenco, Mexico & Universidad Autónoma del Estado de México, Mexico

J. Patricia Muñoz-Chávez
Universidad Tecnológica de la Zona Metropolitana del Valle de México, Mexico

Rigoberto García García-Contreras
National School of Higher Education, National Autonomous University of Mexico, Mexico

ABSTRACT

The metaverse is not just about gaming. It encompasses a wide range of activities, including socializing, education, entertainment, and commerce. It represents an exciting opportunity for companies, as well as consumers, to interact and engage in new ways. It is important to understand the implications of this emerging trend on consumer behavior. This chapter conducts a systematic literature review using the PRISMA methodology, with the goal of understanding how consumer behavior is shaped in the metaverse. The metaverse will allow businesses to reach new customers who are not geographically close and increase the engagement with their current customers. Despite this, it is not all plain sailing, since all types of innovation involve a process of creative destruction. Sectors affected include marketing, education, and healthcare, as well as social effects related to social interaction factors arising from widespread adoption and issues of trust, privacy, bias, misinformation, law enforcement, and psychological aspects related to addiction and the impact on vulnerable people.

DOI: 10.4018/978-1-6684-7029-9.ch001

INTRODUCTION

Emerging technologies, such as deep learning, are increasingly being adopted in both personal and business contexts (Gil-Garcia, Helbig and Ojo, 2014; Valle-Cruz, 2019; Valle-Cruz et al., 2020). These technologies are being used to detect patterns, interact with users, and provide valuable information for decision-making (Valle-Cruz, Fernandez-Cortez and Gil-Garcia, 2022; Garduño et al., 2023; Hernández, Valle-Cruz and Méndez, 2023). The trend is to use these technologies to improve efficiency, reduce time and errors, and perform activities that pose risks to human safety (Criado and Gil-Garcia, 2019). Emerging technologies have facilitated virtuality, that has the potential to perform a variety of tasks without compromising human safety (Nicol, 2022).

Companies are adapting to digital transformation by implementing innovative management and marketing strategies across various areas of commerce, such as e-commerce, social commerce (s-commerce), logistics, and product delivery services, brand influence, product selection, pricing, offer management, promotions, and user recommendations, all of which have the potential to shape consumer behavior (Alderete, 2019; Sohn and Kim, 2020; Erdmann and Ponzoa, 2021). The emergence of digital, virtual, and immersive environments like the metaverse is starting to impact certain cyber user communities (Zallio and John Clarkson, 2022).

Recent years have seen a shift in consumer behavior due to factors such as population growth, changes in lifestyles, and the COVID-19 pandemic (Muñoz-Chávez, Hernández Rivera and Bolaños-Rodríguez, 2021). New technologies have played a crucial role in facilitating the creation of virtual communities and platforms where Internet users can share and exchange experiences and consumer opinions with other users (Liao, Widowati and Hsieh, 2021). These technologies also enable companies to engage with their consumers by gathering feedback on products and services, which helps to measure consumer behavior and satisfaction. This information can provide companies with valuable insights on how to improve their products and services (Qenaj and Beqiri, 2022).

Consumer behavior can be defined as the process by which individuals, groups, or organizations select, purchase, use, and dispose of goods and services to satisfy their needs and wants (Khan et al., 2022). This encompasses the actions and attitudes of consumers when making purchasing decisions, consuming products, and services, and disposing of them. The study of consumer behavior involves analyzing factors such as what consumers buy, why they buy, how often they buy, and how they use the products they purchase (Muñoz-Chávez, García-Contreras and Valle-Cruz, 2022).

Traditionally, consumers go through a process of recognition, information gathering, and evaluation before making a purchase decision (Miah et al., 2022). This process is influenced by various factors, such as social, cultural, economic, and lifestyle factors. Nowadays, social media and technological advancements play a significant role in the marketing environment and have an impact on consumer behavior. Companies that take advantage of these trends are able to achieve their objectives and increase profitability due to the low costs and increased consumer engagement on social media platforms such as Facebook or Twitter (Ajina, 2019).

Making decisions in complex situations can be challenging as it requires thorough evaluation of all available options. In this context, technological advancements have provided consumers with more and more tools to help them find products and services that best meet their needs more accurately, easily and quickly (Zhang et al., 2020; Song et al., 2021). These changes in the way of marketing are resulting in a shift in consumer behavior. One example of this is the use of Non-Fungible Tokens (NFTs) as seen in the case of artist Mike Winkelmann selling a piece of NFT, titled Ocean Front, for \$6 million to combat climate change, indicating the importance of studying digital consumer behavior (Stephen, 2016). Thus, it is important to understand how companies' immersion in the socio-digital era through digital marketing environments and social networks affects consumer behavior, increases their trust, and boosts the purchase and sale of products and services.

Two of the most widely used digital tools today are e-commerce and s-commerce. E-commerce emerged in the 1990s as the first online shopping platform (Wu, Shen and Chang, 2015). and enables companies to improve their efficiency by offering personalized shopping experiences (Molinillo et al., 2021). S-commerce, on the other hand, emerged in 2005 when Internet users started sharing opinions and ratings of products, services, and shopping experiences on Yahoo! (Liao, Widowati and Hsieh, 2021). S-commerce combines commercial and social activities, linking sellers and consumers through websites and social platforms (Abed, 2020). In these contexts, online reviews of products and services posted by consumers on websites are a valuable source of information for Internet users and have an impact on consumer purchasing behavior. These opinions or assessments can be in the form of ratings, reactions, or open text (Gavilan, Avello and Martinez-Navarro, 2018; Song et al., 2021). This evolution has been further enhanced by the metaverse, leading to trends in meta-consumption, purchasing Non-Fungible Tokens, and smart commerce.

The term "metaverse" was first introduced in the computer literature in the 1990s in connection with the developments of interactive worlds, real-time autonomous agents, and virtual human research (Barrera and Shah, 2023). It was first popularized in Neal Stephenson's 1992 novel, Snow Crash, as a black spherical planet accessible to users through terminals with integrated virtual reality capabilities, where users could appear as avatars (Stephenson, 1992). Three decades later, the fictional concept of the metaverse has evolved into a real business consideration for marketing and other applications (Dwivedi et al., 2022; Barrera and Shah, 2023).

Recent definitions of the metaverse have emphasized its interconnectedness, also referred to as interoperability, but in keeping with Wright et al. (2008) argument for a new class of augmented reality interactions, they incorporate the notion that the metaverse is not purely virtual, but rather a convergence of physical and virtual realities. For example, Duan et al. (2021) define the metaverse as "an evolving virtual world with unlimited scalability and interoperability" where technologies such as virtual reality and augmented reality are considered the main interaction interfaces. Similarly, Lee et al. (2021) conceptualize the metaverse as "a virtual environment that blends the physical and digital, facilitated by the convergence between Internet and Web technologies, and Extended Reality (XR)" (Barrera and Shah, 2023).

Large technology companies such as Meta, Microsoft, and Nvidia are investing significant amounts of money in building a digital universe consistent with the concept of the metaverse. Additionally, governments and companies are also undertaking metaverse initiatives at the enterprise and service levels. For instance, Accenture has recently created a digital headquarters to promote collaboration among workers, with the metaverse being seen as a catalyst for business growth. Furthermore, companies are using immersive technology to provide customers with an experience that stimulates the human senses (sight, sound, and touch) through simulations that generate a sense of presence. As a result, companies like H&M have opened their first virtual environment (store) in the CREEK City universe (Shen et al., 2021; Özkaynar, 2022).

The metaverse is a socio-technical phenomenon that is changing the day-to-day interaction between companies and consumers, and as such, it is beginning to have an impact on marketing and consumer behavior. This chapter conducts a systematic literature review using the PRISMA methodology, with the goal of understanding how consumer behavior is shaped in the metaverse. The chapter is divided into five sections, including an introduction, a description of the systematic literature review process based on the PRISMA methodology, a summary of the literature identified, a discussion of consumer behavior in the metaverse, and finally, conclusions and future work.

SYSTEMATIC LITERATURE REVIEW BASED ON THE PRISMA METHODOLOGY

This section outlines the systematic literature review process that was followed to search for studies on consumer behavior in the metaverse, using the PRISMA methodology. The process of identifying relevant articles was conducted in three steps, as outlined in Figure 1. The PRISMA methodology is a widely accepted framework for conducting systematic reviews, which helps ensure that the search process is comprehensive, transparent, and unbiased. Adhering to the PRISMA methodology allows for the identification of the most relevant studies on the topic and allows for a thorough analysis of the literature (Page et al., 2021). By following the PRISMA methodology, the literature review process was able to identify the most current and robust studies on consumer behavior in the metaverse.

Figure 1. Systematic literature review process using PRISMA methodology

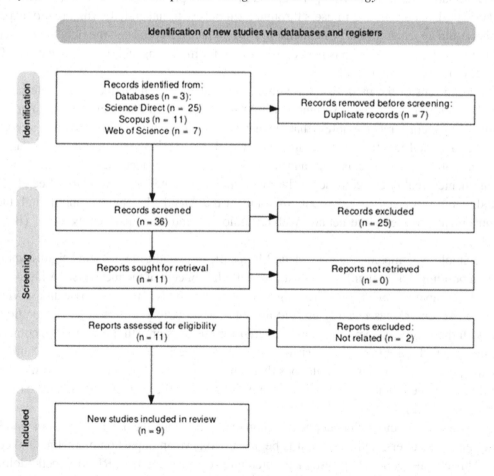

Stage 1: Identification

In the initial stage of the literature review process, the authors conducted a comprehensive search for relevant studies on consumer behavior in the metaverse by searching through three major databases: Science Direct, Web of Science, and Scopus. The authors used the keywords "Metaverse" and "Consumer behavior" to identify literature related to the topic in the titles, abstracts, and keywords of the articles. This search resulted in a total of 43 papers. However, 7 of the articles were duplicates and were subsequently removed, leaving a total of 36 articles that were relevant to the topic of consumer behavior in the metaverse. This initial search helped to identify a broad range of studies that were then further screened and evaluated to ensure their relevance to the research question.

Stage 2: Screening

The authors conducted a thorough review of the titles and abstracts of the articles identified in the previous stage. This step was crucial in identifying articles that were not relevant to the research topic and were therefore excluded from further analysis. After this screening, 25 articles were eliminated for not being related to consumer behavior in the metaverse, leaving a total of 11 articles that were downloaded for in-depth analysis.

The in-depth analysis of the downloaded articles was focused on evaluating the arguments and findings related to consumer behavior in the metaverse. However, after this analysis, 2 papers were eliminated from the final sample as they did not provide sufficient evidence and arguments about consumer behavior in the metaverse. This final screening step helped to ensure that only the most relevant and informative studies on the topic were included in the final sample for analysis. By conducting a thorough review of the literature, we were able to identify the most robust and relevant studies on consumer behavior in the metaverse, providing a strong foundation for the analysis and discussion of the topic.

Stage 3: Inclusion

After the final screening step, a total of 9 articles were included in the final sample for analysis. These articles, which range from 2021 to early 2023, represent the most current and robust studies on consumer behavior in the metaverse (see Table 1). The chosen articles cover a range of topics related to consumer behavior in the metaverse such as, but not limited to, the impact of metaverse on the consumer behavior, the role of social media and virtual reality in shaping the consumer behavior in the metaverse, and the potential of the metaverse in shaping the future of e-commerce.

These 9 articles were analyzed in depth to provide an understanding of the current state of research on consumer behavior in the metaverse. The analysis focus on the main findings and arguments presented in each article, highlighting the key insights and contributions to the field. By conducting an in-depth analysis of these articles, the authors aim to provide a comprehensive understanding of the current state of research on consumer behavior in the metaverse and to identify areas where further research is needed.

Table 1. State of the art of consumer behavior in the metaverse

Year	Authors	Title
2021	Shen B., Tan W., Guo J., Zhao L., Qin P.	How to promote user purchase in the metaverse? A systematic literature review on consumer behavior research and virtual commerce application design.
2022	Branca G., Resciniti R., Loureiro S.M.C.	Virtual is so real! Consumers' evaluation of product packaging in virtual reality
2022	Filimonau V., Ashton M., Stankov U.	Virtual spaces as the future of consumption in tourism, hospitality and events
2022	Gursoy D., Malodia S., Dhir A.	The metaverse in the hospitality and tourism industry: An overview of current trends and future research directions.
2022	Harrisson-Boudreau J.-P., Bellemare J.	Going Above and Beyond eCommerce in the Future Highly Virtualized World and Increasingly Digital Ecosystem
2022	Joy A., Zhu Y., Peña C., Brouard M.	Digital future of luxury brands: Metaverse, digital fashion, and non-fungible tokens
2022	Riar M., Xi N., Korbel J.J., Zarnekow R., Hamari J.	Using augmented reality for shopping: a framework for AR induced consumer behavior, literature review and future agenda
2022	Yogesh K. Dwivedi, Laurie Hughes, Abdullah M. Baabdullah, Samuel Ribeiro-Navarrete, Mihalis Giannakis, Mutaz M. Al-Debei, Denis Dennehy, Bhimaraya Metri, Dimitrios Buhalis, Christy M.K. Cheung, Kieran Conboy, Ronan Doyle, Rameshwar Dubey, Vincent Dutot, Reto Felix, D.P. Goyal, Anders Gustafsson, Chris Hinsch, Ikram Jebabli, Marijn Janssen, Young-Gab Kim, Jooyoung Kim, Stefan Koos, David Kreps, Nir Kshetri, Vikram Kumar, Keng-Boon Ooi, Savvas Papagiannidis, Ilias O. Pappas, Ariana Polyviou, Sang-Min Park, Neeraj Pandey, Maciel M. Queiroz, Ramakrishnan Raman, Philipp A. Rauschnabel, Anuragini Shirish, Marianna Sigala, Konstantina Spanaki, Garry Wei-Han Tan, Manoj Kumar Tiwari, Giampaolo Viglia, Samuel Fosso Wamba	Metaverse beyond the hype: Multidisciplinary perspectives on emerging challenges, opportunities, and agenda for research, practice and policy.
2023	Kevin Giang Barrera, Denish Shah	Marketing in the Metaverse: Conceptual understanding, framework, and research agenda.

ANALYSIS OF THE LITERATURE IDENTIFIED IN THE SYSTEMATIC REVIEW

This section presents the findings of the systematic literature review, which includes both a quantitative and a qualitative analysis of the identified studies on consumer behavior in the metaverse. The quantitative analysis provides an overview of the number of authors, journals, countries of correspondence, and topics covered in the studies. This analysis helps to identify patterns and trends in the literature. The second part of the analysis is a qualitative analysis of the identified papers, which provides a detailed description of the general content of the manuscripts. This analysis focuses on the main findings and arguments presented in each article, highlighting the key insights and contributions to the field. By conducting an in-depth analysis of the studies, this section provides a comprehensive understanding of the current state of research on consumer behavior in the metaverse and to identify areas where further research is needed. The combination of both quantitative and qualitative analyses allows to gain a holistic view of the literature on consumer behavior in the metaverse, which helps to identify the key findings and contributions of each study, and also to identify the areas where more research is needed.

Quantitative Analysis

The topic of the metaverse is relatively new, and studies exploring the analysis of consumer behavior in the metaverse are emerging. The papers identified through the PRISMA methodology were authored by 69 different researchers, who have published their research in 9 different journals, including Applied Sciences (Switzerland), International Journal of Information Management, Internet Research, Journal of Business Research, Journal of Hospitality Marketing and Management, Journal of Tourism Futures, Lecture, Notes in Mechanical Engineering, Psychology and Marketing, and Strategic Change.

The research is also geographically diverse, with authors from ten different countries contributing to the literature. Canada had the highest frequency of publications with 6 articles, followed by Finland with 3, China, Germany, and Italy with 2, and India, Netherlands, Portugal, and Serbia with 1 document each (See Figure 2). This diversity of authors and countries of correspondence highlights the global interest and collaboration in the research on consumer behavior in the metaverse. It also implies that the metaverse is being considered as a phenomenon that has a worldwide impact on the way we interact and consume.

Figure 2. Authors' correspondence countries of consumer behavior in the metaverse

The papers identified in the systematic literature review provide a comprehensive understanding of the current state of research on consumer behavior in the metaverse. The recurring themes found in these papers are related to extended reality, mixed reality, augmented reality, consumer behavior, business models (especially digital), e-commerce, omnichannel media, customer experience, co-creation, co-experiences, and clientelism (See Figure 3). These themes reflect the interdisciplinary nature of the metaverse, as it encompasses various fields such as marketing, business, technology, and psychology.

Figure 3. Word cloud of themes in the systematic literature review of consumer behavior in the metaverse

The theme of extended reality, mixed reality and augmented reality highlights the importance of these technologies in the metaverse and how they are used to create immersive experiences for consumers. Consumer behavior is another recurrent theme, which reflects the importance of understanding how consumers interact and make decisions in the metaverse. Business models and e-commerce, on the other hand, reflect the potential of the metaverse to shape the future of business and commerce. Omnichannel media, customer experience, co-creation, and co-experiences, and clientelism are also relevant themes, they demonstrate the importance of the metaverse in creating personalized, collaborative, and social consumer experiences.

Overall, the recurring themes identified in the literature review demonstrate the significance of consumer behavior in the metaverse and the potential of this technology to shape the future of business, commerce, and consumer experience. The themes also imply that the metaverse is a complex and multi-faceted phenomenon that requires interdisciplinary research to fully understand its impact and potential.

Qualitative Analysis

The literature on consumer behavior in the metaverse identifies the significance of application development in digital business models, digital commerce, and social commerce. It also highlights the importance of understanding consumer behavior based on online tools, multi-sensory experience through multiple channels powered by the metaverse, with the aim of promoting co-experience and co-creation. Furthermore, the literature identifies the most recurrent technologies used in the implementation of the metaverse such as virtual reality, augmented reality, extended reality, immersive technology, and 3D generated products.

Most of the studies are literature reviews, which is understandable given that the area of study is relatively new. The metaverse has the potential to extend the physical world using augmented and virtual reality technologies that enable users to seamlessly interact in real and simulated environments using avatars and holograms. Virtual environments and immersive games (such as Second Life, Fortnite, Roblox, and VRChat) have been described as antecedents of the metaverse and offer insight into the potential socioeconomic impact of a persistent and fully functional cross-platform metaverse (Dwivedi et al., 2022). The metaverse has the potential to change the way we interact and consume, providing a more immersive and personalized experience for consumers. It also has the potential to transform the way businesses operate and connect with their customers, leading to new business models and opportunities.

In the literature on consumer behavior in the metaverse, Barrera and Shah (2023) conducted an extensive literature review across multiple disciplines and gathered expert views from industry leaders to propose a definition and organizational framework for the emerging metaverse. Their analysis highlights that the metaverse brings about significant changes such as hyper-availability of data, virtualization, hyper-connectedness, the blending of virtual and physical, the re-imposition of identity, and new challenges in ownership, privacy, and society. These changes have the potential to induce new implications for marketing, particularly in areas such as intelligence, innovation, communication, experience, consumer behavior, and policy formulation. This highlights the need for further research to understand the impact of the metaverse on consumer behavior and how businesses can adapt to these changes and take advantage of the new opportunities that the metaverse brings.

Dwivedi et al. (2022) conducted a study on the effects of the metaverse on various industries including marketing, education, healthcare, and society using a multiperspective and narrative approach. They analyzed the social interaction factors arising from widespread adoption of the metaverse, including issues of trust, privacy, bias, misinformation, law enforcement, and psychological aspects such as addiction and the impact on vulnerable populations. Their study highlights the need for researchers, practitioners, and policy makers to consider these factors when implementing and designing metaverse technologies. The authors also propose an agenda for further research and action in these areas, emphasizing the need to address these issues in order to fully realize the potential of the metaverse and mitigate its potential negative consequences.

Likewise, Filimonau, Ashton and Stankov (2022) analyzed the potential consumer challenges in the tourism, hospitality and events sectors arising from the implementation of virtual spaces. To achieve this, they conducted an analysis of the academic and grey literature, specifically on the use of the metaverse in the tourism, hospitality, and events industries. The authors conclude that four perspectives representing the various players in the value chain of the tourism, hospitality and events industries should be considered: 1) developers/suppliers, 2) practitioners, 3) customers, and 4) policy makers. The research agenda should also incorporate the broader indirect effects of consuming virtual spaces that may extend well beyond the tourism, hospitality, and events industries. In this context, the metaverse due to technological development such as 5G mobile networks, the Internet of Things and immersive technologies promises to transform the experiences of tourism consumers as well as the management and marketing of the sector. Therefore, tourism consumers will have unprecedented opportunities to interact in an immersive way. For instance, they will be able to know, prior to the purchase, the tourist products or services as well as visit the destinations with which they will obtain real experiences that will allow them to have more elements to make the purchase decision (Buhalis, Leung and Lin, 2023). The expectation is that this anticipated experience will drive the purchase, not replace it.

In their systematic literature review, Shen et al. (2021) aimed to comprehensively examine the current state of research on virtual commerce, with a specific focus on understanding how consumer behavior is affected by the design and promotion of virtual environments. Through their analysis of existing literature, the authors identified key factors that influence consumer behavior and purchase decisions in virtual commerce environments, as well as prominent design elements used in these environments. Furthermore, they identified research gaps and suggested that future research in this area should explore the concept of meta-commerce as a potential trend. Overall, the study provides a comprehensive overview of the current state of research on consumer behavior in virtual commerce environments and highlights areas that warrant further investigation.

The COVID-19 pandemic has greatly impacted consumer habits and accelerated the adoption of digital technologies. Many stores have closed their physical locations and transitioned to online experiences, with consumers now expecting a high level of personalization and convenience in their shopping experiences. This shift in behavior has also led to an increased interest in Extended Reality (ER) technologies such as Augmented Reality (AR) in shopping environments. AR is being used to address the challenges of online shopping, such as providing a more immersive and interactive experience for consumers. Riar et al. (2022) conducted research on the use of AR in shopping environments, and found that AR's capabilities, such as interactivity and vividness, enhance both the pleasure and usefulness of shopping experiences and can increase the likelihood of a consumer purchasing a product or recommending it to others. Therefore, it is crucial for brands and retailers to adopt e-commerce strategies and explore the use of ER technologies to meet the changing needs of consumers.

Tan et al. (2022) recognized that while previous research has examined the factors that influence consumer's green consumption values and ethical purchasing behaviors, and the psychological mechanisms underlying them, there is a gap between consumer's intentions and actions when it comes to sustainable behaviors. In an effort to understand this paradox, the authors conducted research on the consumer values that drive the use of collaborative economy platforms, specifically focusing on the second-hand peer-to-peer platforms. The authors' research draws on consumer values theory and the concept of altruistic-egoistic values, as well as the psychology of affect, to investigate the linkages between context-specific values, green consumption values, and sustainable resale behaviors. The goal of this research is to better understand the underlying motivations and factors that influence consumer behavior in the context of sustainable consumption and the sharing economy. The authors found that economic and practical values for the use of a second-hand peer-to-peer platform negatively affect green consumption values and subsequently weaken consumers' willingness to engage in sustainable resale behavior. In contrast, recreational, generative, social benefit, and protest values positively influence green consumption values and increase consumers' willingness to engage in pro-environmental behavior. The authors also argue that the metaverse and second-hand P2P platforms are part of an expanding sector of the collaborative economy that offers versatile opportunities for both consumers to diversify their consumption practices and for companies to take advantage of extended product life cycles to create sustainable brands. In this sense, metaverse-based platforms can comprise inclusive re-commerce spaces not only between consumer users and sellers, but also between consumers and companies presented by their brands. Therefore, this research suggests that companies should focus on promoting values that align with green consumption values and sustainable behaviors to encourage consumer engagement in sustainable consumption behaviors.

The metaverse, a virtual world where people can interact and engage in various activities, is gaining significant attention from industry professionals and is experiencing an exponential growth in the number of users. In light of this, Harrisson-Boudreau and Bellemare (2021) conducted research to understand consumers' perspectives on the current state of e-commerce and their attitudes towards extended reality commerce. The authors found that consumers view e-commerce experiences as lacking in personalization and desire greater individualization of their brand experiences. They argue that personalization of brand experiences should not be viewed as a mass goal, but from an individual perspective - one-to-one and virtually augmented. Therefore, it is crucial for companies to recognize this new trend and develop strategies to actively participate in this new world and seize this opportunity to build a sustainable competitive advantage. As the metaverse and extended reality commerce continue to gain popularity, companies that can provide personalized and immersive experiences will be better positioned to meet the evolving needs and preferences of consumers.

Gursoy, Malodia and Dhir (2022) developed a conceptual framework for the creation of metaverse experiences, with the goal of identifying research gaps and proposing research agenda items that have the potential to significantly benefit players in the hospitality and tourism industry. In their research, the authors recognized that the metaverse is an emerging trend and that the hospitality and tourism industry has the potential to benefit from its growth. The authors classified the future research agendas into three broad categories. The first category is staging metaverse experiences, which focuses on understanding the technical aspects of creating immersive experiences in the metaverse and the design considerations for creating engaging and memorable experiences. The second category is understanding potential changes in consumer behavior, which aims to understand how the metaverse will change the way consumers engage with the industry and how their expectations will evolve. The third category is marketing and operations strategies in the metaverse, which focuses on how companies can effectively market and operate within the metaverse to reach consumers and create value. Overall, the authors' proposed framework highlights the importance of understanding the metaverse and its potential impact on the hospitality and tourism industry and provides guidance for future research to better understand how companies can effectively leverage the metaverse to improve customer engagement and create sustainable competitive advantages.

Virtual reality (VR) is rapidly changing the way we interact with the world and the metaverse is creating new opportunities for shopping experiences. One area of interest is how consumers evaluate products in a virtual environment compared to a traditional physical environment. To investigate this, Branca, Resciniti and Loureiro (2022) conducted research on consumer evaluation of packaged products in immersive virtual reality. They manipulated structural and haptic cues of the packaging to understand how it impacts consumer's evaluation of the product. The study aimed to understand how consumer's responses in virtual reality differ from their responses in real life. The authors' research highlights the importance of understanding how consumers evaluate products in virtual reality environments and how it differs from traditional physical environments. As the metaverse continues to grow, companies will need to understand how to effectively market their products in virtual reality environments and how to create immersive experiences that will appeal to consumers. The results of this research can inform companies on how to design and present products in virtual reality environments to optimize consumer engagement and purchase intention.

One of the concerns in marketing is that companies may use consumer behavior data for unethical purposes, such as engaging in unethical practices in product, price, place, or promotion. With the advent of the metaverse, it is important to consider the ethical implications of virtual reality, as it is perceived as real, but represents an illusory dimension of the brain. This can make it easier for companies to manipulate consumer perceptions and desires. De et al. (2023) found that consumers' perception of the virtual scenario in the metaverse can be influenced by their own avatar and the social factors such as belonging, reference, and aspiration. Therefore, it is crucial for companies and marketers to take into account the ethical implications of the metaverse and design practices or countermeasures that help prevent the risks of inappropriate use, such as excessive use or consumption, cyberbullying, violence, etc.

Barrera and Shah (2023) also highlighted the importance of considering the ethical implications of the metaverse, specifically the ethical concerns related to biometric data and privacy, hacker attacks, bullying and hate, identity theft, and addiction. In order to ensure the safety and well-being of consumers who interact with the metaverse, it is important for companies and marketers to take these risks into consideration and implement measures to mitigate them. Overall, the research suggests that companies and marketers need to be conscious of the ethical implications of the metaverse and take steps to ensure that consumer interactions with the metaverse are safe and positive.

The metaverse is an emerging technology that has the potential to greatly impact consumer behavior and the way companies interact with consumers. From the qualitative analysis of the main trends and results of the analyzed articles, an underlying structure of the relationship between metaverse and consumer behavior can be proposed. One of the key findings from the research is the potential for the metaverse to provide more personalized and immersive brand experiences for consumers. Consumers desire greater individualization of their brand experiences and companies need to recognize this trend and develop strategies to actively participate in the metaverse.

Another important finding is the need for companies to consider the ethical implications of the metaverse and take steps to mitigate risks. Some of the ethical aspects and risks in the metaverse that were identified in the research include: biometric data and privacy, hacker attacks, bullying and hate, identity theft, and addiction. It is crucial for companies to consider these risks and implement measures to mitigate them to ensure the safety and well-being of consumers who interact with the metaverse.

Overall, the research suggests that the metaverse has the potential to greatly impact consumer behavior and companies need to be aware of the trends and risks associated with it in order to effectively engage with consumers and create sustainable competitive advantages (Figure 4).

Figure 4. Conceptual framework of the relationship between metaverse and consumer behavior

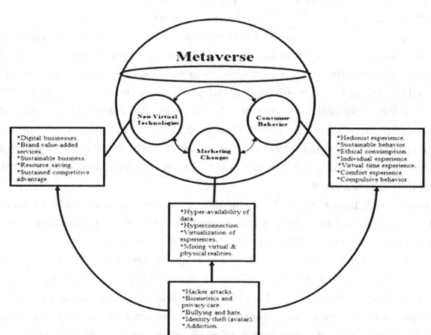

DISCUSSION

The metaverse is a rapidly evolving concept that represents a significant shift in the way we interact with technology and the digital world. At its core, the metaverse refers to the digital representation of reality in an online environment. It is a virtual space in which people can interact and create content, similar to how they do in the real world. However, the metaverse goes beyond the traditional concept of virtual reality, providing a more immersive and interactive experience for users. It blurs the lines between the physical and digital world, enabling users to engage in activities that were previously only possible in the real world. The metaverse is not just about gaming, it encompasses a wide range of activities, including socializing, education, entertainment, and commerce. The metaverse represents an exciting opportunity for companies, as well as consumers, to interact and engage in new ways, and it is important to understand the implications of this emerging trend on consumer behavior.

Initially, the metaverse was considered a quasi-physical and virtual reality world in which participants were represented as avatars (Barrera and Shah, 2023). However, with the incorporation of technologies such as augmented reality, artificial intelligence, the Internet of Things, 3D modeling, and spatial and edge computing, the metaverse has grown to encompass a hyper-connected digital universe that promises to revolutionize the way we interact and transact in virtual spaces (Dwivedi et al., 2022).

The metaverse represents an opportunity for consumers to collaborate and co-participate in virtual spaces, providing an incentive for companies to leverage the metaverse as a disruptive technology. For consumers, the metaverse offers the possibility of experiencing products or services in a virtual environment that is close to reality, which can lead to more informed purchasing decisions. However, it is important to consider that the emotions and behavior of consumers can be influenced by the metaverse. As such, it is crucial for companies to prioritize cybersecurity and the protection of consumer data in order to ensure safe and secure shopping experiences (De et al., 2023).

The metaverse offers a plethora of opportunities for businesses to thrive, such as through the sale of virtual products, provision of services, or promotion of brands. However, it is crucial for these businesses to have a proper means of measuring their performance and progress in order to succeed in this digital realm. Key Performance Indicators (KPIs) play a vital role in determining the success of strategies centered around the creation and distribution of metaverse products and services.

It is essential to note that metrics serve as a means of evaluating the performance of a business and making data-driven decisions. These metrics provide valuable insights into the effectiveness of various business strategies and can be used to identify areas for improvement, track progress over time, and make informed decisions to optimize performance. In the metaverse, utilizing relevant KPIs can be the key to staying ahead of the competition and achieving long-term success.

In the metaverse, businesses must have a clear understanding of their performance and progress in order to succeed. To do this, they must use relevant metrics that can provide valuable insights into the effectiveness of their strategies.

Some common metrics that are particularly useful for conducting business in the metaverse include:

- **Number of Unique Users:** This metric measures the number of individuals who access the metaverse during a given period. It is a crucial metric for understanding the size of the market and the popularity of a product or service.

- **Usage Time:** This metric measures the average amount of time a user spends in the metaverse during a given period. It is an important metric for understanding the attractiveness of a product or service and user loyalty.
- **Conversion Rate:** This metric measures the percentage of users who perform a specific action, such as buying a product or signing up for a service. It is an essential metric for understanding the effectiveness of a marketing campaign or the quality of a product or service.
- **Revenue:** This metric measures the total amount of money a business earns during a given period. It is a key metric for understanding the financial performance of a business.
- **Profitability:** This metric measures the percentage of profits earned in relation to costs incurred. It is an important metric for understanding the long-term viability of a business.

In summary, metrics are an integral tool for evaluating the performance and progress of a business in the metaverse. By measuring the right metrics, businesses can make informed decisions and optimize their performance in this digital realm.

The metaverse represents a transformative tool that can positively affect people in their work, leisure, and social interaction (Dwivedi et al., 2022). The potential impact on how we do business, interact with brands and others, and develop shared experiences is likely to be transformational, as the lines between physical and digital are likely to blur somewhat from current perceptions. However, while the technology and infrastructure necessary to develop new large-scale immersive virtual worlds in which our avatars can transcend platforms does not yet exist, researchers are increasingly examining the transformative impact of the metaverse.

Despite this, it is not all plain sailing, since all types of innovation involve a process of creative destruction, a learning curve, lag, and segregation of some. Only the most innovative can succeed in this type of strategy, but there is always a latent risk in adopting technologies that have been little tested. Sectors affected include marketing, education, and healthcare, as well as social effects related to social interaction factors arising from widespread adoption, and issues of trust, privacy, bias, misinformation, law enforcement and psychological aspects related to addiction and the impact on vulnerable people.

The metaverse can be a space where companies would take advantage of its potential as a new market, new business models can be generated, and revenues can be obtained through advertising in the metaverse. Some of the inherent advantages of the metaverse have to do with the fact that virtual products require fewer processes and resources to manufacture real products, relatively young users can participate in the economic activities, in addition to the fact that the metaverse can simplify the input interface for the elderly. Despite this, there are great challenges, as the metaverse allows for social participation and business aimed at the elderly. Businesses in the metaverse expand when security and privacy are guaranteed. The protection of authored content is also a relevant issue in the metaverse, such as Non-Fungible Tokens (NFTs).

The metaverse can enable a new generation of telecommuting and remote work models in manufacturing and operations management, allowing workers to perform their activities anywhere. Likewise, the metaverse can facilitate the training and education of company employees through digital spaces powered by virtual and augmented reality. With simulation approaches and digital twins, the metaverse will enable operations managers to choose the best resource allocation configurations, considering the characteristics of products, customers, suppliers, etc. The interaction of manufacturing and operations managers with suppliers in metaverse will be more collaborative and transparent (Dwivedi et al., 2022). It will also significantly improve the delivery time of orders. In addition, transactions can be more reliable thanks to blockchain. The metaverse will enable improved interactions with customers and, as a result, they will be able to co-create and provide real-time feedback at all stages of a product's production processes. All of this has the potential to alter consumption patterns in different sectors, such as tourism, hospitality, and events, as the generation of experiences could take place in virtual worlds.

The metaverse is rapidly emerging as a powerful new platform for commerce and communication. It will not replace real-world experiences, but it will fundamentally transform the way consumers interact with products and services. The metaverse offers a unique, immersive, and interactive environment, where customers can experience products and services in ways that were not possible before. The ability to engage customers in a more personal and interactive way, will change the way businesses market and sell their products and services. Furthermore, the metaverse will allow businesses to reach new customers who are not geographically close and increase the engagement with their current customers. The metaverse represents a significant opportunity for businesses to create new revenue streams and increase the overall customer experience.

CONCLUSIONS AND FUTURE WORK

This chapter presents the findings of a comprehensive systematic literature review on consumer behavior in the metaverse. As the metaverse is a relatively new and rapidly evolving field, there is a growing need for research that can provide a deeper understanding of its potential benefits, opportunities, and possible challenges. The literature review shows that while the metaverse is still in its early stages of development, there are several areas that are ripe for further investigation. These include understanding how consumers interact with and experience products and services in the metaverse, identifying the key drivers of consumer behavior in this digital realm, and exploring the potential implications of the metaverse for businesses and society.

Nowadays, most studies on consumer behavior in the metaverse are exploratory in nature, based on literature reviews and theoretical frameworks. However, there is a need for more rigorous empirical research that can provide solid evidence of the potential benefits and challenges of the metaverse. This will be essential for guiding the development of effective strategies for businesses looking to enter the metaverse and for policymakers seeking to regulate this emerging field. The systematic literature review presented in this chapter highlights the need for further research on consumer behavior in the metaverse to fully understand its implications and potential. The metaverse is an ever-evolving field and the need for research to keep pace with its development.

The search for scientific articles on consumer behavior in the metaverse in prominent databases such as Web of Science, Scopus, and Science Direct yielded a limited number of 9 papers. This indicates that the field of research on consumer behavior in the metaverse is still in its nascent stages, and there is a significant need for further exploration and study in this area. The limited number of studies on consumer behavior in the metaverse also highlights the need for more rigorous research to be conducted in the near future. Empirical studies, such as experiments and surveys, can provide valuable insights and evidence on the potential benefits, opportunities, and challenges of the metaverse for consumers and businesses. These studies can help to identify the key drivers of consumer behavior in the metaverse and inform the development of effective strategies for businesses looking to enter this digital realm. The limited number of studies on consumer behavior in the metaverse highlights the need for further research to fully understand its implications and potential. The metaverse is an ever-evolving field and the need for research to keep pace with its development. Therefore, it is crucial to continue researching this topic and to conduct experiments or empirical studies in the near future.

The metaverse is built on advanced technologies such as extended reality, augmented reality, and mixed reality. These technologies have the potential to empower virtual businesses and create ecosystems centered around co-creation and co-experience. This can significantly enhance the user experience, as it allows for the creation of virtual spaces that offer customers a wide range of benefits beyond traditional physical experiences. One industry that is poised to benefit greatly from the metaverse is the tourism sector. Historically, traditional marketing strategies have been challenging for tourism marketers due to the intangible nature of the services they offer. The metaverse presents a solution to this challenge by allowing customers to virtually visit and experience tourist destinations and services before making a real-life trip. This virtual interaction can serve as a powerful motivator for customers and has the potential to significantly promote the tourism sector (Buhalis, Leung and Lin, 2023). The technologies that form the basis of the metaverse, such as extended reality, augmented reality, and mixed reality, have the potential to empower virtual businesses and create ecosystems centered around co-creation and co-experience. The tourism industry is one that is poised to benefit greatly from the metaverse, as it allows for the creation of virtual spaces that offer customers a wide range of benefits beyond traditional physical experiences, such as virtual visit and pre-test of tourist destinations, hospitality, and events. This virtual interaction can serve as a powerful motivator for customers and has the potential to significantly promote the tourism sector.

The metaverse presents an exciting new platform for innovation and experimentation. One of the key advantages of this digital realm is that it allows for the creation of virtual spaces and scenarios that would be impossible or impractical to replicate in the real world. This opens up new possibilities for product development and testing, such as the ability to generate prototypes and launch new products in a virtual environment. In addition to its applications in product development and testing, the metaverse also has the potential to significantly improve collaboration and communication within organizations. By creating virtual environments where team members can interact in real-time, regardless of their physical location, the metaverse can facilitate better communication, coordination, and teamwork. This can lead to improved productivity, creativity, and innovation. The metaverse is a powerful tool that can enable new forms of innovation and experimentation. Its ability to create virtual spaces and scenarios can be used to test new products, generate prototypes, and launch new products. Additionally, it can also improve the collaboration experience for everyone in organizations around the world, leading to improved communication, coordination, and teamwork.

Future research on the metaverse should focus on identifying and developing metrics to evaluate the performance of services and products launched in the digital realm. These metrics will be crucial in determining the success of strategies centered around the creation and distribution of metaverse products and services. Measuring the right metrics will enable businesses to make informed decisions and optimize the performance of their products and services in the metaverse. Identifying the key performance indicators (KPIs) that are relevant to the metaverse, can provide valuable insights into the effectiveness of various business strategies. This will be essential for staying ahead of the competition and achieving long-term success in this emerging technology. In addition, future research should also focus on identifying strategies that can generate competitive advantages in the metaverse. This will require a deep understanding of the unique opportunities and challenges presented by this digital realm, as well as the key drivers of consumer behavior in the metaverse. By understanding these factors, businesses will be able to develop strategies that are tailored to the specific needs of this emerging technology. Future research on the metaverse should focus on identifying and developing metrics to evaluate the performance of services and products launched in the digital realm. Measuring the right metrics will enable businesses to make informed decisions and optimize the performance of their products and services in the metaverse. Additionally, identifying strategies that can generate competitive advantages in the metaverse, will require a deep understanding of the unique opportunities and challenges presented by this digital realm, as well as the key drivers of consumer behavior in the metaverse.

Consumer behavior is constantly evolving, and today's consumers are more in tune with the digital age than ever before. The metaverse presents a unique opportunity to revolutionize consumer experiences by allowing them to "test" products and services before making a purchase. This can provide a deeper understanding of the attributes of products and services, which can increase consumer satisfaction and engagement.

For companies, the metaverse offers a powerful tool to increase profitability and improve brand positioning. The ability to create immersive, interactive virtual spaces where customers can experience products and services in ways that were not possible before, can help to drive sales and customer loyalty. Additionally, the metaverse can also provide valuable insights into consumer behavior, which can be used to inform product development and marketing strategies.

In conclusion, the metaverse offers a unique opportunity to revolutionize consumer experiences and improve business outcomes. By providing consumers with a closer approach and a better understanding of the attributes of products and services, it can increase consumer satisfaction and engagement. For companies, the metaverse offers the possibility of increasing profitability and improving brand positioning. It is an ever-evolving field and companies should adapt to the new possibilities it presents.

REFERENCES

Abed, S. S. (2020). Social commerce adoption using TOE framework: An empirical investigation of Saudi Arabian SMEs. *International Journal of Information Management*, *53*(March), 102118. doi:10.1016/j.ijinfomgt.2020.102118

Ajina, A. S. (2019). The perceived value of social media marketing: An empirical study of online word of mouth in Saudi Arabian context. *Entrepreneurship and Sustainability Issues*, *6*(3), 1512–1527. doi:10.9770/jesi.2019.6.3(32)

Alderete, M. V. (2019). Electronic commerce contribution to the SME performance in manufacturing firms: A structural equation model [Contribución del comercio electrónico al desempeño de las PyMEs industriales: Un modelo structural]. *Contaduría y Administración*, *64*(4), 1–24.

Barrera, K. G., & Shah, D. (2023). Marketing in the Metaverse: Conceptual understanding, framework, and research agenda. *Journal of Business Research*, *155*, 113420. doi:10.1016/j.jbusres.2022.113420

Branca, G., Resciniti, R., & Loureiro, S.M.C. (2022). Virtual is so real! Consumers' evaluation of product packaging in virtual reality. *Psychology & Marketing*.

Buhalis, D., Leung, D., & Lin, M. (2023). Metaverse as a disruptive technology revolutionising tourism management and marketing. *Tourism Management*, *97*(January), 104724. doi:10.1016/j.tourman.2023.104724

Criado, J. I., & Gil-Garcia, J. R. (2019). Creating public value through smart technologies and strategies: From digital services to artificial intelligence and beyond. *International Journal of Public Sector Management*, *32*(5), 438–450. doi:10.1108/IJPSM-07-2019-0178

De, F. (2023). Physical and digital worlds : On implications and opportunities of the 4th International Conference metaverse. *Procedia Computer Science*, *217*, 1744–1754. doi:10.1016/j.procs.2022.12.374

Duan, H. (2021). Metaverse for social good: A university campus prototype. *Proceedings of the 29th ACM International Conference on Multimedia*, 153–161. 10.1145/3474085.3479238

Dwivedi, Y. K., Hughes, L., Baabdullah, A. M., Ribeiro-Navarrete, S., Giannakis, M., Al-Debei, M. M., Dennehy, D., Metri, B., Buhalis, D., Cheung, C. M. K., Conboy, K., Doyle, R., Dubey, R., Dutot, V., Felix, R., Goyal, D. P., Gustafsson, A., Hinsch, C., Jebabli, I., ... Wamba, S. F. (2022). Metaverse beyond the hype: Multidisciplinary perspectives on emerging challenges, opportunities, and agenda for research, practice and policy. *International Journal of Information Management*, *66*, 102542. doi:10.1016/j.ijinfomgt.2022.102542

Erdmann, A., & Ponzoa, J.M. (2021). Digital inbound marketing: Measuring the economic performance of grocery e-commerce in Europe and the USA. *Technological Forecasting and Social Change, 162*. doi:10.1016/j.techfore.2020.120373

Filimonau, V., Ashton, M., & Stankov, U. (2022). Virtual spaces as the future of consumption in tourism, hospitality and events. *Journal of Tourism Futures*.

Garduño, J. C. (2023). Deep Learning Implementation for Pattern and Incidences Identification of Gender Violence in Mexican Contexts. In *Handbook of Research on Applied Artificial Intelligence and Robotics for Government Processes* (pp. 345–371). IGI Global.

Gavilan, D., Avello, M., & Martinez-Navarro, G. (2018). The influence of online ratings and reviews on hotel booking consideration. *Tourism Management*, *66*, 53–61. doi:10.1016/j.tourman.2017.10.018

Gil-Garcia, J. R., Helbig, N., & Ojo, A. (2014). Being smart: Emerging technologies and innovation in the public sector. *Government Information Quarterly*, *31*(Supple), I1–I8. doi:10.1016/j.giq.2014.09.001

Gursoy, D., Malodia, S., & Dhir, A. (2022). The metaverse in the hospitality and tourism industry: An overview of current trends and future research directions. *Journal of Hospitality Marketing & Management, 1–8.*

Harrisson-Boudreau, J.-P., & Bellemare, J. (2021). Going Above and Beyond eCommerce in the Future Highly Virtualized World and Increasingly Digital Ecosystem. In *Towards Sustainable Customization: Bridging Smart Products and Manufacturing Systems* (pp. 789–797). Springer.

Hernández, P. R., Valle-Cruz, D., & Méndez, R. V. M. (2023). Review on the Application of Artificial Intelligence-Based Chatbots in Public Administration. In *Handbook of Research on Applied Artificial Intelligence and Robotics for Government Processes* (pp. 133–155). IGI Global.

Khan, S., Tomar, S., Fatima, M., & Khan, M. Z. (2022). Impact of artificial intelligent and industry 4.0 based products on consumer behaviour characteristics: A meta-analysis-based review. *Sustainable Operations and Computers*, *3*(January), 218–225. doi:10.1016/j.susoc.2022.01.009

Lee, L.-H. (2021). *All one needs to know about metaverse: A complete survey on technological singularity, virtual ecosystem, and research agenda.* arXiv preprint arXiv:2110.05352.

Liao, S. H., Widowati, R., & Hsieh, Y. C. (2021). Investigating online social media users' behaviors for social commerce recommendations. *Technology in Society*, 66(June), 101655. doi:10.1016/j.techsoc.2021.101655

Miah, M. R., Hossain, A., Shikder, R., Saha, T., & Neger, M. (2022). Evaluating the impact of social media on online shopping behavior during COVID-19 pandemic: A Bangladeshi consumers' perspectives. *Heliyon*, 8(9), e10600. doi:10.1016/j.heliyon.2022.e10600 PMID:36127921

Molinillo, S., Aguilar-Illescas, R., Anaya-Sánchez, R., & Liébana-Cabanillas, F. (2021). Social commerce website design, perceived value and loyalty behavior intentions: The moderating roles of gender, age and frequency of use. *Journal of Retailing and Consumer Services*, 63(February), 102404. Advance online publication. doi:10.1016/j.jretconser.2020.102404

Muñoz-Chávez, J. P., García-Contreras, R., & Valle-Cruz, D. (2022). Panic station: Consumer sentiment analysis of the evolving panic buying during the COVID-19 pandemic. Handbook of Research on Consumer Behavior Change and Data Analytics in the Socio-Digital Era, 51–73. doi:10.4018/978-1-6684-4168-8.ch003

Muñoz-Chávez, J. P., Hernández Rivera, A., & Bolaños-Rodríguez, E. (2021). Hacia la adopción del comercio social en micro y pequeñas empresas en México. *Economía Creativa*, (16), 189–211. doi:10.46840/ec.2021.16.07

Nicol, M. J. (2022). Uses, Applications, and Benefits of Virtual Reality Technologies in E-Business. In *Driving Transformative Change in E-Business Through Applied Intelligence and Emerging Technologies* (pp. 209–231). IGI Global. doi:10.4018/978-1-6684-5235-6.ch010

Özkaynar, K. (2022). Marketing strategies of banks in the period of metaverse, blockchain, and cryptocurrency in the context of consumer behavior theories. *Sivas Soft Bilisim Proje Danismanlik Egitim Sanayi ve Ticaret Limited Sirketi*. doi:10.52898/ijif.2022.1

Page, M. J., McKenzie, J. E., Bossuyt, P. M., Boutron, I., Hoffmann, T. C., Mulrow, C. D., Shamseer, L., Tetzlaff, J. M., Akl, E. A., Brennan, S. E., Chou, R., Glanville, J., Grimshaw, J. M., Hróbjartsson, A., Lalu, M. M., Li, T., Loder, E. W., Mayo-Wilson, E., McDonald, S., ... Moher, D. (2021). The PRISMA 2020 statement: An updated guideline for reporting systematic reviews. *Systematic Reviews*, 10(1), 1–11. doi:10.118613643-021-01626-4 PMID:33781348

Qenaj, M., & Beqiri, G. (2022). Marketing in in Hospitality Industry and Its Effect on Consumer Behavior in Industry Behavior in Kosovo and Its Effect on Consumer Social Media Marketing in Hospitality Behavior in Kosovo. *IFAC-PapersOnLine*, 55(39), 66–69. doi:10.1016/j.ifacol.2022.12.012

Riar, M., Xi, N., Korbel, J. J., Zarnekow, R., & Hamari, J. (2022). Using augmented reality for shopping: A framework for AR induced consumer behavior, literature review and future agenda. *Internet Research*. Advance online publication. doi:10.1108/INTR-08-2021-0611

Shen, B., Tan, W., Guo, J., Zhao, L., & Qin, P. (2021). How to promote user purchase in metaverse? A systematic literature review on consumer behavior research and virtual commerce application design. *Applied Sciences (Basel, Switzerland)*, *11*(23), 11087. doi:10.3390/app112311087

Sohn, J. W., & Kim, J. K. (2020). Factors that influence purchase intentions in social commerce. *Technology in Society*, *63*(August), 101365. doi:10.1016/j.techsoc.2020.101365

Song, Y., Li, G., Li, T., & Li, Y. (2021). A purchase decision support model considering consumer personalization about aspirations and risk attitudes. *Journal of Retailing and Consumer Services*, *63*(August), 102728. doi:10.1016/j.jretconser.2021.102728

Stephen, A. T. (2016). The role of digital and social media marketing in consumer behavior. *Current Opinion in Psychology*, *10*, 17–21. doi:10.1016/j.copsyc.2015.10.016

Stephenson, N. (1992). *Snow Crash*. Del Rey.

Tan, T. M., Makkonen, H., Kaur, P., & Salo, J. (2022). How do ethical consumers utilize sharing economy platforms as part of their sustainable resale behavior? The role of consumers' green consumption values. *Technological Forecasting and Social Change*, *176*, 121432. doi:10.1016/j.techfore.2021.121432

Valle-Cruz, D. (2019). Public value of e-government services through emerging technologies. *International Journal of Public Sector Management*, *32*(5), 530–545. Advance online publication. doi:10.1108/IJPSM-03-2018-0072

Valle-Cruz, D., Criado, J. I., Sandoval-Almazán, R., & Ruvalcaba-Gomez, E. A. (2020). Assessing the public policy-cycle framework in the age of artificial intelligence: From agenda-setting to policy evaluation. *Government Information Quarterly*, *37*(4), 101509. doi:10.1016/j.giq.2020.101509

Valle-Cruz, D., Fernandez-Cortez, V., & Gil-Garcia, J. R. (2022). From E-budgeting to smart budgeting: Exploring the potential of artificial intelligence in government decision-making for resource allocation. *Government Information Quarterly*, *39*(2), 101644. doi:10.1016/j.giq.2021.101644

Wright, M. (2008). Augmented duality: overlapping a metaverse with the real world. *Proceedings of the 2008 International Conference on Advances in Computer Entertainment Technology*, 263–266. 10.1145/1501750.1501812

Wu, Y. C. J., Shen, J. P., & Chang, C. L. (2015). Electronic service quality of Facebook social commerce and collaborative learning. *Computers in Human Behavior*, *51*, 1395–1402. doi:10.1016/j.chb.2014.10.001

Zallio, M., & John Clarkson, P. (2022). Designing the Metaverse: A study on Inclusion, Diversity, Equity, Accessibility and Safety for digital immersive environments. *Telematics and Informatics*, *75*(October), 101909. doi:10.1016/j.tele.2022.101909

Zhang, C., Zhao, M., Cai, M., & Xiao, Q. (2020). Multi-stage multi-attribute decision making method based on online reviews for hotel selection considering the aspirations with different development speeds. *Computers & Industrial Engineering*, *143*(143), 106421. doi:10.1016/j.cie.2020.106421

KEY TERMS AND DEFINITIONS

Consumer Behavior: Consumer behavior refers to the actions and decisions made by individuals and households when they acquire, use, and dispose of goods and services.

Emerging Technologies: Emerging technologies are new or rapidly evolving technologies that have the potential to change the way we live, work, and interact with each other.

Metaverse: The metaverse is a term used to describe a virtual world, or collection of virtual worlds, that users can interact with in a manner similar to the real world.

PRISMA: Preferred Reporting Items for Systematic Reviews and Meta-Analyses is a set of guidelines and a checklist for reporting systematic reviews and meta-analyses.

S-Commerce: S-commerce, also known as social commerce, refers to the use of social media platforms and networks to facilitate buying and selling goods and services.

Section 2
Understanding Metaverse and the Virtual World

Chapter 2
Extended Reality–Augmented Technologies in Healthcare

Kevin Sheng-Kai Ma

ⓘ https://orcid.org/0000-0002-9394-4144

Harvard T.H. Chan School of Public Health, Harvard University, USA

ABSTRACT

Extended reality (XR)-facilitated technologies, encompassing augmented reality (AR), virtual reality (VR), and mixed reality (MR), have been actively and increasingly involved in various fields and aspects of healthcare. Practical examples covered in this chapter include XR-facilitated surgical systems, rehabilitation modalities for mental illness, and education modules for clinicians and medical students. In the surgery field, technologies incorporating AR have been increasingly improving the safety and effectiveness of surgery. In mental health rehabilitation, users of head-mounted displays can enter a virtual relaxation world through predesigned VR scenarios. Moreover, AR- and MR-augmented technologies have been incorporated into knowledge platforms and guide simulator practice systems in medical education. Overall, XR-facilitated technologies have promoted personal self-care and patient-centered care, datafication of hospital information, novel disease treatments across various specialties, surgical workflow, and medical education.

1. INTRODUCTION

Virtual Reality (VR) is the use of computer analogy to generate a virtual world of three-dimensional space, providing users with analogy of vision and other senses, allowing users to feel as if they are in the real world, while being able to observe things in three-dimensional space instantly and without restrictions. When the user moves their position, the computer can immediately perform complex calculations and transmit the precise three-dimensional world image back to produce a sense of presence. The technology integrates the latest development achievements of computer graphics, computer simulation, artificial intelligence, sensing, display and network parallel processing and other technologies. It is a high-tech analog system assisted by computer technology.

DOI: 10.4018/978-1-6684-7029-9.ch002

Given the maturity of XR technology and its development in various fields, this chapter aims to discuss the application of XR in the medical field. The concept of VR first came from Stanley G. Weinbaum's science fiction "Pygmalion's Spectacles", which is the first to explore VR. A sci-fi work with short stories detailing virtual reality systems based on smell, touch, and holographic goggles.

In this chapter, introduction to XR technology and its applications were covered. The applications of XR for healthcare would also be emphasized. Lastly, limitations and future trends would be discussed. In the technical introduction, we will introduce the development process of VR/AR from laboratory to commercialization. In the field of application, we will focus on the discussion of XR for healthcare, which is divided into three parts for discussion, namely, education, mental illness and surgical systems. In the challenges and future perspectives section, we will divide into cases of advantages and disadvantages, including the limitations and future trends of XR for healthcare.

1.1 Development of VR in Lab

A general VR device contains at least a screen, a set of sensors and a set of computing elements, which are assembled in the device. The screen is used to display the simulated image, which is projected on the user's retina, the sensor is then used to sense the user's rotation angle, while the computing element collects the sensor's data to determine what the screen displays. In 1968, Ivan Sutherland and his student Bob Sproull created the first VR system. The head-mounted display (HMD) was so primitive and heavy that it had to be suspended from the ceiling. The device was called "The Sword of Damocles". Inventions such as these can only exist in the laboratory and cannot be used by the general public.

1.2 Consumer VR Devices Released

The first widespread commercial release of consumer headphones occurred in the 1990s. In 2007, Google launched Street View, showing a growing number of panoramas around the world, such as roads, buildings, and rural areas. In 2010, Palmer Luckey designed the first prototype of the Oculus Rift. This prototype is built on the shell of another virtual reality headset and can only do rotational tracking. However, its 90-degree field of view was unprecedented in the consumer market at the time (Johnson, 2014).

Google Cardboard is a VR HMD developed by Google in 2014 for use with smartphones. Named for its foldable cardboard helmet, the platform aims to stimulate interest and development in VR applications at a low cost (Perla et al., 2017; BRANSTETTER, 2016). According to the specifications published by Google, users can either make their own helmets using cheap and simple components, or buy pre-made helmets. To use the platform, the user must execute a Cardboard-compatible application on the mobile phone, place the mobile phone on the back of the helmet, and view the content through the lens (Pierce, 2016).

In 2016, HTC Vive was a VR HMD jointly developed by HTC and Valve Corporation. It's also part of Valve's SteamVR project. The HMD is designed to take advantage of "room-scale" technology that uses sensors to turn a room into a three-dimensional space, allowing users to navigate the virtual world naturally, move around, and use motion-tracked handheld controllers with the ability to vividly manipulate objects with sophisticated interaction, communication, and experience in these immersive environments (D'Orazio et al., 2016). Table 1 shows the mainstream VR specifications in the commercial market in more detail. From 2016 to 2020, regardless of the positional tracking method, resolution or FOV has gradually improved.

Table 1. Tethered VR

Name	Released Date	Positional Tracking	Display Type	Resolution (per eye)	Field of View (FOV)
Oculus Rift	2016-03-28	Outside-in	OLED	1080x1200	94°
HTC Vive	2016-04-05	Outside-in	OLED	1080x1200	110°
PlayStation VR	2016-10-01	Outside-in (using the PlayStation Camera)	OLED	960x1080	100°
Samsung Odyssey	2017-11-07	Inside-out markerless	AMOLED	1440x1600	110°
HTC Vive Pro	2018-04-05	Outside-in	AMOLED	1440x1600	110°
Valve Index	2019-05-01	Outside-in	LCD	1440x1600	120°
Oculus Rift S	2019-05-21	Inside-out	LCD	1280x1440	90°
HP Reverb G2	2020-11	Inside-out markerless	LCD	2160x2160	114°

1.3 Portable Device Released (Oculus Quest2)

In order to achieve high-efficiency visual presentation, previous VR devices required high-spec computers for assistance. In 2020, Oculus Quest 2 is a VR HMD launched by Oculus, a brand under Meta Platforms (formerly Facebook). It emphasizes its portable function, relies on optical tracking, installs cameras on the VR headset, allows the device to detect changes in the external environment by itself, and then calculates the spatial position of the camera through the SLAM algorithm. At present, the difficulty of this technology mainly lies in image recognition, which converts the data collected by the camera into spatial data through a visual algorithm. The more front cameras, the more accurate the accuracy. Of course, as the number of cameras increases, the algorithm will be more complex. Oculus Quest 2 can be regarded as the best inside-out tracking positioning headset on the market (Table 2). Oculus Quest 2 is equipped with 4 environmental cameras on the front. When the position of the device changes, it can be reversed by calculating the displacement. Get the motion coordinates of the device in space. Table 2 shows the development trend of VR after 2018, from tethered to standalone. Although the computing performance is not as good as tethered VR, it is favored by more users in terms of its portability and convenience.

Table 2. Standalone VR

Name	Released Date	Positional Tracking	Display Type	Resolution(per eye)	Field of View
HTC Vive Focus	2018-1	Inside-out	AMOLED	1440x1600	110°
Oculus Go	2018-05-01	No	LCD	1280x1440	100°
Oculus Quest 2	2020-10-13	Inside-out	LCD	1832x1920	89°

1.4 AR Glass ® Microsoft Hololens & Google glass

Augmented Reality (AR), also has a translation of the word. Technologies that can integrate and interact with real-world scenarios. This technique was proposed in 1990. With the improvement of the computing power of portable electronic products, the use of AR has become more and more extensive. AR is to superimpose information, images, objects, video, and other content in the real environment in a virtual way. Through the integration of virtual and real, the real environment is enriched, and the public can obtain more information that cannot be provided by physical objects, and even enhance the visual effect and interactive experience, which is the feeling that AR augmented reality hopes to bring to its users.

In 2013, Google released Google Glass, a wearable computer equipped with an optical head-mounted display (OHMD), with the goal of creating a universal computer for the mass consumer market. Google Glass displays various information in a hand-free, smartphone-like manner (Albanesius, 2012). The wearer communicates with internet services through natural language voice commands (Bilton, 2012).

In 2015, Microsoft released Microsoft HoloLens, a smart glasses product that is the main device used by Windows Holographic. It uses advanced sensors, a full-angle high-resolution 3D optical lens head-mounted display, and surround sound, allowing the user interface to communicate with the user through gaze, voice, and gestures in AR. The sensor used by HoloLens is an energy-efficient depth web camera with a 120°×120° field of view (Hempel, 2015). Other functions provided by the sensor include head tracking, video capture, and sound capture. In addition to the high-performance CPU and GPU, HoloLens features a holographic processor (HPU), a co-processor that integrates data from the various sensors described, and handles tasks such as spatial mapping, gesture recognition, and speech recognition.

1.5 Definition of VR / AR / MR

Milgram's reality-virtuality continuum proposed by Paul Milgram and Fumio Kishino in 1994 (Milgram et al., 1994). They take the real environment and the virtual environment as two ends of a continuous system, and the one in the middle is called "mixed reality". The one close to the real environment is augmented reality, and the one close to the virtual environment is augmented virtuality (Figure 1).

Figure 1. The reality-virtuality continuum. (Milgram et al., 1994)

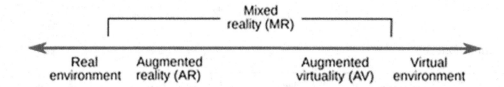

This figure illustrates that to the right side, the surrounding real environment will be completely blocked, presenting a 100% virtual scene to the user. To the left side, virtual objects will be superimposed on the real scene, so that the user can clearly distinguish the real scene from the virtual scene. The middle part is based on the AR device, and further realizes the real-time interaction between virtual objects and the real world.

2. XR FOR HEALTHCARE

2.1 Types of Augmented Reality Technology

The display types of augmented reality are divided into two types of display technologies: Video See-through based on image synthesis technology and Optical See-through based on optical principles. Image-transmissive display technology uses the camera lens to present "image overlay", superimposing digital information or images on real images or objects in the real world, and can be seen in the real state through related applications on mobile phones and tablets. The added images and information are display technologies that combine virtual images with real objects (Rolland et al., 2000)

Optical transmissive display technology is when people's eyes directly see virtual images in three-dimensional space through the lens, and through accurate tracking and precise positioning technology, they can capture or touch virtual graphics in space to generate feedback, which is consistent with synchronization and integration in the real world (Bimber et al., 2005)

. Augmented reality technology builds an augmented reality system based on three principles: the combination of virtual and reality, real-time interaction, and virtual three-dimensional objects, and three technologies of tracking, positioning, and display.

2.2 Application of XR in Different Fields

Applications using XR technology have been widely used on mobile devices such as mobile phones or tablets. As long as the display screen and camera on the device are used, the virtual three-dimensional objects can be displayed simultaneously with the real environment (Bimber et al., 2005); Augmented Reality adds elements of virtual objects or content to the real world, and interacts with users in a situation of use, which is widely used in medical, military, manufacturing, entertainment, robotics, education, marketing, and navigation including path planning, tourism, urban planning and other fields (Mallem, 2010).

In science fiction and interstellar movies, the video content from thousands of miles away is synchronously transmitted to the scene in front of the user, and the penetrating visual system such as the description of the mixed virtual and real life plot is used. The content provides a glimpse into the vision of future life presented by the ideas and technologies of augmented reality technology innovators (Bolluyt, 2015).

2.3 Application of XR in Healthcare

Bringing XR technology to healthcare, powering healthcare organizations to deliver healthcare more efficiently and reduce healthcare resources in clinician and patient consumption, thereby optimizing labor and resources management of medical institutions. Compared to traditional training strategies for healthcare providers, XR-facilitated modules can also reduce training costs. The introduction of AR or VR technology in healthcare has facilitated personal self-care and patient-centered care, digitization of hospital information, new therapies, disease, surgical, and medical education in a variety of specialties.

The next chapter will provide an overview of XR patterns in healthcare, including (1) history and evolving healthcare XR technology trends and (2) state-of-the-art hardware and software to support XR modalities in healthcare. Practical examples covered in the chapter include XR-assisted surgical systems, psychological rehabilitation models disease and education modules for clinicians and medical students.

3. XR IN IN HEALTHCARE (TABLE 3)

3.1 XR in Education System (Gerup et al., 2020)

XR serves as an educational module for clinicians and medical students, implementing different areas of study in various subjects for learners of all levels, especially in anatomy and anesthesiology. These studies are mainly demonstrated by integrating AR and MR technologies into knowledge platforms and simulator practice guide systems. There is claimed significant improvement in AR and MR in multiple studies. Most outcome measures are related to the learning process or part of the task. Some studies have shown that with the assistance of AR/MR, the operation time is significantly shortened. In recent years, virtual augmentation and guidance with AR and MR has been increasingly used for medical topics in healthcare education. However, it is unclear the quality of existing research and applications, including how much educational benefit the technology can achieve. In the following chapter, we will introduce the current research and state of AR and MR based application of health education in medical fields.

3.1.1 Product Description and Its Application (case1) (Aebersold et al., 2018)

The interactive anatomy-augmented virtual simulation training is a good example for nursing students to learn how to administer a nasogastric tube (NGT) on its patients. Sophomore and junior nursing students (N = 69) participated in this mixed methods study. They are randomly assigned either to regular training (control group) or iPad anatomy augmented virtual simulation training group (AR group). Participants' ability to demonstrate the ability to place NGT was assessed using a 17-item ability checklist. After the presentation, students completed a survey to obtain information on student training levels, prior experience with NGT placement, satisfaction with AR technology, and consideration for AR as a potential teaching tool for clinical skills training. The ability to correctly place NGT was statistically significant. There was a significant increase in the AR group compared to the control group (p = 0.011). 86% of participants in AR teams felt AR was better/much better than other procedural training programs they participated in. Only 5.9% of the control group had assessed control procedures much better than (p < .001).

3.1.2 Product Description and Its Application (case2) (Robinson et al., 2014)

In another case, Robinson III, Albert R., et al presents a MR subclavian central venous access (SCVA) simulator, that can help train medical staff. 65 participants participated in three different types of tests, the main test content was the time to complete the SCVA and the SCVA score, which was calculated by the simulator scoring algorithm. Mean SCVA scores improved by 24.5 (n = 65). Repeated measurements ANOVA showed a significant reduction in mean time (F = 31.94, P < 0.0001), number of attempts (F = 10.56, P < 0.0001) and score (F = 18.59, P < 0.0001). SCVA MR Simulator provides realistic representation of subclavian bone central venous access and new possibilities for medical teaching.

3.1.3 Product Description and Its Application (case3) (Wang et al., 2017)

Traditionally, remote areas in many countries have been constrained by a lack of medical resources. Due to a considerable degree of difficulty with the recruitment of medical professionals. Telemedicine, a method of delivering medical care over long distances using communication technology is an economical and efficient way to solve this problem. In Wang, Shiyao, et al.'s study, they used Microsoft HoloLens to enhance telemedicine training. The advantages of AR systems enable distance learners to perform complex medical procedures, such as Point of Care Ultrasound (PoCUS). This study uses HoloLens to capture a first-person view of a simulated rural emergency room (ER) via Mixed Reality Capture (MRC). Use Leap Motion to capture instructor's gestures and visualize them virtually in the HoloLens' AR space. Twelve medical interns were mentored as part of a pilot user who explored learning through simulated ultrasound in a trauma scenario. The study explored the utility of the system from the perspective of different observers and compared the findings with those of traditional multi-camera telemedicine. The results obtained provided valuable insights and support for the development of the telemedicine platform.

3.1.4 Product Description and Its Application (case4) (Rai et al., 2017)

The EyeSI AR BIO simulator is a new AR tool to compare the traditional teaching approach of binocular indirect ophthalmoscopy (BIO). 28 postgraduate year one (PGY1) ophthalmology residents joined this project. 15 people were randomly assigned to traditional teaching (group 1) and the others were assigned to AR simulator training (group 2). There are 3 tasks to be done on the simulator and the results are calculated by the simulator, measuring the total raw score, time, and performance. Group 2 residents showed higher overall scores and performance compared to Group 1 residents. Once Group 1 residents also completed AR BIO training, there was a significant improvement from their baseline scores. Table 3 shows some examples of XR in healthcare education systems, with an overview of research goals and results, and how they are displayed.

Table 3. Consolidation table of XR in education system

Study of a Quantitative Method	Study Aim	Summary of Results	Display System
Aebersold et al. (2018)	Preliminary assessment schedule a training request	Participants agree/strongly agree that AR is more appropriate to visual ($p<.01$) and useful as a tool for skills training($p<.015$)	AR
Robinson et al. (2014)	Evaluate the new MR parts task instructor	Meaningful to all involved, improve SCVA score ($p<.0001$) and time ($p<.0001$). The participants had a significant reduction without trying ($p<.0001$), no skin puncture ($p=.0007$), but no significant difference was found although the success rate increased ($p=.08$). Most 95.4% strong agree on future availability CVC.	MR
Wang et al. (2017)	Feasibility assessment and HMD-based user experience telemedicine guidance platform.	The AR group preferred AR's utility ($p=.065$) and reported lower cognitive load ($p=.28$), but the AR group did not differ significantly.	AR
Rai, Rai, Mavrikakis, & Lam (2017)	Validation and evaluation HMD-based efficacy application	Time spent doesn't matter different ($p=.11$), but The AR group significantly shows advantage Overall Score ($p=.02$) and Performance ($p=.006$).	AR

3.2 XR in Mental Illness (Table 4)

Depression is a common illness worldwide, with an estimated 3.8% of the population affected, including 5.0% among adults and 5.7% among adults older than 60 years. Approximately 280 million people in the world have depression (Tichenor et al., 2019). Poor mental health ranks as one of the costliest forms of sickness for workers and may sap billions of dollars from the country's income growth. Despite strong demand for methods to augment one's psychophysiological state and reduce stress, people are often unwilling to stop their work tasks, decrease productivity, or be forced to consistently maintain behavioral practices (Moraveji et al., 2012).

A challenge faced by many countries is to provide adequate human resources for delivery of essential mental health interventions. Therefore, human-computer interaction (HCI) researchers, designers and technologists started looking at computers not merely as devices to interact with, but as a support for positive changes in users' lives (Roo et al., 2017). Furthermore, in order to solve the above-mentioned problems. AI has been applied to learn, predict and act by observing people's physical and mental state, while also taking some design approaches to explore the content design space.

3.2.1 Product Description and Its Application (case1) (Roo et al., 2017)

Digital technologies are fully integrated into our daily lives, but the use of these technologies to improve the life satisfaction of people is still largely untapped. Mindfulness, the intentional and non-judgmental focus on present-moment behavior, has been shown to have an significant impact on a person's health and subjective well-being. The authors have designed a new tool for mindfulness practice. The tool takes the shape of an augmented sandbox, and by shaping the sand, the user creates a living miniature world that is projected back into the sand. The natural elements of the garden are interconnected real-time physiological measurements, such as breathing, that help users focus on the body. Additionally, users can experience dedicated meditation sessions in their gardens.

The Inner Garden is a mixed reality system that leverages tangible interactions, spatial augmented reality, virtual reality, and physiological computing to support a mindful experience. Preliminary measurements seem to suggest that the system fosters a state of calm and attentiveness to the user. As an engaging way to focus on developing body and breath awareness. It is the first introduction to mindfulness and ideally will guide users through training and developing a conscious perspective that will extend beyond the garden and be integrated into their daily lives. For these purposes, tangible interaction is a promising approach. It has this interesting property of not looking like "real" digital technology, being closer to our bodies and humanity and self.

3.2.2 Product Description and Its Application (case2) (Liang et al., 2018)

This article introduces BioFidget, a biofeedback system that integrates physiological sensing and display into a smart fidget spinner for breathing training. We propose a simple but novel hardware design that transforms a fidget spinner into a non-invasive heart rate variability (HRV) sensor, an electromechanical respiration sensor, and an information display. The combination of these features enables users to design tangible and interaction without wearing additional physiological sensors. The empirical results of this user study show that the breathing training method reduces stress and that the proposed system meets the requirements for perceived effectiveness and engagement in a real environment with 32 participants.

Fidget spinners are a popular toy that was all the rage in 2017. While fun to play, the common perception is that a fidget spinner is a useless machine that has a function but no immediate purpose. BioFidget integrates biofeedback, biosensing and breathing training mechanisms into a fidget spinner. The physical, physiological, and visual design details have been disclosed. Technical and preliminary user result tests also show that the proposed system and method provide an effective and fun experience, turning a popular toy into a useful stress management tool.

3.2.3 Product Description and Its Application (case3) (Amores et al., 2018)

This work introduces a novel wearable olfactory display that releases odors in time based on the wearer's physiological state. The device can release up to three scents and passively capture subtle chest vibrations associated with heartbeat and breathing through clothing. BioEssence is controlled via a custom smartphone app that allows the creation of physiological rules to trigger different scents (for example, releasing the scent of lavender when the heart rate is above 80 beats per minute). Wireless and lightweight, the device is designed to be used in everyday life, clipped to clothing around the breastbone or used as a necklace. We provide a description of the design and implementation of prototypes and potential use cases in the context of mental health.

This work describes BioEssence; a novel wearable olfactory display that passively tracks heart rate and respiratory rate through clothing. Using a smartphone app, users can customize physiological-based rules to automatically trigger odor release in their daily lives. Additionally, physiological data can be used to track the effects of olfactory interventions, which can help tune the user's closed-loop system over time. The authors' recent work will focus on practical deployment and opening the platform to researchers and hospitals. The authors hope that in the future, devices like the BioEssence could be used as a complementary approach to treating anxiety, stress or sleep disorders and improving pain tolerance. Table 4 shows some examples of XR application in mental illness, with an overview of research goals and results, and how they are displayed.

Table 4. Consolidation table of XR application in mental illness

Study of a Quantitative Method	Study Aim	Summary of Results	Display System
Roo et al.	Users can experience a dedicated meditation session in a device developed by the author.	A mixed reality system that utilizes tangible interactions, spatial augmented reality, virtual supported reality and physiological computing for a meditative experience.	VR, projector and sandbox
Liang et al.	Introducing BioFidget, a spinner for smart breathing training, an integrated biofeedback system for physiological sensing and display.	Technical and preliminary user results tests show that the proposed system and method provide effective and fun experience that turns popular toys into a useful stress management tool.	A spinner with physiological sensing
Amores et al.	This work BioEssence introduces a novel wearable olfactory device displays that provide the instant release of scents based on the wearer's physiological state	A novel wearable olfactory device that passively tracks heart rate and respiratory rate. Hopefully, in the future, devices like BioEssence can be used as a supplement to treat anxiety, stress or sleep	A wearable olfactory device with physiological sensing

3.3 XR in Surgical (Vávra et al., 2017) (Table 5)

The development of augmented reality devices allows physicians to incorporate visual data into diagnosis and treatment to improve work efficiency, safety, and cost. Numerous studies have shown that the performance of newly designed augmented reality systems is on par with conventional technologies. However, several issues need to be addressed before augmented reality can be applied to everyday practice.

The first medical imaging experiments were carried out in 1895, when W. C. Röntgen discovered the existence of X-rays. This symbolized the starting point for the use of medical imaging in clinical practice. The subsequent development of ultrasound (USG), computed tomography (CT), magnetic resonance imaging (MRI), and other imaging techniques allowed physicians to use two-dimensional (2D) medical images and three-dimensional (3D) stereoscopic image reconstruction in diagnosis to treat various health problems.

Augmented reality provides surgeons with computer-processed imaging data in real time through specialized hardware and software. AR projection can be achieved by using monitors, projectors, cameras, trackers, or other specialized equipment. The main principle of the basic AR system is shown in Figure 1. The most basic approach is to overlay CG images on real-world images captured by cameras and display the combination of these images on a computer, tablet, or video projector. If a video projector cannot be installed in the operating room, a portable video projection device has been designed. Contrary to common visualization techniques, the main advantage of AR is that the surgeon is not forced to look away from the surgical site.

3.3.1 Product Description and Its Application (case1) (Watanabe et al., 2016)

The invention of the trans-visible navigator system, for example, is a very important technique for brain surgery, previously surgeons needed to rotate the size of MRI/CT to match the surgical field. Additionally, they must frequently alternate between looking at the surgical field and the PC monitor to complete the procedure. Thus tablets are now used for visualization. The patient's head is captured by the tablet's rear camera. Three-dimensional images of intracranial structures were extracted from MRI/CT scans and superimposed on the head. When viewed from all directions of the head, intracranial structures are shown in different orientations. Entire operating room tracking is achieved using the VICON tracking system with 6 cameras.

6 patients who underwent tumor resection, they found that the system can be used to plan skin incisions as well as craniotomy and localization of superficial tumors. The main advantage of this system is that compared to traditional point-to-point navigation, contrastive volumetric navigation adds augmented reality images directly onto real surgical images, helping surgeons to intuitively integrate these two dimensions.

3.3.2 Product Description and Its Application (case2) (Lapeer et al., 2014)

In another case, the researcher found that the major source of error in traditional surgery was the tracking of surgical tools by the navigation system. Mainstream systems typically used optical or electromagnetic tracking techniques, which exhibited an accuracy of 1 mm. The purpose of this study is to introduce a lightweight high precision using a passive coordinate measurement arm for motion tracking of a rigid endoscope for AR. They conducted a series of laboratory experiments to compare the tracking performance of optical tracking devices, passive coordinate measurement arms, and hybrid devices.

The optical device shows overlap errors in the range of 1.5-3 mm. For precision measuring arms, 96% of the overlap error is less than 1 mm. Hybrid settings show overlap errors in the range of 0.8-1.5 mm. Experiments show that a high precision articulated measuring arm can be used as motion tracking device surgical instruments in AR surgical navigation.

3.3.3 Product Description and Its Application (case3) (Sugimoto et al., 2010)

Sugimoto's team applied the new concept of "image overlay surgery", combining VR and AR technology, to superimpose dynamic 3D images on the actual body surface of patients for evaluation of gastrointestinal, hepatobiliary and pancreatic surgery. They had 7 surgeries, including 3 cholecystectomy, 2 gastrectomy and 2 colectomy. The operating room used a Macintosh and a DICOM workstation OsiriX for image analysis. Raw data of preoperative patient information obtained by MDCT were reconstructed as volume renderings and projected onto the patient's body surface during surgery. For accurate registration, first set OsiriX to reproduce the patient's body surface, and fix the position coordinates of the umbilicus, left and right nipples, and groin regions as physiological markers on the body surface to reduce position errors.

The registration process is non-invasive and completed within 5 minutes. Image overlay navigation facilitates 3D anatomical understanding of surgical targets for gastrointestinal, hepatobiliary, and pancreatic anatomy. The surgeon can minimize motion and can utilize image assistance without interfering with forceps manipulation. Accidental organ damage can be avoided. Their non-invasive, label-free registration of surface physiological markers reduces logistics. Image overlay techniques are a useful tool that can provide more information when highlighting hidden structures.

3.3.4 Product Description and Its Application (case4) (Volonté et al., 2013)

One last case about surgery is the author's use of stereoscopic 3D rendered images in the da Vinci surgeon's console. The authors used an OsiriX DICOM workstation to acquire volume-rendered images from the tomography dataset. Using the OsiriX plugin, 3D rendered images can be displayed and volume rendered in the da Vinci Surgeon Console. Display these rendered images in the robot console. The upper part of the screen shows the real endoscopic surgery area, and the lower part shows the stereoscopic 3D rendering image. These are controlled by console-mounted joysticks and updated in real-time.

Five patients underwent robotic augmented reality augmentation procedures. Surgeons are able to switch between classic endoscopic views and combined virtual views. From the results, the addition of rendered images during the dissection stage was found to be helpful. Table 5 shows some examples of XR in surgery, with an overview of research goals and results, and how they are displayed.

Table 5. Consolidation table of XR in surgical

Study of a Quantitative Method	Study Aim	Summary of Results	Display System
Watanabe, Eiju, et al.	To overcome the difficulties of brain surgery, the authors developed an augmented reality-based tracking and navigation system for the whole operating room	It adds augmented reality images directly onto real surgical images, helping surgeons visually integrate both dimensions	AR
Lapeer, Rudy J., et al.	The purpose of this study is to incorporate a lightweight high-precision passive coordinate measurement arm into an augmented reality-based surgical navigation system to track rigid endoscopes.	Experiments show that the high-precision joint measurement arm is very suitable as a motion tracking device for surgical instruments in augmented reality surgical navigation.	AR
Sugimoto, Maki, et al.	The new concept of "image overlay surgery" integrating VR and AR technologies superimposes dynamic 3D images on the actual body surface of the patient as a reference for surgical navigation	Our research reduces the associated logistics. Image overlay techniques are useful tools to highlight hidden structures to provide more information.	VR and AR
Volonté, Francesco, et al.	Describes techniques for rendering images using integrated stereoscopic 3D in the da Vinci Surgeon's Console	Experience projecting 3D rendered images inside a surgical console. Surgeons are finding this mixed reality useful for intraoperative use. The technology will develop rapidly in the next few years.	MR

4. ADVANTAGES / DISADVANTAGES

4.1 Advantages

In terms of advantages, XR for healthcare provides a practice environment for different levels and types of medical learners, and has produced a variety of research and results, and proved the benefits of these tools for learning and practical application in clinical. Four cases are described below.

4.1.1 case 1: Implement Interdisciplinarity Across Different Domains for All Levels of Learner Types

The most frequently studied healthcare education subjects are anatomy and anesthesiology, ladder represented by four studies represented by central venous catheterization. Study participants were divided into 12 different categories: premed, medical, nursing and health science students, novices, residents, fellows, and established clinicians of different professions, technical staff, non-clinician, not specified participants and managers.

4.1.2 Case 2: Rich and Diverse Research and Outcome Focus

A total of six proof-of-concept, pilot or user studies attempted to introduce applications or assess initial effectiveness. Eight studies focused on evaluating the effectiveness of training by applying reinforcement structures. The remaining research focuses on application-based assessments of specific skills or procedures, ultimately linking performance to other outcomes such as cognitive load. Seventeen studies reported technical test results, mainly regarding the accuracy and precision of needle insertion (n = 11). The second most reported technical test results were related to procedure time (n = 9). Nineteen studies investigated learning experience and user acceptance primarily based on Likert scales. Other questionnaire-based outcomes were cognitive load, stress response, adverse health effects and ergonomics. Comprehensive Knowledge Test. Six studies provided questionnaire-based results. One study included an observational approach to determine learning behavior.

4.1.3 Case 3: Growing Evidence to Improve Learning

AR and MR have been found in research to significantly improve the associated learning process or part of the task. Four of the six studies that examined knowledge of anatomy reported significant improvements in learning. Six of the eleven studies found significant positive results, with training in needle insertion skills benefiting both students and sophisticated clinicians. In terms of time, three of the nine studies showed a significant reduction. Some studies used HMD. two studies used foot pedals to interact with the app. One study included switching between AR and MR modes. Eleven studies reported using external cameras and tracking devices. Two studies used projector-based applications, one to identify markers on the phantom, and one to project images directly onto the phantom without the use of tracking devices.

4.2.4 Case 4: Advanced Image in Fusion Using Augmented Reality

Augmented reality can show not only CG images, but also images that are not normally visible. Using this technique, surgeons can detect blood vessels beneath the surface of an organ or detect other tissue abnormalities. AR has been used to visualize areas in laparoscopic surgery that are obscured by surgical instruments, making the tools appear invisible. The system also helps to effectively reduce needle point error during suturing while achieving an average accuracy of 1.4mm and an acceptable latency of 62.4ms

4.2 Disadvantages

In terms of disadvantages, including poor ergonomics, disadvantages of transferability study designs, lack of evidence to improve learning, complex algorithms that require powerful computers and long-term wearing comfort. There are 5 cases described below.

4.2.1 Case 1: Reporting of Prototypes, Technological Limitations and Poor Ergonomics

Sixteen studies presented a prototype, usually as a preliminary. No feasibility study lacks adequate reporting on the educational impact of testing prototypes. Ten studies were conducted on six established applications. Head-mounted display-based applied research (n=8) addresses technical limitations associated with limited computing power, user field-of-view occlusion, and poor head-mounted ergonomics.

4.2.2 Case 2: Disadvantages of Transferability Study Designs

Four studies were only designed as single-group user studies, making it difficult to draw strong conclusions. Twenty-two studies used cohort designs or comparisons, and two studies did not compare AR or

MR with another medium, such as lectures, books, videos, virtual reality, mobile devices, conventional training platforms, and telemedicine suites. Two studies compared media from mobile devices after delivering AR content to one of the groups.

A crossover design was used in both groups of studies.

4.2.3 Case 3: Lacking Evidence for Improving Learning

Eight studies reported descriptive frequency of self-reported assessments and measurements without any statistical analysis important. Seven studies claim to show that technology has no significant impact on improvement. Two studies comparing AR with the same media from mobile devices found no significant differences in any outcome measure. Only one study predicted a significant outcome in the AR group, namely longer time to complete ultrasonography. Potential conflicting factors were addressed in terms of visual misunderstandings, media or technology enthusiasm, motivation, negation of patient discomfort related to patient safety, and lack of performance transfer from simulation to clinical settings.

4.2.4 Case 4: Complex Algorithms Requiring Powerful Computers

All reconstructed images need to be prepared in advance using complex algorithms that require powerful computers. While AR can speed up the surgical procedure, the need to prepare the entire system and perform the required registration and measurements often increases the time required to complete the procedure, the amount of time depending on the type of procedure and the complexity of the augmented reality system. The introduction of a fully automated system will eliminate this problem and reduce the overall time required to complete.

4.2.5 Case 5: Long-Term Wear Comfort

These need to be addressed in the future to better accommodate ergonomics and allow for extended periods of continuous use. Virtual and augmented reality projections in head-mounted displays are known to produce simulator sickness, which in the worst case can lead to nausea, headache, dizziness, or vomiting. The exact reason behind simulator disease is unknown; however, differences between visual, proprioceptive, and vestibular input may be the case.

5. FUTURE TREND

5.1 The Rise of the Metaverse

The future direction of XR is that the metaverse is on the rise. Newly released Meta Quest Pro in 2022, powered by breakthrough high-resolution mixed reality, users can easily interact with virtual worlds while preserving physical spaces in high-definition color. A sleek look with a balanced design creates a more comfortable experience, extending the time for working, creating and collaborating in VR. With the rich and varied VR immersive experience, the virtual world is no longer a static space. Even better, even if you wear glasses, it will not detract from the great immersion experience. Meta Quest Pro has a stereoscopic mixed reality pass-through mode that combines the fields of view of multiple sensors to create a natural 3D world scene. This results in a better quality and more comfortable experience compared to monoscopic see-through solutions, as well as improved depth perception and reduced visual distortion for close-up and walking mixed reality scenarios. Meta Quest Pro will spur more growth in the Metaverse.

5.2 The Improvement of AI Technology

In addition to new product launches, XR and AI will become more closely intertwined. XR applications must constantly gather information about the user's surroundings through multiple sensors. Traditionally, we had to use complex algorithms to make sense of sensor data from the environment. AI can simplify this process and make it more accurate than models made entirely by humans.

6. CONCLUSION

In this chapter, we first introduced the development and history of XR, and then saw its function in healthcare. Taking education, psychotherapy, and surgery as examples, we introduced many related cases. With the advancement of science and technology, technological products have begun to intervene in our lives, of course, including the medical field, being more convenient, with improved efficiency and getting better results for its users. However, in order to realize the full potential and cost-effectiveness of augmented reality, further progress is required.

The future development trends will provide brand-new changes in the field of XR for healthcare or other application fields. The transformation of XR is the current research trend. We need to keep abreast of the latest technological developments to keep up with this rapid development trend.

REFERENCES

Aebersold, M., Voepel-Lewis, T., Cherara, L., Weber, M., Khouri, C., Levine, R., & Tait, A. R. (2018). Interactive anatomy-augmented virtual simulation training. *Clinical Simulation in Nursing, 15*, 34–41. doi: 10.1016/j.ecns.2017.09.008

Albanesius, C. (2012). Google 'project glass' replaces the smartphone with glasses. *PC Mag, 4*.

Amores, J., Hernandez, J., Dementyev, A., Wang, X., & Maes, P. (2018, July). Bioessence: a wearable olfactory display that monitors cardio-respiratory information to support mental wellbeing. In *2018 40th Annual International Conference of the IEEE Engineering in Medicine and Biology Society (EMBC)* (pp. 5131-5134). IEEE.

Bilton, N. (2012). Behind the Google Goggles, virtual reality. *New York Times*, 22.

Bimber, O., & Raskar, R. (2005). *Spatial augmented reality: merging real and virtual worlds*. CRC press.

Bolluyt, J. (2015). *15 Ideas for Augmented Reality From Google-Backed Startup*. The Cheat Sheet.

Branstetter, B. (2016). *Cardboard is everything Google Glass never was*. http://kernelmag. dailydot. com/issue-secti staff-editorials/13490/google-cardboard-review-plus

D'Orazio, D., & Savov, V. (2015). Valve's VR Headset is Called the Vive and it's Made by HTC. *The Verge*.

Gerup, J., Soerensen, C. B., & Dieckmann, P. (2020). Augmented reality and mixed reality for healthcare education beyond surgery: An integrative review. *International Journal of Medical Education*, *11*, 1. doi: 10.5116/ijme.5e01.eb1a

Hempel, J. (2015). Project hololens: Our exclusive hands-on with Microsoft's holographic goggles. *Wired*. Wired. com. Conde Nast Digital, 21.

Johnson, B. (2014). *How the oculus rift works*. Academic Press.

Lapeer, R. J., Jeffrey, S. J., Dao, J. T., García, G. G., Chen, M., Shickell, S. M., ... Philpott, C. M. (2014). Using a passive coordinate measurement arm for motion tracking of a rigid endoscope for augmented-reality image-guided surgery. *International Journal of Medical Robotics and Computer Assisted Surgery*, *10*(1), 65–77. doi: 10.1002/rcs.1513

Liang, R. H., Yu, B., Xue, M., Hu, J., & Feijs, L. M. (2018, April). BioFidget: Biofeedback for respiration training using an augmented fidget spinner. In *Proceedings of the 2018 CHI conference on human factors in computing systems* (pp. 1-12). ACM.

Mallem, M. (2010, July). Augmented Reality: Issues, trends and challenges. In *2010 2nd International Conference on Image Processing Theory, Tools and Applications* (pp. 8-8). IEEE.

Milgram, P., & Kishino, F. (1994). A taxonomy of mixed reality visual displays. *IEICE Transactions on Information and Systems*, *77*(12), 1321–1329.

Moraveji, N., Hagiwara, T., & Adiseshan, A. (2012). BreathTray: Influencing self-regulation without cognitive deficit. *Extended Abstracts of ACM CHI'12*.

Perla, R., & Hebbalaguppe, R. (2017). *Google cardboard dates augmented reality: Issues, challenges and future opportunities*. arXiv preprint arXiv:1706.03851

Pierce, D. (2016). Inside Google's plan to make VR amazing for absolutely, positively everyone. *Wired Magazine*.

Rai, A. S., Rai, A. S., Mavrikakis, E., & Lam, W. C. (2017). Teaching binocular indirect ophthalmoscopy to novice residents using an augmented reality simulator. *Canadian Journal of Ophthalmology*, *52*(5), 430–434. doi: 10.1016/j.jcjo.2017.02.015

Robinson, A. R. III, Gravenstein, N., Cooper, L. A., Lizdas, D., Luria, I., & Lampotang, S. (2014). A mixed-reality part-task trainer for subclavian venous access. *Simulation in Healthcare*, *9*(1), 56–64. doi: 10.1097/SIH.0b013e31829b3fb3

Rolland, J. P., & Fuchs, H. (2000). Optical versus video see-through head-mounted displays in medical visualization. *Presence*, *9*(3), 287–309. doi:10.1162/105474600566808

Roo, J. S., Gervais, R., Frey, J., & Hachet, M. (2017, May). Inner garden: Connecting inner states to a mixed reality sandbox for mindfulness. In *Proceedings of the 2017 CHI conference on human factors in computing systems* (pp. 1459-1470). ACM.

Sugimoto, M., Yasuda, H., Koda, K., Suzuki, M., Yamazaki, M., Tezuka, T., ... Azuma, T. (2010). Image overlay navigation by markerless surface registration in gastrointestinal, hepatobiliary and pancreatic surgery. *Journal of Hepato-Biliary-Pancreatic Sciences, 17*(5), 629–636. doi: 10.1007/s00534-009-0199-y

Tichenor, M., & Sridhar, D. (2019). Metric partnerships: Global burden of disease estimates within the World Bank, the World Health Organisation and the Institute for Health Metrics and Evaluation. *Wellcome Open Research*, 4. doi: 10.12688/wellcomeopenres.15011.2

Vávra, P., Roman, J., Zonča, P., Ihnát, P., Němec, M., Kumar, J., ... El-Gendi, A. (2017). Recent development of augmented reality in surgery: A review. *Journal of Healthcare Engineering, 2017*, 4574172. doi: 10.1155/2017/4574172

Volonté, F., Buchs, N. C., Pugin, F., Spaltenstein, J., Schiltz, B., Jung, M., ... Morel, P. (2013). Augmented reality to the rescue of the minimally invasive surgeon. The usefulness of the interposition of stereoscopic images in the Da Vinci™ robotic console. *International Journal of Medical Robotics and Computer Assisted Surgery, 9*(3), e34–e38. doi: 10.1002/rcs.1471

Wang, S., Parsons, M., Stone-McLean, J., Rogers, P., Boyd, S., Hoover, K., ... Smith, A. (2017). Augmented reality as a telemedicine platform for remote procedural training. *Sensors (Basel), 17*(10), 2294. doi:10.339017102294

Watanabe, E., Satoh, M., Konno, T., Hirai, M., & Yamaguchi, T. (2016). The trans-visible navigator: A see-through neuronavigation system using augmented reality. *World Neurosurgery, 87*, 399–405. doi:10.1016/j.wneu.2015.11.084

Chapter 3
A Concise Review on the Concept of Metaverse:
Types, History, Features, and Technological Perspectives

David Roland Andembubtob

School of Computer Sciences, Universiti Sains Malaysia, Malaysia

Pantea Keikhosrokiani

iD https://orcid.org/0000-0003-4705-2732

School of Computer Sciences, Universiti Sains Malaysia, Malaysia

Nasuha Lee Abdullah

School of Computer Sciences, Universiti Sains Malaysia, Malaysia

ABSTRACT

The advent of metaverse has generated a lot of enthusiasm and opened several opportunities for innovation, revolution, and creative thinking among users, customers, and organisations. The seamless operation of users enabled by the fusion of the physical and digital worlds presents both significant potential and problems for every sector of the actual, imaginable, and even perceived industries. The metaverse is undoubtedly developing as a disruptive future trend that will alter the look of interaction, locations, and organisations, although still in its infancy. For this reason, this chapter aims to provide a concise review on the concept of metaverse, which includes discussions on its types, history, features, and technological perspectives. This chapter can assist the system developers in various industries.

INTRODUCTION

The "metaverse" is described as a persistent virtual space where users can enjoy various entertaining, social, educative, economic, and leisure activities as an extension of their offline life (Oh et al., 2023). This showed that individuals lives whether 'online' or 'offline' would be inseparable and make little

DOI: 10.4018/978-1-6684-7029-9.ch003

or no difference. Metaverse has significant characteristics that makes it unique among other tools in an educational setting including "Corporeity, Interactivity, and Persistence" (Akour et al., 2022).

As the scope of research widens and deepens, the understanding of what the metaverse encompasses continues to evolve and enlarges, so different and diverse perspective and spheres are revealed. The metaverse is a shared digital, virtual space that allows individuals to socialize and interact with each other in the virtual environment. Users dwell in such a space as concrete virtual images called avatars, just like existing in a world parallel to the real world (Braud et al., 2021). In support of this, Wiederhold, (2022) stated that The Wall Street Journal defines the metaverse as "a virtual environment where our digital avatars and those of other people from across the world join together to learn, go to school, work, shop, pursue hobbies, enjoy social gatherings, and do more.

Since existing studies lacks in proper details about metaverse, this chapter aims to conduct a concise review on the concept of metaverse from types, history, features, and technological perspectives. The remaining of this chapter includes definition and history of metaverse. Furthermore, the features, area of applications, and technological aspects of metaverse are discussed. Finally, various platforms of metaverse and difference between simulation, virtual reality and metaverse are discussed and the study is wrapped up with the concluding remarks.

DEFINITIONS OF METAVERSE

To further facilitate the digital transformation of every part of our physical life, the word "metaverse" was developed. The idea of an immersive Internet as a sizable, interconnected, permanent, and shared environment lies at the core of the metaverse. The digital "big bang" of our cyberspace is not far off, despite the metaverse being futuristic and being powered by cutting-edge technology like Extended Reality, Artificial Intelligence, and 5G (Braud et al., 2021). Zhao et al., (2022) agreeing with Braud et al., (2021) that the term "metaverse" refers to a 3D virtual cyberspace that combines the real and virtual worlds. This is made possible by the fusion of Web technologies, Extended Reality (XR), and the Internet. They persisted in considering the metaverse to be a visual realm where the physical and virtual worlds coexist peacefully. In addition, the Metaverse is the convergence of 1) virtually (digital) enhanced physical reality and 2) physically persistent virtual (digital) space. It is a synthesis of both, while permitting users to experience it as either.

Park & Kim, (2022) classified the definitions of the metaverse into four types: (1) environment, (2) interface, (3) interaction, and (4) social value (Cheung et al., 2022). As depicted in Figure 1 the taxonomy or categorization of the metaverse has as its basic components as environment, interface, interaction, and security.

Others have imagined the metaverse from the perspective of the users, where the metaverse can be seen as a cutting-edge internet application, a digital social form, and a virtual world that uses novel, cutting-edge technologies to create an exciting virtual living environment that can be shaped and edited by users and integrates a vibrant social, economic, and identity system (Wang et al., 2021). The creation of digital, virtual, and immersive settings, such as the metaverse, the omniverse, or the multiverse, has lately developed due to the importance of creating, sustaining, and developing meaningful human social relationships and interactions (Zallio & Clarkson, 2022).

Figure 1. Basic components of the metaverse (Park & Kim, (2022)

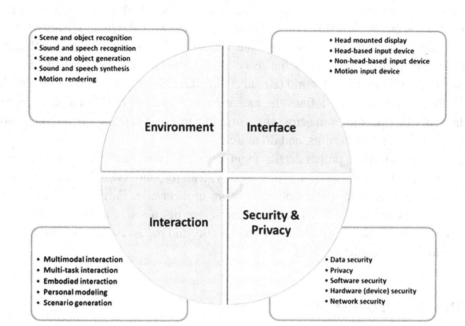

The definition of the Metaverse varies and is diverse, depending on point of view and purpose of the author. Conversely, the widely discussed metaverse is said to be a virtual world that is parallel and like the real world: it is a digital space for interacting with other users and objects (Dwivedi, Hughes, Baabdullah, et al., 2022). One of the current definitions of the metaverse includes a collection of digital spaces, including interconnected and related immersive 3D experiences, that allow users to interact with avatars of people who are not physically present in order to connect, create, socialise, work, learn, and explore scenarios or 3D immersive spaces (Zallio & Clarkson, 2022).

In a metaverse roadmap (taken from Metaverse Roadmap Summit, 2006) categorizes the metaverse into 4 types: (1) augmented reality, (2) lifelogging, (3) mirror world, and (4) virtual reality, as illustrated in Figure 2.

The four categories of the Metaverse (together with their potentials and constraints) as suggested by the Roadmap Summit were defined in an educational way by Kye et al., (2021) as shown in Figure 2. The two axes, Augmentation against Simulation (A vs. S) and External versus Intimate, are used to describe the four categories on the map (E vs I). By projecting digital data onto the perceived real world, augmentation technology enhances the current environment with a new visual function. The Simulation technology, on the other hand, builds and modifies representations of the current actual environment and allows for virtual interactions and experiences. The technology for the External world takes care of the users' external surroundings by providing details about them and how to regulate them. By creating inner worlds for avatars and digital profiles where users have an identity in the digital environment, the intimate world, in contrast, utilises technology that has to do with the identity and behaviour of people or things. The fusion of these two axes results in 4 distinct forms of the Metaverse, to put it simply.

Augmented Reality Metaverse (e.g., Pokémon Go) features building smart environments that are based on location networks. Lifelogging Metaverse (e.g., Facebook or Instagram) features recording daily information about individuals or objects using AR technology. In Mirror Worlds' Metaverse, the technology builds digital models and maps using GPS technology (such as Google Earth or Google Maps). Lastly, Virtual Worlds' Metaverse technology is deals with avatars interacting and reflecting different personas in a virtual environment.

Figure 2. Types of metaverse (Kye et al., 2021)

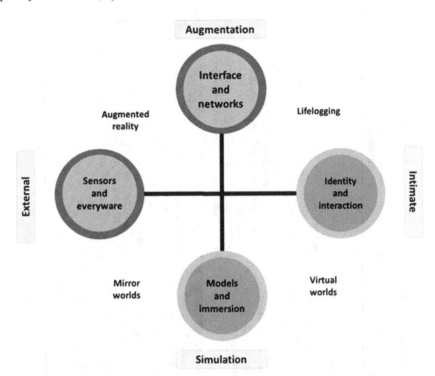

Table 1 outlines the major differences between the various metaverses.

Meta went on to define the metaverse as "a set of digital spaces where you can build and explore with other people who are not in the very same physical space as you." (Meta, 2021). A precise definition of the metaverse is difficult to explain because of its depths, but the majority of technology experts concur, that the metaverse is a gigantic network where individuals by their avatars can interact and interrelate socially and professionally, invest in currency and financial trade, work, take classes and travel in 3-D virtual reality (Folger, 2022).

Table 1. Augmented, Lifelogging, Mirror worlds and Virtual worlds

Augmented Reality	Lifelogging	Mirror worlds	Virtual worlds
• Applications such as Instagram or Tik Tok, Spark AR, Pokemon Go, Pop up 3D emails, Holograms, Google glass, MS Hololens • Use in marketing, tourism, entertainment, design, education, navigation etc. • It is simple to include virtual features into the real-time display modes that our smartphones and digital tablets provide. • Just a small number of programmes let users create this material. • Contextuality, users experience (real world + virtual elements) simultaneously. • Interactivity, interact with AR by manipulation of both real objects and virtual properties, novel possibilities for interaction. • Spatiality, links virtual objects to specific points in space and offers more realistic three-dimensionality of AR visualizations. (Krüger et al., 2019; Prieto et al., 2022)	• Applications such as Exist.io and Twitch apps can monitor it live. • A technology that uses digital sensors to multimodally capture, store, and share the digital record of a person's personal experiences. • An automated biography • Lifelogging is a concept based on wearable sensors and gadgets that tracks everyday activities to better understand human physical condition and behaviour. • An electrocardiogram and electroencephalogram, recorded by wearable devices, gives patient-generated health data which is crucial for diagnosis and treatment for clinicians to engage patients more rapidly and actively. • its use in conjunction with the Internet of Things (IoT) technology, which enables wireless, linked, and fast health data and information to deliver precise medical treatment (Prieto et al., 2022; Wu & Ho, 2022; Kumari et al., 2017; Sila-Nowicka & Thakuriah, 2019; Jung et al., 2019)	• Applications - MS Virtual Earth, Google Earth, Wikipedia, Google Arts & Culture project, Virtual agents / assistants such as Siri and Alexa, Deloitte in real estate and PropTech arena, Autonomous Vehicle Simulation Software, Taking augmented reality into the real world, Spatial Search and Spatial Analytics • The depiction of the real world in digital form. • A simulation of the outside world that gives accurate representations of human surroundings and real-world buildings in virtual reality (VR). • Models or representations of the real world virtualized in order to make content accessible. • Mirrorworld is a 1-to-1 map of almost unimaginable scope, • AI will give your position, time and assess the place, known as SLAM —simultaneous localization and mapping. (Prieto et al., 2022) (Ovunc et al., 2021)	• Software tools for building 3D worlds, including Roblox and Minecraft; video games like Fortnite. • Virtual Worlds are the most prevalent metaverse environment; some of them even let users create and engage in made-up worlds and scenarios. • High quality display Blocks off real world environment. Fully immersive senses controlled by system. Use in medical training, education, entertainmentCyber-sickness, accidents, depersonalization (Prieto et al., 2022)

HISTORY

The Rise of the Metaverse

One may argue that the science fiction writers' and authors' views laid the groundwork for the metaverse in recent history. Table 2 lists the historical occurrences that contributed to the creation of the metaverse (Bale et al., 2022). The word "metaverse" first occurs in Neal Stephenson's science fiction story Snow Crash from 1992, when it is described as a virtual city that encircles a circular plane in all its clearness. Just over ten years later, in 2003, the business Linden Lab from San Francisco created Second Life, a digital, virtual world where users could create avatars and immerse themselves in a second digital existence using a computer with an internet connection.

The metaverse and its associated applications have also flourished in the gaming sector. Several businesses, like ActiveWorlds Inc., Roblox Corp., Epic Games Inc., and many more, have created completely digitalized virtual worlds where users and players may create avatars and engage in intense multiplayer gaming (Zallio & Clarkson, 2022). The metaverse has just evolved into a tool that gives users access to new personified sensory and cognitive situations for work, entertainment, social interaction, and potentially to rethink how people will live in the real world. Indeed, the "metaverse" is a dynamic phenomenon that bears potentials as well as enormous obstacles for the near future, but it is still difficult to locate an accepted description of it (Zallio & Clarkson, 2022).

As a "meta" concept that comprises a wide range of ever-growing enormous virtual-social platforms, the term metaverse is now the trendiest buzzword in the social media industry and the academia (Oh et al., 2023). The expression 'metaverse' was first used in a science fiction novel titled 'Snow Crash' (Sparkes, 2021) to depict an immersive 3D virtual environment. The creation of metaverse was meant to facilitate the day-to-day human communication and social interaction over the Internet (Akour et al., 2022). Despite its fast-growing popularity, it lacks clarity regarding its definition and boundary. It comprises of the prefix "meta," meaning "beyond" and the stem "verse" from the word "universe." It is an infinite virtual space that exists as a computer-generated extension of the physical world (Oh et al., 2023).

In the 90's, and especially in a number of American universities, with the appearance of virtual reality, virtual environments and their manipulation began to be applied, achieving important advancements that have led to enhancement in research through modification in the perception of the modelling, subject, communication processes and the development of 3D digital classrooms. These developments have led to the metaverse, a vibrant environment where humans communicate and interact socially as avatars, and particularly its application in education also, in the fields of tele-education, educational research, learning environments, entertainment, etc (Contreras et al., 2022).

The metaverse changes from concept to reality, and the 'realities of augmentation', 'virtual' and 'mixed' are an indispensable intermediate stage. To a definite extent, virtual environments are the sub technical foundation of the metaverse (Braud et al., 2021). Teng et al., (2022) outlaid that the metaverse is a three-dimensional based virtual environment where users can interact with digital objects, virtual space and people via socially suitable and configurable digital bodies called avatars. Basically, it utilizes multisensory immersive technology known as extended reality (XR), which includes augmented reality (AR), virtual reality (VR), and mixed reality (MR). These recent technologies enable multimodal metaverse interactions with the virtual world and digital avatars, thus allaying the aforesaid problems of 2D e-learning platforms. The idea of the metaverse has been widely debated since 2021. It describes using virtual reality (VR) and augmented reality (AR) glasses to access the internet, and it is considered to be the next-generation mobile computing platform that will be widely utilised in the future (Clark, 2021). The metaverse is a kind of made-up universe with expansive immersive digital places that enables a more virtual and participatory learning environment. The metaverse is a synchronous communication extension that allows a large number of individuals to share a variety of experiences virtually (Akour et al., 2022).

Surely, immersive technologies will shape the new innovative form of immersive internet. Virtual reality will enable users to have a more realistic, pragmatic and specific experience in the networked virtual world, making the digital world operation more akin to the real world. For now, AR/MR can transform the physical world. Consequently, the future of our physical world is more intimately integrated with the metaverse (Braud et al., 2021). Bojic, (2022) outlines several claims made about the metaverse. These are (a) richer ways of self-expression, (b) enhanced immersion, (c) healthier socializing, (d) symmetric relation of physical and virtual spaces, (e) autonomous markets (via NFTs), (f) more efficient user interfaces and (g) soaring need for regulation and governance. The metaverse has the ability to transmit more realism and presence, making it a new and viable route for addressing the social needs of young people left unmet by the decline in the frequency of social encounters and public events (Oh et al., 2023).

Table 2. Historical events that led to the development of the metaverse (Bale et al., 2022)

S/N	Year	Event
1.	1989	Tim Berners-Lee creates the World Wide Web (www).
2.	1992	Neal Stephenson, introduces a science fictional concept of the metaverse to describe a 3-D virtual world
3.	2003	Phillip Rosedale designs the first online virtual world with his team at Liden Lab.
4.	2009	The first successful cryptocurrency and blockchain platform - Bitcoin, is invented
5.	2012	NFTs or non-fungible tokens are introduced which uniquely identify any digital asset over a blockchain network
6.	2014	Facebook acquires virtual reality hardware and platform Oculus
7.	2015	The first iteration of Decentraland's online virtual world was created.
8.	2016	Pokémon Go, the first game to use a virtual environment and augmented reality took the world by storm.
9.	2017	Fortnite, a multiplayer game and social hub is launched. It introduced virtual concerts and tours.
10.	2020	COVID pandemic hits the world and enforces everyone to explore the virtual sphere of interaction and communication.
11.	2021	Microsoft unveils Mesh as an addition to teams to make collaboration fun and personal.
12.	2021	Mark Zuckerberg reveals that Facebook's parent company would adopt the name "Meta" and unveils the plans for the metaverse

The most recent invention, called Metaverse, combines several cutting-edge technologies to provide a sophisticated tool, including blockchain, telecommunications, artificial intelligence, Internet of Things, and augmented reality and virtual reality. Modern technology known as metaverses has much to offer humanity (Bale et al., 2022).

FEATURES

By an exact definition of the metaverse, many applications today are AR or VR rather than the metaverse. In a different way, the quality of these applications determined the direction and potential of the metaverse. Obviously, the following characteristics (shared, durable, and decentralised) must be taken into account in order to implement optimal metaverse applications. A critical examination of the user behaviours and interfaces in the contexts of augmented reality (AR), lifelogging, mirror worlds, and virtual worlds allows us to formulate the following list of quantifiable qualitative criteria for these metaverses.

- **Open designs:** Metaverse design ought to be as open as possible. Young users desire to be free to roam around and interact whenever feasible; they should be included in the planning and modelling of virtual places.
- **Blended contents:** The digitally created material found in metaverses must integrate actual and virtual items in the physical world and show them interacting with one another through layers of metadata and digitally generated content.
- **Creative interfaces:** Metaverse user interfaces should encourage artistic expression, the use of several languages, the application of readily replicable aesthetic principles, and the employment of algorithms. Trends may be spread, and preferences for use patterns might be identified.
- **Massive interactions:** There needs to be a lot of interaction in metaverses. Collaboration and interoperability of environments are insufficient if access is restricted. Moreover, some groups should have access to safety and privacy.
- **Live experiences:** Individual experiences must be broadcast and monitored as live performances in these settings, and the experiences in metaverses must occur in real time. Persistence creates a story that is ongoing, which encourages immersion.
- **Digital identities:** Metaverses ought to support the usage of several, distinct digital identities. The usage of skins and avatars should make it easier to retain privacy, but they shouldn't be used to hide illegal activity. The development of a digital identity has to follow established protocols like the blockchain (Prieto et al., 2022).

Figure 3 shows the ten principles for designing a good metaverse as a manifesto for inclusion, diversity, equity, accessibility, and safety in the metaverse.

Even metaverse fans do not anticipate that this fully immersive vision will be fully fulfilled any time soon because there are currently many barriers in the path. Of course, there must be considerable improvements made to current computer systems and technology if the metaverse is to faithfully represent the real world. While some of the key technologies are already in place, others, including cloud computing, 5G, rapid wireless communications, and artificial intelligence (AI), have just recently reached a state of substantial development. Although if the necessary technology is already available, many of these novel and advanced technologies need to become more accessible, generally cheap, and portable in order for the metaverse to reach its full potential. Beyond system specifics, there are also significant concerns regarding privacy and security that need to be clearly addressed (Wiederhold, 2022).

Figure 3. The ten principles for designing a good metaverse. A Manifesto for Inclusion, Diversity, Equity, Accessibility and Safety in the metaverse (Zallio & Clarkson, 2022)

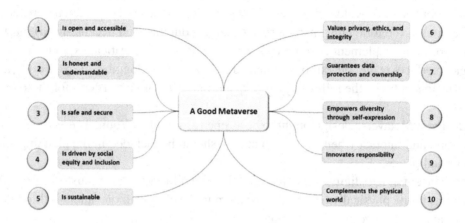

AREAS OF METAVERSE APPLICATION

With the continued advancement of digital technology, people may eventually complete their digital transition from the physical realm to the Metaverse. The Metaverse's scope of applicability will grow with further development, and eventually it may even be incorporated into every part of people's life (Sun et al., 2022). Weinberger, (2022) proposed the following definition of the metaverse after an extensive study of literature in the area, stating: "The Metaverse is an interconnected web of ubiquitous virtual worlds partly overlapping with and enhancing the physical world. These virtual worlds enable users represented by avatars to connect and interact with each other, to experience and consume user-generated content in an immersive, scalable, synchronous, and persistent environment. An economic system provides incentives for contributing to the Metaverse." This underlines the various fields where the metaverse can be effectively deployed as shown in Figure 4.

There are many areas of metaverse application and implementation. Most emerging technologies are ubiquitous in our present day. The development and use of these technologies tend to transcend fields, sectors, geographical regions, physical presence and have moved into the extended and 'unreal' existing virtual worlds. Researchers have related the application of the metaverse based on several perspectives. Park and Kim related that the applications of the metaverse are categorized as "metaverse as a tool" and "metaverse as a target," "Metaverse as a tool" means that the metaverse is used to solve tasks and problems in the real world. While "Metaverse as a target" specifies how the metaverse itself can carry out actions such as developing the metaverse and making profits (Cheung et al., 2022).

Recently, many applications of the metaverse are shown such as in digital games, showcase some new products in advertising, healthcare delivery, education, medical training, simulation of aircraft and spaceflight or to provide virtual experiences and using AR or VR for scientific experimentation, military training and manufacturing training as well as language translation learning (Díaz et al., 2020; Y. Hwang, 2022).

Figure 4. Applications of the metaverse (Sun et al., 2022)

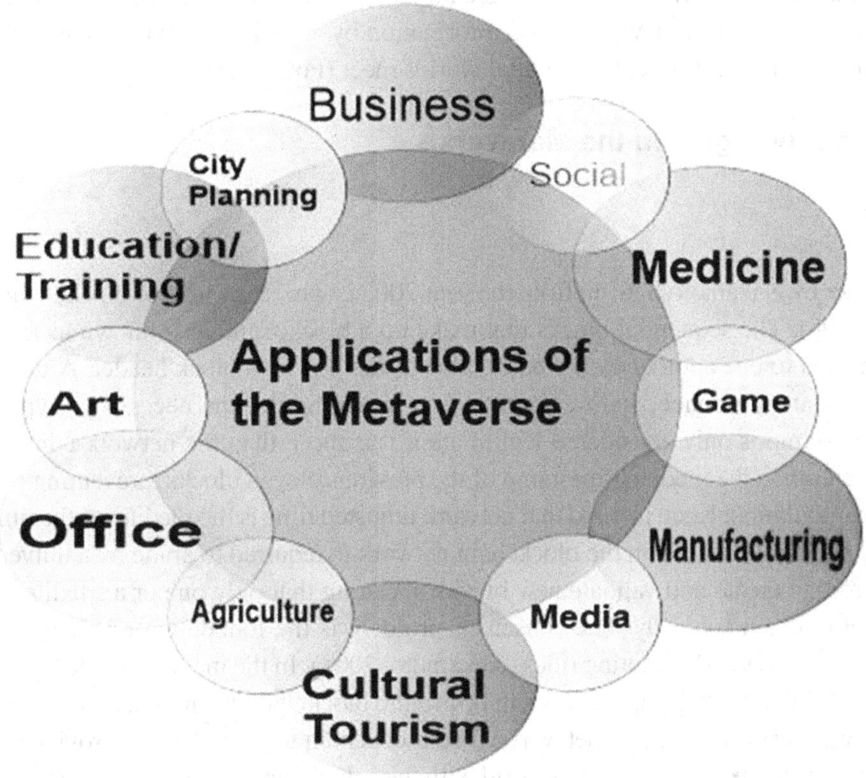

TECHNOLOGICAL PERSPECTIVES

Windows, Tools, and Trending Technologies of the Metaverse

Technical advancements in the metaverse's foundational and basic technologies, such as Virtual Reality (VR), Augmented Reality (AR), and Mixed Reality, are crucial to its growth (MR). The metaverse needs technology that can provide a thoroughly simulated experience in genuine virtual worlds, which the VR, AR, and MR technologies may give in order to produce a fully immersive experience (Teng et al., 2022).

While we currently access the Internet through our smartphones, tablets, and computers—devices that only allow for a minimal level of immersion—innovators and tech leaders believe that in the near future we will be using specialised glasses that are similar to the VR headsets that are currently available, but that are more portable and comfortable. Similar to this, a larger variety of haptic tools will be accessible, enabling users to really "feel" virtual items, as well as equipment like omni-directional treadmills that reflect or mirror the virtual environment by simulating walking, running, and other physical activities (Wiederhold, 2022). The technology to facilitate the creation of the metaverse is rapidly evolving with the use of haptic gloves, VR headsets, AR, and Extended Reality (XR), which enables users to completely experience the lofty levels of interaction and immersive experience (Cheung et al., 2022).

The metaverse is an ongoing digital reality that incorporates aspects of social media, online gaming, cryptocurrencies, augmented reality (AR), and virtual reality (VR), and to enable users to interact virtually. As the metaverse grows, it may provide online communities where user interactions are more multifaceted than what is now possible with technology. Simply said, the metaverse will allow people to experience more than just viewing digital information by allowing them to immerse themselves in a spatial location where the physical and digital worlds meet (Folger, 2022).

Enabling Technologies in the Metaverse

Blockchain

The white paper by Nakamoto Satoshi from the year 2008 is where the idea of blockchain first appeared (Nakamoto, 2008). The sequential blocks that make up a blockchain, also known as a distributed ledger, are connected to one another by the hash value of the previous block header. A block additionally includes a timestamp, a nonce, and transaction data in addition to the necessary cryptographic hash. The block timestamp is only considered legitimate if it is more than the network-adjusted time + two hours and greater than the median timestamp of the previous eleven blocks, preventing potential enemy blockchain manipulation. Keep in mind that network-adjusted time is the median of the timestamps from all the linked nodes. Each node in the blockchain network is required to abide by a universal consensus protocol in order to create and validate new blocks, meaning that only one or a small number of nodes can execute blockchain correctly. The consensus protocol is the foundation of blockchain, regulating both the valid processes and operating rules (Nakamoto, 2008). In the metaverse, the blockchain has two distinct functions. On the one hand, users can utilise the blockchain technology as a store or repository to maintain data everywhere in the metaverse. Yet, blockchain technology can provide a full economic framework to link the metaverse's virtual world with the actual one (Huynh-The, Gadekallu, et al., 2023; Qamar et al., 2023). NFTs (Non-Fungible Tokens) in particular make it possible for virtual products to turn into actual items. Similar to trading in the real world, users are permitted to exchange virtual products. Blockchain therefore serves as a direct link between the actual world and the metaverse's virtual reality (M. Wang & Lau, 2023; Weking et al., 2023).

The blockchain technology is the heart and soul of the metaverse because it can support the efficient economic functioning of the metaverse. The plain motivation behind the incorporation of blockchain into the metaverse are summarized below:

- Ensuring Data Privacy and Security
- Ensuring the Quality of the Data
- Enabling Seamless and Secured Data Sharing
- Enabling Data Interoperability
- Ensuring Data Integrity

Internet of Things

IoT is described as "an infrastructure of linked systems, real systems, people, and information resources, in concert with intelligent services that allow them to manage and act in response to information from both the real world and the virtual world" (International Organization for Standardization, 2018). The Internet of Things (IoT) is also defined as a network of tangible items, or "things," that are outfitted with sensors, networking, communications, and other technologies in order to connect and share data, knowledge, and information with other tools, systems, and gadgets via readily available networking infrastructure (di Martino et al., 2018; Zhou, 2022). In order to provide a foundation and justification for IoT systems, the IoT is therefore composed of physical and virtual states that combine real-world components including sensors, cloud services, actuators, communications, and protocols. Recently, significant developments in sensor and information communication technology have fueled the growth of the IoT, paving the way for the widespread use of connected devices and sensors in a variety of industries, including transportation, health, safety, smart buildings, and auto manufacturing (Baghalzadeh Shishehgarkhaneh et al., 2022; Kor et al., 2022).

Their applications cover every aspect of human life and almost all industrial sectors. They generate colossal data that lead to big data (Zhou, 2022). The IoT-empowered Metaverse has seven key requirements, which are immersion, variety, economy, civility, interactivity, and authenticity and independence (Li et al., 2022) as listed in Table 3.

Table 3. The typical requirements of the Metaverse and technical demands of IoT (Li et al., 2022)

S/N	Requirements of the Metaverse	Technical demands of IoT
1.	Immersion (sustainable)	Real-time computing, massive data monitoring, high synchronisation, low latency, and assurance of network security, privacy, and trust.
2.	Anywhere, anytime and any participant	the network's limitations; the platform's barrier; Guarantee the reliability, security, and privacy of the network; the incompatibility of processing power, electricity, and diversity with light weight; the requirement for resources to operate in this virtual environment.
3.	Variety (heterogeneity, diverse events, places and activities)	Ensure interoperability
4.	Economy (fully functioning and independent creator economy)	Enhance network security, privacy, and trust with high synchronisation, low latency, massive data monitoring, and real-time computation.
5.	Civility (diversity, equality, and inclusiveness)	How can people of different cultures and languages communicate? SemCom: Can we trust them? Comparison of local and cloud semantic knowledge bases (Sem-KB).
6.	Interactivity (seamless connection)	Interoperability is ensured through high synchronisation, low latency, massive data monitoring, and real-time processing.
7.	Authenticity and independence (digital copies of the physical world and parallel space)	The precision with which the physical world was incorporated into the Metaverse.

Digital Twins

Digital Twins are used by Metaverse to totally duplicate the physical world in a virtual "digital" realm. The Metaverse gains a virtual area that is identical to the actual world through real-time communication between Digital Twins and their real-world counterparts, creating a digital space that links the virtual and the real. Digital twins are virtual "clones" created in accordance with real-world entities that are based on computer representations of actual entities or natural processes. We can explore the whole life cycle of physical things and processes by creating digital twins. We can also seamlessly transfer data between the virtual and physical worlds and understand real-time and bidirectional information feedback. Digital Twins first shown versatility, which is seen in their high level of adaptation to numerous industries (Promwongsa et al., 2021; Sodhro et al., 2018). A virtual creature called a "Digital Twin" reconstructs a physical object digitally. It is a straightforward technological method for modelling, forecasting, validating, and regulating the whole life cycle process of a physical entity with the use of real-time data, historical data, and algorithm models. The synchronisation of data and the link between the virtual and physical worlds are the main concerns of digital twins. Compared to Digital Twins, the Metaverse is a larger and more complex system. While the Metaverse grew out of the gaming and entertainment industry, which fosters human-human interaction, and is accelerating from globalisation to urbanisation and industrialization, Digital Twins started from the industrialization of intricate product development and are moving in that direction. Although both the Metaverse and Digital Twins deal with the connection and interaction between the actual and virtual worlds, the Metaverse is fundamentally biassed towards people while Digital Twins are oriented more towards objects. By the use of Digital Twins, the two major technological systems balance one another and help bring about the fourth industrial revolution, as revealed by the Metaverse idea. Future development should simultaneously prioritise a number of different factors, such as the fusion of cutting-edge knowledge from several domains, model building, real-time information flow, and adaptability. Digital twins are emerging digital technologies that turn actual parts into virtual things. Any kind of sensor device may be used to gather data in an appropriate way and create a unique IoT system. A leading system for research and development has been created by combining digital twins, virtual reality, IoT, blockchain, big data, artificial intelligence, and other upcoming technologies. Digital twins that are flexible and can transition from being solid to liquid and from being macroscopic to tiny are possible because to gradual technological advancement. This makes it easier to build the genuine Metaverse (Article & Thomason, 2021; di Martino et al., 2018).

Moreover, a digital twin uses tools and technologies to map the data that is recorded on the physical object, aiding in the creation of information that already exists about the actual object. It operates by synchronised real-time information coordination between the physical object (hardware) and virtual object, just like in cyber-physical systems (software). Digital Twins can transform the real world into a virtual digital area and give technical assistance for building the Metaverse thanks to advancements in new generation information technology (Baghalzadeh Shishehgarkhaneh et al., 2022; Madubuike et al., 2022).

Big Data

Big data deals with formatting, storing, and analysing large datasets. It is also a collection of data that is so large that only specialist software can be used to obtain, manage, and process it. First, at an ACM conference in 1999, Bryson et al. investigated gigabyte data files graphically and in real time (Palaniappan & Fraser, 2001). Additionally, the three Vs—volume, velocity, and variety—were initially proposed by Doug Laney in 2011. Terabyte and petabyte sizes of big data are exceeded. Only high velocity processing can keep up with the transmission of massive data due to the large scale. These enormous amounts of data are utilised to tackle issues that have eluded answers in many areas of life as technology has evolved in recent years. Big data comes in a variety of sources and formats (Samoilenko & Osei-Bryson, 2019). Data is now abundant everywhere in life thanks to the Internet, including e-mails, transaction records, music, photos, movies, software records, etc. Structured, semi-structured, and unstructured data are the three categories into which big data may be generically separated. Relational databases are capable of storing and representing structured data. It may be stated rationally, using two-dimensional tables, etc. Text, photos, audio, and video information are all examples of unstructured data, which is a sort of data without a predetermined structure. Related labels are included in semi-structured data, commonly referred to as self-describing structure. Data contains stages for production, transmission, processing, and display and serves as the link between reality and virtuality (Sun et al., 2022). The Metaverse is an emerging technology of the future, according to Sun et al., (2022) and when merged with other technologies, the gap between virtual online and real-world contact will be reduced. They emphasised how each user in the Metaverse has a unique manner of interacting with the virtual environment. The Metaverse's inter- actions will generate more data, placing strain on the digital world's big data networks and computing power. Hence, in order to implement the Metaverse and understand how the Metaverse is transforming big data and its application, big data processing technology is a crucial technology (Sun et al., 2022). Figure 5 shows the relationship between big data and the metaverse.

Figure 5. The relationship between big data and the Metaverse (Sun et al., 2022)

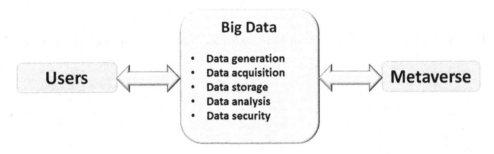

Figure 6 depicts how data transforms and develops to support the metaverse. Through the data in the process of user and device activities of communication, storage, computational power, optical display, data interoperability and data sharing which develops to support the metaverse.

Figure 6. Six aspects of big data are developed to support the Metaverse (Sun et al., 2022)

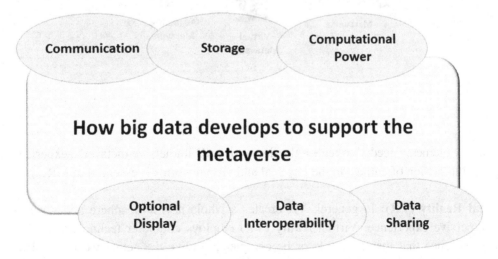

Extended Reality (XR) Apps

XR technologies cover a broad range of immersive technologies, including virtual reality, mixed reality, and augmented reality (VR). The degree to which the outside world is integrated into the experience varies across these technologies, with virtual reality (VR) being at the extreme end of the immersive range and offering consumers a virtually isolated experience. Although while XR technologies have been for a long time, the metaverse would enable us to combine them and make them available to everyone, everywhere, all the time (Plechatá et al., 2022). XR, especially VR, can offer realism experiences that cause actual emotional, cognitive, social, and behavioural reactions (Xi et al., 2022a). By fusing the real and digital virtual worlds in a multilayered and multidimensional way, XR enlarges, drags, and extends the human experiences. Figure 7 illustrates how the word "XR" unifies VR, AR, and MR technologies to enable the development of a sustainable digital environment (Jagatheesaperumal et al., 2022).

Figure 7. The Digital World Realization under the umbrella of XR (Jagatheesaperumal et al., 2022)

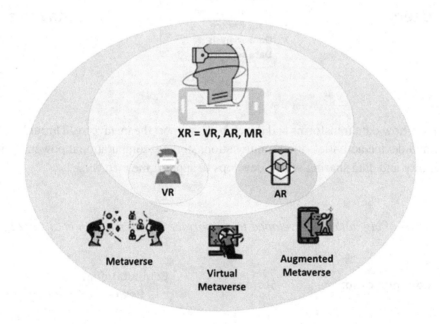

The primary elements needed to realise the dream of a 3D immersive metaverse experience are VR and AR. The interaction of entities in the physical and virtual worlds is essential to MR.

- **Virtual Reality (VR):** In general, VR creates a whole new atmosphere and gives consumers an immersive experience. Virtual reality (VR) employs computer technology to create a virtual experience that may resemble or be completely unlike the actual world. Typical VR systems employ multi-projected environments or headgear to provide lifelike sounds and images (Jagatheesaperumal et al., 2022).

- **Augmented Reality (AR):** The physical environment is not changed by augmented reality; instead, it is covered with layers of digital things. AR systems incorporate three distinct qualities, namely:
  - the integration of the real and virtual world,
  - a real-time interfacing, and (Jagatheesaperumal et al., 2022).
  - exact 3D registration of virtual and real objects. These are the most essential components used for providing rich AR experiences for end-users.
- **Mixed Reality (MR):** The goal of MR is to create new landscapes and representations by fusing the physical and digital worlds. Real-time coexistence and interaction between the physical and digital things (Bec et al., 2021). In contrast to AR, MR lets users to interact with virtual things. Strong tools have been made accessible by MR programmers to bring virtual experiences to life, enabling a range of user experiences from completely immersive to light data layering of settings.

These technologies make it possible to control a digital environment that fosters independent thought and creativity. Holograms are anticipated to be the Metaverse's next major analogue because They are now a crucial component of it. XR impacts the development of technology in a natural way and gives users the freedom to be anywhere in the globe. Recently, augmented reality (AR) apps have been made available for mobile devices, enabling interaction with both virtual and physical items. In the metaverse, this paves the way for mobile augmented reality (MAR) (Bec et al., 2021; Xi et al., 2022b).

6G Technology

5G has recently developed quickly to provide real-time data interchange to IoT devices. Now, 5G offers a higher data throughput than 4G-based systems while providing a high-speed communication architecture that is appropriate for the Metaverse. Particularly, 5G networks support a number of cutting-edge technologies including mmWave, NOMA, and massive MIMO (Li et al., 2022; Temesvári et al., 2019a). Because 5G networks have been widely commercially deployed, it is anticipated that 6G will expand personalised communications to fully realise the machine-to-machine prototype, which connects not only people but also Internet of Things devices, wearable sensors, smart vehicles, and even mobile robots. The dependability of the services, the network capacity, and the density of the Metaverse may all be improved with high-speed data transmission. To meet the needs of ubiquity applications in the Metaverse, 6G can be built based on the current 5G architecture. For instance, given the necessary resources (such as processor speed, graphics power, storage capacity, and connection resources), VR/AR capabilities may be improved with large-scale IoT devices. 6G is being researched to utilise additional frequency bands than 5G and 4G, such as sub-THz and THz, as well as VLC, in order to provide ultra-high data rates and significantly reduce communication latency. Although it is true that a high radio frequency might result in higher data loss, 6G has the advantage of a shorter data transmission distance, allowing it to support more low-latency applications in densely populated areas. 6G also uses ultra-massive MIMO and high-speed, low-latency machine-to-machine communication methods to overcome the issue of restricted coverage (Li et al., 2022; Temesvári et al., 2019b; Yu et al., 2017).

Artificial Intelligence

A variety of cutting-edge technologies have been created in tandem with the Internet's tremendous expansion from the 1990s to the present to provide people amazing experiences with new virtual interactions in cyberspace. There are a lot of virtual environments with immersive experiences and digital transformation that have been developed, but a lot of them are standalone rather than integrated into a platform. In this context, the term "metaverse" refers to a shared virtual environment that is supported by several related emergent technologies. Artificial intelligence (AI), one of these technologies, has demonstrated relevance in increasing immersive experience and simulating human-like intellect in virtual agents. Huynh-The, Pham, et al. (2023) explored the role of AI, adding machine learning algorithms and deep learning architectures, as an essential in the foundation and development of the metaverse. The author's key contributions include a thorough analysis of AI-based techniques pertaining to several technological areas (such as digital twins, blockchain, machine vision, networking, and natural language processing) that have the potential to build virtual worlds in the metaverse. In addition, it is demonstrated that a number of key AI-aided applications, including those for manufacturing, smart cities, healthcare, and gaming, are successfully implemented in virtual environments. The paper also reveals several potential directions for metaverse AI development. This effort, which acts as a main survey, will help researchers, professionals, and non-experts in pertinent disciplines use, develop, and refine AI approaches to improve the calibre of apps created in the metaverse and polish the form of virtual worlds.

As the push toward Metaverse as the future learning platform for society gets more intense, further and new research is considered necessary into new technologies, systems, and methods to support Metaverse learning (Ahuja et al., 2023a; Huynh-The, Pham, et al., 2023; Wesemann, 2022a).

DISCUSSION AND CONCLUSION

With advancement of various technologies such as Blockchain, Internet of Things (Al-rawashdeh et al., 2022; Keikhosrokiani, 2019, 2020a, 2020b, 2020c, 2021a, 2021b; Keikhosrokiani et al., 2020; Keikhosrokiani & Kamaruddin, 2022), Digital Twins, Big Data (Binti Rosli & Keikhosrokiani, 2022; Keikhosrokiani, 2022a), Extended Reality (XR) Apps, 6G technology, and Artificial Intelligence (Abadah et al., 2023; al Mamun et al., 2022; Chu et al., 2022; Jafery et al., 2022a, 2022b, 2022c; Keikhosrokiani, 2022b; Keikhosrokiani & Asl, 2022; Paremeswaran et al., 2022; Sofian et al., 2022; Suhendra et al., 2022; Teoh Yi Zhe & Keikhosrokiani, 2020), metaverse is designed based on different features and using various platforms (Ahuja et al., 2023b). Some leading platforms will cause us to understand the meaning of the Metaverse (Bhat et al., 2023; Haque et al., 2022; Keikhosrokiani & Asl, 2023; Y. Wang & Zhao, 2022; Wesemann, 2022b). Some of the common metaverse platforms are as follows:

- **Decentraland:** Is a blockchain-based virtual social environment. It is used to build, trade in marketplaces for virtual goods, earn money, studying, conduct meetings and explore virtual worlds. It is a digital ledger of indelible records of bitcoin transactions across a computer network.
- **The Sandbox:** It is a 3D virtual world hosted on the Ethereum blockchain where people may interact, build things, and make money. It supports numerous devices, such as Windows phones and smartphones, SandBox has SAND coin based on Ethereum.

- **Bloktopia:** Uses virtual reality to provide users with an immersive experience. It is a 21-story digital structure representing the 21 million Bitcoins being used. It provides a diverse means of revenue-generating potential. Users can design their avatars, explore about crypto-currencies, and purchase virtual "real estate" where using the platform's builder tool and this real estate to make artwork, games, and sequences.

- **Meta Horizon Worlds:** Meta's VR social apps where users can socialize, explore, and participate in virtual activities such as business meetings, and play games. It features functional VR building blocks, such as music, code blocks, and animation effects that help content developers with navigable VR settings. It is also a test platform for virtual users with an invite-only policy.

- **Metahero:** This project offers practical technology that enables users scan real life objects and convey them into the Metaverse instead of a virtual realm. It focuses on bringing physical artifacts into the virtual world using ultra-HD photogrammetric scanning technologies. By their 3D avatars, created by ultrahigh definition from real-world things, including people, users can use explore the NFT, social media, fashion etc.

There are differences between simulation, virtual reality and metaverse as listed in Table 4.

Table 4. Differences between simulation, virtual reality and metaverse (Howell. 2022)

Simulation	Virtual Reality	Metaverse
• To experiment with a simplified copy of an operational system in order to better understand and/or improve that system, simulation is a technique that evokes or mimics significant characteristics of the actual world. • Time use simulation is an indexing variable, simulation objective is to achieve correctness, simulation is computationally intensive, and there is no typical use of simulation • Simulation models components: system entities, input variables, performance measures, and functional relationships. • The eight factors-science, staff, supplies, space, support, systems, success, and sustainability	• Broadly defined, VR is a digitally constructed space that "…perceptually surrounds the user, increasing his or her sense of presence or actually being within it" • Believeable Virtual Reality life-size 3D space, Immersive: non-immersive, semi-immersive, and fully immersive simulations. • Sensory FeedbackInteractive real-time interaction, and self-projection • The brand owns the VR system and all related content. • VR is a limited technology and could only go to the extent of providing simulated 3D environments. • Users are limited to the virtual experience offered in VR systems. • The VR experience of a user stops at the moment they switch off their device.	• The Metaverse is defined as a spatial computing platform that provides digital experiences as an alternative to or a replica of the real world, along with key civilizational aspects like social interactions, currency, trade, economy, and property ownership – founded on blockchain technology. • Layered (Experience, Discovery, Creator economy, Spatial computing, Decentralization, Human interfacing, Infrastructure) • Features of the Metaverse (Incorporation of avatars, Blockchain-based operations, The use of virtual land (parcels), Immersive Experiences (AR/VR), Intersection with artificial intelligence (AI), Decentralized Autonomous Organizations (DAOs) for governance, Reliance on Human-Computer Interface (HCI) technology, A focus on social interactions, Supporting Web3) • Users have complete ownership of their assets and experiences in the metaverse. • Metaverse draws support from technologies such as VR, AR, decentralization, and connectivity technologies, its open to integrate new technologies. • Users can access a wide range of experiences in the metaverse. • The metaverse is a shared and persistent virtual world that exists even when you are not in the metaverse.

The metaverse, which uses augmented reality (AR), virtual reality (VR), mixed reality (MR), and extended reality as its primary technologies, would present virtual environments that facilitate interactions between virtual models and avatars, according to research by Khan et al., (2022) . (XR). To further study and manage physical systems, metaverse will employ cutting-edge technologies including blockchain, computer vision, machine learning, semantic web, network slicing, and natural language processing. The authors presented recent advances, potential applications, and open challenges and the concept of a metaverse as reflected in Figure 8.

Figure 8. Metaverse: Applications, trends, enabling technologies (Khan et al., 2022)

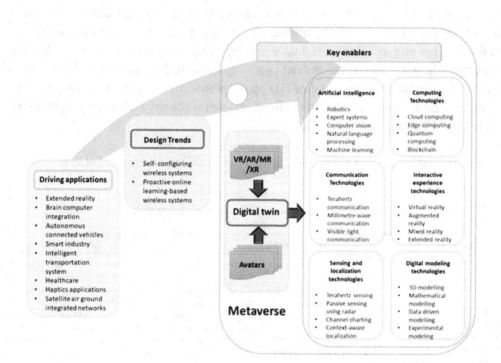

Aburbeian et al. (2022) presented this illustration of metaverse technology as they discussed how personal computers, the internet, and mobile devices—three major technological breakthrough waves—have been seen from consumers' perspectives. Thus, the current fourth wave of computing advances and breakthroughs is being driven by current technologies such as augmented reality, virtual reality, mixed reality, and extended realities. The upcoming wave involves Metaverse technology, as illustrated in Figure 9.

There are various reasons as follows that we consider metaverse as an important technology:

- It is a new technique for interacting with users, promote businesses, build 3D marketing experiences that are immersive and engaging.
- Businesses can find opportunities for virtual events plan a conference or live event that can be seen online and in person. A conference in the Metaverse is a fully-fledged VR experience, with suitable networking and participation where the spectators feel physically present and immersed in the experience.

Figure 9. Illustration of Metaverse technology (Aburbeian et al., 2022)

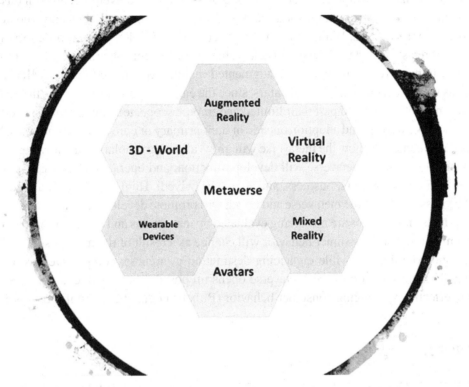

- Companies can advertise and sell their goods, lease shops and showrooms or purchase commercial property.
- The Metaverse introduces a new media of advertising, Brands can engage with a massive global audience through storytelling increasing awareness and identification.
- It is possible to enhance teamwork and the creation of processes and workflows by using the Metaverse and even offer VR workrooms where ability to read one another's body language maintains an emotional bond.
- E-wallets, cryptocurrencies and the Metaverse go hand in hand. Digital wallets are also supported by Metaverse. Blockchain technology and cryptocurrencies have more benefits than drawbacks. No bank account is required, payments take a few clicks, and all transactions are transparent (Hollensen et al., 2022; Rauschnabel et al., 2022).

A recent survey, Ciena found that 78% of business users worldwide would be attracted in leveraging the metaverse. Thus, it is important for enterprises to prepare for this technology, strengthen blockchain capabilities, and embrace a new era of the internet (BasuMallick, 2022).

Concluding Remarks (Metaverse and Consumer Behaviour)

The advent of Metaverse has generated a lot of enthusiasm and opened up several opportunities for innovation, revolution, and creative thinking among users, customers, and organisations. The seamless operation of users enabled by the fusion of the physical and digital worlds presents both significant potential and problems for every sector of the actual, imaginable, and even perceived industries. The Metaverse is undoubtedly developing as a disruptive future trend that will alter how people connect, travel, and organise themselves. With platforms like Second Life, Roblox, and Fortnite serving as what appears to be a foretaste of the metaverse, it is clear that users and consumers have used virtual worlds and interactive, immersive technologies like augmented reality (AR), mixed reality (MR), and virtual reality (VR), as well as experimented with avatars, since the early 2000s. Unfortunately, these pioneering platforms have not yet progressed past their limited geographic scope, technology limits, and functional constraints to achieve widespread adoption outside of their primary or core user communities. Nevertheless, there is no agreement on how the metaverse will grow, allowing scholars and innovators to cogently describe a vision of how the metaverse will develop, function, and operate and discuss the significant ramifications for individual users, business, and society (Dwivedi, Hughes, Wang, et al., 2022; Petit et al., 2022). The possibilities of the metaverse and how it will promote development and increased engagement with products and services are now being evaluated by institutions and organizations. There is little question that marketing and consumer behavior will change as a result of the metaverse. It will improve management and coordination while enhancing destination awareness, competitiveness, positioning, and branding. The introduction of the Metaverse opens up possibilities for interaction, planning, and participation, effectively changing consumer behavior (Buhalis et al., 2023; Trunfio & Rossi, 2022).

REFERENCES

Abadah, M. S. K., Keikhosrokiani, P., & Zhao, X. (2023). Analytics of Public Reactions to the COVID-19 Vaccine on Twitter Using Sentiment Analysis and Topic Modelling. In D. Valle-Cruz, N. Plata-Cesar, & J. L. González-Ruíz (Eds.), *Handbook of Research on Applied Artificial Intelligence and Robotics for Government Processes* (pp. 156–188). IGI Global. doi:10.4018/978-1-6684-5624-8.ch008

Aburbeian, A. M., Owda, A. Y., & Owda, M. (2022). A Technology Acceptance Model Survey of the Metaverse Prospects. *AI, 3*(2), 285–302. doi:10.3390/ai3020018

Ahuja, A. S., Polascik, B. W., Doddapaneni, D., Byrnes, E. S., & Sridhar, J. (2023). The Digital Metaverse: Applications in Artificial Intelligence, Medical Education, and Integrative Health. In Integrative Medicine Research (Vol. 12, Issue 1). Korea Institute of Oriental Medicine. doi:10.1016/j.imr.2022.100917

Akour, I. A., Al-Maroof, R. S., Alfaisal, R., & Salloum, S. A. (2022). A conceptual framework for determining metaverse adoption in higher institutions of gulf area: An empirical study using hybrid SEM-ANN approach. *Computers and Education: Artificial Intelligence, 3*, 100052. Advance online publication. doi:10.1016/j.caeai.2022.100052

al Mamun, M. H., Keikhosrokiani, P., Asl, M. P., Anuar, N. A. N., Hadi, N. H. A., & Humida, T. (2022). Sentiment Analysis of the Harry Potter Series Using a Lexicon-Based Approach. In P. Keikhosrokiani & M. Pourya Asl (Eds.), *Handbook of Research on Opinion Mining and Text Analytics on Literary Works and Social Media* (pp. 263–291). IGI Global. doi:10.4018/978-1-7998-9594-7.ch011

Al-rawashdeh, M., Keikhosrokiani, P., Belaton, B., Alawida, M., & Zwiri, A. (2022). IoT Adoption and Application for Smart Healthcare: A Systematic Review. *Sensors (Basel), 22*(14), 5377. Advance online publication. doi:10.339022145377 PMID:35891056

Article, R., & Thomason, J. (n.d.). *Journal of Metaverse MetaHealth-How will the Metaverse Change Health Care?* https://www.influencive.com/flickplays-3d-social-media-platform-

Baghalzadeh Shishehgarkhaneh, M., Keivani, A., Moehler, R. C., Jelodari, N., & Roshdi Laleh, S. (2022). Internet of Things (IoT), Building Information Modeling (BIM), and Digital Twin (DT) in Construction Industry: A Review, Bibliometric, and Network Analysis. In Buildings (Vol. 12, Issue 10). MDPI. doi:10.3390/buildings12101503

Bale, A. S., Ghorpade, N., Hashim, M. F., Vaishnav, J., & Almaspoor, Z. (2022). A Comprehensive Study on Metaverse and Its Impacts on Humans. In *Advances in Human-Computer Interaction* (Vol. 2022). Hindawi Limited. doi:10.1155/2022/3247060

Bec, A., Moyle, B., Schaffer, V., & Timms, K. (2021). Virtual reality and mixed reality for second chance tourism. *Tourism Management, 83*, 104256. Advance online publication. doi:10.1016/j.tourman.2020.104256

Bhat, J. R., AlQahtani, S. A., & Nekovee, M. (2023). FinTech enablers, use cases, and role of future internet of things. *Journal of King Saud University - Computer and Information Sciences, 35*(1), 87–101. doi:10.1016/j.jksuci.2022.08.033

Binti Rosli, N. H., & Keikhosrokiani, P. (2022). Big medical data mining system (BigMed) for the detection and classification of COVID-19 misinformation. In P. Keikhosrokiani (Ed.), *Big Data Analytics for Healthcare* (pp. 233–244). Academic Press. doi:10.1016/B978-0-323-91907-4.00014-5

Bojic, L. (2022). Metaverse through the prism of power and addiction: what will happen when the virtual world becomes more attractive than reality? In European Journal of Futures Research (Vol. 10, Issue 1). Springer Science and Business Media Deutschland GmbH. doi:10.118640309-022-00208-4

Braud, T., Zhou, P., Lee, L.-H., Wang, L., Xu, D., Lin, Z., Kumar, A., Bermejo, C., & Hui, P. (n.d.). *All One Needs to Know about Metaverse: A Complete Survey on Technological Singularity.* Virtual Ecosystem, and Research Agenda. doi:10.13140/RG.2.2.11200.05124/8

Buhalis, D., Leung, D., & Lin, M. (2023). Metaverse as a disruptive technology revolutionising tourism management and marketing. In *Tourism Management* (Vol. 97). Elsevier Ltd. doi:10.1016/j.tourman.2023.104724

Cheung, C. M. K., Risius, M., Lee, M. K. O., Wagner, C., Malik, O., Karhade, P., Kathuria, A., Jaiswal, A., & Yen, B. (n.d.). *Introduction to Adversarial Coordination in Collaboration and Social Media Systems Minitrack of the Collaboration Systems and Technologies Track.* https://hdl.handle.net/10125/79343

Chu, K. E., Keikhosrokiani, P., & Asl, M. P. (2022). A Topic Modeling and Sentiment Analysis Model for Detection and Visualization of Themes in Literary Texts. *Pertanika Journal of Science & Technology, 30*(4), 2535–2561. doi:10.47836/pjst.30.4.14

di Martino, B., Rak, M., Ficco, M., Esposito, A., Maisto, S. A., & Nacchia, S. (2018). Internet of things reference architectures, security and interoperability: A survey. In Internet of Things (Netherlands) (Vols. 1–2, pp. 99–112). Elsevier B.V. doi:10.1016/j.iot.2018.08.008

Díaz, J. E. M., Saldaña, C. A. D., & Avila, C. A. R. (2020). Virtual world as a resource for hybrid education. *International Journal of Emerging Technologies in Learning, 15*(15), 94–109. doi:10.3991/ijet.v15i15.13025

Dwivedi, Y. K., Hughes, L., Baabdullah, A. M., Ribeiro-Navarrete, S., Giannakis, M., Al-Debei, M. M., Dennehy, D., Metri, B., Buhalis, D., Cheung, C. M. K., Conboy, K., Doyle, R., Dubey, R., Dutot, V., Felix, R., Goyal, D. P., Gustafsson, A., Hinsch, C., Jebabli, I., ... Wamba, S. F. (2022). Metaverse beyond the hype: Multidisciplinary perspectives on emerging challenges, opportunities, and agenda for research, practice and policy. *International Journal of Information Management, 66,* 102542. Advance online publication. doi:10.1016/j.ijinfomgt.2022.102542

Dwivedi, Y. K., Hughes, L., Wang, Y., Alalwan, A. A., Ahn, S. J., Balakrishnan, J., Barta, S., Belk, R., Buhalis, D., Dutot, V., Felix, R., Filieri, R., Flavián, C., Gustafsson, A., Hinsch, C., Hollensen, S., Jain, V., Kim, J., Krishen, A. S., ... Wirtz, J. (2022). Metaverse marketing: How the metaverse will shape the future of consumer research and practice. *Psychology and Marketing.* Advance online publication. doi:10.1002/mar.21767

Haque, S., Eberhart, Z., Bansal, A., & McMillan, C. (2022). Semantic Similarity Metrics for Evaluating Source Code Summarization. *IEEE International Conference on Program Comprehension, 2022-March,* 36–47. 10.1145/3524610.3527909

Hollensen, S., Kotler, P., & Opresnik, M. O. (2022). Metaverse – the new marketing universe. *The Journal of Business Strategy.* Advance online publication. doi:10.1108/JBS-01-2022-0014

Huynh-The, T., Gadekallu, T. R., Wang, W., Yenduri, G., Ranaweera, P., Pham, Q.-V., da Costa, D. B., & Liyanage, M. (2023). Blockchain for the metaverse: A Review. *Future Generation Computer Systems, 143,* 401–419. doi:10.1016/j.future.2023.02.008

Huynh-The, T., Pham, Q. V., Pham, X. Q., Nguyen, T. T., Han, Z., & Kim, D. S. (2023). Artificial intelligence for the metaverse: A survey. In *Engineering Applications of Artificial Intelligence* (Vol. 117). Elsevier Ltd. doi:10.1016/j.engappai.2022.105581

Hwang, G. J., & Chien, S. Y. (2022). Definition, roles, and potential research issues of the metaverse in education: An artificial intelligence perspective. *Computers and Education: Artificial Intelligence, 3,* 100082. Advance online publication. doi:10.1016/j.caeai.2022.100082

Jafery, N. N., Keikhosrokiani, P., & Asl, M. P. (2022). Text Analytics Model to Identify the Connection Between Theme and Sentiment in Literary Works: A Case Study of Iraqi Life Writings. In P. Keikhosrokiani & M. Pourya Asl (Eds.), *Handbook of Research on Opinion Mining and Text Analytics on Literary Works and Social Media* (pp. 173–190). IGI Global. doi:10.4018/978-1-7998-9594-7.ch008

Jagatheesaperumal, S. K., Ahmad, K., Al-Fuqaha, A., & Qadir, J. (2022). *Advancing Education Through Extended Reality and Internet of Everything Enabled Metaverses: Applications, Challenges, and Open Issues.* https://arxiv.org/abs/2207.01512

Jung, S. Y., Kim, J. W., Hwang, H., Lee, K., Baek, R. M., Lee, H. Y., Yoo, S., Song, W., & Han, J. S. (2019). Development of comprehensive personal health records integrating patient-generated health data directly from samsung s-health and apple health apps: Retrospective cross-sectional observational study. *JMIR mHealth and uHealth*, 7(5), e12691. Advance online publication. doi:10.2196/12691 PMID:31140446

Keikhosrokiani, P. (2019). Perspectives in the development of mobile medical information systems: Life cycle, management, methodological approach and application. In *Perspectives in the Development of Mobile Medical Information Systems*. Life Cycle, Management, Methodological Approach and Application. doi:10.1016/C2018-0-02485-8

Keikhosrokiani, P. (2020a). Introduction to Mobile Medical Information System (mMIS) development. In P. Keikhosrokiani (Ed.), *Perspectives in the Development of Mobile Medical Information Systems* (pp. 1–22). Academic Press. doi:10.1016/B978-0-12-817657-3.00001-8

Keikhosrokiani, P. (2020b). *Behavioral intention to use of Mobile Medical Information System (mMIS)*. Academic Press.

Keikhosrokiani, P. (2020c). *Success factors of mobile medical information system (mMIS)*. Academic Press.

Keikhosrokiani, P. (2021a). IoT for enhanced decision-making in medical information systems: A systematic review. In G. Marques, A. Kumar Bhoi, I. de la Torre Díez, & B. Garcia-Zapirain (Eds.), *Enhanced Telemedicine and e-Health: Advanced IoT Enabled Soft Computing Framework* (Vol. 410, pp. 119–140). Springer International Publishing. doi:10.1007/978-3-030-70111-6_6

Keikhosrokiani, P. (2021b). Predicating Smartphone Users' Behaviour Towards a Location-Aware IoMT-Based Information System: An Empirical Study. *International Journal of E-Adoption*, 13(2), 52–77. doi:10.4018/IJEA.2021070104

Keikhosrokiani, P. (2022a). *Big Data Analytics for Healthcare: Datasets, Techniques, Life Cycles, Management, and Applications*. Elsevier Science. https://books.google.com.my/books?id=WbJYEAAAQBAJ

Keikhosrokiani, P. (2022b). *Handbook of Research on Consumer Behavior Change and Data Analytics in the Socio-Digital Era*. IGI Global. doi:10.4018/978-1-6684-4168-8

Keikhosrokiani, P., & Asl, M. P. (2022). *Handbook of research on opinion mining and text analytics on literary works and social media*. IGI Global. doi:10.4018/978-1-7998-9594-7

Keikhosrokiani, P., & Asl, M. P. (Eds.). (2023). *Handbook of Research on Artificial Intelligence Applications in Literary Works and Social Media*. IGI Global. doi:10.4018/978-1-6684-6242-3

Keikhosrokiani, P., & Kamaruddin, N. S. A. B. (2022). IoT-Based In-Hospital-In-Home Heart Disease Remote Monitoring System with Machine Learning Features for Decision Making. In S. Mishra, A. González-Briones, A. K. Bhoi, P. K. Mallick, & J. M. Corchado (Eds.), *Connected e-Health: Integrated IoT and Cloud Computing* (pp. 349–369). Springer International Publishing. doi:10.1007/978-3-030-97929-4_16

Keikhosrokiani, P., Mustaffa, N., Zakaria, N., & Abdullah, R. (2020). Assessment of a medical information system: The mediating role of use and user satisfaction on the success of human interaction with the mobile healthcare system (iHeart). *Cognition Technology and Work*, 22(2), 281–305. doi:10.100710111-019-00565-4

Khan, L. U., Han, Z., Niyato, D., Hossain, E., & Hong, C. S. (2022). *Metaverse for Wireless Systems: Vision, Enablers, Architecture, and Future Directions*. https://arxiv.org/abs/2207.00413

Kor, M., Yitmen, I., & Alizadehsalehi, S. (2022). *An investigation for integration of deep learning and digital twins towards Construction 4.0*. Smart and Sustainable Built Environment. doi:10.1108/SASBE-08-2021-0148

Krüger, J. M., Buchholz, A., & Bodemer, D. (2019). *Human-centred AI in the chemical industry View project Learning with multiple external representations View project Characteristics from a User's Perspective*. https://www.researchgate.net/publication/337900854

Kumari, P., Mathew, L., & Syal, P. (2017). Increasing trend of wearables and multimodal interface for human activity monitoring: A review. In *Biosensors and Bioelectronics* (Vol. 90, pp. 298–307). Elsevier Ltd. doi:10.1016/j.bios.2016.12.001

Kye, B., Han, N., Kim, E., Park, Y., & Jo, S. (2021). Educational applications of metaverse: Possibilities and limitations. In *Journal of Educational Evaluation for Health Professions* (Vol. 18). Korea Health Personnel Licensing Examination Institute. doi:10.3352/jeehp.2021.18.32

Li, K., Cui, Y., Li, W., Lv, T., Yuan, X., Li, S., Ni, W., Simsek, M., & Dressler, F. (2022). *When Internet of Things meets Metaverse: Convergence of Physical and Cyber Worlds*. https://arxiv.org/abs/2208.13501

Madubuike, O. C., Anumba, C. J., & Khallaf, R. (2022). A review of digital twin applications in construction. *Journal of Information Technology in Construction*, 27, 145–172. doi:10.36680/j.itcon.2022.008

Nakamoto, S. (n.d.). *Bitcoin: A Peer-to-Peer Electronic Cash System*. www.bitcoin.org

Oh, H. J., Kim, J., Chang, J. J. C., Park, N., & Lee, S. (2023). Social benefits of living in the metaverse: The relationships among social presence, supportive interaction, social self-efficacy, and feelings of loneliness. *Computers in Human Behavior*, 139, 107498. Advance online publication. doi:10.1016/j.chb.2022.107498

Ovunc, S. S., Yolcu, M. B., Emre, S., Elicevik, M., & Celayir, S. (2021). Using Immersive Technologies to Develop Medical Education Materials. *Cureus*. Advance online publication. doi:10.7759/cureus.12647 PMID:33585133

Palaniappan, K., & Fraser, J. B. (n.d.). *Multiresolution tiling for interactive viewing of large datasets*. Academic Press.

Paremeswaran, P., Keikhosrokiani, P., & Asl, M. P. (2022). Opinion Mining of Readers' Responses to Literary Prize Nominees on Twitter: A Case Study of Public Reaction to the Booker Prize (2018–2020). In F. Saeed, F. Mohammed, & F. Ghaleb (Eds.), Advances on Intelligent Informatics and Computing (pp. 243–257). Springer International Publishing. doi:10.1007/978-3-030-98741-1_21

Park, S. M., & Kim, Y. G. (2022). A Metaverse: Taxonomy, Components, Applications, and Open Challenges. *IEEE Access: Practical Innovations, Open Solutions*, *10*, 4209–4251. doi:10.1109/ACCESS.2021.3140175

Petit, O., Velasco, C., Wang, Q. J., & Spence, C. (2022). Consumer Consciousness in Multisensory Extended Reality. *Frontiers in Psychology*, *13*, 851753. Advance online publication. doi:10.3389/fpsyg.2022.851753 PMID:35529566

Plechatá, A., Makransky, G., & Böhm, R. (2022). Can extended reality in the metaverse revolutionise health communication? In NPJ Digital Medicine (Vol. 5, Issue 1). Nature Research. doi:10.103841746-022-00682-x

Prieto, J. de la F., Lacasa, P., & Martínez-Borda, R. (2022). *Approaching metaverses: Mixed reality interfaces in youth media platforms*. New Techno Humanities. doi:10.1016/j.techum.2022.04.004

Promwongsa, N., Ebrahimzadeh, A., Naboulsi, D., Kianpisheh, S., Belqasmi, F., Glitho, R., Crespi, N., & Alfandi, O. (2021). A Comprehensive Survey of the Tactile Internet: State-of-the-Art and Research Directions. *IEEE Communications Surveys and Tutorials*, *23*(1), 472–523. doi:10.1109/COMST.2020.3025995

Qamar, S., Anwar, Z., & Afzal, M. (2023). A systematic threat analysis and defense strategies for the metaverse and extended reality systems. *Computers & Security*, *128*, 103127. doi:10.1016/j.cose.2023.103127

Rauschnabel, P. A., Babin, B. J., tom Dieck, M. C., Krey, N., & Jung, T. (2022). What is augmented reality marketing? Its definition, complexity, and future. In *Journal of Business Research* (Vol. 142, pp. 1140–1150). Elsevier Inc. doi:10.1016/j.jbusres.2021.12.084

Samoilenko, S., & Osei-Bryson, K. M. (2019). Representation matters: An exploration of the socio-economic impacts of ICT-enabled public value in the context of sub-Saharan economies. *International Journal of Information Management*, *49*, 69–85. doi:10.1016/j.ijinfomgt.2019.03.006

Sila-Nowicka, K., & Thakuriah, P. (2019). Multi-sensor movement analysis for transport safety and health applications. *PLoS One*, *14*(1), e0210090. Advance online publication. doi:10.1371/journal.pone.0210090 PMID:30703128

Sodhro, A. H., Pirbhulal, S., & Sangaiah, A. K. (2018). Convergence of IoT and product lifecycle management in medical health care. *Future Generation Computer Systems*, *86*, 380–391. doi:10.1016/j.future.2018.03.052

Sofian, N. B., Keikhosrokiani, P., & Asl, M. P. (2022). Opinion Mining and Text Analytics of Reader Reviews of Yoko Ogawa's The Housekeeper and the Professor in Goodreads. In P. Keikhosrokiani & M. Pourya Asl (Eds.), *Handbook of Research on Opinion Mining and Text Analytics on Literary Works and Social Media* (pp. 240–262). IGI Global. doi:10.4018/978-1-7998-9594-7.ch010

Suhendra, N. H. B., Keikhosrokiani, P., Asl, M. P., & Zhao, X. (2022). Opinion Mining and Text Analytics of Literary Reader Responses: A Case Study of Reader Responses to KL Noir Volumes in Goodreads Using Sentiment Analysis and Topic. In P. Keikhosrokiani & M. Pourya Asl (Eds.), *Handbook of Research on Opinion Mining and Text Analytics on Literary Works and Social Media* (pp. 191–239). IGI Global. doi:10.4018/978-1-7998-9594-7.ch009

Sun, J., Gan, W., Chen, Z., Li, J., & Yu, P. S. (n.d.). *Big Data Meets Metaverse: A Survey*. https://www.roblox.com/

Temesvári, Z. M., Maros, D., & Kádár, P. (2019). Review of Mobile Communication and the 5G in Manufacturing. *Procedia Manufacturing*, *32*, 600–612. doi:10.1016/j.promfg.2019.02.259

Teng, Z., Cai, Y., Gao, Y., Zhang, X., & Li, X. (2022). Factors Affecting Learners' Adoption of an Educational Metaverse Platform: An Empirical Study Based on an Extended UTAUT Model. *Mobile Information Systems*, *2022*, 1–15. Advance online publication. doi:10.1155/2022/5479215

Teoh Yi Zhe, I., & Keikhosrokiani, P. (2020). Knowledge workers mental workload prediction using optimised ELANFIS. *Applied Intelligence*. Advance online publication. doi:10.100710489-020-01928-5

Trunfio, M., & Rossi, S. (2022). Advances in Metaverse Investigation: Streams of Research and Future Agenda. *Virtual Worlds*, *1*(2), 103–129. doi:10.3390/virtualworlds1020007

Wang, H. N., Lin, Y., Wang, W., Dhelim, S., Farha, F., Ding, J., & Daneshmand, M. (n.d.). *A Survey on Metaverse: the State-of-the-art*. Technologies, Applications, and Challenges.

Wang, M., & Lau, N. (2023). NFT Digital Twins: A Digitalization Strategy to Preserve and Sustain Miao Silver Craftsmanship in the Metaverse Era. *Heritage*, *6*(2), 1921–1941. doi:10.3390/heritage6020103

Wang, Y., & Zhao, J. (2022). *A Survey of Mobile Edge Computing for the Metaverse: Architectures*. Applications, and Challenges., doi:10.1109/CIC56439.2022.00011

Weinberger, M. (2022). What Is Metaverse? A Definition Based on Qualitative Meta-Synthesis. *Future Internet*, *14*(11), 310. doi:10.3390/fi14110310

Weking, J., Desouza, K. C., Fielt, E., & Kowalkiewicz, M. (2023). Metaverse-enabled entrepreneurship. *Journal of Business Venturing Insights*, *19*, e00375. Advance online publication. doi:10.1016/j.jbvi.2023.e00375

Wesemann, A. (2022). Metaverse. *Tanz. Jahrbuch*, *52–55*(1), 486–497. Advance online publication. doi:10.3390/encyclopedia2010031

Wiederhold, B. K. (2021). Ready (or Not) Player One: Initial Musings on the Metaverse. [editorial]. *Cyberpsychology, Behavior, and Social Networking*, *25*(1), 1–2. doi:10.1089/cyber.2021.29234

Wu, T. C., & Ho, C. T. B. (2022). A scoping review of metaverse in emergency medicine. In *Australasian Emergency Care*. Elsevier Australia. doi:10.37766/inplasy2022.5.0159

Xi, N., Chen, J., Gama, F., Riar, M., & Hamari, J. (2022). The challenges of entering the metaverse: An experiment on the effect of extended reality on workload. *Information Systems Frontiers*. Advance online publication. doi:10.100710796-022-10244-x PMID:35194390

Yu, H., Lee, H., & Jeon, H. (2017). What is 5G? Emerging 5G mobile services and network requirements. *Sustainability (Switzerland)*, *9*(10), 1848. Advance online publication. doi:10.3390u9101848

Zallio, M., & Clarkson, P. J. (2022). Designing the metaverse: A study on inclusion, diversity, equity, accessibility and safety for digital immersive environments. *Telematics and Informatics*, *75*, 101909. Advance online publication. doi:10.1016/j.tele.2022.101909

Zhao, Y., Jiang, J., Chen, Y., Liu, R., Yang, Y., Xue, X., & Chen, S. (2022). Metaverse: Perspectives from graphics, interactions and visualization. In Visual Informatics (Vol. 6, Issue 1, pp. 56–67). Elsevier B.V. doi:10.1016/j.visinf.2022.03.002

Zhou, M. (2022). Editorial: Evolution from AI, IoT and Big Data Analytics to Metaverse. In IEEE/CAA Journal of Automatica Sinica (Vol. 9, Issue 12, pp. 2041–2042). Institute of Electrical and Electronics Engineers Inc. doi:10.1109/JAS.2022.106100

Chapter 4
How Will Metaverse and AI Change Traditional Marketing Techniques?

Ozge Doguc

ⓘD https://orcid.org/0000-0002-5971-9218

Medipol University, Turkey

ABSTRACT

The development of technology has transformed the process of product development and customer relationship building. It shows impressive results in deep learning and AI applications. Companies can see farther and make data-driven decisions by leveraging advanced technology solutions managed by AI. Deep learning can be used to analyze and integrate large databases. Considering deep learning activities, it could be a significant opportunity to meet customers' needs and help companies develop profitable new products. Likewise, virtual worlds bring a new approach to marketing. The concept of the metaverse can be described as a simulated reality. Metaverse can enable the creation of virtual reality worlds by integrating online experiences. This chapter discusses how AI and deep learning affect marketing. In this context, industrial opportunities of AI in various marketing activities, AI, strategic marketing, and understanding consumer behaviors will be focused on, and cases of companies using deep learning applications will be included.

INTRODUCTION

There is a growing number of organizations that compete using technology to generate greater impacts on potential consumers. The participation of consumers has a positive impact on the cognitive image and the affective image, likewise, the formation of the image and the purchase intention vary according to the platform used to access the information (Islam et al., 2009). It is a reality that the adoption of artificial intelligence (AI) will accelerate on the digital frontier, reducing the gap between consumers and technology, in such a way that more and more resources are invested in this sector. Following the same line of thought, companies manage their data trough AI, which allowed humans to have more time

DOI: 10.4018/978-1-6684-7029-9.ch004

to carry out other activities that were more useful to the organization, thus generating greater customer satisfaction (Li & Yost, 2000).

Before proceeding with the relationship between AI and marketing, it is important to define marketing as the ability to satisfy consumer needs and wants sometimes, somehow, somewhere, and in some way (Godwin-Jones, 2019). That is why, following the same line of thought, they jump to view between the skills available to AI, machine learning and deep learning.

Concepts that will gradually be used more frequently to improve marketing strategies, thus smoothing out some of the main rough edges between market supply and demand. Likewise, although we are currently experiencing a revolution caused by the different perspectives around technology, this event will have even more great impacts, since it will link totally autonomous devices with others that still require human operation. Marketing, as one of the main business functions, has a large share in the implementation of the business strategy and the realization of its vision, and provides many competitive advantages to businesses in adopting new technologies and adapting to today's conditions. AI is used in market analysis, customer identification, marketing strategy, planning, product management, price strategy, distribution channels and supply chain management, marketing communication, in short, almost all marketing activities.

Metaverse introduces a new world of opportunities for the companies to expand their operations. It is poised to become the next big milestone in the evolution of the internet that will change how private and public-sector businesses work. And, as with many tech revolutions like the cell phone or mobile computing, it will be driven by the consumer, looking for the same digital experience at work that they experience in the home.

The next sections explain how AI has been used in marketing in the recent years and discuss Metaverse's impact on the existing marketing applications. First, concepts of AI, ML and deep learning are provided. Later in the chapter, information about the previous work on AI and metaverse is given. Finally, the future of marketing through metaverse is discussed.

BACKGROUND

Metaverse

Metaverse is attracting the attention of both marketers and consumers. However, many brands have begun to adjust their strategies and approaches to this emerging virtual ecosystem. While some companies watch the evolution of the metaverse with anticipation and curiosity, recent research shows that consumers are ready to engage with brands in new virtual environments. According to Sitecore's "Metaverse Perceptions" report (Sitecore, 2023), 42% of US consumers describe themselves as metaverse enthusiasts. Nearly 9 out of 10 people think the metaverse will play an important role in the way they shop and interact with brands in the future.

While the technology is still evolving, brands are using this time to start exploring virtual environments as another way to reach consumers. To support companies' goals, 57% of marketers use or plan to use the metaverse as an innovation element to excite buyers, and 55% as a way to test products. Half of brands use or plan to leverage the metaverse as a gamification function to engage buyers, with 40% seeing the metaverse as a customer experience tool.

Augmented and virtual realities are enabling brands to create experiences that will reinvent everything from shopping to customer support and employee engagement. Nearly three-quarters of organizations have evaluated the types of experiences they will create on the metaverse.

The most frequently scheduled metaverse features focus on personalized and interactive shopping experiences. Specific tactics may include inspiring users with personalized recommendations based on past preferences, or allowing shoppers to try or test an item using an avatar. To further increase engagement with consumers, marketers are looking to create community environments or forums for users with similar interests (57%), develop inclusive experiences that represent a diverse user group (55%), and win rewards by gamifying experiences (51%) (Sitecore, 2023).

Artificial Intelligence (AI)

The history of the concept of AI is as old as the history of modern computers. In the last several years, there has been a lot of talk about machine learning, deep learning, and data analytics in the context of AI (Keikhosrokiani & Pourya Asl, 2023). Intelligent systems offer certain potential and strengths for supporting the volatile conditions that firms with a strategic character encounter, where good strategic intelligence is necessary (Verma et al., 2021). Machine learning offers the most promising techniques to developing human-level AI, according to AI experts, who are working in this direction. When the parameters of a model are estimated using data, the process is said to "learn" from the data. Machine learning models have a lot of power when it comes to making predictions, especially where a non-theoretical forecast would work well. Therefore scalability, real-time application, and cross-validated predictive accuracy are used to evaluate machine models rather than internal and external validity and theoretical foundations, which are better suited to classical models. A notable advantage of many machine learning tools is that, unlike traditional statistical techniques, they do not make presuppositions about data, which are often restrictive (Syam & Sharma, 2018).

Machine Learning

Machine learning is the discovery of patterns through data analysis without human intervention. In other words, machine learning has been explained as the practice of using algorithms to parse data, learning it, and then deciding or prediction about something in the world (Jordan & Mitchell, 2025). It is generally used in areas that are more dependent on intelligence and do not respond in logical reasoning (Bini, 2018). In machine learning, instead of programming it manually, the model is trained with an existing dataset and then learned tasks are performed on the new data. To learn from data effectively, it is necessary to collect case studies and related input parameters. This feature of machine learning requires the data to be used to train the model to be of sufficient size and quality. Regardless of the differences in learning tasks, machine learning techniques often try to imitate nature based on the knowledge and experience that humans have accumulated since their existence (Kang & Jameson, 2018). Machine learning techniques are driven by human brain function, processes that deal with human evolution, human knowledge acquisition and reasoning theory, and the sociological theory behind human behavior. Machine learning strategies are grouped under three headings. These are supervised, unsupervised and reinforcement learning (Chinnamgari, 2019).

Deep Learning

Deep learning is a recent subfield of AI and machine learning, both of which are extremely popular today. Deep learning is a machine learning technique for learning features and tasks directly from data. Deep learning is the most prevalent approach in AI applications and is systematically at the bottom of AI and machine learning. Deep learning consists of using deep ANN to explore patterns, or in other words, a multi-layered neural network like the human brain. Deep calculations and processing are made on large volumes of data from different sources with learning algorithms in each layer and predict the result as output. Learning and prediction accuracy also increase over time. In other words, deep learning is a simulation of the human brain in the machine learning with a lot of data to more accurately identify objects and perform complex operations without human intervention (Goodfellow et al., 2016).

Deep learning processes unstructured and unspecified data and leverages a multi-layered neural network to automatically discover features and patterns, identify and classify information. In a process, the data from the input layer is then refined through increasingly complex algorithms in the hidden computation layers and the result is estimated at the output layer. (Bini, 2018).

Literature Survey

With the developing technology and digital transformations, the concept of AI has started to take place in all areas of our lives. AI has begun to be used in multiple sectors that have become a part of our lives, such as education, health, tourism, automotive and cyber security, because of the combination of data acquisition, processing, classification, and AI functions. Some sectors where AI is used are mentioned in this section.

Banking and Finance

AI applications are used by banks to collect market information, to supply banking services to consumers, and to facilitate communication. AI applications used in banks are seeking to connect its clients to web and mobile account management tools to improve the bank's image, retain and attract underused clients, reduce queues at branches, and provide faster service to its customers. It should be noted, however, that robust frameworks are required to use these frameworks (Kaya et al., 2019).

Operational tasks such as detecting incompatibilities and fraud transactions can be automated by monitoring the personal data and transaction data of the customers. Analysis of this data enables customer segmentation and personalized marketing campaigns. With the support of natural language processing tools, more effective solutions can be offered in customer services in a shorter time.

The integration of AI technologies into financial advisory services, on the other hand, plays a complementary role for those working in this field and can replace them to a certain extent. Robot-advisors, which have started to be used by various financial institutions, propose personalized portfolios by evaluating customers' expectations, asset structures and risk perceptions by using versatile investment algorithms. It also rearranges the distribution of its portfolios in case market conditions and investor preferences differ (Romao et al., 2019).

Thanks to AI applications, banks attain their clients swiftly and the wide variety of offerings introduced to clients is growing day via way of means of day. Meanwhile, of course, because the race among banks maintains with all its competition, the financial institution that offers the latest and quickest provider takes the lead with inside the race. Therefore, at this factor reached in net and cellular banking, nearly all transactions finished on the department may be finished in those applications.

Health

AI technologies are of great importance in terms of managing processes such as diagnosis and diagnostic tasks in the field of health. Wearable technology with AI systems provides considerable benefits in terms of early disease identification and regular health monitoring. Sensors detect signs such as heart rate, body temperature, cup beat anomalies, and a person's workout habits, and this data can be monitored in real time (Noorbakhsh-Sabet et al. 2019). The data collected and processed with wearable technologies have the potential to improve the health status of users, as well as provide significant benefits for public health. This is especially valuable in terms of developing preventive health policies (Shaw et al. 2019).

In addition, wearable technologies can also be used to improve occupational health and safety controls. For example, jobs that need to be done in areas that pose a risk to human health will be able to be performed by robots. With the developments in the field of robotics and the increase in the speed of internet connection, studies are being carried out for robots to take an auxiliary role in surgeries and even remotely controlled surgery by robots (Panesar et al. 2019).

The use of AI in the health sector has primarily been a development for the use of the most appropriate applications in the flows of treatment, correct diagnosis and correct processing of patient data, and then, with sub-branches such as deep learning and machine learning, which are covered by AI, both reducing costs, measuring the adequacy of personnel and creating a database (Akalın, 2020).

Automotive

Along with the "industry 4.0" developments, transformations continued in the automotive sector as well. AI technologies offer many possibilities in the field of transportation. With the development of the technological infrastructure day by day, the vehicles produced within the scope of AI have also changed. It is possible to make traffic management more effective by equipping vehicles and roads with sensors, GPS, and warnings. Driverless autonomous vehicles are being tested and systems are being developed that can be adapted to fleet management. With the widespread use of autonomous vehicles, the decrease in the number of vehicles in traffic, the decrease in the need for fuel, and the decrease in deaths due to traffic accidents are expected social benefits in this area in the future. Digitalization continues in the estimation of consumer demands, the technological methods and service processes used within the organization. Driverless vehicles and their integration with mobile applications are another example of the use of AI in this sector (Soegoto et al., 2019).

Tourism

AI plays an important role in digitalization in the tourism industry, and it is possible to offer new services with learning robots, big data and analytics, smart signaling systems and cognitive technologies (Zsarnoczky, 2017).

Along with the developing technology, the concept of travel has also become different from the traditional, with online applications, applications used by companies and smart phones, new generation technologies play an important role in tourism activities. It is possible to describe AI as one of the most important systemic inventions that make up the technological revolution today.

Translating applications with AI applications, personalized service, online support applications, accessibility via applications, smart cities, AI-based transportation and health applications, and systems such as online check-in in the tourism sector and AI-based robots offered in accommodation facilities are more professional can be presented in some way. For this reason, it is an important requirement to examine the use of AI technologies in the tourism industry and to reveal their characteristics (Samara, 2020).

It is possible to deliver continuous immediate tourism services 24 hours a day, 7 days a week by utilizing AI's natural language processing and feature identification functions. To provide these services, AI systems such as chatbots and voice customer assistants are deployed (Dittenbach ct al., 2003).

Cyber Security and Defense Industry

The concepts of cyber security and national security have also changed with the development of AI technologies. With the concept of AI, face recognition, autonomous vehicles, tracking of digital footprints, location tracking systems have started to take place in the defense systems of countries (Qiu et al., 2019). The concept of smart war has been put forward and countries have started to give more importance to AI investments for the defense industry and cyber security at the domestic and international level with these developments. With the applications that are tried to be developed for crime detection, the interest in autonomous marine robots and drones has increased.

Cyber defense systems are network defense algorithms developed against cyber-attacks of a website, digital data belonging to public institutions or all foreign networks regarding country security, responding to attacks with AI, minimizing the damage received, and preventing possible attacks with machine learning. The level of security can be increased by modeling attacks, a regular auditing process and research for future attacks, and by using early warning and prevention steps in cyber-attacks (Mosteanu, 2020).

AI in Marketing

Marketing is an organizational process that begins before the production phase and continues after the sales phase. This marketing process is the most important part of a business. Marketing management encompasses all efforts to identify, organize, coordinate, and control these functions (Deepak, 2009). Marketing management has been defined as "the art and science of finding, retaining and increasing the number of customers by selecting target markets, creating, delivering and communicating superior customer value" (Kotler & Keller, 2006). Technology offers businesses a platform where they can address the target market and audience individually and collectively; It enables businesses to convey their promotions with sound, color and moving images. Technology also provides the opportunity to retain existing customers and acquire new customers, together with customer relationship management systems. The advantages of technology and the internet are ease of selection and distribution of the target audience, cheapness, measurable results, interaction with the consumer, instant feedback to the consumer, instant updates, instant sales, and the ability to operate internationally. Communication with customers and potential customers is perhaps the most important feature of the internet for businesses. At the same time, providing competitive advantage significantly affects businesses. For this reason, AI has changed the way businesses do business (Sharma et al. 2007).

Today, AI has been successfully integrated into businesses (Ezimmuo & Keikhosrokiani, 2022; Keikhosrokiani, 2022a; Keikhosrokiani, 2022b; Keikhosrokiani et al., 2019; Xian et al., 2022). Many companies use AI technologies in their production, evaluation, and recruitment processes. At the same time, AI has become an important part of digital marketing strategies. The basic principles of marketing may remain the same, but marketing methods continue to evolve. Businesses use AI solutions to strengthen their marketing strategy and turn target audience interaction into a successful organization. The interaction of marketing strategy and AI is gathered under three main headings as stated in Figure 1. According to Huang & Rust (2021), AI intelligence in marketing is evaluated under three main headings: mechanics, thinking and feeling.

Figure 1. AI & strategic marketing decisions (Huang & Rust, 2021)

Marketing Action
• Standardization (mechanical AI)
• Personalization (thinking AI)
• Relationalization (feeling AI)

Marketing Research
• Data collection (mechanical AI)
• Market analysis (thinking AI)
• Customer understanding (feeling AI)

Marketing Strategy
• Segmentation (mechanical AI)
• Targeting (thinking AI)
• Positioning (feeling AI)

Mechanical AI is used to automate repetitive tasks. Mechanical AI learns the task it is asked to do by assimilating the datasets presented to it. For example, remote sensing, machine translation, classification algorithms, clustering algorithms, and size reduction are examples of mechanical AI (Huang & Rust, 2021).

Thinking AI is designed to make new decisions and process data. For example, text mining is good at recognizing patterns and regularities in data, such as speech recognition and facial recognition. Machine learning, neural networks, and deep learning (neural networks with additional layers) are some of the current ways that thinking AI processes data. AI is the disruptive technology of this age that changes skills and strategies in various industries and creates a new set of interactions between customer and brand (Huang & Rust, 2021).

Feeling AI is used for two-way interactions involving people and to analyze their emotions. Examples of AI technologies are natural language processing, text-to-speech technology, recurrent neural networks (RNN), chatbots, built-in and embedded virtual agents for human interactions, and robots with hardware designed for sensing (McDuff, & Czerwinski, 2018). AI is changing the necessary skills, strategy, and interaction with customers in businesses.

AI-based customer interface is given as an example of the use of this technology in customer relationship management. Analysis of customer behaviors, routines, and tastes with AI technologies; It brings with it more accurate decision making, strategy formation and planning based on the processing results of algorithms (Verma et al., 2020). Thanks to AI, customer awareness has become more pervasive and accurate than ever before. Thus, AI is used to enable the business to obtain information about the customer because of real-time analysis of the data obtained from various channels and, as a result, to enable the marketing managers to achieve their goals. In other words, AI causes marketing to be data-driven, real-time, personalized, and predictive, increasing its performance (Nair, 2021).

AI can significantly impact customer service by managing 85% of customer interactions and providing 24-hour service in the coming years (Fowler & Mönch, 2018). Driven by AI bots that will enable direct interaction with customers, it will be an effective tool to give talented managers time for strategic decision making. It may be an appropriate technological innovation step for business organizations to manage their processes and be successful in day-to-day operations. In addition, companies will be able to gain time, money, and competitive advantage by minimizing the waste of resources. It has the data of all customers using AI applications (Henderson & Venkatraman, 1999).

Thus, customers' search histories and purchased products and services can be viewed. Companies can perform data segmentation and analysis with this data (Vishnoi et al., 2018). AI marketing will contribute to companies increasing the customer experience from creating new sales points, feeding, and following. AI, big data, and machine learning systems integrated together can truly examine these search patterns and assist marketers in identifying critical areas to target. Complementing social models and government initiatives with AI-powered systems that promote justice, openness, and accountability in implementing and monitoring social plans is far more effective. Furthermore, trends will be very helpful in boosting the deployment of AI-powered computers in critical elements of government agencies, such as tax fraud detection, cybersecurity, cybercrime, and cyberwarfare, disease outbreak geographic tracking, and the census bureau for population surveys (Bryant et al., 2008).

AI may give organizations with a lot more intelligence and insight when paired with artificial neural networks, deep learning, natural language processing, picture recognition, and forward-looking personalization technologies. AI, on the other hand, is favored because of the benefits it provides in big data research. AI aims to build models that mimic the intelligent behavior of living things in nature, think like people, and make decisions. Marketing has evolved over time to include new aspects and forms. Yang & Siau, (2018) evaluated the core function of marketing in eight main categories: customer service management, marketing information management, financing, marketing operations, sales, shipping, pricing and product management, and promotion.

Promotion

Customers often differ in demographics, geography, lifestyle and standard. These features also affect the relationship of customers with the brand. Therefore, understanding these differences is especially important in marketing management. Because the message to be conveyed to the customers and the product to be presented must comply with these features. Adapting to this situation increases the return on investment in promotion tools as a whole and contributes to the success of the business.

Existing data is crucial to achieving this goal. By analyzing historical and behavioral data, AI provides the tools for businesses to better understand customers and deliver the most appropriate message through the best channel (Marinchak et al., 2018). AI-powered optimization tools are essential for marketing and customer satisfaction to acquire leads and accelerate business transformation (Miikkulainen et al., 2018). One of the most important reasons for this is that customers prefer to use technologies that can capture their preferences in certain products or services and recommend similar products and services.

Thanks to its algorithms, AI is an expert in scoring according to the click-through rates of the images in the ads and selecting the images used to facilitate brand awareness or encourage consumption (Overgoor et al., 2019). AI technologies analyze the behavior of customers and send customized promotions and campaigns to appropriate customers via social media (Turban et al., 2018). Chatbots and recommendation systems are examples of use of AI to answer questions, make recommendations, and promote the product based on customers' behavioral, demographic, and geographic data. Thus, the click-through rate of business websites will be increased, and their total revenues will increase (Kumar et al., 2020).

Machine Learning-based A/B testing is used to evaluate and optimize the performance of websites, ads, and other online resources in real time. For example, testing static content against dynamic content and adapting it to the HSBC phone app resulted in a 100 percent increase in clickthrough rate (Choi et al., 2020). Purchasing a space to display ads is one of the important processes of the campaign. Unlike traditional methods, doing this automatically makes things easier for marketers in terms of cost, time, efficiency, and customer relevance (Nair, 2021). AI offers new tools and process synchronization to use data, speed, and efficiency to determine customer behaviors and needs on a large scale so that businesses can convey the right message to the right customer in the best and most cost-effective way. Smart methods have the potential to be a good assistant in personalizing the advertisement. Text, image, and video analysis provides the business with the power to select and place advertisements based on the content of the text the customer reads or the video they watch, considering the past behavior and data of the customers (Tuten & Solomon, 2017).

Customer Service Management

AI is dramatically changing the way many different industries work. At the forefront of these processes is customer service. Companies need to gain competitive advantage by correctly perceiving customer expectations and reflecting them in the design and production process. However, to understand customer expectations, businesses need to analyze customer information. Businesses also benefit from databases where customer information is kept confidential. Customer relationship management can be shown as a tool that institutions use for this purpose. By analyzing the data of customers with AI, consumer behavior can be examined, and customized products and services can be offered to the person (Turban et al., 2018).

In CRM studies, it is important not only to bring the customer to the company, but also to make the customer dependent on the company. To achieve this, businesses must first define the customer group they are addressing very well, and thus, care should be taken to ensure that the strategies presented are aimed at both the entire market and individual individuals. Machine learning models used in AI technologies are an important tool for analyzing customer needs and providing advice (Baier, 2020). AI refers to the ability of a system to correctly interpret large amounts of data, learn from that data, and use this learned information to achieve goals (Haenlein et al., 2019). Thanks to the AI-enabled CRM, the storage of customer data in the cloud is used to quickly solve problems to serve customers in real time. Key metrics are analyzed, and data is available 24 hours a day so that companies can make informed business decisions. Data obtained from all customer touch points can be used to create personalized marketing operations, generate new ideas, meet product and service demands and gain competitive advantage.

Marketing Decision Making

The rapid expansion of markets has caused businesses to communicate and operate globally. Technology also makes this process more flexible. In the context of globalization, where the sustainability of operations and the competition between businesses for profit are increasing, discovering customer preferences, understanding the target market depends on the correct analysis and interpretation of the data. Decisions made based on wrong data and wrong analysis have irreversible costs for businesses. In this case, technology plays a life-saving role for businesses to communicate with customers effectively and timely and move towards their goals (Rajagopal, 2019).

The decision-making process in marketing is complex. Analyzing the wishes and needs of the consumers and making the products and services suitable according to these analyzes are important for making the right marketing decisions in the long run. AI modeling techniques can be used to predict consumer behavior. With the decision support system, which is one of the AI systems, data can be collected and analyzed, and help can be obtained to identify trends and make decisions (Moreno, 2009).

To reach the targeted marketing organization, the operational model components should be analyzed based on various layers and efficiency and improvement opportunities for the future situation should be identified. In addition, while all processes are questioned, digitalization levels should be determined, and areas of development should be revealed. Strategic decision-making emerges as a process that allows you to analyze the institutions and their environment in the light of this understanding, considering the expectations of the customer, and to determine a marketing strategy accordingly. While making strategic decisions in marketing, it is necessary to evaluate issues such as determining the sales method, which distribution channels to use, how to determine sales prices and profit margins (Sahaf, 2019).

AI-based decision-making systems can help accelerate strategy development, boost confidence in strategy formulation, improve the quality and quantity of decision-making, and improve the decision's accuracy and precision (Islam et al., 2009). In addition, a hybrid intelligence system is also suitable for developing accurate and appropriate marketing strategies by combining machine-based analysis with human judgment and creativity (Li & Yost, 2000)

Marketing Operations

In marketing management, operations are carried out to meet the supply and demand between producers and consumers. With the change in customer behavior and channels of access to products, marketers use AI to better understand market trends and customers with the data they have, and to meet customer needs through multiple channels. The multiplicity of channels also requires a lot of effort and time to be managed. In this field, AI is also widely used in the form of robots and smart devices (Vlačić et al., 2021). AI is used to offer and recommend personalized products, regardless of customers' comments and behaviors, services, time, place, access type and means, to the extent that they can obtain the products/services they need from these channels in a shorter time and at an affordable price.

The job of marketing operations is to manage an organization's marketing program, campaign planning, and annual strategic planning activities. Internal communications, workflows, and processes are all guided by marketing operations. AI refers to the use of systems that combine machine learning, consumer insights, and other concepts to forecast how your target customers will respond to communications, content, information, products, or services in marketing.

Furthermore, AI enhances managers' creativity and automates boring and repetitive tasks, allowing businesses to devote more time to formulating innovative solutions (Kumar et al., 2020). Some AI applications, such as robots and automated factories, show how AI may automate time-consuming and boring tasks, freeing up people's time for more creative and imaginative work. Furthermore, AI can optimize operational processes by inventing a variety of new types of marketing procedures to meet the many conditions it predicts, as well as implementing certain operational processes automatically and dynamically.

CUSTOMER EXPERIENCE

The acceleration of globalization, the changing technology and the development of AI have brought a new perspective to marketing. It is getting harder and harder for businesses to survive in an intensely competitive environment. Companies have begun to seek ways to establish long-term good relationships that will create value for the customer and make them feel different. With the increase in customer experience, communication tools and touch points, traditional marketing has been replaced by new types of marketing supported by AI (Batra & Keller, 2016).

In general, traditional marketing is referred to as mass marketing. Television, radio, newspapers, brochures placed in mailboxes, and billboards are all examples of mass media used in advertising efforts. Because consumer requirements and habits have evolved, traditional channels are no longer able to accommodate them effectively. Customers are solely seen as rational decision makers in traditional marketing (Schmitt, 1999).

In traditional marketing, it means that they give customer habits and demands based on product features, choosing a product that better meets their needs. Today, with the development of technology and the introduction of new marketing tools such as social media, brands are recognized globally. This means that product features can no longer be evaluated from a single point of view.

Therefore, it is the customer experiences that drive consumption, and they are important for attracting customers and gaining a competitive advantage. In other words, customer experience management is one of the newest methods used by companies to establish an unbreakable bond with their customers. When changing customer demands and needs are added to this situation, new marketing strategies have developed. The concept of experiential marketing has emerged, giving importance to the customer, oriented to the emotions of the customer, and aiming at lasting experiences. It aims to provide different experiences by taking the customer to the focus of marketing. Customer experience is an important concept that enables the benefits of products and services to be considered together with their sensory aspects (Berry et al., 2002).

Customer experience represents the total value a company receives at every touchpoint. Touchpoints cover the customer's thinking, starting before the customer purchases the product or service and continuing throughout the purchase and post-purchase process. During this time, the customer experience has become an important competitive advantage for the enterprise. Companies need to not only provide products and services, but also provide emotional experiences for their customers (Meyer & Schwager, 2007)

Businesses that want to increase the customer experience should pay attention to three important factors (Goodman, 2019):

- Should care about customer needs.
- The relationship with the customer should be memorable.
- It is necessary to embed the customer experience into the business culture.

Due to technological developments and the spread of digital services, customer interactions are moving to online channels. Companies want to invest in online channels to provide better service online and improve customer experience. However, with increasing competition, creating a superior online customer experience is getting harder. One of the most beneficial ways to engage with customers anytime, anywhere and provide an easy and natural interaction is to use a chat-based user interface, namely chatbots. When chatbot systems and chatbots are supported by AI technologies such as natural language understanding, they can more clearly analyze customers' goals.

AI technologies are often used in conjunction with other technologies such as augmented reality, computer vision-based image recognition, and predictive inventory (Saponaro et al., 2018). For AI technologies to adequately enhance customer experiences, they must have a thorough grasp of the customer, including their preferences and experiences. Big data and client profiles are used by AI systems to learn the best ways to engage with customers (Omale, 2019).

An example of the importance of customer experience, Adobe has implemented a comprehensive data strategy called Adobe Dash to solve data correlation problems. Adobe Dash is a commercial AI platform that performs real-time data connections from numerous sources. Due to the weakness of traditional databases in collecting data at a proportional rate, Adobe can quickly combine data from various memories through in-memory computation, providing more tailored customer interactions and a reliable usage experience. For example, when customers click on classified ads online, Adobe presents them with a matching ID and a tailor-made message based on that information. This type of personalized marketing is often aligned with the preferences of its customers (Morabito, 2015).

METAVERSE, A NEW FIELD

Businesses act very interactively to keep up with the rapid steps of the age. They have to respond to the competition and meet the competitive struggle with optimum cost. In recent years, competition has become more challenging in virtual markets, apart from physical ones. While the change in the world reveals that the tendency to virtual markets has increased, it also shows that it is an explanatory feature of consumer trends. Along with the importance of digitalization, businesses are also developing their virtual market strategies. Dominating the virtual markets necessitates changing the known and conventional methods. The most difficult situation in this regard starts with overcoming the trust problems of consumers. The product or service supply of businesses should be shaped according to consumer purchasing behavior. In this context, businesses first must understand the importance of digitalization and then develop new business methods. The most current topic of recent years is seen as Metaverse (Mystakidis, 2022).

Metaverse is defined as a cognitive universe that people can experience using various virtual reality devices without leaving their place, without needing much physical action. Metaverse was first used in the early 1990s to describe a universe beyond dreams in the science fiction writer Neal Stephenson's novel "Snow Crash". In the novel, people participate in the online world through their digital avatars as a way of escaping dystopian reality. However, this concept was criticized a lot in those years because it characterized a very utopian and manipulative understanding of the future. Although it is considered as a more utopian or dystopian dimension away from today's point of view, the motivation to combine the real and the virtual now has made the metaverse universe grow very fast (Kim, 2021).

Metaverse has two components: technology and metaverse ecosystem. These components state that technologies such as hardware, network, cloud technologies, augmented reality lay the foundation for a process extending from the internet to augmented reality and the Metaverse, and this creates the virtual ecosystem that includes avatars, virtual economy, social acceptability, and trust (Lee et al., 2021).

(Ball, 2021), stated that there are eight main elements for the Metaverse:

- Equipment,
- calculation
- networking,
- virtual platforms,
- means of exchange/standards,
- payments,
- content, services, and values,
- user behavior.

Based on these elements, it can be said that a large and powerful technological hardware is used for Metaverse, and a virtual universe is built that can transform human life culturally and economically through digital twins. It also requires having new technological equipment to be able to access the Metaverse.

Metaverse is built as an XR (Extended Reality) extended virtual universe in which VR (Virtual Reality) virtual reality, MR (Mixed Reality) mixed reality and AR (Augmented Reality) augmented reality technologies are used together (Watson, 2021).

In this case, the metaverse needs more technological hardware than the hardware required for internet access. Equipment such as VR headsets, AR glasses, multi-sensor cameras, tactile gloves should be used. In addition, high-speed connections and broadband networks are needed to continue uninterruptedly and quickly in a universe like Metaverse, where large amounts of data and many users are consumed. VR and AR technologies have been used for decades in many applications developed in fields such as military, education, health, marketing, entertainment, and engineering (Choi et al., 2017).

At the same time, the Metaverse is being developed as a universe in which economic and financial transactions can be carried out. Metaverse brings these visualization technologies to another dimension by combining these visualization technologies on the blockchain infrastructure and offering AI support (Nobanee & Ellili, 2023)

Cryptocurrencies such as bitcoin, ethereum and various blockchain technologies allow financial transactions to be carried out smoothly on virtual platforms. It is possible to buy a product or service on Metaverse and pay the price with cryptocurrencies. Metaverse, which aims to immerse users in digital items on screens, seems to have the potential to change not only social media concepts, but also our lives, relationships, behaviors and even our physiology (Kim J., 2021). Metaverse is an expanding universe of assets, services and content created by professionals and users. World-famous popular brands from various sectors such as technology, entertainment, clothing, and education have started their Metaverse investments. Developing products and services for this universe, opening stores and marketing are on the agenda of many big and small brands (Kim, 2021).

FUTURE RESEARCH DIRECTIONS

Metaverse isn't just for socializing or playing digital games; Education emerges as a second universe that includes many activities such as shopping, cultural interaction, and working. Although the virtual universe causes social and psychological criticism and concerns, it is seen as the new reality of the world. Since businesses are affected by many external environmental factors such as technology, competition and politics, marketers take steps to develop new strategies by displaying a proactive attitude.

In our daily life, many technological developments such as telephone, computer networks, internet and mobile phones are reshaping our work and social environment to a great extent. The field of our real and physical world is expanding and intertwining with the electronic world. new lifestyle, new working strategies, new communication and learning methods are required to develop. With the emergence and expansion of the electronic field, it is seen that many activities in the name of e-commerce, e-business, e-government, and e-learning have increased. Such developments require businesses to develop a new generation of organization and management theory.

Businesses that want to take place in the Metaverse world not only have to change their management and organizational theories, but also must improve their understanding of e-business and e-commerce. The world of the Metaverse is leading to the development of a business environment that is much more complex, much more multi-faceted than businesses are used to. The nature and characteristics of this new business environment, which combines the real world and the virtual universe, have economic, social, and political consequences. In this context, businesses need to be systematic and determine their roadmaps in order to take place in the Metaverse world (Hollensen et al., 2022). After Facebook's meta move, world brands such as Microsoft, Nike, Adidas, Zara, H&M, Gucci, Dolce & Gabbana and Dyson started to invest in Metaverse one by one (Yüksel, 2021).

It is known that consumers are an indispensable building block for businesses to survive and compete in the market. Change is experienced in the market first and businesses try to keep up with this change. People every year, compared to the previous one and they spend more time on the internet and establish new relationships and social spaces. Along with the concept of metaverse, the factors affecting purchasing experiences and purchasing preferences will also change.

With the evolution of technology in the market, the features and benefits of products and services lead to creating new experiences for consumers (Schmitt, 1999).

To understand the consumption experiences in the metadata, it is necessary to reveal the determinants of consumers' avatars choices. In the Metaverse, avatars represent a self-concept that the consumer chooses according to his ideal, real, or social self. It can also be said that the avatar reflects the role and personality traits that the consumer chooses to play in the virtual world (Yu et al., 2014).

While evaluating the purchasing habits of consumers, businesses should also research the application designs they use and compare them with consumer behavior. For this reason, the consumption of users should also be encouraged in the Metaverse environment, because it is revealed that the behavior of consumers in the real world and their behavior in the virtual universe are not the same (Shen et al. 2021).

CONCLUSIONS

The rise of AI in marketing does not occur on its own but is in line with the rapid advances in general technology, including front-line operations such as contact centers and resource management. This advance will contribute to the use of AI in marketing by computerizing other aspects of transactions and generating data that can be used to support AI (Stone et al., 2020). This also means that the use of AI needs to be integrated into these applications to automatically collect data and make specific recommendations for both marketers and end users. Thanks to this AI concept, companies that integrate it into their marketing strategies can anticipate customer orientation and preferences, monitor, and analyze buying behavior, and predict the next consumer behavior in this regard. increase.

In addition, the facts discussed in the chapter show that AI has the power to affect the activities of both internal and external businesses. When considered from a wider perspective, AI studies have the power to affect the social structure and social relations in general. However, this situation should be seen as another area that needs to be studied and the literature should be enriched at this point by making more comprehensive studies at this point. Despite the serious problems that must be resolved before they can be rolled out, AI promotes the ability of marketers to create the right value and deliver it to the right people at the right time. It brings great benefits to people and society.

As AI automates repetitive tasks, marketers will be able to focus more and more on value-added activities that improve consumer life, increase workplace satisfaction, and encourage creative thinking (Marinchak et al., 2018). As a result, new developments affect how shoppers choose channels, products, services, and shop. The online and offline worlds are growing together. Knowing what's different, what's similar, and how new technologies affect both two worlds is key to the future of our business. The innovations help customers make the right decisions, reduce time pressure, and increase their confidence and satisfaction in their decisions. Businesses need to take advantage of these new technologies to connect with their customers and make their lives easier.

In addition, Metaverse introduces a very large market, which is a candidate to offer brand new experiences to consumers, is dominated by tough competition conditions, has its own norms, and whose boundaries are unpredictable. The purpose of the Metaverse market is not to interfere with the liberal understanding that constitutes the basic philosophy of the universe, but to provide the most appropriate financial and social conditions for the relations to run freely and healthily at the maximum level.

Adaptation of businesses to the external environment helps them to maintain their presence in the market for a long time. Technological infrastructure and R&D investments correspond to a significant budget of the marketing investments of the enterprises. Because, beyond what they produce or what they offer as a service, what kind of environment and ground they offer this is decisive in their success. Technological developments open many issues to discussion. Today, while it is discussed that time is a relative concept, businesses that come face to face with the fact that space is also relative are adapting to keep up with a new era. Perhaps the most striking example of this is that space travel, which until recently seemed utopian, has become viable.

Being in the Metaverse universe is perceived by the public as a complementary element for personal prestige and corporate image. However, being a qualified avatar in the Metaverse universe is necessary to make the prestige and image stronger. With Metaverse, the meaning of the new generation customer concept is changing. For innovative and hasty customers who are bored with the monotony of classic shopping and spend time on the internet, showing up in the Metaverse market will be adopted as a game-like activity and will become a lifestyle day by day. Marketing actors who want to catch the new generation of customers should improve themselves by constantly chasing new ideas.

A new sector is emerging to meet a series of needs, from providing the necessary tools for users to enter the Metaverse market and adapting to the market, to acquiring a marketing culture; This industry, which is mostly software and hardware, makes a significant contribution to the development of marketing in the Metaverse. To be able to operate successfully in the Metaverse market institutionally, it is of great importance to invest in software and hardware and to follow technology closely.

REFERENCES

Aghion, P. J. (2018). Artificial intelligence and economic growth. In *The economics of artificial intelligence: An agenda* (pp. 237–282). University of Chicago Press.

Akalın, B. (2020). Sağlikta dijitalleşme ve yapay zekâ. *SDÜ Sağlık Yönetimi Dergisi, 2*(2), 128–137.

Alon, I. Q., Qi, M., & Sadowski, R. J. (2001). Forecasting aggregate retail sales: A comparison of artificial neural networks and traditional methods. *Journal of Retailing and Consumer Services, 8*(3), 147–156. doi:10.1016/S0969-6989(00)00011-4

American Marketing Association. (2017). Retrieved from https://www.ama.org/the-definition-of-marketing-what-is-marketing/

André, Q. C., Carmon, Z., Wertenbroch, K., Crum, A., Frank, D., Goldstein, W., Huber, J., van Boven, L., Weber, B., & Yang, H. (2018). Consumer choice and autonomy in the age of artificial intelligence and big data. *Customer Needs and Solutions, 5*(1), 28–37. doi:10.100740547-017-0085-8

Baier, L. K., Kühl, N., Schüritz, R., & Satzger, G. (2020). Will the customers be happy? Identifying unsatisfied customers from service encounter data. *Journal of Service Management, 32*(2), 265–288. doi:10.1108/JOSM-06-2019-0173

Ball, M. (2021). *Framework for the Metaverse*. Academic Press.

Batra, R., & Keller, K. L. (2016). Integrating Marketing Communications: New Findings, New Lessons, and New Ideas. *Journal of Marketing, 80*(6), 122–145. doi:10.1509/jm.15.0419

Berry, L. L., Carbone, L. P., & Haeckel, S. H. (2002). Managing the total customer experience. *MIT Sloan Management Review, 43*(3), 85–89.

Bini, S. A. (2018). Artificial intelligence, machine learning, deep learning, and cognitive computing: What do these terms mean and how will they impact health care? *The Journal of Arthroplasty, 33*(8), 2358–2361. doi:10.1016/j.arth.2018.02.067 PMID:29656964

Bryant, R., Katz, R. H., & Lazowska, E. D. (2008). *Big-data computing: creating revolutionary breakthroughs in commerce, science and society*. Academic Press.

Chinnamgari, S. K. (2019). *Machine Learning Projects: Implement supervised, unsupervised, and reinforcement learning techniques using R 3.5*. Packt Publishing Ltd.

Choi, H. S., & Kim, S. (2017). A content service deployment plan for metaverse museum exhibitions—Centering on the combination of beacons and HMDs. *International Journal of Information Management*, *37*(1), 1519–1527. doi:10.1016/j.ijinfomgt.2016.04.017

Choi, R. Y., Coyner, A. S., Kalpathy-Cramer, J., Chiang, M. F., & Campbell, J. P. (2020). Introduction to Machine Learning, Neural Networks, and Deep Learning. *Translational Vision Science & Technology*, *9*(2), 14. doi:10.1167/tvst.9.2.14 PMID:32704420

Deepak, R. K. (2009). *Marketing management*. Educreation Publishing.

Dittenbach, M., Merkl, D., & Berger, H. (2003). A natural language query interface for tourism information. *ENTER 2003: 10th International Conference on Information Technologies in Tourism*. 10.1007/978-3-7091-6027-5_17

Efraim Turban, E. T., & King Jae Kyu Lee, D. K. J. K. (2015). *Electronic commerce a managerial and social networks perspective.* . doi:10.1007/978-3-319-10091-3

Ezimmuo, C. M., & Keikhosrokiani, P. (2022). Predicting Consumer Behavior Change Towards Using Online Shopping in Nigeria: The Impact of the COVID-19 Pandemic. In P. Keikhosrokiani (Ed.), *Handbook of Research on Consumer Behavior Change and Data Analytics in the Socio-Digital Era* (pp. 210–254). IGI Global. doi:10.4018/978-1-6684-4168-8.ch010

Fowler, J. W., & Mönch, L. (2018). A survey of semiconductor supply chain models Part II: Demand planning, inventory management, and capacity planning. *International Journal of Production Research*, *56*(13), 4546–4564. doi:10.1080/00207543.2018.1424363

Godwin-Jones, R. (2019). In a world of SMART technology, why learn another language? *Journal of Educational Technology & Society*, *22*(2), 4–13.

Goodfellow, I., Bengio, Y., & Courville, A. I. B. (2016). Deep learning. MIT Press.

Goodman, J. (2019). *Strategic customer service: Managing the customer experience to increase positive word of mouth, build loyalty, and maximize profits.* AMACOM.

Haenlein, M., Kaplan, A., Tan, C. W., & Zhang, P. (2019). Artificial intelligence (AI) and management analytics. *Journal of Management Analytics*, *6*(4), 341–343. doi:10.1080/23270012.2019.1699876

Henderson, J. C., & Venkatraman, H. (1999). Strategic alignment: Leveraging information technology for transforming organizations. *IBM Systems Journal*, *38*(2.3), 472-484.

Hollensen, S., Kotler, P., & Opresnik, M. O. (2022, March 17). S. K. (2022). Metaverse–the new marketing universe. *The Journal of Business Strategy*. Advance online publication. doi:10.1108/JBS-01-2022-0014

Huang, M. H., & Rust, R. T. (2021). A strategic framework for artificial intelligence in marketing. *Journal of the Academy of Marketing Science*, *49*(1), 30–50. doi:10.100711747-020-00749-9

Islam, M., Zhou, L., & Li, F. (2009). *Application of artificial intelligence (artificial neural network) to assess credit risk: A predictive model for credit card scoring*. Academic Press.

Jordan, M. I., & Mitchell, T. M. (2015). Machine learning: Trends, perspectives, and prospects. *Science*, *349*(6245), 255–260. doi:10.1126cience.aaa8415 PMID:26185243

Kang, M., & Jameson, N. J. (2018). Machine Learning: Fundamentals. Prognostics and Health Management of Electronics. *Fundamentals, Machine Learning, and the Internet of Things*, 85-109.

Kaya, O., & Schildbach, J., & Schneider, S. (2019). Artificial intelligence in banking. Artificial Intelligence.

Keikhosrokiani, P. (Ed.). (2022a). *Big Data Analytics for Healthcare: Datasets, Techniques, Life Cycles, Management, and Applications*. Elsevier Science., doi:10.1016/C2021-0-00369-2

Keikhosrokiani, P. (Ed.). (2022b). *Handbook of Research on Consumer Behavior Change and Data Analytics in the Socio-Digital Era*. IGI Global., doi:10.4018/978-1-6684-4168-8

Keikhosrokiani, P., Mustaffa, N., Zakaria, N., & Baharudin, A. S. (2019). User Behavioral Intention Toward Using Mobile Healthcare System. In Consumer-Driven Technologies in Healthcare: Breakthroughs in Research and Practice (pp. 429-444). IGI Global. doi:10.4018/978-1-5225-6198-9.ch022

Keikhosrokiani, P., & Pourya Asl, M. (2023). *Handbook of Research on Artificial Intelligence Applications in Literary Works and Social Media*. IGI Global. doi:10.4018/978-1-6684-6242-3

Kim, J. (2021). Advertising in the Metaverse: Research agenda. *Journal of Interactive Advertising*, *21*(3), 141–144. doi:10.1080/15252019.2021.2001273

Kotler, P., & Keller, K. L. (2006). Marketing management (12th ed.). Academic Press.

Kotler, P. A.-M. (2012). *Principles of marketing: An Asian perspective*. Pearson/Prentice-Hall.

Kumar, A., Nayyar, A., Upasani, S., & Arora, A. (2020). Empirical Study of Soft Clustering Technique for Determining Click Through Rate in Online Advertising. In N. Sharma, A. Chakrabarti, & V. Balas (Eds.), *Data Management, Analytics and Innovation. Advances in Intelligent Systems and Computing* (Vol. 1042). Springer. doi:10.1007/978-981-32-9949-8_1

Lee, L. H., Braud, T., Zhou, P., Wang, L., Xu, D., Lin, Z., ... Hui, P. (2021). *All one needs to know about metaverse: A complete survey on technological singularity, virtual ecosystem, and research agenda*. arXiv preprint arXiv:2110.05352.

Li, M., & Yost, R. S. (2000). Management-oriented modeling: Optimizing nitrogen management with artificial intelligence. *Agricultural Systems*, *65*(1), 1–27. doi:10.1016/S0308-521X(00)00023-8

Marinchak, C. M., Forrest, E., & Hoanca, B. (2018). Artificial intelligence: Redefining marketing management and the customer experience. *International Journal of E-Entrepreneurship and Innovation*, *8*(2), 14–24. doi:10.4018/IJEEI.2018070102

Mehta, N. D. (2018). *Amazon changes prices on its products about every 10 minutes—here's how and why they do it*. Academic Press.

Meyer, C., & Schwager, A. (2007). Understanding customer experience. *Harvard Business Review*, *85*(2), 116. PMID:17345685

Miikkulainen, R., Iscoe, N., Shagrin, A., Rapp, R., Nazari, S., McGrath, P., ... Lamba, G. (2018). Sentient ascend: AI-based massively multivariate conversion rate optimization. *Thirty-Second AAAI Conference on Artificial Intelligence*.

Morabito, V. (2015). Managing change for big data driven innovation. In *Big Data and Analytics* (pp. 125–153). Springer. doi:10.1007/978-3-319-10665-6_7

Moreno, J. (2009). Trading strategies modeling in Colombian power market using artificial intelligence techniques. *Energy Policy*, *37*(3), 836–843. doi:10.1016/j.enpol.2008.10.033

Mosteanu, N. R. (2020). Artificial intelligence and cyber security–face to face with cyber attack–a maltese case of risk management approach. *Ecoforum Journal, 9*(2).

Mystakidis, S. (2022). Metaverse. *Metaverse. Encyclopedia*, *2*(1), 486–497. doi:10.3390/encyclopedia2010031

Nair, K., & Gupta, R. (2021). Application of AI technology in modern digital marketing environment. *World Journal of Entrepreneurship, Management and Sustainable Development*. Advance online publication. doi:10.1108/WJEMSD-08-2020-0099

Nobanee, H., & Ellili, N. O. D. (2023). Non-fungible tokens (NFTs): A bibliometric and systematic review, current streams, developments, and directions for future research. *International Review of Economics & Finance*, *84*, 460–473. doi:10.1016/j.iref.2022.11.014

Noorbakhsh-Sabet, N., Zand, R., Zhang, Y., & Abedi, V. (2019). Artificial intelligence transforms the future of health care. The American journal of medicine. *The American Journal of Medicine*, *132*(7), 795–801. doi:10.1016/j.amjmed.2019.01.017 PMID:30710543

Omale, G. (2019). *Improve customer experience with artificial intelligence*. Academic Press.

Overgoor, G., Chica, M., Rand, W., & Weishampel, A. (2019). Letting the Computers Take Over: Using AI to Solve Marketing Problems. *California Management Review*, *61*(4), 156–185. doi:10.1177/0008125619859318

Panesar, S., Cagle, Y., Chander, D., Morey, J., Fernandez-Miranda, J., & Kliot, M. (2019). Artificial intelligence and the future of surgical robotics. *Annals of Surgery*, *270*(2), 223–226. doi:10.1097/SLA.0000000000003262 PMID:30907754

Qiu, S., Liu, Q., Zhou, S., & Wu, C. (2019). Review of artificial intelligence adversarial attack and defense technologies. *Applied Sciences (Basel, Switzerland)*, *9*(5), 909. doi:10.3390/app9050909

Rajagopal, A. (2019). *Managing startup enterprises in emerging markets: Leadership dynamics and marketing strategies*. Springer Nature. doi:10.1007/978-3-030-28155-7

Romao, M., Costa, J., & Costa, C. J. (2019). Robotic process automation: A case study in the banking industry. *2019 14th Iberian Conference on information systems and technologies*. 10.23919/CISTI.2019.8760733

Sahaf, M. A. (2019). *Strategic marketing: making decisions for strategic advantage*. PHI Learning Pvt. Ltd.

Samara, D., Magnisalis, I., & Peristeras, V. (2020). Artificial intelligence and big data in tourism: A systematic literature review. *Journal of Hospitality and Tourism Technology*, *11*(2), 343–367. doi:10.1108/JHTT-12-2018-0118

Saponaro, M., Le Gal, D., Gao, M., Guisiano, M., & Maniere, I. C. M. L. (2018). Challenges and opportunities of artificial intelligence in the fashion world. *International Conference on Intelligent and Innovative Computing Applications.*

Schmitt, B. (1999). Experiential marketing. *Journal of Marketing Management, 15*(1-3), 53–67. doi:10.1362/026725799784870496

Sharma, R. K., Kumar, D., & Kumar, P. (2007). Quality costing in process industries through QCAS: A practical case. *International Journal of Production Research, 45*(15), 3381–3403. doi:10.1080/00207540600774067

Shaw, J., Rudzicz, F., Jamieson, T., & Goldfarb, A. (2019, July 10). Artificial Intelligence and the Implementation Challenge. *Journal of Medical Internet Research, 21*(7), e13659. doi:10.2196/13659 PMID:31293245

Shen, B., Tan, W., Guo, J., Zhao, L., & Qin, P. (2021). How to Promote User Purchase in Metaverse? A Systematic Literature Review on Consumer Behavior Research and Virtual Commerce Application Design. *Applied Sciences (Basel, Switzerland), 11*(23), 11087. doi:10.3390/app112311087

Soegoto, E. S., Utami, R. D., & Hermawan, Y. A. (2019). Influence of artificial intelligence in automotive industry. *Journal of Physics: Conference Series, 1402*(6), 066081. doi:10.1088/1742-6596/1402/6/066081

Stone, M., Aravopoulou, E., Ekinci, Y., Evans, G., Hobbs, M., Labib, A., Laughlin, P., Machtynger, J., & Machtynger, L. (2020). Artificial intelligence (AI) in strategic marketing decision-making: A research agenda. *The Bottom Line (New York, N.Y.), 33*(2), 183–200. doi:10.1108/BL-03-2020-0022

Syam, N., & Sharma, A. (2018). Waiting for a sales renaissance in the fourth industrial revolution: Machine learning and artificial intelligence in sales research and practice. *Industrial Marketing Management, 69*, 135–146. doi:10.1016/j.indmarman.2017.12.019

Tuten, T. L., & Solomon, M. R. (2017). Social media marketing. *Sage (Atlanta, Ga.).*

Verma, N., Malhotra, D., & Singh, J. (2020). Big data analytics for retail industry using MapReduce-Apriori framework. *Journal of Management Analytics, 7*(3), 424–442. doi:10.1080/23270012.2020.1728403

Verma, S., Sharma, R., Deb, S., & Maitra, D. (2021). Artificial intelligence in marketing: Systematic review and future research direction. *International Journal of Information Management Data Insights, 1*(1), 100002. doi:10.1016/j.jjimei.2020.100002

Vishnoi, S. K., Bagga, T., Sharma, A., & Wani, S. N. (2018). Artificial intelligence enabled marketing solutions: A review. *Indian Journal of Economics & Business, 17*(4), 167–177.

Vlačić, B., Corbo, L., Silva, S. C., & Dabić, M. (2021). The evolving role of artificial intelligence in marketing: A review and research agenda. *Journal of Business Research, 128*, 187–203. doi:10.1016/j.jbusres.2021.01.055

Watson A. (2021, May 11). Retrieved from https://www.coinspeaker.com/blockchain-metaverses-vr-headset

Xian, Z., Keikhosrokiani, P., XinYing, C., & Li, Z. (2022). An RFM Model Using K-Means Clustering to Improve Customer Segmentation and Product Recommendation. In P. Keikhosrokiani (Ed.), Handbook of Research on Consumer Behavior Change and Data Analytics in the Socio-Digital Era (pp. 124-145). IGI Global. doi:10.4018/978-1-6684-4168-8.ch006

Yang, Y. &. (2018). A qualitative research on marketing and sales in the artificial intelligence age. *MWAIS 2018 Proceedings, 41.*

Yu, Y., El Kamel, A., Gong, G., & Li, F. (2014). Multi-agent based modeling and simulation of microscopic traffic in virtual reality system. *Simulation Modelling Practice and Theory, 45,* 62–79. doi:10.1016/j.simpat.2014.04.001

YükselY. (2021, November 12). *Webtekno.* Retrieved from https://www.webtekno.com/metaversete-varligini-gostermeye-baslamis-markalar-h117659.html

Zsarnoczky, M. (2017). *How does artificial intelligence affect the tourism industry?* Academic Press.

Chapter 5

A Review on Virtual Reality and Eduverse:
History and Technical Perspectives

David Roland Andembubtob

School of Computer Sciences, Universiti Sains Malaysia, Malaysia

Pantea Keikhosrokiani

iD https://orcid.org/0000-0003-4705-2732

School of Computer Sciences, Universiti Sains Malaysia, Malaysia

Nasuha Lee Abdullah

School of Computer Sciences, Universiti Sains Malaysia, Malaysia

ABSTRACT

Due to the unique ability of making knowledge freely available anywhere at a very cheap cost, ICT is recognised as a key instrument for delivering excellent education. The new, linked virtual world ushers in an easy and unrestricted movement of data, cash, ideas, goods, and people. It is projected that the usage of the metaverse in education would upend current learning methodologies since it will increase learning strategies, the use of technology, and the options available to students, educators, and education providers. Nevertheless, there are presently few systematic studies on how scholars used immersive virtual reality for academic purposes that noted the use of both expensive and inexpensive head-mounted displays. Therefore, this chapter aims to examine virtual reality and Eduverse from a historical and technological standpoint. The success of virtual reality in education will primarily depend on how motivated students, as the main consumers, become and their capacity to recognise the key components required to reach a suitable degree of learning through virtual reality.

DOI: 10.4018/978-1-6684-7029-9.ch005

INTRODUCTION

Son & Amparado (2018) emphasized the importance of Information and Communications Technology (ICT) in every country's developmental plan. ICT has been identified as an important tool to convey quality education and present a radical approach to address developmental needs due to their unrivalled capacity make information readily available at any location globally at a relatively low cost. Consequently, the new interconnected virtual world heralds a fluid and unhindered flow of information, funds, ideas, products, and people. With the convergence technologies, information is no more restricted to text and book form but now includes real-time audio and video (Son & Amparado, 2018).

The critical effort of aligning recent technology in higher education with research is to allow users to get a greater level of virtual reality immersion. This enables users to gain better knowledge with experience both from the new technology and educational assets. In addition, this helps ongoing interaction in an educational, community centred, culturally thoughtful, ethically right, and economically viable environment. Metaverse application in education is anticipated to change the present learning methods since it will elaborate the present learning practices, the use of technology and more opportunities on hand for users, educators, and providers of educational services. Thus, the introduction of emerging technologies into education is a necessity to improve on the delivery, content, construct, and the teaching and learning outcomes of course curriculum. Such technologies are artificial intelligence, virtual reality, 5G network and so on.

Several educators have examined the gains from the various use of digital virtual reality (VR) in diverse situations. It is clear that virtual reality has great potential in its educational application which has drawn considerable interest of late. In spite of this, not many findings are available on how scholars in tertiary institutions have use immersive VR that use of both good and low-cost head-mounted displays (HMDs) (Radianti et al., 2020). Therefore, this chapter aims to review virtual reality and Eduverse from history and technical perspectives. This study can assist system developers to understand how virtual reality and Eduverse can benefit higher education. The remaining section reviewed virtual reality including definition, history, and its applications in education. Furthermore, metaverse and education are discussed from different perspectives. Then, challenges and limitations of virtual reality and Eduverse are discussed, and the chapter ends with discussion and concluding remark.

VIRTUAL REALITY

Definition of Virtual Reality

There are many definitions and perspective to the subject of Virtual Reality, in fact to many other 'realities and several emerging technologies of our times. This depends on the 'who' and 'why' and from the 'where' it is being seen or the context in which it is taken. Augmented, Virtual, Mixed, and Extended Realities are terms frequently used to show how technologies modify or create reality (Rauschnabel et al., 2022). VR is tacitly said to be a technology that creates virtual immersion in a digital environment, using computer simulation which enables users to immerse in an interactive 3D world in which diverse types of emotional and sensory experiences are encountered (Villena-Taranilla et al., 2022). Therefore, VR environment must be digital, immersive, and engaging. Also, virtual reality causes the users to adapt real - time, to a three – dimensional artificial medium using one or more computers. The user's input to the system is by the use of rods and data gloves performed along with verbal and body gestures simultaneously. The outcome is a simultaneous implementation of the movement and application which enables the participants to experience the actual effect of the exercise with complete conformation to the artificial setting (Serin, 2020).

Another perspective is that virtual reality is mostly linked to devices (HMDs, gloves, visors) that are immersive, successfully detaching the user's perceptions from the physical reality by encompassing all or some of the users senses in the virtual world (Falomo Bernarduzzi et al., 2021).

Virtual Reality is an innovative technology which creates a real time, 3D environment, interactive environment, where each user interacts digitally with the platform and experiences real-world interaction (Srimadhaven et al., 2020). Merriam-Webster, (2022) dictionary states virtual reality as 'an digital environment that is experienced via sensory stimuli (such as sounds and sights) made available by a computer and the technology platform the accesses or creates the VR is partially affected by actions of the user. Generally, VR is a 3D environment, generated simulation by a computer that seems very real to the user, using specified electronic equipment. The purpose is to create a strong and real feeling of being in a virtual environment. The VR client puts on an HMDs goggles to look at a stereoscopic three dimensional scenes. By moving your head around, you can see and move about using handheld motion sensors. This engages you in an all immersive experience. The immersiveness makes you feel like you are actually in a virtual world (Glover & Linowes, 2019).

Historical Development of Virtual Reality

VR technology causes virtual experiences look real and unmediated. In the 1960s, VR technology was used via simulations to train health and military personnels, while today it is used as an instrument for evaluating psychological and social metrics in many academic settings. The serene feeling of complete immersion while interacting through body gestures raises interest which also motivates learning. This occurs as users carry out simple tasks and even training practices using the technology. Many research along with empirical experiments which look at the use and effects of VR in the formal educational sector, or have focused on developing the homelictic use of VR in conveying practical skills in engineering and medicine, these studies highlight that VR has effectiveness in the teaching processes, bringing students to reality in digital contexts. Augmented Reality overlays digital information elements onto a real-time display of the physical setting, extending the information presented to the user, and by using equipment such as GPS, compass, digital camera, to detect visual signals that appropriately cover the most significant information. AR technology applications enables the user to bond with the added digital information and physical reality concurrently, giving an efficient and a seamless experience (Bernarduzzi et al., 2021).

How Virtual Reality works

Of late, education, training and teaching have integrated (VR) technologies into several application domains in the sector. Scholars have been attracted to VR, though the technology has been around for a while, due to the current advances in immersive technologies such as in interactions and visualization. Bearing in mind, the use of VR shows prospective learning improvement that is why educators and researchers, have examined this technology passionately, desiring to augment the classroom with an added dimension during learning and teaching (Radianti et al., 2020).

Immersive VR is a key emerging technology in this century which employs head-mounted displays (HMD) has attracted attention from consumers, clients, scholars and practitioners, from different of disciplines (Dincelli and Yayla, 2022).

Figure 1 displays IVR peripherals. Concepts that give complete spatial virtual experience such as immersiveness and presence have been investigated closely by many researchers. These concepts are intimately connected and accounts for the very awareness of reality and virtual space by a user. Immersiveness a major concept refers to the measured of the virtual environment (VE) system's technology quality. Presence tells of the psychological experience of the attribute of existence in a particular virtual plane (Pereira da Silva et al., 2022).

Figure 1. Immersive VR Peripherals (L-R motion controller, lighthouse, tracker, omni-directional treadmill, haptic glove, and suit)

Application of Virtual Reality in Education

AR and VR applications feature prominently in Education. AR and VR application in education is projected to grow and VR is seen to have greater prospect since it needs less real-world stimuli (Wu & Ho, 2022). The present teaching methods lack motivation and are boring as it fails to aid students of all levels to reach the anticipated proficiencies of the relevant courses. Since educational technology has improved and the desire to engross learners of this 21st century, it has become obligatory to alter the classroom standard of tertiary education to be entrenched with novel teaching methods. Through the effectual usage of ICT, the learning - teaching process has been modernised with smart classrooms furnished with useful collaborative activities where the instructors use available online ICT tools along with cloud services for tertiary education (Srimadhaven et al., 2020).

Scholars in universities foresee a more interactive sessions with students via immersive virtual reality (IVR) that makes 3D visualization possible. 360° video study materials can be watched using smartphones inserted in head-mounted displays (HMDs) implanted with motion sensors (Hodgson et al., 2019). Many educators have discovered the gross gains of VR applications in different and diverse scenarios. There is an increase research interest in VR because of its great inherent potential and its educational application (Radianti et al., 2020).

Virtual reality is digital system where users using specialized equipment get a sense of being in a virtual world with which they interact. Virtual reality endowed with this sense of presence can be used in many fields, including education. Through VR applications in education students are able to gain hands on experiences which are life threatening or almost impossible to get in real life but able to learn by doing in the virtual world. Owing to this, in the present, also in future educational settings, virtual reality will play a key role of innovation (Serin, 2020). Research on virtual reality in some fields of education, such as Mathematics, Biology, Health and Business Ethics is available (Haryana et al., 2022; Sholihin et al., 2020).

Educationally, longer memory retention, shorten time of learning, and providing real life observation are some of the affordances of applications of virtual reality. Virtually, students can investigate a hazardous volcano at a close range, learn from history by visiting the roads of an ancient city life through VR. Thus, the training of a pilot is done virtually before going to do the real-life testing on the field for the safety of the person in training, the trainers and the spectators. This scenario is obtainable in medical science when training in medical surgery for dangerous procedures. (Serin, 2020).

In the last two decades, education as seen transformation as the evaluation processes, learning and teaching have been exposed to digital tools (Modgil et al., 2022). Haryana et al., (2022) reiterated what (Y. Zhang et al., 2018) emphasized that "the use of virtual reality not only supports the learning process cognitively but also the learning process constructively. According to constructivist learning theory, learners can learn better when they are actively involved in constructing knowledge".

Haryana et al., (2022), in their study examine how material of learning and media as instructional designs have impacted student learning outcome according to Cognitive Load Theory (CLT). In particular, the study further developed CLT by examining the contrast between audio-visual media (VRM) and virtual reality media (VRM) on the outcome of student learning in the framework of preparing material for accounting equation. The research experimented with a 2x2 factorial design method with 173 participants. Analysis of Variance was used to analyse the data. The result showed VRM gave better student learning outcome than AVM, as a student learning outcome for the use of traditional accounting equation learning materials were lower when using non-traditional accounting equation learning materials. This study showed that the learning outcome of a student were lower when taking AVM and traditional accounting equation learning materials when compared to using VRM and non-traditional accounting equation learning materials. These outcomes substantiate the CLT that a student cognitive load is minimum if they use VRM and non-traditional accounting equation learning materials as maximum learning performance is achieved. The study results show the importance of employing virtual reality technology in developing good learning materials in the learning accounting.

Simply put, in learning, many advantages abound in employing virtual reality, such as enable accommodation of different personalised learning methods, raising motivation for learning, receiving feedback report directly from users, deliver experiences of interest, enrich visual display that excites the imagination and deployment interactive technology (Haryana et al., 2022). Mostly, applications of immersive VR tailored for education and educational purposes are rare, still in the experimental stage, and scarcely have been tried in real learning situations (Radianti et al., 2020).

Radianti et al., (2020), in their paper, focused on tertiary education usage of immersive VR and attempted to give answers to these questions:

- How does tertiary education integrate immersive VR technologies into learning?
- What learning subjects, design features, and immersive technologies are made accessible to aid VR-based learning?
- What possible learning concepts are used to guide VR application design, development, and execution for higher education?
- What assessment techniques have been used to appraise the learning results?
- What tertiary education fields or sphere have used VR application for teaching and learning?

THE EDUVERSE

The concept of the metaverse in education is definitely not new since several educators and researchers have deliberated extensively on its effect on learning. Along this line of thinking, stakeholders in higher education can use the metaverse to actively promote learning and teaching, serving as a spatial avenue for individuals to meet, socially interact as they exchange ideas. Certainly, the growth of the metaverse is relatively young, having the promise of immense potential for further enhancement. In the academia concerning the metaverse little has been done scientifically to direct its growth meanwhile many industries recognising the huge potential, have made investment as they make preparation ahead of time. (Mistretta, 2022; Zhao et al., 2022).

A technology in the present day that has been acknowledged with a huge prospect is the metaverse. Unfortunately, little discussion on the role of the metaverse in education is held. Few scholars are aware of the metaverse, an emerging technology that holds potential in its features and applications (Hwang and Chien, 2022). Without doubt, the metaverse provides learners great opportunities of learning, exploring, and teaching experience in a virtual setting as well as enabling people to interact and work. What users are unable to rehearse, exploit or learn in the actual world can be done in the metaverse (Hwang et al., 2022).

The findings of a recent studies of the metaverse, which were analysed, gave positive result for learning outcomes, concerning its educational use, a good total educational experience of the metaverse' effectiveness in education (López-Belmonte et al., 2022).

Lin et al. (2022) outlined some characteristics of the metaverse that makes it an effective tool for application in the world of teaching and learning to produce desirable lasting learning outcomes that will develop a proposal to improve human development as graphically illustrated in Figure 2.

Figure 2. The characteristics of Metaverse and Education (Lin et al., 2022)

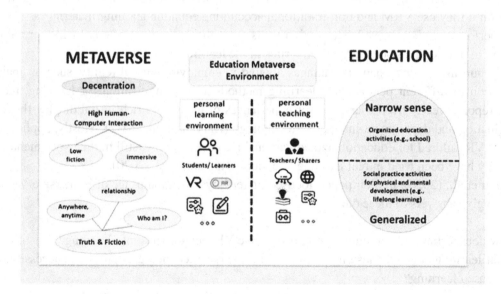

These characteristics include (a) decentralization, meaning the Metaverse becomes co created, co-controlled with co - participation (b) IoT connectivity, the meeting of virtuality and reality, users anywhere and anytime can switch over from the real to the virtual worlds and vice versa (c) Human-computer interaction functions as the boundary between human sense and value and the Metaverse. (d) Digital reality consists of 360o video, augmented, virtual and mixed realities and these remove space and time barrier, giving users immersive experience which enhances understanding and the study skill for learners and (d) Metaverse comes with great monetary gains in education as everyone is empowered to create various digital products with more flexibility exceeds that of traditional method of education (Lin et al., 2022) Godwin-Jones, 2023; Miller et al., 2020; Zhan et al., 2020.).

Tlili et al. (2022), noted in their research that the Metaverse has attracted scholars for a long time. The study uses content and bibliometric analysis to disclose the focus, trends, and research limitations of the topic. A gap was discovered in the metaverse applications of lifelogging in education and it reveals that Metaverse design in education has progressively changed over time, showing generation X and Y have not enjoyed AI technologies as much as generation Z. Few researches have looked at mobile, micro, hybrid learning when it comes to learning scenarios (Tlili et al., 2022). The activities and services delivered by modern metaverse platforms can help the learning and teaching process as clients can show their interactive skills in a safe digital setting, problem solving collectively and assisting other users. The metaverse encourages helpful interactions and the co-learning of constructive social abilities among users to enhance a healthier sense of community presence in the metaverse (Oh et al., 2023).

Tlili et al. (2022), further showed that the instruments and technology of the Metaverse have improved the teaching and practical aid to education, the entire teaching and learning environment, enable immersive learning by students, thereby increasing raising their desire to learn. As shown in Figure 3, technology and tools are grouped into 7 categories, namely wearable, immersive, sensors, artificial intelligence (AI), game application, mobile, educational, simulation and modelling. The metaverse experience gotten by learner promotes teamwork, is immersive, and develops skills, but also involves students in classrooms in diverse means. This technology is a combination of some emerging technologies, including Multi-user Virtual Environment (MUVE), Virtual, Mixed, and Augmented Realities. The technologies are entry points and allow users to engage the Metaverse settings which can enhance student learning and transfer.

Clearly, it is without doubt that metaverse application in education, the pedagogical activities, enhance student-cantered virtual learning experiences as we allow the educational procedure to be carryout in strictly virtual environment (López-Belmonte et al., 2022). "Interactivity, Persistence and Corporeity, are attributes of the Metaverse that positioned it above and beyond similar apparatus in the educational sector. These attributes give users the ability to interact in the virtual world, using the learning platform with each other (Akour et al., 2022).

(López-Belmonte et al., 2022) in their study designed and validated an instrument which enable the assessment, in the metaverse, the formative evaluation and educational experiences from a holistic view point. The design of the research was based on a scale which had been development and used. A purposive sampling technique was used to select 362 Spanish students at secondary schools for the study. At the end, the study developed an evaluation tool which is all-inclusive in nature, made available to scholars interested in the metaverse, a little explored research field practice their educational activities.

Teng et al. (2022) in their study investigated the factors affecting learners' acceptance of a metaverse in education platform using an extended UTAUT model (Keikhosrokiani, 2019, 2020b, 2020c, 2021b; Keikhosrokiani et al., 2020; Keikhosrokiani P, 2021; Lateef & Keikhosrokiani, 2022) and incorporating perceived risk. 495 respondents were surveyed from China and data analysed using structural equation modelling. The results revealed the following (i) PE (performance expectancy), EE (effort expectancy), SI (social influence), and FC (facilitating conditions) had significant positive effects on learners' satisfaction with the Eduverse; (ii) learners' satisfaction had a positive effect on their continued usage intention; (iii) learners' intention to use the Eduverse was reduced after they perceived risks. The study provided practical evidence of the validity of the UTAUT model in explaining learners' adoption of the Eduverse.

Figure 3. Technology and Tools for Metaverse in Education (Tlili et al., 2022)

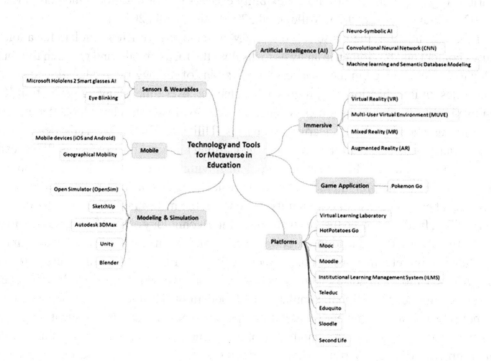

Based on Unicef records, 91% of students learning worldwide, was disrupted by the coronavirus pandemic. As from April 2020, students and educators had to adapt to newly introduced mode of teaching and learning. Without doubt, Technology via the internet has been crucial to the continuation of learning throughout the global lockdowns. Fundamentally, tech experts and educators alike are saying if the internet is beneficial to learning in its contemporary state, would the metaverse not be more advantageous? Thus, the metaverse will improve the following area in education: bring curricula up to date, gamification of learning, promote interdisciplinary learning and encourage practical application of theory and improve test results (Türkiye Bilimler Akademisi et al., 2020; Gutierrez-Bucheli et al., 2022; Sadovets et al., 2022).

There are 14 items according to (Cortés, 2022) in UOC's report which is a commitment to achieving the UN SDG goals that showed how education was disrupted by the metaverse, in context these include:

- Change of environments and content.
- Learning quality enhancement: student's pace matching through personalization.
- Pivoting and leveraging the new, proven possibilities of virtual worlds.

- Transformation from lecturing to gamification.
- Use of technology to reach a greater number of students.
- Closing gap between demand for talent and educational supply.
- Access challenge: digital /generational gaps, investments in technological infrastructure.
- Redesigning educational environments. replica of the physical in the digital world.
- Transforming and redefining the role of student and teacher.
- Comprehending the new ways of capturing attention.
- Solving assessment and monitoring challenges.
- Incorporating new partners in education.
- Outlining and setting appropriate criteria.
- Interoperability, non-fungible tokens and blockchain.

Advantages of Metaverse in Education

Low self-esteem, passive participation, emotional seclusion, lack of attention, and indolence are well known, limitation of 2D e-learning platforms applications in education. Due to compulsive multitasking behaviour, learners face added distractions and give more attention in tutor-supervised classes than to online courses (Teng et al., 2022).

Hwang et al., 2022 outlined in the findings that if generality is not loss, this is why metaverse should be adopted and accepted for educational purposes:

- To able locate students in an intellectual or skill practicing setting maybe unsafe or hazardous in the actual surrounding.
- To always position students in the settings to practice and acquire knowledge deem not possible in the actual environment.
- To allow learners to observe or learn things that require long-term participation and practice.
- Learners can be encouraged to try to build or explore things that cannot be done in the real world for some real reasons, such as cost or lack of materials.
- To expose learners to different thoughts and selections regarding their professions or lives.
- To allow clients to distinguish, practice, or witness things from varied outlooks or roles.
- To cause users to learn to relate and work together people they might not have occasions to work with in the actual world.
- To explore the dormant or higher order thinking of learners by linking them in different, difficult, and realistic tasks.

HCI in the Eduverse

A transformative metaverse is an AI technology. Artificial intelligence (AI) undertakes human based intellectual processes in computers. Educators are strained to regard within learning and teaching, to what extent AI will be allowed. In educational settings, AI have been restricted to instructional software that personalise curriculum materials based on students' particular needs. This is illustrated by Knewton, a platform that is AI driven which develops individualised and adaptive class curriculum for users. Many such platforms which are AI-driven are gradually gaining entry into educational institutions, although they still fall short of the interconnected, virtual social interactivitty of the metaverse experience.

On the other hand, an educationally biased domain of "virtual humans" is emerging. Star Labs, funded and built by Samsung in 2020, made public Neon, an AI Human, the first in the world. Neon can talk, smile and move about making it look so real it's almost impossible to say these are generated by a computer, Neon is a videobot, a photo-realistic human. These robots learn about their clients and serve as educational tutors that speak many language and can be bought.

Furthermore, even in Britain, AV1, an AI teaching instructor robot, helps children with chronic disease to participate in a long distance-learning. The robot represents the student in class where it interacts with classmates by participating in learning activities. In China, a class of 600 kids in kindergarten hear stories read to them, are prompted to give predictions and answer riddles poised by an autonomous robot called Keeko. In addition, Keeko, recognizes faces, remembers conversations, and plays educational games. GPT-3 (Generative Pre-trained Transformer, Version 3) a novel AI tool, accumulates information from the Internet and uses this to composes essays, using language processing, and can describe senses. GPT-3 when prompted can write "impressively" and "human-sounding."

Generally, AI will spice up the metaverse by the use videobots, 3D chatbots, digital humans that interrelate with humans in the virtual world. Education will be impacted in the following ways:

- The metaverse will facilitate students learning in fully immersive and interactive environments harnessing the enriched collaborative setting of both the physical and digital worlds.
- Centralized learning in the metaverse (or "metaverse schools") where physical boundaries or constraints of brick and mortar will no longer exist. Traditional learning methods will be challenged by these novel immersive experiences of learning in the metaverse.
- Progressive gamification of learning and learning activities such as design elements and mechanics along with competition to get rewards and points.

Scholars and parents are concerned about effect of the metaverse on their children as learning and teaching evolves by this technology. When the content of immersive environments is not readily available or apparent to adults combined with exposure to more-and-more "realistic" environments as the difference between reality and fantasy fades, it will cause worry among parents on the effect of these on the children's emotional stability? These will pose a concern related to children in a metaverse environment (Driscoll, 2022).

Complications of Eduverse

Though, challenges subsist from a governance and socio-technical perspective, as providers of digital platform seek to extend the ability for clients to build personal virtual worlds (Cheung, 2022). Zallio & Clarkson, (2022) showed the several and many challenges of using the metaverse to include the necessity to learn and understand a new language and heuristics a scary task as you approach this latest technology. They observed that people connecting to the metaverse using dissimilar devices, in a physical environment, may encounter sensory discomfort or even physical injury. This may be because of the movement wthin the immersive virtual setting as they relate and interact with avatars and objects. In the same vein, the special design with disproportionate mass of wearable gears like VR headsets can restrict movements or bring about discomfort if worn for long.

Apart from bodily discomfort, high numbers of mental cognitive challenges that have to do with the concept of social behaviour may occur. In the metaverse, a cycle of harmful psychological symptoms could occur for diverse users, due to drowning sound, vast info, attitudinal, voiced, or graphic assault which may cause an array of issues such as embarrassment, tiredness, and melancholy. These subsequently may lead to low self-esteem or self-confidence. The use of the technology may not generate these socio-ethical facets but could amplify them. Therefore, careful consideration by designers must be taken into account while designing. Proxemics that is the degree, and effect of the good spatial separation individuals naturally maintain to others that translate into digital proxemics is an important mechanism to ensure good design that will give clients of the metaverse behavioural comfort.

The metaverse is taken and seen as a virtual space, it is a real place where users can develop ideas, express emotions, and feel. While avatars are fictional, digital representations of the users, by building an immersive and virtual world where digital bodies, real-time activities are tracked, and latent digital twins of people are formed and kept; this data can influence the real life, biological, and psychological dimension of real people. Therefore, the ideas of safety, health and inclusion should be given priority, bearing in mind how physical sphere can be affected by psychological wellbeing. (Tiggemann & Anderberg, 2020).

Researchers have also proffered solutions to many of these daunting challenges that tend to mar the progression of the metaverse and its application. Some of these suggestions include the formation of virtual sieves, friction operations or system shields that lower, or momentarily signal and defer or stop the action of avatars. Many have purposed that similar rules and regulations that manage the real world should be applied in the design of the metaverse which does not disorientate behaviour of people and therefore police the affairs of the virtual world. Security and privacy have been pointed out to be vital and key machinery constantly needed to control activities in the metaverse. Hence, privacy and security are to be well thought-out, managed and maintain from installation to decommissioning (Dwivedi et al., 2022).

PRIVACY, HARDWARE, NETWORK AND DATA SECURITY

Security and privacy issues concerning the metaverse have been given little attention in spite of the tons of research about technology of the metaverse. In the metaverse, privacy and security issues are critical as with all platforms of social media. Cybersecurity and privacy concerns must be addressed, if users are to be provided with appropriate services securely and efficiently, because the metaverse is part of the virtual or cyber environment. Malicious users and cyber criminals can observe in real-time and collect metaverse users' behavioural patterns and biometrics identity and use it to harm them (Dwivedi et al., 2022; Z. Zhang et al., 2022). The metaverse harnesses many technologies to enable users enjoy personalised and 3D immersive experiences. A bugging question yet unanswered is how to protect users' content, uniqueness, data and digital identity in the metaverse. Due to this challenge blockchain technology with its unique attributes of immutability, decentralization, and transparency is good solution. Technically, blockchain technology can be used in the metaverse since it is important in data privacy preservation, data storage, acquisition, sharing, and data interoperability. It is also useful in big data, artificial intelligence, digital twins, immersive applications, multi-sensory and Internet-of Things in the metaverse where it impacts key-enabling technologies as mentioned above. The next level of digital evolution is the metaverse that will revolutionize, expand the domain of digital services standardize systems providing online access and service digitization that will lift adopted technology to a staggering height. Truly blockchain will play a pivotal role in the transformation and implementation of the metaverse.

In simple words, blockchain is a storing ledger that keeps dedicated transactions which assist digital asset tracking and security in a financial network. The transactions stored as blocks, are linked jointly using cryptographic measures, or hashing mechanisms, ensures the ledgers' immutability and allows secure sharing capability. One attribute of blockchain is its ability to work on decentralized ledger data devoid of a central authority. In the metaverse context, blockchain brings impose accountability on the virtual or digital eco-system. Blockchain is necessary and imminent, to secure the digital content kept by all the actors in the metaverse. Blockchain ensures user reputation and privacy, accountability of transactions and content in the eco-system of the metaverse on which it depends (Gadekallu et al., 2022).

EDUCATION AT THE ADVENT OF VIRTUAL REALITY AND METAVERSE

Technology and Education

The blending of education and metaverse is known as the Eduverse. Stakeholders, teachers, administrators, and students get digital identities. This allows for collaboration between faculty and students, as it unlocks informal and formal spatial avenue for learning and teaching in a virtual environment (Chen, 2022). Many reasons abound for accepting and application of the metaverse in education. The role of metaverse in education is increasingly drawing attention and steadily possible due to the rapid development of suitable devices for the metaverse, which include wearable apparatus, advanced networks, and computers with appropriate sensing technologies. Every facet of our lives now is increasingly being permeated by the Metaverse. It is essential and important to understand the Metaverse and utilise it fully. Lin et al. (2022) shows the incorporation of the metaverse with education and its interrelationship with the human society as a whole in Figure 4.

The combination of machine learning, blockchain, IoT, and AI improves the real and virtual space interaction and gives a better form of experiences of virtual and augmented reality in the metaverse. When the metaverse is employed in education, better emotional simulation along with cognitive experiences are seen as the traditional classroom scene is recreated more than with earlier versions of technologies and also users and environment interaction is enhanced (Dwivedi et al., 2022). No matter which learning concepts under each model are used by VR researchers, it is essential that the growth and application of VR applications for higher education is consistently rooted on present and current learning models since the concepts offer recommendations on the incentives, noble learning method and results for the learners (Radianti et al., 2020).

Integration of VR/MR into Education

It is predicted that the metaverse in education presently will offer a better form of learning that is above and beyond the current actual classroom simulation (Dwivedi et al., 2022). Polyviou & Pappas (2022) in their contribution state that the social customs and emotional domains of the actual world can be imitated and portrayed through interaction and interrelation of students and scholars as metaverse is employed in education. As students and educators interrelate and interact in the developing educational metaverse there will be seamless operations in the virtual world as students participate actively. As developers engage in the design of the metaverse particularly for use in education the attributes that make up traditional classroom must be rightly understood so as to apply them in the virtual world platforms.

Figure 4. An overview of the Metaverse in education

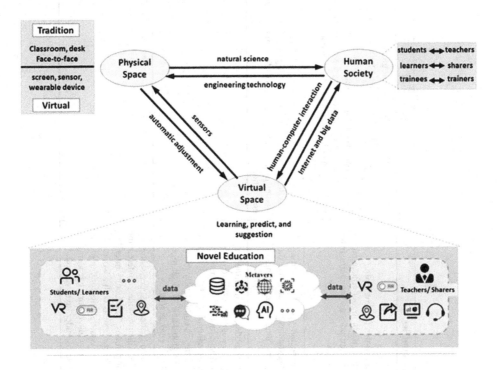

Polyviou & Pappas (2022) subsequently presented five suggestions on the main variations needed to be made for metaverse for learning purposes: Metaverse in education should, for students and scholars mimic the actual world learning settings; enhance the novel methods of teaching and the capabilities of the actual classroom and online apps combined; Scholars must to enhance their instructional styles and curriculum to fit into learning in the metaverse; Viable measurement methods to evaluate learning observations and outcome in the metaverse should be introduced; and Current educational platform suppliers have to develop advance tools as well as tutor the educators on their application for learners in the metaverse (Dwivedi et al., 2022).

These prospective steps are proposed for the use of the metaverse in education: first, educators should cautiously analyse the way learners identify with the metaverse; secondly, educators should plan classes for learners to work out challenges or execute projects creatively in cooperation; and lastly, carefully designed metaverse in education platforms should be developed inhibit abuse of data of learners (Kye et al., 2021).

With the wrong use of digital technology in all spheres of our lives, and the rapid development with deployment of new technologies in the educational setting, the use and teaching of technology in education is an indispensable professional repertoire for teachers to guarantee students' well-being. Good education policy frameworks mandate that teachers acquire competence in the integration of technology for swift delivery of teaching in hybrid online modes and for nurturing students' digital literacy. Future-oriented professional development packages should go beyond individual learning and employ leadership to create conditions for technology-enhanced learning methods at institutional and system levels (Flavin, 2017). Table 1 discusses VR and Metaverse in Education.

Table 1. VR and Metaverse in Education

S/N	Author /Year	Area of Application	Findings/Countries	Limitations
1.	(Jin et al., 2022)	Major stakeholders with instructors and students.	This study offers fresh empirical insights for developing breakthrough VR and HCI technologies in higher education by offering a full overview of existing attitudes and concerns from a multi-stakeholder viewpoint.	A possibly VR-biased participant group because they all attended the same sizable public institution in the Midwest. VR immersion is our top priority. In addition, only eight people are invited to the workshop in order to gain more targeted and in-depth insights.
2.	(Kalinkara & Talan, 2022)	UTAUT-2, UBYS system	Performance expectancy, effort expectancy, enabling settings, and hedonic motivation are among the factors that affect the usage and acceptance of UBYS, according to the findings of SEM.	This study contains age restrictions because it was done with a young participant group. Further studies may look at age as a variable in more diverse populations.
3.	(Ruwodo et al., 2022)	Software Engineering Education: Conceive, Design, Implement and Operate (CDIO) model	We describe how a complementary model for a traditional university, namely a metaversity, can improve software engineering education in Africa. These models were inspired by the CDIO model for engineering education and the CATI model for curriculum reform focusing on contextually relevant education in the Global South. The global and local settings are combined in the teaching of software engineering.	NA
4.	(Hedrick et al., 2022)	College students	For boosting student engagement and academic success, the suggested technological connections include video conferencing, spatial audio, and further app integrations. The faculty intends to let student participants utilise the metaverse as both a workspace and a classroom. Understanding the requirements for conducting a classroom in a virtual environment while ensuring learning occurs is one of the research problems under investigation.	NA

Tertiary Institution, Technology and the Eduverse

For example, it is known that the system of the metaverse is directly associated to the AI technologies and efficient shared learning systems commonly used to boost learning methods and educational approaches (Akour et al., 2022). It is widely proven and accepted that the echelon of higher education is a significant indicator of a country's development level and advancement potential, and how to explore and exploit a more versatile and efficient teaching model is a foremost educational issue common to mankind (Zhu & Liu, 2020). One of the fundamental ways of using these models effectively is to employ related technologies through education platform providers who can deploy AR, VR devices to enhance 'targeted delivery of learning models' at targeted sets of students' for desired learning outcomes. In this regard, many higher education institutions can provide a platform for students, staff and faculty to correspond in a totally elastic atmosphere where the schoolrooms are void of barriers like the normal school classes. Here professors can interact with students in virtual spaces using the computers. Basically, the metaverse can create shared classes, providing learning models where teachers and students move their classrooms to a virtual environment from an actual university campus and institution (Akour et al., 2022; Ando et al., 2013; Tarouco et al., 2013). The metaverse is expected to alter our normal life and livelihood further than the sphere of entertainment and games. It has unbounded prospect as a novel shared community space. With that in focus some imminent jobs are proposed for the metaverse in education: Firstly, tutors should circumspectly analyse the way learners students comprehend the digital world; secondly, educators should organise platforms aimed at problem solving and cooperative and creative project execution; thirdly, prevention of misuse of student data should be a high priority on educational metaverse platforms (Kye et al., 2021).

The paper (Mahmud & Saka, 2020) establishes that by means of research universities and countless higher institutions make significant contributions to the expansion and development of key sectors of a nation. This promotes national and global development. To enable this, ICT is a tool that has catapulted the creation, prompt processing, storage, quick dissemination, accessibility and use of information. Several higher institutions are now accepting the use of ICT and related gadgets such as the Computer Based Instructions (CBI), which is virtually any kind of computer used in the educational sector for instructional delivery such as laptops, electronic white boards, storage devices, video conferencing facilities, software application packages and Management Systems such as Moodle and Google Classroom.

Divjak et al. (2022) and Tor et al., (2021) noted that the availability of ICT facilities is a measure of a society's successive progress and development, which includes communication infrastructure and education. The availability of ICTs enhances students' learning experiences and better academic performance. Studies have shown that Nigeria universities have computers, CDROM, flash drives, inverters, multimedia equipment, printers, Internet equipment, telephones and scanning machines. Others showed that ICT availability in tertiary institutions is quite limited in a similar study. In Tanzania, (Mungwabi, 2018) discovered that mobile phones, the internet, networked PCs, audio devices and YouTube (audio/visual materials) were all available in the university students.

It was discovered that commendable efforts have been put into supplying ICT tools to Nigerian universities and students are engaging them to facilitate various academic activities. Though these ICT tools are available yet grossly inadequate compared to the students' population in the institutions (Tor et al., 2021). Hence, the inadequacy makes it hard for staff and students to derive maximum benefits of integrating ICT in the school system. In Ghanaian universities, lack of infrastructure, sufficient and affordable bandwidth, and little human resource capacity to exploit the technology bedevils the sector (Kwasi & Andrews, 2018).

In the more developed nations new concepts and ideas have emerged in the process of providing ICTs facilities, obtaining, and disseminating cognitive, ethical, and public knowledge. Presently, with the current state of education, equipment, learners, tutors, and the knowledge being transferred are all present, and smart education through available infrastructure has made the process of acquiring knowledge simple and flexible. This is accomplished using smart devices and technologies that are interconnected to access digital resources. These technologies have aided institutions to achieve its educational goals. With good technological solutions, modern technologies are improving the teaching - learning process in today's education in the advanced countries. Thus, the use of modern technologies in education has improved educational quality at the same time making teaching and learning more convenient. For the successful structuring of students' educational processes, the system necessitates the employment of new teaching technology. Of course, in today's digital era, education is becoming increasingly recognized and enthusiastically embraced by younger generations. This highlights the fact that education based on available technology enables more efficient and convenient knowledge transfer to students. Thus, ICTs presents a new age of digital orientation, providing an interactive and collaborative method for the main purpose of increasing learners' engagements. Tutors are also able to understand student skills and learning preferences. ICTs is a means of learning in the modern era of digital orientation to which provide a dynamic, interactive, and better way for enhancing students' attention and enabling instructors to identify student talents and motivation (Omonayajo et al., 2022).

DISCUSSION AND CONCLUSION

New technologies advancement such as artificial intelligences, IoT, big data, analytics, and virtual reality change the way industries works and effect on user behaviour (al Mamun et al., 2022; Al-rawashdeh et al., 2022; Jafery et al., 2022; Keikhosrokiani, 2020a, 2021a, 2022b, 2022a; Keikhosrokiani et al., 2013; Keikhosrokiani & Asl, 2022; Keikhosrokiani & Kamaruddin, 2022; Paremeswaran et al., 2022; Ravichandran & Keikhosrokiani, 2022; Sofian et al., 2022; Suhendra et al., 2022; Teoh Yi Zhe & Keikhosrokiani, 2020).

Generally, the use of VR in education is advantageous, such as make available interactive devices, mental pictures that excites the mind and stimulating experiences, gives correct feedback, increases learning motivation and accommodates different scholarship styles (Haryana et al., (2022). Researchers have learnt that most educators like virtual reality and it makes students to be participate in learning, aids the implementation of information, eases learning, suits learners with graphic and pictorial intelligent approach, which gives them a broad clue and a summary of the course they have studied (Serin, 2020).

Several issues poise as challenges to the use of VR in education and have invariably set limits to the use of 'realities' in the sector. In spite of the seemly gross potentials embedded in its application in the vast domains of teaching and learning especially in higher education. Researchers have discovered a number of gaps in the use of VR in the tertiary education sector, a case in point, learning concepts were not frequently were not taken into account in application of VR curriculum development to help and guide concerning learning output. Moreover, the assessment of educational VR apps has basically paid attention to usability of the VR apps in place of learning output while immersive VR has been frequently a part of investigational and improvement work instead of its application frequently in practical of teaching (Radianti et al., 2020).

A thing of concerned presently is that methodologies and guidelines for VR developers to construct virtual settings don't exist. To prepare a methodology it is critical to have a blueprint to follow when building a design activity that must be repeatable, logical, and portable. The danger of not producing a technique is that of not having procedures when trying to decipher the problem again (Dozio et al., 2022).

Several technological hindrances exist in the use of VR. The cost of VR is exorbitant —at times beyond convincing, if a positive effect on learning is not established with worthy outcomes (Radianti et al., 2020).

Virtual reality (VR) sickness is a challenge that could seriously inhibit extensive adoption. Room-scale VR experiences do not go through the same kinds of simulation sickness issues as seated or automated moving experiences do. VR sickness is also known as cyber or simulator sickness. It is evident as a range of symptoms like drowsiness, nausea, sweating, sickness, headaches, and other symptoms experienced by motion sickness victims who get sick in vehicles, boats, planes, or other moving objects. VR visitors are affected in diverse ways and in different circumstances (Chang et al., 2020; Dozio et al., 2022).

The VR learning platform made possible by educational metaverse easily meets the needs of students who can adopt and adapt to novel, interesting and motivating teaching tools. Therefore, most tertiary educational institutions will make effort to provide study materials as they create metaverse platforms to encourage the propagation of knowledge (Teng et al., 2022). Thus, it is very clear that VR in education is aimed to create learning vehicles that enrich and enhance knowledge acquisition by students in specific areas of learning within a robust educational framework that is applicable to the different academic disciplines which is increasingly important. Based on this, the future of VR in education will largely depend on the motivation generated in students, and the ability to identify the indispensable features to achieve an appropriate level of learning through VR (Rojas-Sánchez et al., 2022).

REFERENCES

Akour, I. A., Al-Maroof, R. S., Alfaisal, R., & Salloum, S. A. (2022). A conceptual framework for determining metaverse adoption in higher institutions of gulf area: An empirical study using hybrid SEM-ANN approach. *Computers and Education: Artificial Intelligence, 3*, 100052.

al Mamun, M. H., Keikhosrokiani, P., Asl, M. P., Anuar, N. A. N., Hadi, N. H. A., & Humida, T. (2022). Sentiment Analysis of the Harry Potter Series Using a Lexicon-Based Approach. In P. Keikhosrokiani & M. Pourya Asl (Eds.), *Handbook of Research on Opinion Mining and Text Analytics on Literary Works and Social Media* (pp. 263–291). IGI Global. doi:10.4018/978-1-7998-9594-7.ch011

Al-rawashdeh, M., Keikhosrokiani, P., Belaton, B., Alawida, M., & Zwiri, A. (2022). IoT Adoption and Application for Smart Healthcare: A Systematic Review. *Sensors (Basel), 22*(14), 5377. Advance online publication. doi:10.339022145377 PMID:35891056

Ando, Y., Thawonmas, R., & Rinaldo, F. (2013). Inference of Viewed Exhibits in a Metaverse Museum. *2013 International Conference on Culture and Computing*, 218–219. 10.1109/CultureComputing.2013.73

Chang, E., Kim, H. T., & Yoo, B. (2020). Virtual Reality Sickness: A Review of Causes and Measurements. *International Journal of Human-Computer Interaction, 36*(17), 1658–1682. doi:10.1080/10447318.2020.1778351

Chen, Z. (2022). Exploring the application scenarios and issues facing Metaverse technology in education. *Interactive Learning Environments*, 1–13. Advance online publication. doi:10.1080/10494820.2022.2133148

Cortés, M. (2022). *Anàlisis i reflexions sobre el potencial impacte del metavers en el sector educatiu.* Academic Press.

Divjak, B., Svetec, B., Horvat, D., & Kadoić, N. (2022). Assessment validity and learning analytics as prerequisites for ensuring student-centred learning design. *British Journal of Educational Technology.* Advance online publication. doi:10.1111/bjet.13290

Dozio, N., Marcolin, F., Scurati, G. W., Ulrich, L., Nonis, F., Vezzetti, E., Marsocci, G., la Rosa, A., & Ferrise, F. (2022). A design methodology for affective Virtual Reality. *International Journal of Human-Computer Studies, 162,* 102791. Advance online publication. doi:10.1016/j.ijhcs.2022.102791

Driscoll, T. (2022). *Making Sense of the Metaverse in Education.* EdTechTeacher. https://edtechteacher.org/making-sense-of-the-metaverse-in-education/

Dwivedi, Y. K., Hughes, L., Baabdullah, A. M., Ribeiro-Navarrete, S., Giannakis, M., Al-Debei, M. M., Dennehy, D., Metri, B., Buhalis, D., Cheung, C. M. K., Conboy, K., Doyle, R., Dubey, R., Dutot, V., Felix, R., Goyal, D. P., Gustafsson, A., Hinsch, C., Jebabli, I., ... Wamba, S. F. (2022). Metaverse beyond the hype: Multidisciplinary perspectives on emerging challenges, opportunities, and agenda for research, practice and policy. *International Journal of Information Management, 66,* 102542. doi:10.1016/j.ijinfomgt.2022.102542

Falomo Bernarduzzi, L., Bernardi, E. M., Ferrari, A., Garbarino, M. C., & Vai, A. (2021). Augmented Reality Application for Handheld Devices: How to Make It hAPPen at the Pavia University History Museum. *Science and Education, 30*(3), 755–773. doi:10.100711191-021-00197-z PMID:33758467

Flavin, M. (2017). *Disruptive technology enhanced learning: The use and misuse of digital technologies in higher education.* Springer. doi:10.1057/978-1-137-57284-4

Gadekallu, T. R., Huynh-The, T., Wang, W., Yenduri, G., Ranaweera, P., Pham, Q.-V., da Costa, D. B., & Liyanage, M. (2022). *Blockchain for the metaverse: A review.* ArXiv Preprint ArXiv:2203.09738. doi:10.48550/arxiv.2203.09738

Glover, J., & Linowes, J. (n.d.). *Complete Virtual Reality and Augmented Reality Development with Unity ... Complete Virtual Rea Complete Virtual Reality and Augmented Reality.* https://books.google.com.my/books?hl=en&lr=&id=xEuTDwAAQBAJ&oi=fnd&pg=PP1&dq=Complete+Virtual+Reality+and+Augmented+Reality++Dev...1/1

Godwin-Jones, R. (2023). Emerging spaces for language learning: AI bots, ambient intelligence, and the metaverse. *Language Learning & Technology, 27*(2). https://hdl.handle.net/10125/73501

Gutierrez-Bucheli, L., Kidman, G., & Reid, A. (2022). Sustainability in engineering education: A review of learning outcomes. In *Journal of Cleaner Production* (Vol. 330). Elsevier Ltd. doi:10.1016/j.jclepro.2021.129734

Haryana, M. R. A., Warsono, S., Achjari, D., & Nahartyo, E. (2022). Virtual reality learning media with innovative learning materials to enhance individual learning outcomes based on cognitive load theory. *International Journal of Management Education*, *20*(3), 100657. Advance online publication. doi:10.1016/j.ijme.2022.100657

Hedrick, E., Harper, M., Oliver, E., & Hatch, D. (2022). Teaching & Learning in Virtual Reality: Metaverse Classroom Exploration. *2022 Intermountain Engineering Technology and Computing*, 1–5. Advance online publication. doi:10.1109/IETC54973.2022.9796765

Hodgson, P., Lee, V. W. Y., Chan, J. C. S., Fong, A., Tang, C. S. Y., Chan, L., & Wong, C. (2019). Immersive Virtual Reality (IVR) in Higher Education: Development and Implementation. doi:10.1007/978-3-030-06246-0_12

Jafery, N. N., Keikhosrokiani, P., & Asl, M. P. (2022). Text Analytics Model to Identify the Connection Between Theme and Sentiment in Literary Works: A Case Study of Iraqi Life Writings. In P. Keikhosrokiani & M. Pourya Asl (Eds.), *Handbook of Research on Opinion Mining and Text Analytics on Literary Works and Social Media* (pp. 173–190). IGI Global. doi:10.4018/978-1-7998-9594-7.ch008

Jin, Q., Liu, Y., Yarosh, S., Han, B., & Qian, F. (2022). How Will VR Enter University Classrooms? Multi-stakeholders Investigation of VR in Higher Education. *Proceedings of the 2022 CHI Conference on Human Factors in Computing Systems*, 1–17. 10.1145/3491102.3517542

Kalinkara, Y., & Talan, T. (2022). Rethinking Evaluating the Use of Distance Learning Systems in the Context of the Unified Theory of Acceptance and Use of Technology-2. *Journal of Learning for Development*, *9*(2), 229–252. doi:10.56059/jl4d.v9i2.617

Keikhosrokiani, P. (2019). Perspectives in the development of mobile medical information systems: Life cycle, management, methodological approach and application. In *Perspectives in the Development of Mobile Medical Information Systems*. Life Cycle, Management, Methodological Approach and Application. doi:10.1016/C2018-0-02485-8

Keikhosrokiani, P. (2020a). Introduction to Mobile Medical Information System (mMIS) development. In P. Keikhosrokiani (Ed.), *Perspectives in the Development of Mobile Medical Information Systems* (pp. 1–22). Academic Press. doi:10.1016/B978-0-12-817657-3.00001-8

Keikhosrokiani, P. (2020b). Behavioral intention to use of Mobile Medical Information System (mMIS). In P. Keikhosrokiani (Ed.), *Perspectives in the Development of Mobile Medical Information Systems* (pp. 57–73). Academic Press., doi:10.1016/B978-0-12-817657-3.00004-3

Keikhosrokiani, P. (2020c). Success factors of mobile medical information system (mMIS). In P. Keikhosrokiani (Ed.), *Perspectives in the Development of Mobile Medical Information Systems* (pp. 75–99). Academic Press., doi:10.1016/B978-0-12-817657-3.00005-5

Keikhosrokiani, P. (2021a). IoT for enhanced decision-making in medical information systems: A systematic review. In G. Marques, A. Kumar Bhoi, I. de la Torre Díez, & B. Garcia-Zapirain (Eds.), *Enhanced Telemedicine and e-Health: Advanced IoT Enabled Soft Computing Framework* (Vol. 410, pp. 119–140). Springer International Publishing. doi:10.1007/978-3-030-70111-6_6

Keikhosrokiani, P. (2021b). Predicating Smartphone Users' Behaviour Towards a Location-Aware IoMT-Based Information System: An Empirical Study. *International Journal of E-Adoption*, *13*(2), 52–77. doi:10.4018/IJEA.2021070104

Keikhosrokiani, P. (2022a). *Big Data Analytics for Healthcare: Datasets, Techniques, Life Cycles, Management, and Applications.* Elsevier Science. https://books.google.com.my/books?id=WbJYEAAAQBAJ

Keikhosrokiani, P. (2022b). *Handbook of Research on Consumer Behavior Change and Data Analytics in the Socio-Digital Era.* IGI Global. doi:10.4018/978-1-6684-4168-8

Keikhosrokiani, P., & Asl, M. P. (2022). *Handbook of research on opinion mining and text analytics on literary works and social media.* IGI Global. doi:10.4018/978-1-7998-9594-7

Keikhosrokiani, P., & Kamaruddin, N. S. A. B. (2022). IoT-Based In-Hospital-In-Home Heart Disease Remote Monitoring System with Machine Learning Features for Decision Making. In S. Mishra, A. González-Briones, A. K. Bhoi, P. K. Mallick, & J. M. Corchado (Eds.), *Connected e-Health: Integrated IoT and Cloud Computing* (pp. 349–369). Springer International Publishing. doi:10.1007/978-3-030-97929-4_16

Keikhosrokiani, P., Mustaffa, N., Sarwar, M. I., & Zakaria, N. (2013). E-Torch: A Mobile Commerce Location-Based Promotion System. *The International Technology Management Review*, *3*(3), 140–159. doi:10.2991/itmr.2013.3.3.1

Keikhosrokiani, P., Mustaffa, N., Zakaria, N., & Abdullah, R. (2020). Assessment of a medical information system: The mediating role of use and user satisfaction on the success of human interaction with the mobile healthcare system (iHeart). *Cognition Technology and Work*, *22*(2), 281–305. doi:10.100710111-019-00565-4

Kwasi, R. A., & Andrews, F. K. (2018). Integrating Information and Communication Technology in Education: Accessibility, Reliability and Convenience in Tertiary Institutions in the Upper West Region of Ghana. *International Journal of Recent Research in Mathematics Computer Science and Information Technology*, *4*(2), 46–54.

Kye, B., Han, N., Kim, E., Park, Y., & Jo, S. (2021). Educational applications of metaverse: Possibilities and limitations. *Journal of Educational Evaluation for Health Professions*, *18*, 18. doi:10.3352/jeehp.2021.18.32 PMID:34897242

Lateef, M., & Keikhosrokiani, P. (2022). Predicting Critical Success Factors of Business Intelligence Implementation for Improving SMEs' Performances: A Case Study of Lagos State, Nigeria. *Journal of the Knowledge Economy*. Advance online publication. doi:10.100713132-022-00961-8

Lin, H., Wan, S., Gan, W., Chen, J., & Chao, H.-C. (2022). *Metaverse in Education: Vision.* Opportunities, and Challenges., doi:10.1109/BigData55660.2022.10021004

López-Belmonte, J., Pozo-Sánchez, S., Lampropoulos, G., & Moreno-Guerrero, A.-J. (2022). Design and validation of a questionnaire for the evaluation of educational experiences in the metaverse in Spanish students (METAEDU). *Heliyon*, *8*(11), e11364. doi:10.1016/j.heliyon.2022.e11364 PMID:36387471

Mahmud, A., & Saka, K. A. (2020). *Application of ICT Facilities for Academic Activities among Engineering Lecturers in University Libraries*. Academic Press.

Miller, M. R., Herrera, F., Jun, H., Landay, J. A., & Bailenson, J. N. (2020). Personal identifiability of user tracking data during observation of 360-degree VR video. *Scientific Reports*, *10*(1), 17404. Advance online publication. doi:10.103841598-020-74486-y PMID:33060713

Mistretta, S. (2022). The Metaverse—An Alternative Education Space. *AI. Computer Science and Robotics Technology*, *2022*, 1–23. doi:10.5772/acrt.05

Modgil, S., Dwivedi, Y. K., Rana, N. P., Gupta, S., & Kamble, S. (2022). Has Covid-19 accelerated opportunities for digital entrepreneurship? An Indian perspective. *Technological Forecasting and Social Change*, *175*, 121415. Advance online publication. doi:10.1016/j.techfore.2021.121415 PMID:36536802

Mungwabi, H. N. (2018). Use of information and communication technologies (ICTs) in learning by undergraduate students at the University of Dar es Salaam library in Tanzania. *University of Dar Es Salaam Library Journal*, *13*(2), 49–64.

Oh, H. J., Kim, J., Chang, J. J. C., Park, N., & Lee, S. (2023). Social benefits of living in the metaverse: The relationships among social presence, supportive interaction, social self-efficacy, and feelings of loneliness. *Computers in Human Behavior*, *139*, 107498. Advance online publication. doi:10.1016/j.chb.2022.107498

Omonayajo, B., Al-Turjman, F., & Cavus, N. (2022). Interactive and innovative technologies for smart education. *Computer Science and Information Systems*, *00*(00), 27. doi:10.2298/CSIS2108170270

Paremeswaran, P., Keikhosrokiani, P., & Asl, M. P. (2022). Opinion Mining of Readers' Responses to Literary Prize Nominees on Twitter: A Case Study of Public Reaction to the Booker Prize (2018–2020). In F. Saeed, F. Mohammed, & F. Ghaleb (Eds.), Advances on Intelligent Informatics and Computing (pp. 243–257). Springer International Publishing. doi:10.1007/978-3-030-98741-1_21

Pereira da Silva, N., Eloy, S., & Resende, R. (2022). Robotic construction analysis: Simulation with virtual reality. *Heliyon*, *8*(10), e11039. Advance online publication. doi:10.1016/j.heliyon.2022.e11039 PMID:36281420

Polyviou, A., & Pappas, I. O. (2022). Chasing Metaverses: Reflecting on Existing Literature to Understand the Business Value of Metaverses. *Information Systems Frontiers*. Advance online publication. doi:10.100710796-022-10364-4 PMID:36589769

Radianti, J., Majchrzak, T. A., Fromm, J., & Wohlgenannt, I. (2020). A systematic review of immersive virtual reality applications for higher education: Design elements, lessons learned, and research agenda. *Computers & Education*, *147*, 103778. Advance online publication. doi:10.1016/j.compedu.2019.103778

Rauschnabel, P. A., Felix, R., Hinsch, C., Shahab, H., & Alt, F. (2022). What is XR? Towards a Framework for Augmented and Virtual Reality. *Computers in Human Behavior*, *133*, 107289. doi:10.1016/j.chb.2022.107289

Ravichandran, B. D., & Keikhosrokiani, P. (2022). Classification of Covid-19 misinformation on social media based on neuro-fuzzy and neural network: A systematic review. *Neural Computing & Applications*. Advance online publication. doi:10.100700521-022-07797-y PMID:36159189

Rojas-Sánchez, M. A., Palos-Sánchez, P. R., & Folgado-Fernández, J. A. (2022). Systematic literature review and bibliometric analysis on virtual reality and education. *Education and Information Technologies*. Advance online publication. doi:10.100710639-022-11167-5 PMID:35789766

Ruwodo, V., Pinomaa, A., Vesisenaho, M., Ntinda, M., & Sutinen, E. (2022). Enhancing Software Engineering Education in Africa through a Metaversity. *2022 IEEE Frontiers in Education Conference (FIE)*, 1–8. 10.1109/FIE56618.2022.9962729

Sadovets, O., Martynyuk, O., Orlovska, O., Lysak, H., Korol, S., & Zembytska, M. (2022). Gamification in the Informal Learning Space of Higher Education (in the Context of the Digital Transformation of Education). *Postmodern Openings*, *13*(1), 330–350. doi:10.18662/po/13.1/399

Sholihin, M., Sari, R. C., Yuniarti, N., & Ilyana, S. (2020). A new way of teaching business ethics: The evaluation of virtual reality-based learning media. *International Journal of Management Education*, *18*(3), 100428. Advance online publication. doi:10.1016/j.ijme.2020.100428

Sofian, N. B., Keikhosrokiani, P., & Asl, M. P. (2022). Opinion mining and text analytics of reader reviews of Yoko Ogawa's The Housekeeper and the Professor in Goodreads. In P. Keikhosrokiani & M. Pourya Asl (Eds.), *Handbook of Research on Opinion Mining and Text Analytics on Literary Works and Social Media* (pp. 240–262). IGI Global. doi:10.4018/978-1-7998-9594-7.ch010

Son, A. L. B., & Amparado, M. A. P. (2018). Integration of Information and Communications Technology (ICT) Tools in the Instructional Program of a University. *International Journal of Social Sciences & Educational Studies*, *5*(1), 63.

Srimadhaven, T., Chris Junni, A., Harshith, N., Jessenth Ebenezer, S., Shabari Girish, S., & Priyaadharshini, M. (2020). Learning analytics: Virtual reality for programming course in higher education. *Procedia Computer Science*, *172*, 433–437. doi:10.1016/j.procs.2020.05.095

Suhendra, N. H. B., Keikhosrokiani, P., Asl, M. P., & Zhao, X. (2022). Opinion Mining and Text Analytics of Literary Reader Responses: A Case Study of Reader Responses to KL Noir Volumes in Goodreads Using Sentiment Analysis and Topic. In P. Keikhosrokiani & M. Pourya Asl (Eds.), *Handbook of Research on Opinion Mining and Text Analytics on Literary Works and Social Media* (pp. 191–239). IGI Global. doi:10.4018/978-1-7998-9594-7.ch009

Tarouco, L., Gorziza, B., Corrêa, Y., Amaral, É. M. H., & Müller, T. (2013). Virtual laboratory for teaching Calculus: An immersive experience. *2013 IEEE Global Engineering Education Conference (EDUCON)*, 774–781. 10.1109/EduCon.2013.6530195

Teng, Z., Cai, Y., Gao, Y., Zhang, X., & Li, X. (2022). Factors Affecting Learners' Adoption of an Educational Metaverse Platform: An Empirical Study Based on an Extended UTAUT Model. *Mobile Information Systems*, *5479215*, 1–15. Advance online publication. doi:10.1155/2022/5479215

Teoh Yi Zhe, I., & Keikhosrokiani, P. (2020). Knowledge workers mental workload prediction using optimised ELANFIS. *Applied Intelligence*. Advance online publication. doi:10.100710489-020-01928-5

Tiggemann, M., & Anderberg, I. (2020). Social media is not real: The effect of 'Instagram vs reality' images on women's social comparison and body image. *New Media & Society*, *22*(12), 2183–2199. doi:10.1177/1461444819888720

Tlili, A., Huang, R., Shehata, B., Liu, D., Zhao, J., Metwally, A. H. S., Wang, H., Denden, M., Bozkurt, A., Lee, L.-H., Beyoglu, D., Altinay, F., Sharma, R. C., Altinay, Z., Li, Z., Liu, J., Ahmad, F., Hu, Y., Salha, S., ... Burgos, D. (2022). Is Metaverse in education a blessing or a curse: A combined content and bibliometric analysis. *Smart Learning Environments*, *9*(1), 24. doi:10.118640561-022-00205-x

Tor, S. F., Gora, R. C., & Ahmed, S. (2021). Identifying of ICT Tools to Improve Project Research by Graduating Undergraduates of a Nigerian Premier University. *Covenant Journal of Informatics & Tongxin Jishu*, *9*(2).

Serin, H. (2020). Virtual reality in education from the perspective of teachers. Amazonia investiga, 9(26), 291-303. doi:10.34069/AI/2020.26.02.33

Wu, T. C., & Ho, C. T. B. (2022). A scoping review of metaverse in emergency medicine. In *Australasian Emergency Care*. Elsevier Australia. doi:10.37766/inplasy2022.5.0159

Zallio, M., & Clarkson, P. J. (2022). Designing the metaverse: A study on inclusion, diversity, equity, accessibility and safety for digital immersive environments. *Telematics and Informatics*, *75*, 101909. Advance online publication. doi:10.1016/j.tele.2022.101909

Zhang, Y., Chen, J., Miao, D., & Zhang, C. (2018). Design and analysis of an interactive MOOC teaching system based on virtual reality. *International Journal of Emerging Technologies in Learning*, *13*(7), 111–123. doi:10.3991/ijet.v13i07.8790

Zhang, Z., Ning, H., Shi, F., Farha, F., Xu, Y., Xu, J., Zhang, F., & Choo, K.-K. R. (2022). Artificial intelligence in cyber security: Research advances, challenges, and opportunities. *Artificial Intelligence Review*, *55*(2), 1029–1053. doi:10.100710462-021-09976-0

Zhan, T., Yin, K., Xiong, J., He, Z., & Wu, S. T. (2020). Augmented reality and virtual reality displays: Perspectives and challenges. *Iscience*, *23*(8), 101397. doi:10.1016/j.isci.2020.101397

Zhao, Y., Jiang, J., Chen, Y., Liu, R., Yang, Y., Xue, X., & Chen, S. (2022). Metaverse: Perspectives from graphics, interactions and visualization. In Visual Informatics (Vol. 6, Issue 1, pp. 56–67). Elsevier B.V. doi:10.1016/j.visinf.2022.03.002

Zhu, X., & Liu, J. (2020). Education in and After Covid-19: Immediate Responses and Long-Term Visions. *Postdigital Science and Education*, *2*(3), 695–699. doi:10.100742438-020-00126-3

Section 3
Metaverse, Consumer Behaviour, and Adoption

Chapter 6
Introduction to Metaverse and Consumer Behaviour Change:
Adoption of Metaverse Among Consumers

Babita Singla
ⓘ https://orcid.org/0000-0002-8861-6859
Chitkara University, India

Saurabh Bhattacharya
ⓘ https://orcid.org/0000-0002-2729-1835
Chitkara University, India

Nithesh Naik
Manipa University, India

ABSTRACT

A virtual digital environment is created using the metaverse, which also connects the real world. The existence of information technology allows us to do new tasks or carry out routine tasks more effectively. The extended reality, or "metaverse," allows for new kinds of captivating telepresence but may also make mundane activities easier. These technologies help us in our employment, education, healthcare, consumption, and entertainment more and more, but they also present a number of obstacles. The concerns discussed in this chapter are why and will customers adopt the fully immersive territory for various activities like shopping and purchasing any products including bank products.

1.0 INTRODUCTION

Utilizing augmented reality and virtual reality, the metaverse has the potential to expand the physical world by enabling users to interact naturally in both real and simulated surroundings using avatars and holograms. Virtual worlds and immersive games "like Second Life, Fortnite, Roblox, and VRChat" have been regarded as the forerunners of the metaverse and provide some insight into the possible socio-

DOI: 10.4018/978-1-6684-7029-9.ch006

economic effects of a fully functional persistent cross-platform metaverse (Dwivedi et al., 2022). By doing jobs that are challenging to undertake in reality, such as exploring isolated locations, providing psychiatric care, and preparing recruits for combat, the metaverse complements the actual world in many ways. It takes the role of familiar settings and enables actions that would be difficult or impossible to complete in reality owing to issues like cost. As a tool, the metaverse reduces complexity ("such as in aircraft engineering") and boosts coherence from a multimodal perspective. Multisensory settings are present in the metaverse. When unwanted and privacy-invasive contents proliferate in the metaverse, they may be perceived as more intrusive and are likely to have a greater negative impact on the users or victims due to complex and sophisticated features such as more graphic, 3D design, and immersive visual and auditory experience. As a result, privacy transgressions in the metaverse are likely to have more severe repercussions, often known as an amplified technological impact. The metaverse has the potential to fundamentally alter how people connect, socialise, and pass their free time, but like every breakthrough that creates new possibilities, it also makes room for the shadowed aspects of human nature (Glavish, 2022).

1.1 Use of Metaverse in the Corporate World

Users in the metaverse are more vulnerable to corporate exploitation. For instance, compared to conventional displays, Virtual reality (VR) headsets can gather more and richer user data. Companies are therefore more motivated to gather user information and share it with other parties so that it may be used for profiling and delivering targeted advertising. As an illustration, Facebook's Meta revealed that it was developing the high-end VR headgear Project Cambria, which will be able to do things that aren't presently feasible with existing headsets. The user's virtual avatar will be able to maintain eye contact and reflect facial emotions thanks to new sensors in the gadget. Businesses' attempts to gather high-velocity data from mobile devices, such as click-stream and GPS data, have encountered significant customer opposition in the present non-metaverse Internet. For instance, a sizable fraction of users disables the location tracking option to safeguard extremely private and sensitive information.

By putting items in a completely realistic virtual reality (VR) shopping environment, businesses have the chance to better engage potential customers. However, little is known about the factors influencing and whether or not consumers would choose to purchase in such immersive settings (Peukert et al., 2019). Users choose virtual and augmented reality (AR)because they allow for actions that, relative to those enabled by actual reality, are either beneficial or impossible. There is a lack of research that fully explains the factors influencing the adoption of VR and AR (Steffen et al., 2019).

1.2 Metaverse in Gamification and Online World

Online worlds like Roblox and Fortnite presently draw up to 400 million users. To express its conviction in a virtual future, Facebook changed its name to Meta. Microsoft is prepared for a future when employees work alongside digital avatars. Clothing and accessories are being created for the metaverse by fashion companies like Nike and Gucci. In Decentraland, J.P. Morgan and Samsung have opened offices (Stackpole, 2022). You can be whatever and anywhere you want to be in the metaverse, and the only limit to how businesses and consumers may profit from the immersive internet is their imagination. With interesting comments on topics like avatars, identity, and digital fashion as well as non-fungible tokens (NFTs), blockchain, and the metaverse's economics (*Step into the Metaverse*, n.d.). In actuality, the metaverse provides a fresh online experience with fresh markets and goods. People want more than just to consume. Gamified, contextual experiences are much more entertaining. People want to maintain their online identity throughout the metaverse and even into the physical world because they value it. People want to have a stake in the places where they choose to spend their time. The emphasis on ownership is what stands out most about the metaverse. Users can participate in almost anything and vote on issues affecting the apps they use and the communities they are a part of. A new economy is created by user ownership, which is a true revolution (*Step into the Metaverse*, n.d.).

Since online learning was originally designed to supplement in-person training, it has evolved in recent years into an essential tool for distance education. The rise of the COVID-19 pandemic, in particular, has speeded up the invasion and importance of online learning. With the advent of Metaverse, learning is being suggested as a powerful instrument for online learning once again, despite existing research restrictions that place both systematic and academic facets into account. The majority of "self-determination theory and information system quality" variables impact learner satisfaction in VR adoption (Gim et al., 2022). One of the characteristics of a metaverse would be that it would encompass the virtual and real worlds, have a full-blown industry, and provide "unprecedented interoperability" — clients will be able to transport one 's avatars and products through one part of such metaverse to the other, regardless of who moves that portion of it. The metaverse will be run by no particular enterprise — it will function as an "embodied internet." (*Mark Zuckerberg Is Betting Facebook's Future on the Metaverse - The Verge*, n.d.). Technology regularly generates unexpected outcomes. The general opinion is that the metaverse is the forthcoming innovation of the web, where we become immersed in it rather than just viewing it. As large sums of money have been engaged, gaming remains to support the arising metaverse, as well as nongaming instances spring up including both businesses and consumers, and the growth of the metaverse gains traction. Although the metaverse can be defined in a variety of ways, it shares several fundamental aspects: "a sense of immersion, real-time interactivity, user agency"(*Value-Creation-in-the-Metaverse.Pdf*, n.d.).Customer use cases are already extending towards truly interactive shopping, leisure, athletics, and academic experience. The eldest Generation Z customers are mostly in their mid-twenties. They are rapidly becoming a significant source of revenue. Such customers are much more acquainted than earlier generations with imaginary spaces, interactions, and commodities. Gaming is laying the groundwork "67 per cent of Roblox's 50 million daily players are under the age of 16, heralding the arrival of a new breed of metaverse natives"(*Marketing in the Metaverse: An Opportunity for Innovation and Experimentation | McKinsey*, n.d.).

Because users recognize businesses in the metaverse to be unique, the threshold for offering unique experiences is significant. Regardless of how well the metaverse emerges, quantities of creativity and consumer acceptance are certain to increase. Customers' affinity to today's metaverse signals a significant change in how individuals utilise technology. To supplement the metaverse, businesses must find the right blend of native advertising, multimedia applications, and genuine promotional events(*Marketing in the Metaverse: An Opportunity for Innovation and Experimentation | McKinsey*, n.d.). The brand-presentation and life-creation system of tomorrow for all types of companies in the three-dimensional digital realm will be called Metaverse. The way we do business in the real world is replicated digitally in the metaverse. All viewers may interact within that 3D virtual environment by using avatars which look like them. How businesses employ the distribution channels and how upcoming generations of people interact with one another will be greatly impacted by this (Hollensen et al., 2022). Technology's widespread use in a variety of fields significantly improves the living standards of people. Now that we are living in the age of industrial innovations, it's become a need. The introduction of desktops, the web, and portable devices are three key technological development waves that have been seen from the viewpoint of end users. The fourth generation of computing breakthroughs is now being driven by innovations like virtual reality and augmented reality. Metaverse systems are part of the next wave. The terms "metaverse" and "universe" are combined; it mixes a variety of virtual environments (a blend of virtual and augmented reality) to portray real life utilising avatars. Although the full metaverse has not yet been created, several systems that make use of the virtual reality idea include metaverse-like qualities. The capabilities of games have been expanded because of this innovation. When a new method is introduced, it's necessary to gauge its user acceptability of it and look into any potential influencing factors (Aburbeian et al., 2022). To organise meetings of avatars, "Meta" ("Facebook renamed to Meta") is focusing on enabling users to build their virtual environments. To underscore its intention to transition out of its controversial social media platform to its interactive virtual vision for the next, Facebook changed the name of its parent Meta in October. With the use of VR gear, prospective network encounters like online conversations with friends might ultimately seem like face-to-face encounters, although Horizon Universes is far from becoming a fully realised metaverse. In response to accusations of abuse, one of the challenging problems for "Facebook parent company Meta's metaverse" vision, it implemented a set length amongst members' avatars in its virtual world Horizon platform early this year. A futuristic web where online interactions like speaking with a buddy might someday seem like face-to-face owing to Head-mounted displays is shown in Horizon Universes, which is far from a fully realised metaverse. However, the site does allow users to socialise, play online games, and indulge themselves in 360° films digitally with colleagues and perhaps other viewers.

1.3 Advantage of Metaverse

Computer animation has improved substantially over time, and at such a quick rate that it now allows the modelling of items and personalities in a virtual world using 3D graphical software. (These virtual items possess enticing properties that make them appear quite genuine.). Users there in the metaverse could explore a "Google Earth-like virtual environment" with this advanced technology enabling them to go to virtually any spot on the planet. Microsoft Corporation began its metaverse adventure through the use of a unique technology named Mesh for Microsoft Teams, which allows customers to access their virtual avatars. Metaverse is an appealing alternative for establishments looking to hold interesting and interactive sessions or seminars with customers and co-workers in an offsite location. This breakthrough has the potential to transform the whole terrain of simulated collaboration and interaction. The replication of realistic events might assist health-conscious folks in digitally enjoying their training regimens without leaving the house, including those in parks, along the seaside, and in a virtual gym. Simulated fitness encounters are a fantastic fit for one's training and exercise regimen, motivating them to achieve their objectives. Even if an awful scenario such as a pandemic forces an individual to sequester themselves at home, one can still enjoy a picturesque activity or gym. Users might even pick a metaverse area to have an enjoyable simulated exercise alongside acquaintances and family. Users can be coached in a simulated gym by a simulated coach allocated to them using artificial intelligence (AI) integrated into a metaverse. The AI coach can easily grasp each individual's strengths and capabilities, allowing them to organise their programmes appropriately. It's an intriguing notion that might entice many gym-goers and health-conscious individuals to explore the virtual sphere and its limitless potential. COVID-19 confinement in severe environments worldwide spurred businesses to investigate virtual reality collaborative domain Schools, universities, organisations, and businesses. To sustain operations, some organizations turned to remote work. their routine or planned work. Metaverses can transform the way experts in sectors like health, technology, emergency responders, defence, combat, and numerous others are trained. A problem may be reproduced in a metaverse that requires certain abilities to handle, and a group of instructors can be enrolled into the metaverse wherein their abilities could be assessed on their capacity to handle the issue. This is all possible in a simulated reality. Surgeons can practise on virtual individuals to improve their medical abilities. Armed personnel can also be assessed in virtual space and experience realistic fights as part of their training. This one-of-a-kind practice knowledge helps organise crises and the demand for service(Bale et al., 2022).

1.2 Consumer Behaviour Study Studies That Use Virtual Reality to Improve Behaviour

According to empirical findings, perceived interaction and augmentation in media have a strong favourable impact on telepresence, which in turn has a positive impact on attitudes and adoption intentions towards AR-based VFRs. Additionally, the relationship between media attributes and consumer sentiments was mediated by telepresence (Lee et al., 2021). Vividness significantly improves perceived enjoyment and utility, which in turn influences attitudes toward virtual reality and behavioural intentions. Perceived utility and enjoyment were not positively impacted by interaction. Through telepresence, it nevertheless indirectly impacted perceived utility and enjoyment. The research also showed a moderating relationship between consumers' prior VR experience and perceived utility and enjoyment of interaction. Additionally favourable was the association between behavioural intentions and attitude (Kim et al., 2021)

Little is known about how consumers feel about using virtual reality as a tool for purchasing. The VR research presented in some of the articles will assist practitioners to comprehend the pressing need for VR adoption in a retail environment.

2.0 LITERATURE REVIEW

Within the metaverse applications most prominent systems, these days are "Twitter, Google, iPhone, and Secondlife (T.G.I.S)". "IP (Internet Protocol) connectivity and iPhone" purchases are the two most commonly used metrics for measuring the uptake of such products/services. The deployment of IT solutions does have a long tradition & remains one of the most prominent subjects in the sector of information systems. Although mobile phones increase social connection, resulting in a sudden increase in Metaverse services along a service adoption process, it would be interesting to learn how to assess such a shift so that consequences may be drawn (Lee et al., 2011).

Tourism and hospitality businesses must deliberately employ the Metaverse to develop hybrid virtual and real experiences that allow customers to interact with them as well as with other visitors before, during, and after their visit (Buhalis et al., 2022)

Through the synchronised delivery of online and metaverse banking services made possible by a variety of cutting-edge technologies, metaverse banking offers users synchronous banking services along with 3D experiences in a virtual world. In the future, there is a strong possibility that metaverse banking will be able to get progressive requests, be promoted aggressively but successfully, and make considerable development (Zainurin et al., 2023)

Intelligent products and artificial intelligence are intended to be viewed as more congruent (Keikhos-rokiani & Pourya Asl, 2023). Gadgets that can learn are expected to be perceived as more compatible. According to a study of literature, adaptability provides the benefit of increasing perceived levels of compatibility and observability. A flexible product is more likely to meet the demands of consumers. Product competence has advantages in that it can lead to new and beneficial brand equity (Rijsdijk & Hultink, 2009)

Someone might claim that we are already located in the metaverse; however, this is just half right, as we explore various cases to back up our claim, taking into account the three-stage metaverse strategic plan. The Earth 3D map provides images of the actual world but without a unique structure apart from GPS data, whereas social networks enable players to create material but are confined to texts, photographs, and videos with specific user involvement choices (e.g., liking a post). Computer games are becoming more real and stunning. Users may enjoy fantastic visuals with in-game dynamics, such as in Call of Duty, that provide a sense of authenticity that closely matches the real universe in many respects. When the metaverse transforms into the most popular place for individuals to manage their time in imaginary spaces, consumer addictions (i.e., excessive usage of digital surroundings) will emerge as a significant problem. Users can utilise the metaverse as a means of 'escape' from the actual world. Cyberspace addictions among users may result in severe issues and mental diseases, including despair, isolation, and aggressive behaviour. COVID-19 being aware Face-to-face communication has changed as a result of the epidemic through a variety of virtual methods, most gatherings or large gatherings. Recent research has revealed that chronic use of such Additional issues might arise from online meetups and seminars. "Abusive Internet usage or Internet addiction". An emotional theory tries to understand why user addiction occurs by explaining how the user's elongated self, which includes their mind, body, material possessions, relatives, companions, and association organisations, motivates them to discover the virtual reality and seek benefits, possibly in an unending remuneration circuit, in fantasy environments. Further research is required to determine whether the community accepts the gadgets that connect users to the metaverse on a community scale. People can construct avatars in the metaverse by utilising comparable personal details like their name, gender, age, or other details, or by creating wholly imaginary personas that have no resemblance to real people in terms of style or anything that might be connected to them. An increasing worry about excessive faith is there on the other hand. Users erroneously place too much faith in items from well-known companies, which is understandable given that human consumers frequently rely on reputation as the primary indicator of a brand's trustworthiness. But in the contemporary statistics society, where consumers' identity is a product, even large businesses have reportedly engaged in tactics geared at learning as much as feasible about the consumer. One of the most important factors in maximising the potential of the metaverse ecosystem is probably responsibilities. Even though "ubiquitous/pervasive" computing is already a reality because, of technological advancements, a lot of the prospective advantages won't be seen until people become accustomed to and supportive of the innovations. The conduct of individuals in the metaverse is reflected in their public acceptance, which is a representation of the general assessments and viewpoints of decisions and policies. The long-term viability of the metaverse would depend on socially acceptable characteristics such as user variety, privacy risks, equality, and habit. Additionally, as both the physical and digital worlds will be impacted by the metaverse, comparable laws and standards should be upheld in both. Everybody will be affected by the coming cyberspace since the metaverse will be incorporated into every area of our lives. Enhancing the huge cyberspace's public acceptance would need developing techniques and technology for combating cybercrime and addressing abuse. Due to the availability of sophisticated smart gadgets and smart devices, our digital tomorrow will now be more participatory, more living, more integrated, and more multi-dimensional. Before the metaverse is fully incorporated into our daily lives and the actual reality, there are still numerous obstacles to be solved (P. Lee et al., 2021). The usage of "augmented reality" (AR) in retail settings is a contemporary technical trend that has lately acquired more pace as a result of the "COVID-19 epidemic". AR is radically changing how customers interact with products by addressing current issues with online buying (such as "experientiality and try-on"). An organised and summarised summary of the most recent studies on AR purchasing is what this study aims to do (Riar et al., 2022). The findings in one of the pieces of literature where Metaverse and its adoption in education were studied showed that I students' fulfilment with the "Eduverse" had a beneficial impact on one 's ongoing utilisation intention; (ii) students' purpose to use the "Eduverse" was lowered after they interpreted risks; and (iii) effort lifespan, hedonic motivation, social influence, and perceived ease had a significantly optimistic impact on learners' gratification with the "Eduverse". The metaverse can usher about a revolutionary change in virtual classrooms. While it is crucial for the growth of the economy and even after several advancements in online technology, academia's formation and methods remain largely intact. It differs from existing "2D e-learning tools" in several ways, including interaction, corporeity, and durability. Although independent learning is also feasible, the "Eduverse" encourages user interaction in a space- and time-free digital online world, which makes training sessions more interactive. "Avatars"—virtual entities that serve as users' representations—help the "Eduverse" community build their online identities. The corporeity factor refers to the fact that, while being a virtual environment, it is nevertheless bound by physical constraints and has finite resources. With "Eduverse", even if the user logs out of the Metaverse platform, the virtual world continues to exist and function, and the stored information can be retrieved upon reconnection. This is the persistent element. Metaverse development relies heavily on advances in the underlying technology. To create fully immersive experiences, the metaverse needs technology that can guarantee fully simulated experiences in virtual environments that can be delivered by VR (Virtual Reality), AR (Augmented Reality), and MR (Mixed Reality) technologies. VR/AR/MR alone does not provide reliable learning outcomes. Applications of the Metaverse in other sectors such as the entertainment industry, government services, tourism industry and agriculture are also being explored (Teng et al., 2022). Flight training takes place in a dynamic learning environment. Because the context of this study focuses on combat training in his pilot school as representative of a dynamic learning environment, understanding the use of immersive simulation training devices for combat training is not possible. Researchers and educators have long advocated the use of flight simulation training devices or simulators as a high-fidelity, low-cost option with many learning benefits for aviation training. Simulators have varying degrees of fidelity and immersion while providing realistic training scenarios to improve procedural memory and performance while reducing the costs associated with combat training. Studies on the use of different simulator levels in terms of fidelity and realism consistently show that combat training in simulated environments is efficient and effective. Numerous studies have shown that training with a computerized flight training device is effective in learning and practicing procedures and manoeuvres, especially when related to instrument combat tasks. Full combat simulators have mainly been used to assess training transitions when introducing movements into the training environment. Empirical evidence suggests that movement does not affect training transmission. Researchers have used the "TAM (Technology Acceptance Model) and TPB (Theory of planned behaviour)" in many literatures to understand the consumer behaviour or adoption pattern (Ezimmuo & Keikhosrokiani, 2022; Keikhosrokiani, 2022b; Keikhosrokiani et al., 2019; Xian et al., 2022). The employment of low-cost, moderate battle simulators employing off-the-shelf equipment and software has been explored by the military. For military pilots to get checklist training in a virtual reality cockpit, an interactive component trainer was developed. VR is still looked into as a possible replacement for flight simulators in pilot schools. Little research has been done utilising objective metrics to assess attitudes toward and intentions for adopting technology for combat training. Consumer experience and metrics across the simulator and VR combat training teams were equivalent, although the intellectual burden was greater for the VR fighters. Researchers frequently get student opinions about how a certain technique can improve combat training. The way people use technology in various situations may depend as to how people view them (Fussell & Truong, 2022). To examine, forecast, and explain human behaviour with a focus on the intention to carry out predicted conduct, "Ajzen introduced the TPB as a derivation of the theory of reasoned action (TRA) in 1991"(Ajzen, 1991). The TPB has been utilised in the aviation sector to evaluate customer behaviour and in the educational industry to evaluate attitudes toward online education. According to a survey of the literature, neither the comprehensive simulation system, much alone VR particularly, nor the aerospace learning atmosphere has utilised the TPB for training or educational objectives. The basic constructions may be modified to use certain technologies for aviation instruction, and TPB structures can be modified and added to expanded TAM models. People with little to no encounter with VR could be less likely to use the new tech for learning than those who have. The ambiguity brought due by the lack of guidelines about the usage of VR for instruction could also have a consequence and make people hesitant to utilize the tech. VR users may be more willing to utilise it if they have confidence in their skills and/or ability to employ the system. The intent will then be affected by this. Interestingly, the TAM has seen a good mix of outcomes from this interaction (Fussell & Truong, 2022). The expanded TAM included new elements that are pertinent to innovation and the educational setting and studied VR technology in a dynamic learning experience. The study's findings have a number of theoretical ramifications. The research adds to the corpus of information about the use of VR in active learning settings. The approach confirmed that existing TAM and TPB parameters may be expanded upon and used to VR and fluid learning settings. The verified model may be further modified to evaluate how users perceive various virtual simulated technologies and dynamic learning and training settings. The model also confirmed variables that could be important for determining if students want to use VR for training. Users' experiences with VR and their ability to contrast their usage of it with other simulation models and training materials may help to strengthen the connection. If learners don't comprehend how virtual reality works or how it will help them learn, probably, they won't use it in a dynamic learning environment. The advantages of VR in a flexible educational context may be required to be demonstrated by teachers and designers (Fussell & Truong, 2022). Although VR can be useful for educating, how it is presented and integrated into the curriculum may influence learners' attitudes, acceptance, and desire to utilise it. Participants admitted to having little experience with virtual reality, and the fact that it may not be easily available to use surely affected their perception of utilising the technology for training. Users may lack confidence in utilising the technology due to their lack of experience with it. Before VR is used as a teaching tool, students may gain by knowing the benefits of VR learning and being comfortable with the technology (Fussell & Truong, 2022).

In the coming ten years, there will be a significant development in demand for the "metaverse" (digital environments where people may learn, enjoy, and purchase). This will increase prospects for electronic service suppliers and metadata producers. The top producers and users of metaverse products, in both the "business-to-business and business-to-consumer" sectors of the market, will come from the top three electronic marketplaces in the globe: "the United States, Europe, and China". Regulation worries concerning data corporate monopolies, security, safety and satisfaction, and cybersecurity will become more widespread as a result of the inclusion of metaverse products. Since China has indeed imposed limitations on network practises, video game usage, influencer marketing, data privacy, localization, and cryptocurrency, it is expected to be the most proactive watchdog (*Emerald Expert Briefings*, 2022). The many behavioural and psychological (cognitive, emotional, and social) effects of using augmented reality when shopping. The research in one of the literatures which was done to understand the acceptance of "metaverse" on shopping experience incorporates the findings into a paradigm for AR-induced customer behaviour in purchasing, giving readers a crucial summary of the characteristics of AR-related shopping and the variables affecting how readily customers will accept the innovation. The superior technology of augmented reality (AR)—such as its interactivity, colourfulness, information quality, etc.—is a source for an improved utilitarian and hedonic buying experience that can endorse motives to choose a product, recycle an augmented reality app, or suggest it to others. Furthermore, this study highlights the need for some future studies (Riar et al., 2022).

The indirect effects of interaction and clarity on user satisfaction and reported pleasure via videoconferencing as well as the mediating influence of customers' past knowledge of VR are also covered, taking into account the dearth of VR empirical studies. The influencing factors of interaction and colourfulness on perceived utility and reported pleasure through videoconferencing as well as the moderating influence of customer significant expertise with VR are also covered, taking into account the paucity of VR empirical studies. Despite the advantages of VR in terms of its utilitarian, hedonistic, and behavioural aspects, little is known about customers' reactions to using VR as a tool for online shopping. The current study may be used as a springboard for evaluating the utility of VR from a customer and management standpoint(J.-H. Kim et al., 2021). In one of the literature reviews about the shopping experience, the observed utility and pleasure of brightness had a strong beneficial impact, which then in turn affected attitudes toward virtual reality and intentions. User satisfaction and gratification were not positively impacted by interaction. The perceived utility and pleasure of videoconferencing were still affected. Additionally, the results demonstrated a moderating relationship among customers' prior VR encounters and both judged usefulness and enjoyment of interaction. Good outcomes also emerged from the link between conduct expectations and disposition (J.-H. Kim et al., 2021).

When the Metaverse system provides the consumer with the joy and interest to discover it, that will assist sense the simplicity of use of Metaverse technology. Perceived interest, perceived joy, and self-efficiency all positively affect usefulness and ease of use. Enjoyment, social convention, and perceived simplicity of use all had a favourable impact on perceived usefulness. In other words, the more enjoyment a user derives from using an item of technology, the more helpful they feel it to be. Additionally, the more usable a technology piece is when it is simple to use. Similar to previous comparable studies, these results indicate that usefulness is highly influenced by social norms, indicating that other people's perspectives have an impact on how much people utilise technology (Aburbeian et al., 2022). The use of technological advancements in a variety of fields significantly improves the quality of human existence. Since we have reached the era of digital breakthroughs, it has evolved into a crucial requirement. From the standpoint of end users, three significant technological development phases have been noted: the introduction of pcs, the web, and portable devices (Aburbeian et al., 2022). Our houses have lately become practically invaded by the web, which now provides automated systems that make our everyday life easier. A smartphone user is all that is needed to operate world wide web gadgets. Due to Internet of Things (IoT) technology, home automation consists of several components and services that operate separately and in concert to communicate with one another and the user. Electricity data systems, assistance that regulates interaction among devices, online payments, lamp controllers, linked smart appliances like fridges and washers and dryers, leisure devices like smart TVs, residential automatons used for numerous household tasks, thermostats and senior living systems and devices, and clever alarm systems with robotic like fire alarms are just a few examples of the offerings and gadgets that enable up the modern smart home. Commercial and retail metaverse products will be most readily adopted in Western and developed Asian economies, which are at the forefront of 5G deployment. Due to the tremendous amount of data that metaverse applications will gather, international tensions around information localization will worsen. The energy demands of the technology sector will rise as a result of metaverse applications, placing more emphasis on the ESG goals of IT companies(*Emerald Expert Briefings*, 2022). The "technology acceptance model" is the most often utilised paradigm for understanding technological adoption, according to many research (Sparkes, 2021). "Perceived utility, perceived comfort, perceived expense, perceived compatibility, perceived social impact, and perceived pleasure" are the most critical variables that has been found by various researchers. Numerous studies have looked at these factors and found that they can all have an impact on how consumers behave(*The Acceptance of Smart Home Technology - the University of Twente Student Theses*, n.d.) (Chang & Nam, 2021). However, the usage of intelligent home care has spread quickly throughout civilization, there are still several issues that must be resolved if these industries are to continue to prosper. Technically speaking, the solutions should minimize several hazards, including those related to system hijacking or security threats that are primarily brought on by the usage of home network capabilities (Park et al., 2018). Having a well-designed consumer experience that enables consumers to view and operate smart home services through an assortment of internet interfaces is also crucial. Due to several problems, such as the challenge of operating home automation services and the dearth of actual info about the house, past research revealed that general consumer contentment for connected devices and household security products is lesser compared to other innovations (H. S. Kim et al., 2015).

According to the direct effect, boredom and place attachment (PA), as well as the indirect effects of loneliness and social presence, were the most significant predictors of intention, followed by perceived conduct and social distance attitude. Additionally, the moderating impact made a substantial contribution by offering a profound understanding of the outcome (Handarkho et al., 2021).

3.0 METHOD

To accomplish the aims of this study, a systematic literature review methodology was used.

This study has the following objectives

1. Identification of factors- What factors influence user's intention to use VR (Virtual Reality) technology.
2. To investigate the feasibility of using virtual reality as a tool for consumer behaviour research.
3. To determine the degree to which a cognitive treatment using virtual reality is effective at changing customer behaviour.

3.1 Selection Standards and Search Tactics

To gain a broad, robust perspective on the methodological validity and success of changing consumer behaviour within virtual reality across numerous consumer domains and forms of behaviour change, I did not concentrate on a particular type of behaviour change or consumer domain. Many measures are typically advised to ensure correctness and clarity in the evaluation. I established the following standards to be used for the search string when implementing these steps: Because changing behaviour is our main focus, the study must have three requirements: (1) An experimental design; (2) Behavioural outcome variable; (3) Application of virtual reality in the behavioural study. Sales figures or actions taken by research subjects are examples of behavioural outcome measures, whereas attitudes and perceptions are types of non-outcome measures (Table 1)

Table 1. Eligibility and selection standards

No	Code	Description	To exclude if	To include if
1	It is Duplicate	The article was found to be duplicated	Google Scholar and Scopus may have their ways of using special characters	
2	It is non-English	Non-English article	Abstract if non-English	
3	It does not have any results	If the paper does not have any results	If the paper does not show significant results and suggests only views	
4	The study is not on VR, AR	The article does not suggest any VR or AR study	Excluded the paper in which there is no study of VR or AR	
5	Consumer behaviour outcome measures not identified	The article which has reference to consumer behaviour	Excluded the article where there is no behavioural or attitude, intention, impact or adoption of VR, AR studied	Included research paper that includes the following: -Sales -Purchase behaviour, -Students, -Preferences, -Intention, -Spending, -Influence
6	Target group	The article has a certain focus on a group	Papers not included in case of the following Children less than 18 years of age, people not aware of the use of Metaverse,	Include articles the following: -Students -Elderly - Any geographical location

3.2 Shortlisting of the Relevant Articles

Through several cycles of publication assessment, I created a method to determine which papers should be included. Then, titles were used to filter out articles. For title checking, I created several inclusion requirements. Publications with titles that stated that the study was only conducted on youngsters (under the age of 18) or a very specific market group. A total of 360 articles were identified via different databases. 219 records were removed which were duplicates, and 87 articles were removed basis the title and language. 48 Articles were excluded for not meeting the eligibility criteria. 84 articles were remaining after screening at the abstract level and further screening of content reduced the article to 30 (Figure 1) which were stored on Mendeley.

Figure 1. Selection flow chart

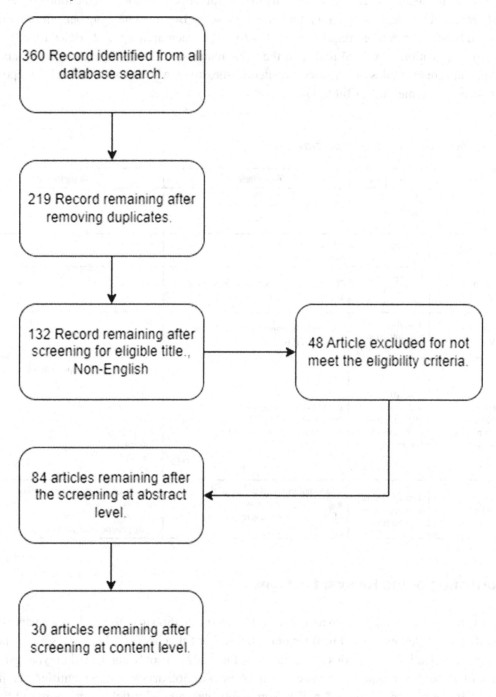

4.0 INTERPRETATION

Some of the studies are only based on personal innovativeness and user satisfaction. Additionally, only two TAM (Technology Acceptance Model) constructs—Perceived ease of use (PEOU) and PU—were employed in one of the articles.

Although the restriction of two variables is important for improving the measuring process, it neglected to take other constructs that might have an impact on the model into account. Various articles studied have used many variables as discussed in Figure 2. Although virtual reality (VR) is gradually becoming more prevalent in the consumer research literature, it is still not a common technique used by academics who investigate consumer behaviour. The question of whether older customers would behave in the same way in VR research that tries to duplicate study findings from real-life or lab research arises as consumers of all ages increasingly use VR in their personal lives, such as for playing games or watching movies. Due to the increased interaction opportunities within the VR environment, VR gives greater opportunities for consumer research. By allowing for these options, the VR world can become even more realistic because real-life users can also engage with their surroundings in this way.

Figure 2. Conceptual framework used in various studies

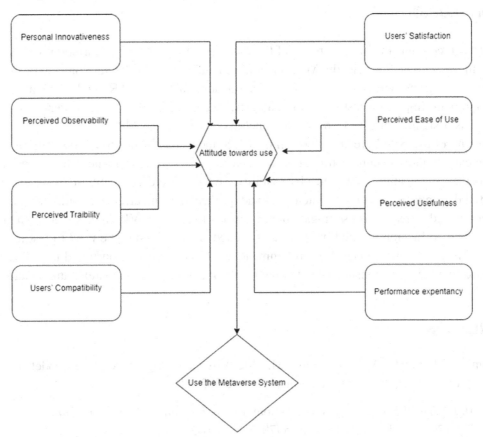

The more widely used VR becomes, the more consumer research will likely incorporate it, and the more the industry will learn about its advantages and unintended expenses.

It is advised that the creation of a VR consumer researchers' toolbox contributes to the development of an easy-to-implement and easy-to-use VR environment, which can encourage consumer behaviour scientists to employ VR in behaviour change research (rather than discouraging them from doing so). The user's propensity to repeat towards the retail environment is found to be affected by engagement along two different paths (a hedonic path and a utilitarian one), which ultimately cancel each other out. The hedonic path is positively impacted by immersion, whereas the utilitarian path is negatively impacted. When compared to activities available in physical reality, our methodology and findings indicate that individuals believe VR and AR give either impossible or favourable activities.

The clever marketing technology of tomorrow, known as Metaverse, will be used to present and breathe life into a variety of companies in the 3D interactive digital environment. The metaverse is a virtual representation of how things are done in actual life. Users can interact with one another in this 3D virtual environment by using avatars that look like them. This would have a significant impact on how businesses use the marketing function going forward as well as the way we interact with one another (Hollensen et al., 2022).

5.0 CONCLUSION

The world will continue to alter as a result of the Metaverse innovation in a variety of fields, including business and academia. Specifically, Metaverse accompanied by other technologies will be crucial in education and learning. The rising creativity and application of VR and AR in educational contexts will have a significant impact on instructional strategies. According to the research, Personal Innovativeness (PI) has a significant effect on people's inclinations for using Metaverse. Perceived usefulness and simplicity of use both have an impact on the PI. Some research adds to the body of knowledge on technological adoption by demonstrating how Metaverse adoption is influenced by adoption qualities such as perceived tribality, perceived observability, and perceived compatibility. user satisfaction is an essential determinant for a user's intention to adopt the use of metaverse. Results from comparable studies conducted in real-world settings typically mirror those from VR environments when it comes to behaviour modification research in consumer-related fields. VR may be used to test interventions in a more effective, more manageable environment. VR has already demonstrated its ability to enable behaviour change in some consumer-related industries, including food, apparel, banking and tourism.

REFERENCES

Aburbeian, A. M., Owda, A. Y., & Owda, M. (2022). A technology acceptance model survey of the metaverse prospects. *AI, 3*(2), 285–302. doi:10.3390/ai3020018

Ajzen, I. (1991). The theory of planned behaviour. *Organizational Behavior and Human Decision Processes, 50*(2), 179–211. doi:10.1016/0749-5978(91)90020-T

Bale, A. S., Ghorpade, N., Hashim, M. F., Vaishnav, J., & Almaspoor, Z. (2022). A comprehensive study on metaverse and its impacts on humans. *Advances in Human-Computer Interaction*, *2022*, 1–11. doi:10.1155/2022/3247060

Chang, S., & Nam, K. (2021). Smart home adoption: The impact of user characteristics and differences in perception of benefits. *Buildings*, *11*(9), 393. doi:10.3390/buildings11090393

Dwivedi, Y. K., Hughes, L., Baabdullah, A. M., Ribeiro-Navarrete, S., Giannakis, M., Al-Debei, M. M., Dennehy, D., Metri, B., Buhalis, D., Cheung, C. M. K., Conboy, K., Doyle, R., Dubey, R., Dutot, V., Felix, R., Goyal, D. P., Gustafsson, A., Hinsch, C., Jebabli, I., ... Wamba, S. F. (2022). Metaverse beyond the hype: Multidisciplinary perspectives on emerging challenges, opportunities, and agenda for research, practice and policy. *International Journal of Information Management*, *66*, 102542. doi:10.1016/j.ijinfomgt.2022.102542

Expert, E. (2022). *Briefings*. Emerald.

Ezimmuo, C. M., & Keikhosrokiani, P. (2022). Predicting Consumer Behavior Change Towards Using Online Shopping in Nigeria: The Impact of the COVID-19 Pandemic. In P. Keikhosrokiani (Ed.), *Handbook of Research on Consumer Behavior Change and Data Analytics in the Socio-Digital Era* (pp. 210–254). IGI Global. doi:10.4018/978-1-6684-4168-8.ch010

Fussell, S. G., & Truong, D. (2022). Using virtual reality for dynamic learning: An extended technology acceptance model. *Virtual Reality (Waltham Cross)*, *26*(1), 249–267. doi:10.100710055-021-00554-x PMID:34276237

Gim, G., Bae, H., & Kang, S. (2022). Metaverse learning: The relationship among quality of VR-based education, self-determination, and learner satisfaction. In *7th International Conference on Big Data, Cloud Computing, and Data Science (BCD), 2022* (pp. 279–284). IEEE Publications/Australasian Center for Italian Studies. 10.1109/BCD54882.2022.9900629

Glavish, M. (2022, March 17). *The dark side of the metaverse, Part I*. https://www.aei.org/technology-and-innovation/the-dark-side-of-the-metaverse-part-i/

Hollensen, S., Kotler, P., & Opresnik, M. O. (2022). Metaverse – The new marketing universe. *The Journal of Business Strategy*. Advance online publication. doi:10.1108/JBS-01-2022-0014

Keikhosrokiani, P. (Ed.). (2022). *Handbook of Research on Consumer Behavior Change and Data Analytics in the Socio-Digital Era*. IGI Global. doi:10.4018/978-1-6684-4168-8

Keikhosrokiani, P., Mustaffa, N., Zakaria, N., & Baharudin, A. S. (2019). User Behavioral Intention Toward Using Mobile Healthcare System. In Consumer-Driven Technologies in Healthcare: Breakthroughs in Research and Practice (pp. 429-444). IGI Global. doi:10.4018/978-1-5225-6198-9.ch022

Keikhosrokiani, P., & Pourya Asl, M. (2023). *Handbook of Research on Artificial Intelligence Applications in Literary Works and Social Media*. IGI Global. doi:10.4018/978-1-6684-6242-3

Kim, H. S., Kim, H. C., & Ji, Y. G. (2015). User requirement elicitation for U-city residential environment: Concentrated on smart home service. *Journal of Society for e-Business Studies, 20*(1), 167–182. doi:10.7838/jsebs.2015.20.1.167

Kim, J.-H., Kim, M., Park, M., & Yoo, J. (2021). How interactivity and vividness influence consumer virtual reality shopping experience: The mediating role of telepresence. *Journal of Research in Interactive Marketing, 15*(3), 502–525. doi:10.1108/JRIM-07-2020-0148

Lee, P., Braud, T., Zhou, P., L., A. W., Xu, D. L., Z., J. L., Kumar, A., B., C., & Hui, P. (2021). *All one needs to know about metaverse: A complete survey on technological singularity, virtual ecosystem, and research agenda.* doi:10.13140/RG.2.2.11200.05124/8

Lee, S.-G., Trimi, S., Byun, W. K., & Kang, M. (2011). Innovation and imitation effects in Metaverse service adoption. *Service Business, 5*(2), 155–172. doi:10.100711628-011-0108-8

Mark Zuckerberg is betting Facebook's future on the metaverse. (n.d.). *The Verge*. Retrieved November 6, 2022. https://www.theverge.com/22588022/mark-zuckerberg-facebook-ceo-metaverse-interview

Marketing in the metaverse: An opportunity for innovation and experimentation. (n.d.). Retrieved November 7, 2022. https://www.mckinsey.com/capabilities/growth-marketing-and-sales/our-insights/marketing-in-the-metaverse-an-opportunity-for-innovation-and-experimentation

Park, E., Kim, S., Kim, Y., & Kwon, S. J. (2018). Smart home services as the next mainstream of the ICT industry: Determinants of the adoption of smart home services. *Universal Access in the Information Society, 17*(1), 175–190. doi:10.100710209-017-0533-0

Peukert, C., Pfeiffer, J., Meißner, M., Pfeiffer, T., & Weinhardt, C. (2019). Shopping in virtual reality stores: The influence of immersion on system adoption. *Journal of Management Information Systems, 36*(3), 755–788. doi:10.1080/07421222.2019.1628889

Riar, M., Xi, N., Korbel, J. J., Zarnekow, R., & Hamari, J. (2022). Using augmented reality for shopping: A framework for AR induced consumer behavior, literature review and future agenda. *Internet Research*. Advance online publication. doi:10.1108/INTR-08-2021-0611

Rijsdijk, S. A., & Hultink, E. J. (2009). How today's consumers perceive tomorrow's smart products *. *Journal of Product Innovation Management, 26*(1), 24–42. doi:10.1111/j.1540-5885.2009.00332.x

Sparkes, M. (2021). What is a metaverse. *New Scientist, 251*(3348), 18. doi:10.1016/S0262-4079(21)01450-0

Stackpole, T. (2022, July 1). Exploring the metaverse. *Harvard Business Review*. https://hbr.org/2022/07/exploring-the-metaverse

Steffen, J. H., Gaskin, J. E., Meservy, T. O., Jenkins, J. L., & Wolman, I. (2019). Framework of affordances for virtual reality and augmented reality. *Journal of Management Information Systems, 36*(3), 683–729. doi:10.1080/07421222.2019.1628877

Step into the metaverse: How the immersive Internet will unlock a trillion-dollar social economy. (n.d.). Retrieved November 5, 2022. https://www.wiley.com/en-ie/Step+into+the+Metaverse%3A+How+the+Immersive+Internet+Will+Unlock+a+Trillion+Dollar+Social+Economy-p-9781119887591

Teng, Z., Cai, Y., Gao, Y., Zhang, X., & Li, X. (2022). Factors affecting learners' adoption of an educational metaverse platform: An empirical study based on an extended UTAUT model. *Mobile Information Systems, 2022*, 1–15. doi:10.1155/2022/4663740

The acceptance of smart home technology—University of Twente Student Theses. (n.d.). Retrieved November 9, 2022. https://essay.utwente.nl/75338/ Value-creation-in-the-metaverse.pdf

Xian, Z., Keikhosrokiani, P., XinYing, C., & Li, Z. (2022). An RFM Model Using K-Means Clustering to Improve Customer Segmentation and Product Recommendation. In P. Keikhosrokiani (Ed.), Handbook of Research on Consumer Behavior Change and Data Analytics in the Socio-Digital Era (pp. 124-145). IGI Global. doi:10.4018/978-1-6684-4168-8.ch006

Chapter 7
Understanding Consumer Behavior in Virtual Ecosystems:
Adoption of Immersive Technologies in Metaverse Among Consumers

Princi Gupta
JECRC University, India

ABSTRACT

This chapter outlines the understanding of consumer behavior in the virtual ecosystem and the adoption of immersive technologies in the metaverse among consumers. The metaverse is based on the convergence of technologies that enable multisensory interactions with virtual environments, digital objects, and people such as virtual reality (VR) and augmented reality (AR). This chapter covers the impact of consumer behavior in metaverse followed by the strategies adopted by entrepreneurs to work in metaverse to reach consumers. This chapter outlines the metaverse market size, trends, growth, and forecast. This chapter offers a comprehensive framework that examines the metaverse development under the dimensions of metaverse ecosystem. This chapter further aims at identifying the challenges and issues faced in adoption of immersive technologies in metaverse. The metaverse also poses numerous problems to our customary modes of communication and teamwork. The metaverse is significant for retailers for a number of reasons in addition to remaining on the bleeding edge of technology.

INTRODUCTION

Since the Internet became widely used in the 1990s, cyberspace has continued to develop. In addition to social networks, video conferencing, virtual 3D worlds (like VR Chat), augmented reality software (like Pokemon Go), and non-fungible token games, we have also developed other computer-mediated virtual environments (e.g., Upland). These virtual spaces, albeit transient and unconnected, have enabled different levels of digital transformation for us. To accelerate the digital transformation of every part of our physical life, the term "metaverse" has been developed. The idea of an immersive Internet as a vast,

DOI: 10.4018/978-1-6684-7029-9.ch007

contiguous, lasting, and shared domain is at the heart of the metaverse. The digital "big bang" of our cyberspace is not far off, despite the metaverse's seemingly futuristic appearance, which is being fueled by cutting-edge technology like Extended Reality, 5G, and Artificial Intelligence (Keikhosrokiani & Pourya Asl, 2023; MacCallum, 2019). Researchers and computer scientists want to quickly expand some fields in virtual environments. The proliferation of social media platforms and the Internet provide for easy and affordable access to technology and software, enabling the development of superior digital material represented by three-dimensional (3D) virtual environments (Parsons, 2019). According to V'azquez-Cano and Sevillano-Garca (2017), the metaverse is an immersive, 3D virtual environment where people interact socially and economically through computation that is independent of where they are located. Virtual reality has recently made it feasible to experience things like making a loop on a roller coaster or being at a beach resort while lying on a sofa at home (VR) (V'azquez-Cano & Sevillano-Garca, 2017). Users can experience three-dimensional settings that resemble artificially manufactured spaces thanks to the relatively new technology known as virtual reality (VR) (Nelson, 2020).

These computer-generated virtual environments may feature interactive elements that are felt from a first-person perspective, giving users the chance to feel as though they are physically present at a different area. Technology-wise, virtual reality is advancing quickly and increasingly successful in giving consumers seemingly realistic virtual surroundings at a relatively low price (Siegrist et al., 2019).

Figure 1. Framework for Metaverse Development under the dimensions of metaverse ecosystem (Lee et al., 2021)

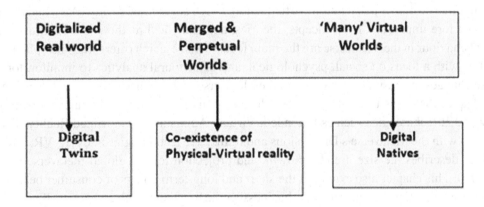

Figure 1 illustrates 'digital twins-native continuum' on the basis of duality. Three stages of evolution can be seen in this metaverse vision. The digital twins are a good place to start because they have the physical environments digitalized and can update their virtual siblings on a regular basis (Doolani, 2020). According to the physical world, digital twins produce "many" virtual worlds that are digital replicas of the real world, and human users who use their avatars to create new things in these virtual worlds are considered "digital natives". In the beginning, these virtual worlds will experience limited connectivity with one another and the real world, or an information silo (Berg, 2019). Then, amid a vast landscape, they will gradually come together. The final stage of the coexistence of physical-virtual reality, which is related to surreality, will eventually see the digitised physical and virtual worlds mix. The demands for an everlasting, 3D virtual cyberspace known as the metaverse are unique in a connected physical-virtual universe. The metaverse is a virtual setting that combines the physical and digital worlds that is made possible by the fusion of Extended Reality and Internet and Web technology (XR). According to the *Milgram and Kishino's Reality-Virtuality Continuum* (Laudon, 2016), XR, which includes virtual reality, mixed reality, and augmented reality, merges the digital and physical worlds to varying degrees (VR). Similar to this, Snow Crash's metaverse scene depicts the contrast between the real world and a replica of digital settings. Each individual user in the metaverse is the owner of their own unique avatar, which functions as an analogue to the user's physical self and allows them to experience a different life in a virtuality that is a metaphor for their actual reality (Becker, 2020).

The development of the metaverse must go through three consecutive phases to attain this duality: (I) digital twins; (II) digital natives; and finally (III) the coexistence of physical and virtual reality, or more specifically, surreality. The link between the three stages is shown in Figure 1. Large-scale, very accurate digital replicas of real-world objects and entities are known as "digital twins." (Grieves, 2017).

The book aims to compile and analyse virtual retail in the metaverse in terms of extended reality technologies, immersive visualisation systems, and customer behaviour analytics. Understanding whether digitised retail products and augmented reality shopping tools in virtual malls can integrate consumers' intelligence, contextual awareness, and brand perception metrics to improve computational efficiency is crucial given the growing evidence of consumer values on blockchain-based metaverse platforms. The book focuses on seeing how customer behaviour changes as the Metaverse is adopted. The emergence of the Metaverse has had a significant impact on consumer behaviour, influencing everything from decision-making and brand relationships to feelings of self-worth and wellbeing. Investigating the Metaverse themes like customer behaviour in virtual reality (VR), augmented reality (AR), and mixed reality (MR) is therefore important. The concepts, theories, and analytical methods used to track changes in consumer behaviour in the Metaverse are the main focus. This research offers transdisciplinary research and practise with a focus on social, psychological, and behavioural analytics to monitor, forecast, and categorise changes in consumer behaviour in the Metaverse and enhance commercial decision-making.

This chapter discusses the history of the Metaverse, its scope and its features, as well as a brief overview of XR technologies such as Extended, Virtual, Augmented, and Mixed Reality. This chapter is concerned with the Metaverse's Dimensions and immersive technologies like XR, VR, AR, and MR. The chapter describes the size, trends, growth, and projection for the global metaverse market from 2022 to 2030. This chapter also examines the short and long-term effects of consumer behaviour in the metaverse, as well as the strategies used by businesspeople to interact with consumers there. The goal of this chapter is to find instances of businesses employing the metaverse and to highlight the difficulties and problems associated with the adoption of immersive technologies in the metaverse as well as with the future areas of research.

LITERATURE REVIEW

Metaverse

The word "metaverse" was first applied to a virtual environment where users could engage with one another in many real-world scenarios while assuming the identities of avatars or pseudonyms. In the immersive, 3D virtual world known as the Metaverse, users can connect socially and economically in a computational manner from anywhere in the world (Díaz et al., 2020; V´azquez-Cano & Sevillano-García, 2017). Virtual commerce is business activity carried out in a fully immersive virtual setting. It is one of the most recent advancements in e-commerce, the colossal commercial tool of the past 20 years driven by technology progress, commercial innovation, and social uptake (Laudon, 2016). Virtual commerce, from a technical standpoint, comprises of e-commerce infrastructures, such as electronic product catalogues (Kovacs, 2015) and electronic payment that utilises immersive technologies to produce new settings for commercial activity (Kou, 2013). Immersive technology consists of computer software and hardware that stimulate the five senses of humans (i.e., vision, hearing, touch, smell, and taste) in an artificial environment to give users the impression that they are actually present. This is known as the "feeling of presence" (Xue et al., 2019). It has caught the interest of both business and academia. Gaming has widely embraced immersive technology in the form of augmented reality (AR) and virtual reality (VR). The findings from user behaviour literatures must be effectively translated into design artefacts (broadly defined as a construct, a model, a method, or an instantiation of application design research and development) in order for immersive technology to be used in virtual commerce applications (Vasarainen et al., 2021). While research on application design develops and evaluates design artefacts to engage users and promote user consumption through the patterns discovered from consumer behaviour studies, consumer behaviour research empirically evaluates the consumer behavioural responses (e.g., level of acceptance and purchase intention) impacted by certain design artefacts (Vasarainen et al., 2021).

A virtual environment called the metaverse is developed by artificial reality (AR) and allows users to interact as avatars from virtual reality (VR) in these two interconnected universes. In other words, this can be seen as a video game simulation of the actual world in which the user assumes the role of a virtual character while acting and behaving realistically (Giulio, 2021). Due to the synchronisation of the Metaverse chronology with the actual world time, this interaction is seamless. The modern customer has grown weary of companies bragging about themselves in static online displays and pop-up adverts and longs for rich, immersive experiences where they can take part and make decisions. Such an experience is provided by the Metaverse in 3D and even 4D. It is similar to a virtual marketplace where one may invite virtual representations of actual customers to one's own virtual shop, tavern, disco, or performance from the comfort of their homes and let them test and enjoy the goods (Moi, 2020).

Virtual reality (VR), non-fungible tokens (NFTs), gaming, community and shared experiences, geo-enabled virtual locales, and virtual commerce are all characteristics of the connected, global metaverse. The metaverse is a form of made-up universe with expanding immersive digital places that make learning environments more participatory. The metaverse is an enlargement of the synchronous communication that embraces an effective number of participants to share varied experiences (Sohaib et al., 2019).

Brief History of XR Technologies; Extended, Virtual, Augmented and Mixed Reality

A broad term known as "extended reality" or "cross reality" (XR) refers to a number of immersive technologies that create electronic, digital settings in which data are represented and projected. Virtual Reality (VR), Augmented Reality (AR), and Mixed Reality are all parts of XR (Slater, 2016). VR is a different, entirely artificial environment that has been produced digitally (Milgram, 1995). Users of VR feel engrossed, as though they are in a new environment, and behave similarly to how they would in the real world (Slater, 2021). This experience is enhanced by the senses of sight, hearing, touch, movement, and the organic interaction with virtual things with the aid of specialised multisensory apparatus such as immersion helmets, virtual reality headsets, and omnidirectional treadmills (Pellas et al., 2021).

AR takes a distinct approach to actual spaces; it incorporates digital inputs and virtual features into the real world to improve it (Ibanez, 2018). It geographically combines the real world and the digital one (Klopfer, 2008). The result is a layer of digital artefacts that are spatially projected and are mediated by tools like smart phones, tablets, glasses, contact lenses, or other transparent surfaces (Mystakidis, 2021). Additionally, by showing input from built-in camera sensors in VR headsets with pass-through mode, AR can be applied there as well. The definition of MR has changed over time to reflect changing technology advancements, as well as the predominate verbal meanings and narratives (Vasilevski, 2020). When the physical environment and the projected digital data interact in real time, MR is frequently referred to as an enhanced version of AR (Vasilevski, 2020). For instance, in an MR game, a scripted non-player character would be aware of the actual environment and might hide behind a desk or a couch. Similar to VR, MR calls need specialised eyewear. But for the sake of this essay, we accept the definition of MR as any fusion of augmented reality and virtual reality, as well as any intermediate versions like augmented virtuality (Pellas et al., 2021). This choice is made in light of the long-term technological development and advancement of augmented reality to include interactive affordances. As a result, MR is a blend of AR and VR that continue to be the two core technologies. We use Milgram's and Kishino's one-dimensional reality-virtuality continuum to understand and visualise how these immersive technologies interact with the environment (Pellas et al., 2021). An illustration of this continuum looks like a straight line with two endpoints. The natural, physical environment is at the far left end of the line. The user experiences a wholly virtual, fake environment at the right end as opposed to a real one (Mystakidis, 2021). As a result, VR is located at the right extremum of the spectrum, while AR is close to the left end. Both are supersets of MR (Mystakidis, 2021). Definitions of AR, VR, MR, and VW are mentioned in Table 1.

Table 1. Definitions of AR, VR, MR, and VW

Concept	Definition
AR	Realtime display of computer-generated content over a real-world scene
VR	Computer-simulated, interactive, and immersive virtual environments that isolate the user from the surrounding physical environment, using various immersion methods
MR	The dynamic coexistence of virtual and real content in the same space.
XR	An umbrella term for AR, VR, and MR.
VW	Synthetic, persistent, immersive, and networked multi-users environments, allowing users represented as avatars to interact with other users and in-world content in (nearly) realtime.

Source: Shen et al. (2020)

GLOBAL METAVERSE: MARKET SIZE, SHARE, TRENDS, FORECAST 2022-30

In 2021, it was predicted that the worldwide metaverse market would be worth USD 38.85 billion. From 2022 to 2030, it is anticipated to increase at a compound annual growth rate (CAGR) of 39.4%. The rise in interest in using the Internet to integrate the physical and digital worlds, the popularity of mixed reality (MR), augmented reality (AR), and virtual reality (VR), and the COVID-19 outbreak and the developments that follow as outcomes of the situation are some of the key factors anticipated to drive the revenue growth. As one of the hottest technology platforms, the Metaverse is luring industry heavyweights from the worlds of social networks, technology, and online game development to the market. With a significant user penetration rate for a variety of applications—including gaming, content creation, social interaction, learning and training, and online virtual shopping—the metaverse is a rapidly expanding trend.

The potential business opportunity or the total addressable market is estimated at more than USD 1 trillion in yearly revenues, and industry analysts predict that the metaverse will permeate a wide range of industries in the upcoming years (Size, 2018).

Additionally, the global digital economy accounted for 15.5% of all GDP in 2018, according to the UN, which led to a prediction of 15% to 16.8% by 2021. The potential market opportunity for the metaverse is estimated to be between USD 3.75 trillion and USD 12.46 trillion, according to C-level executives of the top providers of metaverse solutions. This would depend on the percentage of the digital economy shifting to the metaverse and the percentage of the total addressable market expansion. In order to experience the immersive nature of the digital world, numerous end-user players, including Walmart, Nike Inc., Gap Inc., Verizon, Hulu, LLC, Adidas, and Atari, Inc., are entering the metaverse in various ways. After Facebook Inc. announced that the company would change its name to Meta Platforms Inc. or simply "Meta", the concept or idea of the "metaverse" gained traction effectively immediately. The business would be devoted to building the virtual world known as the metaverse. It is widely employed as a real-time virtual environment to create and exploit vast opportunities for brand connection (share & Trend Analysis report, 2022). Meta Platforms Inc., Epic Games Inc., Nvidia Corporation, Tencent Holdings Ltd., ByteDance Ltd., Lilith Games, Unity Technologies Inc., Roblox Corporations, NetEase Inc., and Nextech AR Solutions Corp. are important industry participants. It is projected that the industry would grow in the future thanks to the release of cutting-edge hardware supporting the metaverse of virtual worlds. The Sandbox and Warner Music Group announced a collaboration in January 2022 to introduce the first planet in The Sandbox metaverse with a musical theme. With this agreement, Warner Music Group (WMG) would formally enter the metaverse and the NFT space. Tencent Holdings Ltd. declared a partnership with The Asian Institute of Digital Finance in November 2021. To promote Asia's fintech sector, the businesses will work together in the fields of entrepreneurship, research, and education. Epic Games Inc. bought Harmonix Music Systems Inc. in November 2021. The Harmonix team will collaborate closely with Epic Games Inc. to create musical adventures and gameplay for Fortnite while continuing to support current products like Rock Band 4. According to estimates from October 2021, Facebook Reality Labs will invest at least USD 10 billion in the creation of hardware, software, and content for augmented reality (AR) and virtual reality (VR). The section of Meta Platforms Inc., formerly Facebook Inc., is called Facebook Reality Labs.

Table 2 illustrates the report that forecasts revenue growth at the global, regional, and country levels and provides an analysis of the latest industry trends and opportunities in each of the sub-segments from 2017 to 2030. Grand View Research divides the worldwide metaverse market report into segments for this study based on the following criteria: product, platform, technology, offering, application, end use, and region.

It includes the most important market participants and is probably created specifically to meet the needs of the customer. Within the projected period of 2021–2027, this phase investigates the complexity of the company enterprise's fiercest rivalry as well as its current market characteristics. The Metaverse market file includes a financial hit on important global market players, which includes an analysis of the company's operations, financial statements, product description, and strategic goals.

Table 2. An analysis of the latest industry trends and opportunities in each of the sub-segments from 2017 to 2030

R Report Attribute	Details
Market size value in 2022	USD 47.48 billion
Revenue forecast in 2030	UDS 678.8 billion
Growth Rate	CAGR of 39.4% from 2022 to 2030
Base year for estimation	2021
Historical Data	2017-2021
Forecast period	2022-2030
Quantitative units	Revenue in USD Million and CAGr from 2022 to 2030
Report Coverage	Revenue forecast, company ranking, competitive landscape, growth factors, and trends.
Segments Covered	Component, platform, offering, application, technology, end use, region.
Regional scope	North America; Europe; Asia pacific; south America; Middle East & Africa
Country Scope	US; Canada; Mexico; U.K; Germany; France; China; India; Japan; South Korea; Brazil
Key companies profiled	Meta Platforms Inc.; Tencent Holdings Ltd.; Epic Games Inc.; Nvidia Corporation; Unity Technologies Inc.
Customization scope	Free report customization (equivalent up to 8 analysts working days) with purchase. Addition or alteration to country, regional & segment scope.
Pricing and purchase options	Avail customized purchase options to meet your exact research needs.

Source: share & Trend Analysis report, 2022

METAVERSE: IT'S EFFECT ON CONSUMER BEHAVIOUR

Around the world, there is a lot of excitement about the metaverse. But how will this virtual environment affect how customers shop, and how can brands benefit from it?

A consumer is someone who recognises a need or want, makes a purchase, and then discards the item after using it. The utility of a typical consumer depends on their consumption of industrial and agricultural commodities, services, housing, and money (Ezimmuo & Keikhosrokiani, 2022; Keikhosrokiani, 2022; Kotler, 2019; Xian et al., 2022). Since everyone is influenced by various internal and external elements that shape consumer behaviour, no two of them are alike. Consumer behaviour includes the process of looking for, selecting, paying for, utilising, reviewing, and discarding goods and services (Valaskova et al., 2015). A 3D virtual world called the metaverse offers varied and compelling experiences outside of gaming. People can develop, purchase, and sell goods and services in a digital economy. The metaverse can be used by users for social interactions, teamwork, and educational endeavours (Arnold, 2017).

We are already observing the early stages of how the metaverse affects our engagement with technology, despite the fact that this virtual environment may appear in far future. By designing personalised avatars and vehicles, developing virtual relationships, buying digital real estate, and meeting friends at virtual events and concerts, users are reproducing their everyday routines and hobbies in the virtual world. The relationship between brands and customers will start to change as the metaverse prepares the path for new interactions between users and technology. Brands will need to adapt and better understand their customers' behaviour in this digital environment if they want to stay ahead of rivals (Barbosa Escobar, 2021).

It is safe to conclude that most customers will eventually shift to the metaverse, and consumer habits will adjust as new kinds of content, consumption, and commerce become available. Over three-quarters of global consumers rely on technology throughout their everyday lives. Although digital commerce and video games already interact, the metaverse elevates buying through virtual goods and services, opening up new revenue streams for businesses and providing marketers with the opportunity to reach out to younger consumers (Basu, 2021).

Consumers are already adopting this parallel universe to reproduce their physical daily routines in the digital world, especially by developing new routines where they own high-value digital assets like real estate, vehicles, and other goods. According to reports, the average value of a digital home is $76,000, the average value of an original work of art is $9,000, and the average value of a digital designer handbag is over $2,900. Fashion-only digital brands are increasingly becoming well-known. The company RTFKT, which makes virtual collectibles like sneakers, garnered $3.1 million in sales in just 7 minutes (Boursier, 2020).

The majority of younger shoppers want to be able to purchase their favourite brands wherever they go online, even on platforms for the metaverse. According to a study by Obsess, 70% of customers who visit an online retailer make a purchase. According to the report, almost 75% of Gen Z consumers have bought a digital good within a video game, and 60% of them believe that firms should sell their goods in the metaverse (Elder, 2022). 54% of Gen Z consumers believe that consumers should be able to shop anywhere they go online, while 45% think that metaverse retail spaces should resemble malls. Almost half (41%) of Gen Z consumers believe that companies should offer goods in the metaverse because it gives customers a place to purchase digital goods like nonfungible tokens (NFTs). There are a few things brands can do right away to make the shift to the virtual world easier with the growth of the metaverse:

Create a Brand Experience for the Metaverse

As the metaverse expands, brands that establish their presence there today will be in the lead. But compared to other digital media, metaverse branding, marketing, and commerce tactics will be different. Users can interact with 3D representations of companies, "try on" virtual clothing, and even visit digital replicas of stores with the integration of AR and VR technologies, for instance, to get completely engaged in the brand. Instead of only concentrating on brand exposure and awareness, the ultimate goal of opening up shop in the metaverse will be to "offer the most fascinating digital experience" (Flavián, 2019).

Learn About Your Brand's Metaverse Audience and How They Interact With It

Marketers will have a new chance to study audience demographics, but they need to be aware that customers' interactions with brands and purchases of goods in the virtual world can be very different from those in the physical world. To flourish in the metaverse, brands will need to comprehend the complexities of the relationships between users and NPCs (non-playable characters) (Shen, 2021).

Reframe Your Customer Journey to Take the Metaverse Into Account

Brands must anticipate that the metaverse will add yet another stage to the consumer journey, just as it took years for them to comprehend how digital channels complimented brick-and-mortar. By incorporating metaverse platforms into their current consumer journey, following their audience into the digital domain, and focusing on new user communities, brands can get a jump start on the competition (Shen, 2021).

Adapt Visual Search Optimization to Your Online Strategy

For the metaverse, brands will need to optimise themselves similarly to how they do so for Google. A significant factor in a brand's future digital success in the metaverse will be visual search optimization, which has already made waves in the retail sector (Elder, 2022). In the metaverse, the options are limitless. Branding, marketing, and commercial innovation have room to grow in the metaverse. Brands have countless options for engaging with consumers virtually throughout the world—whether through interactive ads, virtual billboards, videos, or experiences. Figure 2 shows the factors affecting consumer behavior in the metaverse based on the study done by Domina (2012).

Figure 2. Factors affecting consumer behavior in the metaverse (Domina, 2012)

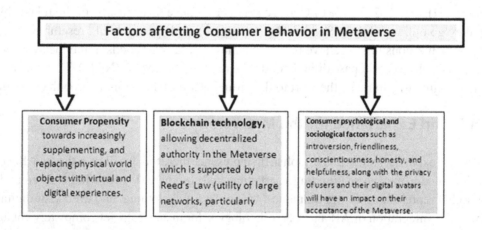

These elements include consumer inclination, blockchain technology, and social and psychological aspects of consumers. Consumers will gradually transpose their physical daily routines into the digital world, engaging in financial investments, employment opportunities, and entertainment as well as owning assets like real estate, vehicles, and NFTs. In order to flourish in the Metaverse, brands are looking into customer behaviour in terms of demographics, ethnicity, gender, and the complexities of the relationships between users and their NPCs/avatars. The tendencies of consumers are to substitute virtual experiences for tangible products and to safeguard their interests. The next platform on the internet, called Metaverse, uses the open-source technology layer to construct private augmented places where users can experience virtual reality. Blockchain enables users to build applications and take part in online commerce through a decentralised open-source environment (Domina, 2012). A metaverse often combines a user-friendly DUI, a decentralised wallet, and a decentralised exchange as an open-source blockchain technology.

EVOLVING USERS AND ROLE OF BUSINESS BEHAVIOR IN METAVERSE: SHORT-TERM AND LONG-TERM IMPACT

Observable changes in consumer and business behaviour (including spending and investing, paying attention and decision-making, as well as spending and investing time and resources) that are either directly related to the Metaverse, or that in some other way support it or reflect its guiding principles (Shen, 2021). When they first occur, these behaviours almost invariably appear to be 'trends' (or, more derogatorily, 'fads'), but are eventually revealed to be enduring global social significance.

Short-Term Behavioral Changes

The increase in our online and virtual world usage over the past year has been the most noticeable behavioural change. But the destigmatization of this period is more crucial. Making "fake" avatars, "gamers" have been spending their free time in virtual worlds performing random jobs and pursuing non-game-like goals like decorating a room in Second Life for decades (versus killing a terrorist in Counter-Strike). If not the majority of society, a sizable section of it think that such attempts are odd, pointless, or anti-social (if they do not look down on it overtly). Some perceive it as the contemporary equivalent of a grown man constructing a train set in their basement (Flavián, 2019).

It is difficult to think of anything else that might have altered this perception more quickly than COVID-19. Millions of the aforementioned sceptics have since engaged in (and loved) virtual worlds and activities (like Roblox, Animal Crossing, or Fortnite) as they look for things to do, go to events that are originally scheduled for the real world, or attempt to spend time with their children indoors (Shen, 2021). This has not only destigmatised virtual reality and "the Metaverse", but it may also encourage participation from younger generation.

Millions of customers have been aware of the service for years, but they have been reluctant to use it because they think that if they do not choose their own food, they would come rotten, broken, or otherwise unsatisfactory. Even if the apples were not damaged, they would still appear "wrong" to these customers. Importantly, no amount of marketing or Net Promoters could make up for this (Barbosa Escobar, 2021). However, many of these holdouts have been compelled to use food delivery for months due to the coronavirus. These clients have learned that their foods are fine, and the process is not only simple but pleasant as a result. Some people will resume making in-person purchases, but not everyone or always (MacCallum, 2019).

Increased user engagement and revenue for developers inevitably results in increased spending and improved products. However, "Metaverse revenues" have received two further substantial injections over the past year. The first is the quick legalisation of and investment in wholly virtual assets, most prominently through cryptocurrencies and NFTs. The second is financial support from well-known non-gaming companies and celebrities, like Neymar Jr., Travis Scott, Prada, Ford, and Gucci (Heller, 2019a). This investment also enables virtual platforms to shift their historical emphasis away from "game-like" goals like win, shoot, kill, lose, and score in favour of more universally appealing pursuits like creation, exploration, identification, expression, collaboration, and socialization (Javornik, 2021).

In order to support the Metaverse, many organisations are changing their technology pipelines, operations, and investments. Hollywood, for instance, is quickly converting its movies to real-time rendering platforms like Unreal and Unity or creating their own engine, as Disney has done with its Helios engine. These changes allow for unlimited reuse and iteration of anything created for the actual world—like a

Ford F150, or previously for a specific purpose, like Moff Gideon's light cruiser, with relative ease and little financial outlay. It would be tough to understate the effect here. Virtual content must be added to the Metaverse, but it is expensive to generate and frequently has no immediate short-term business rationale. Although many of us might desire to ride bikes on planet Endor using Zwift, bringing it to fruition would be pricey (Barbosa Escobar, 2021). However, if Disney has already made it, all that is needed is some customising. Disney's capacity to capitalise on its virtual Endor ought to encourage a higher investment in its caliber as well.

Virtual platforms like Roblox, Fortnite, and Minecraft have evolved into social places that shape culture, and they are now an essential component of consumer marketing, brand creation, and multi-media franchise experiences. The NFL and FIFA, Disney's Marvel Comics, Star Wars and Alien, Warner Bros., DC Comics, Legendry's John Wick, Microsoft's Halo, Sony's God of War and Horizon Zero Dawn, Capcom's Street Fighter, Hasbro's G.I. Joe, Nike and Michael Jordan, Travis Scott, and more have all been featured in Fortnite over the past three years (Shen, 2021).

However, in order to partake in these experiences, brand owners must embrace three things that they virtually never permit in an activation or marketing partnership: unlimited-term licences (players can keep in-game attire for life), overlapping marketing windows, and little to no editorial control. These add up to the fact that you may now explore Stark Industries while dressed as Neymar, carrying Aquaman's Trident, and wearing a Baby Yoda or Air Jordan bag. These franchise owners want it to take place (Bibri, 2022).

Finally, Epic is beginning to drive blatant cross-title achievements and virtual goods through the Epic Online Series. Rocket League from Psyonix would transition to Epic's account systems and go free-to-play shortly after Epic acquired Psyonix. Epic announces the first of multiple "Llama-Rama" events a few months later. With the help of these "LTMs", Fortnite players may accomplish Rocket League challenges and unlock exclusive outfits and achievements that can be used in both games (Heller, 2022).

Fall Guys creator Tonic Games Group was acquired by Epic earlier this year as part of its "investments in constructing the Metaverse". It is clear that Epic will incorporate its Rocket League trials into all of Tonic's games as well as those from Epic Games Publishing, which funds, publishes, and sells independent studio games through the Epic Games Store. Given that Houseparty now uses Epic Online Services, which makes it possible to stream one's Houseparty audio and video into one's Fortnite game, it is improbable that other games utilising EOS and Epic's account system will not also have access to this feature (Heller, 2022). Additionally, it goes without saying that Epic will incorporate Houseparty streaming into its real-time human rendering features and user's avatar collection. As a result, players will be able to import their assets, identities, and physical likeness into any game running on the EOS network (Bibri, 2022).

Long-Term Behavioral Changes

Despite the importance of each of the aforementioned changes, the impact of generational transition is greater. It is typical to witness press accounts and YouTube videos of newborns and young children picking up "analogue" magazines or books and attempting to "swipe" their nonexistent touchscreen for the first two or so years after the arrival of iPad. These are variously cute, funny, and popular. We are able to comprehend what was going on with ease, but we are unable to fully comprehend how these frames of reference are different from our own (Javornik, 2021). Those infants are now between ten and twelve years old. In 2011, a four-year-old was close to becoming an adult. These once illiterate media customers now directly pay for content. Some people already produce their own stuff (Heller, 2022).

These children now comprehend why we think their frames of reference hilarious, but we still find it difficult to comprehend how they differ from our own. Industries change as a result of these maturing consumers (Nagaraj, 2021).

The online game Roblox serves as a prime illustration here. A decade has passed after Roblox's 2006 inception before it attracted a sizable audience. Before any non-players truly paid attention to the title, another three years elapsed. It was one of history's most significant media events two years later. Today, it is altering the world. Compared to generations before it, the iPad generation has drastically different social norms, expectations, and habits. When those outside the "iPad Native" cohort do look at Roblox, they do not notice much (Ozkara, 2021). Visually, Roblox was and is uninspiring. Comparatively, if not objectively, its narratives lack interest. Even its social features are lagged behind those used by Gen Y, Gen X, and baby boomers—like FaceTime, Snapchat, Instagram, and even highly developed games like Fortnite. How could a platform for socialising have fewer effective tools for socialising?

To many in the entertainment industry, playing with Roblox is more like watching Nickelodeon or building with Legos—a largely primitive format that promotes learning from which we eventually progress to more "practical" pursuits like home improvement or car maintenance, or "produced" pursuits like HBO or The Last of Us. These are all excellent ways to spend time, equally as good as Roblox. But this reasoning rarely works.

Hollywood has long predicted that millennials will either lose interest in YouTube or adapt to linear Pay-TV package. And even if they now watch Netflix and Disney+, the percentage of leisure time spent watching videos is declining across generations. Children of today use interactive, collaborative virtual environments to express themselves, learn a lot of different things, and socialise continuously (Nagaraj, 2021). That will not end any time soon. Instead, these virtual worlds' capacities will increase, their usability will get better, and their importance will rise. Additionally, the generation that is "iPad Native" (or perhaps "virtual world native" generation) will keep developing. There are few creators and hardly any business owners, whereas the majority are still consumers. The changes they will bring about will be transformative (Ozkara, 2021).

METAVERSE FOR CUSTOMER EXPERIENCE AND RETAIL-APPLICATIONS

The metaverse is rapidly evolving from a platform for hobbyists to an ecosystem where people interact, influence, and live online. Additionally, one's brand must be present wherever clients go online. The metaverse is significant for retailers for a number of reasons in addition to remaining on the bleeding edge of technology (Ozkara, 2021).

Enables Conversational Marketing

The metaverse offers one a method to interact with customers in a two-way manner at scale rather than shouting at them.

Trackable

Does one feel depressed about the extinction of cookies? No issue. One can control all of their first-party data thanks to rich data from the metaverse, which simplifies the process of personalising marketing.

Immersive

On social media, marketers are competing for the attention of customers. However, it is far simpler to keep someone's interest during a branded game or in a virtual dressing room.

And certainly, a number of companies have already gotten on board with the metaverse.

- IKEA's Place app lets one see an augmented reality representation of how its furniture will appear in one's flat.
- Both L'Oréal and Avon let one virtually test on cosmetics so they can always pick the appropriate colour.
- One can try on sunglasses at Bolle to see how they look on one's face. One can also peek behind the lenses to see how they would seem when worn frequently!

ENTREPRENEURS ENTERING THE METAVERSE: STRATEGIES

Although the metaverse may still be in its infancy, it is obvious that immersive shopping is the direction the world is moving in. Marketing to avatars, developing NFTs, and embracing non-traditional selling platforms are all necessary if a marketer wants to stay ahead of the competition (MacCallum, 2019).

Market to Avatars

Right now, we are presumably using a business-to-consumer (B2C) approach. However, the metaverse uses the B2A (business-to-avatar) paradigm. To make avatars that better reflect everyday consumers and are more relatable, incredible strides have been made. One will need to master the art of marketing to avatars in an online space because every user creates an avatar to explore the metaverse. B2A is a low-cost method of interacting with customers in an online environment that replicates actual encounters. With avatar-friendly marketing techniques like virtual tours, events, and games, one can even go further. Disney is already creating a fully virtualized version of its theme parks for avatars to enjoy in the metaverse. One has the opportunity to design unique experiences that clients cannot wait to tell their friends about because the laws of physics do not apply in the metaverse (Petit, 2019).

However, it all begins with having a fundamental grasp of one's target avatar, which calls for knowing the platforms, game preferences, and VR/AR/3-D technology used by one's customers. Reconstruction algorithms, like the one created by graphics expert Dr. Fangyang Shen, are currently available and they can quickly transform tangible goods into lifelike 3-D models with exact appearances at a record-breaking low price. These technologies lay the foundation for a mass-appealing online shopping experience.

Create NFTs.

NFTs, or non-fungible tokens, appear to be difficult to comprehend, but they are actually quite straightforward. Users own them in the metaverse as digital goods. An NFT may occasionally be a digital rendition of a physical good, but it may also be a digital good in and of itself, such as Roblox clothing. The foundation of the metaverse economy will be NFTs. As a result, customers will purchase both one's physical products and their digital counterparts.

Consider Non-Traditional Selling Platforms

Many businesses have happily adopted metaverse platforms like Facebook, Instagram, and TikTok in recent years, but there are a few other sites to take into account such as:

- Rec Room.
- DressX.
- Twitch.
- Clubhouse.
- Microsoft Mesh.
- Horizon.

Get Ready for Metaverse Retail

Despite the fact that this technology is not perfect, it is still a good idea for users to understand how it operates. One has the chance to establish oneself early in the next wave of retail as the metaverse develops and branding opportunities arise.

IMPORTANCE OF COMPANIES USING THE METAVERSE- EXAMPLES

The web's changes and the evolution of marketing are related. When web 1.0 first emerged, the aim of marketing was to create a website containing a business's contact details. Then Web 2.0 began bringing people together and aggregating their search histories to tailor the user experience (Vasilevski, 2020). According to Griffin LaFleur, senior marketing operations manager at Swing Education and a B2B marketing consultant, Web 3.0 now offers a more immersive experience. A report from the consultancy firm, Metaversed on LinkedIn, claims that 400 million distinct and active users utilise a metaverse platform each month. Companies must follow their generational audiences into the metaverse in order to connect with these consumers. Businesses are interested in the metaverse for a number of reasons. It allows businesses to interact with customers in unique ways (Wang, 2021). Nevertheless, reaching for Gen Z and millennials is one of the key reasons businesses are focusing on the metaverse. The decentralisation of the metaverse is an intriguing feature, according to LaFleur. Contrary to Facebook, when businesses and individuals use a platform owned by another company, they have the opportunity to choose the surroundings they view (Mystakidis, 2021). The gaming sector is the first to fully embrace the metaverse, despite the fact that businesses are just beginning to enter it. The metaverse's early adopters are discovering its potential and reaping the greatest rewards (Petit, 2019).

"The metaverse is unfinished business. You can create everything you can imagine," LaFleur declared. Gucci is one business that makes use of the metaverse's e-commerce component. The Gucci Virtual 25 are a special pair of computerised sneakers that Gucci released in March 2021.

Another example include Microsoft's Mesh for Teams (Wang, 2021). Employing mixed reality applications to simulate physical presence, the new meeting platform will allow users to share experiences. Holographic 3D pictures for sharing and visualisation allow employees to train together from anywhere in the world, which can reduce travel costs. A restricted free preview of Mesh for Teams is presently available.

There is a block party by Warner Bros. to promote "In the Heights" featured interactive games, dancing, and scavenger hunts. Another example of immersive entertainment is concerts in Fortnite. Another example is Nike's digital NFT collection for new digital, one-of-a-kind products (Ibanez, 2018).

METAVERSE: CHALLENGES AND ISSUES

Instead of just pushing their products, businesses are letting customers try them out so that they can talk about and recommend them on their own. The way brands communicate with their customers online has undergone a paradigm shift thanks to engagement marketing, which gives them greater opportunity to exploit customer interactions for a more targeted advertising and brand development. Regardless, the metaverse has some unique difficulties (Slater, 2021).

i. Digital Trembling

Despite the enthusiastic reception it has gotten from all sides since its launch, novelty could be a significant barrier to the adoption of the Metaverse. Metaverse is likely to continue to be a very specialised urban phenomenon for a very long time in nations like India with low levels of internet penetration and what appears to be a reluctance towards digital adoption (Sohaib et al., 2019).

ii. Plan Long Term

It implies that businesses must make long-term plans. In this new world, having the first mover advantage will be essential. Large companies like Nike, Coca-Cola, McDonald's, and P&G are aware of this as they swarm there in large numbers. However, the adoption of the Metaverse may still be years away because of consumer habit familiarity. Educating consumer is essential and will require perseverance and preparation (Allam, 2022).

iii. Abundant Creativity

Businesses can now be more innovative and experimental in their consumer outreach thanks to augmented reality in the Metaverse. Daler Mehndi, a singer, has recently made history by being the first man to own property in the Metaverse. He has given the area the moniker Balle Balle Land and even held a concert there. In the days to come, expect addition of such experiments from even more well-known and well-sized companies (Moi, 2020).

iv. Keep it Real

The vibrant Metaverse Marketplace is home to a variety of cafes, eateries, bars, and hangout spots that are in high demand as locations for events like weddings, fashion shows, festivals, sales, and other gatherings. Brand, though, must remember that the only virtual aspect of it is the market. Only the marketing and promotions, not the claims, may be virtual because the brand, its customers, and their interactions are all actual (Papagiannidis, 2010).

v. Hook'em Up

The Metaverse is not a needs-based market where repeat visits will just happen. One, only young people who are adept with technology are likely to be its early adopters. Two, it will take some persuasion to get them to visit a certain brand's virtual store again after their initial visit. The key will be in the hook (Giulio, 2021).

vi. Co-Create

The data generated in the metaverse will be continuous and available around-the-clock. Brands will have more opportunities thanks to consumer interactions to collaborate on innovative products and services with their customers (Grieves, 2017). For instance, in fashion shows, fashion businesses can use actual customers as models for their products. To promote the brand, these models will interact with their friends and family.

vii. Risks Galore

On the internet, data has always been an issue. It is as if data were loaded into a hypersonic rocket in the Metaverse without being informed where to stop. The hazards are increased by a million, making users cautious. These issues must be resolved before anything else. It is all actually just becoming meta until that happens (Papagiannidis, 2013).

FUTURE RESEARCH DIRECTIONS

Customer journey analytics (CJA) is a cutting-edge technique for locating target consumers by comprehending their wants and demands. Artificial intelligence (AI) is the main topic. A comparable concept known as avatar journey analytics (AJA) will soon rule marketers' plans in the metaverse. AI will change the metaverse and Web3 into a stunning universe of marketing potential through the use of these four principles (Nelson, 2020).

Extending Business Intelligence: The Metaverse

By utilising data management, data warehousing, and well-synchronized procedures, organisations may gather enormous amounts of client data. The collected data are then examined by AI and human analysts to cross-reference registered clients between the physical and the virtual worlds. Marketers and brands need to start thinking about how to integrate data from virtual platforms into the structures they are familiar with in order for this to function in the metaverse.

KPI Selection and Analytics for Avatar Journey

Omnichannel metaverse KPIs can be set and gathered through the many touchpoints and channels of each avatar's journey thanks to continual analysis. The data are then put via AI analysis to provide a single view of the trip of the avatar. Even though the metaverse is still in its infancy, implementing these tools now will assist in lowering the difficulty of brand alignment between marketing and IT in the future (Becker, 2020). The brand's real and metaverse ecosystems will benefit from more effective revenue growth, nimbler marketing operations, and stronger customer experiences thanks to comprehensive analytics tools.

Automated Journey Stages to Identify Cross-Metaverse Demand

Marketers can identify an avatar's need and direct it toward the brand's metaverse platform by using a journey analytics tool. A clickstream model that automatically generates a list of the engagement stages that each consumer is in can then be operated by AI and automation. The optimal course of action can then be decided for each customer's avatar.

For Metaverse Orchestration, Marketers Must "Think One-To-Avatar"

The metaverse presents marketers with the best chance to plan the client journey. With automated activities distributed through a variety of media, brands can precisely meet the needs of their customers. As time goes on, orchestration will merely spread to metaverse locales like Sandbox and Decentraland. A new paradigm of customer journey orchestration where preferences are linked to individual avatars, not just persons, should emerge as the network effect takes root. Imagine that while one enjoys Pepsi in the real world, one's avatar enjoys Coca-Cola in a certain metaverse. Customer journey orchestration will recognise this detail in the next-generation metaverse and use it to provide the appropriate product to the appropriate avatar or person, in the appropriate reality (MacCallum, 2019)

As the metaverse and Web3 revolution take shape, contemporary marketing strategies can aid in preparing for functional marketing. Metaverse marketing strategies can mimic contemporary design cues to create intelligent technologies.

However, more users must engage with the metaverse and offer insightful comments. People will eventually be forced to use Web3 and the emerging metaverse economy instead of conventional browsers.

FINDINGS AND CONCLUSIONS

The chapter is essential for understanding the Consumer behavior in Virtual Ecosystem: Adoption of Immersive Technologies in Metaverse among Consumers. The contribution of this chapter offers a comprehensive framework that examines the metaverse development under the dimensions of metaverse ecosystem. According to the literature review, results from comparable studies conducted in real-world settings often mirror those from VR environments when it comes to behaviour modification research in consumer domains. VR may therefore be used to test interventions in a more effective, more manageable context. But it is crucial to remember that consumer domains still do not have a lot of these kinds of studies. The metaverse system is a type of technology that will alter the world from a variety of angles, including engineering, economics, and consumer behaviour. To progress the field of consumer studies that seek to encourage behaviour change, the use of VR for consumer research appears to be particularly relevant. Technology behemoths like Apple and Google have grand aspirations to bring the metaverse to life. In the future years, the appearance of our virtual worlds (or "digital twins") will significantly change as a result of the application of developing technologies and the steady growth and refinement of the ecosystem. Now that powerful computer devices and intelligent wearables are available, our digitised future will be more interactive, alive, embodied, and multidimensional. Before the metaverse is fully incorporated into the physical world and our daily lives, there are still many obstacles to be overcome.

This chapter focuses on the dimensions and immersive technologies of Metaverse such as XR, VR, AR & MR. The post-reality world, or the metaverse, is a continuously existing multiuser environment that combines physical reality and digital virtuality. It is built on convergence of technologies, such as virtual reality (VR) and augmented reality (AR), that allow for multimodal interactions with digital objects, virtual surroundings, and people. The idea of the Metaverse is not new. It can combine social media connectivity with the distinctive benefits of immersive VR and AR technologies in the context of MR. It has the potential to alter many different industry areas if the interaction between them is imaginatively unleashed. As technology develops and more people use the Metaverse, an increasing amount of data is generated as acts comparable to those in reality are carried out. In and of itself, the metaverse data are valuable. The amount of data in the Metaverse are growing, along with their value and the demand for security and dependability.

This chapter further studies the impact of consumer behavior in the metaverse, followed by the strategies adopted by entrepreneurs in the metaverse to reach out to consumers. Consumer and corporate behaviour changes are either directly related to the Metaverse, support it in some other ways, or reflect its tenets and philosophies. When they first occur, these behaviours almost always appear to be "trends", but they are eventually revealed to have a persistent global social significance.

This chapter outlines the metaverse market size, trends, growth and forecast. This chapter aims at identifying examples of how companies are using the metaverse. This chapter highlights the challenges and issues faced in adoption of immersive technologies in the metaverse as well as future research directions.

REFERENCES

Agnusdei, G. P., Elia, V., & Gnoni, M. G. (2021). A classification proposal of digital twin applications in the safety domain. *Computers & Industrial Engineering*, *154*, 107137. doi:10.1016/j.cie.2021.107137

Allam, Z., Sharifi, A., Bibri, S. E., Jones, D. S., & Krogstie, J. (2022). The Metaverse as a virtual form of smart cities: Opportunities and challenges for environmental, economic, and social sustainability in urban futures. *Smart Cities*, *5*(3), 771–801. doi:10.3390martcities5030040

Arnold, G., Spence, C., & Auvray, M. (2017). A unity of the self or a multiplicity of locations? How the graphesthesia task sheds light on the role of spatial perspectives in bodily self-consciousness. *Consciousness and Cognition*, *56*, 100–114. doi:10.1016/j.concog.2017.06.012 PMID:28712507

Barbosa Escobar, F., Petit, O., & Velasco, C. (2021). Virtual terroir and the premium coffee experience. *Frontiers in Psychology*, *12*, 586983. doi:10.3389/fpsyg.2021.586983 PMID:33815192

Basu, T. (2021). *The metaverse has a groping problem already*. MIT Technology Review.

Becker, V., Rauchenstein, F., & Sörös, G. (2020). Connecting and controlling appliances through wearable augmented reality. *Augment Hum Res*, *5*(1), 2. doi:10.100741133-019-0019-0

Berg, C., Davidson, S., & Potts, J. (2019). Blockchain technology as economic infrastructure: Revisiting the electronic markets hypothesis. *Frontiers in Blockchain*, *2*, 22. doi:10.3389/fbloc.2019.00022

Bibri, S. E., & Allam, Z. (2022). The Metaverse as a virtual form of data-driven smart urbanism: On post-pandemic governance through the prism of the logic of surveillance capitalism. *Smart Cities, 5*(2), 715–727. doi:10.3390martcities5020037

Boursier, V., Gioia, F., & Griffiths, M. D. (2020). Objectified body consciousness, body image control in photos, and problematic social networking: The role of appearance control beliefs. *Frontiers in Psychology, 11*, 147. doi:10.3389/fpsyg.2020.00147 PMID:32158409

Díaz, J., Saldaña, C., & Avila, C. (2020). Virtual world as a resource for hybrid education. *International Journal of Emerging Technologies in Learning, 15*(15), 94–109. doi:10.3991/ijet.v15i15.13025

Domina, T., Lee, S. E., & MacGillivray, M. (2012). Understanding factors affecting consumer intention to shop in a virtual world. *Journal of Retailing and Consumer Services, 19*(6), 613–620. doi:10.1016/j.jretconser.2012.08.001

Doolani, S., Owens, L., Wessels, C., & Makedon, F. (2020). Vis: An immersive virtual storytelling system for vocational training. *Applied Sciences (Basel, Switzerland), 10*(22), 8143. doi:10.3390/app10228143

Elder, R. S., & Krishna, A. (2022). A review of sensory imagery for consumer psychology. *Journal of Consumer Psychology, 32*(2), 293–315. doi:10.1002/jcpy.1242

Ezimmuo, C. M., & Keikhosrokiani, P. (2022). Predicting Consumer Behavior Change Towards Using Online Shopping in Nigeria: The Impact of the COVID-19 Pandemic. In P. Keikhosrokiani (Ed.), *Handbook of Research on Consumer Behavior Change and Data Analytics in the Socio-Digital Era* (pp. 210–254). IGI Global. doi:10.4018/978-1-6684-4168-8.ch010

Flavián, C., Ibáñez-Sánchez, S., & Orús, C. (2019). The impact of virtual, augmented and mixed reality technologies on the customer experience. *Journal of Business Research, 100*, 547–560. doi:10.1016/j.jbusres.2018.10.050

Grieves, M., & Vickers, J. (2017). Digital twin: Mitigating unpredictable, undesirable emergent behavior in complex systems. In J. Kahlen, S. Flumerfelt, & A. Alves (Eds.), *Transdisciplinary perspectives on complex systems*. Springer. doi:10.1007/978-3-319-38756-7_4

Heller, J., Chylinski, M., de Ruyter, K., Mahr, D., & Keeling, D. I. (2019). Touching the untouchable: Exploring multi-sensory augmented reality in the context of online retailing. *Journal of Retailing, 95*(4), 219–234. doi:10.1016/j.jretai.2019.10.008

Heller, J., Hilken, T., Chylinski, M., de Ruyter, K., Keeling, D. I., & Mahr, D. (2022). Embracing falsity through the Metaverse: The case of synthetic customer experiences. *Business Horizons, 65*(6), 739–749. doi:10.1016/j.bushor.2022.07.007

Ibáñez, M. B., & Delgado-Kloos, C. (2018). Augmented reality for STEM learning: A systematic review. *Computers & Education, 123*, 109–123. doi:10.1016/j.compedu.2018.05.002

Jason, J. (2016). *The VR book: Human centered design for virtual reality*. ACM Books.

Javornik, A., Marder, B., Pizzetti, M., & Warlop, L. (2021). Augmented self – The effects of virtual face augmentation on consumers' self-concept. *Journal of Business Research, 130*, 170–187. doi:10.1016/j.jbusres.2021.03.026

Keikhosrokiani, P. (Ed.). (2022). *Handbook of Research on Consumer Behavior Change and Data Analytics in the Socio-Digital Era*. IGI Global. doi:10.4018/978-1-6684-4168-8

Keikhosrokiani, P., & Pourya Asl, M. (2023). *Handbook of Research on Artificial Intelligence Applications in Literary Works and Social Media*. IGI Global. doi:10.4018/978-1-6684-6242-3

Klopfer, E. (2008). *Augmented learning: Research and design of mobile educational games*. MIT Press. doi:10.7551/mitpress/9780262113151.001.0001

Kotler, P. (2019). The market for transformation. *Journal of Marketing Management, 35*(5-6), 407–409. doi:10.1080/0267257X.2019.1585713

Kou, W. (Ed.). (2013). *Payment technologies for E-commerce*. Springer Science & Business Media.

Kovács, P. T., Murray, N., Rozinaj, G., Sulema, Y., & Rybárová, R. (2015). Application of immersive technologies for education: State of the art. *2015 International Conference on Interactive Mobile Communication Technologies and Learning (IMCL)*. 10.1109/IMCTL.2015.7359604

Laudon, K. C. (2016). *E-commerce: Business, technology*. Pearson India.

Lee, L. H., Braud, T., Zhou, P., Wang, L., Xu, D., Lin, Z., & Hui, P. (2021). *All one needs to know about metaverse: A complete survey on technological singularity, virtual ecosystem, and research agenda*. arXiv preprint arXiv:2110.05352. doi:10.48550/arXiv.2110.05352

MacCallum, K., & Parsons, D. (2019). Teacher perspectives on mobile augmented reality: The potential of metaverse for learning. In *World Conference on Mobile and Contextual Learning* (pp. 21-28). Academic Press.

Milgram, P., Takemura, H., Utsumi, A., & Kishino, F. (1995). Augmented reality: A class of displays on the reality-virtuality continuum. *Telemanipulator and Telepresence Technologies, 2351*, 282-292. doi:10.1117/12.197321

Mohammadi, N., & Taylor, J. (2017). Smart city digital twins. *IEEE Symposium Series on Computational Intelligence (SSCI)*. 10.1109/SSCI.2017.8285439

Moi, T., Cibicik, A., & Rølvåg, T. (2020). Digital twin based condition monitoring of a knuckle boom crane: An experimental study. *Engineering Failure Analysis, 112*, 104517. doi:10.1016/j.engfailanal.2020.104517

Mystakidis, S., Christopoulos, A., & Pellas, N. (2021). A systematic mapping review of augmented reality applications to support STEM learning in higher education. *Education and Information Technologies*, 1–45. doi:10.1080/0144929X.2022.2079560

Nagaraj, S. (2021). Role of consumer health consciousness, food safety and attitude on organic food purchase in emerging market: A serial mediation model. *Journal of Retailing and Consumer Services, 59*, 102423. doi:10.1016/j.jretconser.2020.102423

Nelson, K. M., Anggraini, E., & Schlüter, A. (2020). Virtual reality as a tool for environmental conservation and fundraising. *PLoS One, 15*(4), e0223631. doi:10.1371/journal.pone.0223631 PMID:32251442

Ozkara, B. Y., & Bagozzi, R. (2021). The use of event related potentials brain methods in the study of conscious and unconscious consumer decision making processes. *Journal of Retailing and Consumer Services, 58*, 102202. doi:10.1016/j.jretconser.2020.102202

Papagiannidis, S., & Bourlakis, M. A. (2010). Staging the new retail drama: At a Metaverse near you! *Journal of Virtual Worlds Research, 2*(5), 425–446. doi:10.4101/jvwr.v2i5.808

Papagiannidis, S., Pantano, E., See-To, E. W., & Bourlakis, M. (2013). Modelling the determinants of a simulated experience in a virtual retail store and users' product purchasing intentions. *Journal of Marketing Management, 29*(13-14), 1462–1492. doi:10.1080/0267257X.2013.821150

Pellas, N., Dengel, A., & Christopoulos, A. (2020). A scoping review of immersive virtual reality in STEM education. *IEEE Transactions on Learning Technologies, 13*(4), 748–761. doi:10.1109/TLT.2020.3019405

Pellas, N., Mystakidis, S., & Kazanidis, I. (2021). Immersive virtual reality in K-12 and higher education: A systematic review of the last decade scientific literature. *Virtual Reality (Waltham Cross), 25*(3), 835–861. doi:10.100710055-020-00489-9

Petit, O., Velasco, C., & Spence, C. (2019). Digital sensory marketing: Integrating new technologies into multisensory online experience. *Journal of Interactive Marketing, 45*, 42–61. doi:10.1016/j.intmar.2018.07.004

Shen, B., Tan, W., Guo, J., Cai, H., Wang, B., & Zhuo, S. (2020). A study on design requirement development and satisfaction for future virtual world systems. *Future Internet, 12*(7), 112. doi:10.3390/fi12070112

Shen, B., Tan, W., Guo, J., Zhao, L., & Qin, P. (2021). How to promote user purchase in metaverse? A systematic literature review on consumer behavior research and virtual commerce application design. *Applied Sciences (Basel, Switzerland), 11*(23), 11087. doi:10.3390/app112311087

Siegrist, M., Ung, C. Y., Zank, M., Marinello, M., Kunz, A., Hartmann, C., & Menozzi, M. (2019). Consumers' food selection behaviors in three-dimensional (3D) virtual reality. *Food Research International, 117*, 50–59. doi:10.1016/j.foodres.2018.02.033 PMID:30736923

Size, D. I. M., & Growth, D. I. M. S. (2018). *Share & trends analysis report by product (Titanium Implants, Zirconium Implants), by region (North America, Europe, Asia Pacific, Latin America, MEA), and segment forecasts, 2018-2024.* Personalized Medicine Market Analysis by Product and Segment Forecasts to 2022.

Slater, M., & Sanchez-Vives, M. V. (2016). Enhancing our lives with immersive virtual reality. *Frontiers in Robotics and AI, 3*, 74. doi:10.3389/frobt.2016.00074

Sohaib, O., Hussain, W., Asif, M., Ahmad, M., & Mazzara, M. (2019). A PLS-SEM neural network approach for understanding cryptocurrency adoption. *IEEE Access: Practical Innovations, Open Solutions, 8*, 13138–13150. doi:10.1109/ACCESS.2019.2960083

Suh, A., & Prophet, J. (2018). The state of immersive technology research: A literature analysis. *Computers in Human Behavior, 86*, 77–90. doi:10.1016/j.chb.2018.04.019

Valaskova, K., Kramarova, K., & Bartosova, V. (2015). Multi criteria models used in Slovak consumer market for business decision making. *Procedia Economics and Finance*, *26*, 174–182. doi:10.1016/S2212-5671(15)00913-2

Vasarainen, M., Paavola, S., & Vetoshkina, L. (2021). A systematic literature review on extended reality: Virtual, augmented and mixed reality in working life. *The International Journal of Virtual Reality: a Multimedia Publication for Professionals*, *21*(2), 1–28. doi:10.20870/IJVR.2021.21.2.4620

Vasilevski, N., & Birt, J. (2020). Analysing construction student experiences of mobile mixed reality enhanced learning in virtual and augmented reality environments. *Research in Learning Technology*, *28*(0). Advance online publication. doi:10.25304/rlt.v28.2329

Vázquez-Cano, E., & Sevillano-García, M. L. (2017). Lugares y espacios para el uso educativo y ubicuo de los dispositivos digitales móviles en la Educación Superior. *Edutec. Revista Electrónica de Tecnología Educativa*, (62), 48–61. doi:10.21556/edutec.2017.62.1007

Wang, Q. J., Escobar, F. B., Da Mota, P. A., & Velasco, C. (2021). Getting started with virtual reality for sensory and consumer science: Current practices and future perspectives. *Food Research International*, *145*, 110410. doi:10.1016/j.foodres.2021.110410 PMID:34112413

Xian, Z., Keikhosrokiani, P., XinYing, C., & Li, Z. (2022). An RFM Model Using K-Means Clustering to Improve Customer Segmentation and Product Recommendation. In P. Keikhosrokiani (Ed.), Handbook of Research on Consumer Behavior Change and Data Analytics in the Socio-Digital Era (pp. 124-145). IGI Global. doi:10.4018/978-1-6684-4168-8.ch006

Xue, L., Parker, C. J., & McCormick, H. (2019). A virtual reality and retailing literature review: Current focus, underlying themes and future directions. In M. C. tom Dieck & T. Jung (Eds.), *Augmented Reality and Virtual Reality* (pp. 27–41). Springer. doi:10.1007/978-3-030-06246-0_3

ADDITIONAL READING

Akhondan, H., Johnson-Carroll, K., & Rabolt, N. (2015). Health consciousness and organic food consumption. *Journal of Family and Consumer Sciences*, *107*(3), 27–32.

Çöltekin, A., Lochhead, I., Madden, M., Christophe, S., Devaux, A., Pettit, C., Lock, O., Shukla, S., Herman, L., Stachoň, Z., Kubíček, P., Snopková, D., Bernardes, S., & Hedley, N. (2020). Extended reality in spatial sciences: A review of research challenges and Future Directions. *ISPRS International Journal of Geo-Information*, *9*(7), 439. doi:10.3390/ijgi9070439

Lombart, C., Millan, E., Normand, J. M., Verhulst, A., Labbé-Pinlon, B., & Moreau, G. (2020). Effects of physical, non-immersive virtual, and immersive virtual store environments on consumers' perceptions and purchase behavior. *Computers in Human Behavior*, *110*, 106374. doi:10.1016/j.chb.2020.106374

Paul Odenigbo, I., AlSlaity, A., & Orji, R. (2022, June). Augmented and virtual reality-driven interventions for healthy behavior change: A systematic review. In *ACM International Conference on Interactive Media Experiences* (pp. 53-68). 10.1145/3505284.3529964

Weise, M., Zender, R., & Lucke, U. (2019). A comprehensive classification of 3D selection and manipulation techniques. *Proceedings of Mensch und Computer*, *2019*, 321–332. doi:10.1145/3340764.3340777

KEY TERMS AND DEFINITIONS

Augmented Reality (AR): By enabling users to see the actual environment through the screens of their phones or tablets or by using smart glasses and making virtual modifications to it on the screen, augmented reality (AR) appears on top of our physical world.

Customer Journey Analytics (CJA): Is a cutting-edge strategy for attracting target audiences by learning about their wants and needs.

Extended Reality (XR): Includes the ideas of mixed, virtual, and augmented reality in addition to other immersive experiences.

Mixed Reality (MR): MR, also known as hybrid reality, is the blending of the virtual and real worlds to create a new setting where real-time interactions between virtual and real-world items are possible.

Non-Fungible Tokens (NFTs): The necessary tokens or goods needed for trading within the metaverse are non-fungible tokens. Within the metaverse, NFTs act as proxies for asset ownership.

Virtual Reality (VR): Virtual reality (VR) describes a 3D, computer-generated environment that can either match the real world or an imaginative one.

Virtual World (VW): Virtual reality (VR) and augmented reality (AR) headsets are used to create this virtual environment.

Chapter 8
Customer Experience in the E-Commerce Market Through the Virtual World of Metaverse

Kamaladevi Baskaran
Amity University, Dubai, UAE

ABSTRACT

The present study critically analyses the online shopping experience of consumers and suggests the firm change the operations to adopt the virtual retail world of metaverse and the contribution of e-commerce towards economic growth. All the sectors, including transportation, education, and infrastructure, as well as employment and government, have potential impact on e-commerce. The obstacles to electronic commerce that influence sellers and shoppers will be diminished due to the transformation to the virtual world of metaverse. As UAE is the place for successful implementation of business innovations, a case study of Souq.com acquired by Amazon has been discussed in this study. This case study focuses on fruitful contribution of e-commerce market towards UAE's economic growth and the elements that drive e-commerce development. The study concludes with the identification of e-commerce factors, which has an impact on online shopping experience of metaverse consumers, and addressing the issues that stimulate economic growth through virtual world of metaverse.

INTRODUCTION

Innovations in everyday life has significant impact on social relationships, communication, and human interaction. Three significant technological innovation waves have been identified from individual customer's perspective, and they were successively centered on the emergence of personal computers, the Internet, and mobile devices. Virtual reality (VR) and augmented reality (AR) are two spatial immersive technologies that are core of fourth wave of computing innovation. This wave is anticipated to create the subsequent paradigm for ubiquitous computing, which has the power to revolutionize (online) business, education, remote work, and entertainment. The Metaverse is this new paradigm. The Greek prefix meta, which means post, after, or beyond, and universe combined to form the closed compound

DOI: 10.4018/978-1-6684-7029-9.ch008

word "metaverse." The Metaverse is, in other words, a post-reality universe that combines the physical world with digital virtual world in a continuous and enduring multiuser environment. Consumer 'browse the internet' but 'live in Metaverse'.

Due to rapid technological advancement, most nations have been urged to take advantage of the possibilities offered by the digital economy. E-commerce has a significant influence on United Arab Emirates (UAE) economy. The link between e-commerce and economic growth plays a vital role. The e-commerce business in UAE has undergone a huge transformation accomplished through developing innovative consumer experiences, changes in shopping trends, challenging company models, and leveraging the emergence of small online businesses and e-commerce companies.

The Dubai Metaverse Strategy intends to build advanced ecosystems through accelerators and incubators that draw businesses and projects to Dubai by promoting innovation, and increase the economic contributions of the Metaverse through R&D collaborations. By giving the required support to developers, content creators, and users of digital platforms in the Metaverse community, Metaverse education can fosters talent and attracts investment in future capacities. In addition, it develops Web3 technology and its applications to build new governmental work models and advance key industries including tourism, education, retail, remote work, healthcare, and the legal industry. (Dubai Metaverse Strategy, 2022)

UAE has become a global leader in e-commerce over the past decade. The GCC's e-commerce industry was valued at $5.3 billion in 2015 with UAE's e-commerce sector accounting for about half of all regional sales. UAE's success in e-commerce could be attributed in part to its early adoption of technological advancements compared to other Middle East countries. During the mid 2000, the UAE government took steps to open up new opportunities to boom the e-commerce. Many companies were able to take benefit of the UAE's customer base familiar to local e-commerce sites as well as the concept of online payment. (Emara, 2019)

UAE's e-commerce market has grown significantly over the years. Customers have gained trust and comfortable using credit cards and other payment methods to do online shopping. A strong commitment by government agencies is also responsible for the UAE's growth in e-commerce. It outlines several policies initiated by the government to encourage the growth of the e-commerce sector. Dubai Electricity and Water Authority (DEWA), for example, established an e-commerce portal for consumers to pay for their services. (Emara, 2019)

The UAE's e-commerce industry has seen a significant increase in internet and mobile penetration. UAE is the leader in smartphone penetration and internet usage in the GCC and MENA regions. According to 2017 government economic report, 91.9 percent of the country's population had access to the internet. The smartphone penetration rate was 73.8 percent. The higher volume of online shopping of goods is due to penetration of smartphone and high internet access. Gulf Today, 2019, shows that at least 80 percent of internet users in the country visit e-commerce websites to buy goods. It is predicted that the UAE's e-commerce market, which includes digital retail platforms like Namshi, Souq, Ounass and Noon, will grow tremendously with the rise of digital retailers such as Namshi, Souq and Ounass. Computers, electronics, and jewelry are the most popular products that generate the most revenue through e-commerce sites. In the last few years, clothing has seen the greatest popularity. (Abu Bakar, Ahmad & Ahmad, 2019)

The private and public sectors are driving growth in UAE's e-commerce market. The UAE's e-commerce sector will be improved by changes in its regulatory framework, including lower export and import tariffs, and easier company setup (Seetharaman et al., 2017). The industry will expand as long as local governments continue to invest in innovation, and to update their policies. The strong growth in the UAE's e-commerce sector is attributed to several factors. One of them is the government's adoption of e-commerce payment on various platforms. Other categories driving up the e-commerce market in UAE are the transport sector and fast service restaurants. The thriving shopping mall culture and retail sector in UAE have also been supporting its e-commerce sector. The crucial factors for customers purchasing in e-commerce sites are customer engagement, price and ease of use (Seetharaman et al., 2017). Despite high rates of internet access and mobile penetration in UAE, online sales only account for 5 percent of all sales in the retail sector. As such, the untapped potential of the e-commerce market is huge. Most traditional retailers operating in brick and mortar stores have now focused their attention on integrating online retail platforms to their businesses to boost their revenues (Seetharaman et al., 2017). For instance, the largest retailers in UAE, Lulu Group and Carrefour added online shopping portals to boost customer experience.

In recent years, e-government initiatives in UAE have been launched to build trust in online commerce. The initiatives involve integrating paper-based information services such as traffic services, billing payments, visa issuance and licensing. The migration of these services to online platforms and later integrating them to online payment platforms has enabled local governments to provide residents and citizens with more effective and faster public services (Ma et al., 2019). The e-government initiatives have attracted immense foreign direct investment to UAE hence boosting its economy. (Ahmed et al., 2022)

Local governments are also taking up initiatives to ensure they provide a conducive environment for the e-commerce sector. For instance, new e-commerce regulations for free zones were put in place by the Dubai Free Zones Council (DFZC). The regulations are aimed at attracting greater foreign direct investment to Dubai's e-commerce sector. Most of DFZC's initiatives focus on establishing e-commerce controls through collaboration with the Dubai Government (Ma et al., 2019). The cooperation is informed through joint workshops and teams to ensure crucial proposals and procedures are adopted. DFZC is also aiming at examining mechanisms for the e-commerce sector to adopt block chain technology that will speed up the automation of procedures and enhance transparency (Ma et al., 2019). The foreign direct investment will certainly boost Dubai's economic growth and the larger UAE.

Dubai Metaverse Strategy also aims to benchmark international standards in building secure user friendly platforms and develop Metaverse infrastructure and regulate to accelerate the adoption of Extended Reality, Augmented Reality, Virtual Reality, Mixed Reality and Digital Twins (a virtual representation of an object or system) technologies. Using Machine learning, Internet of Things, Artificial Intelligence simulation and block chain technology, the Metaverse aims to enhance human thinking process using real-time data. Data, network, cloud, edge computing and 5G are pillars of Metaverse technology. (Dubai Metaverse Strategy, 2022).

The identified factors influencing customer shopping experience includes Quality digital experience content, shopping cost, asset ownership, privacy/security, customer engagement and delivery service quality. Such factors gives the outline to analyse the online shopping experience of consumers in the virtual world of Metaverse. The present study critically analyses the online shopping experience of consumers, suggest the firm in changing the operations to adopt the virtual retail world of Metaverse and the contribution of e-commerce towards economic growth. The purpose of this research is to analyze the online factors influencing consumers experience in the virtual retail world of Metaverse.

BACKGROUND

The theoretical background explores the pragmatic output specified by erstwhile researchers with the case study of Souq.com.

Company Background

Souq was the leading online retailer in the UAE. The company was established in 2005 by Samih Toukan and Ronaldo Mouchawar. Its website (Souq.com) was initially an action site but transformed its business model to become an e-commerce site in 2011. The company raised capital from several investors with its largest shareholders being Naspers Limited and Tiger Global Management. As of 2014, the company had raised $150 million which was the largest amount any internet based business had raised in the Gulf region. In 2015, it was valued at $1 billion during another round of fundraising (El Sawy, 2019). During that period, the website was receiving 10 million visitors. Souq's e-commerce site has more than 35 categories of products including household goods, consumer electronics, health and beauty, fashion and baby categories. In 2017, the company localized its operation in UAE, Saudi Arabia and Egypt. It also set-up semi-automated fulfillment centers such in Kuwait and Saudi Arabia. As of 2018, the company has about 3,000 employees across the Middle East (Rusell, 2017). The scale of operations the company had initiated increased its influence in the Gulf region.

Souq.com Initial Success

Souq.com was launched at a fortuitous period. Initially, the company focused on electronic devices which accounted for 40 percent of total sales. The site then began tapping into opportunities from UAE's young population who at the time had high disposable income. This led to the site's massive success because it was able to ride on the smartphone boom and the initial launch of tablets (Benmamoun et al., 2018). Despite the boom fizzling after two years, Souq.com still had a huge outlay of smartphone sales compared to global e-commerce sites such as Amazon.

The huge growth in internet penetration in the UAE has also been crucial for its success. Despite Souq.com posting tremendous growth over the years, it faces challenges of scalability and provision of quality customer services. As a result, the company initially sought investors to boost its infrastructure. This enabled it expand to other Gulf regions such as Kuwait, Saudi Arabia and Egypt. These markets added the company over 120 million customers (AlSharji et al., 2018). With the company seeking to expand its operations to more countries such as Bahrain, Jordan, Qatar and Lebanon, its overall influence and customer numbers will only continue to surge.

Souq.com Acquisition by Amazon

Amazon, a major international e-commerce retailer, purchased Souq.com in 2017 for $580 million so that the business may take advantage of the Middle Eastern market's prospects. After acquiring Souq, Amazon decided to keep it as a local subsidiary rather than dissolve it. Following the completion of the deal, the two merged their activities. Customers could access Souq.com using their Amazon account credentials (El Sawy, 2019). The sole distinction was that users of Souq.com were redirected to Amazon. ae. The 30 million products that were being sold on the Souq.com platform were carried over to the new website, along with five million additional products that users could access through Amazon in the United States. Once clients make purchases on Amazon.ae, the new things are dispatched from the U.S. (El Sawy, 2019). Amazon decided to keep the Souq.com brand in the UAE because of its favorable customer reputation. Amazon had a negligible footprint in the UAE prior to purchasing Souq. It ran the Middle East's Amazon Web Services, which provided cloud computing services. In the UAE and other Middle Easter region, Amazon uses Souq as its public face.

Effect of Amazon's Acquisition on UAE's Economy

The entry of Amazon into UAE's e-commerce market will reverberate the country's retail industry and the entire Middle East region. It will boost the country's potential to have the fastest growing e-commerce industry globally. Currently, e-commerce contributes only 0.4 percent to UAE's GDP. However, Amazon's entry is expected to quadruple the market value by 2020 if the government puts in place the right enablers (Okasha, 2020). Amazon's acquisition of Souq.com gives other global e-commerce players an opportunity to invest in the country. The acquisition also gives UAE's emerging e-commerce industry a vote of confidence. It recognizes that the digital and technology industry in UAE is sustainable and can grow in value.

The acquisition could also increase consolidations between local and multinational e-commerce players. Small online companies will have to be creative to ensure they can compete favorably and stay in the market. However, Amazon entry will help the small e-commerce companies gain crucial experience from the company undertakings such as logistics planning, innovation and customer service (Okasha, 2020). UAE's economy will be harnessed from digital transformation and adoption by several e-commerce players.

Amazon Metaverse

Amazon Metaverse opens an entry into the virtual destination of Amazon universe where users can experience as musician, meet the favorite influencer, play games and explore vast selection using virtual reality and augmented reality headsets in Amazon categories. It gives businesses the freedom to create experiences free from the limitations of the real world and creates a whole new universe for interaction. (Metamandrill, 2022)

Penetration of Mobile Payments

The growing e-commerce sector presents UAE with tremendous opportunities that will drive its economy. The e-commerce transactions are expected to grow by 23 percent each year from 2018 to 2021. Most online retailers in the UAE continue to report high revenues after integrating digital payments such as Visa and mobile wallets as one of the payment methods. The growth in its e-commerce industry attracted global mobile service providers such as Samsung Pay, Google Pay and Apple Pay (TheNational, 2019a). Their entry into the UAE markets alongside other local players such as Beam Wallet and Etisalat Wallet boosted the country's e-commerce industry particularly the emerging online retailers.

The mobile wallet market in the UAE is projected to develop exponentially in future. The top priority for the UAE government has been integrating cashless and digital commerce payments through the Smart Government Initiative. UAE's Vision for 2021 is to significantly reduce the use of cash payments by 2020 (TheNational, 2019a). This vision could be realized since the country's population has eagerly embraced technology driven solutions.

It will also increase the use of digital payments. The value many e-commerce transactions in the UAE average at $144. This is sizable compared to most transactions in emerging and mature markets that range at $26 and $79 respectively. For e-commerce sites such as Souq.com that have millions of transactions monthly, the tax fees charged on customers are remitted to the government (TheNational, 2019a). This will certainly boost economic growth because the government will re-invest in other sectors of the economy.

If the metaverse follows the growth path of mobile technology, it may add $360 billion to the GDP in the Middle East, North Africa, and Turkey in 10 years, according to analysis group research cited by Meta, the company that owns Facebook and other social media giants.(AlArabia News, 2022)

Importance of Logistics in E-Commerce

The country's online market is projected to grow tremendously in the coming years. The exponential growth will be boosted by logistic providers. UAE is currently one of the leading emerging markets in the logistics industry after India and China. The demand for professional logistic service providers has continued to surge in UAE because of the growth in e-commerce. Qualified logistics providers are required to meet the customers' diverse logistic requirements (Gulf Today, 2019). Different aspects logistics such as packaging, handling, inventory management, billing, transportation, product return, cash on delivery and warehousing are in great demand.

Many e-commerce sites tie their success to having an efficient, reliable and timely logistics system. However, some e-commerce giants such as Souq that can afford vertical integration have begun building a logistics arm and creating partnerships with major logistics providers to ensure speedy and reliable delivery services to their customers. Large e-commerce players can support an in-house logistics and delivery network because they have a significant volume of shipments. However, small e-commerce players are compelled to rely on external logistic firms that specialize in e-commerce delivery (Gulf Today, 2019). E-commerce continues to fuel logistic opportunities in UAE with reputed logistic companies setting up operations in the country to grab the opportunities.

E-Commerce Industry's Contribution Towards UAE's Economic Growth

The e-commerce industry in the UAE is getting a significant boost from Souq.com's acquisition by Amazon. In 2017, Souq.com purchased Wing.ae, an e-commerce delivery marketplace in UAE (Staff, 2017). The purchase enabled Souq to connect with merchants and ensure delivery couriers were made through an on-demand basis. Souq's investment in Wing boosted UAE's e-commerce industry by accelerating investments in technology, infrastructure and innovative delivery solutions. For Souq.com's merchants and customers, the investment made online shopping more convenient. Greater convenience boosted UAE's e-commerce retail sales because online shoppers could have their purchases delivered on the same or next day (Staff, 2017). The investment also enabled Wing to connect popular e-commerce sites in the Middle East.

In 2017, Souq.com and SAP (Systems, Applications and Products) partnered to improve digital transactions of online shoppers. The partnership was successful since it accelerated real time transactions in UAE's online market. Most e-commerce companies in the UAE were compelled to improve their websites to ensure digital transactions were on real-time. Real-time has over the years become the major driver of e-commerce. Most online businesses use real-time to identify new customer trends or complete transactions. Souq's partnership with SAP and Amazon will enable local online businesses to borrow global best practices. This will improve UAE's digital economy and create more economic opportunities for millions of buyers and sellers. Today, Enterprise Resource Planning (ERP) solutions are integrated into most e-commerce sites to allow real-time transactions (Staff, 2017). Most ERP solutions run on cloud computing platforms.

In addition, Souq.com market leader status enables UAE's emerging small and medium enterprises (SMEs) to develop and grow their online business using the company's technical assistance, solid technology platform and market exposure. Most of the SMEs using Souq.com's platform have enjoyed unparalleled success in the last few years (Staff, 2017). As a result, the business to business market in the UAE will be a major economic driver because of the government's SME backed e-commerce growth. UAE government supports the e-commerce market to benchmark in the global online market. The country boosts wealthy individuals and a tech savvy population with significant disposable income. Therefore, Souq's partnership with SAP will provide SMEs with a secure, robust and real-time e-commerce platform that will facilitate their growth (Staff, 2017). This will boost UAE's online businesses and boost overall economic growth.

With the entry of Singapore-based Metapolis, which claims to be the world's first "metaverse-as-a-service" (MaaS) venture - a la Software-as-a-Service (SaaS) for web2 companies, the UAE is poised to witness the next stage in Metaverse development. Metapolis has ambitious plans to support businesses from various industries into the virtual world.

Consumers may navigate the appropriate, accurate, and timely information on online stores with the aid of high-quality digital experience content (Baskaran, K. 2022). The product's comprehensive information provides an overall picture of its features, consumer feedback, product FAQs, and service information, all of which increase consumers' experience with their purchase of the product. Customers who are dissatisfied with the quality of the information will not make purchases from online stores (Majji, K. C. 2021). Online transactions are predicated on product pricing, delivery cost, discounts, and offers, despite the fact that e-commerce has risen enormously in the post-Covid age. With up-to-date information, this target market concentrates on sales volume and cost reduction (Baskaran, K. 2019). Retailers of jewelry should prioritize product variety, value for money, product packaging, image quality, transaction security, and product delivery in their online stores (Moncey, A. A., 2020).

Website design should draw attention to online transaction security measures (Baskaran, K. 2019b). Online shoppers worry about the information gathered at the moment of purchase and the use of such personal data without their consent. Online shops should strengthen their policies to secure the private information that customers provide while conducting an online transaction. (Baskaran, K. 2014) Privacy concerns are only an individual's perceptions of the threats and potential drawbacks of disclosing private information (Baskaran, K., & Rajavelu, S., 2020).

In an online store, customer service features like home delivery, a return policy, and easiness of online transaction completion are particularly crucial. Online shoppers' top priority is prompt product delivery (Cyriac, 2020). Online retailers should provide fast delivery, transaction accuracy, and prompt delivery parameters to give consumers a higher level of service. Such delivery characteristics significantly affect customer happiness, which encourages additional online product purchases (Cyriac, N. T. 2021).

According to Ariff and colleagues, online shoppers in Malaysia are concerned about seven different types of risks while doing business online: financial risk, product performance risk, time or convenience risk, privacy risk, psychological risk, social risk, and delivery risk (Ariff, 2014). Importantly, the post-purchase delivery service is crucial in emphasizing the status of product delivery, accurate product delivery, timely product delivery, dependability of service provision, and the potential for returning items via cargo in the event of damage (Baskaran, 2014 & 2019). Such factors, which are included in the survey questionnaire to meet the research hypothesis, are crucial for efficient delivery options.

Based on the case study and the literature review, the research gap has been identified. As shown in Figure 1, the factors influencing customer shopping experience includes Quality digital experience content, shopping cost, asset ownership, privacy/security, customer engagement and delivery service quality. This study focuses on influence of such factors with reference to the purchase decision in the virtual world of Metaverse.

Figure 1. Conceptual framework of factors affecting online shopping experience

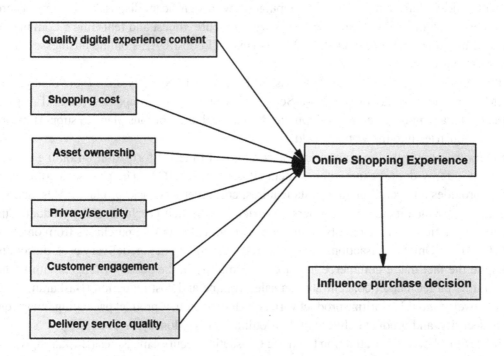

RESEARCH METHODOLOGY

The purpose of this research is to analyze the online factors influencing consumers experience in the virtual retail world of Metaverse which includes Quality digital experience content, shopping cost, asset ownership, privacy/security, customer engagement and delivery service quality. Descriptive research design has been applied, as the research is focused to study the characteristics of population. Google Forms was developed as a survey tool to obtain primary data from UAE residents. Then, data analysis has been done using SPSS and Amos. 161 samples obtained through Simple Random Sampling from online customers who reside in UAE. The first segment of the survey questionnaire covers the demographic factors, second segment covers the usage of internet, frequency of consumer purchase over internet and the last segment focuses on the factors influencing customer shopping experience using Likert Scale. The hypothesis have been framed to analyze the online shopping experience of consumers using Statistical Package for Social Science (SPSS) version 28 and AMOS. The hypothesis for this research is constructed as follows:

Hypothesis One:

$H_0 1$: Online shopping experience factors does not influence the purchase decision in the virtual world of Metaverse.

$H_a 1$: Online shopping experience factors influence the purchase decision in the virtual world of Metaverse.

Hypothesis Two:

$H_0 2$: There is no significant relationship between number of years of internet usage and frequency of online purchase.

$H_a 2$: There is significant relationship between number of years of internet usage and frequency of online purchase.

DATA ANALYSIS AND INTERPRETATION

The online shopping experience of consumers' survey questionnaire has been tested using Reliability analysis which allows to study the properties of measurement scales and the items that compose the scales.

Table 1 highlights the Reliability Statistics that provides the actual value for Cronbach's alpha of 0.900. It indicates a high level of internal consistency for the scale with the given set of sample.

Table 1. Reliability statistics

Cronbach's Alpha	Cronbach's Alpha Based on Standardized Items	N of Items
.900	.906	6

Table 2, which includes Item-Total Statistics, presents the "Cronbach's Alpha if Item Deleted" and "Corrected Item-Total Correlation". The Corrected Item-Total Correlation values are ranging from 0.67 to 0.84 and Cronbach's Alpha if Item Delete is between 0.86 and 0.90. Hence, removal of any question would result in a lower Cronbach's alpha.

Table 3 includes descriptive statistics, which presents the values of mean, standard deviation and variance. Table 4 indicates R Square equals 0.576, which is a good fit. 57% of frequency of online purchase is explained by the independent variables Quality digital experience content, shopping cost, asset ownership, privacy/security, customer engagement and delivery service quality.

Table 5 presents the significance level of F (<.001) which is less than 0.05 at F value of 12.775, then the independent variables looks fine and the null hypothesis is rejected. Hence, it concludes that Online shopping experience factors influence the purchase decision in the virtual world of Metaverse.

Table 2. Item-total statistics

	Scale Mean if Item Deleted	Scale Variance if Item Deleted	Corrected Item-Total Correlation	Squared Multiple Correlation	Cronbach's Alpha if Item Deleted
Quality digital experience content	19.009	11.294	.703	.529	.887
Shopping Cost	19.022	11.153	.667	.545	.892
Asset Ownership	18.957	10.457	.783	.643	.874
Privacy/security	18.887	10.689	.846	.738	.867
Customer Engagement	19.025	9.978	.675	.515	.898
Delivery Service Quality	18.834	10.802	.756	.593	.879

Table 3. Descriptive statistics

	N	Mean	Std. Deviation	Variance
Quality digital experience content	161	3.738	.7090	.503
Shopping Cost	161	3.724	.7652	.585
Asset Ownership	161	3.790	.7999	.640
Privacy/security	161	3.860	.7137	.509
Customer Engagement	161	3.722	.9844	.969
Delivery Service Quality	161	3.913	.7589	.576
Valid N (listwise)	161			

Table 4. Model summary table for ANOVA

Model	R	R Square	Adjusted R Square	Std. Error of the Estimate
1	.576ª	.332	.306	.995
a. Predictors: (Constant), Quality digital experience content, shopping cost, asset ownership, privacy/security, customer engagement, delivery service quality.				
b. Dependent Variable: Frequency of online purchase				

Table 5. ANOVA

	Model	Sum of Squares	df	Mean Square	F	Sig.
1	Regression	75.810	6	12.635	12.775	<.001ᵇ
	Residual	152.314	154	.989		
	Total	228.124	160			
a. Dependent Variable: Frequency of online purchase						
b. Predictors: (Constant), Quality digital experience content, shopping cost, asset ownership, privacy/security, customer engagement, delivery service quality.						

Hypothesis One Result:

Online shopping experience factors influence the purchase decision in the virtual world of Metaverse.

Table 6 shows the frequency of online shopping done by UAE customers. 2.5% of male aged above 50 years never shopped online but 6.8% of female aged above 50 years shop more than 10 times yearly. 8.7% of female aged between 30-39 years are doing online shopping once yearly. 6.2% of male aged between 40-49 years are shopping online 2-4 times yearly and 6.2% of female age group of 40-49 years shop 5-10 times yearly.

Table 6. Frequency of online shopping done by UAE customers

| | | | | Frequency of online purchase | | | | | | | | | |
| | | | | Never shopped online | | Once Yearly | | 2-4 times yearly | | 5-10 times yearly | | More than 10 times yearly | |
				Count	Table N %	Count	Table N %	Count	Table N %	Count	Table N %	Count	Table N %
Age	Below 20	Gender	Male	0	0.0%	2	1.2%	2	1.2%	2	1.2%	0	0.0%
			Female	0	0.0%	0	0.0%	4	2.5%	0	0.0%	0	0.0%
	20-29	Gender	Male	0	0.0%	1	0.6%	0	0.0%	3	1.9%	0	0.0%
			Female	0	0.0%	8	5.0%	2	1.2%	2	1.2%	5	3.1%
	30-39	Gender	Male	0	0.0%	8	5.0%	3	1.9%	3	1.9%	10	6.2%
			Female	0	0.0%	14	8.7%	5	3.1%	5	3.1%	4	2.5%
	40-49	Gender	Male	0	0.0%	0	0.0%	10	6.2%	9	5.6%	6	3.7%
			Female	0	0.0%	0	0.0%	7	4.3%	10	6.2%	4	2.5%
	Above 50	Gender	Male	4	2.5%	1	0.6%	6	3.7%	0	0.0%	7	4.3%
			Female	0	0.0%	1	0.6%	2	1.2%	0	0.0%	11	6.8%

Table 7 shows the relationship between number of years of internet usage and frequency of online purchase. Here, the P value is less than the standard significance level of 0.05, so reject the null hypothesis. Hence, there is no strong evidence to at 5% level to accept that there is no statistically significant relationship between number of years of internet usage and frequency of online purchase.

Table 7. Chi-square test

	Value	df	Asymptotic Significance (2-sided)
Pearson Chi-Square	111.230[a]	16	<.001
Likelihood Ratio	106.945	16	<.001
Linear-by-Linear Association	50.512	1	<.001
N of Valid Cases	161		
a. 15 cells (60.0%) have expected count less than 5. The minimum expected count is .05.			

Hypothesis Two Result:

There is a significant relationship between number of years of internet usage and frequency of online purchase.

SOLUTIONS AND RECOMMENDATIONS

Contribution of E-Commerce Towards UAE's Economic Growth

The UAE, which has a history of ambitious huge projects like the 830-meter (2,723-foot) Burj Khalifa, expects the Metaverse may boost the country's GDP by $4 billion and create 40,000 new employment opportunities by 2030. By easing visa requirements for independent contractors, business owners, and creatives, Dubai hopes to attract 1,000 blockchain and similar technology focused enterprises as part of its effort to rank among the top 10 Metaverse economies in the world. (AlArabia News, 2022)

Adoption of information technology and the internet will power UAE's economic growth. E-commerce presents the country with a "new economic paradigm" that will help it deliver higher rates of inflation free growth. The collapse of many online startups in mature markets such as the United States during the e-commerce boom of mid-2000s led to skepticism about the sustainability of the "new economy" (Okasha, 2020). However, the success of various e-commerce companies such as Amazon and eBay demonstrates that ICT has long term effect on a country's economy. The triumph of the e-commerce market will have an affirmative effect on macroeconomic and productivity growth of the UAE. For instance, technological revolutions in the United States generated productivity gains in the economy and the long run, it helped improve the country's living standards (Seetharaman et al., 2017). In the UAE, induced change to e-commerce and ICT will accelerate productivity growth and incentivize improvement of e-commerce elements such as production, corporate organization, logistics, marketing and marketing. (Ashok, 2022)

E-commerce industry success will support economic growth through the reduction of computing power. Many businesses will be compelled to reorganize their operations to leverage the benefits of e-commerce. Even if the sector's growth in the UAE fails to maintain the current pace of development, its positive effect on the economy will still be felt. However, sustainable economic growth from the e-commerce industry will only be realized when internet businesses catch up technologically with those of mature markets (Benmamoun et al., 2018). Currently, UAE's e-commerce industry has multiple misgivings and the challenges need to be addressed to ensure the sector has a broader impact on the country's economy.

E-commerce success will create an opportunity for business to business (B2B) e-markets to flourish in the UAE. In the future, B2B e-markets are expected to outstrip business to consumer (B2C) e-commerce. The highest growth in those markets will be in sectors such as food, utilities, computing and electronics and office products. The B2B e-markets are also likely to undergo consolidation in order to have greater focus on provision of specialized and differentiated products and services. The growth in B2B and B2C e-commerce will boost economic growth in UAE. (Mohan, 2021)

E-commerce industry success in UAE will certainly create more opportunities for economic development and growth. The application of e-commerce technologies particularly SAP will bring down transaction costs incurred by businesses through the adoption of remote delivery of goods and services. Businesses with access to e-commerce ICT platforms increase their potential to reach out to more domestic and foreign customers at a lower cost. They will also incur lower delivery costs particularly for electronically provided content (Staff et al., 2017). As a result, the productivity of businesses across the UAE will be harnessed. Productivity gains lead to more profitability, job opportunities and economic growth.

The digital economy offers UAE more opportunities for innovation and entrepreneurship. For instance, UAE currently has many e-commerce start-ups that are attracting foreign direct investment and creating jobs for the citizens. Even though most of the start-ups are yet to attain a significant scale and become profitable, the current pace of e-commerce growth will boost their revenues within a few years. New digital payment solutions have also emerged in recent years to offer payment solutions to e-commerce startups (Seetharaman et al., 2017). In the future, the startup and payment solutions players could boost economic growth through innovative logistics and job creation. In addition to accepting major cryptocurrency exchange platforms, the UAE has already passed legislation controlling virtual assets and established a cryptocurrency regulatory agency. One of the first private-sector Metaverse initiatives in the UAE is termed 2117, after Dubai's ruler Sheikh Mohammed bin Rashid's desire to conquer Mars in 100 years. Users of the Metaverse can now purchase tickets for a virtual shuttle transporting settlers to Mars. (Forbes India, 2022)

E-commerce industry success will also help SME's overcome the barriers of expansion. Emerging e-commerce startups could leverage on peer to peer collaboration in alternative funding mechanisms and innovation to grow their influence and size of their operations. Cloud based solutions will reduce the need by SMEs in the UAE to invest in in-house expertise and information technology equipment (Ma et al., 2019). As a result, SME's will be able to scale-up by using verifiable online transactions records to seek financing opportunities and attract new customers.

The rural economy in the UAE will be enhanced if the e-commerce industry is successful. It will enable rural communities to leverage on opportunities presented by e-commerce platforms. For instance, they could sell their local products on the country's e-commerce sites. This will boost rural development and incentivize e-commerce players to develop logistics infrastructure in rural areas. Enterprises that embrace e-commerce platforms can boost their productivity with small enterprises realizing the greatest benefits. For instance, the total factor productivity growth for the UAE's SME's that used e-commerce sites to market their goods was 1.7 percentage points higher in 2018 compared to businesses that did not sell through online platforms (Abu Bakar, Ahmad & Ahmad, 2019). This indicates e-commerce gives businesses more opportunities to scale up.

Challenges in Implementation of Metaverse

Despite the digital economy creating more opportunities for economic growth in the UAE, it still poses a number of potential challenges and risks. The full realization of Metaverse benefits requires that all players have equal access for affordable information and technology platforms. This ensures that digital divides in businesses are minimized. However, there is increased risk amongst businesses to adopt e-commerce at the same pace because literacy levels amongst business owners on e-commerce and the digital economy are quite low in UAE (Grab et al., 2018). Therefore, government needs to adopt mechanisms that will sensitize business owners and consumers on digitalization. This will ensure that enterprises leverage the opportunities of digitalization.

The expected growth in digitalization in UAE is likely to have a disruptive impact on employment and skills. Embracing Metaverse will lead to new types of jobs, changes in skills' requirements, alteration of conditions and nature of work and the functioning of UAE's labor markets. Increased technological innovation will increase demand for other labor skills. Consequently, there could be mass layoffs because of job redundancies or employees lacking requisite skills (Kirkcaldy & Furnham, 2016). Furthermore, it will lead to a greater concentration of market power and growing income inequalities. The increased scope of automation, computerization and use of artificial intelligence expose more occupations in UAE to the risk of disappearing despite a potential rise in productivity, output and greater returns to capital in the e-commerce industry (Grab et al., 2018). This will disrupt economic growth and increase resentment of the e-commerce industry.

Reliance on the digital economy to drive economic growth could have adverse effects on existing industries. The industries that are well organized in terms of operations could be disrupted. For instance, the UAE's banking sector will be compelled to upgrade its systems and operations to ensure it meets the financial demands of the e-commerce sector. Banks will be expected to introduce mobile applications and other automated payment systems to facilitate payments in the e-commerce sector (Ma et al., 2019). Such disruptions could lead to losses in the banking sector because they will be compelled to make significant investments in their banking and payment systems. Consequently, other sectors of the economy relying on banks for loans will be adversely affected because banks could reduce uptake of loans from its customers to make up for the sudden disruption (Grab et al., 2018). This could hinder economic growth because the productivity of other economic sector is negatively affected.

Metaverse consumers face potential risks from big data, automation and artificial intelligence that are relied upon by Metaverse players. Online platform owners are likely to use purchasing and prior shopping histories of customers to set product prices hence negatively affecting the bargaining power of consumers. Consumers using connected applications to access Metaverse applications could also lose their bargaining power and privacy because these sites can retrieve data from their devices. Smartphone applications that are free to use such as music streaming services, map navigation and online purchases services create added risk to consumers because they allow app developers and e-commerce players to retrieve detailed information about their preferences, personal habits, relationships and whereabouts without the consumers knowing (Al-Alawi & Al-Ali, 2015). Metaverse companies can use information obtained from the online activities of consumers to assemble dossiers on them such as target advertisements. This could adversely affect public trust in Metaverse shopping hence limiting the number of people willing to purchase products through Metaverse.

Metaverse players and e-government initiatives embracing digitalization face the risk of hacking, financial information theft, industrial sabotage and identity theft of customer information. The sabotage can result from public infrastructure, industry system, cloud computing platforms and private communication networks. Such risks could discourage SME's from embracing Metaverse platforms to prevent negative consequences on the businesses. Consequently, this could hurt Metaverse success and the overall economy.

Despite the e-commerce sector being lucrative in UAE, several barriers hinder additional activities from being integrated into the e-commerce market. The barriers include the prevalence of cash on delivery by customers instead of digital payments, inadequate logistics, lack of consumer trust on Metaverse and lack of unified address which in turn creates challenges during delivery.

CONCLUSION

The adoption and implementation of Metaverse activities by online retailers will benefit customers, organizations and government. It will also boost the UAE's overall economy. For organizations, Metaverse will reduce their overall business costs by reducing operation process and lead time. Customers will save costs and valuable time by purchasing from Metaverse. The e-commerce industry in UAE generated $10 billion in 2018. Despite this value being much lower compared to what other regions generate, e-commerce in UAE is becoming a major inclination for local enterprises (Ma et al., 2019). As the value of the e-commerce industry will continue to growth through Metaverse, more new job and business opportunities across UAE will be created.

Moreover, Metaverse will help economic sectors such as transport, wholesale trade, business and financial services to save business and operation costs. Productivity growth amongst businesses could be realized through cost savings in services. It will also allow the government to analyze macroeconomic variables such as wages, gross domestic product, terms of trade and welfare (Benmamoun et al., 2018). Through this, the government will be able to determine whether UAE's economic model can meet its economic development agenda.

The general outlook of the Metaverse in e-commerce market in the UAE looks bright. The country's digitally savvy customers are incentivized for new shopping experiences and broader online product selection. Metaverse is viewed as one of the retailers' core strategies and this has encouraged e-commerce players to expand product categories and venture into new market strategies. Despite the few challenges facing the country's e-commerce industry, several components of the e-commerce system such as logistics and payments have come a long way.

The success of Amazon gives new e-commerce players something to emulate as they venture into business. The strong momentum of the industry in the last few years will continue to create opportunities for businesses, consumers, ecosystem players and investors in the virtual world of Metaverse. However, the pace of growth will rely on how fast the Metaverse players improve on product selection, product delivery and payments. Currently, other e-commerce elements such as digital media investments and consumer internet adoption are favorable. Metaverse players have to come together to educate consumers and invest in enabling infrastructure to boost the growth of the online market and its impact on the economy.

REFERENCES

Abu Bakar, A. R., Ahmsad, S. Z., & Ahmad, N. (2019). SME social media use: A study of predictive factors in the United Arab Emirates. *Global Business and Organizational Excellence*, *38*(5), 53–68. doi:10.1002/joe.21951

Ahmed, A., Moncey, A., Mohan, M., Cyriac, N. T., Ali, S. A., Mariam, S., Lyu, M., & Baskaran, K. (2020). Journey of education technology towards innovation. *2020 Advances in Science and Engineering Technology International Conferences (ASET)*. 10.1109/ASET48392.2020.9118334

Al-Alawi, A. I., & Al-Ali, F. M. (2015). Factors affecting e-commerce adoption in SMEs in the GCC: An empirical study of Kuwait. *Research Journal of Information Technology*, *7*(1), 1–21. doi:10.3923/rjit.2015.1.21

AlArabia News. (2022). *UAE sets up economy ministry in the metaverse*. Retrieved from: https://english.alarabiya.net/News/gulf/2022/10/03/UAE-sets-up-economy-ministry-in-the-metaverse

AlSharji, A., Ahmad, S. Z., & Abu Bakar, A. R. (2018). Understanding social media adoption in SMEs: Empirical evidence from the United Arab Emirates. *Journal of Entrepreneurship in Emerging Economies*, *10*(2), 302–328. doi:10.1108/JEEE-08-2017-0058

Ariff, M. S. M., Sylvester, M., Zakuan, N., Ismail, K., & Ali, K. M. (2014). Consumer perceived risk, attitude and online shopping behavior : Empirical evidence from Malaysia. *Proceedings of the 2014 International Conference on Manufacturing, Optimization, Industrial and Material Engineering.*

Ashok, S., & Baskaran, K. (2022). The prominence of corporate governance in banking sector with reference to UAE. In *Pervasive Computing and Social Networking* (pp. 417–430). Springer Singapore. doi:10.1007/978-981-16-5640-8_33

Baskaran, K. (2019). An Interpretive Study of Customer Experience Management towards Online Shopping in UAE. *International Journal of Mechanical Engineering and Technology*, *10*(02), 1071–1077. https://iaeme.com/MasterAdmin/Journal_uploads/IJMET/VOLUME_10_ISSUE_2/IJMET_10_02_112.pdf

Baskaran, K. (2019b). The impact of digital transformation in Singapore e-tail market. *International Journal of Innovative Technology and Exploring Engineering*, *8*(11), 2320–2324. doi:10.35940/ijitee. I8046.0981119

Baskaran, K. (2022). E-Consumer Behavioral Analytics: Paradigm Shift in Online Purchase Decision Making. In P. Keikhosrokiani (Ed.), *Handbook of Research on Consumer Behavior Change and Data Analytics in the Socio-Digital Era* (pp. 192–209). IGI Global. doi:10.4018/978-1-6684-4168-8.ch009

Baskaran, K., & Rajavelu, S. (2020). Digital innovation in industry 4.0 era – rebooting UAE's retail. *2020 International Conference on Communication and Signal Processing (ICCSP).* 10.1109/ICC-SP48568.2020.9182301

Baskaran, K., & Vanithamani, M. R. (2014). E-Customers Attitude towards E-Store Information and Design Quality in India, Applied Research in Science, Engineering and Management. *Applied Research in Science, Engineering and Management. World Applied Sciences Journal*, 51–56. doi:10.5829/idosi. wasj.2014.31.arsem.555

Benmamoun, M., Singh, N., Lehnert, K., & Lee, S. B. (2018). Internationalization of e-commerce corporations (ECCs) Advanced vs emerging markets ECCs. *Multinational Business Review*. Retrieved from https://www.emeraldinsight.com/doi/abs/10.1108/MBR-02-2018-0010

Cyriac, N. T., & Baskaran, K. (2020). A study on the effectiveness of non-monetary retention strategies in UAE. *2020 8th International Conference on Reliability, Infocom Technologies and Optimization (Trends and Future Directions) (ICRITO).* 10.1109/ICRITO48877.2020.9197867

Cyriac, N. T., & Baskaran, K. (2021). Predictive Analytics in a Post Covid-19 World: India's Travel and Tourism Industry. *Proceedings of International Conference on Advances in Technology, Management & Education.* 10.1109/ICATME50232.2021.9732706

Dubai Metaverse Strategy. (2022). Retrieved from UAE Government Portal: https://u.ae/en/about-the-uae/strategies-initiatives-and-awards/local-governments-strategies-and-plans/dubai-metaverse-strategy

El Sawy, N. (2019). *Souq becomes Amazon.ae in the UAE*. Retrieved from https://www.thenational.ae/business/technology/souq-becomes-amazon-ae-in-the-uae-1.855759

Emara, S. (2019). *UAE the fastest growing e-commerce market in the Middle East and North Africa*. Retrieved from tellerreport.com: https://www.tellerreport.com/business/2019-07-23---uae-the-fastest-growing-e-commerce-market-in-the-middle-east-and-north-africa-.B1L0BU-HfB.html

Forbes India. (2022). *UAE's economy ministry to set up shop in the metaverse*. Retrieved from https://www.forbesindia.com/article/news/uaes-economy-ministry-to-set-up-shop-in-the-metaverse/80255/1

Grab, B., Gavril, R. M., & Bothe, J. (2018, May). Managing the challenges and opportunities of e-commerce platforms in the Gulf region. In *ICMLG 2018 6th International Conference on Management Leadership and Governance* (p. 368). Academic Conferences and Publishing Limited.

Gulf Today. (2019). *UAE's e-commerce market is estimated to hit $27.1b by 2022*. Retrieved from https://www.gulftoday.ae/business/2019/06/18/uaes-e-commerce-market-is-estimated-to-hit-$27-1b-by-2022

Kirkcaldy, B., & Furnham, A. (2016). The Changing Face of Education and Work: Attitudes toward Work and Its Impact on Economic Growth and the Wealth of Nations. In The Aging Workforce Handbook: Individual, Organizational, and Societal Challenges (pp. 135-157). Emerald Group Publishing Limited.

Ma, S., Guo, J., & Zhang, H. (2019). Policy analysis and development evaluation of digital ttrade: An international comparison. *China & World Economy*, *27*(3), 49–75. doi:10.1111/cwe.12280

Majji, K. C., & Baskaran, K. (2021). Artificial intelligence analytics—virtual assistant in UAE automotive industry. In *Inventive Systems and Control* (pp. 309–322). Springer Singapore. doi:10.1007/978-981-16-1395-1_24

Metamandrill. (2022). *Amazon Metaverse; Amazon's Vision Entering the Metaverse*. Retrieved from: https://metamandrill.com/amazon-metaverse/

Mohan, M., & Baskaran, K. (2021). Financial analytics: Investment behavior of middle income group in south India. *2021 11ᵗʰ International Conference on Cloud Computing, Data Science & Engineering (Confluence)*. 10.1109/Confluence51648.2021.9377029

Moncey, A. A., & Baskaran, K. (2020). Digital marketing analytics: Building brand awareness and loyalty in UAE. *2020 IEEE International Conference on Technology Management, Operations and Decisions (ICTMOD)*. 10.1109/ICTMOD49425.2020.9380579

Okasha, A. A. (2020). Entrepreneurship in the United Arab Emirates. In *Entrepreneurial Innovation and Economic Development in Dubai and Comparisons to Its Sister Cities* (pp. 158–182). IGI Global. doi:10.4018/978-1-5225-9377-5.ch008

Rusell, J. (2017). *Amazon completes its acquisition of Middle Eastern e-commerce firm Souq*. Retrieved from https://techcrunch.com/2017/07/03/amazon-souq-com-completed/

Seetharaman, A., Niranjan, I., Saravanan, A. S., & Balaji, D. (2017). A Study of the Moderate Growth of Online Retailing (E-commerce) In the UAE. *Journal of Developing Areas*, *51*(4), 397–412. doi:10.1353/jda.2017.0109

Staff, A. (2017). *SOUQ.com and SAP to boost GCC e-commerce*. Retrieved from https://www.logistic-smiddleeast.com/article-12995-souqcom-and-sap-to-boost-gcc-e-commerce

TheNational. (2019a). *UAE e-commerce transactions to reach $16bn in 2019, study says*. Retrieved from https://www.thenational.ae/business/technology/uae-e-commerce-transactions-to-reach-16bn-in-2019-study-says-1.889835

TheNational. (2019b). *Souq becomes Amazon.ae in the UAE*. Retrieved from https://www.thenational.ae/business/technology/souq-becomes-amazon-ae-in-the-uae-1.855759

KEY TERMS AND DEFINITIONS

Augmented Reality (AR): An interactive experience that superimposes virtual objects over the physical environment.

Digital Economy: The use of information technology to create or adapt, market or consume goods and services.

E-Commerce or Electronic Commerce: A trading of goods and services over the internet.

Logistics: It manages the flow of commodities between the place of origin and the place of consumption with effective transportation and storage.

Metaverse: A virtual world where users can communicate with each other and a computer-generated environment.

Mixed Reality (MR): It creates a new environment that enables users to become immersed in the real world while interacting with the virtual one by fusing real and digital surroundings together that coexist and interact with each other.

Virtual Reality (VR): A fully artificial digital environment which gives a simulated experience using position tracking and 3D near-eye displays to offer an immersive sense of a virtual world.

Chapter 9
The Critical Success Factors of Metaverse Adoption in Education:
From the Consumer Behaviour Perspective

David Roland Andembubtob

School of Computer Sciences, Universiti Sains Malaysia, Malaysia

Pantea Keikhosrokiani
ⓘ https://orcid.org/0000-0003-4705-2732
School of Computer Sciences, Universiti Sains Malaysia, Malaysia

Nasuha Lee Abdullah

School of Computer Sciences, Universiti Sains Malaysia, Malaysia

ABSTRACT

Metaverse is considered one of the platforms that can be used for teaching and learning in higher education. In order to develop, adopt, and use an innovative application or system, the critical success factors are crucial. Consumer behaviours and adoption are crucial to the development of a proposed system based on the metaverse in order to improve the system's usefulness. Consequently, the goal of this study is to evaluate various theories, models, and previous research related to the innovation adoption in order to draw conclusions about the critical success factors for the adoption of the metaverse in education and consumer intention to use.

INTRODUCTION

Critical success factors (CSFs) are the few major areas of activity in which good results are necessary for a specific individual or institution to reach its goals (Bullen & Rockart, 1981). CSFs are the restricted number of areas in which acceptable results will guarantee successful competitive performance for the

DOI: 10.4018/978-1-6684-7029-9.ch009

individual, institution, or organization. CSFs are often the selected crucial issues on which a management or organization should concentrate their efforts. The phrase "important success factors" is carefully chosen in light of this. They portray the few key "factors" that are "critical" to the "success" of the institution concerned. It is crucial to identify the CSFs that will have the most impact on whether the organization's goals are achieved. However, the environment might alter sometimes, and certain issues or possibilities may present themselves for a certain firm. Consequently, it is important to grasp what CSFs are not in this context. They are not a special set of measures, sometimes known as "key indicators," which can be applied to all divisions of an institution, company, or organization. CSFs are the areas of major value to a particular system, in a specific division, at a particular point in time (Bullen & Rockart, 1981).

A metaverse platform is a crucial resource for enhancing learners' immersion and motivation. It gives them the chance to think critically about the use of cutting-edge teaching methods and get first-hand knowledge of self-directed learning. Moreover, Farjami et al. (2011), Han (2020), and Kanematsu et al. (2013) showed the importance of employing the metaverse system in many academic domains throughout the world. The goal of these experiments was to develop real-world scenarios in which the metaverse system is used to find answers to problems. This demonstrates the necessity for a conceptual model to be created that can explain to pupils the vital role the metaverse system plays. The conceptual model is required to assess the effectiveness and adoption of the metaverse system by concentrating on consumers' perceptions from a particular angle (Alfaisal et al., 2022a). In order to propose a proper conceptual model for assessing metaverse adoption among consumers and to consumers' behavioural intention, identifying the success factors are required (Ezimmuo & Keikhosrokiani, 2022; Humida et al., 2021; Keikhosrokiani, 2020a, 2022b; Keikhosrokiani, Mustaffa, Zakaria, & Baharudin, 2019). Furthermore, to develop a proper system based on metaverse, consumer adoption and behaviour are very important to increase the usability of the system. Therefore, this study aims to review different theories, models, and existing studies related to the adoption of innovations to conclude the critical success factors of metaverse adoption in education and consumer behavioural intention to use.

CRITICAL SUCCESS FACTORS

Critical success factors (CSFs) have been employed extensively in information system deployments since the late 1970s. CSFs give a thorough knowledge of the various components and range of implementation success (Ashworth, 2020; Rabaa', 2009; Rockart, 1982). Critical Success Factors are defined from different perspectives, such as: "The several elements that directly adds to the success of an organization or institution and without which, the institution can fail. One puts it this way, "It is a cluster of organizational activities that, if appropriately used, will correctly lead to the achievement of the planned success of the institution" and "Elements and components that need to be applied well to attain the desired success." Ashworth, (2020) and Rockart, (1982) indicate that 20% of critical factors can define and mirror 80% of an institution's performance. Fong Yew & Jambulingam, (2015) stated that critical success factors are of different importance, since are related to time and change over time, therefore should be evaluated over time to keep in tune with continuous changes. Critical Success Factors (CSFs), in its simplest term refers to the main requirements that ensure the educational institution takes the right direction to realize the goals and the desired value, and the very standards of higher education worth that go to elucidate the elements of the educational institution's continued existence and its adaptation to environmental changes.

A vast number of studies have been carried out during the last several decades attempting to discover and identify those factors that significantly contribute to information systems success (Keikhosrokiani, 2020; Keikhosrokiani et al., 2012, 2018; Keikhosrokiani, Mustaffa, Zakaria, & Abdullah, 2019; Lateef & Keikhosrokiani, 2022; Al-Fraihat et al., 2020; Alqahtani & Rajkhan, 2020; Keikhosrokiani, Mustaffa, Zakaria, & Baharudin, 2019). The CSFs described are proven to be crucial elements for carrying out improvement activities and are completely supported by evidence-based research. When implemented collectively, each of these thoroughly researched approaches is essential to ongoing school development. These elements help raise academic achievement, which is a fundamental Critical Success Factor. By ensuring the Critical Success Factors of (i) teacher quality, (ii) effective leadership, (iii) data driven instructional decisions, (iv) productive community and parent involvement, (v) efficient use of learning time, and (vi) maintaining a positive school climate, these can increase performance for all students. Table 1 shows several critical success factors are outlined for various applications in higher education institutions.

Table 1. Critical success factors for technological applications in higher education

Author(s)	Area	Critical Success Factors
(Priatna et al., 2020)	e-Learning implementation	"Organizational factors, Technology, human resources."
(Castro-Lopez et al., 2022)	Adapt Fuzzy Inference Systems	S"atisfaction with the degree choice, study self-regulation and social adaptation"
(Clark et al., 2020)	Learning analytics (LA)	"Strategy and policy at organizational level, information technological readiness, performance and impact evaluation, people's skills and expertise and data quality."
(Kokkinou & van Kollenburg, 2022)	Lean implementation in HE	"Employee empowerment, Sharing success stories and Training."
(König et al., 2022)	Individual Digital Study Assistant (IDSA)	"Skilled and Reliable HEI personnel, Well-organized and Useful content, Cross-platform usability, Ease of use, and Students' social factors"
(Shatat & Shatat, 2021)	Virtual migration E- learning	"Technological factors (usefulness, ease of use, technical support, security, privacy, quality) Psychological factors (trust, culture, engagement, self-efficacy, responsibility, motivation, and awareness)"
(Abu Madi et al., 2022)	Enterprise Resource Planning (ERP) implementation in higher education institutions (HEIs)	"Organizational factors (change management, training and education, and process reengineering) Technical factors (IT infrastructure, information quality, system compatibility, and system quality) Social factors (top management support, qualified IT staff, and vendor relations) Project factors (project management, time, and budget selection of the appropriate) ERP system."
(Fernandes et al., 2022)	General Data Protection Regulation (GDPR) implementation	"Empower workers, Commit Top management, Implement the GDPR, Data protection, Security of information, Adapt the Information Systems to the GDPR, Use a progressive approach Start, Surveying, Adapt, Conduct security audits, Guarantee the necessary resources, Create a decentralized team of pivots for data protection, Create institutional communication channels, Adopt a computer application, Implement a change management process"
(MacIel-Monteon et al., 2020)	Application Six Sigma	"Top Management Involvement and Commitment (TM), Training and Education (TE), Select Team Members and Teamwork (TW), Link SS with Institutional Strategy (LI), Cultural Change (CC), Link SS with Human Resources (HR), Clear Performance Metrics (CM), Link SS with Costumers (LC), Communication (C), Link SS with Suppliers (LS) and Benefits (B)."
(Soleimani et al., 2022)	Applying and evaluating online delivery methods	"Benefits of the eLearning system, educational system quality, information quality, instructor quality, learner quality, service quality and technical system quality."
(Milic & Simeunovic, 2021)	Exploring e-learning on the basis of the students' perceptions	"Quality learning materials, student's attitude toward e-learning, teacher's attitude toward e-learning, technological support, classroom interaction, student's activities, and teacher's attitude towards students."
(Francescatto et al., 2023)	Applying the Lean Six Sigma methodology,	"Leadership and management involvement, project management and organizational infrastructure, training, and education. data accessibility, LSS competence"

continues on following page

Table 1. Continued

Author(s)	Area	Critical Success Factors
(VanDerSchaaf & Daim, 2020)	Perspectives on student success technology	"Navigation, Tactical funding, Personalization, and planning. funding, is not significant."
(Chaiya & Ahmad, 2021)	Policy process of quality assurance	"The achievement of graduates, university ranking, and the country's competitiveness."
(Atıcı et al., 2022)	The interval type-2 fuzzy Analytical Hierarchy Process determining the efficiency of e-learning systems	"Adaptation, Framework, Function, Security, Content, Cooperation and Communication, Quality, Learning, Assessment and Evaluation, Technical specifications, and Support."

Success Factor that Can be Used Virtual Reality and Metaverse in Education

The knowledge economy, the information age, and the information society now seem to be the main factors influencing the future of higher education. Today's higher education landscape is changing as national boundaries blur, resources flow fast across borders, and international human resource mobility is on the rise in particular. Higher education institutions must use their resources to achieve worldwide recognition while also helping to create an information economy because they are one of the primary actors in the information society (Carayannis & Morawska-Jancelewicz, 2022; Saykili, 2019).

Theories and Models

Many dictionary definitions state that the word theory can take on several meanings, including "a mental view" or a "contemplation," a "conception or mental scheme of something to be done, or the method of doing it; a systematic statement of rules or principles to be followed," a "system of ideas or statements held as an explanation or account of a group of facts or phenomena; a hypothesis that has been confirmed or established by observation or experiment, and is propounded or accepted as accounting for the known facts; statements of what are held to be the general laws, principles, or causes of something known or observed," a "mere hypothesis, speculation, conjecture" (Gregor, 2006).

In general, scientists who write in the tradition of the physical or natural sciences are inclined to view theory as providing justifications and predictions in addition to being testable. A taxonomy is a concept that groups ideas of information systems according to how four key objectives are handled: (1) analysis, (2) explanation, (3) prediction, and (4) prescription. In the same vein, the five different types of Information System (IS) theory distinguished are labelled: (i) theory for analysing, (ii) theory for explaining, (iii) theory for predicting, (iv) theory for explaining and predicting (EP theory), and (v) theory for design and action. Theory is a must for understanding IS because it connects the very natural world, the local social world, and the constructed artificial world. Hence, compared to other disciplinary domains, IS theory may have a distinct character. The fact that IS is concerned with the use of objects in human-machine systems sets it apart from other related subjects. Information systems research looks into more than only the current technology system, the popular social system, or even the two systems side by side (Abubakre et al., 2022; Kesharwani, 2020); additionally, it examines the phenomena that emerges when the two interact (Gregor, 2006).

Information System Success Models and Theories

Information systems are said to collect, process, store, analyze and disseminate information for a definite purpose. The reason of information systems has been defined as getting the correct information to the right people, at the needed time, in the right proportion and in the wanted form (George & Gnanayutham, 2010; Szymkowiak et al., 2021). An information system is a set of interconnected and interrelated components that work as one to collect, process, store and disseminate information. This data and information support basic business operations, accurate data reporting and visualization, proper data analysis, timely decision making, good communications, and coordination within an organization. A well designed and developed information system has some form of feedback mechanism to check and control its operation. This feedback loop ensures that the system operates in an efficient manner. Basically, Information systems are of four types based on their field of influence: (i) personal, (ii) workgroup, (iii) enterprise and (iv) inter-organizational information systems (Abdul Aziz et al., 2020).

Information system success (ISS) has been the subject of several studies in recent years (DeLone & McLean, 2016; Jeyaraj, 2020a; Stair & Reynolds, 2020) many of which have relied heavily on the models developed by DeLone and McLean (DM) in 1992 and 2003. Many links revealed in the DM models have been occasionally validated in empirical study however the whole DM models have not been always utilized. Several research evaluated links between ISS characteristics not mentioned in the DM models and looked into relationships between ISS dimensions and other variables. Some studies also traded relationships between the 1992 and 2003 models.

Nine success indicators were suggested by Sela & Sivan (2009) Nine success indicators were suggested by Sela & Sivan (2009) for an enterprise-wide e-learning research. These elements were discovered through analysis, literature research, and conversations with e-learning project managers. These elements were discovered through analysis, literature research, and conversations with e-learning project managers. To determine the optimum success elements required to establish an e-learning program, interviews were performed, twelve semi-structured questionnaires were created and distributed, and the results were evaluated. These criteria were identified and then divided into two groups: "must-have" factors and "nice-to-have" factors. The first set of essential elements were practical and user-friendly e-learning technologies, management support, marketing, the appropriate organizational culture, and the presence of a genuine need for the organisation. Second, there were a few "good to have" elements including learning time, required learning, assistance, and incentives. As a result, a checklist of e-learning success elements is offered for effective implementation of Information system platform based on the research's findings. In a special supplement, the elements in recessionary periods were examined as well as their significance and character.

Information management (IM) and information system (IS) research provide unique opportunities due to the extensive use of ICT, which has had a significant impact on the development of several new research findings and ideas. The evolution of IM and IS research has somehow been impacted throughout time by the fragmentation of basic ideas. In particular, even though IM and IS research has a wealth of ideas accessible, it is not practical to include every theory. Hence, based on the examination of empirical studies conducted in the IM and IS fields over the past 20 years, there are even ideas that are relatively important but less well-researched. These seven ideas are: "Transactive Memory System (TMS), Flow Theory (FT), Impression Management Theory (IMT), Structural Holes Theory (SHT), Social Presence Theory (SPT), Resource Dependence Theory (RDT), Illusion Of Control (IC)" (Wu et al., 2022).

Online learning was originally designed to support in-person instruction, but it has since developed into an essential tool for distance education. In particular, the COVID-19 pandemic's arrival has boosted online education's popularity and significance. The lack of research on the fundamentals of how online education should be methodically delivered and which educational factors should be taken into account to increase learner satisfaction in an online setting has been made clear by the explosion of innovation in the education sector. Notwithstanding current limits in study findings that take into account both systemic and instructional worlds, VR education is once again advocated as a significant tool for online learning in light of the most recent appearance of the Metaverse. In order to examine factors that influence learner satisfaction by mediating the flow theory, Gim et al., (2022) proposed and described a research model that converges the technological acceptance model, information systems success model, and self-determination theory. The study's findings demonstrated that the majority of factors related to self-determination theory and the effectiveness of the information system in VR education had an effect on student satisfaction. Learners' flow, or total absorption in the learning process, specifically serves as a key mediating variable for learner pleasure. These results clearly imply that in order to introduce the finest educational techniques into the Metaverse, it is essential to create and manage a systematic platform that encourages self-directed learning. Table 2 and Table 3 summarize some information system theories and models.

Table 2. Information system theories/models

S/N	Theory/Model/Title/Author	Area of Application/ Constructs	Findings
1.	**Task-Technology Fit** A meta-regression of task-technology fit in information systems research, (Jeyaraj, 2020b)	"TTF predicts individuals' perceptions, intentions, and behaviours as well as performance impacts due to technology use."	"This study shows that the variation in TTF effects is explained by type of respondents, type of dependent variable, and type of TTF variable."
2.	**"Transactive memory systems (TMS)** Communication in theory and research on transactive memory systems: A literature review" (Peltokorpi & Hood, 2019)	"Cognitive, organizational, and social psychology; communication; information science; and management."	The crucial role of communication in TMS theory, theoretical extensions, and empirical research is detailed in this paper's survey of the literature on the connections between communication, TMS, and outcomes in dyads, groups, and teams.
3.	**"Impression Management Theory (IMT)** Impression Management After Image-Threatening Events: A Case Study of JUUL's Online Messaging" (Eng, 2020)	"Impression management tactics of self-promotion, exemplification, and supplication."	This study uses impression management theory to examine how JUUL engaged in positive impression management online in response to these image-threatening events. Results suggest that JUUL made both textual and visual changes in its messaging over time to engage in positive impression management, while using the impression management tactics of self-promotion, exemplification, and supplication.
4.	**"Cognitive fit theory** When cognitive fit outweighs cognitive load: Redundant data labels in charts increase accuracy and speed of information extraction" (Kopp et al., 2018)	"Cognitive fit theory emphasizes that a chart's efficiency depends on its correspondence to the mental representation of the task."	In the online experiment presented in this paper, the authors investigated the effect of data labels in line and bar charts on users' accuracy and speed in solving chart-related business tasks dependent on different task types. The findings show that users judge redundant labelled charts to be much more effective and respond to associated questions with significantly more accuracy and speed, which we explain with the aid of cognitive fit theory.
5.	**"Activity theory** Understanding digitalization and educational change in school by means of activity theory and the levels of learning concept" (Pettersson, 2021)	"Cultural–historical activity theory (CHAT) including the concepts of object, change, and transformation is used"	Study reveals that the digitalization's target harbours a notion that affects how it is anticipated and implemented inside the educational setting. The way schools perceive digitalization—what it means both conceptually and practically—influences how they manage their budget, staff development, and organisational transformation.

continues on following page

Table 2. Continued

S/N	Theory/Model/Title/Author	Area of Application/ Constructs	Findings
6.	**"Socio-Technical Systems Theory** Industry 4.0 integration with socio-technical systems theory: A systematic review and proposed theoretical model" (Sony & Naik, 2020)	"People, infrastructure, technology, processes, culture and goals."	Socio-Technical Systems theory considered while designing the horizontal, vertical and end-to-end integration for sustainable implementation of Industry 4.0. the integration is also suggested for analysis on the impact of stakeholders, economic situation and regulatory frameworks around which the operating organizations are operating
7.	**"Diagrammic Reasoning Framework** Challenges in Learning Unified Modelling Language: From the Perspective of Diagrammatic Representation and Reasoning" (Z. Shen et al., 2018)	"In this study, a cognitive technique is used to investigate students' challenges in learning UML. The constructed concept maps provide empirical evidence of the difficulties that novices experience in learning UML."	The study used a concept-mapping methodology to pinpoint the difficulties associated with learning UML notational features. It demonstrates that some technical aspects of the UML diagrammatic representation, when combined with the cognitive characteristics of the students, obstruct learning by impeding perceptual and conceptual processes involved in finding, identifying, and inferring visual information.
8.	"Information System Model Success Success of IoT in Smart Cities of India: An empirical analysis" (Chatterjee et al., 2018)	"Perceived Information Quality (PIQ), Perceived System Quality (PSQ) and Perceived Service Quality (PESQ) influence different impacts of IoT policy implementation in proposed SCI."	IoT and AI must be combined to create "Smart Machines" that replicate intelligent behaviour in order to make decisions that are accurate and trustworthy without the need for human interaction. Identification of the elements influencing an information system is crucial for its success. According to the study, perceived information quality has a beneficial impact on perceived IoT use intentions in SCI. According to the study, perceived net benefits of IoT use have a favourable impact on perceived intentions to use IoT in SCI.
9.	"Integrating Technology Acceptance Model with Innovation Diffusion Theory: An Empirical Investigation on Students' Intention to Use E-Learning Systems," (Al-Rahmi et al., 2019)	"Six perceptions of innovation characteristics, observability, trialability, perceived compatibility, complexity, and perceived enjoyment on the perceived ease of use, complexity, trialability, observability, perceived compatibility, perceived enjoyment, perceived usefulness"	Innovation diffusion theory (IDT) and an integrating TAM have both been used to evaluate and assess an extended TAM. The integrated approach between TAM and IDT is well supported by the empirical findings. The results point to an expanded TAM with IDT model that can be used by decision-makers in higher education, universities, and colleges to evaluate, plan, and implement the use of e-learning systems. This model is intended to increase the acceptance of the use of e-learning systems to improve students' learning performance.

Table 3. List of information system theories / models

S/N	Information System Models / Theories
1.	Flow Theory (FT)
2.	Structural Holes Theory (SHT)
3.	Resource Dependence Theory (RDT)
4.	Social Presence Theory (SPT)
5.	Illusion Of Control (IC) .
6.	Deterrence theory
7.	Theory of open systems
8.	Learning theory
9.	Toulmin's model of argumentation
10.	Production theory
11.	Bourdieu's theory of practice
12.	Bayesian decision theory
13.	The theory of metagraphs
14.	Pricing theory
15.	Helson's adaptation-Level Theory

S/N	Information System Models / Theories
16.	Diagrammic reasoning framework
17.	Theory of image processing
18.	Organizational memory
19.	Theory of breakpoints
20.	Control theory
21.	Systems theory
22.	Is design theory
23.	Decision theory
24.	Graph-theory
25.	Cognition theory
26.	Agency theory
27.	Theory of coordination
28.	Multi-attribute utility theory
29.	Representation model
30.	Theory of decomposition
31.	Semantic network theory
32.	Representation model
33.	Reputation mechanisms

Technology of Adoption Theories and Models

Information Systems (IS) research uses a variety of theories and models to examine the factors influencing how companies and institutions embrace new technology (Alaba et al., 2022; McLeod & Dolezel, 2022; Puleng Modise & Van Den Berg, 2021). Technology adoption is one of the prime areas of research in information systems (Rathod, 2014; Sharma and Mishra, 2014). It's worth mentioning that Adoption refers to "the point in which a technology is chosen for use by an individual or an organization" (Carr, 1999). The proper assessment of the demands and the effective variables for the adoption of new technology are aspects that should be considered in connection with the creation of new technology. As a result, several academics have studied the issue and created a variety of frameworks for simulating the idea that people adopt a technology (Yadegari et al., 2022). An important study area in the world of information technology is understanding the elements that influence technological adoption and providing the foundation for such acceptance. Moreover, one of the most important issues in the field of information systems is why individuals choose and utilise certain technologies, or do not. It is possible to define technology adoption as the acceptance and acknowledgement of the use of that technology. The first ideas and models of technology adoption first appeared in the 1960s. The introduction of computers and their subsequent rise in popularity among humans can be connected to the development and use of technology acceptance models (Yadegari et al., 2022).

According to Kang et al., (2021), a leading theory that was employed, the Technology Acceptance Model (TAM), the character of the institution has an influence on IT adoption. Using the Institution-based Technology Acceptance Model, the study investigates how institutions affect the adoption of new Technologies (ITAM). Data from a survey of 300 public sector workers was used to run an empirical test. The suggested ideas were put to the test using structural equation modelling (SEM). The findings demonstrated that institutions have a favourable and considerable impact on individuals' intentions to utilise new Technologies. Second, it can be shown that different types of institutions have an influence on IT adoption; external institutions have a greater impact than internal ones on factors like perceived utility (PU), perceived ease of use (PEOU), and intention to use. Thirdly, perceived ease of use and perceived usefulness play mediating roles between institution and IT adoption. Fourthly, results from the base model were corroborated by an alternate enlarged model, to which other human and organisational components were also incorporated. As a result, they came to the conclusion that institutions have a significant influence on the desire to use IT in terms of perceived utility and convenience of use (Kang et al., 2021).

The Technology Acceptance Model (TAM) has been used by numerous researchers to predict the acceptance of the visitors towards the use of interactive technology in Information System (IS) studies. The consistency and validity of the TAM model are proven by many types of research in various of discipline. The evolution of TAM also has shown that contribution in development of TAM can be made by adding external factors, testing in different sites, different subjects, and different users. The purpose of this study is to explore the evolution of Technology Acceptance Model. Data were obtained from the various related literature review in technology adoption research. This paper provides fundamental knowledge for researchers in understanding the direction of the Technology Acceptance Model for any extension or modification model in future research.

According to (Abdul Aziz et al., 2020), many researchers frequently employ the Technology Acceptance Model (TAM) to predict how users and visitors would react to the deployment of interactive technology in Information System (IS) investigations. The validity and reliability of the TAM model have been shown by numerous research in numerous domains. The dynamic growth of TAM has also demonstrated that numerous contributions to its development are produced by incorporating outside variables and conducting tests across a variety of locations, subjects, and users. The development of TAM was examined in the study. Data were obtained from multiple reviews of related literature in many studies on technology adoption. This paper provided basic knowledge for researchers in comprehending the direction of the TAM for any extension or modification in the model for future research. Several of these models and frameworks have been developed to elucidate user adoption of new technologies and these establish factors that influence user acceptance (Taherdoost, 2018).

The goal of technology acceptance theories and models is to explain how people may relate to, accept, and make use of new technologies. Consequently, it is important to make some significant related research of the history of technology acceptance and its use in order to know how they developed and evolved over the years (Table 4), outlining the similarities and differences between them in Figure 1 (Momani et al., 2017).

Table 4. Evolution of technology acceptance theories/models

S/N	Theory / Model / Author
1.	Cognitive Dissonance Theory 2 (CDT)
2.	Theory of Reasoned Action (TRA)
3.	Theory of Interpersonal Behaviour (TIB) (Triandis, 1978)
4.	Uses and Gratifications Model (U&G) (Blumler, 1979)
5.	Expectation Disconfirmation Theory (EDT) (Oliver, 1980)
6.	Social Cognitive Theory (SCT)
7.	Technology Acceptance Model (TAM)
8.	Technology Organizational Environment Framework (TOE) (Tornatzky et al., 1990)
9.	Theory of Planned Behavior 3 (TPB)
10.	Perceived Characteristics of Innovation (PCI) (Moore and Benbasat, 1991)
11.	Model of Personal Computer Utilization (MPCU) (Thompson et al. 1991)
12.	Motivation Model (MM) (Davis, Bagozzi, and Warshaw 1992)
13.	Diffusion Of Innovations 4 (DOI)
14.	Decomposed Theory of Planned Behavior (DTPB) (Taylortodd, 1995)
15.	Task Technology Fit Model (TTF)
16.	Combined TAM And TPB (C-TAM-TPB) (Taylortodd, 1995)
17.	Division Theory of Planned Behavior (DTPB) (Taylortodd, 1995)
18.	Igbaria Model 5 (IM)
19.	Technology Acceptance Model 2 (TAM 2) (Venkatesh & Davis, 2000)
20.	Unified Theory of Acceptance and Use of Technology (UTAUT)
21.	Technology Acceptance Model 3 (TAM 3) (Venkatesh & Bala, 2008)
22.	Unified Theory of Acceptance and Use of Technology 2 (UTAUT 2)
Source: (Yadegari et al., 2022), (Momani et al., 2017), (Shehzad et al., 2022)	

Technology acceptance/adoption models and theories have long sought to explain and forecast how people would use technology. The user may examine the factors influencing technology acceptability from a variety of angles thanks to these models and ideas. Even in two separate settings, using these models for a technology can occasionally produce the opposite effects. So, improved outcomes may follow from understanding the key influencing factors of an acceptance model, identifying them rather than interpreting the model's components, and adapting the model to the circumstance. Researchers believe that a specific model cannot be used to explain the adoption of a wide variety of technologies, which is seen as a serious drawback and a restriction for academics who rely on a single model. However, many academics believe that merging many theories offers better study grounds for examining the acceptability and adoption of technologies while gaining a deeper understanding of that technology. Consequently, the model or theory used might produce various results depending on the kind of the stated technology. As a result, the first step in using any model is to have a thorough grasp by deriving the technical attributes. The research goal can then be achieved using a model or collection of models depending on the knowledge that has been gained. Based on the Pareto principle, the theory of Diffusion of Innovation (DOI), the Theory of Planned Behavior (TPB), the Social Cognition Theory (SCT), the Technology Acceptance Model (TAM) as well as the Unified Theory of Acceptance and Use of Technology (UTAUT), are among the most popular models/theories in the field of technology acceptance. Also, among the constructs which form the models/theories of technology acceptance, the following 10 constructs of 'perceived ease of use', experience', 'attitude towards behavior', ''perceived usefulness', 'subjective norms', 'result demonstrability', 'utilization voluntariness', 'social influence', 'image' and 'perceived behavioral control' are the most applicable variables (Yadegari et al., 2022)Momani et al., 2017 Shehzad et al., 2022) Figure 1 gives an overview of Technology Adoption/ Acceptance models that are commonly used by researchers and how they relate to one another.

Figure 1. An overview of adoption / acceptance models

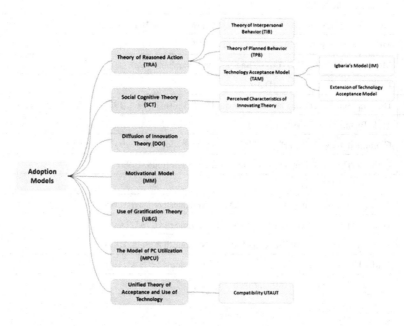

An Overview of Individual Adoption / Acceptance Models

Diffusion of Innovations (DOI)

According to Rogers & Singhal, (2003), theory of diffusion of innovations points to the processes of acceptance and rejection of practices, ideas and environments that are perceived as new by individuals or institutions. The theory of diffusion of innovations is defined by four main elements. Innovation, Communication channels, Time and Social system and consists of five steps: Knowledge, Persuasion, Decision, Implementation and Confirmation (Sahin, 2006). Figure 2 illustrates the innovation-decision process which consists of knowledge, persuasion, decision, implementation, and confirmation.

Figure 2. The innovation-decision process

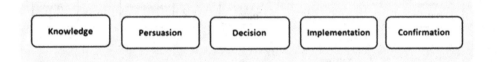

Reasoned Action Theory

In this theory, intention is important in the appearance of an individual's behavior. Attitudes and subjective norms influence the intention. Attitudes comprises of beliefs and outcomes for the right behavior. Subjective norms are expressed as beliefs about motivation and rules. Figure 3 shows the overall view of theory of reasoned action.

Figure 3. Theory of Reasoned Action

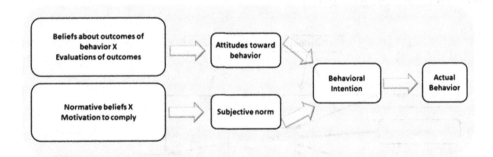

Technology Acceptance Model

There are models about how technology is adopted as innovation and transformed into human behaviour. TAM and other models are important in the context of innovation diffusion and adoption. TAM originates from the theory of reasoned action. TAM presents a model that determines user behaviour and the level of technology acceptance based on a small number of variables such as ease of use, perceived usefulness, attitude toward using, behavioural intention to use, and actual system use. Figure 4 shows technology acceptance model.

Figure 4. Technology Acceptance Model

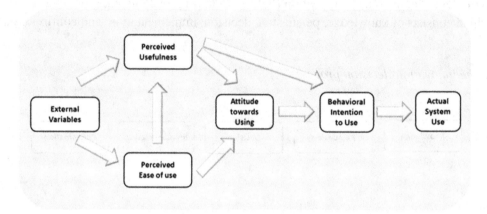

Technology Acceptance Model-2

TAM model gave birth to a new model by updating the existing model. Venkatesh & Davis, (2000) in their study, referred to as Technology Acceptance Model-2 (TAM-2), added various components to the model to overcome the limitations of the TAM. Technology acceptance model-2 is illustrated in Figure 5.

Figure 5. Technology Acceptance Model-2

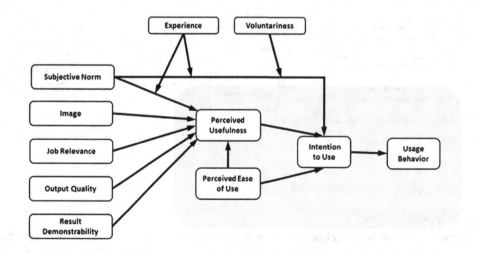

Unified Theory of Acceptance and Use of Technology

The different rules for the TAM, led proposing of a Unified Theory of Acceptance and Use of Technology (UTAUT) by altering the weaknesses and strengths of the models previously presented in their study. The four key components of usage and intention in the UTAUT are performance expectancy, effort expectancy, social influence, and enabling factors. Age, gender, experience, and voluntariness of use were explored in the model along with use behaviour and behavioural intention, which played the role of major moderators. Figure 6 shows the unified theory of acceptance and use of technology.

Figure 6. Unified theory of acceptance and use of technology

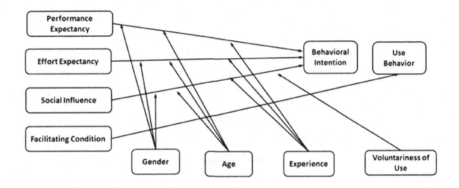

The versatile nature of the Unified Theory of Acceptance and Use of Technology (UTAUT) model is illustrated in Figure 7 where it is deployed in studies to resolve unanswered questions in the previous versions of the earlier Technology adoption/acceptance models.

The abbreviations shown in Figure 7 stands for:

1. "TRA - The theory of reasoned action"
2. "IDT - The innovation diffusion theory"
3. "TPB - The theory of planned behaviour"
4. "MM - The motivational model"
5. "TAM - The technology acceptance model"
6. "SCT - The social cognitive theory"
7. "TAM-TPB - A combined TPB and TAM"
8. "MPCU - The model of PC utilization"

Unified Theory of Acceptance and Use of Technology-2

The UTAUT was remodelled by Venkatesh and others in 2012 and called the Unified Theory of Acceptance and Use of Technology-2 (UTAUT-2). The new model excluded the voluntariness of use. The variables price value, hedonic motivation, and habit were brought into the new model. Behavioural Intention explained 56% and 74% of the variance in the old and new models respectively (Arpaci et al., 2022; Yu et al., 2021a, 2021b). UTAUT-2 helps to understand the use and adoption of such technologies like distance education. Figure 8 shows the unified theory of acceptance and use of technology 2.

Figure 7. The Unified theory of acceptance and use of technology (UTAUT) model

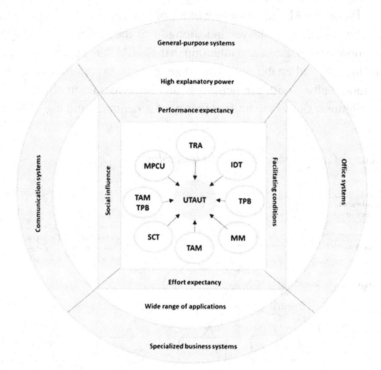

Figure 8. Unified Theory of Acceptance and Use of Technology-2

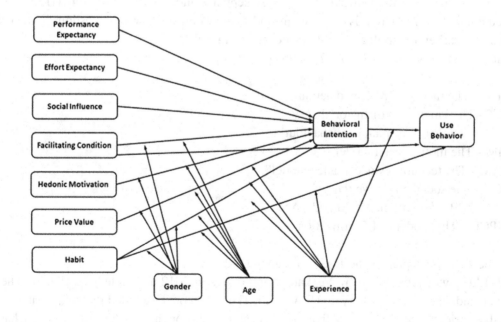

These theories and models are used in the context of technology integration in the classroom and conducted studies that provide generalizable results. Table 5 summarize the related works which focused on the success factors of innovation adoption among consumers. Metaverse is also considered as one of those innovations.

Table 5. Technology of Adoption Theories and Models

S/N	Author/Title/Year	Model/Theory /Constructs
1.	User Acceptance of Metaverse: Insights from Technology Acceptance Model (TAM) and Planned Behaviour Theory (PBT) (Toraman, 2018)	**TAM, PBT, SEM** Attitude Towards Use; Perceived Behavioural Control; Perceived Ease of Use; Perceived Usefulness; Subjective Norms
2.	Measuring Technology Acceptance Model to use Metaverse Technology in Egypt. (Mostafa, 2022)	**TAM, (ETAM), TAM 3** (Perceived usefulness, Perceived ease of use, Social Influence, Security, Technology availability and Trust)
3.	A conceptual framework for determining metaverse adoption in higher institutions of gulf area: An empirical study using hybrid SEM-ANN approach. (Akour et al., 2022)	**TAM** trialability, observability, compatibility, and complexity, users' satisfaction, personal innovativeness, TAM constructs, SEM, ANN
4.	Feeling displeasure from online social media postings: A study using cognitive dissonance theory (Jeong et al., 2019)	**Cognitive Dissonance Theory 2** Covariance based structural equation modelling (CB-SEM) methodology
5.	Predicting students' intention to adopt mobile learning: A combination of theory of reasoned action and technology acceptance model. (Buabeng-Andoh, 2018)	(TAM) (TRA)
6.	An investigation of cyberloafing in a large-scale technology organization from the perspective of the theory of interpersonal behaviour. (Elciyar & Simsek, 2021)	Theory of Interpersonal Behaviour (TIB)
7.	"Exploring the application of the uses and gratifications theory as a conceptual model for identifying the motivations for smartphone use by e-tourists" (Moon et al., 2022)	Uses and gratifications theory U&G theory
8.	Wearable health information systems intermittent discontinuance: A revised expectation-disconfirmation model. (X. L. Shen et al., 2018)	This study proposes a revised expectation-disconfirmation model by incorporating four new theoretical constructs, i.e. neutral disconfirmation, attitudinal ambivalence, neutral satisfaction, and intermittent discontinuance
9.	Blockchain Technology for Supply Chains operating in emerging markets: an empirical examination of technology-organization-environment (TOE) framework(Chittipaka et al., 2022).	TOE
10.	Extending the theory of planned behaviour (TPB) to explain online game playing among Malaysian undergraduate students. (Alzahrani et al., 2017)	Theory of Planned Behaviour (TPB)

Research by Wisdom et al. (2014) primarily aims to understand what it is about innovation adoption that works in companies, even for people, as well as when adoption works and under what conditions. It also explores how and why the processes that have been found encourage adoption (Wisdom et al., 2014). Understanding why people accept, reject, or adopt any new technology is one of the most crucial topics in the information technology industry in the modern day. Since the 1970s, it has been recognised that studying how people and organisations embrace, accept, and use information systems (IS) and information technologies (IT) is an essential component of software engineering in the field of computer sciences (Momani et al., 2017)

Teng et al., (2022) investigated the factors affecting users' adoption of an educational metaverse platform using an extended UTAUT model and incorporating perceived risk. A survey of 495 respondents was taken, students from a Chinese university and analysed using structural equation modelling. The results from the data revealed that (i) performance expectancy (PE), effort expectancy (EE), social influence (SI), and facilitating conditions (FC) had a significantly positive effects on learners' satisfaction with the Eduverse platform; (ii) learners' satisfaction had a positive effect on their continued usage intention; (iii) learners' intention to use the Eduverse was decreased after they perceived risks. The study reported empirical evidence of the validity of the UTAUT model in amplifying learners' adoption of the Eduverse platform. The findings have considerable practical implications for educational institutions, enterprises, and governments.

The study included a number of shortcomings that call for further fruitful investigation in the future. First off, because Chinese university students were employed in the study, conclusions may not be relevant to students at other educational levels. Therefore, next study may desire to examine the variables impacting students' intentions to continue utilising Eduverse platforms at subsequent levels of educational settings. Second, because women made up the majority of the respondents (68.9%), gender bias may be present in the findings. The proportion of the genders in future research should be more evenly distributed. Thirdly, pupils in the educational environment have little exposure to technology relevant to the metaverse. Those with greater expertise with Eduverse technology should participate in future research, and another approach is to look at how or to what extent the Eduverse influences lesson plans. An experimental group that uses Eduverse technology and a control group that uses conventional educational tools may both be evaluated longitudinally in this situation. Fourth, since students at the same university are exposed to the same hardware, it is presumed that their prior experiences with Eduverse are on par. In order to examine aspects that influence learner satisfaction in the experimental metaverse setting, it is therefore challenging to regulate the level of current relevant experiences. As several studies have demonstrated that users with varying levels of experience placed emphasis differently on the drivers of usage and intention, it is well recognised that experience level is an important moderating variable in technology acceptability and adoption. As a result, additional research on the role of experience is necessary (Teng et al., 2022). Table 6 summarizes the use of technology of adoption theories and models in higher education.

Technology Adoption Models /Theories in Virtual Reality

Virtual reality (VR) offers a variety of uses, but, Sagnier et al., (2020) discovered that just a small number of research have looked at how well-liked this immersive technology is among users. An expanded version of the Technological Acceptance Model (TAM) that takes a closer look at several features of VR is suggested in the study. The TAM was used to generate the model's variables, which drew on user experience, user attributes, and variables unique to VR. The model was tested with 89 individuals who performed an aeronautical assembly exercise in VR. Results show that intention to use VR is positively (+) impacted by perceived usefulness and negatively (-) influenced by cyber-sickness. Moreover, personal inventiveness and hedonic quality-stimulation are indicators of perceived utility. It was observed that pragmatic quality was the sole factor influencing perceived ease of use, which did not significantly affect usage intention. These results therefore have a variety of ramifications for how users will react to virtual reality.

Table 6. Technology of adoption theories and models in higher education

S/N	Author/Title/Year	Model/Theory /Constructs	Findings	Limitation
1.	"Influencing Factors of Usage Intention of Metaverse Education Application Platform: Empirical Evidence Based on PPM and TAM Models" (Wang & Shin, 2022)	"PPM (push–pull–mooring) model and the TAM (technology acceptance model); SEM (structural equation model) and fsQCA (fuzzy-set qualitative comparative analysis)"	The study discovered that the propensity to utilise the metaverse education platform is significantly positively influenced by customised learning, contextualised teaching, perceived utility, perceived ease of use, social needs, and social effect. According to the results, there are three potential guides for improving usage intentions: the experience-led community-driven mode, personality-led community-driven mode, and social-led utility-driven mode.	Time and geographic restrictions applied to this investigation. In the future, methodical study can be conducted over a certain period of time to examine the evolution of the elements that affect users' desire to utilise the platform for metaverse education at various phases. In the future, individuals from various nations might be chosen for study to examine users' cognitive variations when utilising the metaverse education platform across nations.
2.	"Factors Affecting Learners' Adoption of an Educational Metaverse Platform: An Empirical Study Based on an Extended UTAUT Model" (Teng et al., 2022)	"UTAUT"	The results revealed that "(i) performance expectancy, effort expectancy, social influence, and facilitating conditions had significantly positive effects on learners' satisfaction with the Eduverse; (ii) learners' satisfaction had a positive effect on their continued usage intention; (iii) learners' intention to use the Eduverse was reduced after they perceived risks. Our study provided empirical evidence of the validity of the UTAUT model in explaining learners' adoption of the Eduverse."	The use of the metaverse in other industries, such as the entertainment sector, governmental services, the tourist sector, and the agriculture sector, needs further study. Women (68.9%) could be subject to gender prejudice. The Eduverse tools were not widely used by the students that responded to our poll. Further research on the role of experience is warranted.
3.	"A conceptual framework for determining metaverse adoption in higher institutions of gulf area: An empirical study using hybrid SEM-ANN approach" (Akour et al., 2022)	"The conceptual model comprises the adoption properties, namely trialability, observability, compatibility, and complexity, users' satisfaction, personal innovativeness, and Technology Acceptance Model (TAM) constructs. Deep-learning-based analysis of structural equation modelling (SEM) and artificial neural network (ANN)"	Perceived Usefulness (PU) was shown in the study to be a crucial predictor of the factor of users' intention to use the metaverse system (MS).	First, just two important variables—personal innovativeness and user satisfaction—are included in the conceptual model. In order to measure the TAM construct, it was required to restrict it to two constructs—PEOU and PU—and to concentrate on two pertinent characteristics that influence personal innovation. Third, the poll was disseminated via the web and social media, and fourth, the metaverse may be applied in a variety of contexts. The focus of this study is on educational settings because that is where the metaverse system will have the most impact on the teaching and learning environments.
4.	"Metaverse system adoption in education: a systematic literature review" (Alfaisal et al., 2022b)	"Technology Acceptance Model (TAM) SmartPLS (PLS-SEM)"	The primary study findings demonstrated that the Technology Acceptance Model (TAM) is acknowledged as the most often utilised model in predicting people's intentions to support the metaverse system. Additionally, a typical technique for verifying metaverse models was found to be SmartPLS (PLS-SEM). Studying how students embrace or accept the metaverse system and the technology that underpins it is another important aspect of the reviewed research.	At the beginning, just four scientific databases were used. Second, the exclusive focus of this research was the application of IS theories and models to the adoption of the metaverse. Third, only journal papers and conference proceedings were used. Future research may examine additional works.

continues on following page

Table 6. Continued

S/N	Author/Title/Year	Model/Theory /Constructs	Findings	Limitation
5.	"An analysis of the technology acceptance model in understanding university students' behavioral intention to use metaverse technologies" (Misirlis & Bin Munawar, 2023)	"Technology Acceptance Model (TAM) intention to use Attitude (ATT), Perceived Usefulness (PU), Perceived Ease of Use (PE), Self-efficacy (SE) Subjective Norm (SN)"	According to preliminary findings, university students are reluctant to adopt MetaEducation technology. Self-efficacy and Subjective Norm have a favourable impact on attitudes and perceived usefulness, but there is no clear relationship between perceived ease of use or perceived usefulness and attitudes.	The poor connections between the study's constructs, according to the authors, are a result of a lack of understanding of what MetaEducation actually is.
6.	"Prediction of User's Intention to Use Metaverse System in Medical Education: A Hybrid SEM-ML Learning Approach" (Almarzouqi et al., 2022a)	"Technology Acceptance Model (TAM), Personal innovativeness (PI), Perceived Compatibility (PCO), User Satisfaction (US), Perceived Triability (PTR), and Perceived Observability (POB) Machine Learning (ML) algorithms and Structural Equation Modelling (SEM)"	A strong association between PU and PEOU was discovered by the study. The results demonstrate that respondents' perceptions of MS were impacted by personal and technological factors. MS adoption increases with increased PU and PEOU. The study reveals that the US is a crucial factor in predicting users' inclination to use the metaverse (UMS). In order to evaluate the significance and performance of the elements, the current study also uses the Importance Performance Map Analysis (IPMA).	Because it is only dependent on PI and US, the conceptual research model has several limitations. Moreover, only two TAM constructs—PEOU and PU— were employed in the current investigation. A skewed response can also be the result of the questionnaire being sent online. As the study's exclusive focus was on educational settings, its findings might not be relevant in other contexts.
7.	"Factors Affecting Medical Students' Acceptance of the Metaverse System in Medical Training in the United Arab Emirates" (Alawadhi et al., 2022)	A conceptual model comprising the adoption properties of personal innovativeness, perceived enjoyment, and Technology Acceptance Model concepts was utilised.	The relationships between Personal Innovativeness (PI), which is impacted by both perceived ease of use (PEOU) and perceived usefulness (PU), were shown to be statistically significant (PU). More evidence was provided for the statistically significant relationships between perceived enjoyment (EJ), PEOU, and PU. Moreover, PEOU was associated with. Finally, the participants' propensity to adopt the metaverse technology was strongly impacted by PEOU and PU, respectively.	The study has a number of drawbacks, including its sole dependence on the two variables PI and EJ. While the survey URL was circulated on social media, there was a chance that respondents would submit skewed data because the TAM constructs only employed the two constructs of PEOU and PU.
8.	"Factors Affecting the Adoption of Digital Information Technologies in Higher Education: An Empirical Study" (Almaiah et al., 2022)	"Technology Acceptance Model (TAM) and Digital Information in Education (DIE)"	The findings show that users' perceptions of the value of DIE may depend on several extrinsic conditions that improve their experiences of learning and teaching. The user's traits, such as technological preparedness, are vital in determining perceived ease of use. In some cultures, the superior quality of the tutor may further increase perceptions of the technology's perceived usefulness. The intention to adopt technology may also be highly influenced by other variables such as information flow.	This study narrowed its attention to learning environments in schools where DIE significantly affects the atmosphere for teaching and learning. Future writings could focus on monetary or health-related institutions. The conceptual model is first constrained to a subset of external variables that may explicitly correlate with the TAM components. Second, the sample is limited to a group of college students who have selected a variety of majors. Finally, social media and the internet were used to spread the survey.

DISCUSSION AND CONCLUSION

Summary of Findings

Various theories, models, and studies were reviewed in this study to find the critical success factors of adoption of metaverse in education. Several constructs are deployed in the many models such as technology adoption/acceptance models, thus it becomes necessary to define the meaning of the constructs so as give clearer picture of what they represent in the models. Table 7 presents a number of the constructs that can be used for the assessment of metaverse adoption in education.

Table 7. Definitions of Constructs

S/N	Construct	Meaning
1.	Attitude Toward Behaviour	"An individual's positive or negative feelings (evaluative affect) about performing the target behaviour" (Tan, 2013)
2.	Subjective Norm	"The person's perception that most people who are important to him think he should or should not perform the behaviour in question" (Tan, 2013)
3.	Beliefs	"The individual's subjective probability that performing the target behaviour will result the consequence i".
4.	Evaluation	"An implicit evaluative response" to the consequence (Tan, 2013)
5.	Normative Beliefs	"Normative beliefs refer to the perceived behavioural expectations of important referent individuals or groups".
6.	Perceived Behavioural Control	"The perceived ease or difficulty of performing the behaviour". In the context of information systems research, "Perceptions of internal and external constraints on behaviour".
7.	Actual Behavioural Control	"It refers to the extent to which a person has the skills, resources, and other prerequisites needed to perform a given behaviour".
8.	Behavioural Beliefs	"A behavioural belief is the subjective probability that the behaviour will produce a given outcome"
9.	Control Beliefs	"Control beliefs have to do with the perceived presence of factors that may facilitate or impede performance of a behaviours"
10.	Perceived Usefulness	"The degree to which a person believes that using a particular system would enhance his or her job performance" (Venkatesh & Davis, 2000)
11.	Perceived Ease of Use	"The degree to which a person believes that using a particular system would be free of effort" (Venkatesh & Davis, 2000)
12.	Image	"The degree to which use of an innovation is perceived to enhance one's status in one's social system" (Venkatesh & Davis, 2000)
13.	Job Relevance	"Individual's perception regarding the degree to which the target system is relevant to his or her job" (Venkatesh & Davis, 2000)
14.	Output Quality	"The degree to which an individual believes that the system performs his or her job tasks well" (Venkatesh & Davis, 2000)
15.	Result Demonstrability	"Tangibility of the results of using the innovation".(Venkatesh & Davis, 2000)
16.	Experience	"The degree knowledge or skill that individual has in using technologies or particular technology in addition to the period of time with this skill."
17.	Voluntariness	"The extent to which potential adopters perceive the adoption decision to be non-mandatory" (Venkatesh & Davis, 2000)
18.	Job-fit	"The extent to which an individual believes that using (a technology) can enhance the performance of his or her job". (Thompson et al., 1991)
19.	Complexity	"The degree to which an innovation is perceived as relatively difficult to understand and use". (Thompson et al., 1991)
20.	Long-term Consequences	"Outcomes that have a pay-off in the future". (Thompson et al., 1991)

continues on following page

Table 7. Continued

S/N	Construct	Meaning
21.	Affect Towards Use	"Feelings of joy, elation, or pleasure, or depression, disgust, displeasure, or hate associated by an individual with a particular act". (Thompson et al., 1991)
22.	Social Factors	"The individual's internalization of the reference group's subjective culture, and specific interpersonal agreements that the individual has made with others, in specific social situations". (Thompson et al., 1991)
23.	Facilitating Conditions	Objective factors in the environment that observers agree to make an act easy to accomplish. For example, returning items purchased online is facilitated when no fee is charged to return the item. In an information system context, "Provision of support for users of PCs may be one type of facilitating condition that can influence system utilization" (Thompson et al., 1991)
24.	Relative Advantage	"The degree to which an innovation is perceived as being better than its precursor". (Moore and Benbasat, 1991)
25.	Ease of Use	"The degree to which an innovation is perceived as being difficult to use". (Moore and Benbasat, 1991)
26.	Image	"The degree to which use of an innovation is perceived to enhance one's image or status in one's social system". (Moore and Benbasat, 1991)
27.	Visibility	The degree to which one can see others using the system in the organization. (Moore and Benbasat, 1991)
28.	Compatibility	"The degree to which an innovation is perceived as being consistent with the existing values, needs, and past experiences of potential adopters". (Moore and Benbasat, 1991)
29.	Results Demonstrability	"The tangibility of the results of using the innovation, including their observability and communicability". (Moore and Benbasat, 1991)
30.	Voluntariness of Use	"The degree to which use of the innovation is perceived as being voluntary, or of free will". (Moore and Benbasat, 1991)
31.	Extrinsic Motivation	"The perception that users will want to perform an activity because it is perceived to be instrumental in achieving valued outcomes that are distinct from the activity itself, such as improved job performance, pay, or promotions".
32.	Intrinsic Motivation	"The perception that users will want to perform an activity for no apparent reinforcement other than the process of performing the activity per se".
33.	Outcome Expectations Performance	The performance-related consequences of the behaviours. Specifically, performance expectations deal with job-related outcomes.
34.	Outcome Expectations Personal	The personal consequences of the behaviours. Specifically, personal expectations deal with the individual esteem and sense of accomplishment.
35.	Self-efficacy	"Judgment of one's ability to use a technology (e.g., computer) to accomplish a particular job or task".
36.	Affect	"An individual's liking for a particular behaviour (e.g., computer use)".
37.	Anxiety	"Evoking anxious or emotional reactions when it comes to performing a behaviour (e.g., using a computer)".
38.	Usage	The degree of use of the technology.
39.	Innovation	Element is the ideas, practices, or environments that an individual or community encounters for the first time and that individuals or organisations define as new.
40.	Communication channels	Refer to communication between individuals who know about the innovation and those who do not.
41.	Time	Refers to the time that elapses before individuals adopt and begin to use the innovation.
42.	Social system	Means that the diffusion, adoption, or rejection of innovation affects the social system.
43.	Knowledge	This is the step in which the innovation is perceived, and the individual is aware of the innovation.
44.	Persuasion	This is the step in which the individual's attitude toward the innovation decreases and uncertainty about the results of the innovation decreases.
45.	Decision	This is the step in which the individual's behaviour is observed to accept or reject the innovation.
46.	Implementation	This is the step where the individual begins to use the innovation. Although the previous steps are mostly mental processes, this step shows that the individual uses the innovation itself.
47.	Confirmation	In this step, the individual uses the innovation for a short period of time and then continues to use it or discards it permanently.

Source: (Momani et al., 2017; Shehzad et al., 2022)

Metaverse, HCI, and Its Future

The metaverse is a large real time, online computing platform comprised of large-scale individual users with their devices on different platforms. The attainment of this goal depends to a great extent on the application of human-computer interaction (HCI) in the growth and development of the Metaverse, that is, how to supply the user's actions into the digital world. HCI is a method of information trade between a human and a computer in a given way to achieve certain tasks. The fundamental principle of the Metaverse is chiefly to blur and close the boundaries that exist between the virtual world and the real world, enabling users to accomplish anything and everything in the physical world through technological devices in virtual space. This is possible based on human-computer interaction, developed and launched into an online network of virtual worlds. The metaverse as known is a concept and technology that is a combination of many of today's interactive technologies. It vigorously requires HCI-related technology support base, as it involves transmitting human actions to the computer and feeding them into the virtual world. (Tan, 2022).

Science fiction has traditionally included the ability to instantly morph into anything we choose travel to planets that are only imagined to humans and explore. With the wide availability of new technologies, such as augmented and virtual reality, and the rise of free development tools, anyone may now create an alluring, fascinating, and engaging virtual experience place (Makransky & Petersen, 2021).

Metaverses and associated emerging technologies are the new interfaces and platforms that are expected to be used to carry out the many and several types of human-computer interaction. Therefore, it is a new prototype model hinged on technologies such as augmented reality, lifelogging, mirror worlds and virtual worlds (Prieto et al., 2022). Table 8 listed the human computer interaction theories and models which can be used for the assessment of metaverse adoption in education.

Table 8. Human computer interaction theories and models

S/N	Theory/Model/ Author/Year	Area of Application	Constructs
1.	Split Attention Effects (George & Gnanayutham, 2010; Mayer & Moreno, 1998)	Multimedia incorporates animations and text on screen; interaction design	audio and visual elements
2.	Anchored Instruction CTGV (1993, p52) (George & Gnanayutham, 2010)	Psychological	"The use of interactive videodisc technology makes it possible for students to easily explore the content"
3.	GOMS Model (George & Gnanayutham, 2010.; GOMS and Keystroke-Level Model, 2002)	GOMS is a theory of the cognitive skills involved in human-computer tasks.; text editing tasks; planning of interactivity.	"According to the GOMS model, cognitive structure consists of four components: (1) a set of goals, (2) a set of operators, (3) a set of methods for achieving the goals, and (4) a set of selection rules for choosing among competing methods"
4.	Activity Theory Soviet Union in 1920 (Poursoltan et al., 2021)	intelligent and interconnected systems; computer, engineering, social sciences	"Activity, action, and operation; motives, goals, conditions, or context change; object, subject, mediating artifact, community, division of labour, rules outcomes"
5.	Cognitive Model of Trust (Hill et al., 2006)	socio-technical system; software products	"Relationship initiated by trustor; Assess need for relationship; Evaluate reputation; Evaluate power relations; Monitor and assess; experience; Trust and actions"

User experience is one of the Human Computer Interaction (HCI) notions that is frequently contested. It has been observed that the Technological Acceptance Model and user experience models are rarely combined. Of course, research has shown the need for such mixed models, such as in the straightforward setting of a web-based encyclopaedia (Van Schaik & Ling, 2011). Sagnier et al., 2020) documented that to their knowledge, user experience has not yet been combined with Technology Acceptance Model in the context of VR.

Severally, it is shown that researchers have deem it necessary to incorporate or combine two or three theories in their studies to be able get the results or findings they set out to seek. It is very clear that most models are inadequate in their available variables, constructs, and moderators to sufficiently provide studies with enough tools to cover the scope of their research. For example, Yuyang et al, (2023) in research titled A Hybrid SEM – ANN Approach for Intention to Adopt Metaverse Using C-TAM-TPB and IDT in China. The study tried to identify factors affecting university students' intention to adopt or accept the metaverse due to the 4th industrial revolution and the ravaging COVID-19 pandemic in China, based on the integration of C-TAM-TPB model and IDT theory. A questionnaire survey was conducted among the university students and a sample of the valid data was analysed by T - test and SEM – ANN analysis performed. Thus, the combination of the models was applied for effective research outcome (Lai, 2023). Table 9 includes some research that have combination of theories and models in the studies (Shehzad et al., 2022).

Table 9. Research that used combination of theories/models

S/N	Reference	Theory/Model
1.	(Tsai et al., 2013)	DOI + TAM
2.	(Borr, 2015)	TAM + TPB
3.	(Ahmed & Kassem, 2018; Ahuja et al., 2016; Kassem & Succar, 2017)	DOI + INT
4.	(Gong et al., 2019)	TAM + TOE
5.	(Nita, 2014)	DOI + TAM + UTAUT + TPB

The way that humans live has drastically changed as a result of the rapid advancement of wireless technology. For their use at home, they employ complex equipment based on cutting-edge technology. Access to this pricey service is particularly available to those living in contemporary cities throughout the globe. An example of this is how the Indian government declared the development of 100 Smart Towns where residents will reportedly utilise ICT while connected to the internet. Greater use of internet by the citizens would increase more internet penetration and here Internet of Things (IoT) (Al-rawashdeh et al., 2022; P. Keikhosrokiani, 2021; P. Keikhosrokiani & Kamaruddin, 2022) plays a critical role. However, exploiting and tapping into the IoT is small a part of the story. It is indispensable to combine IoT with Artificial Intelligence (AI) (Al Mamun et al., 2022; Asri et al., 2022; Elmi et al., 2023; Fasha et al., 2022; Jafery et al., 2022, 2023; Jinjri et al., 2021; P. Keikhosrokiani, 2022a; P. Keikhosrokiani et al., 2023; P. Keikhosrokiani & Asl, 2022; Kng et al., 2023; Paremeswaran et al., 2022; Sofian et al., 2022a, 2022b; Suhendra et al., 2022; Teoh Yi Zhe & Keikhosrokiani, 2020) in 'Smart Machines' to replicate intelligent behavior (HCI) to arrive at a correct and reliable decision without human intervention. A crucial pre-requisite for the development of information systems is now the integration of AI and IoT technologies. Identification of the elements affecting an information system is crucial for its success.

The metaverse is projected to be the new transaction and marketing universe. Nevertheless, we cannot negate that every transformational change comes with its challenges and benefits. Despite the opportunities and privileges that the metaverse presents to the teeming users, scholars, developers, consumers and various industry actors, several challenges are acknowledged from the study, calling for further research to tackle them. These challenges are classified, namely (a) regulation, (b) security and ethical issues, (c) technical knowledge, (d) design choices, (e) accessibility and health concerns, (f) digital literacy, and (g) sustainability (Tlili et al., 2023). Digitalization is without a doubt one of the most notable changes to occur in the previous 20 years. Numerous companies, institutions, and groups have changed how they operate by using digital or traditional methods. Moreover, corporations, academics, and practitioners have faced both possibilities and problems as a result of the digital transition (Rana et al., 2022; Trunfio & Rossi, 2022). The metaverse system is a kind of technology that has emerged as a result which will change the world from several perspectives including economical, entertainment, engineering, and educational. It is enabled by innovative technologies, which form a crucial part of educational practices. Considering the great advantages, the metaverse system can bring to teaching and learning, this paper explored the factors that are influencing the intentions to the educational world to adopt it (Akour et al., 2022) 2022). The findings of this chapter suggested that users and students' willingness to adopt and to use metaverse is expressively associated and influenced by the innovativeness, along with perceived ease of use and perceived usefulness. Other critical factors that impact consumer behavior towards the acceptability of the metaverse are especially in education include the adoption of new technology by the culture within a given community, the cooperation of colleagues and willingness of the top management of businesses and institutions (Almarzouqi et al., 2022b; Du et al., 2022).

REFERENCES

Abu Madi, A., Ayoubi, R. M., & Alzbaidi, M. (2022). Spotting the Critical Success Factors of Enterprise Resource Planning Implementation in the Context of Public Higher Education Sector. *International Journal of Public Administration*, 1–17. Advance online publication. doi:10.1080/01900692.2022.2085300

Abubakre, M., Zhou, Y., & Zhou, Z. (2022). The impact of information technology culture and personal innovativeness in information technology on digital entrepreneurship success. *Information Technology & People*, *35*(1), 204–231. doi:10.1108/ITP-01-2020-0002

Ahmed, A. L., & Kassem, M. (2018). A unified BIM adoption taxonomy: Conceptual development, empirical validation and application. *Automation in Construction*, *96*, 103–127. doi:10.1016/j.autcon.2018.08.017

Ahuja, R., Jain, M., Sawhney, A., & Arif, M. (2016). Adoption of BIM by architectural firms in India: Technology–organization–environment perspective. *Architectural Engineering and Design Management*, *12*(4), 311–330. doi:10.1080/17452007.2016.1186589

Akour, I. A., Al-Maroof, R. S., Alfaisal, R., & Salloum, S. A. (2022). A conceptual framework for determining metaverse adoption in higher institutions of gulf area: An empirical study using hybrid SEM-ANN approach. *Computers and Education: Artificial Intelligence*, *3*, 100052. Advance online publication. doi:10.1016/j.caeai.2022.100052

Al-Fraihat, D., Joy, M., Masa'deh, R., & Sinclair, J. (2020). Evaluating E-learning systems success: An empirical study. *Computers in Human Behavior*, *102*, 67–86. doi:10.1016/j.chb.2019.08.004

Al Mamun, M. H., Keikhosrokiani, P., Asl, M. P., Anuar, N. A. N., Hadi, N. H. A., & Humida, T. (2022). Sentiment Analysis of the Harry Potter Series Using a Lexicon-Based Approach. In P. Keikhosrokiani & M. Pourya Asl (Eds.), *Handbook of Research on Opinion Mining and Text Analytics on Literary Works and Social Media* (pp. 263–291). IGI Global. doi:10.4018/978-1-7998-9594-7.ch011

Al-Rahmi, W. M., Yahaya, N., Aldraiweesh, A. A., Alamri, M. M., Aljarboa, N. A., Alturki, U., & Aljeraiwi, A. A. (2019). Integrating Technology Acceptance Model with Innovation Diffusion Theory: An Empirical Investigation on Students' Intention to Use E-Learning Systems. *IEEE Access: Practical Innovations, Open Solutions*, *7*, 26797–26809. doi:10.1109/ACCESS.2019.2899368

Al-rawashdeh, M., Keikhosrokiani, P., Belaton, B., Alawida, M., & Zwiri, A. (2022). IoT Adoption and Application for Smart Healthcare: A Systematic Review. *Sensors (Basel)*, *22*(14), 5377. Advance online publication. doi:10.339022145377 PMID:35891056

Alaba, O., Abass, O., & Igwe, E. (2022). Mobile Learning via Mobile Devices in Nigeria Higher Education: Usage Analysis Based on Utaut Model. *The Journal of the Southern Association for Information Systems*, *9*(1), 64–80. doi:10.17705/3JSIS.00022

Alawadhi, M., Alhumaid, K., Almarzooqi, S. Sh. A., Aburayya, A., Salloum, S. A., & Almesmari, W. (2022). Factors Affecting Medical Students. *Acceptance of the Metaverse System in Medical Training in the United Arab Emirates*, *25*. Advance online publication. doi:10.11576eejph

Alfaisal, R., Hashim, H., & Azizan, U. H. (2022). Metaverse system adoption in education: a systematic literature review. *Journal of Computers in Education*. doi:10.1007/s40692-022-00256-6

Almaiah, M. A., Alhumaid, K., Aldhuhoori, A., Alnazzawi, N., Aburayya, A., Alfaisal, R., Salloum, S. A., Lutfi, A., Al Mulhem, A., Alkhdour, T., Awad, A. B., & Shehab, R. (2022). Factors Affecting the Adoption of Digital Information Technologies in Higher Education: An Empirical Study. *Electronics (Switzerland)*, *11*(21), 3572. Advance online publication. doi:10.3390/electronics11213572

Almarzouqi, A., Aburayya, A., & Salloum, S. A. (2022). Prediction of User's Intention to Use Metaverse System in Medical Education: A Hybrid SEM-ML Learning Approach. *IEEE Access: Practical Innovations, Open Solutions*, *10*, 43421–43434. doi:10.1109/ACCESS.2022.3169285

Alqahtani, A. Y., & Rajkhan, A. A. (2020). E-learning critical success factors during the covid-19 pandemic: A comprehensive analysis of e-learning managerial perspectives. *Education Sciences*, *10*(9), 1–16. doi:10.3390/educsci10090216

Alzahrani, A. I., Mahmud, I., Ramayah, T., Alfarraj, O., & Alalwan, N. (2017). Extending the theory of planned behavior (TPB) to explain online game playing among Malaysian undergraduate students. *Telematics and Informatics*, *34*(4), 239–251. doi:10.1016/j.tele.2016.07.001

Arpaci, I., Karatas, K., Kusci, I., & Al-Emran, M. (2022). Understanding the social sustainability of the Metaverse by integrating UTAUT2 and big five personality traits: A hybrid SEM-ANN approach. *Technology in Society*, *71*, 102120. Advance online publication. doi:10.1016/j.techsoc.2022.102120

Ashworth, S. J. (2020). *The evolution of facility management (FM) in the building information modelling (BIM) process: An opportunity to use critical success factors (CSF) for optimising built assets.* Academic Press.

Asri, M. A. Z. B. M., Keikhosrokiani, P., & Asl, M. P. (2022). Opinion Mining Using Topic Modeling: A Case Study of Firoozeh Dumas's Funny in Farsi in Goodreads. In F. Saeed, F. Mohammed, & F. Ghaleb (Eds.), *Advances on Intelligent Informatics and Computing* (pp. 219–230). Springer International Publishing. doi:10.1007/978-3-030-98741-1_19

Atıcı, U., Adem, A., Şenol, M. B., & Dağdeviren, M. (2022). A comprehensive decision framework with interval valued type-2 fuzzy AHP for evaluating all critical success factors of e-learning platforms. *Education and Information Technologies*, *27*(5), 5989–6014. doi:10.100710639-021-10834-3 PMID:35095324

Blumler, J. G. (n.d.). *The role of theory in uses and gratifications studies.* Academic Press.

Borr, M. L. (2015). Miller, M.D. (2014). Minds Online: Teaching Effectively with Technology. Cambridge, MA: Harvard University Press. ISBN: 978-0674368248. 279 pp. (hardcover). *Family and Consumer Sciences Research Journal*, *44*(2), 234–236. doi:10.1111/fcsr.12137

Buabeng-Andoh, C. (2018). Predicting students' intention to adopt mobile learning. *Journal of Research in Innovative Teaching & Learning*, *11*(2), 178–191. doi:10.1108/JRIT-03-2017-0004

Bullen, C. V, & Rockart, J. F. (1981). *A primer on critical success factors.* Academic Press.

Carayannis, E. G., & Morawska-Jancelewicz, J. (2022). The Futures of Europe: Society 5.0 and Industry 5.0 as Driving Forces of Future Universities. *Journal of the Knowledge Economy*, *13*(4), 3445–3471. doi:10.100713132-021-00854-2

Carr, A. R. (1999). *Predicting College of Agriculture professors' adoption of computers and distance education technologies for self-education and teaching at the University of Guadalajara.* Iowa State University.

Castro-Lopez, A., Cervero, A., Galve-González, C., Puente, J., & Bernardo, A. B. (2022). Evaluating critical success factors in the permanence in Higher Education using multi-criteria decision-making. *Higher Education Research & Development*, *41*(3), 628–646. doi:10.1080/07294360.2021.1877631

Chaiya, C., & Ahmad, M. M. (2021). Success or failure of the thai higher education development— Critical factors in the policy process of quality assurance. *Sustainability (Switzerland)*, *13*(17), 9486. Advance online publication. doi:10.3390u13179486

Chatterjee, S., Kar, A. K., & Gupta, M. P. (2018). Success of IoT in Smart Cities of India: An empirical analysis. *Government Information Quarterly*, *35*(3), 349–361. doi:10.1016/j.giq.2018.05.002

Chittipaka, V., Kumar, S., Sivarajah, U., Bowden, J. L. H., & Baral, M. M. (2022). Blockchain Technology for Supply Chains operating in emerging markets: An empirical examination of technology-organization-environment (TOE) framework. *Annals of Operations Research*. Advance online publication. doi:10.100710479-022-04801-5

Clark, J.-A., Liu, Y., & Isaias, P. (n.d.). Critical success factors for implementing learning analytics in higher education: A mixed-method inquiry. In Australasian Journal of Educational Technology (Vol. 2020, Issue 6). doi:10.14742/ajet.6164

DeLone, W. H., & McLean, E. R. (2016). Information Systems Success Measurement. *Foundations and Trends® in Information Systems, 2*(1), 1–116. doi:10.1561/2900000005

Du, H., Ma, B., Niyato, D., Kang, J., Xiong, Z., & Yang, Z. (2022). *Rethinking Quality of Experience for Metaverse Services: A Consumer-based Economics Perspective.* https://arxiv.org/abs/2208.01076

Elciyar, K., & Simsek, A. (2021). An investigation of cyberloafing in a large-scale technology organization from the perspective of the theory of interpersonal behavior. *Online Journal of Communication and Media Technologies, 11*(2), e202106. Advance online publication. doi:10.30935/ojcmt/10823

Elmi, A. H., Keikhosrokiani, P., & Asl, M. P. (2023). A Machine Learning Approach to the Analytics of Representations of Violence in Khaled Hosseini's Novels. In P. Keikhosrokiani & M. Pourya Asl (Eds.), *Handbook of Research on Artificial Intelligence Applications in Literary Works and Social Media* (pp. 36–67). IGI Global. doi:10.4018/978-1-6684-6242-3.ch003

Eng, N. (2020). Impression Management After Image-Threatening Events. *The Journal of Public Interest Communications, 4*(2), 32. doi:10.32473/jpic.v4.i2.p32

Ezimmuo, C. M., & Keikhosrokiani, P. (2022). Predicting Consumer Behavior Change Towards Using Online Shopping in Nigeria: The Impact of the COVID-19 Pandemic. In P. Keikhosrokiani (Ed.), *Handbook of Research on Consumer Behavior Change and Data Analytics in the Socio-Digital Era* (pp. 210–254). IGI Global. doi:10.4018/978-1-6684-4168-8.ch010

Farjami, S., Taguchi, R., Nakahira, K. T., Fukumura, Y., & Kanematsu, H. (2011). W-02 Problem Based Learning for Materials Science Education in Metaverse. *JSEE Annual Conference International Session Proceedings, 2011*, 20–23. 10.20549/jseeen.2011.0_20

Fasha, E. F. B. K., Keikhosrokiani, P., & Asl, M. P. (2022). Opinion Mining Using Sentiment Analysis: A Case Study of Readers' Response on Long Litt Woon's The Way Through the Woods in Goodreads. In F. Saeed, F. Mohammed, & F. Ghaleb (Eds.), *Advances on Intelligent Informatics and Computing* (pp. 231–242). Springer International Publishing. doi:10.1007/978-3-030-98741-1_20

Fernandes, J., Machado, C., & Amaral, L. (2022). Identifying critical success factors for the General Data Protection Regulation implementation in higher education institutions. *Digital Policy, Regulation & Governance, 24*(4), 355–379. doi:10.1108/DPRG-03-2021-0041

Fong Yew, O., & Jambulingam, M. (2015). Critical Success Factors of E-learning Implementation at Educational Institutions. In Journal of Interdisciplinary Research in Education (Vol. 5, Issue 1).

Francescatto, M., Neuenfeldt Júnior, A., Kubota, F. I., Guimarães, G., & de Oliveira, B. (2023). Lean Six Sigma case studies literature overview: critical success factors and difficulties. In International Journal of Productivity and Performance Management (Vol. 72, Issue 1, pp. 1–23). Emerald Publishing. doi:10.1108/IJPPM-12-2021-0681

George, J., & Gnanayutham, P. (2010). Human computer interaction and theories. In M. Sarrafzadeh & P. Petratos (Eds.), *Strategic advantage of computing information systems in enterprise management* (pp. 255–272). Atiner.

Gim, G., Bae, H., & Kang, S. (2022). Metaverse Learning: The Relationship among Quality of VR-Based Education, Self-Determination, and Learner Satisfaction. *Proceedings - 2022 IEEE/ACIS 7th International Conference on Big Data, Cloud Computing, and Data Science, BCD 2022*, 279–284. 10.1109/BCD54882.2022.9900629

Gong, P., Zeng, N., Ye, K., & König, M. (2019). An Empirical Study on the Acceptance of 4D BIM in EPC Projects in China. *Sustainability (Switzerland), 11*(5). doi:10.3390/su11051316

Gregor, S. (2006). The Nature of Theory in Information Systems The Nature of Theory in Information Systems. *Management Information Systems Quarterly, 30*(3).

Han, H.-C. (2020). From Visual Culture in the Immersive Metaverse to Visual Cognition in Education. In R. Z. Zheng (Ed.), *Cognitive and Affective Perspectives on Immersive Technology in Education* (pp. 67–84). IGI Global. doi:10.4018/978-1-7998-3250-8.ch004

Hill, C. A., & O'Hara, A. (2006). *A Cognitive Theory of Trust* (Vol. 84). Academic Press.

Humida, T., Al Mamun, M. H., & Keikhosrokiani, P. (2021). Predicting behavioral intention to use e-learning system: A case-study in Begum Rokeya University, Rangpur, Bangladesh. *Education and Information Technologies*. doi:10.1007/s10639-021-10707-9

Jafery, N. N., Keikhosrokiani, P., & Asl, M. P. (2022). Text Analytics Model to Identify the Connection Between Theme and Sentiment in Literary Works: A Case Study of Iraqi Life Writings. In P. Keikhosrokiani & M. Pourya Asl (Eds.), Handbook of Research on Opinion Mining and Text Analytics on Literary Works and Social Media (pp. 173–190). IGI Global. doi:10.4018/978-1-7998-9594-7.ch0088

Jafery, N. N., Keikhosrokiani, P., & Asl, M. P. (2023). An Artificial Intelligence Application of Theme and Space in Life Writings of Middle Eastern Women: A Topic Modelling and Sentiment Analysis Approach. In P. Keikhosrokiani & M. Pourya Asl (Eds.), Handbook of Research on Artificial Intelligence Applications in Literary Works and Social Media (pp. 19–35). IGI Global. doi: 10.4018/978-1-6684-6242-3.ch002

Jeong, M., Zo, H., Lee, C. H., & Ceran, Y. (2019). Feeling displeasure from online social media postings: A study using cognitive dissonance theory. *Computers in Human Behavior, 97*, 231–240. doi: 10.1016/j.chb.2019.02.021

Jeyaraj, A. (2020). DeLone & McLean models of information system success: Critical meta-review and research directions. *International Journal of Information Management, 54*. doi:10.1016/j.ijinfomgt.2020.102139

Jinjri, W. M., Keikhosrokiani, P., & Abdullah, N. L. (2021). Machine Learning Algorithms for The Classification of Cardiovascular Disease- A Comparative Study. *2021 International Conference on Information Technology (ICIT)*, 132–138. doi:10.1109/ICIT52682.2021.9491677

Kanematsu, H., Kobayashi, T., Ogawa, N., Barry, D. M., Fukumura, Y., & Nagai, H. (2013). Eco Car Project for Japan Students as a Virtual PBL Class. *Procedia Computer Science*, *22*, 828–835. doi: 10.1016/j.procs.2013.09.165

Kang, Y., Choi, N., & Kim, S. (2021). Searching for New Model of Digital Informatics for Human-Computer Interaction: Testing the Institution-Based Technology Acceptance Model (ITAM). *International Journal of Environmental Research and Public Health*, *18*(11). doi: 10.3390/ijerph18115593

Kassem, M., & Succar, B. (2017). Macro BIM adoption: Comparative market analysis. *Automation in Construction*, *81*, 286–299. doi: 10.1016/j.autcon.2017.04.005

Keikhosrokiani, P. (2020a). *Behavioral intention to use of Mobile Medical Information System (mMIS)*. Academic Press. doi:10.1016/B978-0-12-817657-3.00004-3

Keikhosrokiani, P. (2020b). *Success factors of mobile medical information system (mMIS)*. Academic Press. doi:10.1016/B978-0-12-817657-3.00005-5

Keikhosrokiani, P. (2021). IoT for enhanced decision-making in medical information systems: A systematic review. In G. Marques, A. Kumar Bhoi, I. de la Torre Díez, & B. Garcia-Zapirain (Eds.), Enhanced Telemedicine and e-Health: Advanced IoT Enabled Soft Computing Framework (Vol. 410, pp. 119–140). Springer International Publishing. doi:10.1007/978-3-030-70111-6_6

Keikhosrokiani, P. (2022a). Big Data Analytics for Healthcare: Datasets, Techniques, Life Cycles, Management, and Applications. Elsevier Science. doi:10.1016/C2021-0-00369-2

Keikhosrokiani, P. (2022b). Handbook of Research on Consumer Behavior Change and Data Analytics in the Socio-Digital Era. IGI Global. doi: 10.4018/978-1-6684-4168-8

Keikhosrokiani, P., Naidu, A. B., Iryanti Fadilah, S., Manickam, S., & Li, Z. (2023). Heartbeat sound classification using a hybrid adaptive neuro-fuzzy inferences system (ANFIS) and artificial bee colony. *Digital Health, 9*. doi:10.1177/20552076221150741

Keikhosrokiani, P., & Asl, M. P. (2022). Handbook of research on opinion mining and text analytics on literary works and social media. IGI Global. doi:10.4018/978-1-7998-9594-7

Keikhosrokiani, P., & Kamaruddin, N. S. A. B. (2022). IoT-Based In-Hospital-In-Home Heart Disease Remote Monitoring System with Machine Learning Features for Decision Making. In S. Mishra, A. González-Briones, A. K. Bhoi, P. K. Mallick, & J. M. Corchado (Eds.), Connected e-Health: Integrated IoT and Cloud Computing (pp. 349–369). Springer International Publishing. doi: 10.1007/978-3-030-97929-4_16

Keikhosrokiani, P., Kianpisheh, A., Zakaria, N., Limtrairut, P., Mustaffa, N., & Sarwar, M. I. (2012). A Proposal to Measure Success Factors for Location-Based Mobile Cardiac Telemedicine System (LMCTS). *International Journal of Smart Home*, *6*(3).

Keikhosrokiani, P., Mustaffa, N., & Zakaria, N. (2018). Success factors in developing iHeart as a patient-centric healthcare system: A multi-group analysis. *Telematics and Informatics, 35*(4). doi:10.1016/j.tele.2017.11.006

Keikhosrokiani, P., Mustaffa, N., Zakaria, N., & Abdullah, R. (2019). Assessment of a medical information system: the mediating role of use and user satisfaction on the success of human interaction with the mobile healthcare system (iHeart). *Cognition, Technology and Work*. doi:10.1007/s10111-019-00565-4

Keikhosrokiani, P., Mustaffa, N., Zakaria, N., & Baharudin, A. S. (2019). User Behavioral Intention Toward Using Mobile Healthcare System. In *Consumer-Driven Technologies in Healthcare: Breakthroughs in Research and Practice* (pp. 429–444). IGI Global. doi:10.4018/978-1-5225-6198-9.ch022

Kesharwani, A. (2020). Do (how) digital natives adopt a new technology differently than digital immigrants? A longitudinal study. *Information & Management, 57*(2). doi:10.1016/j.im.2019.103170

Kng, C. K., Keikhosrokiani, P., & Asl, M. P. (2023). Artificial Intelligence and Human Rights Activism: A Case Study of Boochani's No Friend But the Mountains and His Tweets on Justice and Equality. In P. Keikhosrokiani & M. Pourya Asl (Eds.), Handbook of Research on Artificial Intelligence Applications in Literary Works and Social Media (pp. 114–141). IGI Global. doi:10.4018/978-1-6684-6242-3.ch006

Kokkinou, A., & van Kollenburg, T. (2022). Critical success factors of Lean in Higher Education: an international perspective. *International Journal of Lean Six Sigma*. doi:10.1108/IJLSS-04-2022-0076

König, C. M., Karrenbauer, C., & Breitner, M. H. (2022). Critical success factors and challenges for individual digital study assistants in higher education: A mixed methods analysis. *Education and Information Technologies*. doi:10.1007/s10639-022-11394-w

Kopp, T., Riekert, M., & Utz, S. (2018). When cognitive fit outweighs cognitive load: Redundant data labels in charts increase accuracy and speed of information extraction. *Computers in Human Behavior, 86*, 367–376. doi: 10.1016/j.chb.2018.04.037

Lateef, M., & Keikhosrokiani, P. (2022). Predicting Critical Success Factors of Business Intelligence Implementation for Improving SMEs' Performances: A Case Study of Lagos State, Nigeria. *Journal of the Knowledge Economy*. doi:10.1007/s13132-022-00961-8

MacIel-Monteon, M., Limon-Romero, J., Gastelum-Acosta, C., Tlapa, Di., Baez-Lopez, Y., & Solano-Lamphar, H. A. (2020). Measuring Critical Success Factors for Six Sigma in Higher Education Institutions: Development and Validation of a Surveying Instrument. *IEEE Access: Practical Innovations, Open Solutions, 8*, 1813–1823. doi: 10.1109/ACCESS.2019.2962521

Makransky, G., & Petersen, G. B. (2021). The Cognitive Affective Model of Immersive Learning (CAMIL): A Theoretical Research-Based Model of Learning in Immersive Virtual Reality. *Educational Psychology Review, 33*(3), 937–958.

Mayer, R. E., & Moreno, R. (n.d.). *Multimedia learning 1 A Cognitive Theory of Multimedia Learning: Implications for Design Principles*. Academic Press.

McLeod, A., & Dolezel, D. (2022). Information security policy non-compliance: Can capitulation theory explain user behaviors? *Computers and Security, 112*. doi:10.1016/j.cose.2021.102526

Milic, S., & Simeunovic, V. (2021). Exploring e-learning critical success factors in digitally underdeveloped countries during the first wave of the COVID-19. *Interactive Learning Environments*. doi:10.1080/10494820.2021.1990965

Misirlis, N., & Bin Munawar, H. (n.d.). *An analysis of the technology acceptance model in understanding university students' behavioral intention to use metaverse technologies*. Academic Press.

Momani, A. M., Jamous, M., & Jamous, M. M. (2017). The Evolution of Technology Acceptance Theories. In *International Journal of Contemporary Computer Research (IJCCR)* (Vol. 1, Issue 1). https://www.researchgate.net/publication/316644779

Moon, J.-W., An, Y., & Norman, W. (2022). Exploring the application of the uses and gratifications theory as a conceptual model for identifying the motivations for smartphone use by e-tourists. *Tourism Critiques: Practice and Theory, 3*(2), 102–119. doi:10.1108/trc-03-2022-0005

Mostafa, L. (n.d.). *Measuring Technology Acceptance Model to use Metaverse Technology in Egypt*. https://jsst.journals.ekb.eg

Abdul Aziz, M. N., Harun, S., Baharom, M., & Kamaruddin, N. (2020). The Evolution of The Technology Acceptance Model (TAM). 242.

Nita, K. (2014). Building Information Modelling Penetration Factors in Malaysia. *International Journal of Advances in Applied Sciences, 3*(1), 47–56.

Oliver, R. L. (1980). A congitive model of the antecedents and consequences of satisfaction decisions. In Journal of Marketing Research (Vol. 17). Academic Press.

Paremeswaran, P., Keikhosrokiani, P., & Asl, M. P. (2022). Opinion Mining of Readers' Responses to Literary Prize Nominees on Twitter: A Case Study of Public Reaction to the Booker Prize (2018–2020). In F. Saeed, F. Mohammed, & F. Ghaleb (Eds.), *Advances on Intelligent Informatics and Computing* (pp. 243–257). Springer International Publishing. doi:10.1007/978-3-030-98741-1_21

Peltokorpi, V., & Hood, A. C. (2019). Communication in Theory and Research on Transactive Memory Systems: A Literature Review. *Topics in Cognitive Science, 11*(4), 644–667. doi:10.1111/tops.12359

Pettersson, F. (2021). Understanding digitalization and educational change in school by means of activity theory and the levels of learning concept. *Education and Information Technologies, 26*(1), 187–204. doi:10.1007/s10639-020-10239-8

Poursoltan, M., Pinède, N., Traore, M. K., & Vallespir, B. (2021). A new descriptive, theoretical framework for cyber-physical and human systems based on activity theory. *IFAC-PapersOnLine, 54*(1), 918–923. doi:10.1016/j.ifacol.2021.08.109

Priatna, T., Maylawati, D. S., Sugilar, H., & Ramdhani, M. A. (2020). Key success factors of e-learning implementation in higher education. *International Journal of Emerging Technologies in Learning, 15*(17), 101–114. doi:10.3991/ijet.v15i17.14293

Prieto, J. de la F., Lacasa, P., & Martínez-Borda, R. (2022). Approaching metaverses: Mixed reality interfaces in youth media platforms. *New Techno Humanities*. doi:10.1016/j.techum.2022.04.004

Puleng Modise, M., & Van Den Berg, G. (n.d.). *Covid-19 as an Accelerator for Training and Technology Adoption by Academics in Large-Scale Open and Distance Learning Institutions in Africa*. doi:10.25159/UnisaRxiv/000016.v1

Rabaai, A. (2009). Identifying critical success factors of ERP Systems at the higher education sector. In *Proceedings of the Third International Symposium on Innovation in Information and Communication Technology* (pp. 133-147). British Computer Society.

Rana, S., Udunuwara, M., Dewasiri, N. J., Kashif, M., & Rathnasiri, M. S. H. (2022). Editorial: Is South Asia ready for the next universe – metaverse? Arguments and suggestions for further research. *South Asian Journal of Marketing*, *3*(2), 77–81. doi:10.1108/sajm-10-2022-141

Rockart, J. F. (1982). *The changing role of the information systems executive: A critical success factors perspective*. Academic Press.

Rogers, E. M., & Singhal, A. (2003). Empowerment and Communication: Lessons Learned From Organizing for Social Change. *Annals of the International Communication Association*, *27*(1), 67–85. doi:10.1080/23808985.2003.11679022

Sagnier, C., Loup-Escande, E., Lourdeaux, D., Thouvenin, I., & Valléry, G. (2020). User Acceptance of Virtual Reality: An Extended Technology Acceptance Model. *International Journal of Human-Computer Interaction*, *36*(11), 993–1007. doi:10.1080/10447318.2019.1708612

Sahin, I. (2006). Detailed review of rogers' diffusion of innovations theory and educational technology-related studies based on rogers' theory. In The Turkish Online Journal of Educational Technology (Vol. 5). Academic Press.

Saykili, A. (2019). Higher Education in The Digital Age: The Impact of Digital Connective Technologies. *Journal of Educational Technology and Online Learning*, 1–15. doi:10.31681/jetol.516971

Sela, E., & Sivan, Y. (2009). Enterprise e-learning success factors: An analysis of practitioners' perspective (with a downturn addendum). *Interdisciplinary Journal of E-Learning and Learning Objects*, *5*(1), 335–343.

Shatat, A. S., & Shatat, A. S. (2021). Virtual migration of higher education institutions in times of crisis: Major challenges and critical success factors. *Human Systems Management*, *40*(5), 653–667. doi:10.3233/HSM-201160

Shehzad, H. M. F., Ibrahim, R., Khaidzir, K. A. M., Alrefai, N., Chweya, R. K., Zrekat, M. M. Y., & Hassan, O. H. A. (2022). A Literature Review of Technology Adoption theories and Acceptance models for novelty in Building Information Modeling. *Journal of Information Technology Management*, *14*, 83–113.

Shen, X. L., Li, Y. J., & Sun, Y. (2018). Wearable health information systems intermittent discontinuance: A revised expectation-disconfirmation model. *Industrial Management & Data Systems*, *118*(3), 506–523. doi:10.1108/IMDS-05-2017-0222

Shen, Z., Tan, S., & Siau, K. (2018). Challenges in learning unified modeling language: From the perspective of diagrammatic representation and reasoning. *Communications of the Association for Information Systems*, *43*(1), 545–565. doi:10.17705/1CAIS.04330

Sofian, N. B., Keikhosrokiani, P., & Asl, M. P. (2022a). Opinion mining and text analytics of reader reviews of Yoko Ogawa's The Housekeeper and the Professor in Goodreads. In P. Keikhosrokiani & M. Pourya Asl (Eds.), Handbook of Research on Opinion Mining and Text Analytics on Literary Works and Social Media (pp. 240–262). IGI Global. doi:10.4018/978-1-7998-9594-7.ch010

Sofian, N. B., Keikhosrokiani, P., & Asl, M. P. (2022b). Opinion Mining and Text Analytics of Reader Reviews of Yoko Ogawa's The Housekeeper and the Professor in Goodreads. In P. Keikhosrokiani & M. Pourya Asl (Eds.), Handbook of Research on Opinion Mining and Text Analytics on Literary Works and Social Media (pp. 240–262). IGI Global. doi:10.4018/978-1-7998-9594-7.ch010

Soleimani, S. M., Jaeger, M., Faheiman, A., & Alaqqad, A. R. (2022). Success factors of recently implemented eLearning methods at higher education institutions in Kuwait. *Quality in Higher Education*. doi:10.1080/13538322.2022.2132702

Sony, M., & Naik, S. (2020). Industry 4.0 integration with socio-technical systems theory: A systematic review and proposed theoretical model. *Technology in Society, 61*. doi:10.1016/j.techsoc.2020.101248

Stair, R., & Reynolds, G. (2020). *Principles of information systems*. Cengage Learning.

Suhendra, N. H. B., Keikhosrokiani, P., Asl, M. P., & Zhao, X. (2022). Opinion Mining and Text Analytics of Literary Reader Responses: A Case Study of Reader Responses to KL Noir Volumes in Goodreads Using Sentiment Analysis and Topic. In P. Keikhosrokiani & M. Pourya Asl (Eds.), Handbook of Research on Opinion Mining and Text Analytics on Literary Works and Social Media (pp. 191–239). IGI Global. doi: 10.4018/978-1-7998-9594-7.ch009

Szymkowiak, A., Melović, B., Dabić, M., Jeganathan, K., & Kundi, G. S. (2021). Information technology and Gen Z: The role of teachers, the internet, and technology in the education of young people. *Technology in Society, 65*. doi:10.1016/j.techsoc.2021.101565

Taherdoost, H. (2018). A review of technology acceptance and adoption models and theories. *Procedia Manufacturing, 22*, 960–967. doi:10.1016/j.promfg.2018.03.137

Tan, P. J. B. (2013). Applying the UTAUT to understand factors affecting the use of english e-learning websites in Taiwan. *SAGE Open, 3*(4). doi:10.1177/2158244013503837

Tan, Z. (2022). *Metaverse*. HCI, and Its Future.

Teng, Z., Cai, Y., Gao, Y., Zhang, X., & Li, X. (2022). Factors Affecting Learners' Adoption of an Educational Metaverse Platform: An Empirical Study Based on an Extended UTAUT Model. *Mobile Information Systems*. doi:10.1155/2022/5479215

Teoh Yi Zhe, I., & Keikhosrokiani, P. (2020). Knowledge workers mental workload prediction using optimised ELANFIS. *Applied Intelligence*. doi:10.1007/s10489-020-01928-5

Thompson, R. L., Hlgglns, C. A., & Howell, J. M. (n.d.). *Utilization of Personal Computers Personal Computing: Toward a Conceptual Model of Utilization*. Academic Press.

Tlili, A., Huang, R., & Kinshuk. (2023). Metaverse for climbing the ladder toward 'Industry 5.0' and 'Society 5.0'? *Service Industries Journal*. doi:10.1080/02642069.2023.2178644

Toraman, Y. (2018). *User Acceptance of Metaverse: Insights from Technology Acceptance Model (TAM) and Planned Behavior Theory (PBT), 7*(2). doi:10.5195/emaj.2018.134

Triandis, H. C. (1978). 43 Cross-Cultural Social and Personality Psychologyl The paper will provide, first, definitions of ecology and the subsistence, cultural, social, individual, interindividual and projective systems. Second, the most plausible dimensions along which such systems. In *Triandis and Brislin.* Przeworski and Teune.

Trunfio, M., & Rossi, S. (2022). Advances in Metaverse Investigation: Streams of Research and Future Agenda. *Virtual Worlds, 1*(2), 103–129. doi:10.3390/virtualworlds1020007

Tsai, J. T., Fang, J. C., & Chou, J. H. (2013). Optimized task scheduling and resource allocation on cloud computing environment using improved differential evolution algorithm. *Computers & Operations Research, 40*(12), 3045–3055. doi:10.1016/j.cor.2013.06.012

VanDerSchaaf, H., & Daim, T. (2020). Critical Factors Related to Student Success Technology. *International Journal of Innovation and Technology Management, 17*(06), 2050045. doi:10.1142/S0219877020500455

Van Schaik, P., & Ling, J. (2011). An integrated model of interaction experience for information retrieval in a Web-based encyclopaedia. *Interacting with Computers, 23*(1), 18–32. doi:10.1016/j.intcom.2010.07.002

Venkatesh, V., & Bala, H. (2008). Technology acceptance model 3 and a research agenda on interventions. *Decision Sciences, 39*(2), 273–315. doi:10.1111/j.1540-5915.2008.00192.x

Venkatesh, V., & Davis, F. D. (2000). Theoretical extension of the Technology Acceptance Model: Four longitudinal field studies. *Management Science, 46*(2), 186–204. doi:10.1287/mnsc.46.2.186.11926

Wang, G., & Shin, C. (2022). Influencing Factors of Usage Intention of Metaverse Education Application Platform: Empirical Evidence Based on PPM and TAM Models. *Sustainability (Switzerland), 14*(24). doi:10.3390/su142417037

Wisdom, J. P., Chor, K. H. B., Hoagwood, K. E., & Horwitz, S. M. (2014). Innovation adoption: A review of theories and constructs. *Administration and Policy in Mental Health, 41*(4), 480–502. doi:10.1007/s10488-013-0486-4

Wu, C., Huang, S., & Yuan, Q. (2022). Seven important theories in information system empirical research: A systematic review and future directions. *Data and Information Management, 6*(1). doi:10.1016/J.DIM.2022.100006

Yadegari, M., Mohammadi, S., & Masoumi, A. H. (2022). Technology adoption: an analysis of the major models and theories. *Technology Analysis and Strategic Management.* doi:10.1080/09537325.2022.2071255

Yu, C. W., Chao, C. M., Chang, C. F., Chen, R. J., Chen, P. C., & Liu, Y. X. (2021). Exploring Behavioral Intention to Use a Mobile Health Education Website: An Extension of the UTAUT 2 Model. *SAGE Open, 11*(4). doi:10.1177/21582440211055721

Chapter 10
Understanding User Experience in the Metaverse

Rajeshwari Krishnamurthy
Great Lakes Institute of Management, Chennai, India

Shagun Trivedi
Great Lakes Institute of Management, Chennai, India

ABSTRACT

Despite its growing popularity, the understanding of user experience in the metaverse is limited. In-depth interviews were conducted in a comparative context between gamers and metaverse users to understand their experience in the medium, and NVivo software was used to analyze the findings with Csikszentmihalyi's flow theory as a framework. While most of the flow antecedents and flow outcomes were intact, the 'skill' aspect of flow seems to be different in metaverse, compared to gaming. Aspects such as ease of use, speed, vividness were felt highly by those familiar with metaverse, whereas the gamers more frequently used the medium and found it stimulating and trustworthy. The study offers rich perspectives for metaverse designers, ad agencies, marketing practitioners, and media personnel.

INTRODUCTION

The idea of the Metaverse is intricate. The phrase has expanded in recent years beyond Stephenson's *Snow Crash* (1992) concept of an immersive 3D virtual world to encompass elements of the actual world. This includes objects, actors, interfaces, and networks that create and engage with virtual worlds. One of the definitions of the Metaverse reads as follows: the merging of 1) virtually improved physical reality and 2) physically persistent virtual space is known as the metaverse. It combines the two while giving people the option to perceive it in any manner. The major dimensions of the Metaverse are augmentation, simulation, external and intimate (Songlee & Yangjin, 2021). Virtual worlds, mirror worlds, augmented reality, and lifelogging are the four main elements of the future of the Metaverse resulted from the combination of augmentation and simulation. *Virtual worlds* (VW) enhance economic and social life of communities in the actual world (Hendaoui et al., 2008; Papagiannidls et al; 2008). Users' avatars that

DOI: 10.4018/978-1-6684-7029-9.ch010

serve as the users' personification in VW are a crucial part in the Metaverse. The social and economic capacities of avatar can advance more quickly here (Songlee & Yangjin, 2021; Lee et al., 2011). *Mirror worlds* (MW) are virtual representations of the real world that is virtually enhanced models and actual "reflections" of the physical world. Their creation uses cutting-edge geospatial, virtual modeling, annotation, and lifelogging tools as well as other sensors (Lee et al., 2011). *Augmented reality* (AR) uses location-aware systems and interfaces to process network layers of information on top of our ordinary vision of the world to improve people's perception of physical environments. (Adner and Kapoor, 2010). The goal of *lifelogging* is to enhance object and self-memory, observation, and behaviour modelling by recording and reporting objects' and users' intimate states and life histories (Chu & Choi, 2011; Chung et al., 2017; Kang & Schuett, 2013). The Bored Ape franchise's US-based creator, Yuga Labs, has reportedly raised

$320 million from the sale of 55,000 virtual plots of land in the other side metaverse, bringing down Ethereum network in the process.

The Metaverse may also be thought of as a virtual representation of the world that we live in. Users interact with one another and their surroundings, which replicate the real world, using avatars that mirror them and duplicate their actions in this three-dimensional digital environment. By 2026, Gartner, Inc. predicts that 25% of people will spend at least one hour per day engaging in work, shopping, learning, socialising, and doing entertainment activities in the metaverse (Rimol, 2022). Users may interact with friends in the metaverse, buy and sell digital goods, travel virtually to fully built or analogous real-world locales, and much more. Only the user's imagination serves as a limit in the metaverse's universe of boundless possibilities (Mileva, 2022). It is anticipated that it will have a significant influence on several industries including marketing, fashion, technology, and gaming in the future. Before accessing the metaverse, which combines the worlds of physical reality with digital virtuality, it is essential to have knowledge of the medium. The authors of "Metaverse - the new marketing universe" (Hollensen et al., 2022) claim that the Metaverse will not entirely replace the Internet or social media networks, but rather build upon and continuously change them into a virtual 3D social media world consisting of many new and fascinating user experiences.

The metaverse, according to some critics (Robertson, 2021; Wankhede, 2022; MacDonald, 2022), is a vague concept that virtually signifies nothing even within science fiction. The term "metaverse" is only a lofty term for a certain sort of virtual or augmented reality activity in its most basic form (Bogost, 2021). The mystery that surrounds the metaverse has led to a fair amount of skepticism about it. The lack of a tangible product or goal means that the notion is perhaps nothing more than a trendy phrase. Despite the advantages that have been associated with the metaverse, there is not one yet that is open and linked. This shows that, in contrast to well-established and well-defined technologies, these technologies are typically either hypotheses or early prototypes.

Because most customers nowadays are homogeneous and there is fierce competition in both local and global marketplaces, merely satisfying them with the best products and services is no longer adequate (Israfilzade, 2021). The typical user could infer that in the metaverse, people use avatars to represent themselves, interact/engage with one another, and virtually establish a community based on how the media and the first metaverse firms have promoted and portrayed the metaverse to the audience. In addition, digital cash is used in the metaverse to buy goods from businesses, such as apparel, artefacts, and stuff for video games. It may sound like science fiction in a brief statement, but when broken down, we can see that we already have such technology and have been utilising them for years (e.g., the gaming industry). The metaverse, according to some, is a 3D version of the Internet. It is thought to be the inevitable next development and, in an ideal world, would be reachable via a single access point. The Metaverse, according to writers Hollensen, Kotler, and Opresnik (2022), is a second 3D layer on top of the traditional 2D Internet. As the metaverse is still in its early stages of development, no research has been noted to systematically summarise the technical framework for its full visual construction and investigation. In addition, nor have graphics, interactions, and visualisation been studied separately from the perspective of the metaverse, according to the authors of the paper "Metaverse: Perspectives from graphics, interactions, and visualization" (Zhao et al., 2022). Our skepticism regarding four important categories—consumer experiences, customer trust, customer involvement, and advertising in the metaverse—is closely related to the current research.

Virtual worlds are developing toward Stephenson's idea of a metaverse, where social and economic interactions are the primary drivers, beyond the entertainment and gaming aspects. One of the best examples of this evolution right now is Second Life, an SVW where users (referred to as residents) can interact, work together, and exchange real as well as virtual goods and services (like clothing and real estate) through their personalised virtual spaces and avatars. The creators of Second Life have added an important feature that sets it apart from most previous virtual worlds, where content is created and managed by software specialists. Users are now able to create and customise their avatars, private virtual spaces (lands), and objects (houses and clothes) using a robust and user-friendly interface. In addition, recent voice communication enhancements made by developers have created intriguing new possibilities for learning and training applications. From 64 acres in 2003 to 65,000 acres now, and from 2 million inhabitants in December 2006 to more than 9 million inhabitants today, Second Life has experienced significant population growth. Approximately 500,000 individuals use Second Life on a regular basis.

USE CASES IN THE METAVERSE

Over the last few months, some use cases have emerged across the world. For examples: VR (Roblox, Zepeto, Animal Crossing), mirror worlds (Kakao Map, Baemin), lifelogging (Instagram, Facebook), and AR (Pokémon Go, Snow App) (Songlee & Yangjin, 2021). Leading IT companies are embracing the metaverse craze—Nvidia Omniverse, Facebook Horizon, and Microsoft's corporate metaverse, to mention a few. Nonfungible Tokens (NFTs) from consumer brands like Gucci and Coca-Cola are being sold on the metaverse marketplaces like Decentraland. The authors are already observing the development of the metaverse ecosystem, in which numerous people of different sizes collaborate to build a second world that closely resembles the real one (Caulfield, 2021). The participants in the metaverse ecosystem, according to Newzoo's 2021 Global Games Market Report, include the metaverse gateways that offer platforms and content (such as Roblox, Zepeto, Fortnite, Sandbox, and Decentraland), feature suppliers (e.g., avatar tech e.g., Tafi), social media, user interface and immersion (e.g., Oculus), and economy (e.g., Coinbase), and infrastructure (e.g., cloud, artificial intelligence, ad tech, and connectivity). Based on who generates the material and whether the experience is centralised (like Fortnite) or decentralised (like other games), these gamers can be segmented (e.g., Decentraland). Just as one company cannot control the Internet, neither can one or a small number of tech titans control the metaverse (Brown, 2021). *Social VR* enables users to collaborate and communicate with one another as if they were in the real world by using their avatars to represent them. It is viewed as social media of the future and is a crucial element of the metaverse. Social VR also offers a clear practical advantage. The worldwide

COVID-19 epidemic has forced many individuals to stay at home and limit their social connections, which has increased demand for creative social media apps.

The Study Set Up

The metaverse offers an experience like no other before. The users of this medium are transported into an alternate reality. While there are studies that focus on the various examples and how the medium can be used for different sectors ranging from education to medical training to retail shopping and brand building, there is very little understanding of how exactly users feel during the metaverse experience. There have been cases where users are "exposed to abusive behaviour every seven minutes," according to Platforms Metaverse, which finds that this includes instances of bullying, the display of explicit sexual content, racism, threats of violence, and the grooming of children (CCDH, 2022).

This research aims to fill the gap of understanding the user experience phenomenon in the Metaverse medium.

The Flow Concept

Csikszentmihalyi (2000) defines flow as "the comprehensive experience that people sense when they operate with absolute participation." Flow may be used to gauge how strongly players intend to keep playing an online game, leading to repeated plays. A crucial element of online games' appeal is flow (Weibel et al., 2008). Players value online games based on whether they deliver a flow experience (Sherry, 2004). Players are more inclined to play online games that encourage flow than those that do not (Chen, 2007; Holt, 2000; Sherry, 2004). There is a direct connection between flow and gaming, according to researchers.

Application to games is simple and follows a well-established paradigm for analysing experience in any setting (Cowley et al., 2008). The level of a player's "immersion" is determined by how integrated they feel with the gaming environment (Taylor, 2002). According to research, fluidity is a key element for online gaming players (Hsu & Lu, 2004; Wan & Chiou, 2006). The metaverse as a medium comes closest to an online gaming experience. Even the early adopters are those who are video gamers. Hence, studying the user experience of metaverse may be akin to understanding how online gamers feel during a 'game'. While there may be differences between the Metaverse and an online game, the flow theory can be used as a framework and the metaverse user experience can be understood in that context.

According to Csikszentmihalyi (2000), the idea of flow refers to a "peculiar dynamic condition, the holistic sense that individuals have when they operate with entire engagement" and an "ordered, negentropic state of awareness" (Csikszentmihalyi, 2000). People that are in flow are completely absorbed in what they are doing. The acts seamlessly flow into one another, exhibiting their own internal logic and fostering harmony. The actor, in this case an online shopper, goes through a smooth transition and has uninterrupted absolute control over the activities, which causes the actor/user to lose interest in what they are doing. Recently, flow has been recognised as a key concept for comprehending consumer behaviour in online settings and online customer experiences (Hoffman & Novak, 1996; Novak et al., 2000). Negentropic is a phrase that describes harmony and a lack of disorder. The actor or user feels completely in control of his or her actions without being interrupted throughout transitions. Participants in Csikszentmihalyi's study invent the word "flow."

Flow may be defined as the pleasurable sensation people (such as gamers) get while fully absorbed in an activity (such as online shopping) (Hung et al., 2012). It is essential to having fun, enjoying yourself, and having the best experience possible. Researchers and practitioners alike concur that an important idea for explaining consumer behaviour in online contexts is flow (Huang et al., 2012; Teng et al., 2012). The following traits of flow are present— awareness, absolute control, and attention and immersion—which are related to intense concentration on an activity. When a user is in flow, time seems to move more quickly or slowly than it would in other situations, and this sensation is seen as intrinsically pleasant (Csikszentmihalyi, 1988). Information systems researchers look at how consumers experience flow since it is thought that flow might be useful in understanding online experiences (e.g., Agarwal & Karahanna, 2000; Chen, 2006; Hausman & Siekpe, 2009; Huang, 2003; Siekpe, 2005; Skadberg & Kimmel, 2004; Wu & Chang, 2005). Online environments have been shown to link flow experiences to a range of outcomes including behavioural intentions like loyalty and plans to return and repurchase (Hausman & Siekpe, 2009; Siekpe, 2005; Wu & Chang, 2005), positive affects (Chen, 2006; Agarwal & Karahanna, 2000; Huang, 2003; Chen, 2006), favourable evaluations of and attitudes about websites, and exploratory activity with greater learning (Skadberg & Kimmel, 2004). The examination of flow as the best online customer experience in the context of e-commerce is a promising but immature area, according to a review of earlier studies. Furthermore, there is disagreement on how flow is measured, its causes, and its effects in online contexts (Novak et al., 2000; Lee & Chen, 2010; Voiskounsky, 2008). A key distribution channel, the Internet, has changed how consumers purchase (see Hoffman & Novak, 1996; Butler & Peppard, 1998; Schlosser, 2003). Because of this, understanding how the Internet affects consumer behaviour has become crucial, making this a crucial area of research (Barwise et al., 2002). Customers in e-commerce include both consumers and Internet users (Koufaris, 2002). Similar to this, in the realm of gaming, players contribute to the co-creation of gaming platforms through frequent input. As a result, co-creation of the online consumer experience emerges as a key topic of study. Hoffman and Novak (1996) contend that in order to comprehend the aforementioned dual function of online consumers, it is critical to research flow experience in interactive, computer-mediated environments. Understanding flow as the ideal experience would help explain how e-commerce businesses get a competitive edge (Hoffman & Novak, 1996) as the creation of experiences lead to competitive advantage in contemporary marketplaces.

Given the different ways of defining flow, it is not surprising to notice various ways of garnering empirical data on flow. Among others, questionnaire surveys have been the most popular method of collecting data, although the scale of measurement varies from study to study depending upon the working definitions adopted and the tasks concerned with individual studies. For instance, Trevino and Webster (1992) summed up the scores of sub constructs such as 'control', 'attention', 'curiosity' and 'interest' to gauge one's level of flow. Whereas Skadberg and Kimmel (2004) asked users of tourism websites to report the degree to which they experienced 'time distortion' as well as the 'enjoyment' that they felt while taking the virtual tour.

Flow experiences generally extend Internet and website use (Nel et al., 1999; Rettie, 2001). The flow sensation is highly associated with good behavioural goals, according to Hsu and Lu (2004). Studies have also revealed that being in the flow has a favourable impact on one's behavioural intentions, significantly increasing the chance of making an online purchase (Korzaan, 2003).

The relevant flow experience antecedents and effects from e-commerce literature are shown in Figure 1 (this has been used as a framework for our study).

Figure 1. Conceptual model of online learner's flow experience

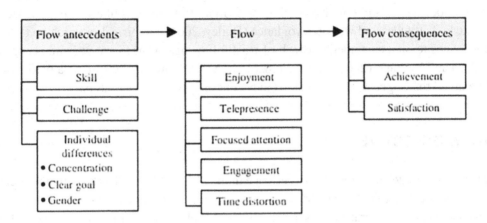

The main components of Figure 1 show that flow experience is reflected in five subconstructs of "enjoyment," "telepresence," "focused attention," "engagement," and "time distortion." These five subconstructs are chosen as the most appropriate to the present research from a total of 13 subconstructs that appear in the work of Novak et al. (1998). Given their potential significance in predicting the flow level, variables of individual differences such as the general tendency of "concentration," "having a clear goal" for taking online courses, and "gender" are also included as flow antecedents (Finneran & Zhang, 2005). The authors have further broken down the above flow antecedents and consequences into smaller factors—addictiveness, perceived utility, usability, objectives that are clear, interaction, speed, information richness, challenges, and vividness. These precursors can be divided into two categories: hedonic (experiential) and utilitarian (functional). Features on hedonistic websites encourage compulsive Internet usage and produce flow (Bridges & Florsheim, 2008). By boosting the enjoyment of online experience, user interfaces that make purchasing exciting, appealing, and gratifying have a significant impact on flow experience. Hedonic characteristics, either as a forerunner to flow or as a part of the Technology Adoption Model, have been widely employed in research on the acceptance and usage of websites (Agarwal & Karahanna, 2000; Davis et al., 1992; Koufaris, 2002; Koufaris et al., 2001). Flow experiences are also produced by hedonic website features (Se'ne'cal et al. 2002). According to Ghani and Deshpande (1994), Koufaris (2002), Novak et al. (2000), Skadberg and Kimmel (2004), and Trevino and Webster (1992), flow experiences are more likely to be attained when there is a greater impression of interaction. The utilitarian performance of a website, which is determined by whether the specific goal is achieved, is connected to its utilitarian characteristics (Davis et al., 1992; Venkatesh, 2000). According to Huang (2003), fluidity induces positive online assessments for the utilitarian elements. According to earlier study, the likelihood of achieving flow increases with user perception of utilitarian aspects (such as faster navigation) in online environments (Ghani & Deshpande, 1994; Koufaris, 2002; Novak et al., 2000; Skadberg & Kimmel, 2004; Trevino & Webster, 1992). According to Choi et al. (2007), utilitarian aspects encourage the sensation of flow. Trust, brand equity, contentment, compulsive behaviours, buy intent, intention to use, and desire to return are outcomes of the flow experience in e-commerce. Fredrickson et al. (2003) state that experiencing flow expands users' attention and thinking by causing them to engage in more exploratory and playful behaviours (Ezimmuo & Keikhosrokiani, 2022; Keikhosrokiani, 2022; Keikhosrokiani et al., 2019; Xian et al., 2022). The favourable feelings that result from a user's interaction with an e-commerce website help customers learn more about the brand and cement their associations with it. Online settings with more flow are less likely to experience negative outcomes like bad attitudes and website avoidance (Dailey, 2004). Empirical research on the impact of a company's website on a customer's growth of trust following a visit to the website is conducted by Hampton-Sosa and Koufaris (2005). In e-commerce websites, flow is proven to be a predictor of trust. It should be noted that suggested relationships may contain possible moderators.

RESEARCH OBJECTIVE

This chapter aims to understand the user experience in the Metaverse, by investigating the social behaviour and psychological factors during a Metaverse experience. The chapter is interdisciplinary in nature and the results pertain to several fields such as consumer behaviour, AIML, Visual arts, ARVR, data science, brand management, marketing communications and business studies.

The study intends to enable marketers, ad agencies, and technology leaders to make a more informed decision about using the metaverse medium for their brand strategies. It also has important implications for students, educators of higher education, researchers, academicians, technology leaders, and data scientists.

RESEARCH METHODOLOGY

Data is primarily collected from people using a semi-structured questionnaire (Refer Appendix 1), which is formulated using the literature on Flow Theory.

Interviews are conducted by the authors across different segments that majorly comprised of gamers and metaverse users (including tech vendors). There are also respondents who have played games in tech cafes that provide their users with VR gear. All the samples are graduates who are fluent in English and have had exposure to technology. The respondents are majorly male, but some females are also parts of the sample. The interviews that the authors carry out are transcribed into a word document. Refer to Figure 2 for a sample set of respondents who are interviewed.

Secondary data containing used cases are analysed to add richness to understanding.

As the findings are qualitative in nature, the authors use NVivo Software for analysis. Interview transcripts are fed into the software where key themes are identified. The authors expand on the themes to arrive at a modified framework of flow theory with reference to the Metaverse.

NVivo

The primary goal of analysis of qualitative data is transformation of data into conclusions and judgments (Patton, 2002). NVivo helps researchers manipulate data records, browse them, code them, annotate them, and rapidly and precisely retrieve data records (Richards, 1999). Tools in NVivo may be used to "capture and link thoughts in many different ways, as well as search for and examine trends in data and ideas" . The numerous activities include linking, coding, and shaping in sets for the documents and nodes, as well as proxy documents, nodes, and attributes that assign values to the attributes.

Figure 2. Sample set of respondents

Name	Age	Gender	Qualification	Familiarity with digital devices	Familiarity with technology	Gamer or not	Fluency in English	Have they used metaverse before?
Anandu Sreenivas	25	Male	Graduate	Yes	Yes	Yes	Good	Yes
Aniruddh	24	Male	Graduate	Yes	Yes	Yes	Good	Yes
Mehlam Tumsa	21	Male	Graduate	Yes	Yes	Yes	Good	No
Monish Saravanan	21	Male	Graduate	Yes	Yes	Yes	Good	No
Tanisha Jadhav	24	Male	Graduate	Yes	Yes	Yes	Good	Yes
Vishal N	22	Male	Graduate	Yes	Yes	Yes	Good	Yes
Rosemary Reggie	23	Female	Graduate	Yes	Yes	No	Good	Yes
Srinivasan (Grishas Laboratory)	.	Male	Technology entrepreneur	Yes	Yes	.	Good	Yes

The authors develop codes that in turn help them generate themes and a Cross Matrix Query. The interviews that the authors carry out are transcribed and fed in the software as codes. Codes, also known as nodes earlier, are containers for categories and codes that represent abstract ideas, concepts, people, locations, processes, or any other category specified in project papers. Any quantity of document coding can be found in codes. As concepts arise and merge inside codes, researchers can rearrange and alter the indexing system. Information regarding a research study is stored in attributes such as data sources, an organisation, the personnel, a place, the year in which a document is created, gender of a respondent, and other aspects of codes. The transcripts are converted to word trees with the help of Text Search Query which allows the authors to identify the labels for codes. Then, using the same tool, every interview is manually scanned and fed in the system leading the authors to an output that helps in the modulation of Flow Theory.

FINDINGS

The findings have been classified according to the following sections, as per the Flow Theory:

1.   Flow antecedents and flow consequences in the Metaverse.

The antecedents of the flow theory comprise skills and challenges. Most of the respondents of the survey are adept at basic technology and even if they do not have exposure to the metaverse, they are able to explore the stimulus provided. They also express that the metaverse interface is easy enough for anyone with basic experience of technology and that no specific skill set is required to experience flow either through metaverse or gaming.

Achievement and customer satisfaction are resulted from flow even in the Metaverse, just like on any other online mediums. However, satisfaction does not lead to any specific behaviour (such as purchase etc.). This area will be dealt with later in detail.

2. Connection between the flow state (skill challenge) and a person's rate of flow

Flow state refers to the skill set a person might have when he or she engages in a specific task. While challenges are activities that correspond to a player's skill level in an online game, skills relate to a player's ability to participate in specific levels of activity in those games (Hoffman & Novak, 1996). Customers' online experiences, attitudes, and behaviour are impacted by their IT abilities and limitations (Udo et al., 2010). Only when individuals believe that the tasks on the web are compatible with their abilities can the flow possibly happen (Csikszentmihalyi & Csikszentmihalyi, 1988). Otherwise, kids can get worried or bored (Ellis et al., 1994). A game's challenge level is appropriate when it is balanced with the player's abilities (Fu et al., 2009). A particular activity has to create a balance between the intrinsic difficulty of that activity and the player's capacity to deal with and surpass it while maintaining the flow during the gameplay. To keep players in the flow state, a game must have a proper ratio of difficulty level and player ability (Chen, 2007). High perceived skills and difficulty levels directly lead to flow in a person. Considering this, players of online games that experience a high degree of skill and difficulty in a game are more likely to experience flow, and as a result, they are more likely to seek participation in online games. However, this aspect is modified in the flow theory—showing that people might have an experience at flow despite not having a specific level of skill set. The samples that have prior experience of the metaverse can elaborate more on how they experience a certain aspect of the metaverse, in comparison to the gamers who barely have any experience. A few research have theoretically and experimentally investigated how utilitarian goals might act as a moderator. People play online games for utilitarian reasons involving extrinsic incentives in addition to enjoyment (e.g., upgrades, prizes, experience points, and money). Diverse levels of utilitarian incentive have resulted in very different relationships between flow and replay intention. The significance of flow to a player's intention to keep playing an online game is determined by such reasons. In order to better understand the link between flow and desire to repeat online games, this study tries to specifically evaluate the moderating impact of player utilitarian motivation levels.

In our study, the challenges that most users face are either because of internet bandwidth or due to bugs that are present in the platform (as the medium is in its infancy stage). As the respondents have some prior exposure to the metaverse, they do not face any skill challenge. So 'skill' per se does not determine the rate of flow for the users.

Most of the people use the platform for either gaming purpose or office work. There are respondents who quote that there have been instances where surgery is performed by medical students through the metaverse. They also specify that they find the experience on the metaverse to be more useful than in real life as they could maneuver here to get their desired result.

Engagement as quoted by the respondents is good as their overall experience is free from any sort of hassle. Most of the people find the platform to be user-friendly which increases their engagement hours.

3. Do individual differences' (social/ psychological) affect a person's level of flow?

In the study, individual differences do not affect the flow in the Metaverse. Technology adeptness seems to be the only driving factor that largely affecting the usage of the Metaverse.

Some also add that the experience might be so immersive that people might lose track of time while they are on the platform. About a year ago, an experiment was conducted by a woman who tried staying on the metaverse through Google Oculus for Wall Street Journal. She experienced a bunch of different activities where she attended meetings, played games, and went to a campfire with the editor of Meta. She defined her experience to be too real—when she saw other avatars on the metaverse for the first time, to her it felt like being in any room with a bunch of people. She also noted that there were women who were coughing, and there was a noise of babies crying too. One very interesting thing that she noticed while being on the metaverse was that the avatars did not have legs. Reason being that the Oculus headset can catch signal from one's head—the gears then help in catching signals from one's hand, but there is no device as of now which can help getting signal from one's legs. She enjoyed her time there, but soon after, the entire experience started feeling a little too overwhelming. She also complained of having back and neck ache as well as sore eyes. She was feeling sick by the end of the experiment.

CHANGE IN THE FLOW THEORY FRAMEWORK

The flow theory framework is modified on the basis of skill and purchase intent (deriving from customer satisfaction). Even though it is stated initially that a specific skill set is required for any user to experience flow, the sample that the authors use for their research suggests that even if a person is not a gamer but has basic exposure to technology, it is easy enough for anyone who wishes to explore the metaverse to do so without any prerequisites. As long as the users have the gear and adequate bandwidth connection, they will be able to navigate the metaverse easily. This finding is based on the assumption that the people who have access to the metaverse have basic exposure to technology and are willing to explore further.

The modified flow theory based on this research can be seen in Figure 3.

Figure 3. Modified Flow Theory

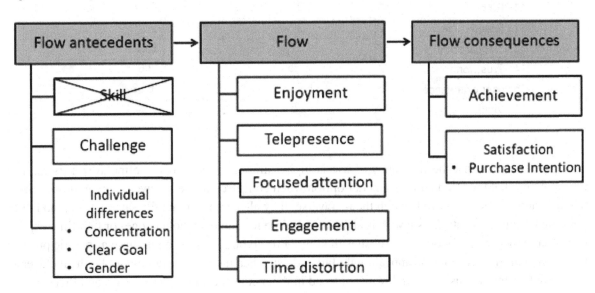

Understanding User Experience in the Metaverse

Other User Experience Aspects in the Metaverse

Figure 4 captures the output from NVivo software. Analysis is shown across two broad categories: gamers or the metaverse users. Gamers are the ones who have more experience in gaming and have been exposed to the metaverse only through social media, such as YouTube or VR cafes. The metaverse users are those who are frequently exposed to the metaverse platforms. The research is conducted to understand the experience of these different sets of users on the Metaverse medium. The Metaverse users themselves serve as the benchmark of the experience measurement.

Figure 4. NVivo output

	A : Metaverse User	B : Gamer
1 : Addictive	4.27%	2.38%
2 : Challenges	1.27%	2.13%
3 : Ease of use	11.98%	5.55%
4 : Frequency of use	6.58%	8.57%
5 : Interactive	8.47%	7.23%
6 : Mentally Stimulating	3.1%	8.12%
7 : Objective	1.41%	1.24%
8 : overwhelming	5.54%	6.98%
9 : Platforms Exposure	8.51%	5.5%
10 : Purchase intention	3.1%	0.15%
11 : Rich	3.99%	5.99%
12 : Speed	7.37%	2.77%
13 : Standard met	4.27%	6.69%
14 : Trustworthy	10.85%	13.67%
15 : user experience	6.78%	16.69%
16 : Vivid	12.5%	6.34%

Figure 4 shows that the frequency of use is higher among gamers than the metaverse users. The reason being that they find gaming a better option when compared to the metaverse. Even if they enjoy the experience that they have through the metaverse, they also mention that the satisfaction (and hence possible purchase intention) is low. It is almost negligible for gamers who had one- or two-time experience on the metaverse. Hedonistic websites that might try to budge users to purchase a specific product based on their gratification and appeal might fail to do so when it comes to gaming under the metaverse. The reason being that users see a downward trend in the metaverse gaming as of now, and therefore investing and purchasing a product just for enjoyment purpose is not something that they seek to do. Also, the availability of the metaverse gears is extremely difficult which hampers the frequency of its usage.

Gamers find the use of the metaverse to be more overwhelming. The reason for this can be due to the comparatively high frequency of use and exposure to such platforms for the metaverse users. Vividness is experienced more by gamers in the metaverse as they have been previously exposed only to screens as a medium of playing games. Also, trustworthiness levels are higher for the metaverse users than gamers as they may have had better experience at it.

CONCLUSIONS

This study has provided an overview of what the user experience is in the Metaverse. The findings have been analysed through Flow Theory framework, as well as other psychological and behavioural aspects. The Metaverse is a disruptive medium that promises to rewrite the rules of brand communication. According to a paper published by Wisnu Buana (2022), people who believe the metaverse is only a passing fad have plenty of doubts at the moment. Here are some reasons in support of the medium:

1. Ongoing developments in technology – Each Meta's Horizon Worlds and The Sandbox has a high number of participants. Technical obstacles must be addressed before the metaverse experiences can become entirely widespread. But as processing power continues to advance, bigger virtual worlds are now possible. Extensive large-data tasks, such as producing graphics, may be moved off local devices thanks to cloud and edge computing. Mobile devices may now access these vast worlds more quickly and simply thanks to the quick deployment of 5G. In addition, gear for augmented and virtual reality is becoming less expensive to produce. In 2021, Meta delivered 10 million Oculus Quest 2 headsets as additional innovative products like haptic gloves and bodysuits enter the market.

2. A broader range of usage scenarios – Metaverse gaming has already gained widespread popularity. New immersive retail, entertainment, sports, and instructional experiences are already being developed for consumer use cases. Then there are the significant—but less publicized—business prospects and uses of the metaverse, such as virtual employee training and team collaboration using avatars, virtual prototyping in building and manufacturing, and virtual showroom displays for goods like vehicles. Even governmental organisations are testing the metaverse. Creating a virtual Mayor's Office and Seoul Campus Town will be the first two phases of the five-year Metaverse Seoul Basic Plan which is unveiled by the city of Seoul in South Korea.

3. Online shopping is commonplace – Since payment credentials are frequently built in the hardware and software they use; Omni channel commerce is already a second nature to the majority of the metaverse customers. More than 40% of the $1 billion in gaming sales worldwide are produced by the virtual goods industry. Future criteria to create cryptocurrency wallet accounts on the metaverse platforms will become less of a barrier as a result of the long-term growth of cryptocurrencies. As an example, purchasing Domino's pizza in Decentraland and having it delivered in the real world is an example of how physical-to-virtual and virtual-to-physical transactions are already becoming more innovative.

4. Demographic advantage – The eldest members of Gen Z are adults in their mid-20s. They are a force to be reckoned with when it comes to money generation. Compared to prior generations, these customers are more familiar with virtual worlds, transactions, and products. Leading the way is gaming, considering the fact that 67% of Roblox's 50 million daily users are under the age of

16. This may herald the birth of a brand-new generation of people who are born into the age of the metaverse.

5. Brand involvement and marketing are increasingly consumer-driven – The more than 50% increase in influencer marketing over the previous five years on platforms like WeChat and Pinduoduo in China, and YouTube and Instagram in the West, is proof of the shift toward independent content creators (McKinsey & Co, 2022)

IMPLICATIONS

This research has tremendous implications for marketing practitioners, students, higher education instructors, researchers, academics, tech leaders, and data scientists. The Metaverse designers and ad creators will now know the elements that need emphasis in order to enhance user experience in the Metaverse. Technology innovators may improve the usability of the metaverse and make it available to companies that might be prepared to invest in the technology. They can thereby work on making the VR lenses and gears functional and portable enough for users as this might arouse their interest to purchase them in years to come.

Students will learn about how the metaverse has changed flow theory. Then they will be able to carry out further experiment in this area. In the last thirty years, academics and scholars have cited, examined, and theorized about customer experience. Customer experience has been described in a number of ways because it has so many different meanings. One of the first definitions of hedonic consumer experiences was offered by Holbrook and Hirschman (1982), who emphasised the sensory, emotional, and imaginative components of consumption. This paper might be of help for academicians and higher education personnel who can work on the Metaverse as a brand building medium in the intersection of marketing and technology. As for the researchers, they can validate the findings here with more sample.

REFERENCES

Adner, R., & Kapoor, R. (2010). Value creation in innovation ecosystems: How the structure of technological interdependence affects firm performance in new technology generations. *Strategic Management Journal*, *31*(3), 306–333. doi:10.1002mj.821

Agarwal, R., & Karahanna, E. (2000). Time flies when you're having fun: Cognitive absorption and beliefs about information technology usage. *Management Information Systems Quarterly*, *24*(4), 665–694. doi:10.2307/3250951

Azeem, M., Salfi, N. A., & Dogar, A. H. (2012). Usage of NVivo software for qualitative data analysis. *Academic Research International*, *2*(1), 262–266. doi:10.4135/9781412957397.n71

Barwise, P., Elberse, A., & Hammond, K. (2002). *Marketing and the Internet: A research review*. London Business School. doi:10.4135/9781848608283.n22

Brown, D. (2021, October 28). Big Tech wants to build the 'metaverse.' What on Earth does that mean? *The Seattle Times*. https://www.seattletimes.com/business/technology/big-tech-wants-to-build-the-metaverse-what-on-earth-does-that-mean/

Caulfield, B. (2022, November 3). *What is the metaverse?* NVIDIA Blog. https://blogs.nvidia.com/blog/2021/08/10/what-is-the-metaverse/

Chen, H. (2006). Flow on the net–detecting web users' positive effects and their flow states. *Computers in Human Behavior, 22*(2), 221–233. doi:10.1016/j.chb.2004.07.001

Chen, H., Wigand, R. T., & Nilan, M. (2000). Exploring web users' optimal flow experiences. *Information Technology & People, 13*(4), 263–281. doi:10.1108/09593840010359473

Chen, J. (2007). Flow in games (and everything else). *Communications of the ACM, 50*(4), 31–34. doi:10.1145/1232743.1232769

Choi, H. S., & Kim, S. H. (2017). A content service deployment plan for metaverse museum exhibitions-Centering on the combination of beacons and HMDs. *International Journal of Information Management, 37*(1), 1519–1527. doi:10.1016/j.ijinfomgt.2016.04.017

Chu, S. C., & Choi, S. M. (2011). Electronic word-of-mouth in social networking sites: A cross-cultural study of the United States and China. *Journal of Global Marketing, 24*(3), 263–281. doi:10.1080/08911762.2011.592461

Chung, N., Tyan, I., & Chung, H. C. (2017). Social support and commitment within social networking site in tourism experience. *Sustainability, 9*(11), 2102. doi:10.3390u9112102

Cowley, B., Charles, D., Black, M., & Hickey, R. (2008). Toward an understanding of flow in video games. *Computers in Entertainment, 6*(2), 1–27. doi:10.1145/1371216.1371223

Csikszentmihalyi, M. (2000). *Beyond boredom and anxiety.* Jossey-Bass. doi:10.2307/2065805

Dastin, J., & Chmielewski, D. (2022, October 13). *Metaverse could accelerate manufacturing as well as social ills.* The Star. https://www.thestar.com.my/tech/tech-news/2022/10/13/metaverse-could-accelerate-manufacturing-as-well-as-social-ills

Davis, F. D., Bagozzi, R. P., & Warshaw, P. R. (1992). Extrinsic and intrinsic motivation to use computers in the workplace. *Journal of Applied Social Psychology, 22*(14), 1111–1132. doi:10.1111/j.1559-1816.1992.tb00945.x

Dickey, M. D. (2005). Engaging by design: How engagement strategies in popular computer and video games can inform instructional design. *Educational Technology Research and Development, 53*(2), 67–83. doi:10.1007/BF02504866

Ellis, G. D., Voelkl, J. E., & Morris, C. (1994). Measurement and analysis issues with explanation of variance in daily experience using the flow model. *Journal of Leisure Research, 26*(4), 337–356. doi:10.1080/00222216.1994.11969966

Ezimmuo, C. M., & Keikhosrokiani, P. (2022). Predicting Consumer Behavior Change Towards Using Online Shopping in Nigeria: The Impact of the COVID-19 Pandemic. In P. Keikhosrokiani (Ed.), *Handbook of Research on Consumer Behavior Change and Data Analytics in the Socio-Digital Era* (pp. 210–254). IGI Global. doi:10.4018/978-1-6684-4168-8.ch010

Finneran, C. M., & Zhang, P. (2005). Flow in computer-mediated environments: Promises and challenges. *Communications of the Association for Information Systems*, *15*(1), 4. doi:10.17705/1CAIS.01504

Fredrickson, B. L., Tugade, M. M., Waugh, C. E., & Larkin, G. R. (2003). What good are positive emotions in crisis? A prospective study of resilience and emotions following the terrorist attacks on the United States on September 11th, 2001. *Journal of Personality and Social Psychology*, *84*(2), 365–376. doi:10.1037/0022-3514.84.2.365 PMID:12585810

Ghani, J. A., & Deshpande, S. P. (1994). Task characteristics and the experience of optimal flow in human—Computer interaction. *The Journal of Psychology*, *128*(4), 381–391. doi:10.1080/00223980 .1994.9712742

Hampton-Sosa, W., & Koufaris, M. (2005). The effect of web site perceptions on initial trust in the owner company. *International Journal of Electronic Commerce*, *10*(1), 55–81. doi:10.1080/10864415 .2005.11043965

Han, S., & Noh, Y. (2021). Analyzing Higher Education Instructors' perception on Metaverse-based Education. *Journal of Digital Contents Society*, *22*(11), 1793–1806. doi:10.9728/dcs.2021.22.11.1793

Hendaoui, A., Limayem, M., & Thompson, C. W. (2008). 3D social virtual worlds: Research issues and challenges. *IEEE Internet Computing*, *12*(1), 88–92. doi:10.1109/MIC.2008.1

Hoffman, D. L., & Novak, T. P. (1996). Marketing in hypermedia computer-mediated environments: Conceptual foundations. *Journal of Marketing*, *60*(3), 50–68. doi:10.1177/002224299606000304

Hollensen, S., Kotler, P., & Opresnik, M. O. (2022). Metaverse–the new marketing universe. *The Journal of Business Strategy*. Advance online publication. doi:10.1108/JBS-01-2022-0014

Hsu, C. L., & Lu, H. P. (2004). Why do people play on-line games? An extended TAM with social influences and flow experience. *Information & Management*, *41*(7), 853–868. doi:10.1016/j.im.2003.08.014

Huang, Y. C., Backman, S. J., & Backman, K. F. (2012). Exploring the impacts of involvement and flow experiences in second life on people's travel intentions. *Journal of Hospitality and Tourism Technology*, *3*(1), 4–23. doi:10.1108/17579881211206507

Israfilzade, K. (2022). Marketing in the Metaverse: A Sceptical Viewpoint of Opportunities and Future Research Directions. *The Eurasia Proceedings of Educational and Social Sciences*, *24*, 53–60. doi:10.55549/epess.1179349

Kang, M., & Schuett, M. A. (2013). Determinants of sharing travel experiences in social media. *Journal of Travel & Tourism Marketing*, *30*(1-2), 93–107. doi:10.1080/10548408.2013.751237

Keikhosrokiani, P. (Ed.). (2022). *Handbook of Research on Consumer Behavior Change and Data Analytics in the Socio-Digital Era*. IGI Global. doi:10.4018/978-1-6684-4168-8

Keikhosrokiani, P., Mustaffa, N., Zakaria, N., & Baharudin, A. S. (2019). User Behavioral Intention Toward Using Mobile Healthcare System. In Consumer-Driven Technologies in Healthcare: Breakthroughs in Research and Practice (pp. 429-444). IGI Global. doi:10.4018/978-1-5225-6198-9.ch022

Keikhosrokiani, P., & Pourya Asl, M. (2023). *Handbook of Research on Artificial Intelligence Applications in Literary Works and Social Media*. IGI Global. doi:10.4018/978-1-6684-6242-3

Korzaan, M. L. (2003). Going with the flow: Predicting online purchase intentions. *Journal of Computer Information Systems*, *43*(4), 25–31. doi:10.1057/palgrave.ejis.3000445

Koufaris, M. (2002). Applying the technology acceptance model and flow theory to online consumer behavior. *Information Systems Research*, *13*(2), 205–223. doi:10.1287/isre.13.2.205.83

Koufaris, M., Kambil, A., & LaBarbera, P. A. (2001). Consumer behavior in web-based commerce: An empirical study. *International Journal of Electronic Commerce*, *6*(2), 115–138. doi:10.1080/1086441 5.2001.11044233

Lee, S. G., Trimi, S., Byun, W. K., & Kang, M. (2011). Innovation and imitation effects in Metaverse platform adoption. *Service Business*, *5*(2), 155–172. doi:10.100711628-011-0108-8

Lee, S. M., & Chen, L. (2010). The impact of flow on online consumer behavior. *Journal of Computer Information Systems*, *50*(4), 1–10. doi:10.1080/08874417.2013.11645645

MacDonald, K. (2022, January 25). I've seen the metaverse – And I don't want it. *The Guardian*. https://www.theguardian.com/games/2022/jan/25/ive-seen-the-metaverse-and-i-dont-want-it

Nel, D., van Niekerk, R., Berthon, J. P., & Davies, T. (1999). Going with the flow: Web sites and customer involvement. *Internet Research*, *9*(2), 109–116. doi:10.1108/10662249910264873

Novak, T. P., Hoffman, D. L., & Duhachek, A. (2003). The influence of goal-directed and experiential activities on online flow experiences. *Journal of Consumer Psychology*, *13*(1-2), 3–16. doi:10.1207/S15327663JCP13-1&2_01

Novak, T. P., Hoffman, D. L., & Yung, Y. F. (2000). Measuring the customer experience in online environments: A structural modeling approach. *Marketing Science*, *19*(1), 22–42. doi:10.1287/mksc.19.1.22.15184

Papagiannidis, S., Bourlakis, M., & Li, F. (2008). Making real money in virtual worlds: MMORPGs and emerging business opportunities, challenges and ethical implications in metaverses. *Technological Forecasting and Social Change*, *75*(5), 610–622. doi:10.1016/j.techfore.2007.04.007

Patton, M. Q. (2002). Learning in the Field: An Introduction to Qualitative Research (G. B. Rossman & S. F. Rallis, Eds.). Sage.

Richards, L. (1999). *Using NVivo in qualitative research*. Sage Publication Ltd.

Rimol, M. (2022, February 7). *Gartner predicts 25% of people will spend at least one hour per day in the metaverse by 2026*. Gartner. https://www.gartner.com/en/newsroom/press-releases/2022-02-07-gartner-predicts-25-percent-of-people-will-spend-at-least-one-hour-per-day-in-the-metaverse-by-2026

Robertson, H. (2021, December 25). *Wall street is pumped about the metaverse. but critics say it's massively overhyped and will be a regulatory minefield*. Business Insider. https://markets.businessinsider.com/news/stocks/metaverse-outlook-overhyped-regulations-facebook-meta-virtual-worlds-genz-2021-12

Schlosser, A. E. (2003). Computers as situational cues: Implications for consumers product cognitions and attitudes. *Journal of Consumer Psychology*, *13*(1-2), 103–112. doi:10.1207/S15327663JCP13-1&2_09

Senecal, S., Gharbi, J. E., & Nantel, J. (2002). *The influence of flow on hedonic and utilitarian shopping values*. ACR North American Advances.

Sherry, J. L. (2004). Flow and media enjoyment. *Communication Theory, 14*(4), 328–347. doi:10.1111/j.1468-2885.2004.tb00318.x

Siekpe, J. S. (2005). An examination of the multidimensionality of flow construct in a computer-mediated environment. *Journal of Electronic Commerce Research, 6*(1), 31. doi:10.120715327744joce15024

Skadberg, Y. X., & Kimmel, J. R. (2004). Visitors' flow experience while browsing a Web site: Its measurement, contributing factors and consequences. *Computers in Human Behavior, 20*(3), 403–422. doi:10.1016/S0747-5632(03)00050-5

Taylor, L. N. (2002). *Video games: Perspective, point-of-view, and immersion*. Academic Press.

Venkatesh, V. (2000). Determinants of perceived ease of use: Integrating control, intrinsic motivation, and emotion into the technology acceptance model. *Information Systems Research, 11*(4), 342–365. doi:10.1287/isre.11.4.342.11872

Wan, C. S., & Chiou, W. B. (2006). Psychological motives and online games addiction: Atest of flow theory and humanistic needs theory for taiwanese adolescents. *Cyberpsychology & Behavior, 9*(3), 317–324. doi:10.1089/cpb.2006.9.317 PMID:16780399

Wankhede, C. (2022, August 1). *What is the metaverse and why is it so controversial?* Android Authority. https://www.androidauthority.com/what-is-the-metaverse-3107774/

Webster, J., Trevino, L. K., & Ryan, L. (1993). The dimensionality and correlates of flow in human-computer interactions. *Computers in Human Behavior, 9*(4), 411–426. doi:10.1016/0747-5632(93)90032-N

Weibel, D., Wissmath, B., Habegger, S., Steiner, Y., & Groner, R. (2008). Playing online games against computer-vs. human-controlled opponents: Effects on presence, flow, and enjoyment. *Computers in Human Behavior, 24*(5), 2274–2291. doi:10.1016/j.chb.2007.11.002

Wisnu Buana, I. M. (2023). Metaverse: Threat or Opportunity for Our Social World? In understanding Metaverse on sociological context. *Journal of Metaverse, 3*(1), 28–33. doi:10.57019/jmv.1144470

Xian, Z., Keikhosrokiani, P., XinYing, C., & Li, Z. (2022). An RFM Model Using K-Means Clustering to Improve Customer Segmentation and Product Recommendation. In P. Keikhosrokiani (Ed.), Handbook of Research on Consumer Behavior Change and Data Analytics in the Socio-Digital Era (pp. 124-145). IGI Global. doi:10.4018/978-1-6684-4168-8.ch006

Zhao, Y., Jiang, J., Chen, Y., Liu, R., Yang, Y., Xue, X., & Chen, S. (2022). Metaverse: Perspectives from graphics, interactions and visualization. *Visual Informatics, 6*(1), 56–67. doi:10.1016/j.visinf.2022.03.002

APPENDIX 1 (SEMI-STRUCTURED QUESTIONNAIRE)

Name

Age

Gender

Educational Qualifications Familiarity with Digital Devices Familiarity with technology

Are they a video gamer? Fluency in English

Have they used metaverse before? If yes, for what?

What is the specific Metaverse usage, recently or currently they use (for the purpose of answering this questionnaire)?

Figure 5.

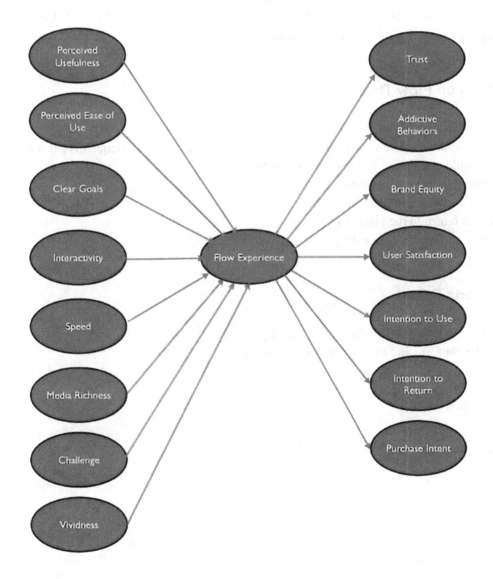

For all questions, please give options to describe the answer? Give provision for explanations. As why or why not after each question.

Antecedents

Q1. What are the platforms that you have used that exposed you to metaverse? Q2. How useful did you find the metaverse platform for your job?

Q3. How easy was it for you to use metaverse?

Q4. What was the objective or goal for the use of metaverse?

Q5. Was the objective or goal met by using the platform that used metaverse?

Q6. Was the platform interactive? Were you happy with the speed of the platform? Q7. Would you define the experience on the platform to be rich? Why?

Q8. How vivid was the experience on the platform?

Q9. Did you find the platform to be mentally stimulating? How? Why not? Q10. What were the challenges you faced while being on the platform?

Questions on Flow Theory

Q1. Did you find the platform to be trustworthy?

Q2. Do you think you'll be visiting the platform frequently? If yes, how frequently? If no, why?

Q3. How would you define your experience on the platform?

Q4. Did brand meet the standards it had set?

Q5. Was your intention to use fulfilled?

Q6. Will you return to the platform?

Q7. If the platform offers something for sale, would you purchase?

Discomforts Faced

Q1. Did you find the platform to be user friendly? How?

Q2. Was the platform and experience overwhelming?

Open Ended

Q3. Anything you wish to add, about the MV experience?

Section 4
The use of Metaverse in Different Disciplines

Chapter 11
Metaverse Concepts and Marketing

Ibrahim Halil Efendioglu
https://orcid.org/0000-0002-4968-375X
Gaziantep University, Turkey

ABSTRACT

Metaverse is a virtual reality world where users can interact with each other, buy and sell things, and fulfil their dreams through virtual reality or augmented reality. This technology allows people to participate in social activities and entertainment like never before, providing a different dimension of participation, socialization, and digital living space. In the development process of technology, social media has changed the habits of use and involvement, and this change has revolutionized many areas, from personal space to commercial applications. This chapter reviews and discusses metaverse concepts and marketing. The study findings show that metaverse offers businesses a new way to reach their target audience. Integrating the metaverse into future marketing strategies will be the way forward and for the brand to exist for a long time because metaverse offers brands of all kinds the chance to seamlessly combine the accessibility and convenience of the digital world with the immersive experiences of the physical world.

INTRODUCTION

Metaverse, one of the essential concepts that have entered our lives in recent years, is expected to precede the internet revolution in the future. The Metaverse is a three-dimensional virtual universe where people interact with each other through their avatars. The real world is a metaphor in this immersive universe, and there is no physical limitation (Chalmers et al., 2022). Therefore, the Metaverse is a new visual world that combines the physical and digital worlds (Zhao et al., 2022). Metaverse is an environment where people experience augmented reality, virtual reality, mixed reality, and extended reality together. It will be a turning point in our lives when users can have fun, socialize, shop, play games, chat with their friends, spend time and navigate easily with their avatars in this three-dimensional virtual universe. With Web 3.0, based on the concept of decentralization, it is predicted that storing our records on the blockchain, not on a single server, will move many stones.

DOI: 10.4018/978-1-6684-7029-9.ch011

Metaverse is a virtual reality world where users can interact with each other, buy and sell things and fulfill their dreams through virtual reality or augmented reality. Marketing success in today's digital age is about more than embracing modern technology and making the most of it. It is also about keeping up with upcoming developments such as metadata storage. In the marketing context, Metaverse can be defined as a permanent, 3D virtual space where users can spend their time while being used as a target with brand-related content and sales activation tactics (Yazıcı, 2022). Metaverse's proposal for marketing is to provide exclusive access to consumers who primarily value innovation, using technologies that combine virtual reality, augmented reality and mixed reality in addition to artificial intelligence as part of their digital marketing strategy (Yassin, 2022). Metaverse marketing allows brands to maximize their creativity and reach their target audience in the most compelling way. That's why, one by one, brands are turning their faces to the Metaverse world for digital marketing.

Along with the importance of digitalization, businesses are also developing their virtual market strategies. Dominating the virtual markets necessitates changing the known and conventional methods. The most challenging situation in this regard starts with overcoming consumers' trust problems. Businesses' products or service supply should be shaped according to consumer purchasing behavior. In this context, companies must first understand the importance of digitalization and then develop new business methods. In line with this information, the necessity of planning the steps businesses need to take emerges. Many factors (social, psychological, economic, personal) affect the purchasing behavior of consumers, and the most determinant of these factors is seen as psychological factors. Using the advantages of technological developments has an advantageous effect on consumer behavior. Especially with the understanding of post-modern consumption, the demands and expectations of consumers differ. The most critical rule brought by this differentiation makes it necessary to develop new simulations compatible with change (Çelikkol, 2022). In the Metaverse world, businesses' adoption of immersive technologies are expected to cause significant changes in consumer behavior. Following a specific plan for this will accelerate businesses' entry into the Metaverse. The behavioral responses of consumers will depend on the method businesses use. Therefore, Metaverse is a determinant for exchanging virtual world elements with consumer behavior (Shen et al., 2021).

This section aims to explain the important concepts frequently used in Metaverse such as augmented reality, virtual reality, mixed reality, extended reality, blockchain, cryptocurrency, non-fungible token, Web 3.0, mirror-world, meatspace, digital twins, multiverse, internet of things, avatar, human computer interaction, three dimension, artificial intelligence, massive multiplayer online game, non-player character, digital identities, lifelogging, smart contracts. In addition, Metaverse marketing, consumer behavior that will change with Metaverse, and brands entering Metaverse will be examined and marketing strategies for the future will be explained. Thus, it is aimed to contribute to the literature by understanding the concept of Metaverse in detail, which is rapidly expanding its awareness and usage area, and to be a guiding study for brands to start their marketing studies.

METAVERSE

The concept of Metaverse was first introduced by Neal Stephenson in 1992 with the novel "Snow Crash". In 2003, software developers inspired by Snow Crash designed a game called "Second Life". In the game, everyone has an avatar as a cartoon, and the players communicate with each other in virtual environments (Hollensen et al., 2022). Within the game, some activities are similar to reality, such as conversations, physical interaction, trade, and construction that should be in society (Lv et al., 2022). Metaverse is a combination of the words meta and universe. It is expressed as a new internet generation where users can communicate and interact with each other through avatars and special software (Duan et al., 2021). Metaverse, in other words, is also defined as convergence. This convergence: creates a virtual enhanced physical reality and a physically permanent virtual space, allowing users to experience both simultaneously (Kutlu, 2022). The concept of the Metaverse is used to express a virtual universe based on daily life where both the real and the virtual coexist (Akour et al., 2022). It describes three-dimensional structures in which avatars in this universe engage in political, economic, social, and cultural activities (Park & Kim, 2022). Metaverse, which refers to this entirely or partially virtual universe where individuals can live under the rules defined by their creative ideas, is the post-reality universe that combines physical reality and digital virtuality with permanent, permanent, and multi-user features. The virtual universe stages effectively reached the augmented reality dimension of this universe (Hwang & Chien, 2022; Mystakidis, 2022).

The biggest misconception about the Metaverse is that there is only one Metaverse. However, there is not only one Metaverse, and any number of Metaverses can be created. Today, companies have Metaverses of different sizes and various features. Metaverse is a new world where three-dimensional visuality is more important, and the real world and virtuality are blended. That is why an umbrella is used as a concept. Platforms such as Horizon, Roblox, Fortnite, The Sandbox, Alien Worlds, Decentraland, Zepeto, Somnium Space, Axie Infinity, My Neighbor Alice, Hyper Verse, Super World, and Star Atlas can be given as examples. In Metaverse, people can be represented virtually with their avatars, socialize, buy and sell products, services, real estate, and land, and share with users (Akkus et al., 2022). It is also possible to pay, watch concerts, attend exhibitions, shop, visit museums, verify identity, and conduct recruitment interviews in the Metaverse world. Metaverse is not an independent world parallel to reality and can replace reality, but a symbiotic world intertwined with real life. It is a choice created not to separate the real from the virtual but to complete the reality with the virtual (Pu & Xiang, 2022). Metaverse combines the real and virtual worlds with various technological tools and software. It offers the option to customize them by creating avatars, participating in various social activities, financially acquiring virtual property, and recording them with tools such as NFT, blockchain, and trade. It can be defined as a vast network of interconnected virtual worlds rather than a single virtual world, designed to complement reality with virtual, offering the sense of an immersive three-dimensional experience where profits can be made (Özel, 2022).

The structure of Metaverse allows the presentation of the current information status to all users at the same time at all times. Therefore, it is a persistent virtual system with real-time computing capabilities. Metaverse, in terms of computer architecture, is a decentralized platform that offers a high degree of interoperability to enable the mobility of digital identities, experiences, and properties from one place, event, or event to another. It is also possible for users to develop their perceptions and assets. From the sensory point of view, it increases human interaction and makes human qualities more realistic (Efendioğlu, 2022).

It has been stated that the Metaverse consists of three structures for its architecture. These; are infrastructure, interaction, and ecosystem. Metaverse facilitates convergence between internet technologies and extended reality (Duan et al., 2021).

Infrastructure describes the multimedia system corresponding to the data storage and computation required for the virtual universe. On the other hand, interaction refers to the inclusion of users from the physical world into the virtual universe through their avatars. For this, an immersive user experience and content must be created. An immersive user experience is made possible by digital twins. Thus, users can interact within the virtual ecosystem through their avatars. The ecosystem consists of user-generated content, artificial intelligence, and the economy. User-generated content is necessary for the economy to function. Thus, it will be possible to create a vibrant community (Gadekallu et al., 2022).

The long-term Covid-19 pandemic has dramatically changed the way people live and work. Various online meetings and activities have gradually replaced face-to-face meetings. Such virtual events and events encompass the concept of Metaverse, attracting interest in academia and industry as of 2019. With the Covid-19 pandemic, the spread of remote and hybrid work in the public and private sectors, the increase in the use of digital communication technologies, and the fact that the events organized in the Metaverse have begun to be seen can be considered as an indicator of the place of virtual communication and virtual universes in people's lives (Han et al., 2021).

Although the idea of Metaverse has existed for thirty years as a speculative fictional narrative in which users are represented as avatars in disconnected virtual spaces, it has recently come to the forefront with Facebook's rebranding as "Meta" (Bibri et al., 2022). Furthermore, after Mark Zuckerberg announced in October 2021 that he started working to focus on integrating Metaverse into daily life, the word Metaverse became the most searched word in the last quarter of 2021 (Google Trends, 2022). The fact that an American couple created an avatar and participated in the first wedding held in Metaverse with their avatars, likewise holding concerts and organizing events in Metaverse, can be counted among the factors that increase the interest in the idea of Metaverse.

Metaverse offers many affordances. These are immersion, embodiment, presence and identity construction. Metaverse provides these with avatars. This creates a superior sense of self as participants control their own avatars. Because it reflects the freedom of self-expression of users and looks human-like gives them confidence. On the other hand, there are some challanges encountered in Metaverse. These are physical well-being, health and safety, psychology, morality and ethics, and data privacy. On a physical level, apps distract users and cause harmful accidents. In addition, information overload is a psychological problem that should be prevented. Morally, it leads to unauthorized magnification of preconceived views and manipulation of facts. Finally, data poses many risks in terms of privacy. The basic principles of Metaverse are based on interoperable, open, hardware agnostic and network (Mystakidis, 2022). Metaverse technologies offers consumers a very realistic experience. Users can experience mixed environments via headset, phone, or tablet. It can also interact by placing or moving digital objects into the physical world. Thus, with mixed reality, real and virtual objects are mixed and presented on a single screen. Technologies is the fusion of virtual and augmented reality to create new environments and visualizations where real and virtual objects coexist in real-time (Flavián et al., 2019). Metaverse affordances, challenges, technologies and principles are shown Figure 1 (Mystakidis, 2022).

Different platforms such as Decentraland, The Sandbox, Superworld, Somnium Space, games such as Roblox and Fortnite exist with their own platforms. While the number of platforms participating in the Metaverse universe is increasing day by day, many global brands operating in real life, from cosmetics to clothing, from automotive to food, have also started to take place here with their own platforms or by collaborating with existing platforms.Some big global brands that take a proactive attitude, that is, take a position and take action in the face of new developments, have started marketing, advertising, and brand communication activities on the Metaverse platform (Efendioglu, 2022).

Figure 1. Metaverse technologies, principles, affordances and challenges

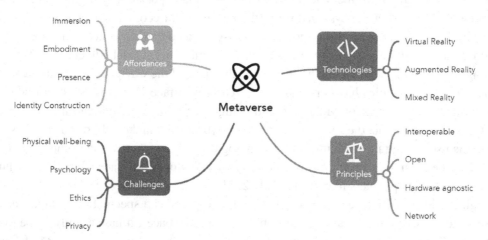

METAVERSE CONCEPTS

Augmented Reality (AR)

AR is a real-time display of computer-generated content on a real-world scene. With AR, an experience emerges where virtual elements are added to the real world (Shen et al., 2021). AR is a real-time interactive, three-dimensional system formed by superimposing a virtual component on a real space or object (Azuma, 1997). In other words, AR is the process of superimposing computer-generated information on reality, whether it is a geographical location or an object. Users benefit from tools such as smartphones, cameras, and wireless wristbands to perceive both reality and information presented virtually (Çelikkol, 2022). An image processed in AR is superimposed on a real-world image. With the world-famous mobile game Pokémon GO, which made AR widespread, players are walking around. During this ride, players capture computer-generated monsters using AR. AR can be viewed through smartphones and tablets, providing users with an interactive creative experience. Today, a navigation system is installed on vehicles with AR. Simulated arrows on the glass direct the driver to exactly where to turn. In this way, the driver does not need to follow the map; it is sufficient to follow the arrows superimposed on the road view. On the other hand, AR is the blending of digital with reality, designed to increase the user's experience or understanding (Berryman, 2012).

A concept called Augmented Reality Marketing (ARM) has also emerged with the emblem of AR's use in the marketing field. It is a new concept for today, and studies on it continue. ARM's customer experiences differ from traditional marketing (Chylinski et al., 2020). Within ARM, some strategies and examples can be applied to different sectors. For example, customers of a make-up brand can wear AR glasses and apply make-up to themselves in a virtual environment and see how they look. Wearable technologies and ARM offer powerful possibilities to maximize the experience of consumers (Rauschnabel et al., 2022). At this point, the use of neuro-marketing will bring a distinct advantage. By observing the movements of the avatars with the help of virtual reality equipment, and using body temperature and heart rate monitors, the reactions of individuals can be measured. Improvements and arrangements can be made in marketing and brand communication applications accordingly (Çelikkol, 2022).

Virtual Reality (VR)

VR is an artificial environment experienced through computer-provided sensory stimuli, such as images and sound, where one's actions partially determine what is happening in the environment. VR technology aims to integrate users with a completely artificial environment with various forms of technology to appeal to one or more senses (Scavarelli et al., 2021, p. 258). VR is the technology that enables the person to interact with the artificial three-dimensional visual and sensory environment using computer modeling. With the advanced technological methods used, the user is isolated from the physical environment. Thus, it can enter interactive and immersive virtual environments with computer simulation. So VR is the experience of fully immersing in a different environment to interact with virtual objects. VR headsets should be worn to experience VR (Shen et al., 2021). Recently, VR technologies have made environments look like the real world. For example, additional senses such as touch, sound, and smell are added to VR. Using VR technology, players can manipulate a video game with all their senses while architects review building projects before starting construction. The difference between VR from AR. AR enables embedding visual elements and sounds in a real-world environment to enhance the user experience, while VR is purely virtual and sensorial and enhances fictional realities. AR can be accessed with smartphones, and users can control real-world assets. In contrast, VR-specific headsets and glasses equipment is required.

VR allows users to access the Metaverse by bridging the apparent gap between the physical and digital worlds. Users provide experiences through digital selves or avatars. Metaverse can incorporate augmented reality and virtual reality to allow users to experience the experience of being inside the internet, digitally interacting with other individuals, objects, entities, and environments. In the Metaverse, it can be said intuitively that the soul is outside the body. Assuming that the body is viewed as a shell of our consciousness, the Metaverse allows us to break the physical and natural world with the body as the boundary and integrate human consciousness into the virtual computer world through a brain-computer interface (Bal, 2022).

Metaverse VR glasses, which are examined as examples of head-mounted displays and wearable technologies, are among the essential digital devices in the world. The ideal goal of display development in AR and VR devices is to deliver lifelike crystal clear images that can simulate, merge or recreate the surrounding environment and avoid disturbance simultaneously (Zhan et al., 2020). By observing the movements of the avatars with the help of virtual reality equipment, and using body temperature and heart rate monitors, the reactions of individuals can be measured. Improvements and arrangements can be made in marketing and brand communication applications accordingly (Çelikkol, 2022). It will take time for virtual reality products to become widespread, as the market is still tiny. In addition, these products are expected to be easy to use, affordable, stylish, and ergonomic. However, it is necessary to strengthen technological infrastructures so that hundreds of millions of users can simultaneously connect to Metaverses with high data (Topsümer & Toktop, 2022).

Mixed Reality (MR)

MR refers to the combined use of augmented and virtual reality technology (Tayfun et al., 2022). It can also be defined as the intersection between two extremes of mixed reality, realistic and unrealistic (Park & Kim, 2021). AR and VR apps may be the most popular way to experience the Metaverse, but these apps are only one way to access the Metaverse (Ball, 2022; Park & Kim, 2022). MR is the dynamic coexistence of virtual and real content in the same space. Physical and digital objects both coexist and interact in real-time. Real and virtual worlds can merge to create new environments and visualizations with MR (Shen et al., 2021). Mixed reality combines the physical and digital worlds, linking computer and environmental interactions. Its infrastructure includes computer vision, graphics processing, imaging technologies, and cloud computing. MR is beneficial for consumers and businesses. By adding virtual objects or characters to a live video stream of the real world, MR provides the user with an experience where both environments can seamlessly coexist and interact (Farshid et al., 2018, p. 660). Thanks to glasses and wearable devices that support MR technology, a movie or a football match can offer a holographic and three-dimensional experience that can be entered into the moment without the need for any screen.

Major factors expected to drive the growth of the Metaverse market include media and entertainment, increased demand in the gaming industry, and opportunities and partnerships from virtual markets. Furthermore, digitization in MR, art, fashion, and retail is increasing scope, reach and offerings to industries and end users. In addition, the meta database for promotions of brands using gamification and virtual world simulators creates a growing increase in restructuring state-of-the-art infrastructure design (Yazıcı, 2022).

Extended Reality (XR)

Extended Reality includes AR, VR, and MR technologies. The technological interaction between humans and machines begins at the point of Extended Reality (Shen et al., 2021). Thanks to extended Reality, it is possible for people to use multi-sensory wearable technologies (Mystakidis, 2022). Metaverse is recognized as one of the technologies with the most significant potential for the future. In Metaverse with Extended Reality, people can participate in activities such as discussing a topic, collaborating on a project, and learning by experiencing some problems. A person's friends in the Metaverse can be real or virtual characters. Like in the real world, various activities can occur in the Metaverse, such as economic activities, political events, and natural disasters (Hwang & Chien, 2022). High-quality Extended Reality is becoming more and more common. Consumers worldwide enjoy Extended Reality experiences ranging from immersive gaming to distance learning and virtual education. One of the trends in recent years is to broadcast Extended Reality experiences via 5G from the cloud. This eliminates the need to depend on servers or limit experiences to just one domain (Singh et al., 2021).

On the other hand, XR can be expressed as an umbrella term covering all VR/AR/MR technologies. In the last five years, XR has become a technology that has received significant interest in the scientific and industrial world, as technological developments have led to the development of more economical and ergonomic devices and allow to use of significantly more powerful software than previous generations (Çöltekin et al., 2020). Furthermore, the simulation capability offered by XR technology, which can be defined as the creation of an artificial but highly realistic form of a system's model (Maria, 1997), can be considered a kind of training ground (Kaplan et al., 2021). Metaverse handles different using AI and reality techniques. Figure 2 shows the extended reality in Metaverse (Mozumder et al., 2022).

Reality covers all realities from an umbrella perspective in the Metaverse environment. Therefore, it covers all virtual and real environments realized with computer technology and hardware. Along with the perception of mixed Reality as computer technology, it is also possible to express it as an experience that distinguishes between the simulation and the physical to the individual indistinguishably, with hardware wearable technology. In marketing, the virtual environment provides a competitive advantage in experiencing products and services and ensuring the interaction between the producer and the consumer. This brings a new perspective to marketing strategies as a force that ensures sustainability..

Figure 2. Metaverse extended reality

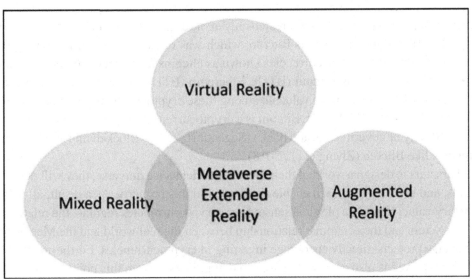

Blockchain

Blockchain is a digital, decentralized, and distributed ledger where transactions are recorded and added chronologically to create permanent and unauthorized access-protected records. Blockchain securely records transactions related to money, property, information, and authorization rights without needing a third-party intermediary such as a bank or government (Peres et al., 2022). Blockchain, not only financial transactions but also attributed value; It can be applied in many areas to record almost everything, such as education information, health reports, birth, and marriage records (Kahraman, 2022). A blockchain is a distributed database shared in ledgers between the ends of a computer network. This database stores information electronically in digital form in ledgers at each endpoint. Each block in the chain contains all transactions made. If a new transaction occurs on the blockchain, this transaction record is added to the ledger of all participants. Deletion and editing are not possible. Blockchain technology; has essential features such as decentralization, permanence, anonymity, security, and suitability. In addition, blockchain technology is becoming compatible with next-generation internet interaction systems such as smart contracts, utilities, IoT, and reputation management (Zheng et al., 2018).

Blockchain technology stores, processes, shares, and determines the originality of the metadata formed in the Metaverse. For example, blockchain technology will come to the fore in voting, determining ownership, creating an economic structure, and processing health data in the Metaverse environment. Metaverse's technologically fundamental infrastructure is vital because it is based on the decentralized blockchain without needing third-party providers. Blockchain technology is necessary for data security and economic transactions to continue securely. Therefore, Metaverse is expected to establish assertive communication with the real-world economy. Blockchain technology has also become the most significant guarantee of copyright in the digital world. Blockchain is needed because it primarily secures the digital content owned by all users in the Metaverse. Metaverse relies on the blockchain to ensure user integrity, privacy, and reputation and to account for their content and transactions (Gadekallu et al., 2022).

Cryptocurrency

Cryptocurrency is encrypted digital assets created only in the digital environment and traded in the digital environment. The first cryptocurrency is Bitcoin, which was released in 2008. Following the success of Bitcoin, several alternative cryptocurrencies known as altcoins have emerged rapidly. The most used cryptocurrencies; It is known as Bitcoin (BTC), Ethereum (ETH), Binance Coin (BNB), and Tether (USDT). However, Bitcoin is the most valuable among these cryptocurrencies because it is produced in a certain number (Wu et al., 2022, p. 3). Bitcoin is a cryptocurrency designed for anonymous payments created independently of governments and banks (Segendorf, 2014). Blockchain is formulated to create cryptocurrencies like Bitcoin (Zheng et al., 2018).

For the characters to design a world of their own in the Metaverse universe, they will need land, property, materials, and inventory that will enable them to build this property. As a result, all these services have a monetary value, if not in a physical sense. Here, cryptocurrencies regulate the relationship in the Metaverse ecosystem and the economic relationship between the real world and the Metaverse. For this reason, Metaverse projects directly encourage investing in cryptocurrencies. Furthermore, a Metaverse cryptocurrency received is also a key to the door to that universe. From this point of view, the most severe cryptocurrencies working on the Metaverse universe are Decentraland (MANA), Sandbox (SAND), Theta Network (THETA), Axie Infinity (AXS), Enjin Coin (ENJ), CEEK VR (CEEK). These Metaverse coins are also an alternative to Bitcoin and the largest altcoin, Ethereum (Toktay, 2022).

Non Fungible Token (NFT)

NFT is a digital asset trading with cryptocurrencies, and its infrastructure is based on the blockchain. NFT secures assets as royalty. All items that need copyright have been converted to digital, such as artwork, music, games, images, or videos. Because NFTs have unique and unique properties, they cannot be changed. NFT is a cryptocurrency derived from Ethereum's intelligent contracts (Wang et al., 2021). NFT is an encrypted, unchangeable, unique, and original asset that cannot be used interchangeably on the blockchain network. NFTs are transferable rights to digital assets such as art, in-game items, collections, or music. NFT secures the selling prices of intellectual property-related products and non-tradable virtual assets (Ante, 2022). In line with these explanations, it seems possible to express NFT as a fingerprint that has a different structure from each other.

NFT, a part of the Ethereum blockchain platform, is mainly used in Metaverse, which is offered to users. NFT is a type of technology that proves that any digital media is unique. NFT, which stands for the immutable digital asset, is a unit of data stored in a digital ledger called a blockchain, which confirms that a digital asset is unique and, therefore, not interchangeable. For example, the global gaming industry is valued at $300 billion, with $200 billion in direct spending and $100 billion in indirect revenue. Metaverse and blockchain-based games use NFTs to offer players a different experience. Thus, digital property is brought to the fore, and new business models and opportunities to earn money are created using crypto money (Rijmenam, 2022).

All marketing authorities agree that the metaverse universe will create an economy worth trillions of dollars due to its unique products and services. Digital objects such as NFTs will form the cornerstone of the Metaverse economy. It will be possible for an avatar to meet virtual hardware, virtual wishes, and needs, or to engage in some virtual activities, by using NFTs or other digital objects that it can buy according to its economic power (Anıl & Alankuş, 2022).

Web 3.0

Metaverse is the next phase of digital evolution and could revolutionize the internet space at a significant level. This is why most services can go beyond standard systems with online access (Gadekallu et al., 2022). When the InternetInternet first emerged, all interactions with the user with Web 1.0 were text-based. For example, emails, messages, and usernames are text-based, and the user cannot edit what is written on the website. The internet user is just a reader. Agents in Web 1.0 were servers. We needed servers to interact with someone. In Web 2.0, these servers have been replaced by platforms, and we have come to communicate only by registering. Then the multimedia-based Internet Internet emerged. These; include photos, videos, and live broadcasts. Now, users can add and edit multimedia on the InternetInternet, thanks to Web 2.0 technology. Finally, in the next step of the user experience on the Internet, a different dimension was introduced with Web 3.0.

Web 3.0 is the idea of being decentralized without being dependent on a service provider. Metaverse represents the world, the three-dimensional layer introduced with Web 3.0. The creation of economic value by blockchain technology and virtual currencies without being dependent on any authority can only become possible and operational with Web 3.0 technology. For this reason, Metaverse needs Web 3.0 technology to ensure the coexistence of digital worlds (Çelik, 2022).

The early Metaverses of Web 3.0 are predominantly virtual games where users own and trade digital assets such as land, fashion, and NFT (Murray et al., 2022). Web 3.0 will allow for a decentralized connection without any intermediaries. Again, cryptocurrencies with a decentralized system have recently become a viral subject. This brought the possibility of Web 3.0 to the agenda again and led us to an involuntary expectation. This new internet network is called the semantic network. In the Web 3.0 system, people can carry out this information entirely by connecting two people. Web 3.0 refers to the entire blockchain-supported and personalized version of the InternetInternet that can be used as Peer to Peer.

It is a prerequisite for the Web 3.0 Metaverse. Because Web 3.0 will reveal a new social contract around data and identity. Building Metaverse on the Web 3.0 infrastructure will allow it to move away from corporate surveillance. Of course, this will reduce the risk of data falling into the wrong hands to a certain extent and allow people to have complete control over their data and identities (Rijmenam, 2022). Metaverse provides an embodied user experience with real-time and dynamic interactions with digital artifacts as it connects multi-user platforms. (Mystakidis, 2022).On a closer look, Metaverse and Web 3.0 are quite relevant entities. Web 3.0 will be an infrastructure for Metaverse. VR devises to be used for Metaverse can accelerate the transition to Web 3.0. This process can be easily achieved if an open-source system, a reliable infrastructure, and verifiable communication methods are provided.

Web 3.0 is a decentralized network centered around the idea of being user-centric, offering unprecedented levels of security and privacy to user data. This web is an internet based on blockchain technologies, basically defined as a decentralized and distributed permanent digital ledger, with various cryptocurrencies that are predominantly created and traded digitally only and immutable NFTs, each of which is different from the other (Nath, 2022).

Mirror-World (MW)

The metaverse proposes 3D surroundings via glasses, headsets, and connected watches. Consequently, the metaverse is both a mirror of reality and a new universe, allowing the formation of an advanced reality with imaginative scenarios. Professionals call this digital copy of reality the mirror world. Modeling the physical world, MW captures, stores, analyzes, and manages reflections with the help of virtual mapping and sensors. A mirror world can be defined as a Metaverse where the appearance, knowledge, and structure of the real world are transferred to virtual reality as if they were mirrored. In other words, mirror worlds are digital creations that imitate the physical and social structures of the real world in a VR environment (Anderson & Rainie, 2022). An example of a mirror world is Google Earth, which collects satellite images worldwide and periodically updates the photos to reflect the ever-changing view of the real world (Lee & Kwon, 2022). Among the basic phenomena of Metaverse platforms, virtual reality technologies also show parallelism with the concept of the mirror world, which is expressed as reflecting real-world information to the virtual world in the most realistic way (Park & Kim, 2022).

Meatspace

Meatspace is the physical world or real life as opposed to cyberspace or virtual environment. It was invented in opposition to the emergence of cyberspace, the interconnected virtual world of computers with which we interact. In a modern context, cyberspace would be online, while meatspace would be offline. Metaverse transforms this type of mapping on a large scale with comprehensive, interactive user modeling by mapping and simulating all our daily activities into cyberspace. The communication formulas between people in cyberspace tend to completely change the human subject status in the content and identity transformations created in media environments. Individuals; play an active role in creating user, consumer, content provider, media opinion leadership, and communicative action areas. This new era also lays the foundation for the issue of inter-media through user accounts and applications, in which interaction and transitions between media are integrated with convergent technologies. For example, from a consumer perspective, Metaverse has opened up a new distribution channel for retailers and fashion companies when shopping for real-life products (WSJ, 2022). Users can also use 3D versions of clothing stores in Metaverse to purchase fashion items for their real-life personalities. This way, a different shopping experience has been created with real-life and online shopping characteristics. The user can act as if visiting the real-life counterpart in the three-dimensional representation of the store, go shopping with friends, and the store staff can track the person's movement and interest in the store and accordingly offer recommendations based on the product of interest to the person. This creates a service that existing online stores cannot copy.

Digital Twins

A digital twin is a digital copy of a physical asset; it updates and stores all information about its physical counterpart. Intelligent devices can be expressed as enabling objects to exchange data with other objects via the internet (Yang et al., 2022). Thanks to the IoT, every asset can theoretically emit real-time data to its digital twin (Batty, 2018). The digital twin can reduce or even prevent these risks by providing comprehensive information about real-world asset status, history, and maintenance needs (Dietz & Pernul, 2020). Furthermore, digital twins are used to predict the consequences of situations that may occur in real life through simulations (Park & Kim, 2022). Thanks to the Digital Twins applications, which are expressed as a virtual model of the product or service in Metaverse, with the creation of virtual twins of physical objects, it will be possible to decide how to make production with minimum time, movement and cost. Thus, the production time will be shortened, contributing to the preparation of the final products (Far & Rad, 2022). From a different perspective, the development process of Metaverse can be explained in three stages. These; are digital twins, digital natives, and surrealism. In the first stage, which is defined as digital twins, the physical and virtual worlds are explained as two wholly separate and independent areas; In the second stage, which is defined as digital natives, the physical and virtual worlds are explained as two separate areas that are interconnected and intertwined, with joint points. In the last stage, the physical and virtual worlds are defined as surrealism, and it is seen that the physical and virtual universes are not separated. Instead, the physical and virtual spaces are intertwined (Wang et al., 2022). Figure 3 shows presented four classification criteria for types of Metaverse (Park & Kim, 2022).

Figure 3. Types of Metaverse

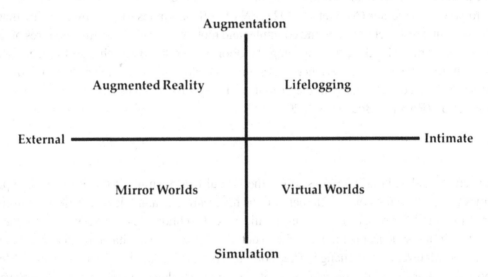

Multiverse

The definition of the Multiverse usually refers to many different universes operating independently. In the context of technology/internet/social media, this is Horizon, Minecraft, Roblox, Twitch, Fortnite, Discord, and any other virtual social media and gaming place where people socialize, play, and shop. In theory, the Metaverse could gather all these multiverses in one place. However, the concept of the Multiverse creates a large ecosystem of unconnected and different digital worlds. These digital ecosystems within the Multiverse may not allow users to switch between digital worlds seamlessly. Therefore, the fact that experiences belong to different Metaverses instead of a single Metaverse may cause this concept to be called Multiverses. From this point of view, a real Metaverse infrastructure and the development of global standards and protocols are required for Multiverses to become a single Metaverse (Rostami & Maier, 2022). The difference between the Multiverse and the Metaverse is misunderstood, as they each consist of several different ecosystems in their own right. In the case of Multiverse, a user can discover an unlimited number of different ecosystems that are unrelated to each other.

Internet of Things (IoT)

Within the Metaverse ecosystem, avatars, content production, virtual economy, and social acceptance. Metaverse's technological infrastructure includes augmented reality, human-computer interaction, blockchain, image processing, IoT, cloud computing, and artificial intelligence. IoT is a system that can transfer data over a network without needing a computer and consists of interrelated computing devices. Devices can directly connect and share data with other devices and systems over the internet. For this purpose, sensors, software, and other embedded technologies work together in the same network. These devices can be simple household appliances or advanced industrial tools. While IoT enables Metaverse to analyze and interact with the real world, Metaverse will act as a 3D user interface for IoT devices, paving the way for a new and tailored IoT user experience. Thus, Metaverse and IoT will help the world make data-driven decisions with minimal training and mental energy. As a result, Metaverse and IoT are likely to power each other (Ning et al., 2021). While IoT continues to develop in a way that renews itself daily, semantic web technologies and computer and mobile device-compatible features offer virtual worlds different from each other, thus opening the door to a new type of change for users. Real-time IoT supports immersive digital experiences with wireless and seamless connectivity. To map this IoT data from real life to a digital reality in the virtual world, Metaverse takes advantage of the advantages created by the IoT (Roxin & Bouchereau, 2017).

Avatar

Avatar is users' visual and digital expression in the virtual world, similar to their physical appearance. Many games and applications offer different options for creating avatars. It is effortless for users to create avatars similar to their physical appearance with current technologies. However, we still have a long time to create mimics, synchronization, and facial details. If people are imitated precisely, the perception of reality in the Metaverse will change. Therefore, the Avatar has an essential role in the Metaverse. The purpose of avatars, virtual representations of people in simulated environments, in Metaverse is to embody the user's desired features on a virtual character. This sense of embodiment within the fun and play in the Metaverse enhances the overall perceptual experience and interaction with the environment. In addition, the fact that the avatars are personal increases the users' motivation and positively affects public participation. Approaching ideal similarity, avatars identify with the characters of the users and create a perception of awareness around them (Rahill & Sebrechts, 2021). Besides, the relationship between Avatar and the real person in Metaverse will play an essential role in social behavior in the virtual world because a lifelike avatar will have a strong identity and facilitate social interaction. All these sensory and image similarities between people and avatars will enable the person to stand out more quickly in virtual environments (Takano & Taka, 2022).

Contrary to the use of origin, which means the manifestation of a deity on earth, Avatar is used today to mean the reflection of the human body in the digital environment. From this point of view, Avatar is used to express digital users in the virtual world (Dionisio et al., 2013). In other words, avatars are visual reflections that individuals can create to represent themselves in the virtual world. Avatars, which can be designed to look flexible and suitable for a specific scenario, as in the real world, have a significant impact on the views and perceptions of other users on digital platforms such as Metaverse (Lemenager et al., 2020).

Human Computer Interaction (HCI)

Metaverse offers new opportunities to bring human-computer interaction to life. HCI is an interdisciplinary field that studies how people interact with computers. HCI aims to make computer features as close to humans as possible. The design, evaluation, and implementation of interactive technologies are among the functions of HCI. In this respect, HCI is a new paradigm for the virtual world based on ergonomics, user experience, and interface design. (Prieto et al., 2022). In Metaverse, a three-dimensional environment where it is possible to engage in social and financial interactions, users can easily participate in daily life activities, play highly realistic games, and shop faster with the improvement of HCI (Skalidis et al., 2022). For Metaverse to take an innovative form in the future, human-computer interaction should be used in parallel with technological developments.

Three Dimension (3D)

3D can be defined as an environment where all perceptions, such as width, height, and depth, are together. It will positively affect the perception of objects' width, length, and depth in the 3D environment, which is inevitable for the Metaverse. Through 3D, the Metaverse feels like the physical world, and objects are perceived as in real life (Ljungholm, 2022).

Three dimensions, which users use to feel themselves in the virtual universe, make the interaction more realistic. For Metaverse to exist, it must be built on a three-dimensional platform. This is possible by developing the real world as virtual and three-dimensional. Today there are 3D environments such as Apple LIDAR Scanner and Microsoft Hololens.

Artificial Intelligence (AI)

AI imitates real-life experiences and tasks of individuals on a computer. It is possible to use AI in Metaverse thanks to personalized digital avatars. AI is the technology that enables machines to perform tasks by more intelligent beings using knowledge learned from previous experiences. With Metaverse, big data belonging to users will be processed, and very different AI applications will be developed. In particular, artificial intelligence will be used to create the digital twin of the physical world. Artificial intelligence can give Metaverse users real-time and essential information. Thus, the user participates more effectively in systems sensitive to people, objects, and actions with this information. Artificial intelligence-supported intelligent assistants are indispensable for digital interaction. It is planned to enter the Metaverse universe with virtual reality helmets or smart glasses, and it is stated that these will be replaced by intelligent lenses soon. Technological infrastructure studies continue on many sensory issues such as walking, running, using hands and mimics effectively, perceiving odor, and eyesight that will be strengthened with smart lenses (Gümüş, 2022). Metaverse uses 3D digital objects and avatars in a very complex way while mimicking the real world with artificial intelligence. This environment is basically defined as a virtual space that can interact. Figure 4 shows the five AI stages in the Metaverse (Mozumder et al., 2022).

Figure 4. Five Artificial Intelligence use cases in the Metaverse

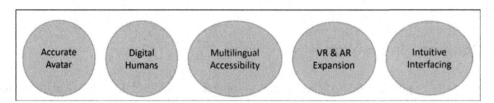

Massive Multiplayer Online Game (MMOG)

MMOGs are video games that allow multiple players to join the game simultaneously over an internet connection. This game genre connects thousands of players within the virtual world. With MMOGs, many players can use and enhance their avatars (Kong et al., 2012). There is also social interaction in these environments where the players interact with each other. These games usually take place in a shared world that players have access. These games can have thousands of players on the same server. Players can join MMOGs from anywhere worldwide with a smartphone, tablet, or computer. With MMOG, users can simultaneously play with other users from different parts of the world in various new and fictionally created digital universes. This role-playing experience, which was previously performed with simple hardware tools such as a computer interface, keyboard, and mouse, has brought the players to be included in the environment where the characters they play in the game are located with the development of wearable technologies. Thus, users have come to control it more effectively as they own a body in the fictional universe. Virtual freedoms have replaced the restrictions created by some physical necessities in the real world to the extent the software allows. However, Metaverse has a complex structure beyond the subjects such as games, entertainment software, etc., that have been produced individually until now. Devices and hardware are suitable for the interfaces, the software, and the algorithms in the background, and the developers make great efforts to make them work in harmony with each other. On the other hand, for such an intensive and application-based data flow to be uninterrupted throughout the world, the transmission and distribution infrastructures of the internet must be adapted to this.

Non Player Character (NPC)

NPC is a game character controlled by the computer and displaying intelligence. Especially in some games, people want to be friends with the artificial intelligence-driven NPC. Thus, the player has completely different social experiences from the real world (Duan et al., 2021). It can change the story in the game with NPCs acting as the player's partner. The player cannot directly control NPCs. These characters can interact with the player through text or voice. In addition, NPCs can give the player tips, cheats, and information. NPCs can serve as guides, assistants, or customer service in the Metaverse.

Moreover, in most games, machine learning algorithms are used to improve the intelligence of NPCs and artificial intelligence agents in the tactical planning and strategy of actions (Huynh-The, 2023). On the other hand, Avatars in Metaverse have much interaction with NPC. In this case, scenarios may inevitably arise that make some people feel inappropriate due to cultural differences (Zhao et al., 2022).

Digital Identities

Today, most transactions are carried out digitally. Depending on this situation, some digital identity or authentication, that is, the digital identity, enables individuals or companies to identify people, devices, or objects in the virtual world (Ante et al., 2022). Identity is a concept that defines people in general terms and uniquely distinguishes them from others. Digital identity can also be defined as the digital version of identity that uniquely distinguishes individuals digitally from others. Digital identity is the compilation of the complete information of an object or entity that exists digitally (Varma et al., 2022). The Metaverse is the evolution of the social experiment that connects our physical and digital identities. This new phygital world allows us to create ourselves as much as we want. Digital identities will not be limited to our physical bodies but will continue to exist in phygital social life in the immortality of digitalization. Digital identity is an online and technology-based form of identity designed to be equivalent to the real identity of individuals or institutions. In other words, digital identities can be defined as an identity type that is at the intersection of technology and identity, which includes many components such as biometric information, online profiles, social media shares, and self-presentations, which are defined as digital footprints of individuals, created with information transferred and recorded in digital forms has defined. Digital identities offer advantages to users. An example of these advantages is providing citizens with the opportunity to benefit from intelligent city facilities such as health, transportation, finance, and energy quickly and efficiently with a digital identity. Individuals, also known as digital users or citizens, use digital identities in all online platforms, such as social media, online shopping, digital banking, digital games, and e-commerce. With digital identity, personal digital traces are formed on the internet, and this provides many functions, such as travel, tourism, food, entertainment, and public services. It can be explained as a technology-based identity form that contributes to individuals' digital reputations, self-presentations, and personalities, that includes biometric data such as tone of voice, signature, retina, and facial expressions and is integrated into living spaces with the development of communication technologies (Mitra et al., 2022).

Lifelogging

The proliferation of ubiquitous intelligent devices such as biometric devices, smartphones, wearable fitness devices, and smartwatches has enabled us to capture, store, process, and analyze activities of daily living. In recent years, these smart devices have been equipped with various lifelogging tools and applications mainly to record and store all daily movements of users (Khan et al., 2022). Lifelogging allows people to keep digital archives of their daily lives, including footage, location tracking, attending activities, listening, reading, watching, body measurements, and internet browsing history (Belli et al., 2019). People record every moment of their lives with the applications of smart devices. Lifelogging is a technology that captures, stores, and describes everyday experiences and information about objects and people. Users capture every moment of their daily life via text, video, and audio, and then the contents are stored on the server, edited, and shared with other users (Lee, 2022).

On social media, people share their lives very freely. With the attraction of connecting with others, expectations are formed in people after posting posts. People record their life through words, pictures, videos and post it on these contributions and then wait for their community to comment on the same words, pictures and videos after the post. Predicting the reactions of friends and followers plays an important role in the lives of many people today (Kim, 2021). Lifelogging is used to improve current reality practice. The aim is to build on the current experience of everyday life. It becomes easier with the wearing of wearable devices to capture what's going on in people's lives. The most common use case for lifelogging is uploading items from someone's life for the world to see. Life diary happens when someone creates a video on YouTube, shares a picture on Instagram, posts an update on Facebook, posts a video on Tiktok, or writes their own blog post (Bolger, 2021). Lifelogging will be a core part of Metaverse in the future. Because it is truly a turning point for humanity that so many people have the ability to disclose the intimate details of their lives with such a large global community. Any environment that allows one to see the world through another's eyes and offers an insight into how others see their daily reality is a potential opportunity for everyone (Delio, 2020).

Smart Contracts

A smart contract is a contract between the buyer and the seller that works by writing the contract directly into the lines of code. The code and contracts here are distributed; It is located on a decentralized blockchain network. The code controls execution; Transactions are traceable and irreversible. With this technology, a digital contract is made within a network that can be exchanged, unchangeable, reliable, traceable, and digital without the participation of a different party (Varma et al., 2022). Smart contracts are predefined digital contracts that will be executed automatically when certain conditions are met. Contracts are stored on a blockchain, which offers a shared and trusted decentralized ledger system for parties to manage their terms of agreement through a distributed and encrypted peer-to-peer network. Traditional contracts often rely on the physical presence of the parties or electronic signature if signed remotely. Because of this, traditional contracts can be slow to execute and have inflexible terms that must be enforced by law when being adopted. Smart contracts, on the other hand, can automatically and reliably function as legally binding contracts.Thus, smart contracts are crucial for regulating in the Metaverse and helping to solve the hassle of transactions made in the Metaverse (Gilmour, 2022). Smart contracts are a method for implementing direct democracy in virtual worlds. However, it is not clear whether voting preferences in the virtual world reflect real-world voting preferences. Policies implemented by smart contracts thus offer an effective and democratic way of managing virtual worlds. Smart contracts also offer conveniences not common in the physical world, such as weighted voting in elections. In our study, we investigate the second case. For example, community voting decisions in Decentraland are enforced by smart contracts, which are programs that run when predetermined conditions are met. The most popular platform for writing smart contracts is known as Ethereum. Because in the context of the Ethereum blockchain, it is designed as a mutual fund where investors can vote on possible investments. It allows cryptographic token holders to vote on decisions that affect the community. These decisions include banning usernames, creating processes, and adding terms to the list of banned words (Oppenlaender, 2022).

METAVERSE MARKETING

It is expected that new rules will be added to the digital marketing efforts with Metaverse. For example, marketing studies in the two-dimensional digital environment are similar to traditional environments, using formats such as text, audio, video, and pictures. However, in three-dimensional virtual worlds, these studies are carried out with the help of AR applications, also called wearable technologies, and VR glasses and tactile gloves. Thus, all marketing elements are readily displayed to target users on Metaverse platforms that can be accessed (Topsümer & Toktop, 2022). Metaverse marketing allows brands to interact with customers in different ways to stand out from their competitors. Prioritizing new forms of interactive content increases the likelihood of starting a conversation with the brand's target audience. Registering the brand's place in the virtual world not only increases its exposure in the metadata store, but also increases its conversions in the real world. Marketing in metadata expands brand awareness and adapts to the capabilities of virtual environments. Metaverse provides new and different environments to create an immersive story that users can participate in while telling the stories of brands in marketing campaigns (Yazıcı, 2022). Because Metaverse is comprehensive, it offers branded installations and events that users can interact with, rather than just placing simple ads. In the Metaverse, brands have recently discovered new revenue streams through collaborations. A perfect integration between the brand and Metaverse is very important for this to happen. The placement of the brand in the Metaverse world and the selection of the messages it gives require good planning, the right choice and a good integration.

It is seen that the tendency of consumers toward innovative businesses has increased in recent years. Consumers expect innovation in the services and products offered and management styles that affect the customer experience. The consumer profile, which wants to stay within the usual consumer behaviors and be limited by the environment they live in, directs the future of the enterprises. We must know that we are faced with consumers who do not want to be imprisoned in time limits, geographical boundaries, and even administrative boundaries that will determine the rules of life. The metaverse world offers the opportunity to create a life form beyond the perceptions of place and space. It offers a libertarian space for the consumer to go to the concert they want with one click, travel anywhere in the world, and own land in the country they want (Çelikkol, 2022). Besides its potential to create a new technological revolution, Metaverse is expected to provide a shared environment and economy for humanity regardless of where people live, their occupational position, gender, race, and even disability (Duan et al., 2021). Metaverse, which is thought to affect consumer behavior, consumption patterns, and working life by changing the structure of society, is seen as a great opportunity (Pu & Xiang, 2022).

On the other hand, traditional marketing is to communicate directly with existing or potential customers and to get an instant reaction from customers in return for this communication. Metaverse is a candidate to be a typical traditional marketing site. Metaverse is seen as the first option of businesses aiming to hold on to the market in the future. Sponsored ads, an activity that facilitates marketing, is another method used to ensure promotion in Metaverse markets, and its roots are based on physical reality (Avila, 2022). Sponsorship is much more effective when used in an integrated way with other marketing communication elements. In addition, it provides the opportunity to eliminate the multiplicity and durability of messages in traditional advertising environments and draw attention to the message. As the end point of digitalization, Metaverse brings a new dimension to many marketing concepts, such as distribution, supply, and delivery. Despite this, the distinction between goods and services remains valid in the metaverse market, and the ethical principles that dominate physical distribution are also observed in virtual reality. These principles and other Metaverse-specific rules will likely develop and settle over time. At this point, the concept of Metaverse law emerges. Predictably, a decentralized life will be maintained in parallel with the blockchain mentality in the metaverse universe (Vergne, 2021, p.8). However, the establishment of this life on a chaotic plane is not considered. Metaverse, which is a big market as well as opening a new digital age, has some general rules to give confidence to investors, standard contracts on issues such as usage, trading, smart contracts necessary to operate in the market, ethical codes, and even basic norms that all users must comply with them. It is evaluated to have a meta-law that includes the rights and freedoms specific to the universe (Anıl & Alankuş, 2022). Because the Metaverse is a significant investment arena where large volumes of money are invested, each user acts as a potential trader.

FUTURE CONSUMER BEHAVIOUR WITH METAVERSE

In Metaverse, which is also called the future of the internet by many users, consumers will soon be able to perceive the virtual world with their five senses thanks to wearable technologies (Doko, 2021). Over the years, people have started to take more place in the digital environment. As a result, the number of people shopping online has also increased. While in classical e-commerce sites, consumers make a purchase decision by looking at the photo of the product and the comments under the product, this situation has started to change with Metaverse. Consumers will begin to have an easier buying experience, for example, by trying on an outfit. In addition, in Metaverse, people will not only consume products, but will interact with brands constantly. As a result, brands will be able to keep in touch with their customers and manage the process more effectively (Çelikkol, 2022).The use of the internet by brands and businesses to promote and present their products or services to consumers has led to the rapid development of digital practices of consumer behavior, which is an important dimension of communication (Zhu, et al., 2017). Thus, in the marketing of products or services, it will change consumer behavior in Metaverse in line with digital marketing strategies. Because Meteverse will facilitate the digital experience of the products or services in the ecosystem of businesses, the ability to shop and the organization of virtual event organizations. It is seen that the target consumer groups are working hard to be included in the Metaverse ecosystem in order to reach them through new communication channels. In this context, Metaverse, which is predicted to be the internet of the future, will reveal new consumer behavior practices (Yılmaz, 2022).

With consumers using previous internet-based systems, companies entering Metaverse, Metaverse is a crucial opportunity to bring products and services together. Therefore, many leading global brands have already been included in the Metaverse trend (Hackl et al., 2022). As a result of these big investments that will shape the future, it is thought that the current two-dimensional internet environment will be replaced by three-dimensional virtual worlds that can be accessed with the help of wearable technologies (Sanaç, 2022). These created virtual worlds are multi-user, permanent platforms of the future. Consumers who normally live far from each other can interact with Metaverse in real-time in virtual worlds to shop and socialize. With all these innovations, there will be a situation where the real and the virtual can no longer be completely separated from each other. Metaverse eliminates the distinction between real and virtual, making it possible to bring social relations, entertainment and shopping together in 3D to the digital environment (Topsümer & Toktop, 2022).

Global brands use digital marketing practices in line with their digital communication strategies in order to establish and maintain their communication with their target audiences online. While social media channels are used intensively today in order to produce a unique, participatory and interactive consumer experience between the brand and the target audience, Metaverse, which is described as the internet and social media of the future, is expected to be used in the coming years. Therefore, today's marketing communication practices will initiate a new marketing approach in the Metaverse environment in the digital marketing understanding of the future.

BRANDS ENTERING METAVERSE

By starting to use Metaverse, brands will reach their target audiences more efficiently and cost-effectively, develop digital marketing strategies and make their work continuous. The most important feature of this process is that brands start to receive feedback from customers virtually. Comments that most people can witness in the Metaverse environment will make consumer feedback very remarkable for brands. In recent years, international product or service brands have been implementing Metaverse marketing practices in line with their marketing digital communication strategies. The Hyundai Mobility Adventure application, realized in the Roblox metaspace, an online game programming, production and playing system in partnership with Hyundai, a manufacturer brand in the automotive industry, and Roblox, one of the Metaverse platforms, is the festival square of the application, the mobile city of the future, the eco-forest with customizable avatar user characters. offers the opportunity to experience the future applications of the products and services of the Hyundai brand, play game ads and participate in social activities in the themes of race park and smart technology campus. The QVerse virtual reality application, produced as a result of the partnership of Qatar Airways, a brand in the transportation industry, and Epic Games, a video game production and development company, offers a service called Sama, the first meta-human cabin crew among global airline companies, and provides individuals with a digital interactive customer experience in their air travels. . The Nikeland application, realized in the Roblox metaspace in partnership with Nike, a brand in the textile industry, and Roblox company, enables individuals to experience Nike products in a digital sports format in a game advertisement format through avatar characters that can be personalized using Nike products (Yılmaz, 2022).

Global brands such as Pizza Hut, Dolce & Gabbana, Balenciaga, Nike, Zara, Adidas, Coca Cola have stepped into the world of Metaverse. The world-famous pizza restaurant chain Pizza Hut produced the world's first NFT pizza with a project called "1 Byte Favorites". This virtual pizza slice was sold in cryptocurrency (0.0001 Ethereum). On the other hand, the Coca-Cola brand offered the NFT product named "Coca-Cola Bubble Jacket" for sale through OpenSea. Luxury fashion brand "Gucci" has built a virtual and permanent town named "Gucci Town" in the "Roblox" universe. This town has a Gucci online store, a cafe, and a playground.

According to Gucci officials, twenty million users visited this town in two weeks. Gucci also continues its activities in augmented reality applications. When they point a mobile phone camera at their feet, they can see how the virtually fabricated shoes look on their feet. Gucci also sells its products, such as shoes and bags, as NFT, and users also get virtual products at considerable prices compared to the actual products. Another clothing brand, Nike, launched an NFT collection of 20,000 shoes. Developing digital add-ons in addition to shoes, Nike has also offered its customers the experience of how shoes look on their feet through camera filters using AR. A digital fashion event was held for the first time on "Decentraland," another Metaverse platform. In the "Metaverse Fashion Week 2022" event, catwalk walks, parties, and clothing exhibitions were open to everyone. Users could purchase products in NFT format and could try those products beforehand (Türk et al., 2022). Figure 5 shows experience, discovery, creator economy, spatial computing, decentralize, human interface and infrastructure for Metaverse market map (Radoff, 2021).

Metaverse platforms also provide vast opportunities in terms of marketing methods known as "interactive marketing" or "experiential marketing," which enable brands to connect with their target customers by designing and creating personal experiences. Thanks to the "realistic experience" feature of Metaverse, brands have had the opportunity to have their consumers test their products in a virtual environment.

Brands have also started to move their stores to the 3D digital environment. Brands that enter the Metaverse can offer new customer purchasing experiences by appealing to the senses with various wearable technology equipment such as virtual reality glasses, tactile gloves, and sensor heads. With the help of virtual glasses, customers can visit 3D stores and try products with their avatars. Purchased products can be used as NFTs and can be dressed as avatars (Topsümer & Toktop, 2022).

Figure 5. Metaverse market map

DISCUSSION AND CONCLUSION

Today, with the introduction of Web 3.0 technology, the two-dimensional internet environment is evolving into three-dimensional virtual worlds. Metaverse, which is the most talked about one of these today, is predicted to be an advanced version of the social media platforms that everyone knows today. As a result of this, new rules and dynamics will naturally be added to the marketing activities carried out in the digital environment. While marketing communication works in the two-dimensional digital environment are carried out using forms such as text, audio, video, and images in a way that we can say similar to traditional environments, these works in three-dimensional virtual worlds are delivered to target users on Metaverse platforms, which can be entered with the help of augmented reality glasses, also called wearable technologies, and tactile gloves. will be displayed. 21st century businesses face many changes. Among these, it is the technological changes that provide the most benefit to the business. In the digital age, where Industry 5.0 is being talked about, businesses need to be ready for change and transformation. Because consumer demands and needs are also affected and differentiated by technology. Since the main founding philosophy of the enterprises is to meet the needs, the enterprises should present their products to the market within the framework of the demands and needs required by today's technological conditions.

Metaverse has created its own system in terms of both participation and economic values and created a new market. This phenomenon, which is expressed as the Metaverse market, has its own components. Brands and businesses need to implement some techniques and strategies in order to exist in the Metaverse marketing world and to continue the opportunities they have obtained before. For this, the Metaverse marketing strategy should be set up correctly, and then evaluation, planning, training and influencing steps should be applied. Metaverse marketing strategy, which has started to be used effectively as a new generation representation of digital marketing, has created both its own usage area and an economic system. Although this new generation participation method has various disadvantages and risks, it will reach a wide user base effectively and rapidly in the world. Metaverse offers a promising future for computing and technology for participants, businesses and brands alike. When evaluated within the brand and marketing relationship, digital marketers need to keep up with the latest technological developments. Metaverse is shown as the new platform of digital marketing. In terms of brands and marketing, the meta universe is expanding very fast. Metaverse world, the last point of digital transformation, is a platform designed on augmented virtual reality. Metaverse is a digital universe where you can buy and sell products and communicate with customers, as well as providing entertainment, education and information. In this context, Metaverse is a virtual world where physically existing businesses can show themselves, as well as hosting completely virtual businesses. Metaverse business consists of various sub-systems such as production, management and marketing so that the business can continue its activities, just like in the physical organization. Thanks to the technology used in the Metaverse world, communication with all stakeholders as well as customers in business management will be fast and easy. Thanks to technological designs, the promotion of products will be easier and the number of the target audience of the enterprise will increase rapidly. For example, with the Digital Twin application, the ability of a physically existing business to observe its activities in the Metaverse world in three dimensions will contribute to the development of the business.

Metaverse users will exist on Metaverse platforms through their avatars. In other words, users need to carefully design their avatars in order to present themselves in such a new marketing environment and to be permanent in that environment. In this way, users in the Metaverse world can create their own avatars as they wish. The person can create an image of himself as if he were in real life and feel that he belongs to the social class he wants to be. For this reason, new consumers will be created and spending in the virtual world will not be avoided. There is no doubt that this provides an advantage for brands and businesses as well.Metaverse marketing consists of many trends already making much noise and should be noticed. With the increasing interest and knowledge of companies and investors, the future of this industry is evident. Metaverse provides opportunities to create memorable, immersive experiences for audiences of users and customers. With virtual webinars and events, concerts, launch parties, and more to be used in event marketing strategies, Metaverse is a technology where consumers can interact with a brand like never before and experience an emotion they will never forget. Marketing professionals and businesses need to understand and evaluate the full potential of the metaverse universe. Because if we look at the digitalized world, it is possible to say that the Metaverse and similar technologies will take place in the lives of individuals for a long time. This situation shows that marketing will be an essential element in the metaverse world day by day. The first thing digital marketers who want to improve themselves in metaverse marketing should do is to determine a target audience. Considering the Metaverse and marketing, the companies determining the target audience should turn to the Y and Z generations at this point because it would be correct to say that the individuals who will adapt most quickly to the metaverse technology are the members of the Y and Z generation. In addition, marketers who want to adapt to Metaverse need to take specific training and have a little knowledge of blockchain technology, having information about which universes are used and how it makes it easier to adapt to the Metaverse here. In addition, examining the brands that stepped into the metaverse world and discovering what kind of discourse they developed will make things easier. It is well known that branding and advertising opportunities will grow in Metaverse. Located in the metaverse world, virtual billboards, commercial products, and NFTs will play an active role in metaverse marketing in the future. They will facilitate the branding process of brands in Metaverse. At this point, brands will create virtual content for their customers over time in order to be able to market in the Metaverse, and this will affect their brand awareness. In the Metaverse universe, brands need to reach their target audience and develop a community after reaching this target audience. At this point, it is essential to respect the community's management and individuals' decisions.

It is expected that a certain time will pass for the Metaverse to take a strong place in our lives. It will take time for virtual reality products to become widespread, as the market is still small. In addition, these products are expected to be easy to use, affordable, stylish and ergonomic. In addition, it is necessary to strengthen technological infrastructures in order for hundreds of millions of users to simultaneously connect to Metaverses with high data. It is very important for businesses to be able to catch up with the ever-changing technology and see opportunities in order to survive and stay ahead of the competition. Businesses that cannot keep up with the times, cannot be open to technological innovations, and cannot develop strategies for potential future situations are in a way doomed to be defeated. The sooner and consciously the businesses adapt to the changes in the external environment, the more they can be successful the more they attach importance to technological research and infrastructure. This situation actually enables businesses, brands and businesses to enter the Metaverse world. Because in Metaverse, it has become possible not only to play games, but also to virtual tours, artistic activities and shopping. Metaverse users want to exist in the Metaverse world, experience shopping and service by using virtual and augmented reality equipment. As a result, businesses have directed their investments to this technology. The fact that brands offer a realistic shopping experience creates significant advantages for Metaverse consumers. Businesses using virtual and augmented reality technologies have a high chance of being successful in the market. Creating NFT products and virtual-only collections and offering them for sale in virtual stores will be strategies that reinforce this experience.

Metaverse offers consumers, businesses and brands a promising future for information marketing. When evaluated in this relationship, digital marketers need to keep up with the latest technological developments offered with Metaverse. When the general structure of Metaverse and digital marketing are evaluated together, it is seen that the concept of creative content comes to the fore. Metaverse marketing shows that it can be effective in creating awareness for a certain product and service category, helping to promote new products and services in the market, and repositioning a product in the market. It is very important for manufacturers and brands to get acquainted with Metaverse without wasting time and to understand its dynamics in terms of opening the way for strategies that can be produced in marketing communication in the future. The more target consumers and potential consumers are encountered in the relevant environment, the more closely their expectations and needs in the environment will be followed and analyzed. For this reason, Metaverse marketing strategy is an area that needs to be studied in detail.

REFERENCES

Akkus, H. T., Gursoy, S., Dogan, M., & Demir, A. B. Metaverse and Metaverse Cryptocurrencies (Meta Coins): Bubbles or Future?. *Journal of Economics Finance and Accounting, 9*(1), 22-29. doi:10.17261/Pressacademia.2022.1542

Akour, I. A., Al-Maroof, R. S., Alfaisal, R., & Salloum, S. A. (2022). A conceptual framework for determining metaverse adoption in higher institutions of gulf area: An empirical study using hybrid SEM-ANN approach. *Computers and Education: Artificial Intelligence, 3*, 100052. doi:10.1016/j.caeai.2022.100052

Anderson, J., & Rainie, L. (2022). *The metaverse in 2040*. Pew Research Center.

Anıl, F., & Alankuş, Z. (2022). Metaverse Evreninde Pazarlama: 7P Pazarlama Karmasi Üzerinden Bir Değerlendirme. *Uluslararası Halkla İlişkiler ve Reklam Çalışmaları Dergisi, 5*(1), 134–168.

Ante, L., Fischer, C., & Strehle, E. (2022). A bibliometric review of research on digital identity: Research streams, influential works and future research paths. *Journal of Manufacturing Systems, 62*, 523–538. doi:10.1016/j.jmsy.2022.01.005

Avila, A. (2022). Prophetic Churches for the Metaverse: Communities who sing the melody of hope. *Indonesian Journal of Theology, 10*(2), 209–230. doi:10.46567/ijt.v10i2.250

Azuma, R. T. (1997). A survey of augmented reality. *Presence (Cambridge, Mass.), 6*(4), 355–385. doi:10.1162/pres.1997.6.4.355

Bal, F. (2022). Metaverse'de Duygusal ve İkili İlişkiler. A. Güven & M. S. Tam (Ed.), Alternatif Dijital Evren Metaverse-I Kavramsal Tartışmalar, Sosyoloji, Psikoloji, Sanat ve Etik (123-138). Necmettin Erbakan Üniversitesi Yayınları

Ball, M. (2022). *The metaverse and how it will revolutionize everything*. Liveright Publishing.

Belli, K., Akbaş, E., & Yazici, A. (2019). Activity learning from lifelogging images. *In International Conference on Artificial Intelligence and Soft Computing* (pp. 327-337). Springer, Cham.

Berryman, D. R. (2012). Augmented reality: A review. *Medical Reference Services Quarterly, 31*(2), 212–218. doi:10.1080/02763869.2012.670604 PMID:22559183

Bibri, S. E., Allam, Z., & Krogstie, J. (2022). The Metaverse as a virtual form of data-driven smart urbanism: Platformization and its underlying processes, institutional dimensions, and disruptive impacts. *Computers & Urban Society, 2*(1), 1–22. doi:10.100743762-022-00051-0 PMID:35974838

Bolger, R. K. (2021). Finding wholes in the metaverse: Posthuman mystics as agents of evolutionary contextualization. *Religions, 12*(9), 768. doi:10.3390/rel12090768

Çelik, R. (2022). Metaverse Nedir? Kavramsal Değerlendirme ve Genel Bakış. *Balkan ve Yakın Doğu Sosyal Bilimler Dergisi, 8*(1), 67–74.

Çelikkol, Ş. (2022). Metaverse Dünyasi'nin, Tüketici Satin Alma Davranişlari Açisindan Değerlendirilmesi. *İstanbul Kent Üniversitesi İnsan ve Toplum Bilimleri Dergisi*. 3 (1). 64-75.

Chalmers, D., Fisch, C., Matthews, R., Quinn, W., & Recker, J. (2022). Beyond the bubble: Will NFTs and digital proof of ownership empower creative industry entrepreneurs? *Journal of Business Venturing Insights, 17*, e00309. doi:10.1016/j.jbvi.2022.e00309

Chylinski, M., Heller, J., Hilken, T., Keeling, D. I., Mahr, D., & de Ruyter, K. (2020). Augmented reality marketing: A technology-enabled approach to situated customer experience. [AMJ]. *Australasian Marketing Journal, 28*(4), 374–384. doi:10.1016/j.ausmj.2020.04.004

Çöltekin, A., Lochhead, I., Madden, M., Christophe, S., Devaux, A., Pettit, C., Lock, O., Shukla, S., Herman, L., Stachoň, Z., Kubíček, P., Snopková, D., Bernardes, S., & Hedley, N. (2020). Extended reality in spatial sciences: A review of research challenges and future directions. *ISPRS International Journal of Geo-Information, 9*(7), 439. doi:10.3390/ijgi9070439

Delio, I. (2020). *Re-Enchanting the Earth: Why AI Needs Religion*. Orbis.

Dietz, M., & Pernul, G. (2020). Digital twin: Empowering enterprises towards a system-of-systems approach. *Business & Information Systems Engineering, 62*(2), 179–184. doi:10.100712599-019-00624-0

Dionisio, J. D. N., III, W. G. B., & Gilbert, R. (2013). 3D virtual worlds and the metaverse: Current status and future possibilities. *ACM Computing Surveys (CSUR), 45*(3), 1-38. doi:10.1145/2480741.2480751

Doko, E. (2021). Alternatif bir dünya arayışı: Metaverse. *Lacivert., 85*, 79–81.

Duan, H., Li, J., Fan, S., Lin, Z., Wu, X., & Cai, W. (2021, October). *Metaverse for social good: A university campus prototype*. In *Proceedings of the 29th ACM International Conference on Multimedia* (pp. 153-161). 10.1145/3474085.3479238

Efendioglu, I. H. (2022). Metaverse Platformları, Metaverse Oyunları ve Metaverse'e Giriş Yapan İşletmeler. A. Güven & M. S. Tam (Ed.), Alternatif Dijital Evren Metaverse-I Kavramsal Tartışmalar, Sosyoloji, Psikoloji, Sanat ve Etik (101-126). Necmettin Erbakan Üniversitesi Yayınları

Far, S. B., & Rad, A. I. (2022). Applying Digital Twins in Metaverse: User Interface, Security and Privacy Challenges. *Journal of Metaverse, 2*(1), 8–16.

Farshid, M., Paschen, J., Eriksson, T., & Kietzmann, J. (2018). Go boldly!: Explore augmented reality (AR), virtual reality (VR), and mixed reality (MR) for business. *Business Horizons, 61*(5), 657 663. doi:10.1016/j.bushor.2018.05.009

Flavián, C., Ibáñez-Sánchez, S., & Orús, C. (2019). The impact of virtual, augmented and mixed reality technologies on the customer experience. *Journal of Business Research, 100*, 547–560. doi:10.1016/j.jbusres.2018.10.050

Gadekallu, T. R., Huynh-The, T., Wang, W., Yenduri, G., Ranaweera, P., Pham, Q. V., . . . Liyanage, M. (2022). *Blockchain for the Metaverse: A Review*. arXiv preprint arXiv:2203.09738. doi:10.48550/arXiv.2203.09738

Gilmour, P. M. (2022). *Smart Contracts and the Metaverse*. The Company Lawyer.

Google Trends. (2022). https://trends.google.com/trends/explore?q=metaverse Access Date: 11.12.2022

Gümüş, B. (2022). Modadan Dijital Modaya – Modanin Teknolojik Dönüşümü. A. Güven & M. S. Tam (Ed.), Alternatif Dijital Evren Metaverse-I Kavramsal Tartışmalar, Sosyoloji, Psikoloji, Sanat ve Etik (269-286). Necmettin Erbakan Üniversitesi Yayınları

Hackl, C., Lueth, D., & Di Bartolo, T. (2022). *Navigating the metaverse: A guide to limitless possibilities in a Web 3.0 world*. John Wiley & Sons.

Han, J., & Heo, J., ve You, E. (2021). *Analysis of metaverse platform as a new play culture: Focusingon roblox and zepeto*. In Proceedings of the 2nd International Conference on Human centered Artificial Intelligence (Computing 4 Human 2021). CEUR Workshop Proceedings, Da Nang, Vietnam

Hollensen, S., Kotler, P., & Opresnik, M. O. (2022). Metaverse–the new marketing universe. *The Journal of Business Strategy*. Advance online publication. doi:10.1108/JBS-01-2022-0014

Huynh-The, T., Pham, Q. V., Pham, X. Q., Nguyen, T. T., Han, Z., & Kim, D. S. (2023). Artificial intelligence for the metaverse: A survey. *Engineering Applications of Artificial Intelligence, 117*, 105581. doi:10.1016/j.engappai.2022.105581

Hwang, G. J., & Chien, S. Y. (2022). Definition, roles, and potential research issues of the metaverse in education: An artificial intelligence perspective. *Computers and Education: Artificial Intelligence, 100082*, 100082. Advance online publication. doi:10.1016/j.caeai.2022.100082

Kahraman, M. E. (2022). Blok zincir, Deepfake, Avatar, Kripto para, NFT ve Metaverse ile Yaygınlaşan Sanal Yaşam. [UKSAD]. *Uluslararası Kültürel ve Sosyal Araştırmalar Dergisi, 8*(1), 149–162. doi:10.46442/intjcss.1106228

Kaplan, A. D., Cruit, J., Endsley, M., Beers, S. M., Sawyer, B. D., & Hancock, P. A. (2021). The effects of virtual reality, augmented reality, and mixed reality as training enhancement methods: A meta analysis. *Human Factors, 63*(4), 706–726. doi:10.1177/0018720820904229 PMID:32091937

Khan, M., Khusro, S., & Alam, I. (2022). Smart TV-based lifelogging systems: current trends, challenges, and the road ahead. *Information and Knowledge in Internet of Things*, 31-58. doi:10.1007/978-3-030-75123-4_2

Kim, S.. 2021. The Metaverse: The Digital Earth—The World of Rising Trends. Kindle Edition. Paju: SPlanB Design.

Kong, J. S. L., Kwok, R. C. W., & Fang, Y. (2012). The effects of peer intrinsic and extrinsic motivation on MMOG game-based collaborative learning. *Information & Management, 49*(1), 1–9. doi:10.1016/j.im.2011.10.004

Kutlu, M. (2022). Metaverse Kapisini Aralayan Reklamlar. A. Güven & M. S. Tam (Ed.), Alternatif Dijital Evren Metaverse-II Reklam, Pazarlama, Marka ve İşletme Yönetimi (33-56). Necmettin Erbakan Üniversitesi Yayınları

Lee, J., & Kwon, K. H. (2022). Novel pathway regarding good cosmetics brands by NFT in the metaverse world. *Journal of Cosmetic Dermatology, 21*(12), 6584–6593. doi:10.1111/jocd.15277 PMID:35894837

Lemenager, T., Neissner, M., Sabo, T., Mann, K., & Kiefer, F. (2020). "Who am i" and "how should I be": A systematic review on self-concept and avatar identification in gaming disorder. *Current Addiction Reports, 7*(2), 166–193. doi:10.100740429-020-00307-x

Ljungholm, D. P. (2022). Metaverse-based 3D visual modeling, virtual reality training experiences, and wearable biological measuring devices in immersive workplaces. *Psychosociological Issues in Human Resource Management, 10*(1), 64–77. doi:10.22381/pihrm10120225

Lv, Z., Shang, W. L., & Guizani, M. (2022). Impact of Digital Twins and Metaverse on Cities: History, Current Situation, and Application Perspectives. *Applied Sciences (Basel, Switzerland)*, *12*(24), 12820. doi:10.3390/app122412820

Mitra, A., Bera, B., Das, A. K., Jamal, S. S., & You, I. (2023). Impact on blockchain-based AI/ML enabled big data analytics for Cognitive Internet of Things environment. *Computer Communications*, *197*, 173–185. doi:10.1016/j.comcom.2022.10.010

Moro-Visconti, R. (2022). ESG-compliant Metaverse Ecosystems: Clues for Impact Investing. http://www.morovisconti.com/en Access date: 22.01.2022

Mozumder, M. A. I., Sheeraz, M. M., Athar, A., Aich, S., & Kim, H. C. (2022). Overview: Technology roadmap of the future trend of metaverse based on IoT, blockchain, AI technique, and medical domain metaverse activity. In 2022 24th International Conference on Advanced Communication Technology (ICACT) (pp. 256-261). IEEE.

Murray, A., Kim, D., & Combs, J. (2022). The promise of a decentralized Internet: What is web 3.0 and HOW can firms prepare? *Business Horizons*. Advance online publication. doi:10.1016/j.bushor.2022.06.002

Mystakidis, S. (2022). Metaverse. *Encyclopedia*, *2*(1), 486–497. doi:10.3390/encyclopedia2010031

Nath, K. (2022). *Evolution of the Internet from Web 1.0 to Metaverse: The Good*. The Bad and The Ugly.

Ning, H., Wang, H., Lin, Y., Wang, W., Dhelim, S., Farha, F., . . . Daneshmand, M. (2021). *A Survey on Metaverse: the State-of-the-art, Technologies, Applications, and Challenges*. arXiv preprint arXiv:2111.09673. doi:10.48550/arXiv.2111.09673

Oppenlaender, J. (2022). The Perception of Smart Contracts for Governance of the Metaverse. In *Proceedings of the 25th International Academic Mindtrek Conference* (pp. 1-8). 10.1145/3569219.3569300

Özel, N. G. (2022). *Metaverse ve Pazarlama Uygulamalarinin Değerlendirilmesi* (M. Saygılı, Ed.). Sürdürülebilirlik Güncel Konular ve Tartışmalar. Efe Akademi.

Park, S., & Kim, S. (2022). Identifying World Types to Deliver Gameful Experiences for Sustainable Learning in the Metaverse. *Sustainability*, *14*(3), 1361. doi:10.3390u14031361

Peres, R., Schreier, M., Schweidel, D. A., & Sorescu, A. (2022). Blockchain meets marketing: Opportunities, threats, and avenues for future research. *International Journal of Research in Marketing*. Advance online publication. doi:10.1016/j.ijresmar.2022.08.001

Prieto, J. de la F., Lacasa, P., & Martínez-Borda, R. (2022). *Approaching Metaverses: Mixed reality interfaces in youth media platforms*. New Techno Humanities., doi:10.1016/j.techum.2022.04.004

Pu, Q., & Xiang, W. (2022). The metaverse and its influence and transformation on human society. *Metaverse*, *3*(1), 15. doi:10.54517/met.v3i1.1796

Radoff, J. (2021). Market map of the metaverse Medium, https://medium.com/ building-the metaverse/market-map -of-the-metaverse-8ae0cde89696 Access Date: 20.01.2022

Rahill, K. M., & Sebrechts, M. M. (2021). Effects of Avatar player-similarity and player-construction on gaming performance. *Computers in Human Behavior Reports*, *4*, 100131. doi:10.1016/j.chbr.2021.100131

Rauschnabel, P. A., Babin, B. J., tom Dieck, M. C., Krey, N., & Jung, T. (2022). What is augmented reality marketing? Its definition, complexity, and future. *Journal of Business Research*, *142*, 1140–1150. doi:10.1016/j.jbusres.2021.12.084

Rijmenam, V. M. (2022). *Step into the Metaverse: How the Immersive Internet Will Unlock a Trillion Dollar Social Economy*. John Wiley & Sons.

Rostami, S., & Maier, M. (2022). The Metaverse and Beyond: Implementing Advanced Multiverse Realms With Smart Wearables. *IEEE Access: Practical Innovations, Open Solutions*, *10*, 110796–110806. doi:10.1109/ACCESS.2022.3215736

Roxin, I., & Bouchereau, A. (2017). Introduction to the Technologies of the Ecosystem of the Internet of Things. *Internet of Things: Evolutions and Innovations*, *4*, 51–95. doi:10.1002/9781119427391.ch3

Şahin, D., & Mutlu, S. (2022). Meta Influencer: Dünyada Yer Alan Meta Influencer Örneklerinin Değerlendirilmesi. A. Güven & M. S. Tam (Ed.), Alternatif Dijital Evren Metaverse-II Reklam, Pazarlama, Marka ve İşletme Yönetimi (101-126). Necmettin Erbakan Üniversitesi Yayınları

Scavarelli, A., Arya, A., & Teather, R. J. (2021). Virtual reality and augmented reality in social learning spaces: A literature review. *Virtual Reality (Waltham Cross)*, *25*(1), 257–277. doi:10.100710055-020-00444-8

Segendorf, B. (2014). What is bitcoin. *Sveri ges Riksbank. Economic Review (Kansas City, Mo.)*, *2014*, 2–71.

Shen, B., Tan, W., Guo, J., Zhao, L., & Qin, P. (2021). How to promote user purchase in metaverse? A systematic literature review on consumer behavior research and virtual commerce application design. *Applied Sciences (Basel, Switzerland)*, *11*(23), 11087. doi:10.3390/app112311087

Singh, A. K., Liu, J., Tirado Cortes, C. A., & Lin, C. T. (2021, May). *Virtual global landmark: An augmented reality technique to improve spatial navigation learning*. In *Extended Abstracts of the 2021 CHI Conference on Human Factors in Computing Systems* (pp. 1-6).

Takano, M., & Taka, F. (2022). Fancy avatar identification and behaviors in the virtual world: Preceding avatar customization and succeeding communication. *Computers in Human Behavior Reports*, *6*, 100176. doi:10.1016/j.chbr.2022.100176

Tayfun, A., Silik, C. E., Şimşek, E., & Dülger, A. S. (2022). Metaverse: Turizm İçin Bir Fırsat Mı? Yoksa Bir Tehdit Mi?(Metaverse: An Opportunity. *Journal of Tourism and Gastronomy Studies*, *10*(2), 818–836. doi:10.21325/jotags.2022.1017

Toktay, Y. (2022). Metaverse Evrenlerinde Kripto Paralarin Rolü. A. Güven & M. S. Tam (Ed.), Alternatif Dijital Evren Metaverse-II Reklam, Pazarlama, Marka ve İşletme Yönetimi (59-78). Necmettin Erbakan Üniversitesi Yayınları

Topsümer, F., & Toktop, O. (2022). Metaverse Platformlarinda Pazarlama, Reklam ve Marka İletişimi. A. Güven & M. S. Tam (Ed.), Alternatif Dijital Evren Metaverse-II Reklam, Pazarlama, Marka ve İşletme Yönetimi (59-78). Necmettin Erbakan Üniversitesi Yayınları

Türk, G. D., Bayrakci, S., & Akçay, E. (2022). Metaverse ve Benlik Sunumu. *Turkish Online Journal of Design Art and Communication, 12*(2), 316–333. doi:10.7456/11202100/008

Varma, P., Nijjer, S., Kaur, B., & Sharma, S. (2022). Blockchain for transformation in digital marketing. In Handbook of Research on the Platform Economy and the Evolution of E-Commerce (pp. 274 298). IGI Global.

VergneJ. P. (2021). The Future of Trust will be Dystopian or Decentralized: Escaping the Metaverse. *Available at* SSRN. doi:10.2139/ssrn.3925635

Wang, Q., Li, R., Wang, Q., & Chen, S. (2021). Non-fungible token (NFT): Overview, evaluation, opportunities and challenges. *arXiv preprint arXiv:2105.07447.*

Wang, Y., Kang, X., & Chen, Z. (2022). A survey of digital twin techniques in smart manufacturing and management of energy applications. *Green Energy and Intelligent Transportation, 100014*(2), 100014. Advance online publication. doi:10.1016/j.geits.2022.100014

WSJ. (2022). From Meatspace to Metaverse: Two Books on Virtual Reality. https://www.wsj.com/articles/from-meatspace-to-metaverse-review-books-on-virtual-reality 11663870672. Access Date: 20.12.2022

Yang, B., Yang, S., Lv, Z., Wang, F., & Olofsson, T. (2022). Application of Digital Twins and Metaverse in the Field of Fluid Machinery Pumps and Fans: A Review. *Sensors (Basel), 22*(23), 9294. doi:10.339022239294 PMID:36501994

Yassin, A. K. (2022). The Metaverse Revolution and Its Impact on the Future of Advertising Industry. *Journal of Design Sciences and Applied Arts, 3*(2), 131–139. doi:10.21608/jdsaa.2022.129876.1171

Yazıcı, T. (2022). Dijital Pazarlamanin Yeni Evreni: Metaverse. A. Güven & M. S. Tam (Ed.), Alternatif Dijital Evren Metaverse-II Reklam, Pazarlama, Marka ve İşletme Yönetimi (79-98). Necmettin Erbakan Üniversitesi Yayınları

Yılmaz, A. (2022). Evren Ötesi Reklamcilik: Metavertising. A. Güven & M. S. Tam (Ed.), Alternatif Dijital Evren Metaverse-II Reklam, Pazarlama, Marka ve İşletme Yönetimi (3-29). Necmettin Erbakan Üniversitesi Yayınları

Zhan, T., Yin, K., Xiong, J., He, Z., & Wu, S. T. (2020). Augmented reality and virtual reality displays: Perspectives and challenges. *iScience, 23*(8), 101397. doi:10.1016/j.isci.2020.101397 PMID:32759057

Zhao, Y., Jiang, J., Chen, Y., Liu, R., Yang, Y., Xue, X., & Chen, S. (2022). *Metaverse: Perspectives from graphics, interactions and visualization.* Visual Informatics., doi:10.1016/j.visinf.2022.03.002

Zheng, Z., Xie, S., Dai, H. N., Chen, X., & Wang, H. (2018). Blockchain challenges and opportunities: A survey. *International Journal of Web and Grid Services, 14*(4), 352–375. doi:10.1504/IJWGS.2018.095647

Zhu, X., Tao, H., Wu, Z., Cao, J., Kalish, K., & Kayne, J. (2017). *Fraud Prevention in Online Digital Advertising.* Springer. doi:10.1007/978-3-319-56793-8

Chapter 12
Metaverse Librarians:
A New Profession for Intelligent Libraries

Mohammad Daradkeh
https://orcid.org/0000-0003-2693-7363
University of Dubai, UAE & Yarmouk University, Jordan

ABSTRACT

Intelligent libraries have been a hot topic in academia, and scholars have offered many insights into the future development of library intelligence. However, there has been little research on the concept and competency characteristics of intelligent librarians as an important driver of library intelligence, which is viewed as a new profession. Meanwhile, the emergence of metaverse has opened up new ideas and impetus for the development of library intelligence, while demanding the professional competence of intelligent librarians. Based on previous research, this chapter examines the evolution of metaverse, its application in libraries, and its advantages. It also discusses the requirements and training routes for intelligent librarians, as well as the concept of intelligent librarians in the context of metaverse. Intelligent libraries, in effect, create a new need for increased cooperation and collaboration between librarians and users. Each party must be aware of their respective roles, responsibilities, and privileges.

INTRODUCTION

At the beginning of the 21st century, the concept of intelligent libraries was proposed by university libraries and initial practical experiments were carried out worldwide. Since then, with the development of smart cities and social informatization, countries have gradually carried out theoretical research and practical exploration of intelligent library construction (Awasthi, Ahuja, & Sharma, 2022). Since 2019, academic terms related to library development transformation and intelligent library construction have been selected as the top ten academic hotspots in the field of graphic archives for three consecutive years (Asemi, Ko, & Nowkarizi, 2021; Kwanya, Stilwell, & Underwood, 2012). In March 2021, the Outline of the 14th Five-Year Plan for National Economic and Social Development of the People's Republic of China and Vision 2035 first proposed to develop intelligent libraries and provide intelligent and convenient public services (Sanji, Behzadi, & Gomroki, 2022). Some scholars have called 2021 the year of

DOI: 10.4018/978-1-6684-7029-9.ch012

intelligent libraries (Harisanty, Anna, Putri, Firdaus, & Noor Azizi, 2022). Over the years, librarianship researchers have thought deeply about the key issues surrounding the development of intelligence. While the existing research focus varies, it is generally accepted that intelligent librarians are the driving force behind library development and represent the core elements of intelligent libraries (Duncan, 2021).

The year 2021 is also known as the year of the metaverse. In March 2021, the first metaverse share, Roblox, was listed on the New York Stock Exchange, and the metaverse concept quickly became the focus of public attention (Noh, 2022), and librarianship and related fields began to focus on and study the service transformation and technology applications in the metaverse era (Njoku, Nwakanma, Amaizu, & Kim, 2022). As an emerging concept, metaverse is built on and gradually formed by technologies such as virtual reality, augmented reality, cloud computing, blockchain, 5G, and digital twin (Kesselman & Esquivel, 2022); it is a comprehensive application scenario formed by a new generation of information technology through different permutations and combinations, ultimately pointing to a virtual platform highly correlated and interoperable with reality (Tait & Pierson, 2022).

In general, metaverse is an emerging scientific concept and there is no clear definition that can clearly explain what metaverse actually means. The current mainstream definition considers the metaverse to be a collection of virtual space-time consisting of a series of virtual reality (VR), augmented reality (AR), mixed reality (MR), extended reality (XR), and the Internet. Through AR, VR, MR, XR, 5G, artificial intelligence and wearable hardware facilities, people can break the dimensional wall and create new universes and civilizations in the metaverse. The current public perception of the metaverse is to use various existing technological means to interconnect and create a new living space with a high degree of interoperability between reality and virtual, and to establish a sound social system. Strictly speaking, metaverse is not a technology but an artificial interactive space beyond the universe, which integrates XR, 3D, 5G, artificial intelligence, big data, blockchain, cloud computing, digital twin and other technologies to fuse reality with reality and integrate all resource platforms. Internet 3.0 era belongs to the era of metaverse, where users can be in the space they need anytime and anywhere, and feel the interaction between reality and virtual through.

At present, metaverse is in its infancy in terms of technology, content supply and user experience, and the research on metaverse is also in its initial stage. However, library services have been developed in the virtual world Second Life, which is the predecessor of metaverse. For example, McMaster University Library opened a space in Information Island in 2006 and established the world's first virtual library, and then the University of California, Berkeley, Stanford University, and Harvard University also began to establish branches on the Second Life platform (Tait & Pierson, 2022), which laid the foundation for theoretical research and practical application of library intelligence services into the metaverse era. It lays the foundation for theoretical research and practical application for the library intelligent services to enter the metaverse era.

A truly intelligent library environment can only be achieved when all stakeholders acknowledge and play their part in the development of a facilitated information ecosystem. Unfortunately, the current discussion of intelligent libraries focuses primarily on the responsibilities and competencies required of librarians to implement this paradigm. Little, if any, attention has been paid to the responsibilities and skills that library users must have in order to effectively participate in a disintermediated intelligent library environment. Indeed, metaverse create new demands for greater cooperation and collaboration between librarians and users. Each party must be aware of their respective roles, responsibilities, and privileges. They must also recognize that some of the functions they have performed in the past may have changed or must change in the new information ecology. Therefore, they must understand which boundaries need to be defended and which boundaries need to be abandoned. All stakeholders must be involved in the creation of the ideal information environment. This process requires certain competencies, attitudes, and behaviors that everyone must be willing and able to acquire and develop. Building on previous research, this chapter investigates the emergence of metaverse, its implementation in libraries, and its benefits. It also examines the prerequisites and training routes for smart librarians, as well as the concept of smart librarians in the context of metaverse.

The remainder of this chapter is structured as follows. The following section gives an overview of the current state of metaverse applications in the library community. The next section provides an overview of smart librarian research and discusses the internal competencies of smart librarians. The next section provides new professional competencies for smart librarians in the metaverse era. Finally, this chapter concludes by offering suggestions and insights into emerging approaches to developing professional competencies for intelligent librarians.

CURRENT STATUS OF METAVERSE APPLICATIONS IN THE LIBRARY COMMUNITY

At present, all industries are actively looking for technological innovation breakthroughs in their own industries, trying to take advantage of this new technological means as soon as possible to strive for industry leadership. The library community is in the exploration stage for the use of metaverse. Throughout the history of library development, from traditional libraries, digital libraries, intelligent libraries, to the current metaverse libraries, the breakthroughs in libraries will be reflected in the service targets, service methods, and comprehensive management.

In fact, the initial exploration of metaverse libraries was carried out in the early stages of the Second Life platform. In November 2006, the American Library Consortium system united all online libraries to create the first library in the Second Life platform, called Cybrary City, meaning information island, to provide library services in a virtual world (Duan et al., 2021). In the same month, the platform launched Second Life Library 2.0 to provide online communication, reference consultation, collection search, and document delivery (Kwanya et al., 2012). In 2006, McMaster University Library in Canada opened a space to explore the provision of library services in a virtual world. Subsequently, McMaster University, University of California at Berkeley, Harvard University, and Stanford University have set up branches in Second Life to provide patrons. In September 2009, the Second Life Library of the Hong Kong Polytechnic University was officially established. In September 2009, the YK Pao Library of the Hong Kong Polytechnic University established a virtual library in Second Life (Maddahi & Chen, 2022).

In 2008, the National Library explored the interaction between virtual and reality by using VR technology and set up a special 3D experience area, where the real-time 3D spatial representation and human-machine interactive operating environment brought readers an immersive experience (Harisanty et al., 2022). The second phase of the new library project specifically set up a virtual digital library experience area, which is an upgraded version of the 3D experience area. Through virtual technology and digital means, it can bring readers a better experience, and readers can visit the National Library online through special VR equipment and freely visit the virtual world.

Prospects for the Metaverse Library

The development of libraries is driven by the needs of patrons and innovations in technology. The core of library development is people-oriented and dedicated to providing targeted humanized and personalized services to readers. In the current social environment and economic situation, the stickiness between libraries and readers is gradually decreasing, and the traditional business and offline activities of libraries are greatly reduced, which has accelerated the pace of library transformation. Therefore, libraries must make drastic changes, actively explore and implement them. In this context, metaverse may become one of the epochal opportunities for libraries to break through the bottleneck.

(1) Making the Most of Space

The key service of the library is to provide equal reading services for readers. Taking the National Library of China as an example, the annual collection of various Chinese and foreign language documents and ancient books reaches more than 1.2 million volumes, and the number of paper documents in the collection is on the rise (Kwanya et al., 2012). After the introduction and application of green energy-saving concepts such as carbon neutrality and carbon peaking, libraries should pay more attention to how to deal with the contradiction between the growing collection of documents and the space of the collection. Digital images are easy to reproduce, easy to store, and easy to manage. Readers can log in to the platform anytime, anywhere, easily and quickly to instantly satisfy their reading and knowledge acquisition needs, while reducing the management costs of libraries. In the future, the technology of metaverse can be used to present the accessioned documents in digital form in the virtual library, so that various documents can be integrated into a three-dimensional structure with real sensory quality.

(2) Optimization of Service System

Metaverse library can provide a combination of online and offline library services, including traditional offline position services, online new media services, services in virtual space, and library services with high interoperability between virtual space and real world. The services include offline exhibitions, lectures and national reading activities. The same diversified services above can be truly experienced in Metaverse library. At the same time, the back-end management relies much less on manual labor, and librarians can complete the corresponding work through the metaverse platform.

(3) Effective Integration of Resources

At present, library literature resources are mainly physical and digital resources. Libraries in various countries and regions mostly adopt the traditional model to develop resources and provide services to readers through offline venues, online official websites, self-media or self-built databases. The metaverse library can integrate library resources from different countries and regions, so that library resources can be presented in a metaverse library space, where readers can access and use resources of any country, any language and with legal copyright that they are interested in. Readers can enjoy library services in an immersive way.

(4) Strengthen the Protection and Utilization of Precious Documents

Precious documents include ancient books, good books, public opinion maps, gold and stone toppings, oracle bones, manuscripts of famous people, calligraphy and paintings. There are three main ways for ordinary readers to make use of these precious documents in real libraries: one is for readers to provide a series of applications, and the other is to apply for microfilms of the corresponding documents. The third is to use the digital images of the literature database provided through the official platform of the library. However, in the current reality, libraries have very strict requirements for the use of these precious documents, and many of them have aged badly. In order to maximize the preservation and service life of these precious documents, most libraries do not easily take out the originals for readers to view. The emergence of metaverse library can effectively solve the contradiction between conservation and utilization of precious documents. If libraries establish a metaverse library platform, all countries and branches can build virtual venues on the platform and use advanced technology to process precious documents to simulate the original paperback effect. All the books that readers read on this platform are virtual, and they do not need to touch the original paper and the reproduction films in their collections, thus achieving the purpose of preserving precious documents.

(5) Enhancing the Interactivity of Libraries and Readers

Nowadays, libraries tend to be composite in function, not only providing library lending services to readers, but also integrating services such as events, exhibitions, lectures, learning exchanges, and interactive experiences, allowing readers to experience learning and knowledge exchange in a one-stop manner. However, most of these experiences are limited to offline field venues, and many offline services are not well developed in the current global outbreak of the new crown epidemic, which accelerates the pace of library development to the next stage. In the metaverse library, readers only need to enter the metaverse library through the network or external devices, where they can realize the barrier-free communication and interaction between people in different spaces. At the same time, they can participate in various exhibitions, lectures, learning and exchange activities in virtual space. It can also rely on existing technologies such as big data and blockchain to analyze readers' needs, making it possible for librarians to provide various services to meet readers' needs in the metaverse library for each reader. This will greatly improve the stickiness of readers and libraries and enhance the interaction between readers and libraries.

At present, the development of metaverse libraries is still in its nascent stage, and the library community is gradually exploring metaverse libraries. As a position for the construction of human spiritual civilization, meta-space libraries may become the next stage of library development in the future. Libraries need to actively transform and adapt to changes in order to better serve readers and meet their needs. In particular, the technological integration of metaverse expands the domain and boundaries of intelligent library services, but also places higher demands on librarians' digital literacy and information literacy. On this basis, this chapter explores the professional competence requirements and cultivation paths of the new profession of intelligent librarian in the context of the metaverse era.

AN OVERVIEW OF INTELLIGENT LIBRARIAN RESEARCH

In recent years, a large number of research results have been generated in the research boom of intelligent libraries (Noh, 2022). However, specialized research on intelligent librarians is relatively weak, and there is no consensus on the concept of intelligent librarians among academics. Bi et al. (2022) summarized and analyzed the research on intelligent librarians in China and the United States in the past decade. They classified the definitions from both macro and micro perspectives. They found that most of the existing studies started from the micro level and revolved around the overall concept of what kind of people are intelligent librarians and what kind of work intelligent librarians should do. Most of the existing studies start from the micro level and explain the overall concept around what kind of person a smart librarian is and what kind of work they should do, emphasizing the capabilities and practical utility of smart librarians (Bi et al., 2022). Combing the years of publication of existing studies, the number of relevant studies has been steadily increasing since 2017, and the research topics have become more focused.

Based on previous research, this chapter provides an analysis of the concept of intelligent librarianship in the last five years and finds that the concept of intelligent librarianship has changed, and its competencies and functions have been adjusted as the research progresses, which can be viewed from two perspectives: types and roles. From the perspective of types, intelligent librarians are considered as research librarians, technical librarians, embedded librarians and business librarians (Duncan, 2021), smart innovative research librarians, smart applied technical librarians and smart embedded subject librarians (Bolger, 2021). From the perspective of roles, intelligent librarians are identified as consulting librarians and subject librarians (Duan et al., 2021), no longer in an intermediary role, but as a team of expert librarians with high education, quality, service and research capabilities (Jamil, Rahman, & Fawad, 2022; Jin, Xu, & Leng, 2022; Nguyen, 2022).

While researchers have offered their insights on the understanding of intelligent librarianship from different perspectives, no research has been conducted to explore the concept and competency dimensions of intelligent librarianship from the perspective of a new career in intelligent libraries. In November 2021, the Action Plan for Digital Literacy and Skills Enhancement for All People (hereinafter referred to as the Action Plan) proposed to basically build a strong digital talent country by 2035. Digital literacy and skills for all people reach a high level, and high-end digital talents play a leading role. Digital innovation and entrepreneurship are prosperous and active, promoting the construction of a strong network country, and providing strong support for building a strong network country and a smart society (Ahn, Kim, & Kim, 2022). Intelligent librarians in the perspective of digital power and smart city are highly qualified, efficient, and high-level knowledge workers who fully master digital technology, and intelligent people who participate in public services and work affairs of libraries (Allam, Sharifi, Bibri, Jones, & Krogstie, 2022; Hassani, Huang, & MacFeely, 2022).

However, the professional level and ability of existing librarians cannot keep up with the pace of library intelligence (Asemi et al., 2021), which becomes a factor that restricts the development of intelligent libraries. Therefore, it is imperative to strengthen the training of intelligent librarians and reserve talents for the construction and development of intelligent libraries. It should be clarified that the new occupation in this study does not refer to a new position added to the existing library system, and the qualities and competencies of smart librarians are not a pile-up or supplement to the traditional occupational requirements, much less simply adding the title of intelligence in front of the existing competency guidelines. Rather, it refers to a new type of librarian who is engaged in intelligent library operations, adapts to the development needs of intelligent services and management, masters digital technologies, and connects service and security, patrons and resources (Alpala, Quiroga-Parra, Torres, & Peluffo-Ordóñez, 2022).

INTERNAL CAPABILITIES OF INTELLIGENT LIBRARIANS

Intelligence has brought great changes to society. From VR/AR to metaverse, intelligent development has become the focus of attention and research from all walks of life. As a new form of library development, intelligent libraries integrate the concept of intelligence into management and services, and introduce the concept of sustainable development into the front and back of the library, so as to maximize the effectiveness, efficiency and effect of library system development (Awasthi et al., 2022). The operation of intelligent library system requires intelligent librarians to play a key role, and the quality and ability of librarians directly determine the level of library intelligence, and intelligent librarians become the core force of library intelligence, which is the law of library intelligence.

The concept of people-oriented has always been the service concept and purpose of library work. In the context of intellectualization, libraries play a greater role of cultural value and mission, and digital intelligence technology gradually becomes the core of library culture. However, this does not weaken the key role of people in the framework of library elements, but rather promotes libraries to pursue the harmonious symbiosis of humanity, technology, and people and things. Some scholars point out that the elemental framework of intelligent libraries includes two basic elements of resources and services and two auxiliary elements of facilities and management, while people are the core elements related to these four elements (Bibri, 2022). Among them, intelligent librarians are the core force in the development of intelligent library theory and practice and the providers of quality library services.

Libraries have evolved from initial collections to today's intelligent libraries, during which they have experienced two forms: composite libraries and digital libraries. In line with this, the professional competencies of librarians have changed from simple cataloging to digital services, research information and knowledge, and the titles of librarians have been restructured, undergoing a transition and evolution from reference librarians and subject librarians to digital humanities librarians and intelligent librarians. Reference librarianship began with the development of reference consulting services, which required librarians to have the ability to screen, organize, synthesize, and innovate library information. At the end of the 20th century, the special needs of professional disciplines for library information about specialized literature increased, and the system of subject librarians in universities came into existence due to the inability of the knowledge background of reference consulting librarians to perform this work (Bibri & Allam, 2022). Today, in the era of mobile Internet and even in the era of metaverse, the access to information resources, transmission channels and user needs have changed fundamentally. Digital humanities has become a new direction for libraries to provide knowledge services (Bolger, 2021). Therefore, digital humanities librarians who have received professional training in library intelligence have become librarians who meet the new professional competence requirements of libraries.

This chapter focuses on intelligent librarians, who are the core of library intelligence and perform the duties of reference librarians and subject librarians. At the same time, they combine high level of professional background knowledge with digital science and information technology to achieve intelligent links between readers and resources, front and back office, so as to better fulfill the cultural mission of libraries and provide more intelligent patron services (Figure 1).

Figure 1. Generation and mechanism of intelligent librarian empowerment in metaverse

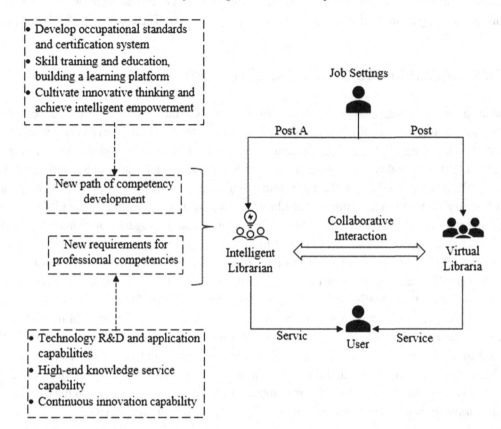

New Occupational Competencies for Intelligent Librarians in the Metaverse Era

Metaverse is a digital space that seamlessly combines the virtual with the real and can generate value beyond the real world (Rahaman, 2022). Metaverse is an inevitable product of a certain stage of technological development. As a sign of the beginning of a new era, it has the following basic characteristics: (1) immersive experience combining reality with reality (2) user-produced content (3) complete social systems of law, economy, and services (4) gradually growing civilization (5) social networks (6) integration of new technologies (Buhalis, Lin, & Leung, 2022). The contemporary character of it puts new demands on the professional competence of librarians in digital literacy and information literacy. Librarians should not only have the ability to serve the real world, but also need to be familiar with virtual scenarios and skilled in relevant technological tools. Metaverse technology needs to go through a long process from theoretical implementation to practical application. In this process, smart librarians, as a new profession, need to continuously enhance the literacy and competencies they should possess. In this context, this chapter puts forward the following three new requirements for the professional competencies of intelligent librarians.

Technical Capabilities for Achieving Intelligent Universality

(1)   Technology Development Capability

The 2019 World 5G Conference was held in Beijing, and the Minister of Science and Technology pointed out that 5G technology continues to develop (Duan et al., 2021), realizing the Internet of everything through ubiquitous sensing, ubiquitous connectivity, and ubiquitous intelligence. Combined with big data (Keikhosrokiani, 2022a), cloud computing, and artificial intelligence (Keikhosrokiani & Pourya Asl, 2023), 5G technology has promoted the information and digital transformation of the entire society, changed social governance and production methods, and gradually moved from the communications industry to cultural services Expansion. The library community actively explores the application of 5G technology in intelligent libraries, arguing that 5G+intelligent technology drives the development of intelligent library services (Duncan, 2021). By analyzing the current research related to intelligent librarians, this chapter identifies that both the exploration of librarians' professional capacity enhancement paths and the research on the cultivation strategy of intelligent librarians' creativity are inseparable from the in-depth application of 5G technology (Njoku et al., 2022; Pamucar, Deveci, Gokasar, Tavana, & Köppen, 2022; Rahaman, 2022). However, the development of 5G has entered the fast lane, and the research and development of 6G technology has been launched globally (Dahan et al., 2022), with China at the forefront of 5G technology in the world (Eom, 2022). Intelligent libraries need intelligent librarians with the ability to realize intelligent services with technological empowerment in the 5G era and the expertise to realize an intelligent and ubiquitous digital model with 6G technology and various technologies such as virtual reality, augmented reality, cloud computing, and blockchain.

(2) Technology Evaluation Capability

The continuous establishment and extensive and in-depth application of 5G technology has propelled the development of intelligent libraries into the boosting phase. Technology, as a means and utility, plays an important role in the development of smart libraries. With the advent of the Metaverse era, the practical challenge for librarians is which new technology to choose to build a smart library? This first step is to use professional skills to evaluate each technology. In order to evaluate technologies, we need to develop evaluation metrics, specify the technology and its applicability, and select the technology that is more beneficial to the library's business. Thus, it is possible to select the technology that is more helpful for the library business and make the technology work for the business (Erdei, Krakó, & Husi, 2022).

(3) Technology Application Capability

Development and evaluation are the paths of library application of intelligent technologies (Ezimmuo & Keikhosrokiani, 2022; Keikhosrokiani, 2022b; Xian et al., 2022), which are reflected in the development of intelligent classrooms in universities. In 2011, Shanghai Jiaotong University pioneered the intelligent ubiquitous classroom, i.e., the library took the initiative to push the corresponding electronic resources for each student's course and provide personalized teaching materials (Dahan et al., 2022). This is an important practice for libraries to apply intelligent technology and explore intelligent ubiquitous services.

The metaverse cannot be described as a technology, but rather as an idea or concept. The 6G technology provides the infrastructure for the development and implementation of the metaverse and empowers it. At the same time, the metaverse is also a key focus and basic requirement for 6G technology. It can be argued that 6G technology is mutually reinforcing, evolving, driving and iteratively developing with the metaverse. 6G will open a digital twin and intelligent ubiquitous world for human beings. Flexible, minimalist, intelligent endogenous, security endogenous and digital twin intelligent librarians become the key factors for libraries to achieve an intelligent and ubiquitous digital model (Faraboschi, Frachtenberg, Laplante, Milojicic, & Saracco, 2022).

Knowledge Capabilities for Service Transformation and Promotion

(1) Intelligence Analysis Capability

To meet the needs of innovative society and national science and technology innovation construction, collaborative innovation has become a new trend pursued by various disciplines and institutions, and libraries are no exception. In addition, libraries, as public cultural service institutions, support to meet a large number of information and research needs (Harisanty et al., 2022). Therefore, in-depth analysis of information and user needs by librarians has become a basic professional skill that requires librarians to acquire intelligence analysis skills and carry out intelligence analysis services. For example, sensing the social needs and environment to locate the future direction of libraries; providing accurate customized services based on deep mining and analysis of user information needs by cloud computing technology; and conducting specialized demand intelligence analysis in conjunction with user loan and return data collated by libraries.

(2) Scientific Evaluation Capability

Scientific evaluation ability is a basic requirement for librarians in the metaverse era. Scientific evaluation aims to promote better development of libraries, takes scientific evaluation system as a guideline, comprehensively examines librarians' service ability and their own level, pays attention to both work differences between departments and users' satisfaction with library use, and evaluates and pays attention to all aspects of intelligent library development. As professionals within the library, the level of librarians' scientific evaluation ability affects the level of the library. Therefore, in order to promote the transformation of library services, the evaluation principles of diversity, openness, progressiveness, generativity and motivation of evaluation are used to promote library development (Hassani et al., 2022).

(3) Intellectual Service Capability

Intelligence is closely related to knowledge, and knowledge is the raw material of intelligence. After experiencing three stages of document service, information service and knowledge service (Jamil et al., 2022), libraries have evolved to the stage of intelligence. As a result, users' needs have gradually changed from traditional lending services to more efficient intelligent mining and software updating services (Jin et al., 2022). The updating of readers' needs has put forward higher requirements on the competence quality of librarians, which is to cultivate intelligent librarians into high-end digital talents with the ability to absorb knowledge quickly in the new era, and finally identify knowledge services as the basis and intelligent librarians as the key to creatively integrate literature, information and resources, so as to provide high-level intellectual services (Keshmiri Neghab, Jamshidi, & Keshmiri Neghab, 2022). Intellectual services do not mean abandoning the existing knowledge services, but require librarians to be flexible in their personal abilities and participate in various tasks within the library based on professional knowledge services. Intellectual knowledge is the use of cerebral abilities (Kwanya et al., 2012), and the transformation of library knowledge services to intellectual knowledge services reflects the improvement of librarians' professional abilities and the upgrade of their cognitive level in the intellectualization stage.

Innovation Capabilities to Meet User Needs

(1) Theoretical Innovation Capability

The traditional management theory of libraries lacks innovation and reflexivity. All along, library research librarians have been relying on existing theories for scientific research and research services. As a result, their thinking has gradually solidified, making it more difficult to support the transformation of library functions and services in the metadata era. At this time, it is especially important to strengthen the innovation of management and service theories, to put forward new requirements for librarians' key knowledge literacy and research innovation ability, to break the shackles of the original theories, to plan key research topics, to abandon empiricism, and to achieve new innovations (Kesselman & Esquivel, 2022). Theoretical innovation is used to meet the innovation of intelligent library management and user services.

(2) Management Innovation Capability

The operating model of a library changes as the environment and society evolves. As an organization, management is essential. Librarians in the metaverse era need innovative management skills. At the same time, intelligent management should be added to digital and networked management, with business management and human resource management as the central focus, and intelligent hardware and software management as the means to improve the efficiency of library services and maximize the satisfaction of users.

(3) Service Innovation Capability

Providing services to users is the responsibility and commitment of librarians. In the past, the traditional reference lending service of libraries could hardly meet the needs of readers in smart libraries. Therefore, with artificial intelligence and cloud computing technology as the background and smart services as the model, establishing accurate user portraits and providing personalized and customized services are necessary for librarians to innovate their service capabilities and meet the needs of users in the metaverse era. Therefore, the first task of intelligent librarians is to improve data processing and analysis capabilities and to accurately grasp readers' preferences by relying on the intelligent facilities of libraries. At the same time, more, deeper and more valuable information can be mined to meet the actual needs of the majority of users and provide personalized and quality services (Kwanya et al., 2012).

(4) Branding and Innovation Capabilities

Branding is common in the business world and has since been emphasized by the library community as a new service concept and innovative capability. Library branding is a special form of strategy to build a socially recognized image and show its uniqueness, which leads to differentiated competitive capabilities. Branding is a characteristic and label for library development, while brand design and innovation capabilities are key to library branding (Maddahi & Chen, 2022). Intelligent libraries require librarians to flexibly use cloud computing and blockchain technologies to conduct comprehensive and systematic research on user and social needs, research, analyze, and evaluate library images, update library connotations, design library brands, form distinctive brand services, and establish an intelligent image.

EMERGING APPROACHES FOR CULTIVATING PROFESSIONAL COMPETENCIES OF INTELLIGENT LIBRARIANS

As a new profession, intelligent librarians are not intended to eliminate the existing librarians, but to cultivate a new type of librarian who can engage in the intelligent library business based on the existing librarians. Based on the current situation and development considerations, the library's intelligent librarian team will be composed of three parts. Firstly, new librarians will be recruited according to the professional competence needs of intelligent librarians. New librarians with new technical skills and intelligent literacy will play a key role in the construction of intelligent libraries. The library should give priority to meet the needs of intelligent library construction and development when recruiting. Secondly, based on the existing reference librarians, subject librarians, and digital humanities librarians, they should be the key training targets of the library to build a backbone of intelligent librarians and become the first echelon of intelligent librarians. Third, besides reference librarians, subject librarians and digital humanities librarians, other librarians in libraries should also be trained according to the development needs of intelligent libraries and a group of them should be selected to enter the second echelon. To help libraries establish standardized training paths and better develop librarian competencies, three focuses of training paths are discussed in this chapter.

Building Professional Competency Standards and Intelligent Librarian Certification System

Several standards have been developed internationally for the professional competencies of librarians. In the United States, more than twenty professional competency standards for librarians have been promulgated and implemented (Magalhães et al., 2022). Most of the competency standard texts emphasize information technology, subject skills, professionalism, and research skills for librarians (Magalhães et al., 2022). The knowledge system of the Library and Information Association of New Zealand Aotearoa (LIANZA, the Library and Information Association of New Zealand Aotearoa) uses information as a vein to demand professional competencies for librarians based on the flow of information and IT skills such as cloud computing and big data as Librarians. The professional competence of librarians is judged by IT skills such as cloud computing and big data (Nguyen, 2022; Zhang et al., 2022). Although China has introduced professional skills standards in some industry fields, many factors have led to the fact that the standards related to the professional competence of librarians in China have not been landed (Njoku et al., 2022). Nowadays, intelligent librarians, as a new model in the library industry, urgently need to construct relevant professional competency standards and realize standard-oriented intelligent training.

Relying on the development of standards alone cannot support a new path for intelligent librarian training. Intelligent libraries can take advantage of library resources to open up talent enhancement channels, promote the establishment of a librarian certification system that adapts to the development of intelligence, and conduct regular assessments and evaluations. At the same time, libraries can design training systems and supporting resources that meet the new professional standards for librarians to provide reliable and feasible dimensional support for the development of intelligent librarians.

Education And Skills Training for The Three Major Literacies and The Establishment Of A Lifelong Knowledge Learning Platform

According to the current extensive information literacy education in libraries, librarians have improved their information literacy skills while providing information services, and librarians engaged in information literacy education are in a position to become information literacy teachers (Noh, 2022). In August 2017, IFLA released the IFLA Statement on Digital Literacy, which states that digital literacy should be positioned as a core library service to support the implementation of digital literacy and innovative spaces in libraries (Pamucar et al., 2022). The introduction of the Framework for Action provides new opportunities for libraries to expand their social impact and achieve quality development. It shows that libraries have great potential to improve digital literacy and skills for all (Park & Kim, 2022; Yang et al., 2022). Libraries improve digital literacy education and skills training is a need for libraries to keep their integrity. High-end digital talent training system and rich vocational skills training courses are important for intelligent libraries to cultivate innovative and complex digital talents.

It is still not enough for intelligent librarians to have high information literacy and digital literacy, especially data literacy is also needed. Therefore, it is necessary to scientifically design data literacy education and skills training programs for librarians, strengthen their theoretical knowledge of data science, and cultivate their ability of data analysis, processing and dissemination, especially big data analysis and big data service. Conducting such training activities is not only a requirement for librarians by intelligent libraries, but also a need for libraries themselves to adapt to the paradigm shift of data research and serve the national big data strategy.

The lifelong learning platform is an effective way to accelerate the training of digitally excellent librarians and narrow the capability gap between librarians of all levels and types. The establishment of a smart learning platform can basically meet the training needs of smart librarians; in other words, it can achieve full coverage of online and offline resources, combine technical means and policy texts, strengthen the interconnection among librarians, and make up for the deficiencies in the lifelong learning process. In the era of metaverse, libraries and smart librarians should show new roles and responsibilities to better serve the development of smart cities.

Cultivating Computational and Innovative Thinking for Intelligent Cloud-Enabled Energy

The formation of librarians' computational and innovative thinking has an important role in promoting the development of intelligent libraries. Intelligent libraries should rely on cloud computing technology and consider the setting of intelligent librarian training system comprehensively. By dismantling and analyzing the problems that may be encountered in the actual service process layer by layer, librarians should master the computational principles of intelligent services, develop new service ideas, and improve their ability to use artificial intelligence knowledge flexibly.

Currently, 5G edge cloud technology has been applied to the teaching field to solve social problems such as unbalanced educational resources (Popescu, Dragomir, Popescu, & Dragomir, 2022; Y. Wang et al., 2022). As a cultural and educational center, the library is a continuation, integration and sublimation of the concept and practice of digital and composite library development (Rahaman, 2022), and should make full use of 5G technology to create intelligent cloud librarians, improve the digital competitiveness of librarians, and explore a new paradigm driven by intelligence (see Figure 2).

Figure 2. Intelligent librarian competency development model in metaverse

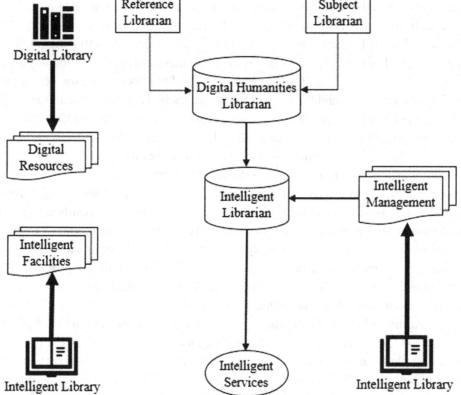

Based on the application of virtual chatbots in library business work, a new type of librarian, virtual librarian, was proposed by Ruiz Mejia and Rawat (2022). With the increasing level of artificial intelligence technology and machine intelligence, there is an urgent need to develop virtual intelligent librarians with computational capabilities as an aid and support for intelligent librarians with computational thinking in the cultivation of intelligent librarians (Wang, Yu, Bell, & Chu, 2022). In the future, in the post planning of intelligent librarians, AB posts of each post can be set, with intelligent librarians as A posts and virtual intelligent librarians as B posts, cooperating and supporting each other to realize 24-hour real-time intelligent services for each patron of the library. With the assistance and support of virtual intelligent librarians, it can break through the current time and space limitations faced by libraries and combine human intelligence and machine intelligence to better achieve the goals of library services (Salem & Dragomir, 2022).

Intelligent librarians are public cultural service providers with a sense of self-spiraling, a new profession oriented to intelligent libraries born from the changes in the overall social environment and the rapid development of intelligent technologies. From VR/AR to metaverse, technological innovation and transformation have brought new opportunities and challenges to the development of intelligent libraries, and have raised higher requirements for intelligent librarians. In this context, this chapter explores the new concept, new needs and new cultivation paths of the new profession of intelligent librarians, and injects new power into the cultural theory research of intelligent libraries (Tait & Pierson, 2022; Vishkaei, 2022).

5. CONCLUSION

In the information age, with the emergence of big data, artificial intelligence, the Internet of Things and other high technologies, libraries conform to the development of the times and begin to move towards a new era of open and autonomous intelligent libraries based on data resources. The library is no longer just a simple physical space, but also an intelligent service space. In the process of information socialization, the role of intelligent librarian has been given more new connotations. In the era of information explosion, information is proliferating, libraries have started to increase the acquisition of digital resources year by year to meet the needs of academic research, and the use of metaverse technology has increased the demand for digital resources. However, at the same time, the risk of copyright infringement is increasing, users are still at the level of fetishism in accessing resources, and intelligent library services have increased the risk of copyright problems.

From smart societies to smart libraries, smart people play an important role. Intelligent librarians are the core driving force of intelligent library development and the most important element in the intelligent library system. Intelligent librarians are public cultural service providers with a sense of self-motivation, a new profession oriented to intelligent libraries arising from the changes in the overall social environment and the rapid development of intelligent technologies. From VR/AR to metaverse, technological innovations and transformations have brought new opportunities and challenges to the development of intelligent libraries and raised higher requirements for intelligent librarians. In this context, this chapter explores new concepts, new requirements, and new cultivation paths for the new profession of intelligent librarian, providing a new impetus to the cultural theory research of intelligent libraries.

REFERENCES

Ahn, S., Kim, J., & Kim, J. (2022). The Bifold Triadic Relationships Framework: A Theoretical Primer for Advertising Research in the Metaverse. *Journal of Advertising*, *51*(5), 592–607. doi:10.1080/0091 3367.2022.2111729

Allam, Z., Sharifi, A., Bibri, S., Jones, D., & Krogstie, J. (2022). The Metaverse as a Virtual Form of Smart Cities: Opportunities and Challenges for Environmental, Economic, and Social Sustainability in Urban Futures. *Smart Cities*, *5*(3), 771–801. doi:10.3390martcities5030040

Alpala, L., Quiroga-Parra, D., Torres, J., & Peluffo-Ordóñez, D. (2022). Smart Factory Using Virtual Reality and Online Multi-User: Towards a Metaverse for Experimental Frameworks. *Applied Sciences (Basel, Switzerland)*, *12*(12), 6258. doi:10.3390/app12126258

Asemi, A., Ko, A., & Nowkarizi, M. (2021). Intelligent libraries: A review on expert systems, artificial intelligence, and robot. *Library Hi Tech*, *39*(2), 412–434. doi:10.1108/LHT-02-2020-0038

Awasthi, S., Ahuja, R., & Sharma, S. (2022). Leadership and Emotional Intelligence: A Comparative Study. In D. Bathla & A. Singh (Eds.), *Applying Metalytics to Measure Customer Experience in the Metaverse* (pp. 99–110). IGI Global. doi:10.4018/978-1-6684-6133-4.ch009

Bi, S., Wang, C., Zhang, J., Huang, W., Wu, B., Gong, Y., & Ni, W. (2022). A Survey on Artificial Intelligence Aided Internet-of-Things Technologies in Emerging Smart Libraries. *Sensors (Basel)*, *22*(8), 2991. doi:10.339022082991 PMID:35458974

Bibri, S. (2022). The Social Shaping of the Metaverse as an Alternative to the Imaginaries of Data-Driven Smart Cities: A Study in Science, Technology, and Society. *Smart Cities*, *5*(3), 832–874. doi:10.3390martcities5030043

Bibri, S., & Allam, Z. (2022). The Metaverse as a Virtual Form of Data-Driven Smart Urbanism: On Post-Pandemic Governance through the Prism of the Logic of Surveillance Capitalism. *Smart Cities*, *5*(2), 715–727. doi:10.3390martcities5020037

Bolger, R. (2021). Finding Wholes in the Metaverse: Posthuman Mystics as Agents of Evolutionary Contextualization. *Religions*, *12*(9), 768. doi:10.3390/rel12090768

Buhalis, D., Lin, M., & Leung, D. (2022). Metaverse as a driver for customer experience and value co-creation: implications for hospitality and tourism management and marketing. *International Journal of Contemporary Hospitality Management*. doi:10.1108/IJCHM-05-2022-0631

Dahan, N., Al-Razgan, M., Al-Laith, A., Alsoufi, M., Al-Asaly, M., & Alfakih, T. (2022). Metaverse Framework: A Case Study on E-Learning Environment (ELEM). *Electronics (Basel)*, *11*(10), 1616. doi:10.3390/electronics11101616

Duan, H., Li, J., Fan, S., Lin, Z., Wu, X., & Cai, W. (2021). Metaverse for Social Good: A University Campus Prototype. *Proceedings of the 29th ACM International Conference on Multimedia*. 10.1145/3474085.3479238

Duncan, A. (2021). Opportunities for academic smart libraries in the Caribbean. *Library Hi Tech News*, *38*(5), 9–12. doi:10.1108/LHTN-06-2021-0035

Eom, S. (2022). The Emerging Digital Twin Bureaucracy in the 21st Century. *Perspectives on Public Management and Governance*, *5*(2), 174–186. doi:10.1093/ppmgov/gvac005

Erdei, T., Krakó, R., & Husi, G. (2022). Design of a Digital Twin Training Centre for an Industrial Robot Arm. *Applied Sciences (Basel, Switzerland)*, *12*(17), 8862. doi:10.3390/app12178862

Ezimmuo, C. M., & Keikhosrokiani, P. (2022). Predicting Consumer Behavior Change Towards Using Online Shopping in Nigeria: The Impact of the COVID-19 Pandemic. In P. Keikhosrokiani (Ed.), *Handbook of Research on Consumer Behavior Change and Data Analytics in the Socio-Digital Era* (pp. 210–254). IGI Global. doi:10.4018/978-1-6684-4168-8.ch010

Faraboschi, P., Frachtenberg, E., Laplante, P., Milojicic, D., & Saracco, R. (2022). Virtual Worlds (Metaverse): From Skepticism, to Fear, to Immersive Opportunities. *Computer*, *55*(10), 100–106. doi:10.1109/MC.2022.3192702

Harisanty, D., Anna, N., Putri, T., Firdaus, A., & Noor Azizi, N. (2022). Leaders, practitioners and scientists' awareness of artificial intelligence in libraries: a pilot study. *Library Hi Tech*. doi:10.1108/LHT-10-2021-0356

Hassani, H., Huang, X., & MacFeely, S. (2022). Impactful Digital Twin in the Healthcare Revolution. *Big Data and Cognitive Computing*, *6*(3), 83. doi:10.3390/bdcc6030083

Jamil, S., Rahman, M., & Fawad, M. (2022). A Comprehensive Survey of Digital Twins and Federated Learning for Industrial Internet of Things (IIoT), Internet of Vehicles (IoV) and Internet of Drones (IoD). *Applied System Innovation*, *5*(3), 56. doi:10.3390/asi5030056

Jin, J., Xu, H., & Leng, B. (2022). Adaptive Points Sampling for Implicit Field Reconstruction of Industrial Digital Twin. *Sensors (Basel)*, *22*(17), 6630. doi:10.339022176630 PMID:36081088

Keikhosrokiani, P. (Ed.). (2022a). *Big Data Analytics for Healthcare: Datasets, Techniques, Life Cycles, Management, and Applications*. Elsevier Science. doi:10.1016/C2021-0-00369-2

Keikhosrokiani, P. (Ed.). (2022b). *Handbook of Research on Consumer Behavior Change and Data Analytics in the Socio-Digital Era*. IGI Global. doi:10.4018/978-1-6684-4168-8

Keikhosrokiani, P., & Pourya Asl, M. (2023). *Handbook of Research on Artificial Intelligence Applications in Literary Works and Social Media*. IGI Global. doi:10.4018/978-1-6684-6242-3

Keshmiri Neghab, H., Jamshidi, M., & Keshmiri Neghab, H. (2022). Digital Twin of a Magnetic Medical Microrobot with Stochastic Model Predictive Controller Boosted by Machine Learning in Cyber-Physical Healthcare Systems. *Information (Basel)*, *13*(7), 321. doi:10.3390/info13070321

Kesselman, M., & Esquivel, W. (2022). Technology on the move, Consumer Electronics Show 2022: The evolving metaverse and much more. *Library Hi Tech News*, *39*(5), 1–4. doi:10.1108/LHTN-03-2022-0038

Kwanya, T., Stilwell, C., & Underwood, P. (2012). Intelligent libraries and apomediators: Distinguishing between Library 3.0 and Library 2.0. *Journal of Librarianship and Information Science*, *45*(3), 187–197. doi:10.1177/0961000611435256

Maddahi, Y., & Chen, S. (2022). Applications of Digital Twins in the Healthcare Industry: Case Review of an IoT-Enabled Remote Technology in Dentistry. *Virtual Worlds*, *1*(1), 20–41. doi:10.3390/virtualworlds1010003

Magalhães, L., Magalhães, L., Ramos, J., Moura, L., de Moraes, R., Gonçalves, J., Hisatugu, W. H., Souza, M. T., de Lacalle, L. N. L., & Ferreira, J. (2022). Conceiving a Digital Twin for a Flexible Manufacturing System. *Applied Sciences (Basel, Switzerland)*, *12*(19), 9864. doi:10.3390/app12199864

Nguyen, T. (2022). Toward Human Digital Twins for Cybersecurity Simulations on the Metaverse: Ontological and Network Science Approach. *JMIRx Med*, *3*(2), e33502. doi:10.2196/33502

Njoku, J., Nwakanma, C., Amaizu, G., & Kim, D. (2022). Prospects and challenges of Metaverse application in data-driven intelligent transportation systems. *IET Intelligent Transport Systems.* doi:10.1049/itr2.12252

Noh, Y. (2022). A study on the discussion on Library 5.0 and the generation of Library 1.0 to Library 5.0. *Journal of Librarianship and Information Science.* Advance online publication. doi:10.1177/09610006221106183

Pamucar, D., Deveci, M., Gokasar, I., Tavana, M., & Köppen, M. (2022). A metaverse assessment model for sustainable transportation using ordinal priority approach and Aczel-Alsina norms. *Technological Forecasting and Social Change, 182*, 121778. doi:10.1016/j.techfore.2022.121778

Park, S., & Kim, Y. (2022). A Metaverse: Taxonomy, Components, Applications, and Open Challenges. *IEEE Access: Practical Innovations, Open Solutions, 10*, 4209–4251. doi:10.1109/ACCESS.2021.3140175

Popescu, D., Dragomir, M., Popescu, S., & Dragomir, D. (2022). Building Better Digital Twins for Production Systems by Incorporating Environmental Related Functions—Literature Analysis and Determining Alternatives. *Applied Sciences (Basel, Switzerland), 12*(17), 8657. doi:10.3390/app12178657

Rahaman, T. (2022). Into the Metaverse – Perspectives on a New Reality. *Medical Reference Services Quarterly, 41*(3), 330–337. doi:10.1080/02763869.2022.2096341 PMID:35980623

Ruiz Mejia, J., & Rawat, D. (2022). *Recent Advances in a Medical Domain Metaverse: Status, Challenges, and Perspective.* Paper presented at the 2022 Thirteenth International Conference on Ubiquitous and Future Networks (ICUFN). 10.1109/ICUFN55119.2022.9829645

Salem, T., & Dragomir, M. (2022). Options for and Challenges of Employing Digital Twins in Construction Management. *Applied Sciences (Basel, Switzerland), 12*(6), 2928. doi:10.3390/app12062928

Sanji, M., Behzadi, H., & Gomroki, G. (2022). Chatbot: An intelligent tool for libraries. *Library Hi Tech News, 39*(3), 17–20. doi:10.1108/LHTN-01-2021-0002

Tait, E., & Pierson, C. (2022). Artificial Intelligence and Robots in Libraries: Opportunities in LIS Curriculum for Preparing the Librarians of Tomorrow. *Journal of the Australian Library and Information Association, 71*(3), 256–274. doi:10.1080/24750158.2022.2081111

Vishkaei, B. (2022). Metaverse: A New Platform for Circular Smart Cities. In P. De Giovanni (Ed.), *Cases on Circular Economy in Practice* (pp. 51–69). IGI Global. doi:10.4018/978-1-6684-5001-7.ch003

Wang, M., Yu, H., Bell, Z., & Chu, X. (2022). Constructing an Edu-Metaverse Ecosystem: A New and Innovative Framework. *IEEE Transactions on Learning Technologies*, 1–13. doi:10.1109/TLT.2022.3226345

Wang, Y., Su, Z., Zhang, N., Xing, R., Liu, D., Luan, T., & Shen, X. (2022). A Survey on Metaverse: Fundamentals, Security, and Privacy. *IEEE Communications Surveys and Tutorials*, 1–1. doi:10.1109/COMST.2022.3202047

Xian, Z., Keikhosrokiani, P., XinYing, C., & Li, Z. (2022). An RFM Model Using K-Means Clustering to Improve Customer Segmentation and Product Recommendation. In P. Keikhosrokiani (Ed.), Handbook of Research on Consumer Behavior Change and Data Analytics in the Socio-Digital Era (pp. 124-145). IGI Global. doi:10.4018/978-1-6684-4168-8.ch006

Yang, C., Tu, X., Autiosalo, J., Ala-Laurinaho, R., Mattila, J., Salminen, P., & Tammi, K. (2022). Extended Reality Application Framework for a Digital-Twin-Based Smart Crane. *Applied Sciences (Basel, Switzerland)*, *12*(12), 6030. doi:10.3390/app12126030

Zhang, Z., Wen, F., Sun, Z., Guo, X., He, T., & Lee, C. (2022). Artificial Intelligence-Enabled Sensing Technologies in the 5G/Internet of Things Era: From Virtual Reality/Augmented Reality to the Digital Twin. *Advanced Intelligent Systems*, *4*(7), 2100228. doi:10.1002/aisy.202100228

ADDITIONAL READING

Akour, I., Al-Maroof, R., Alfaisal, R., & Salloum, S. (2022). A conceptual framework for determining metaverse adoption in higher institutions of gulf area: An empirical study using hybrid SEM-ANN approach. *Computers and Education: Artificial Intelligence*, *3*, 100052. doi:10.1016/j.caeai.2022.100052

Batat, W., & Hammedi, W. (2022). The extended reality technology (ERT) framework for designing customer and service experiences in phygital settings: a service research agenda. *Journal of Service Management*. doi:10.1108/JOSM-08-2022-0289

Buhalis, D., O'Connor, P., & Leung, R. (2022). Smart hospitality: from smart cities and smart tourism towards agile business ecosystems in networked destinations. *International Journal of Contemporary Hospitality Management*. doi:10.1108/IJCHM-04-2022-0497

Dubey, R., Gupta, M., Mikalef, P., & Akter, S. (2022). Incorporating blockchain technology in information systems research. *International Journal of Information Management*, *102573*. Advance online publication. doi:10.1016/j.ijinfomgt.2022.102573

Dwivedi, Y., Hughes, L., Baabdullah, A., Ribeiro-Navarrete, S., Giannakis, M., Al-Debei, M., Dennehy, D., Metri, B., Buhalis, D., Cheung, C. M. K., Conboy, K., Doyle, R., Dubey, R., Dutot, V., Felix, R., Goyal, D. P., Gustafsson, A., Hinsch, C., Jebabli, I., ... Wamba, S. (2022). Metaverse beyond the hype: Multidisciplinary perspectives on emerging challenges, opportunities, and agenda for research, practice and policy. *International Journal of Information Management*, *66*, 102542. doi:10.1016/j.ijinfomgt.2022.102542

Gupta, P., Prashar, A., Giannakis, M., Dutot, V., & Dwivedi, Y. (2022). How organizational socialization occurring in virtual setting unique: A longitudinal study of socialization. *Technological Forecasting and Social Change*, *185*, 122097. doi:10.1016/j.techfore.2022.122097

Koo, C., Kwon, J., Chung, N., & Kim, J. (2022). Metaverse tourism: Conceptual framework and research propositions. *Current Issues in Tourism*, 1–7. doi:10.1080/13683500.2022.2122781

Polyviou, A., & Pappas, I. (2022). *Metaverses and Business Transformation*. Paper presented at the Co-creating for Context in the Transfer and Diffusion of IT, Cham.

Yu, J. (2022). Exploration of Educational Possibilities by Four Metaverse Types in Physical Education. *Technologies*, *10*(5), 104. doi:10.3390/technologies10050104

KEY TERMS AND DEFINITIONS

Augmented Reality: Augmented Reality (AR) superimposes digitally generated images onto the real world. Users can use devices such as their phones or tables to superimpose graphics and sounds onto their real-life environment.

Avatar: An avatar is a digital character that represents you in a computer-generated world, such as metaverse. Avatars can be static or animated, and many of us already have some experience with avatars.

Extended Reality: Extended Reality (or XR) is a general term for computer-generated environments that blend the physical and virtual worlds, or create a fully virtual experience for the user.

Metaverse: Simply put, a metaverse is a set of shared three-dimensional virtual environments where people can engage in everyday activities such as working, socializing and playing as if they were in the real world.

Virtual Reality: Often also written as VR, virtual reality is an immersive experience in an environment generated entirely through computer technology.

Chapter 13
Virtual World and the Teaching of Literature Studies in IR 4.0 Era:
Learning Behaviour and Challenges of Malaysian University Students

Saravanan P. Veeramuthu
School of Humanities, Universiti Sains Malaysia, Malaysia

Mohamad Luthfi Abdul Rahman
Universiti Sains Malaysia, Malaysia

Moussa Pourya Asl
iD https://orcid.org/0000-0002-8426-426X
School of Humanities, Universiti Sains Malaysia, Malaysia

Manonmani Devi M. A. R. Annamalai
Universiti Perguruan Sulthan Idris, Malaysia

ABSTRACT

The rapid innovations in computer sciences and the emergence of technologies such as virtual reality (VR), augmented reality (AR), metaverse, and similar cyberspaces have greatly impacted the field of education. The radical changes that IR4.0 has made in the teaching approaches and learning behaviours have posed new challenges for students of literary studies in academia. This chapter aims to examine the learning behaviours and challenges of literature students in Malaysian tertiary education in the context of IR4.0. Specifically, the study explores how digital and virtual world has impacted the teaching and learning of literature in academia and thereby seeks to suggest ways to overcome them. It is concluded that effective instruction of literature courses in IR4.0 era requires a combination of pedagogical approaches, technological tools, and cultural sensitivity as well as an effective convergence of the real and the virtual worlds.

DOI: 10.4018/978-1-6684-7029-9.ch013

INTRODUCTION

The rapid innovations in computer sciences and the emergence of technologies such as Virtual Reality (VR), Augmented Reality (AR), Metaverse and similar digitized worlds have greatly impacted the field of education. The potentials and limitations of the educational applications of virtual world are matters of ongoing debate among scholars whose research examine the multiple ways in which the Fourth Industrial Revolution (IR4.0) is transforming human life and behaviour—that is, how we live, work, and communicate. In this chapter, we argue that the radical changes that IR4.0 has made in the teaching approaches and learning behaviours have posed new challenges for students of literary studies in academia. For centuries, the study of literature has been a crucial aspect of education (Gurcaglar, 2020). Through the study of literature, students can gain a profound understanding of the human experience (Anderson, 2016), the complexities of language, and the power of storytelling. In Malaysia, literature studies have always played an important role in higher education (Mustaffa & Nordin, 2017).

This chapter aims to examine learning behaviour and challenges of Malaysian university students of literature studies in the context of IR4.0. Our aim is to investigate how digital and virtual world has impacted the teaching and learning of literature in Malaysian universities. On the one hand, the integration of technology in education has helped students with access to an ever-expanding range of resources. On the other hand, the rapid changes and advancements have presented considerable challenges. Understanding literature students' learning behaviour in IR 4.0 era will help to better support them in their studies and create a more inclusive learning environment. We will begin by providing an overview of the Fourth Industrial Revolution and its impact on education. The chapter will then discuss the challenges faced by literature students in Malaysian tertiary education, including the difficulty in balancing the use of traditional and digital resources, the need for critical thinking and analysis in a rapidly changing world, and the impact of technology on language use and communication. The literature review will examine various approaches used by educators to address the challenges of teaching literature in the digital age, such as the integration of technology in the classroom, critical thinking skills in the curriculum, and the promotion of multilingualism and intercultural communication.

To understand these challenges, the study will employ a qualitative research approach using interviews with literature educators in Malaysian universities. The interviews aim to gain insights into the challenges faced by educators in teaching literature in the context of IR4.0 and the strategies they use to overcome these challenges. The data collected from the interviews will be analysed using thematic analysis. In conclusion, this chapter will provide insights into the challenges faced by Malaysian students in their literature studies in the context of IR4.0. The study will contribute to the existing literature on the teaching of literature in the digital age and provide recommendations for educators on how to better support students in their literary studies. The findings of this study will be of interest to literature educators, policymakers, and researchers interested in the intersection between literature studies and technology in education. Additionally, the chapter will address the cultural diversity of the country and the importance of creating an inclusive learning.

Problem Statement

The integration of technology in education has brought significant changes to the way literature is studied, taught, and learned in universities. Previous studies indicate that the advent of artificial intelligence techniques and approaches such as machine learning, sentiment analysis, and opinion mining has opened new possibilities for the objective analysis of literary texts (Asri et al., 2022; Chu et al., 2022; Elmi et al., 2023; Fasha et al., 2022; Jafery et al., 2022, 2023; Keikhosrokiani et al., 2023; Kng et al., 2023; Paremeswaran et al., 2022; Sofian et al., 2022). However, the Fourth Industrial Revolution (IR4.0) has also presented new challenges for students and educators alike. In Malaysia, literature studies have always played a significant role in higher education, but Malaysian students face unique challenges in their literature studies due to the rapid technological advancements in their country. To improve students' learning behaviour and provide better support for them, it is essential to identify the challenges they face and develop effective strategies to overcome them.

As Yap and Zainol (2021) observe in "Teaching Literature Studies in Universities and Challenges Malaysian Students Face in IR4.0", there is a need to examine the challenges faced by Malaysian students in their literature studies in the context of IR4.0. The authors argue that the impact of IR4.0 on education has created new challenges for literature educators in Malaysia, and it is essential to identify these challenges and develop effective strategies to address them. The article highlights that the integration of technology in education has led to an expansion in the range of resources available to students, but this has also created difficulties in balancing the use of traditional and digital resources. Additionally, the authors point out that the rapidly changing world requires students to develop critical thinking and analysis skills to make sense of the overwhelming amount of information available to them. Furthermore, the impact of technology on language use and communication is another challenge faced by Malaysian students in their literature studies.

Apart from this there are few other articles related to teaching literature studies and the challenges faced by students in the context of IR4.0. Liu's (2018) study has examined the teaching of literature in the digital era through online discussion forums. This article examines the use of online discussion forums in a literature classroom and their impact on student engagement and learning outcomes. The study found that the use of online discussion forums can enhance student engagement and critical thinking skills in literature studies. Another study by Petrilli and Salomoni (2019) discusses the challenges and opportunities presented by the integration of digital literacy in literature studies. The authors argue that digital literacy can enhance student engagement and learning outcomes in literature studies, but it also requires educators to adapt their teaching methods to accommodate the changing needs of students. Likewise, Olaosebikan and Osime (2020) discuss the challenges faced by Nigerian undergraduate students in their literature studies due to the prevalence of distractions created by the virtual world. The study found that students' use of digital devices can impact their reading comprehension and critical thinking skills, and that educators need to be aware of these challenges and to develop strategies to mitigate their impact.

In "Integrating digital technology into the teaching of literature: A case study of a Malaysian university", Ismail et al. (2019) examine the challenges and benefits of integrating digital technology in the teaching of literature in a Malaysian university. The study found that while the integration of technology can enhance student engagement and learning outcomes, it also requires educators to adapt their teaching methods and to be aware of the potential cultural barriers to the use of digital technology in education. The findings of this study are interesting because they suggest that the benefits of digital technology in education are not automatic and that the successful integration of technology requires careful planning and execution.

Based on previous studies mentioned above, the Fourth Industrial Revolution (IR4.0) has brought significant changes to the teaching and learning of literature, posing unique challenges for students and educators alike. Malaysian students face specific challenges in their literature studies due to the rapid technological advancements in their country (Yap & Zainol, 2021). The integration of technology in education has transformed the way students learn and access information, presenting challenges such as the difficulty in balancing traditional and digital resources, the need for critical thinking and analysis in a rapidly changing world, and the impact of technology on language use and communication (Chin & Tan, 2019; Wong & Noor, 2019). The integration of digital technology in literature studies presents both challenges and opportunities for educators (Mahfodz, 2019). While the use of online discussion forums and digital literacy can enhance student engagement and critical thinking skills, it also requires educators to adapt their teaching methods to accommodate the changing needs of students. Additionally, cultural barriers and digital distractions can impact students' learning outcomes and comprehension (Zainuddin & Attaran, 2016). While various approaches have been used to address these challenges, such as the use of technology in the classroom, the integration of critical thinking skills in the curriculum, and the promotion of multilingualism and intercultural communication (Ng & Tan, 2019), it is still unclear how effective these approaches are in addressing the challenges faced by Malaysian students in their literature studies.

The integration of IR 4.0 with literary studies also has implications for the teaching of literary studies. With the increasing availability of digital resources and tools such as virtual world and metaverse, educators of literary studies are presented with new opportunities to engage students in the study of literature. However, the integration of technology into the classroom also requires careful consideration of pedagogical approaches and the potential impacts on student learning behaviour (Cordle & Thompson, 2021). Incorporating digital tools and resources into literary studies classrooms can provide students with access to a broader range of texts and perspectives. For example, digital archives and databases allow students to explore literary texts from different historical periods and cultural contexts, while online discussion forums and social media platforms provide opportunities for students to engage in literary analysis and discussion beyond the classroom.

At the same time, the integration of technology into the classroom also raises questions about the impact of digital distractions and the potential for a loss of focus on close reading and critical thinking. Additionally, there is a need for careful consideration of the ethical implications of data collection and analysis in the classroom, particularly with regard to student privacy and data security. Overall, the integration of IR 4.0 with literary studies presents both opportunities and challenges for the teaching of literature. As educators navigate the changing landscape of literary studies in the digital age, careful consideration of pedagogical approaches and ethical considerations will be essential in ensuring that students receive a well-rounded and meaningful education in literature.

In addition to the challenges mentioned above, the integration of IR 4.0 with literary studies also raises questions about the role of the reader in the digital age. With the rise of e-books, audiobooks, and other digital formats, the traditional relationship between reader and text has been disrupted (Schreibman & Siemens, 2016). Furthermore, the use of algorithms and machine learning in literary analysis has the potential to diminish the interpretive role of the reader and reduce literary analysis to a series of quantitative metrics (Keikhosrokiani & Asl, 2022, 2023a, 2023b; Suhendra et al., 2022; Tammi, 2020; Ying et al., 2022; Zainol et al., 2023).

Moreover, the integration of IR 4.0 with literary studies also has implications for the preservation of literary heritage. As literary texts become increasingly digitized and dispersed across various platforms, there is a risk of losing important cultural artifacts and historical records (Ovenden, 2015). Additionally, the use of digital technologies in literary studies may require new standards for archiving and preserving digital materials to ensure their longevity (Tammi, 2020).

To address the above-mentioned issues, this study aims to explore the challenges faced by Malaysian students in studying literature in IR4.0 era and to identify effective strategies that can be employed to overcome these challenges. Therefore, there is a need to explore the challenges faced by students and educators in teaching literature in the digital age and to develop strategies to overcome these challenges. This study aims to contribute to the existing literature by examining the impact of digital technology on literature studies and identifying effective teaching strategies that can enhance student engagement and learning outcomes.

LITERATURE REVIEW

The impact of Industry 4.0 on literary studies has received increasing attention in recent years. Scholars argue that the convergence of advanced technologies such as artificial intelligence, big data analytics, and the Internet of Things has the potential to revolutionize literary studies in unprecedented ways (Al Mamun et al., 2022; Malik et al., 2021; Tammi, 2020; Ying et al., 2021). However, this integration also poses several challenges, including the need for new approaches to literary analysis, the ethical implications of data collection and analysis, and the potential for a loss of humanistic inquiry. Other scholars have also explored the implications of Industry 4.0 on literary studies. For instance, Guo and Huang (2019) discuss the potential of big data analytics to enhance the study of Chinese literature. They suggest that big data can be used to identify patterns and connections that were previously difficult to discern, leading to new insights and discoveries. Similarly, in a study on Jane Austen's novels, Kao and Lee (2020) use natural language processing and machine learning techniques to analyse the sentiment and themes of the texts, revealing previously hidden patterns and insights. However, the integration of technology with literary studies also raises questions about the role of the reader and the preservation of literary heritage. As Devi and Veeramuthu (2020) note, the rise of digital formats and the use of algorithms in literary analysis may diminish the interpretive role of the reader and reduce literary analysis to a series of quantitative metrics. Additionally, the digitization of literary texts may require new standards for archiving and preserving digital materials to ensure their longevity.

Overall, the integration of Industry 4.0 with literary studies presents both opportunities and challenges. While advanced technologies have the potential to enhance the study of literature, they also require careful consideration of their ethical and practical implications. The integration of digital technology in literature studies has brought both challenges and opportunities for students and educators. Challenges include the difficulty in balancing traditional and digital resources, the need for critical thinking and analysis in a rapidly changing world, and the impact of technology on language use and communication (Chin & Tan, 2019; Petrilli & Salomoni, 2019). These challenges have been further complicated by the need to adapt teaching methods to accommodate the changing needs of students and to address cultural barriers and digital distractions (Ismail et al., 2019; Olaosebikan & Osime, 2020; Zainuddin & Attaran, 2016).

One challenge that has been noted in literature studies is the difficulty in balancing traditional and digital resources. While digital technology has made literature more accessible, students may face difficulties in navigating the vast number of online resources available to them (Ng & Tan, 2019). Additionally, students may struggle with the shift from print to digital literature, which may require different reading and analytical strategies (Chin & Tan, 2019). Another challenge is the need for critical thinking and analysis in a rapidly changing world. Digital technology has transformed the way information is disseminated and consumed, and students must learn to critically evaluate sources of information and analyse texts in light of changing cultural, social, and political contexts (Petrilli & Salomoni, 2019). Additionally, the integration of digital technology in literature studies requires educators to adapt their teaching methods to incorporate digital literacy and to promote critical thinking skills (Liu, 2018). The impact of technology on language use and communication is another challenge faced by students and educators in literature studies. The use of digital devices can impact students' reading comprehension and critical thinking skills (Olaosebikan & Osime, 2020). Additionally, the use of digital communication platforms can lead to a deterioration in language proficiency and communication skills (Zainuddin & Attaran, 2016).

Despite these challenges, literature studies have also seen opportunities for enhancing student engagement and learning outcomes using digital technology. Online discussion forums and digital literacy help to promote critical thinking skills and student engagement (Liu, 2018). Furthermore, the integration of technology in the classroom has been used to address these challenges and to promote multilingualism and intercultural communication (Ng & Tan, 2019).

To address these challenges and seize opportunities for enhanced student engagement and learning outcomes, effective teaching strategies must be identified. Strategies that have been proposed in the literature include the integration of digital technology in the classroom, the integration of critical thinking skills in the curriculum, and the promotion of multilingualism and intercultural communication (Ismail et al., 2019; Ng & Tan, 2019; Petrilli & Salomoni, 2019). Further research is needed to determine the effectiveness of these strategies in addressing the challenges faced by students and educators in teaching literature in the digital age.

Digital technologies have transformed the way we teach and learn literature, providing new opportunities and challenges for educators and students alike. Review of few studies that explore the impact of digital technologies on the teaching and learning of English literature. The studies focus on the use of e-readers, digital humanities, online courses, and the integration of digital technologies in literature education. The findings of these studies suggest that while digital technologies can enhance engagement and critical thinking skills, they also present challenges such as the need for digital literacy skills, the potential for distraction, and the shift in traditional literary scholarship.

Nashwa (2019) explores the impact of digital technologies on the teaching and learning of English literature. The study found that the integration of digital technologies can enhance students' critical thinking skills and engagement with literature. However, it also presents challenges such as the need for digital literacy skills and the potential distraction of technology. Nashwa suggests that educators need to balance the use of traditional and digital resources and provide training for students to develop digital literacy skills. Geaghan-Breiner and Bach (2018) examine the impact of e-readers on students' reading habits and engagement with literature. The findings suggest that e-readers can enhance access to literature and offer a personalized reading experience. However, they also present challenges such as the potential for distraction and the loss of the physical experience of reading. Geaghan-Breiner and Bach recommend that educators consider the pros and cons of e-readers and provide guidance on how to use them effectively. Pettersson and Berg (2020) discuss the potential of digital humanities for literary studies and the challenges it presents. The study found that digital humanities can enhance research and analysis of literature, but it also requires a shift in traditional literary scholarship and the development of new skills and methods. Pettersson and Berg suggest that educators need to provide training for students to develop digital literacy skills and encourage collaboration between scholars from different disciplines. Yildiz and Sahin (2020) examine the challenges and possibilities of literature education in the digital age. The findings suggest that the integration of digital technologies can enhance student engagement and learning outcomes. However, it also requires the development of new skills and methods for educators and the need to balance traditional and digital resources. Yildiz and Sahin recommend that educators provide guidance on how to use digital technologies effectively and offer training for students to develop digital literacy skills. Juntunen (2019) discusses the benefits and challenges of teaching literature through online courses. The study found that online courses can enhance access to literature and offer flexibility for students. However, they also require careful planning and design to ensure effective teaching and learning outcomes. Juntunen recommends that educators provide guidance on how to use online courses effectively and offer training for students to develop digital literacy skills.

The studies reviewed in this article suggest that digital technologies have the potential to enhance the teaching and learning of literature. However, they also present challenges such as the need for digital literacy skills, the potential for distraction, and the shift in traditional literary scholarship. Educators need to consider the pros and cons of digital technologies and provide guidance on how to use them effectively. Therefore, this study aims to explore the challenges faced by Malaysian students in studying literature in the context of IR 4.0 and provide insights for educators on students' learning behaviour and how to better support them in their literary studies.

METHODOLOGY

To investigate the challenges that Malaysian students encounter while studying literature in the context of Industry 4.0 (IR4.0), a qualitative research design and mixed-methods approach are adopted in this study. In this regard, a thorough literature review was carried out to explore the existing research on teaching literature studies in universities, students' learning behaviour, and the challenges that Malaysian students face in the context of IR4.0. This entailed searching databases for relevant articles and books which helped in determining the current state of knowledge in the field while also identifying gaps that this study could address. An informal interview would also be conducted to obtain information on the teaching methods and materials that are presently employed in literature studies courses, as well as the challenges faced by students in comprehending and engaging with literary texts in the context of IR4.0. The interviews would provide more in-depth insights into the experiences and perspectives of both students and lecturers. Qualitative methods would be utilized for data analysis. The findings of this study would be presented in a report that discusses the current state of literature studies in Malaysian universities, the challenges faced by students in the context of IR4.0, and potential solutions to address these challenges. This article would also include recommendations for future research and improvements to literature studies courses in Malaysian universities.

Challenges Faced by Malaysian Students in IR4.0

The challenges faced by Malaysian students in studying literature in the context of IR4.0 have been the subject of various studies. In a study conducted by Abdul Mutalib and Mohd Nor (2021), it was found that limited exposure to technology is one of the most significant challenges faced by Malaysian students. Many students come from economically disadvantaged backgrounds and do not have access to the latest technology, hindering their ability to engage with the subject matter. This can be particularly problematic if digital resources are required for the course.

Furthermore, the language barrier is another challenge faced by Malaysian students. Most literature courses in Malaysia are taught in English or Malay, which can be a significant barrier to comprehension and engagement for students who are not proficient in the language. This finding is supported by the study conducted by Shaari and Kassim (2019), who found that language proficiency is one of the major challenges faced by students in studying literature in Malaysia. Furthermore, efforts could be made to improve the Malay and English language proficiency of Malaysian students. This could involve providing additional language support services or offering literature courses in alternative languages, such as Tamil or Mandarin.

In addition to language barriers, the cultural diversity of Malaysia presents another challenge for literature instruction. As a multi-ethnic and multi-religious society, some students may be unfamiliar with the cultural references in a particular text, which can hinder their comprehension. Moreover, some texts may be offensive or inappropriate for some students due to cultural or religious differences. To address the challenges faced by Malaysian students in studying literature in the context of IR4.0, it is crucial to develop effective strategies and interventions that can enhance their engagement and comprehension of literary texts. One such strategy is to promote cultural sensitivity and inclusivity in literature instruction. This can be achieved by incorporating a wider range of texts from diverse cultures and backgrounds and providing more context and explanation of cultural references. Additionally, instructors can create a more inclusive classroom environment that respects and values the diversity of their students. These suggestions are in line with the findings of Tammi et al. (2021) and Tengku Putri Norishah and Abdullah (2018) who highlight the importance of incorporating technology and cultural sensitivity in literature instruction in the Malaysian context (Tammi et al., 2021; Tengku Putri Norishah & Abdullah, 2018). To address the challenges faced by Malaysian students in studying literature in IR4.0, it is important to develop strategies and interventions that can improve their engagement and comprehension of literary texts. One potential solution is to provide more training and resources to students on the use of technology in literature studies. This could involve providing access to digital resources and tools, as well as training on how to effectively use these resources.

To address the challenges faced by Malaysian students in studying literature in the context of IR4.0, it is necessary to develop new approaches to teaching and learning that consider the unique needs and circumstances of these students (Ng & Lee, 2019). This may involve incorporating more digital resources into literature studies courses and providing students with access to technology and training to use it effectively. It may also involve developing new pedagogical approaches that address the cultural diversity of Malaysia and the need for more inclusive instruction (Abdullah & Othman, 2017). In addition, efforts should be made to improve students' proficiency in English, as this is the language in which most literature is taught in Malaysia (Ariffin & Rahman, 2019).

Finally, it may be useful to conduct further research on the challenges faced by Malaysian students in studying literature in IR4.0, as well as the effectiveness of different strategies and interventions (Tengku & Abdullah, 2018). By better understanding these challenges and developing evidence-based interventions, it may be possible to improve the quality of literature education in Malaysia and enhance the learning experiences of students. Overall, these challenges demonstrate the need for educators to be aware of the diverse backgrounds and experiences of their students, and to adapt their teaching methods and materials accordingly. By addressing these challenges, literature studies in Malaysian universities can be made more accessible and engaging for all students, regardless of their background or level of technological proficiency.

Teaching Strategies

To overcome the challenges faced by Malaysian students in studying literature in IR4.0, literature instructors can adopt a range of pedagogical approaches, technological tools, and cultural sensitivity. One effective approach is to incorporate diverse literature into the curriculum. This can expose students to a range of cultural and linguistic perspectives, which can enhance their understanding and appreciation of different literary forms. The argument for adopting a range of pedagogical approaches, technological tools, and cultural sensitivity to overcome challenges faced by Malaysian students in studying literature in IR4.0 is well-supported by existing literature. For instance, Tammi et al. (2021) suggest that incorporating diverse literature in the curriculum can help students develop critical thinking skills and broaden their perspectives. Moreover, Tengku Putri Norishah and Abdullah (2018) emphasize the importance of using technology to enhance student learning experiences.

Instructors can also use online resources, such as e-books, audiobooks, and online discussion forums to enhance student engagement. In addition, instructors can adopt a range of technological tools to enhance student learning. For example, instructors can use social media platforms to facilitate online discussions and collaboration, as well as tools such as virtual reality to create immersive learning experiences. Furthermore, the use of technology in literature education has been found to be effective in enhancing student engagement and learning outcomes (Hirsh, 2019; Yulianto et al., 2020). Social media platforms, for instance, can be used to facilitate online discussions and collaboration, which can help students develop their communication skills and broaden their perspectives (Shu & Liang, 2021). Additionally, virtual reality technology has been found to enhance student engagement and understanding of literary texts (Zainuddin & Mohamad, 2020). Such tools can help to overcome the limitations of traditional classroom settings, particularly for students who have limited access to technology.

In addition to the strategies mentioned above, there are a few other methods literature instructors can use to enhance their teaching and help students overcome challenges in IR4.0. One effective approach is to use active learning strategies, such as group work and peer review, to encourage student engagement and collaboration. These methods have been shown to improve student learning outcomes in literature studies (Mofidi, 2014). Another approach is to incorporate multimedia elements into the curriculum, such as videos, podcasts, and interactive online content. These tools can help to enhance student engagement and provide additional context for understanding the literature being studied (Mahmod et al., 2017). Furthermore, instructors can use data-driven approaches to analyse student learning outcomes and adjust their teaching strategies accordingly. By collecting and analysing data on student performance, instructors can identify areas of weakness and adjust their teaching methods to better meet the needs of their students (Sebesta & Apostolova, 2020).

Finally, cultural sensitivity is essential in creating an inclusive learning environment. Cultural sensitivity is also a key component of effective literature instruction. Instructors should be aware of the cultural and religious diversity of their students and should work to create an inclusive learning environment that respects and values this diversity. Instructors should be aware of the cultural and religious diversity of their students and be sensitive to any potential conflicts or issues that may arise. For example, they can provide alternative texts or resources for students who find a particular text offensive or inappropriate. This can involve providing alternative texts or resources for students who may find a particular text offensive or inappropriate (Al-Haj, 2018). Moreover, instructors should be sensitive to any potential conflicts or issues that may arise in the classroom due to cultural or religious differences (Chua, 2018).

In conclusion, a combination of pedagogical approaches, technological tools, and cultural sensitivity can help to overcome the challenges faced by Malaysian students in studying literature in IR4.0. Effective literature instruction in IR4.0 requires a combination of pedagogical approaches, technological tools, and cultural sensitivity. Malaysian students face a range of challenges in studying literature in this era, but these challenges can be overcome by adopting these strategies. By creating an inclusive and engaging learning environment, literature instructors can help to ensure that students have a positive and enriching experience with literature in the era of IR4.0 and are better equipped with the skills and knowledge needed to succeed in the rapidly evolving landscape of the 21st century. It is important to acknowledge that the nature of literature has changed in the era of IR4.0, and this has significant implications for how literature is taught and studied. As noted by Widerhold (2019), IR4.0 is characterized by the integration of digital technologies, such as artificial intelligence and the Internet of Things, which are transforming the ways in which we access and interact with literature. Therefore, literature instructors need to adapt their pedagogical approaches to ensure that they are equipping students with the skills and knowledge needed to engage with literature in this new context.

Industrial Expectation

In the era of the Fourth Industrial Revolution (IR 4.0), industries have a growing demand for employees with skills in creativity, critical thinking, and adaptability (World Economic Forum, 2018). These skills are not only important for success in the workforce but are also essential for the study of literature. Literature allows students to develop these skills by providing opportunities to analyse complex ideas, think critically, and engage with diverse perspectives. Furthermore, industries in the digital age require employees who are proficient in digital communication and content creation. By incorporating digital literature, multimedia resources, and new pedagogical approaches, literature courses can equip students with the digital literacy skills needed for success in the modern workforce. For example, students can learn to create digital content, analyse online discourse, and use social media for collaborative learning and research. In addition to digital literacy, industries in the IR 4.0 era also require employees who have a deep understanding of global and cultural perspectives. Literature courses can provide students with opportunities to explore different cultures and perspectives through reading and analysis of literary texts. By incorporating literature from diverse cultural backgrounds, literature courses can help students develop cultural awareness and sensitivity, essential skills for success in a globalized workforce.

The industrial expectations for literary studies in the IR 4.0 era (Ibrahim, 2020) are high, and it is crucial for literature educators to adapt to the changing needs of industries. This means that literature courses should not only focus on developing critical thinking and analytical skills but also equip students with practical skills that are in demand in the job market. Some of these skills include digital literacy, communication skills, and the ability to work in teams. By incorporating these skills into literature courses, educators can ensure that students are well-prepared for the demands of the IR 4.0 era. Overall, the study of literature in the IR 4.0 era can prepare students for the demands of the modern job market by providing opportunities to develop creativity, critical thinking, digital literacy, and cultural awareness.

A Need for New Syllabus for Literature

Restructuring the curriculum is one of the potential solutions to address the challenges faced by Malaysian students studying literature in the context of IR4.0. By incorporating IR4.0 technologies into the curriculum, students can gain practical experience and develop the necessary digital literacy skills to succeed in their academic pursuits and future careers. A revised curriculum can also help bridge the gap between students who have access to technology and those who do not, thus promoting equal learning opportunities. Kabilan and Nambiar's (2019) study has proposed the implementation of a new curriculum in Malaysian universities that integrates digital literacy skills and strategies to enhance the quality of teaching and learning. The proposed curriculum includes various digital tools such as e-books, virtual reality, and social media, which can be used to create engaging learning experiences for students. Another study by Lee (2019) has proposed the use of e-learning platforms in teaching literature courses, which can facilitate collaboration, peer review, and interactive learning experiences. The use of these platforms can help overcome the constraints of time and space, as students can access course materials and participate in discussions from any location.

Overall, restructuring the curriculum to integrate IR4.0 technologies can be an effective way to address the challenges faced by Malaysian students studying literature. By providing students with practical experience and digital literacy skills, they can develop the necessary competencies to succeed in the 21st-century workforce. One way to achieve this is by introducing a new syllabus for literature studies that reflects the changing nature of literature in IR4.0. This could involve incorporating new forms of literature, such as digital literature and interactive fiction, as well as exploring the ways in which technology is transforming the production, distribution, and reception of literature. In addition, a new syllabus could also incorporate pedagogical approaches that are more engaging and interactive, such as flipped classrooms and gamification.

To address the challenges faced by Malaysian students in studying literature in IR4.0, Ling and Wah (2019) suggest that literature instructors need to incorporate new media and address industrial needs in their syllabus. This includes incorporating new media forms, such as graphic novels and online literature, into the curriculum. Instructors can also teach students how to critically analyze media and popular culture, which are becoming increasingly important in the era of IR4.0. Furthermore, instructors should address the industrial needs of the current job market by teaching students' practical skills related to literature, such as editing, publishing, and digital content creation.

Furthermore, instructors should address the industrial needs of the current job market by teaching students' practical skills related to literature, such as editing, publishing, and digital content creation (Levy, 2016). This can help students to better prepare for careers in fields related to literature and communication. Overall, the incorporation of new media and addressing industrial needs can not only improve student engagement and comprehension of literary texts but also better prepare them for the demands of the modern job market. Moreover, a new syllabus could also consider the changing demands of the job market in IR4.0, such as the need for creativity, critical thinking, and adaptability (Lim, 2019). By incorporating literature that addresses contemporary social issues and technological advancements, students can gain a better understanding of the evolving societal and cultural context in which they will work. For example, instructors can incorporate literature that explores the ethical implications of emerging technologies, such as artificial intelligence and biotechnology, or literature that addresses social justice issues, such as race and gender inequality in the digital age (Scherer, 2018). Such literature can help students to develop critical thinking skills and cultural awareness that are essential for success in the modern workforce.

In conclusion, the challenges faced by Malaysian students in studying literature in IR4.0 call for a new syllabus that reflects the changing nature of literature and addresses the specific needs of Malaysian students. By incorporating new forms of literature, addressing language proficiency and cultural sensitivity, and adopting more engaging pedagogical approaches, literature instructors can equip students with the skills and knowledge needed to succeed in the era of IR4.0.

Facilities for Teaching Literature in the Era of IR 4.0

The era of IR 4.0 has brought about significant changes in the way we teach and learn. With the rise of digital technology, educators are presented with new opportunities and challenges in teaching literature. In this article, we will explore the facilities available for teaching literature in the era of Industry 4.0 and their potential impact on literature education.

One of the most significant facilities available for teaching literature in the era of IR 4.0 is digital libraries (Hu et al., 2019). Digital libraries allow students to access a vast array of literature from anywhere in the world, without being limited to physical locations. The rise of digital libraries has been facilitated by advancements in digital technology, which has made it possible for libraries to provide online access to their collections. Another facility available for teaching literature in the era of Industry 4.0 is e-books (Maleki & Shahbazinia, 2017). E-books offer a convenient and cost-effective way to provide literature to students. They can be accessed on laptops, tablets, or smartphones and offer interactive features such as highlighting, note-taking, and search functions. E-books can also be used to support language learning by providing models of pronunciation and intonation. Audio books are another facility available for teaching literature in the era of Industry 4.0 (Moore & Tschang, 2017). They provide an alternative way for students to engage with literature, particularly for students who struggle with reading or have visual impairments. Audio books can also be used to support language learning by providing models of pronunciation and intonation. Virtual reality technology can be used to create immersive experiences that bring literature to life. For example, students can use VR technology to explore the setting of a story or to experience a character's perspective. This facility provides a unique way for students to engage with literature and can help to enhance their understanding of literary texts (Chen, 2020). Social media platforms can be used to create online communities of literature enthusiasts. Educators can use social media to share literature recommendations, facilitate discussions, and provide feedback to students. This facility can help to foster a love of literature and create a sense of community among students who share a passion for reading (Shen, 2019).

The facilities available for teaching literature in the era of Industry 4.0 are diverse and offer many opportunities for educators to enhance their teaching practices. Digital libraries, e-books, audio books, virtual reality, and social media can all be used to create engaging and immersive learning experiences that inspire a love of literature in students. As we continue to embrace digital technology, educators will need to adapt their teaching practices to meet the evolving needs of their students.

By incorporating diverse literature into the curriculum, using technology to enhance student engagement, and creating an inclusive learning environment that respects cultural and religious diversity, instructors can improve student learning outcomes and enhance the quality of literature education in Malaysia.

Overcoming Perceptions and Embracing Innovation

The emergence of the Fourth Industrial Revolution (IR 4.0) has brought significant changes to the way we live, work, and learn. In the field of education, these changes have challenged traditional pedagogical approaches, particularly in teaching and studying literature. Many students perceive literature as outdated and irrelevant in the era of digital media, where instant gratification and visual stimulation dominate.

This perception has resulted in a decline in student enrollment in literature courses, as well as a lack of interest and engagement in literary texts. However, there are ways to overcome this perception and reinvigorate the study of literature in the IR 4.0 era.

One of the main challenges in teaching literature in the IR 4.0 era is the perception that literature is irrelevant to the modern world. This perception stems from the misconception that literature is solely concerned with the past and does not address contemporary issues. To overcome this perception, literature instructors need to incorporate new forms of literature that address current social and technological issues. For example, science fiction literature can be used to explore the ethical implications of emerging technologies, while digital literature can provide an interactive and engaging experience for students (Vint, 2016). By incorporating these new forms of literature, instructors can demonstrate the relevance of literature to the modern world and capture the interest of students.

Another challenge is the perception that literature is difficult to understand and requires a high level of language proficiency. This perception is particularly prevalent among non-native speakers in Malaysia. To overcome this challenge, literature instructors need to adopt pedagogical approaches that address language proficiency and cultural sensitivity. For example, instructors can use simplified versions of literary texts, provide vocabulary lists, and incorporate multimedia resources such as audio and video to aid comprehension (Lee, 2015). By adopting these approaches, instructors can help students overcome language barriers and develop a deeper appreciation of literary texts.

The challenge of engaging students in the study of literature can be overcome by adopting more engaging pedagogical approaches. One such approach is to use technology to create interactive and immersive learning experiences. For example, virtual reality can be used to create a simulated environment that allows students to explore literary texts in a more engaging and interactive manner (Hoffman, 2017). Another approach is to use social media platforms to create a collaborative and participatory learning experience. For example, instructors can use social media to create online discussion forums and collaborative projects that allow students to interact with literary texts in a more dynamic and engaging way (Wang et al., 2011).

Facilities for teaching literature in the era of Industry 4.0 is also an important aspect to be considered. Digital libraries and online databases can provide access to a wider range of literary texts, and technology can be used to enhance the reading and learning experience. For example, e-books and audiobooks can be used to provide students with different options for accessing literary texts, while interactive whiteboards and online discussion forums can facilitate classroom discussions and collaboration (Ibrahim, 2020).

Furthermore, there is a need for new syllabus for literature to keep up with the demands of the IR 4.0 era. The new syllabus should include literature that explores contemporary issues and emerging technologies. It should also incorporate new pedagogical approaches and technological tools that can enhance the learning experience for students. This will ensure that the study of literature remains relevant and engaging for students in the era of IR 4.0.

Finally, to meet the industrial expectations, it is important to prepare students with skills and knowledge that are relevant to the IR 4.0 era. Literature studies can help develop critical thinking, communication, and analytical skills that are in high demand in the digital age. In addition, incorporating emerging technologies such as virtual reality and social media platforms into the study of literature can help students develop digital literacy and adaptability skills that are crucial for success in the era of IR 4.0.

In the era of the Fourth Industrial Revolution (IR4.0), literature studies face new challenges as traditional approaches to teaching literature must be adapted to keep pace with changing technologies and cultural shifts. This is particularly true for Malaysian students, who face a unique set of challenges in their pursuit of literature studies in IR4.0. One of the key challenges facing Malaysian students is the need to bridge cultural gaps between traditional literary texts and contemporary society. As noted by Abdul Rashid Mohamed (2015), Malaysian students often struggle to relate to classic literary texts because of cultural differences, leading to disinterest in literature studies. Furthermore, the rapid pace of technological change in IR4.0 presents additional challenges for literature studies, as students must learn to navigate digital tools and resources while maintaining a critical perspective on their use. To address these challenges, literature instructors must adopt new pedagogical approaches and incorporate technological tools that enhance student engagement and foster critical thinking skills.

In conclusion, the challenges of teaching literature in the IR 4.0 era can be overcome by incorporating new forms of literature, adopting pedagogical approaches that address language proficiency and cultural sensitivity, providing adequate facilities, introducing a new syllabus and preparing students for the industrial expectations of the digital age. By overcoming these challenges, literature instructors can help students develop a deeper appreciation of literary texts and equip them with the skills and knowledge needed to succeed in the era of IR 4.0.

CONCLUSION

In conclusion, the challenges faced by Malaysian students in studying literature in the era of IR4.0 call for innovative and creative teaching strategies. The integration of new pedagogical approaches and technological tools, as well as a cultural sensitivity, can significantly enhance student engagement and comprehension of literary texts. The need for new facilities for teaching literature in the era of IR4.0 is also evident, as students require access to the latest technologies and digital resources. Overcoming perceptions and embracing innovation are key to ensuring that literature instruction remains relevant and effective in the digital age. As such, the introduction of a new syllabus for literature studies that reflects the changing nature of literature and addresses the specific needs of Malaysian students is essential. Ultimately, effective literature instruction in IR4.0 requires a collaborative effort among students, instructors, and educational institutions to ensure that literature continues to be a valuable and meaningful area of study in the digital age.

REFERENCES

Abdul Mutalib, N., & Mohd Nor, N. A. (2021). Teaching literature studies in universities and challenges Malaysian students face in IR4.0. *International Journal of Academic Research in Business & Social Sciences, 11*(3), 76–88.

Abdullah, M. N., & Othman, N. (2017). Multi-culturalism and diversity in Malaysian education. In J. Zajda, S. Majhanovich, & V. Rust (Eds.), *Education and social transition: societal change, public policy and curriculum development* (pp. 327–342). Springer.

Al-Haj, H. (2018). Reading literature in a multicultural society: Cultural sensitivity and literary appreciation. *Intercultural Education, 29*(3), 297–309.

Al Mamun, M. H., Keikhosrokiani, P., Asl, M. P., Anuar, N. A. N., Hadi, N. H. A., & Humida, T. (2022). Sentiment analysis of the Harry Potter series using a lexicon-based approach. In P. Keikhosrokiani & M. P. Asl (Eds.), *Handbook of research on opinion mining and text analytics on literary works and social media* (pp. 263–291). IGI Global. doi:10.4018/978-1-7998-9594-7.ch011

Anderson, K. (2016). Digital media in the literature classroom: A critical evaluation. *English Teaching*, *15*(1), 7–23. doi:10.1108/ETPC-10-2014-0081

Ariffin, N. M., & Rahman, N. A. (2019). Challenges of English language teaching and learning in Malaysia. *English Language Teaching*, *12*(1), 55–63.

Asri, M. A. Z. B. M., Keikhosrokiani, P., & Asl, M. P. (2022). *Opinion mining using topic modeling: A case study of Firoozeh Dumas's Funny in Farsi in Goodreads*. Advances on Intelligent Informatics and Computing. doi:10.1007/978-3-030-98741-1_19

Chen, X. (2020). Application of digital technology in literature teaching in the age of industry 4.0. In *2020 International Conference on Modern Educational Technology and Computer Science (METCS)* (pp. 248-252). IEEE.

Chin, L. S., & Tan, C. Y. (2019). Multimodal pedagogy in the Malaysian ESL classroom: The role of digital technology in enhancing student literacy. *Malaysian Journal of Learning and Instruction*, *16*(1), 1–33.

Chu, K. E., Keikhosrokiani, P., & Asl, M. P. (2022). A topic modeling and sentiment analysis model for detection and visualization of themes in literary texts. *Pertanika Journal of Science & Technology*, *30*(4), 2535–2561. doi:10.47836/pjst.30.4.14

Chua, R. Y. (2018). Diversity and inclusion in the classroom: A case study of cultural sensitivity in teaching literature. *Journal of Language, Identity, and Education*, *17*(5), 276–287.

Cordle, D., & Thompson, S. (2021). Teaching in the age of industry 4.0: Opportunities and challenges for literary studies. *College Literature*, *48*(2), 343–365.

Devi, M., Annamalai, M. A. R., & Veeramuthu, S. P. (2020). Literature education and industrial revolution 4.0. *Universal Journal of Educational Research*, *8*(3), 1027–1036. doi:10.13189/ujer.2020.080337

Elmi, A. H., Keikhosrokiani, P., & Asl, M. P. (2023). A machine learning approach to the analytics of representations of violence in Khaled Hosseini's novels. In P. Keikhosrokiani & M. P. Asl (Eds.), *Handbook of research on artificial intelligence applications in literary works and social media* (pp. 36–67). IGI Global. doi:10.4018/978-1-6684-6242-3.ch003

Fasha, E. F. B. K., Keikhosrokiani, P., & Asl, M. P. (2022). *Opinion mining using sentiment analysis: A case study of readers' response on Long Litt Woon's The Way Through the Woods in Goodreads*. Advances on Intelligent Informatics and Computing. doi:10.1007/978-3-030-98741-1_20

Geaghan-Breiner, C., & Bach, A. (2018). Reading literature in the digital age: An exploration of e-readers and reading habits. *Journal of Adolescent & Adult Literacy*, *62*(4), 395–404.

Guo, L., & Huang, Y. (2019). Application of big data analysis in Chinese literature research. *Journal of Digital Information Management*, *17*(4), 255–260.

Gurcaglar, S. S. (2020). Integrating technology in the teaching of literature: A survey of undergraduate English language and literature programs in Turkey. *Journal of Language and Linguistic Studies*, *16*(1), 1–14. doi:10.17263/jlls.717274

Hirsh, S. G. (2019). Technology in the literature classroom: Exploring new pedagogical approaches. *Journal of Interactive Technology and Pedagogy, 14.*

Hoffman, J. (2017). Virtual reality and education: Opportunities and challenges. *Computers & Education*, *110*, 1–2. doi:10.1016/j.compedu.2017.03.013

Hu, J., Guo, Y., & Wang, Y. (2019). The impact of digital technology on teaching and learning in higher education. *Education Sciences*, *9*(2), 100. doi:10.3390/educsci9020100

Ibrahim, M. A. (2020). The Fourth Industrial Revolution (4IR) and the higher education landscape: A systematic review of the literature. *Education Sciences*, *10*(7), 173. doi:10.3390/educsci10070173

Ismail, H. B., Yusoff, N. M., & Saad, N. F. M. (2019). Integrating digital technology into the teaching of literature: A case study of a Malaysian university. *International Journal of Emerging Technologies in Learning*, *14*(02), 157–170.

Jafery, N. N., Keikhosrokiani, P., & Asl, M. P. (2022). Text analytics model to identify the connection between theme and sentiment in literary works: A case study of Iraqi life writings. In P. Keikhosrokiani & M. P. Asl (Eds.), *Handbook of research on opinion mining and text analytics on literary works and social media* (pp. 173–190). IGI Global. doi:10.4018/978-1-7998-9594-7.ch008

Jafery, N. N., Keikhosrokiani, P., & Asl, M. P. (2023). An artificial intelligence application of theme and space in life writings of Middle Eastern women: A topic modelling and sentiment analysis approach. In P. Keikhosrokiani & M. P. Asl (Eds.), *Handbook of research on artificial intelligence applications in literary works and social media* (pp. 19–35). IGI Global. doi:10.4018/978-1-6684-6242-3.ch002

Juntunen, M. (2019). Teaching literature in the digital age: The pros and cons of online courses. *Scandinavian Journal of Educational Research*, *63*(4), 601–614.

Kabilan, M. K., & Nambiar, R. M. K. (2019). The integration of digital literacy in English language curriculum in Malaysian universities. *English Teaching*, *48*(1), 1–17.

Kao, C. H., & Lee, H. J. (2020). Natural language processing and machine learning techniques for literary studies: A case study of Jane Austen's novels. *Journal of English for Academic Purposes*, *45*, 100873.

Keikhosrokiani, P., & Asl, M. P. (Eds.). (2022). *Handbook of research on opinion mining and text analytics on literary works and social media*. IGI Global. doi:10.4018/978-1-7998-9594-7

Keikhosrokiani, P., & Asl, M. P. (Eds.). (2023a). *Handbook of research on artificial intelligence applications in literary works and social media*. IGI Global. doi:10.4018/978-1-6684-6242-3

Keikhosrokiani, P., & Asl, M. P. (2023b). Introduction to artificial intelligence for the analytics of literary works and social media: A review. In P. Keikhosrokiani & M. P. Asl (Eds.), *Handbook of research on artificial intelligence applications in literary works and social media* (pp. 1–17). IGI Global. doi:10.4018/978-1-6684-6242-3.ch001

Keikhosrokiani, P., Asl, M. P., Chu, K. E., & Anuar, N. A. N. (2023). Artificial intelligence framework for opinion mining of netizen readers' reviews of Arundhati Roy's The God of Small Things. In P. Keikhosrokiani & M. P. Asl (Eds.), *Handbook of research on artificial intelligence applications in literary works and social media* (pp. 68–92). IGI Global. doi:10.4018/978-1-6684-6242-3.ch004

Kng, C. K., Keikhosrokiani, P., & Asl, M. P. (2023). Artificial intelligence and human rights activism: A case study of Boochani's No Friend But the Mountains and his tweets on justice and equality. In P. Keikhosrokiani & M. P. Asl (Eds.), *Handbook of research on artificial intelligence applications in literary works and social media* (pp. 114–141). IGI Global. doi:10.4018/978-1-6684-6242-3.ch006

Lee, C. K. (2015). *Teaching literature to ESL students: A teacher's guide.* Pearson Malaysia.

Lee, L. S. (2019). E-learning in the teaching of literature: A case study of Malaysian tertiary students. *Arab World English Journal, 10*(2), 115–127.

Levy, M. (2016). The impact of the digital age on editing and publishing. *Publishers Weekly, 263*(15), 20–21.

Lim, J. (2019). The impact of Industry 4.0 on education: What students need to succeed in Industry 4.0. *Journal of Education and Learning, 8*(1), 1–10. doi:10.5539/jel.v8n1p1

Ling, L. M., & Wah, L. L. (2019). Facing the challenges of the Fourth Industrial Revolution: A literature review. *International Journal of Academic Research in Business & Social Sciences, 9*(2), 400–417.

Liu, Y. (2018). Teaching literature in the digital age: A study of online discussion forums in a literature classroom. *Educational Media International, 55*(4), 301–315.

Mahfodz, N. A. (2019). Challenges and opportunities in teaching literature in the digital age: A Malaysian perspective. *Advances in Language and Literary Studies, 10*(1), 26–35.

Maleki, A., & Shahbazinia, M. (2017). The role of e-books in developing reading habits among university students. *International Journal of Research in English Education, 2*(3), 1–7. doi:10.29252/ijree.2.3.1

Malik, E. F., Keikhosrokiani, P., & Asl, M. P. (2021). Text mining life cycle for a spatial reading of Viet Thanh Nguyen's The Refugees (2017). *2021 International Congress of Advanced Technology and Engineering (ICOTEN)*, 1-9. 10.1109/ICOTEN52080.2021.9493520

Moore, T., & Tschang, F. (2017). Reading and language learning with audio books: Raising the bar on reading strategies. *Reading in a Foreign Language, 29*(2), 240–254.

Mustaffa, R., & Nordin, N. M. (2017). The challenges of teaching literature in the era of the Fourth Industrial Revolution: The Malaysian context. *Advanced Science Letters, 23*(7), 6356–6358. doi:10.1166/asl.2017.9807

Nashwa, A. (2019). The role of digital technologies in the teaching and learning of English literature. *International Journal of Education and Research, 7*(1), 219–228.

Ng, C. S., & Lee, S. S. (2019). Teaching literature studies in universities and challenges Malaysian students face in IR4.0. *International Journal of Social Science and Humanity, 9*(8), 215–219.

Ng, E. M. W., & Roslan, S. (2020). Challenges in teaching literature to Malaysian students in the era of IR 4.0. *Journal of Language and Communication, 7*(1), 46–57.

Ng, S. H., & Tan, Y. S. (2019). Developing critical thinking skills in Malaysian ESL classrooms: An exploratory study. *English Language Teaching, 12*(2), 68–79.

Olaosebikan, J., & Osime, A. (2020). Challenges of teaching literature in the age of digital distraction: A case study of Nigerian undergraduate students. *International Journal of English Linguistics, 10*(5), 267–277.

Ovenden, R. (2015). The digital archive as a research tool: An overview of archival theory, practice and technology. In J. Drucker & P. D. Juhl (Eds.), *History of the digital humanities: A reader* (pp. 331–348). Routledge.

Paremeswaran, P. p., Keikhosrokiani, P., & Asl, M. P. (2022). *Opinion mining of readers' responses to literary prize nominees on Twitter: A case study of public reaction to the Booker Prize (2018–2020).* Advances on Intelligent Informatics and Computing. doi:10.1007/978-3-030-98741-1_21

Petrilli, D., & Salomoni, P. (2019). Literature and digital literacy: New challenges and opportunities for teaching and learning. *Journal of Education and Training Studies, 7*(3), 47–54.

Pettersson, A., & Berg, L.-O. (2020). Digital humanities and literary studies: Challenges and opportunities. *Journal of English Studies, 18*, 65–85.

Scherer, M. (2018). Technological advances and their impact on literature: Exploring ethical and societal implications. *Journal of Digital and Social Media Marketing, 6*(2), 173–181. doi:10.1080/24702405.2 018.1480987

Schreibman, S., & Siemens, R. (2016). A short history of digital humanities. In S. Schreibman, R. Siemens, & J. Unsworth (Eds.), *A new companion to digital humanities* (pp. 3–13). John Wiley & Sons.

Shaari, N. N., & Kassim, N. A. (2019). Enhancing the teaching and learning of literature in ESL classroom: A study on the implementation of technology. *Journal of Nusantara Studies, 4*(2), 105–119.

Shen, L. (2019). The use of social media in teaching literature. *Journal of Language Teaching and Research, 10*(2), 368–375.

Sofian, N. B., Keikhosrokiani, P., & Asl, M. P. (2022). Opinion mining and text analytics of reader reviews of Yoko Ogawa's The Housekeeper and the Professor in Goodreads. In P. Keikhosrokiani & M. P. Asl (Eds.), *Handbook of research on opinion mining and text analytics on literary works and social media* (pp. 240–262). IGI Global. doi:10.4018/978-1-7998-9594-7.ch010

Suhendra, N. H. B., Keikhosrokiani, P., Asl, M. P., & Zhao, X. (2022). Opinion mining and text analytics of literary reader responses: A case study of reader responses to KL Noir volumes in Goodreads using Sentiment Analysis and Topic. In P. Keikhosrokiani & M. P. Asl (Eds.), *Handbook of research on opinion mining and text analytics on literary works and social media* (pp. 191–239). IGI Global. doi:10.4018/978-1-7998-9594-7.ch009

Tammi, M. M., Baki, R., & Siraj, S. (2021). Teaching literature studies in universities and challenges Malaysian students face in IR4.0. *Journal of Language and Cultural Education, 9*(2), 176–191.

Tammi, P. (2020). Industry 4.0 and the future of literature. *Journal of the Association for the Study of Australian Literature, 20*(2), 1–13.

Tammi, T., Käpylä, M., Vainio, L., & Sutinen, E. (2021). Promoting critical thinking in literature education: A systematic literature review. *Education Sciences, 11*(1), 36.

Tengku Putri Norishah, T. M., & Abdullah, N. (2018). Issues and challenges in teaching English literature at Malaysian higher education institutions. *Journal of Nusantara Studies, 3*(2), 47–64.

Vint, S. (2016). Science fiction and the Fourth Industrial Revolution. *The European Journal of Science Fiction Research, 2*, 2–10. doi:10.5281/zenodo.45537

Wang, Q., Chen, W., & Liang, Y. (2011). The effects of social media on college students. *Journal of Educational Technology Development and Exchange, 4*(1), 1–14.

Widerhold, B. K. (2019). The Fourth Industrial Revolution: Healthcare in the digital age. *Healthcare Technology Letters, 6*(6), 163–165.

Wong, F. K., & Noor, N. M. (2019). Integrating digital technology in ESL classrooms: Opportunities and challenges. *Journal of Nusantara Studies, 4*(2), 91–102.

World Economic Forum. (2018). *The future of jobs report 2018*. World Economic Forum. https://www.weforum.org/reports/the-future-of-jobs-report-2018

Yap, C. H., & Zainol Abidin, N. A. (2021). Teaching literature studies in universities and challenges Malaysian students face in IR4.0. *The Journal of Asia TEFL, 18*(1), 192–206.

Yildiz, Y., & Sahin, M. (2020). Literature education in the digital age: Challenges and possibilities. *Journal of Language and Linguistic Studies, 16*(1), 238–248.

Ying, S. Y., Keikhosrokiani, P., & Asl, M. P. (2021). Comparison of data analytic techniques for a spatial opinion mining in literary works: A review paper. In F. Saeed, F. Mohammed, & A. Al-Nahari (Eds.), *Innovative Systems for Intelligent Health Informatics* (pp. 523–535). Springer International Publishing. doi:10.1007/978-3-030-70713-2_49

Yulianto, A., Mulyono, H., & Riyadi, R. (2020). Online discussion forum as a tool for developing critical thinking and social interaction among EFL students. *English Teaching & Learning, 44*(3), 351–369.

Zainol, A. F., Keikhosrokiani, P., Asl, M. P., & Anuar, N. A. N. (2023). Artificial intelligence applications in literary works: Emotion extraction and classification of Mohsin Hamid's Moth Smoke. In P. Keikhosrokiani & M. P. Asl (Eds.), *Handbook of research on artificial intelligence applications in literary works and social media* (pp. 93–113). IGI Global. doi:10.4018/978-1-6684-6242-3.ch005

Zainuddin, Z., & Attaran, M. (2016). Malaysian teachers' readiness for teaching with technology: Implications for further policy planning and curriculum development. *Journal of Educational Technology & Society, 19*(3), 37–48.

Zainuddin, Z., & Mohamad, M. M. (2020). The impact of virtual reality on students' engagement and understanding in literature class. *International Journal of Emerging Technologies in Learning, 15*(16), 140–153.

Chapter 14
Application of Metaverse in the Healthcare Sector to Improve Quality of Life

Md. Ashrafuzzaman
 https://orcid.org/0000-0002-3366-9144
Military Institute of Science and Technology, Bangladesh

Rayesa Haque Rupanti
Military Institute of Science and Technology, Bangladesh

Nawrin Tasnim
Military Institute of Science and Technology, Bangladesh

Tasnuba Tabassum Mourin
Military Institute of Science and Technology, Bangladesh

ABSTRACT

The Healthcare sector is expected to undergo a disruptive change as a result of metaverse technology, which will open the doors for newer treatment possibilities and greater surgical accuracy while enhancing patient outcomes. Since the healthcare industry is one of those most vulnerable industries to technological change, this chapter reviews the applications of Metaverse in healthcare sector. Metaverse has the potential to revolutionize healthcare by fusing robots with AI, VR, AR, the Internet of Medical Devices, Web 3.0, intelligent clouds, edge computing, and quantum computing. Telepresence, digital twinning, and blockchain are three significant technological advances that are converging in the metaverse. Doctors and specialists are using VR to train other medical professionals as they create new ways to improve patient aftermaths. The metaverse continues to develop with the help of 4IR technologies that provide the means to address some of the most fundamental barriers to equitable access to digital healthcare.

DOI: 10.4018/978-1-6684-7029-9.ch014

INTRODUCTION

According to multiple peer-reviewed scientific studies, the term "metaverse" has attracted a lot of interest recently from both business and academia. The 1992 science fiction book, *Snow Crash*, is where the word was first used. Oxford English Dictionary describes the term as a computer-generated virtual world in which users can interact with one another and their surroundings. However, this explanation falls short of capturing the complexity and the development of the idea. Some people have the incorrect impression that the metaverse is simply a social networking and computer game progression, or possibly just a hyped-up rebranding of virtual and augmented reality.

It is essential to combine all the elements of cutting-edge technologies on a massive social and economic scale—including high-speed internet, VR, AR, MR, XR, digital twins, haptics, holography, secure computation, and AI—in order to fully benefit from the advantages that metaverse promises to offer. People will be able to communicate with each other, AI agents, algorithms, and medical equipment and facilities thanks to this. The goal of the metaverse is to provide a parallel experience, not to take the place of the real world. This entails a medical technology and AI (MeTAI) ecosystem, which includes secure access to medical data, virtual comparative scanning with digital twins, and a new regulatory framework. To enhance performance and accessibility, a metaverse that goes beyond current medical VR, AR, and telemedicine is being developed. The MeTAI metaverse should now begin to take shape. The "metaverse" in medicine refers to the medical Internet of Things, which is made possible by the usage of AR and VR glasses. It is changing in the metaverse.

By combining robots with AI, VR, AR, the Internet of Medical Devices, Web 3.0, intelligent clouds, edge computing, and quantum computing, they have the potential to revolutionize healthcare. There are three key technological developments that are merging in the metaverse—telepresence, digital twinning, and blockchain—where each has the potential to have an impact on healthcare. Digital twinning will emerge as a result of our expanding understanding of each person's genetic makeup and capacity to map it. Blockchains are actually encrypted, decentralized databases that enable secure data storage (Thomason, 2021). The risk of data theft is increased by the frequent centralized storage of health records. In order to manage their caseloads more effectively, doctors and nurses are now employing video conferences or phone conversations to identify minor medical issues. Patients are no longer limited to receiving care from particular clinicians because of their physical location thanks to the use of virtual reality in the field of telemedicine. Virtual reality also helps train medical professionals to create entirely new treatment modalities that could lower costs and greatly improve patient results. In the metaverse, where VR and AR technology is already gaining swift popularity, treatments like cognitive therapy, support groups, psychiatric evaluations, rehabilitation, and even physical therapy using haptic sensors are all made possible. The metaverse is expected to be a helpful tool for carrying out difficult surgical procedures and enhancing patient care (Science Direct, 2021).

Complex surgeries will soon incorporate augmented reality (AR), just as surgical procedures presently use robotics. Also, for effective diagnosis (Ashrafuzzaman, Mahmudul Haque Milu, et al., 2022), the use of technology like smart glasses could bring extraordinary results. The immersive visual capabilities of the metaverse will undoubtedly improve the fields of radiology and medical imaging, unlocking new opportunities. However, every opportunity comes with difficulty. The same is true for the metaverse. The healthcare sector is frequently a high-value and vulnerable target for hackers, and in order to fully utilize the metaverse in healthcare, a vast infrastructure with solicitous investment is required (Mystakidis, 2022).

The basic objectives of this book chapter can be summarized as follows;

- To evaluate the metaverse's limitations as a tool for healthcare. It will assist us in understanding why not everyone has utilized the metaverse as of yet.
- To list the advantages of the metaverse so that we can increase awareness and disseminate the benefits of using the metaverse in healthcare.
- To briefly go through the uses of the metaverse and the industries where it is already in use.
- To describe the difficulties that might be encountered when using the metaverse, as it is not a technology that is frequently and widely used.

We shall break the discussion into a few different categories in this chapter according to Figure 1. We will try to concentrate on the constraints first. Limitations will help us find the reasons why the metaverse is still only partially deployed. The benefits will then be discussed, so that we can inform and inspire others about the metaverse and its uses. Later, we will try to look for any challenges we may encounter when utilizing the metaverse.

Figure 1. Growth Tree of Metaverse in Healthcare

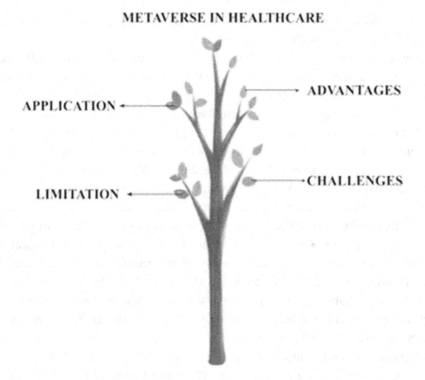

Figure 2 shows the metaverse effect and applications worldwide. Based on the map, Netherlands and Singapore are considered as number one in using Metaverse in healthcare while New Zealand is number six.

Figure 2. Metaverse Effect on World wide

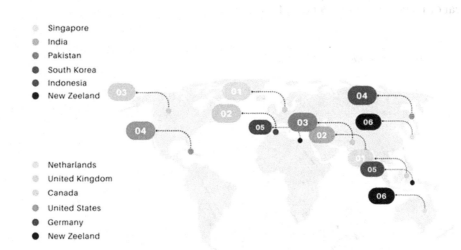

Metaverse in Healthcare

The current healthcare system is inadequate. Due to the "Sick-Care" delivery system's infrastructure, public faith in the healthcare system has decreased. Chronic lifestyle disorders like diabetes, cardiovascular disease, stroke, and cancer are on the rise (Al Mamun & Keikhosrokiani, 2022; Keikhosrokiani, 2022a). Since patients need to alter their behavior as part of a new self-care lifestyle, patient therapies are now a big issue because they are frequently linked with high levels of uncertainty. Does there exist a remedy that can close this gap? All the aforementioned problems can be resolved with the help of the metaverse.

The metaverse has the potential to fundamentally alter how we view healthcare. It will be a more engaging, close-knit, and enticing medical experience with a sense of support for those who most need it. Particularly in small towns and cities, adaptive intelligent solutions can assist lower the boundaries between hospitals and patients, improving availability to healthcare services and increasing patient satisfaction.

The metaverse might create new opportunities for doctors to interact with patients in more intimate ways, such as leading patients through a three-dimensional model of the human body while discussing a diagnosis and a course of therapy. This will allow medical personnel to model the effects of a prescribed treatment before applying it, as opposed to what is currently possible with two-dimensional visuals on a screen.

An adaptable ecosystem will be required for effective deployment of the metaverse in order to allow for smooth integration of technologies that produce various immersive experiences. This ecosystem will encompass scalable and secure computing environments—5G, AI, IoT, VR, XR, and other upcoming technologies.

The framework shown in Figure 3 is modified for the healthcare industry based on Jon Radoff's "The seven layers of the metaverse" creative commons figure. The methodology shows that before "developing the edge for hyper-scale," enterprises must "Shore the key technology." We suggest a six-part metaverse Health architecture that combines cutting-edge core technologies, AI-driven experiences, and spatial computing across all consumer touchpoints to deliver immersive and hyper-personalized treatment in whatever physical or metaverse reality a patient chooses.

Figure 3. Metaverse Health Framework (Exarta, 2022)

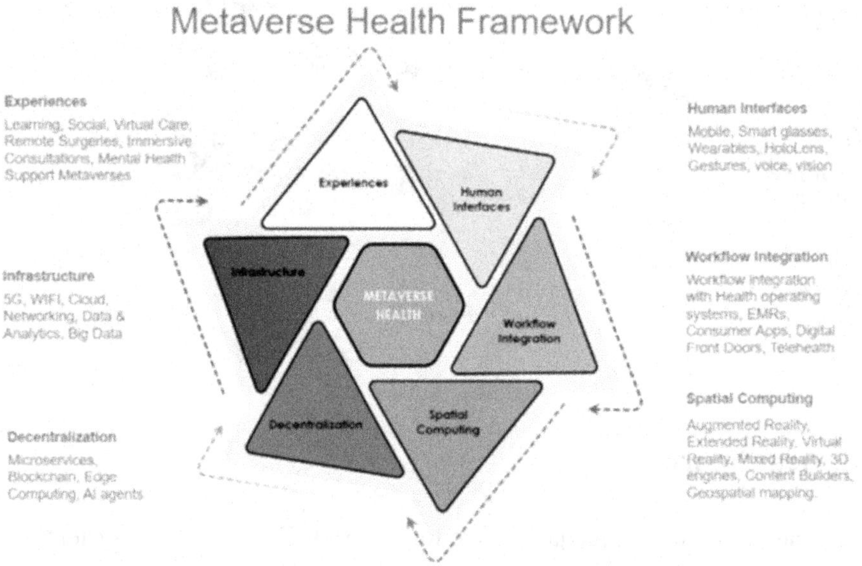

Metaverse in Digital Transformation

The dearth of knowledge about the metaverse is due to the fact that people do not yet have access to it. It is undeniable that the metaverse ushers in a new age for the digital world. Social media was a topic of conversation until quite recently. However, the metaverse is now a topic of conversation. People could not participate in the process because Web-1 only had one dimension. Then came Web-2, which made it possible for people to interact with the digital world. One of the biggest human innovations, social media, arrived with Web-2. Stanley Milgram discovered in late 1960s that it takes six handshakes to get to someone you don't know. People connect with one another, express their opinions, and produce material.

Recently, there has been a rise in smartphone usage, which has an impact on how frequently people use social media. Daniel Miller claims that smartphone is no longer just a tool we use; it has become the location where we live. People swiftly adapt to the digital world, and the vast majority of them are now unable to live without social media or a smartphone. Currently, 5.27 billion people worldwide use mobile phones, 4.80 billion use the internet, and 4.48 billion routinely use social media. According to these facts, the adoption of the metaverse will come swiftly, so society needs to be prepared. Every product is said to have a life cycle in the literature. According to the product life cycle, a product is born with pains because firms invest a lot of time and money into it. The product then develops into an adult and eventually passes away. Each product has a different lifetime. As a result, social media is considered to be in its decline in the digital world. The cause for that is because a new product that will challenge the status quo is now in development. The metaverse is this brand-new item.

Impact of Metaverse in Healthcare Sector

The health metaverse will be the next major disruptor in the coming years. Virtual reality (VR), augmented reality (AR), and mixed reality are currently being used for medical training and surgical operations. Healthcare practitioners will be able to deliver more collaborative treatment plans in the health metaverse because the current healthcare system's siloed structure would not be an obstacle. The rapid exchange of information between physicians and clinicians will also be advantageous because it will make it easier to identify the root causes of health problems. Monitoring patient activities in the metaverse allows for easier tracking of variables like compliance, which helps with disease diagnosis and treatment.

One can make his/her own digital avatar, put on a headset, and meet a doctor in avatar form in this parallel digital reality environment. Without leaving the house, one can describe his/her symptoms, perhaps in conjunction with uploaded health information, and get an evaluation for additional therapy. Sessions can be recorded for playback later if anyone wants to go back and review them. Even fees can be paid via blockchain using cutting-edge new payment methods. Avatar can engage in physical activities, games, and social interactions with friends and new people. To stay healthy and fit, one's digital avatar will follow the same exact routine as oneself, just like in science fiction movies.

Artificial Intelligence (AI) in Healthcare

Artificial intelligence (AI) technologies are widely used in contemporary commerce and everyday living and are steadily expanding in the healthcare industry. Artificial intelligence can help doctors and physicians in rendering patient care as well as improving surgical techniques. It helps them to expand on developed solutions and uncover ways to address issues more efficiently (Yang et al., 2022). Even though a large number of them are crucial to the healthcare industry, hospitals and other healthcare organizations may employ a variety of tactics to incorporate AI and healthcare technologies. It will be a while before AI in healthcare is extensively employed, despite claims made in a number of articles on its usage that it is capable of performing some activities just as well as or better than humans, such as detecting illness.

Each year, 100,000 hospitalized patients sustain needless harm, and 400,000 of them pass away as a result. This makes the potential use of AI to improve diagnostics as one of the most fascinating applications in healthcare. Human errors that are lethal can be caused by heavy caseloads and insufficient medical histories. AI can recognize and foresee disease more promptly than the majority of medical professionals since it is immune to these influences (Ong, 2019). Figure 4 shows evolution of intelligent systems.

Robotics in Digital Healthcare

The long-term viability and profitability of healthcare systems can be significantly boosted by automation driven by digital healthcare technology like robotics and artificial intelligence. Robots greatly boost the productivity of the healthcare industry by taking over monotonous, repetitive tasks that require constant attention to detail. Robots are transforming medical operations, accelerating the delivery of supplies and sterilizing, and freeing staff members to focus on engaging and providing care for patients. Intel offers a wide spectrum of technology for development of medical robots, including configurable and autonomous mobile robots. Robotics and digital technologies are not only altering the way we work and communicate, but they also give us new ways to track, monitor, and operate more effectively. They also assist in enhancing care coordination, reducing the risk and expense of surgery, and emphasizing self-care. We shall discover how technology affects our life and the healthcare system in this section.

Figure 4. Evolution of the Intelligent Systems

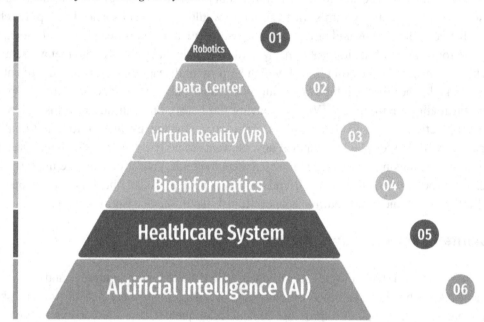

Virtual World

A virtual world created by computers allows us to communicate with one another and utilize and create objects in an online community. The phrase has generally evolved to mean interactive 3D virtual environments where users can be seen by others as avatars—a full simulation of the physical world. Avatars of players and virtual representations of characters from virtual worlds fill this realm (bots). Virtual worlds can replicate real-world settings or create whole new ones with entirely separate people and natural laws. A virtual world has the following characteristics:

- Three dimensions are involved.
- It is inhabited by beings that fulfill certain functions chosen by the world's creator.
- It changes in some ways in response to the user's presence and activity.
- It is handled by a computer system.

Development of Metaverse for Intelligent Healthcare

People and their digital representations can interact in a setting made possible by technologies such as high-speed internet, VR, AR, MR, blockchain, digital twins, and AI that have all been augmented by massive amounts of data thanks to the metaverse, which merges the physical and the virtual worlds.

Although it began as a social networking and entertainment platform, its usage in healthcare has the potential to make a big impact on how people are treated and how they feel about themselves.

Researchers from a wide range of disciplines including academics, business, medicine, and law see enormous potential for metaverse in healthcare. Metaverse for medical technology and AI has the potential to advance and enhance AI-based medical practices, notably in the areas of diagnosis and treatment based on medical imaging (Wang et al., 2022).

A virtual comparison image is illustrated in Figure 5 which shows: (a) to determine the most effective imaging technique in a particular scenario). (b) Data sharing in raw form (to provide regulated access to tomographic raw data). (c) Improved regulatory science using technology (to expand the coverage and duration of virtual clinical trials). (d) Using metaverse to provide medical assistance (to carry out medical procedures with the aid of the virtual world).

Figure 5. Metaverse Ecosystem with Four Major Healthcare Applications (Wang et al., 2023)

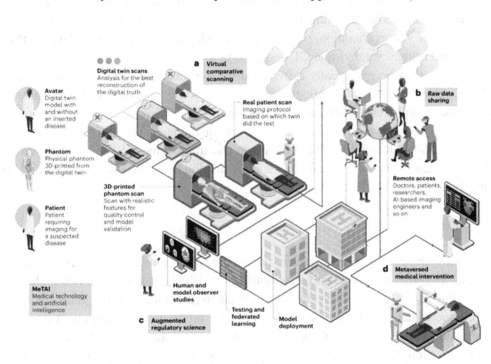

Before a patient receives a genuine CT scan, virtual simulations of the scan are conducted on several machines to identify the best imaging outcome. This is an example of the metaverse system in operation. This information is used to guide the actual scan. The patient's medical team is then informed about the metaverse photos, and with the patient's permission and in accordance with strict security procedures, researchers may have access to them for research purposes. In virtual clinical trials, the metaverse is utilized to aggregate all of the real and simulated images, data, and other medical information. If required, the patient can have a remote surgery assisted by the metaverse, with rehabilitation and follow-up treatment taking place in the virtual world (Prova et al., 2022; Wang et al., 2022).

The metaverse ecosystem has been recognized as the four primary areas where the metaverse can have a substantial impact on healthcare, with a concentration on medical imaging. These include virtual comparative scanning, raw data sharing, virtual regulatory scientific advancement, and virtual medical intervention. The new opportunities provided by metaverse are wide, inclusive, and original in terms of the breadth, scale, and level of integration, despite the fact that comparable concepts have been put up in the past (Wang et al., 2022).

a.   Virtual Comparative Scanning

The concept of a "digital twin" which combines information from real-world and virtual objects has emerged as a result of the development of highly complex computer models of the human body and the imaging technologies used to create them. We need to develop virtual tomographic scanners tailored to each vendor, individualized computational avatars with anatomy that can be resolved by the scanners, and AI-powered graphical tools to add, remove, and modify medical conditions within the avatars in order to further advance medical imaging using these innovations. For instance, if a patient is referred for a CT scan because of a heart condition, possible health problems can be simulated within the patient's avatar and scanned using several virtual CT scanner types.

The images can then be realistically recreated using several deep reconstruction techniques, and they can be examined with AI diagnostic tools. In order to mimic genuine scans and enhance the accompanying models and analysis, physical avatars can also be 3D-printed and scanned. The benefit of Metaverse ecosystem-powered extended reality over standalone extended reality is the capacity for extensive collaboration, allowing for fair comparison and improvement of various hardware and software manufacturers, as well as direct and rapid communication between patients and medical providers (Sutherland et al., 2019).

b.   Raw Data Sharing

Medical tomographic scanners are the main source of the multi-dimensional data used to create medical imaging, which is then converted into images using sophisticated algorithms. Researchers have long had trouble getting access to the raw data from these scanners, including CT sinograms, and this problem is only getting more challenging as AI is used more and more in medical imaging. This is so because not all information can be retained following image reconstruction, and as raw data are necessary for algorithm optimization. Recent efforts have been made by numerous groups to employ an end-to-end deep learning method known as "Rawdiomics," which necessitates access to raw data.

Metaverse includes building virtual replicas of real-world CT scanners so that they may scan digital patients and provide digital raw data. The virtual data and visuals can then be subjected to AI analysis. This simulated data is a useful tool for researchers because it can be easily shared without disclosing private information about the actual CT scanner. Although deep learning-based rawdiomics in the raw data domain may disclose even more information, image-domain modeling and simulation techniques like HeartFlow currently offer useful diagnostic information. MeTAI, for instance, makes it possible to minimize motion abnormalities in reconstructed pictures that are brought on by irregular heartbeats from atrial fibrillation. This helps to enhance the quantification of coronary artery stenosis in the sinogram domain. Metaverse makes it possible to use AI to analyze both actual and realistically simulated raw data.

c.   Augmented Regulatory Science

Medical imaging has been greatly enhanced by the use of artificial intelligence, particularly deep learning. However, the limitations of regulatory science in assessing these AI-powered medical devices are also brought up by these developments. To guarantee their advantages and security, problems like generalizability and susceptibility to hostile attacks must be resolved. The FDA has developed a framework for the regulation of AI-based software as medical devices in order to allay these worries (SaMDs). This plan's regulatory mechanisms for detecting algorithm bias and enhancing robustness are to be improved, which is a crucial component. Large and varied datasets are required in order to optimize the entire medical imaging procedure, from data collecting to diagnostic results. The downside of this is that it costs a lot of money to compile these huge clinical databases. In this situation, virtual and simulated scans can be quite useful in streamlining the approval process for AI-based medical equipment.

d.   Metaverse Medical Intervention

The metaverse will have a big impact on how patients and healthcare providers use medical data. Using computer simulations, the metaverse enables healthcare practitioners to perform sophisticated surgeries, radiotherapies, and other medical techniques. As a result of being able to test various treatment strategies on virtual avatars, healthcare personnel will be able to improve treatments and work more efficiently. The metaverse will broaden the use of patient-specific computer simulations in all medical treatments, enabling remote surgery from a distant site or from a room nearby using high-speed internet.

The metaverse has the potential to significantly alter how patients, medical professionals, and other stakeholders' approach and comprehend diseases, interventions, and treatments. Virtual simulations allow for practice and optimization of medical operations, including surgeries and radiotherapies, before they are carried out on actual patients. By simulating biological reactions to radiation using a patient's genetic information and prior patient data, the metaverse can also increase the accuracy of treatment regimens and lower the risk of organ toxicity during therapy.

Health care is just one of the many uses for the metaverse, which combines technological and social improvements. The metaverse may eventually become a reality given the current increase in telemedicine during the COVID-19 epidemic. In order to make the metaverse affordable, user-friendly, dependable, safe, equitable, and ethical, it is crucial that everyone works together to temper hype with reasonable expectations.

APPLICATION OF METAVERSE IN HEALTHCARE SECTOR

Medical Training

Healthcare professionals are constantly looking for new and creative ways to advance their knowledge and sharpen their abilities. They now have access to an innovative method of immersive learning by means of development of the metaverse which gives an online virtual environment. Doctors and surgeons can now practice new techniques in a very realistic setting. Learners can obtain experience in a range of medical specialties and hone their abilities in a secure environment by participating in interactive simulations.

The metaverse provides educational opportunities outside of the traditional classroom. Professionals can access interactive challenges, classes, and tutorials from any device at any time. As a result, students may stay updated on industry trends and stay on top of their industries. Nowadays medical practitioners have a multitude of options to further their education in the virtual world of the metaverse. Without the hazards associated with conventional approaches, students can get a thorough understanding of medical procedures through interactive role-playing situations and anatomical models. Additionally, students can work together virtually and receive insightful criticism from professionals.

The user-immersion features of the metaverse make it the ideal environment for medical staff training. Surgery training, in particular, has traditionally been an elevated game in the medical field. In other words, it is challenging to become comfortable with the body without having exposure to actual bodies. When patient lives are at stake, surgery is not always easy to perform. Overall, healthcare professionals wishing to expand their knowledge have a lot to gain from training in the metaverse. The metaverse can deliver an incredibly immersive learning experience thanks to its believable landscapes and interesting challenges.

Digital Therapeutic Applications

New possibilities are also emerging in the metaverse in therapeutic applications. The metaverse enables users to experience various digital therapies including cognitive behavioral therapy. Cognitive Behavioral Therapy (CBT) is referred to as a psychological treatment that has already been used to treat several conditions like depression, anxiety, drug addiction, eating disorders etc. Virtual reality-assisted cognitive behavioral therapy, often known as VRCBT, is a specific kind of therapy used to treat depression and anxiety in people with anxiety disorders. Researchers have evaluated the therapeutic effects of VRCBT on conventional cognitive behavioral therapy (CBT) in order to assess VRCBT's long-term effectiveness (Ashrafuzzaman, Rishat, et al., 2022). The Cochrane risk of bias tool and the Grading of Recommendation, Assessment, Development, and Evaluation tool (GRADE) are used to assess the methodological quality. Eventually, it has been deduced that people with anxiety disorders or other mental conditions may get specific benefits from VRCBT therapy.

Telemedicine

Telehealth represents a substantial change in the way services are delivered to healthcare. Healthcare workers' participation in virtual, immersive, and interactive online environments not only improves interdisciplinary physician collaboration but also fosters improved medical expertise. To remain competitive, telehealth providers must adapt to what consumers want and need.

One industry where the application of the metaverse technology is expected to have a positive impact is medicine. With the Covid-19 pandemic barely behind us, the world has experienced the fragility of our current healthcare systems (Binti Rosli & Keikhosrokiani, 2022; John & Keikhosrokiani, 2022). As a result, patients with severe medical conditions fail to receive the usual medical treatment from hospitals due to unmanageable outbreak of the disease. During the peak of the pandemic, telemedicine gains popularity as the sole way for most patients and caregivers to visit or consult a healthcare practitioner. However, the need for telemedicine gradually decreases with the introduction of vaccination, even though telemedicine is considered the safest way of communication in times of epidemics and pandemics.

In modern settings, the metaverse can be viewed as an opportunity that enables users to have a virtual presence in the digital world, allowing them to socialize and engage with the manufactured environment through their senses. For instance, Facebook is developing haptic gloves that transmit pressure from the fingertips and palms when interacting with virtual objects. In a similar way, digital avatars allow medical personnel to approach a broad range of healthcare services. The consumers of telemedicine find it to be an easily accessible way to reach healthcare professionals and caregivers in emergency, epidemics or pandemics. The need of telemedicine is a perpetual feature in the healthcare sector as the consumers like the expediency. The advancements in the technological perspective of the metaverse can definitely enhance the scopes of telemedicine, resulting in better interaction between the medical personnel, doctors and the patients.

Patients and doctors can meet in a 3D clinic or any other places as part of the metaverse's virtual office that will support telemedicine visits. A new platform "virtual reality medical environment" that uses the metaverse to provide live, free mental health care to members of the armed forces is unveiled by metaverse platform 2B3D. Veterans-owned and -operated 2B3D is utilizing modern technology to deliver treatment that might significantly enhance veterans' physical and emotional health. Unity, a tool for creating real-time content, has served as the primary design platform for 2B3D's metaverse projects. A sophisticated real-time tool for creating next-generation 3D experiences and contents, Unreal Engine 5, is another technology the organization is interested to investigate (2B3D Metaverse, 2022).

Augmented Reality (AR)

Augmented Reality (AR) allows us to interact with our surroundings by superimposing a digital augmentation on top of them. It works by seamlessly incorporating digital data into a user's surroundings. In augmented reality, real-world objects are enhanced with computer-generated capabilities. To improve user experience, AR incorporates graphics, effects, sounds, texts, and touch feedback. This technology helps its users to easily communicate with virtual materials in real time in the physical world.

Robotic-Assisted Surgery (RAS) systems have grown into fame in recent years due to their increased availability to minimally invasive techniques and enhanced surgical accuracy. Combining robotic-assisted surgery with augmented reality creates a sophisticated interface that improves user perception. AR helps to visualize health conditions that assist physicians to make better surgical decisions. Robotic hepatic surgery, intraoperative reconstruction systems, robotic liver resections, preoperative imaging, intraoperative robotic ultrasound techniques and other RAS disciplines are some of the RAS fields that will be altered by AR in upcoming years.

Traditional wound parameter assessment methods have been found to be inaccurate, and in some cases, painful for the patient. AR enables non-invasive wound parameter approach by providing visual feedback on the wound healing status. A 3D model of the wound is used to visualize the depth of injury where AR features are integrated based on a miniaturized projector. The result is a more accurate patient data which allows doctors to recommend the most applicable treatment plans and procedures. It also permits nurses to go for wound dressing properly. In short, AR-based wound healing techniques provide patients with a better understanding of the condition of the wounds, which improves compliance with doctors' advice in an effective and significant way (Sutherland et al., 2019).

On top of its game changing benefits in the mentioned fields, AR shows unique advancements in physiotherapy as well. The data collected from each session in physiotherapy enable therapists to better evaluate patients' outcomes. Besides, behavioral treatment plans are also slowly becoming more apparent in healthcare industry. AR opens the door for a novel mode of intervention in both motor and cognitive rehabilitation by giving patients a secure platform to practice movements and organize their activities. It makes patients more enthusiastic and enables caregivers to provide affordable physiotherapy at home (Uppot et al., 2019).

The Electronic Medical Record (EMR) system is a new intervention made possible by the use of augmented reality. It is referred as the digital version of clinical charts used in clinics and hospitals. Doctors can use AR technology to obtain patient records from the EMR system while treating a patient and project the information into their field of sight. Correlative AR charts can save medical professionals from having to sift through mountains of paperwork. As a result, patient records can be kept confidential to protect their privacy. In addition, the information can be prevented from getting stolen and damaged. Physicians can view the entirety of a patient's history that AR retrieves from the EMR database by simply scanning the patient's hospital wristband. It promotes a better interaction between patients and doctors while shortening the time required for diagnosis and decision-making.

Multiple floors and buildings make indoor and outdoor wayfinding in large hospital facilities difficult for patients, visitors, and new medical trainees. The development of calibrated smartphone cameras, as well as recent advances in computer graphics algorithms, can aid in a better understanding of AR infrastructure in multi-story buildings. Augmented reality inserts virtual arrows on the images of patients' environment in real time, enabling patients to easily access medical amenities. Patients can explore a hospital building with comfort and get where they need to go promptly by following the quickest route (2B3D Metaverse, 2022).

The first augmented reality surgery was performed on June 8th, 2020 by John Hopkins neurosurgeons. In order to cure a patient's acute, debilitating back pain, screws were placed into the patient's spine to fuse three vertebrae. Medical students have been trained in procedures like penile implant surgery and blood clot removal using augmented reality for a number of years. It is taking a little longer to transition from training to routine use in surgery. While Stanford University is creating its own gadget, the University of Alabama and Emory University test an orthopedic shoulder replacement using Google Glass (Johns Hopkins Medicine, 2021).

Blockchain Technology

A blockchain network is utilized in the healthcare industry to store and transmit patient data across hospitals, clinical laboratories, pharmacy companies, and doctors. Applications of blockchain technology in the medical sector can reliably detect serious and even deadly errors. As a result, it may enhance efficiency, safety, and openness of the exchange of medical data throughout healthcare amenities. Medical organizations can acquire insight and enhance medical record analysis with the use of this technology.

Blockchain is essential in addressing fraud in clinical trials; this technology has the ability to enhance data efficiency for healthcare industry. By permitting a unique data storage pattern with the highest level of security, it can aid in easing the concern about data tampering in healthcare. It provides flexibility, connectivity, liability, and attestation for data access. For several reasons, health records need to be kept private and safe. Blockchain helps to prevent specific dangers and adds to the decentralized protection of data in healthcare. Companies like BurstIQ and Healthvariety are utilizing this technology to help healthcare institutions solve issues like risk assessment, patient engagement, and secure management of individualized health information that is the largest concern in this revolution (Wu et al., 2021).

Radiology

Virtual reality is already being used in diagnostic and interventional radiology practice, training, and patient education. Radiologists have traditionally relied on two-dimensional imaging, but VR can supplement slice-based imaging. It has been shown that VR systems can deliver three-dimensional, hypnotic experiences that support assessment techniques. The metaverse can also be used to facilitate collaboration.

VR environments can be designed so that physicians and other healthcare professionals can share a virtual space. Users can discuss medical data that are represented as a mutually interactable visualization in front of them while in the metaverse. While this can be accomplished in the real world by occupying the same physical space, the metaverse allows for collaborative experiences between remote locations.

Medical Wearables

Medical wearables are nothing but the use of sensors, actuators and appropriate software in order to monitor the health condition of patients. The development of various medical wearables and electronic equipment in the age of the metaverse aids in detecting important physical parameters. This technology can be worn on the body to track vital signs, such as oxygen saturation levels, heart rate, blood pressure via health related smart devices by means of Internet of Things (IoT).

One significant application of the medical wearables is Chronic Obstructive Pulmonary Disease (COPD) monitor. It is used to notify doctors and caregivers to provide routine checks if a patient has a COPD emergency. Additionally, wearables are anticipated to give doctors not only improved data but also to boost virtual consultations in the metaverse with collected and actual data.

Digital Twins

An avatar-like computer generated depiction of a person is known as a digital twin. In a therapeutic context, this image might stand in for a patient. One benefit of creating a digital twin in healthcare industry is the capacity to enhance patient care and research. By correctly recreating a patient's brain, for instance, scientists can better understand disorders and discover how medicines affect human cells. Hospitals can also save money on personnel expenditures and research projects by substituting digital twins for real patients. Digital twins are a trending topic in healthcare industry. They help hospitals save money on research projects while also improving patient care and research.

Digital twins are virtual replicas of physical things or systems, such as the brain of a patient or an automobile engine. They are produced via computer manipulation. By allowing researchers to examine what would happen if particular parameters were altered, they help researchers to understand better on how things function. For instance, a digital twin that accurately duplicates a patient's brain structure may be used to test out various treatments on the patient's brain without actually providing them.

Digital twins have been used by researchers for many years to examine conditions like cancer, but they have only recently started being employed in place of actual patients. When conducting clinical trials, doctors might cut costs by utilizing virtual patients rather than actual ones. Hospitals can also utilize digital twins to replace actual people during procedures, saving money by delaying hiring new staff or equipment until they are certain that it will function properly in practice.

Twins who were conjoined can be separated via virtual reality. Brazilian twins with a combined head were successfully separated with the use of virtual reality. The three-year-old Bernardo and Arthur Lima underwent surgery in Rio de Janeiro under the direction of Great Ormond Street Hospital in London (BBC News, 2022). Through the use of virtual reality twin projections based on CT and MRI data, the researchers had evaluated a number of techniques over the course of several months. It was one of the most challenging separation operations ever completed according to Gemini Untwined, the nonprofit organization Mr. Jeelani founded in 2018 (GE Healthcare, 2022).

In order to choose the best course of action, GE Healthcare provides a platform that allows users to assess potential changes in operational strategy, capacity, staffing, and care delivery models. To achieve this, a digital twin of a hospital and its related ambulatory services is built. The GE Healthcare Command Center, which evaluates the effects of various decisions on changes in overall organizational performance, is an important endeavor to virtualize hospitals.

Virtual Hospitals

Virtual hospitals are a part of healthcare organizations to provide continuous remote patient care without significant physical interaction between doctors and patients. They make use of IoT, digital therapeutics, and caregiving technologies for performing in order to do that. Virtual hospitals do not necessarily reflect telemedicine technology. Rather, it serves as a major component to render a holistic approach in the field of telemedicine.

Increased hospital capacity is one of the main advantages of virtual hospitals during pandemics like COVID-19. Virtual hospital solutions can help with boosting inpatient capacity because the number of positive cases and those needing inpatient care is rapidly rising. In addition to reducing exposure to other patients and healthcare personnel, the use of virtual hospitals can enhance daily monitoring and care for COVID-19-infected patients (Tan et al., 2022).

Due to how infrequently they necessitate emergency medical attention, the divisions of mental health, allergies, physiotherapy, and chronic diseases are especially ideally adapted to the establishment of a virtual hospital. A virtual hospital can help medical professionals spread out their burden, speed up patient care, and monitor more patients at once. The COVID-19 outbreak has led to an upsurge in hospital admissions, and as a result, hospital resources including beds and exam gloves are in high demand and always in short supply.

Patients who do not require immediate hospital admission can use a virtual hospital to receive care at home while saving money on diagnostic and therapeutic procedures. For instance, remote triage, which involves a video chat with a primary care doctor, increases access to healthcare while reducing the expense of ER visits (Dionisio et al., 2013).

Medical Education

The metaverse can encourage hands-on, active learning while embracing a number of successful educational strategies including problem-based learning, simulations, augmented reality and virtual reality (AR/VR), extended reality (XR) (Zweifach & Triola, 2019) and game-based learning. Numerous studies have been carried out over the past 20 years to evaluate levels of satisfaction and performance improvement for the metaverse instructional activities across a range of subjects. The construction of an inpatient psychiatric unit in Second Life in 2006 gave users the opportunity to simulate hallucinations, which helped them grasp both visual and aural hallucinations. The same decade saw the rise in popularity of computer-based or electronic virtual patients that simulated actual clinical circumstances.

These patients allowed students to conduct anamnesis and physical exams, make diagnoses, and decide on treatments in a secure setting to sharpen their clinical abilities. The training simulations and surgical procedures have been changed by AR and VR approaches paired with machine learning tools, giving students real-world training, hyper-realistic simulations, and fast feedback. Most students who used VR anatomy training strongly agreed or agreed with the statement "I feel less afraid with the complexity of neuroanatomy" after the VR training, and they were in favor of incorporating VR training into the curriculum. Recently, an AR smartphone was used to teach the neuroanatomy of the ascending and descending tracts of the medulla, and it improved students' performance. Additionally, the fields of cardiology, dentistry, fetal medicine, obstetrics, and oncology have all embraced immersive instruction with headsets and glasses.

It is quite evident that the metaverse is now conquering the world with its fascinating applications, especially in the medical, biomedical, and clinical engineering fields. Table 1 shows different metaverse applications in healthcare sector in terms of their types, methods, users, and technologies (Boulos et al., 2007).

Virtual Reality

Virtual reality has the ability to transport oneself within and beyond the body, enabling oneself to view areas that are often inaccessible. Clinical experts can use virtual models that are displayed in real-time with hyper-realistic computer-generated images to provide patients with important information in more depth. Patients may visualize their illnesses better and comprehend how therapies and treatments will work. Without the need to travel, the best level of medical consultations may be provided to the furthest of places, freeing up crucial medical staff in the process. In the comfort of their homes, patients are able to understand better and learn about their issues. In comparison to the outdated cadaver and book-based methods of teaching human anatomy, interactive digital models provide educators and students cutting-edge visualization capabilities. To fulfill curricular requirements, clinical tests can be replicated, taught, and evaluated. Additionally, it is possible to duplicate certain surgical techniques without endangering the patient, creating safer environments and making far better use of both time and resources while boosting learning.

Virtual copies can also react dynamically in a way that no preserved specimen can, allowing students and teachers to smoothly shift between the macro level (such as a virtual full-body cardiovascular evaluation) and the micro level (CGI lipid molecules contributing to luminal occlusions). They all aid in our ability to understand physiology more comprehensively. When the Mechanisms of Action are shown, even complex pharmaceutical concepts are easier to comprehend (Wang et al., 2023).

Unity framework allows for creation of virtual worlds and 360-degree video, which may be used to deliver mental health in settings and ways that go well beyond traditional approaches. A client no longer needs to have a therapist following them to a crowded mall or up a flight of stairs. A fear of flying or traumatic events that may be the root of PTSD can be produced with a click of a mouse in conditions that are challenging or impossible to replicate. Now that the simulations and exposures are being controlled, the consultation room can offer in-person coaching that is beneficial in resolving many problems. One of the most effective outcomes of virtual immersion is the development of empathy. The pharmaceutical research and development company AbbVie creates an experience to teach medical professionals about the difficulties individuals with Parkinson's disease encounter every day.

People may put on a headpiece and watch in real time as a Parkinson's sufferer moves through a virtual supermarket, facing awkward circumstances and interacting with others. At a business expo, the experience is presented.

The positive impacts of AR and VR on immersive learning throughout the healthcare spectrum have been demonstrated, making them more than simply intriguing new tools. In the next few years, immersive technology like augmented surgery will be used more frequently to improve the accuracy and efficacy of current surgeries. People will be able to take care of themselves and others better, and they will have access to vital information and skills in ways that no other technology can match.

Twins who were conjoined can be separated via virtual reality. Brazilian twins with a combined head were successfully separated with the use of virtual reality. The three-year-old Bernardo and Arthur Lima underwent surgery in Rio de Janeiro under the direction of Great Ormond Street Hospital in London. Using virtual reality twin projections based on CT and MRI data, the researchers had evaluated a number of techniques over the course of several months. It was one of the most challenging separation operations ever completed according to Gemini Untwined, the nonprofit organization Mr. Jeelani founded in 2018 (GE Healthcare, 2022).

In order to choose the best course of action, GE Healthcare provides a platform that allows users to assess potential changes in operational strategy, capacity, staffing, and care delivery models. To achieve this, a digital twin of a hospital and its related ambulatory services is built. The GE Healthcare Command Center, which evaluates the effects of various decisions on changes in overall organizational performance, is an important endeavor to virtualize hospitals. A comparison between different Metaverse applications in healthcare sector is presented through Table 1.

Table 1. Different Metaverse Applications in Healthcare Sector

No.	Types	Methods	Users	Technology	Technology Providers
1	Medical Training	Interactive simulations, online virtual environment	Doctors, surgeons and students	Virtual Reality (VR), Extended Reality	MetaMedicsVR, Osso VR, Spineology, Ghost Productions (Medical Device Network, 2022)
2	Digital Therapeutic Applications	Clinically evaluated software and devices used to treat an array of diseases and disorders.	Healthcare professionals and patients	Internet of Things (IoT)	Omada, Virta Health, Biofourmis, Akili Interactive, Pear Therapeutics (Insider Intelligence, 2022)
3	Telemedicine	Live video conferencing, Asynchronous Video (AKA Store-and-Forward), Remote Patient Monitoring (RPM)	Doctors and patients	Artificial Intelligence (AI), Internet of Things (IoT), Virtual Reality (VR), Nanotechnology	Google, Alihealth, 2B3D, Utility (2B3D Metaverse, 2022) (Unity, n.d.)
4	Augmented Reality (AR) and Virtual Reality (VR)	Multimedia, 3D-modelling, real-time tracking and registration, intelligent interaction, sensing	Surgeons, doctors and medical students	Neural Network, Machine Learning	Augmedics, EchoPixel, Medivis, OxfordVR (HIT Consultant, 2020)
5	Blockchain Technology	Record-keeping, clinical trial, patient monitoring, improves safety, display information and transparency.	Healthcare professionals	Cryptographic keys a peer-to-peer network, computing	BurstIQ, MedicalChain, ProCredEx, Nebula Genomics (Built in, 2022)
6	Radiology	Image visualization, manipulation, reconstruction, collaboration in a 3D format	Radiologists	Augmented Reality (AR), Virtual Reality (VR)	VoxelCloud, Behold.ai, IBM Watson (AI Multiple, 2020)

continues on following page

Table 1. Continued

No.	Types	Methods	Users	Technology	Technology Providers
7	Digital Twins	Replacing patients in clinical setting to study diseases	Scientists, researchers and doctors	Artificial Intelligence and Machine Learning (AI/ML)	NUREA, PrediSurge, Optimo Medical, GE Healthcare, Philips Healthcare, Siemens (Delveinsight, 2022)
8	Medical Wearables	3D body scans and voice tone analysis to provide the status of our health	Patients, players and general people	Automatic speech recognition (ASR), Natural Language Processing (NLP), Bluetooth Wireless Technology	Apple, Amazon, Proteus, Neurotech, Augmedix (Insider Intelligence, 2023)

METAVERSE ECOSYSTEM

By becoming an integral component of healthcare, medical technology and AI metaverse have the potential to change healthcare in the same way that social media has. Because of the enormous quantity and variety of datasets, the big scale, and the emphasis on user involvement, interaction, and cooperation, it differs from conventional medical imaging simulation methodologies. As a result, it needs a well-thought-out infrastructure that connects patients, physicians, researchers, AI algorithms, medical devices, and data in an efficient manner. However, given its innovative character, there are issues that must be rapidly resolved to ensure its successful development (Wang et al., 2023).

Privacy and Security

A key component of the metaverse is privacy. Privacy rules, such as HIPAA in the US, must be applied to the medical data gathered in the metaverse. Blockchains and other secure computing methods are required to provide privacy in a secure setting. Raw data can be used by a secure metaverse system while still protecting sensitive or private information. Federated learning is a starting step towards achieving this objective, but there are many additional ways to advance healthcare while protecting patient data privacy. In order for patients to share their digital healthcare information as they see fit, it is crucial that they have control of their own data and avatar through blockchain technology.

As it is for all digital systems, cybersecurity is essential for the metaverse. In social metaverses, there have already been cases of harassment and bad behavior; this might potentially happen in metaverse, too. New approaches and regulations are being created to deal with these problems. To stop VR harassment, for instance, personal space has been established. In order to protect against hostile attacks, methods for stabilizing picture reconstruction in medical imaging have also been developed. However, there are still issues with safety, such as how explainable AI models are to small input perturbations. Despite these obstacles, it is anticipated that the quality of the evidence obtained through the metaverse will quickly increase, resulting in clinical translation of numerous advances (Wang et al., 2022).

Management and Investment

The adoption of metaverse technology in the healthcare industry will present new difficulties and obligations as well as opportunities for cost- and revenue-saving measures. The information offered by the metaverse may become more valuable for directing healthcare as AI advances and the need for human inspection of metaverse-based images and analysis declines. Cloud and edge computing solutions are well adapted to handle the vast amount of data generated.

Future datasets for other diseases and imaging modalities should be developed using the same methodology as the current Medical Imaging and Data Resource Center (MIDRC) endeavor. Creating a comparable dataset would cost less than previously estimated, roughly between $3 million and $6 million. Legislation regarding data sharing and metaverse development will be necessary, nevertheless. For instance, there can be demands that a dataset or method not be deleted before a specific time. Although blockchain technology is still being researched and may not be required for the metaverse, it is being regarded as a desired element of the metaverse. However, evidence of labour, stake, or history can still be used to demonstrate data provenance.

Technology, hardware, and infrastructure investments will be necessary for MeTAI implementation. MeTAI development will be financed throughout multiple stages. Funding for the exploratory phase, which is where the technologies that will enable metaverse are being developed, will mostly come from business and grants from the government. Once viability has been proved, the metaverse moves into an early adoption phase where established businesses and venture capitalists will adopt and support apps that promise cost savings. Venture financing will be used to fund high-risk metaverse innovations with significant upside during the following phase. Early adopters and innovators in the field of technology will be essential in the creation, testing, and presentation of the metaverse's advantages to entice investment. Methods that have been modified from other contexts can be used to calculate the metaverse's value (Wang et al., 2022).

Disparity Reduction

The use of metaverse to choose the best scanner for a patient may be constrained in some areas due to the lack of availability of multiple scanning devices. However, by increasing data capture, reconstruction, and post-processing, the imaging procedure can still be optimized with the current hardware. By advocating for fair access to healthcare, academia and business must address this disparity. There are ongoing efforts to provide affordable imaging equipment, including low-cost CT scanners, MRI machines, and tablet-based ultrasound systems, as well as management software for these equipment. The creation and marketing of affordable products in nations like India demonstrate how medical imaging companies are attempting to make their devices more widely available. MeTAI's development offers a beneficial atmosphere for continued research and development.

It is anticipated that the advancement of the metaverse technology will help to lessen healthcare inequities. There are currently differences in the accessibility of top-notch imaging technology and qualified professionals in low-income nations. MeTAI offers a platform where professionals and AI models can remotely monitor the operation of imaging equipment wherever it is being used. The use of inexpensive scanners can be enhanced by this technique, potentially enhancing their performance. The metaverse will make the process of enhancing medical devices and algorithms quicker, less expensive, and more efficient. The knowledge gathered by MeTAI will also aid in removing obstacles that prevent low- and middle-income countries from accessing human skills. The ultimate objective is to end healthcare inequities, with MeTAI helping to achieve this (Wang et al., 2022).

METAVERSE TOOLS /ALGORITHMS IN HEALTH CARE SECTOR

Artificial Intelligence (AI)

The replication of human intelligence functions by machines, particularly computer systems, is known as artificial intelligence. Building autonomous systems that could exhibit human-like intelligence was the original inspiration for artificial intelligence (AI). It is widely believed that the field of artificial intelligence is indeed ready to have a substantial impact on society as a whole given the rapid growth of AI technology over the past ten years.

Given that much of what humanity has accomplished is a result of human intelligence, it is abundantly evident that the notion of enhancing cognitive capacities with AI offers great potential for attaining revolutionary advances in important fields like healthcare, renewable energy, finance, etc. AI is already being used in areas such as biomedical information processing, biomedical research, disease diagnosis and prediction, healthcare, bladder volume prediction, epileptic seizure prediction, living assistance etc.

Virtual Reality (VR)

The use of computer simulation and modeling to enable interaction with a three dimensional (3D) visual or other sensory world is known as virtual reality (VR). Through the use of interactive, wearable devices that send and receive information—such as goggles, headsets, gloves, or bodysuits—VR applications immerse users in a virtual environment that resembles reality. Users can experience animated pictures of a virtual environment while wearing a helmet with a stereoscopic screen in a conventional VR format (Kyaw et al., 2018).

A technology known as virtual reality (VR) allows users to explore and interact with artificial or computer-generated three-dimensional (3D) multisensory worlds in real time. Different levels of immersion enable first-person active learning, which is the perception of the virtual environment as real and the capacity to interact with things and/or carry out a series of actions there. Avatars are virtual representations of users that can be used to create virtual worlds or 3D settings in VR. Patients or medical professionals can be portrayed by avatars used in virtual reality for health professions education. VR is very helpful for training related to clinical and surgical procedures since it allows simulation (2B3D Metaverse, 2022). Figure 6 shows the list of metaverse tools.

Augmented Reality (AR)

The technique of integrating or enhancing video or photographic displays by superimposing pertinent computer-generated data over the pictures is known as augmented reality in computer programming. The "heads-up displays" (HUDs) used in military aircraft and tanks are probably the first use of augmented reality. These gadgets allow a crew member to see the outside world through the same cockpit canopy or viewfinder while receiving information from an instrument panel. Real-time video can now be combined with such data displays thanks to faster computer processors.

Through the magnificent perspective of the actual and the digital worlds, Augmented Reality is used by metaverse businesses to capture their clients' attention. This aids in increasing physical interaction with digital tools and acclimating consumers to new technologies. There is a considerable market need for products that can enhance present clinical practice in the healthcare industry, as shown by the rise in publications on augmented reality (AR) for treatment, medication, and rehabilitation. This special issue aims to provide software engineers and end users with an overview of the potential of augmented reality technologies in fostering the development of practical applications in the near future and to guide academic research toward resolving the technological and biological challenges still present among the most prevalent techniques for enhancing the visual experience with computer-generated elements. During an operation, a surgeon can monitor a patient's vitals using an AR-enabled head-mounted device without fumbling with several different gadgets or displays. They are less likely to mistake or misinterpret the data if they do this.

Figure 6. Metaverse Tools

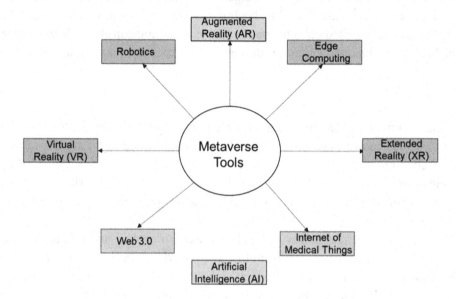

Extended Reality (XR)

Extended reality, sometimes known as XR, describes settings created by computers that merge real and virtual worlds or provide users a completely virtual experience. XR is a combination of virtual reality (VR), augmented reality (AR), and mixed reality (MR). Combining all of these elements allows for a wide range of novel opportunities in real-world and virtual environments. Programs for training residents using surgical simulation have become increasingly popular in recent years. One innovative way to bring simulation into effect is through the use of extended reality (XR) technology.

By enabling interaction with virtual 3D objects positioned in either real-world imagery or virtual environments, these technologies enable students to improve their skills. The ultimate consumer of XR technology in medical education is medical student or trainee. Although XR may address a number of issues in anatomical and procedural teaching, including ubiquitous access and real-time feedback, it will not be included in medical curricula unless it can demonstrate that it has educational value and that students are eager to use it. Medical student input should be solicited continuously throughout the development of a product like XR for it to become an engaging, effective medical training aid (Yu et al., 2018).

Internet of Medical Devices (IoMT)

The Internet of Medical Things (IoMT) is a network of application programs, hardware architecture, and healthcare devices connected to the Internet with the goal of integrating healthcare information technology. It is made up of a variety of software operating systems, clinical devices, and a range of services associated with health. Because it enables patients to share medical data online, which can reduce the number of hospital visits, it has a patient-centric approach. These devices frequently have an impact on how people live, as well as how fast and convenient things become for them.

The Internet of Medical Things is the collective name for various equipment and systems (IoMT). All the relevant sensors, information processing software, and specialized architecture are becoming more and more a part of it. IoMT enhances patient care while also enhancing clinic operations and financial metrics. Healthcare professionals and patients alike have a lot of innovative monitoring opportunities thanks to IoT devices. As a result, the variety of wearable IoT devices present opportunities as well as challenges for healthcare providers and their patients. The usage of IoT has already been shown in the monitoring of glucose levels, remote patient monitoring, heart rate, ingestible sensors, connected contact lenses, robotic surgery, connected inhalers, Parkinson's disease monitoring, depression and mood monitoring, and other devices.

Web 3.0

Web 3.0 or Web3 refers to the third generation of the World Wide Web. It is an idea that is still under development for a more usable, autonomous, and universal Web. Web alludes to the World Wide Web (WWW), the main information search engine on the internet. The most recent Internet technology uses blockchain, AI, and machine learning to facilitate in-person human connection. The most significant feature of web 3.0 is that users will get paid for their online time in addition to being able to own their data. Web 3.0 is characterized by decentralization, openness, and amazing user utility.

The term "decentralized autonomous organization" (DAO) refers to a model of automated computer network organization that is managed by its community as a whole rather than by a single entity, such as the government or a financial institution, and whose transaction records are kept on a blockchain. The semantic web is intended to comprehend and interpret the context and concept of the data. As a result, when a user searches for an answer, web 3.0 provides the most precise and pertinent result.

Remaking electronic health records (EHRs), a cornerstone of Web 1.0 healthcare technology, is the core healthcare application for Web 3.0. Many issues could be resolved by moving EHRs from centralized, compartmentalized software to interoperable, patient-owned, immutable records. The dispersed nature of one's medical data makes it impossible for anyone intending to alter or use it without one's consent.

Intelligent Cloud

The term "Intelligent Cloud" describes brand-new cloud applications created with enhanced functionality or artificial intelligence in mind. In order to focus on artificial intelligence applications, major IT companies like Microsoft are developing key technologies that go beyond the first-generation cloud technologies of the previous 10 or 15 years. Doctors and patients may interact with each other due to the advancement of intelligent cloud computing. They have online access to test and analysis findings, the ability to follow the dynamics of the treatment, and notice any updates.

Edge Computing

Edge computing is a distributed computing platform that brings business applications closer to data sources like IoT devices or adjacent edge servers. To quickly give in-depth analysis and predictions, edge computing makes use of the growing capacity of in-device computing. Innovators can be inspired by improved analytics capabilities in edge devices to increase value and boost quality (Keikhosrokiani, 2022b). Edge computing increases the value of the enormous volumes of untapped data produced by connected gadgets. We can identify new business opportunities, increase operational effectiveness, and provide customers with quicker, more consistent service. The most effective edge computing models can help us boost performance by performing local data processing. Edge computing should be used carefully to protect privacy, keep workloads up to date and compliant with established standards, and adhere to data residency rules and regulations. Edge computing reduces end-to-end congestion, the restrictions of irregular connectivity and data broadband connections over long distances, and hazards to privacy and data protection.

Robotics

Science, engineering, and technology are combined in robotics to produce robots, or machines that replicate or replace humans in activity. Robots have motions that have been pre-programmed in order for them to move in specific directions or patterns. Thanks to artificial intelligence, robots can now evaluate data and learn; they can get information about their surroundings through electronic sensors and make judgments based on that knowledge. Thanks to medical robots, the healing process is becoming more efficient, safe, and intelligent for both patients and caregivers. By lowering stress and staffing shortages, medical robots benefit nurses and healthcare teams. Robots offer companionship, mobility, and specialized care to patients. This metaverse robot system aids in integrating and connecting synchronously displayed virtual and physical robots.

By using robotics technologies and artificial intelligence, the "Unity" platform based in San Francisco aims to design and train the metaverse. With the help of the metaverse technology, Meta is concentrating on creating a thin, disposable robotics skin that will enable robots to physically interact with their surroundings in the future. This robot is made of magnetic particles, a rubbery material that is less than three millimeters thick, and artificial intelligence. It can be sensed through touch. In this robotics application, the plastic deforms after the robotic skin hits any surface, altering the magnetic field. China has the first metaverse robot system in the world thanks to the inclusion of cutting-edge technologies including digital twins, augmented reality, virtual reality, artificial intelligence, the Internet of Things, and many more. The metaverse has a long way to go before it matches how prevalent the internet is in our lives. However, the concept will inevitably see an exponential surge if it finds success in the market. It will completely penetrate society and substantially alter how society runs, just like the internet did.

CHALLENGES

The metaverse has many life-changing benefits, such as increased social connections and lifelike interactions in various fields, but it also presents certain frightening concerns that we should evaluate and find solutions to. Using the metaverse will allow people to learn through doing rather than just passively absorbing information, but we also need to consider the fact that metaverse is extensively dependent on a number of sophisticated technologies. These technologies are out of reach for most people, especially in places like ours that are considered third-world nations. It will take some time to adopt and adjust to this technology. Additionally, following adoption, a number of controversial issues may come up (Chengoden, 2022).

a. Security & Privacy for Data

In order to provide its patients and health-care personnel with their unique perks, the metaverse will need to keep all of their personal information. The metaverse will keep all of personal information, not just email address. Physiological data, personality, identity, and behavior will be stored in the metaverse. With this massive data mining, the metaverse must include strong security measures; otherwise, a single data breach will compromise everyone's personal security (Wang et al., 2022).

b. Defining the Technology

We face one of the biggest problems in trying to define the metaverse. There is no clarity on what it actually is or will become, since it will cause so much uncertainty among individuals on what it theoretically usually implies (Petrigna & Musumeci, 2022).

c. Lack of Willingness to Adopt

People are generally not very welcoming of new technology, especially in healthcare industry. Before investing, they want the technology to be checked by trustworthy sources. It will take a very long time for them to become accustomed to it and even accept it as a reliable technology to depend on when addressing medical issues. Additionally, it is dangerous to provide them services without verifying sufficient maturity in adopting all the delicate technologies. It is essential to raise awareness about the metaverse and conduct a minimal training program before deploying it in the healthcare sector. It is important to validate our understanding of the metaverse technology before continuing with the use-case section.

d. Addiction and Psychological Health

The metaverse has surely solved many health conditions by using its miraculous features and technologies. But it is also possible that the metaverse has an effect on our psychological health. Due to the sedentary manner of working, addiction to the virtual world can lead to weight gain and cardiac complications in addition to mental health problems like anxiety and depression.

e. Hardware

The technologies and tools used in virtual reality (VR), augmented reality (AR), and mixed reality (MR) are essential to the metaverse's operation. Most of them are neither lightweight nor transmissible or affordable; therefore, metaverse cannot be utilized every now and then. The problems with highly equipped technologies are that very few models can meet the expectation for a holistic virtual environment with proper pixel density and retina display. The accessibility of the hardware and devices in every location of the world is also a questionable subject in the aspect of the metaverse.

f.   Defining Identity

In addition to the sustaining challenges of the metaverse, another difficulty in proving our identification is that our appearance, data, behavior, and entire identity may be copied by bots. For authentication, we will need a variety of verification techniques such as speech recognition, retinal scanning, and face scanning. In the contemporary world, we occasionally question if our social media friends are quite as engaging in person as they are online. The metaverse, which we will be able to access through our avatars, may experience a similar thing.

g.   Social Conventions and Jurisdiction

Social media has already been used to report virtual offenses, so there will be plenty of wrongdoings in the metaverse as well. It will be insufficient to disable an account using the policies and guidelines. There must be establishment of appropriate law as the metaverse has no physical location and the virtual environment will span international borders. To offer consumers a secure environment, the nations and authorities must define their own spheres of influence.

h.   Currency and Online Payments

A new global online market linking billions of people will emerge if the metaverse is used to support healthcare system. There will be a requirement for rapid and simple exchanges due to the large number of currencies and cryptocurrencies.

i.   Lack of feasibility

A key component of traveling securely in the healthcare ecosystem is our digital identity and interoperability, which is also one of the hardest goals to fulfill with evolving technology. The ease with which some devices may be moved across platforms and networks may be significantly and unexpectedly affected by the introduction of a novel element, such as the metaverse. Technology may only be available to those who can afford it since hardware is still expensive and cannot be purchased by the entire population. When it comes to surgery, the infrastructure for healthcare practitioners needs to be of the highest caliber, like 5G.

FUTURE SCOPES

Healthcare practitioners will be able to provide a range of highly integrated, deliberate, and individualized care due to the convergence of the metaverse, free from the limitations imposed by the fragmented structure of current healthcare models. Telepresence, digital twinning, and blockchain are three significant technological advancements that are converging in the metaverse and have the potential to individually make an influence on healthcare. Our growing capacity to map and comprehend each person's genetic makeup will lead to the development of digital twinning. In reality, blockchain technology in the medical sector can reliably detect serious and even deadly errors. As a result, it may enhance the efficiency, safety, and openness of the exchange of medical data throughout healthcare amenities (Chengoden, 2022).

Healthcare is rapidly changing from one size fits all to the value-based, consumer-focused competitive marketplace with new entrants from other industries with heavy technology investments. In order to stay competitive, healthcare industry needs to revitalize through successful transformation of services and experience it provides to consumers. This can be achieved through intelligent investment in emerging technologies and leading the development of health metaverse.

Additionally, physicians and nurses have found that using a phone call or video conference enables them to quickly and efficiently diagnose a variety of minor conditions accounting for the majority of their workload. The crucial issue, however, is how customers will react to this type of implementation in healthcare system. There is no guarantee that it will function effectively or that it will not harm us in the future. We cannot guarantee that people will adopt and effectively use this cutting-edge technology. However, if we take the right steps, we can use it to improve the entire healthcare technology. Applications of the metaverse in healthcare might greatly enhance patient outcomes by creating whole new avenues for the delivery of affordable medicines. It can develop a patient-specific health care plan that will provide us with the most effective course of action for treating them. The same holds applicable for training sessions.

CONCLUSION

The metaverse improves health 4.0 by merging AI, AR, and VR—demonstrated through improving of patient safety outcomes, allowing patients to participate, and providing them with a clear image of their health status. It can be thought of as the next version of the internet, leveraging cutting-edge connectivity like 5G networks, AI, AR, and VR to create online experiences that are more immersive, interactive, and experiential. One of the important technologies is the metaverse, which would expand the serviceable area to a larger patent base globally by introducing novel services such as service delivery methods and payment schemes. The metaverse will be the primary means of internet communication in the future. This technology is therefore expected to see a significant growth in healthcare sector in near future.

Healthcare system appears unstable as a result of growing demands of contemporary issues such as autoimmune illnesses, increasing life expectancy, a lack of health professionals and resources, as well as rising costs. It is clear that the metaverse has the greatest potential to revolutionize healthcare sector. Five sectors will make use of the technology: clinical care and wellness, teamwork, healthcare education, and monetization. Despite the metaphorical metaverse's numerous layers, it may be summed up as an online environment that is exponentially more experienced, interactive, and distinguished by its immersive nature rather than one that is gradually more of these things. It stands for the "second coming of the internet," a reinvention that is enhanced and created with components of hyperconnectivity, augmented and virtual reality, and artificial intelligence.

These technological foundations in healthcare have the potential to completely rethink doctor-patient relationship. They have already proven to be incredibly beneficial as healthcare has developed over the past ten years. It appears that the metaverse will eventually replace our current reality in all spheres of life, including healthcare.

REFERENCES

3D Metaverse. (2022). *2B3D Metaverse*. 2B3D Metaverse. https://2b3d.com/

Al Mamun, M. H., & Keikhosrokiani, P. (2022). Predicting onset (type-2) of diabetes from medical records using binary class classification. In P. Keikhosrokiani (Ed.), *Big Data Analytics for Healthcare* (pp. 301–312). Academic Press., https://doi.org/https://doi.org/10.1016/B978-0-323-91907-4.00012-1

Multiple, A. I. (2020). *AI Multiple*. AI Multiple.

Ashrafuzzaman, M., Mahmudul Haque Milu, M., Anjum, A., Khanam, F., & Asadur Rahman, M. (2022). Big data analytics techniques for healthcare. In P. Keikhosrokiani (Ed.), *Big Data Analytics for Healthcare* (pp. 49–62). Academic Press.

News, B. B. C. (2022). *BBC News*. BBC News.

Binti Rosli, N. H., & Keikhosrokiani, P. (2022). Big medical data mining system (BigMed) for the detection and classification of COVID-19 misinformation. In P. Keikhosrokiani (Ed.), *Big Data Analytics for Healthcare* (pp. 233–244). Academic Press., https://doi.org/https://doi.org/10.1016/B978-0-323-91907-4.00014-5

Boulos, M. N., Hetherington, L., & Wheeler, S. (2007). Second life: An overview of the potential of 3-D virtual worlds in medical and Health Education. *Health Information and Libraries Journal*, *24*(4), 233–245. doi:10.1111/j.1471-1842.2007.00733.x

Built in. (2022). *Built in*. Built in.

Chengoden, R. V.-T. (2022). *Cornell University*. Cornell University.

Delveinsight. (n.d.). *Delveinsight*. Delveinsight Website. https://delveinsight.com

Dionisio, J. D., III, W. G., & Gilbert, R. (2013). 3D virtual worlds and the metaverse. *ACM Computing Surveys, 45*(3), 1–38. https://doi.org/ doi:10.1145/2480741.2480751

Exarta. (2022, November 17). *The 7 layers of the Metaverse*. Exarta. https://exarta.com/blog/the-7-layers-of-the-metaverse/

Healthcare, G. E. (2022). *GE Healthcare*. GE Healthcare.

Consultant, H. I. T. (2020). *HIT Consultant*. HIT Consultant.

Insider Intelligence. (2022). *Insider Intelligence*. Insider Intelligence.

Insider Intelligence. (2023, January 25). *Here are the top health tech companies and startups developing wearable medical devices in 2023*. Insider Intelligence. https://www.insiderintelligence.com/insights/wearable-tech-companies-startups/

Johns Hopkins Medicine. (2021). *Johns Hopkins Medicine*. Johns Hopkins.

Keikhosrokiani, P. (Ed.). (2022a). *Big Data Analytics for Healthcare: Datasets, Techniques, Life Cycles, Management, and Applications*. Elsevier Science., doi:10.1016/C2021-0-00369-2

Keikhosrokiani, P. (Ed.). (2022b). *Handbook of Research on Consumer Behavior Change and Data Analytics in the Socio-Digital Era.* IGI Global., doi:10.4018/978-1-6684-4168-8

Kyaw, B. M., Saxena, N., Posadzki, P., Vseteckova, J., Nikolaou, C. K., George, P. P., Divakar, U., Masiello, I., Kononowicz, A. A., Zary, N., & Tudor Car, L. (2019). Virtual reality for health professions education: Systematic review and meta-analysis by the Digital Health Education Collaboration. *Journal of Medical Internet Research, 21*(1). Advance online publication. doi:10.2196/12959

Medical Device Network. (2022). *Medical Device Network.* Medical Device Network.

Mystakidis, S. (2022). Metaverse. *Encyclopedia, 2*(1), 486–497. doi:10.3390/encyclopedia2010031

Ong, Y. S. (2019). AIR5: Five pillars of artificial intelligence research. *IEEE Transactions on Emerging Topics in Computational Intelligence, 3*(5), 411–415. doi:10.1109/TETCI.2019.2928344

Petrigna, L., & Musumeci, G. (2022). The metaverse: A new challenge for the healthcare system: A scoping review. *Journal of Functional Morphology and Kinesiology, 7*(3), 63. doi:10.3390/jfmk7030063

Prova, O. S., Ahmed, F., Sultana, J., & Ashrafuzzaman, M. (2022). Big medical data analytics for diagnosis. In P. Keikhosrokiani (Ed.), *Big Data Analytics for Healthcare* (pp. 111–124). Academic Press., https://doi.org/https://doi.org/10.1016/B978-0-323-91907-4.00013-3

Sparkes, M. (2021). What is a metaverse. *New Scientist, 251*(3348), 18. doi:10.10160262-4079(21)01450-0

Sutherland, J., Belec, J., Sheikh, A., Chepelev, L., Althobaity, W., Chow, B. J., Mitsouras, D., Christensen, A., Rybicki, F. J., & La Russa, D. J. (2019). Applying modern virtual and augmented reality technologies to medical images and models. *Journal of Digital Imaging, 32*(1), 38–53. doi:10.100710278-018-0122-7

Tan, T. F., Li, Y., Lim, J. S., Gunasekeran, D. V., Teo, Z. L., Ng, W. Y., & Ting, D. S. W. (2022). Metaverse and virtual health care in ophthalmology: Opportunities and challenges. *Asia-Pacific Journal of Ophthalmology, 11*(3), 237–246. doi:10.1097/apo.0000000000000537

Thomason, J. (2021). How will the Metaverse change health care? *Journal of Metaverse, 1*(1), 13–16.

Unity. (n.d.). *Unity.* Unity Website.

Uppot, R. N., Laguna, B., McCarthy, C. J., De Novi, G., Phelps, A., Siegel, E., & Courtier, J. (2019). Implementing virtual and augmented reality tools for Radiology Education and training, communication, and clinical care. *Radiology, 291*(3), 570–580. doi:10.1148/radiol.2019182210

Wang, G., Badal, A., Jia, X., Maltz, J. S., Mueller, K., Myers, K. J., Niu, C., Vannier, M., Yan, P., Yu, Z., & Zeng, R. (2022). Development of metaverse for Intelligent Healthcare. *Nature Machine Intelligence, 4*(11), 922–929. doi:10.103842256-022-00549-6

Wang, Y., Su, Z., Zhang, N., Xing, R., Liu, D., Luan, T. H., & Shen, X. (2023). A survey on Metaverse: Fundamentals, security, and privacy. *IEEE Communications Surveys and Tutorials, 25*(1), 319–352. doi:10.1109/comst.2022.3202047

Wu, J., Sun, Y., Zhang, G., Zhou, Z., & Ren, Z. (2021). Virtual reality-assisted cognitive behavioral therapy for anxiety disorders: A systematic review and meta-analysis. *Frontiers in Psychiatry, 12.* Advance online publication. doi:10.3389/fpsyt.2021.575094

Yang, Q., Zhao, Y., Huang, H., Xiong, Z., Kang, J., & Zheng, Z. (2022). Fusing blockchain and AI with metaverse: A survey. *IEEE Open Journal of the Computer Society, 3*, 122–136. doi:10.1109/ojcs.2022.3188249

Yu, K.-H., Beam, A. L., & Kohane, I. S. (2018). Artificial Intelligence in healthcare. *Nature Biomedical Engineering, 2*(10), 719–731. doi:10.103841551-018-0305-z

Zweifach, S. M., & Triola, M. M. (2019). Extended reality in medical education: Driving adoption through provider-centered design. *Digital Biomarkers, 3*(1), 14–21. doi:10.1159/000498923

Section 5
Future Directions

Chapter 15
The Metaverse and Web 3.0:
Revolutionising Consumption and Communication for the Future

Ali B. Mahmoud

(iD) https://orcid.org/0000-0002-3790-1107

St John's University, USA & London South Bank University, London, UK

ABSTRACT

The metaverse is a new frontier in consumption. It is a digital place where people can buy and consume anything they want, whenever they want. It is an oasis of freedom and choice, and it has the potential to change the way we live and work. The future of the metaverse is placed where data and technology merge to create an experience that's both unique and engaging. With information overload becoming a weekly reality, it is crucial for businesses to understand how their consumers are engaging with their offerings. This chapter synthesised the current research and practice to answer the following questions: How is the metaverse changing the way we consume and communicate? How is Web 3.0 empowering and transforming the metaverse? What are the threats Web 3.0 is bringing to our privacy on the internet?

INTRODUCTION

The digital landscape is changing rapidly, with more and more emerging technologies connecting us in ways that were not possible even a few years ago (Keikhosrokiani, 2022). We are on the brink of a revolutionary era in how we use the internet. Web 3.0, also known as the Metaverse, is a new version of the internet powered by blockchain technology and data. Web 3.0 is bringing about a change in how we interact with information online and, more importantly, a dramatic shift in the power dynamics between consumers and companies.

The Metaverse, an online world made up of data and technology, is the latest frontier in this digital revolution. Conceived in the minds of science-fiction novelists (The Economist, 2022), the Metaverse, or virtual worlds, has the potential to revolutionise marketing by providing brands with new ways to engage with consumers and deliver immersive experiences. In the Metaverse or the *new market uni-*

DOI: 10.4018/978-1-6684-7029-9.ch015

verse, as termed by Hollensen et al. (2022), brands can create virtual storefronts and product displays (Darbinyan, 2022), host virtual events and promotions (Chen, 2022), and even create virtual versions of their products for customers to try on or test drive (Lim et al., 2022). Additionally, the Metaverse can allow for more targeted and personalised marketing (Dwivedi et al., 2022), as brands can gather data on consumer behaviour and preferences in virtual environments (Hazan et al., 2022). A 2021 study (Netcore Cloud, 2021) comparing the conversion rates of U.S. e-commerce websites revealed that a greater proportion of sales were completed when the shopping experience was personalised to individual consumers. Though conversion rates increased in a number of e-commerce subsegments, marketplaces demonstrated the largest difference in conversion rates before and after personalisation (see Table 1). Overall, the Metaverse has the potential to create more engaging and interactive brand experiences that can build stronger connections with consumers who can use Web 3.0 to shop, pay bills, communicate with friends and family, and even participate in digital marketing activities. Therefore it is no wonder that the Metaverse is considered to be shaping the real-world ambitions of the leading brands worldwide (The Economist, 2022).

Table 1. Online shopping conversion rate in select verticals before and after offering personalised shopping experience in the United States in 2021

	Pre-personalisation	Post-personalisation
Marketplace	1.2%	1.75%
Brand	1.04%	1.5%
Fashion/Apparel	1.32%	1.78%
Groceries	1.31%	1.79%
Jewelry	1.43%	1.78%
Books	1.22%	1.66%
Cosmetics	1.29%	1.75%

Web 3.0 is the latest iteration of the internet, allowing us to access more and more data and information on the Web. From digital marketing to media and blockchain, the implications of Web 3.0 on the Metaverse are far-reaching. The precursors to the modern Metaverse emerged during the Web 2.0 era, primarily concentrating on the gaming industry (Dwivedi et al., 2022). With the advent of web 3.0 technology, metaverse platforms now provide users with an augmented reality extension of traditional platforms, paving the way for more natural discussions between users (Solakis et al., 2022). The implications of the Metaverse for digital marketing are vast. With the ability to target specific audiences, businesses can now engage consumers with highly relevant content reversing long-held negative attitudes towards digital marketing, especially the one delivered via e-mail (Mahmoud, 2015; Mahmoud et al., 2019). This includes connecting with potential customers through social media, personalising e-mail campaigns, and offering customised product recommendations. Therefore, this chapter delves into the Metaverse's past, present and future, looking at how the Metaverse is changing the way we consume and communicate and what that signifies for the future of communication, highlighting how Web 3.0 is empowering and transforming the Metaverse—it discusses the technologies necessary to power the Metaverse and explores the benefits, challenges, and privacy concerns that come with Web 3.0.

BACKGROUND

Web 3.0 is a concept that refers to the next evolution of the internet, characterised by a shift towards a more decentralised and user-driven web (Choudhary, 2022). Web 3.0, commonly referred to as the Metaverse, is a concept where the entire Web operates as a single, interconnected virtual world (Salar et al., 2023). It refers to an interconnected network that includes the internet, data and technology, information, media, and digital marketing (Kumar, 2021). Theoretically, Web 3.0 could bring together the entire world in a shared online experience.

At the heart of Web 3.0 is the idea of decentralisation. By removing the reliance on a single platform, Web 3.0 encourages a more open, accessible web. For example, blockchain technology is being used to decentralise services and create a more secure environment for data transactions (Yli-Huumo et al., 2016). Additionally, Web 3.0 is set to create a more personalised experience for users (Ferrari, 2016), giving them greater control over who and what they interact with online. Therefore, Web 3.0 refers to the next stage of the World Wide Web, where the internet is more intelligent, decentralised, and user-centric.

Overall, Web 3.0 is working towards creating a more secure, user-centric web experience. Albeit primarily visible in the finance sector (see Figure 1), by decentralising services and creating a more personalised experience, however, Web 3.0 is beginning to revolutionise the way people interact with and consume information online. This could potentially create a new era of digital marketing and media, where consumers have more control over what information and services they can access. Web 3.0 is anticipated to bring several benefits, but legitimate privacy worries about it exist. To that end, this chapter argues that businesses and governments need to take measures to safeguard users' privacy so that we can keep the Metaverse private and safe through ethical data collection and solid policy frameworks.

Figure 1. Top sectors in Web 3.0 panorama in India as of April 2022
Source: (Fleishman-Hillard & Website (eleve.co), 2022)

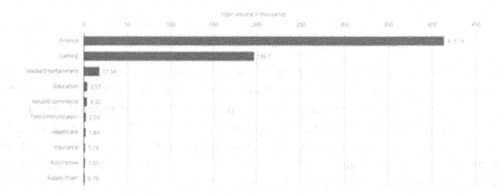

METHODOLOGY

As a general review (e.g. Mahmoud, 2021; Mohr et al., 2022a), this chapter synthesised and summarised existing research on the Metaverse and Web 3.0 concerning consumption and communication patterns. Therefore, the methodology for conducting this work involved the following steps (Templier & Paré, 2015):

1. The work identified the research objectives that steered the scoping of previous research. It sought to answer the following questions: How is the Metaverse changing the way we consume and communicate? And how is Web 3.0 empowering and transforming the Metaverse? Moreover, what are the threats Web 3.0 is bringing to our privacy on the internet?
2. A comprehensive search of academic databases, journals, and other good sources was conducted to determine relevant research studies, articles, and books. The ultimately deemed-relevant literature was carefully and critically read and analysed to synthesise the information into a coherent narrative.
3. The assistance of three independent expert peers was solicited to guarantee that the source selection method was devoid of bias.
4. This chapter synthesised the fragmented pieces of knowledge that informed the discussions and conclusions presented in this work.

THE METAVERSE

The term "Metaverse" has become increasingly popular in the world of technology and information-related industries. It is a combination of the words "meta", which refers to an abstraction layer, and "universe", which is used to describe a wide variety of virtual worlds. In essence, the Metaverse is a collective virtual shared space created by the convergence of virtually enhanced physical reality, virtual reality, and the internet (Falchuk et al., 2018). The Metaverse is poised to represent a virtual world that is created when the internet, data, and technology are combined. In the Metaverse, people are no longer limited by physical distance or time zones, allowing them to access and consume information and media anytime, anywhere in the world (Armstrong, 2023).

As technology advances and the internet expands, the Metaverse is becoming a reality, becoming an important part of the communications, entertainment, and digital marketing industries (Babu & Mohan, 2022). This new virtual environment promises to provide a space for people to interact and engage in ways not possible in the physical world, creating a new, more immersive experience (Solakis et al., 2022). The Metaverse is quickly becoming an integral part of our digital lives and our access to information and media, with an estimated global market size surging from 47.48 billion U.S. dollars in 2022 to 678.8 billion U.S. dollars in 2030 (Figure 2). As we move into this new era of digital transformation, it is important to consider how consumers may be responding to the Metaverse and what we can expect to see in the near future.

Consumption in Metaversial Realms

Consumers are becoming increasingly aware of how the internet, data, and technology are impacting how we shop, communicate, and interact. The Metaverse allows for a wide range of activities, from online social networking to gaming and even virtual shopping. As the Internet of Things (IoT) expands, the Metaverse will become increasingly connected to the internet, allowing for the storage and sharing of data across different platforms and allowing for new technologies to be developed (Gadekallu et al., 2022). This is all made possible by the usage of blockchain technology and its associated data-processing protocols (Jeon et al., 2022).

Figure 2. Metaverse market revenue worldwide from 2021 to 2030 (in billion U.S. dollars)
Source: (Grand View Research, 2022)

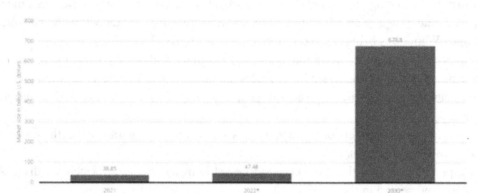

The Metaverse, empowered by Web 3.0 technologies, is already transforming the way consumers interact with companies, services, and entertainment. For instance, retailers are now able to offer virtual product demonstrations, where customers can try out products before making a purchase (Read, 2022). Customers can also receive virtual consultations with customer service representatives and access real-time product information. The construction of avatars for realistic consultations, tailored care through data interconnection, the use of digital twins, and future clinical uses in teaching, diagnostics, and therapies are all examples of applications of the Metaverse in ophthalmology (Tan et al., 2022). In the entertainment industry, the Metaverse is being used to create immersive gaming experiences, allowing players to interact with each other in virtual environments (Kharjule, 2022). For instance, Decentraland (see Figure 3) is a browser-based three-dimensional world platform. Using the Ethereum blockchain-based MANA cryptocurrency, users can purchase non-fungible tokens (NFTs) representing virtual plots of land on the platform.

Figure 3. Decentraland's marketplace
Source: Current study and Decentraland (2023)

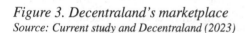

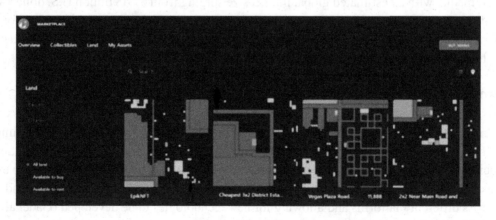

The Metaverse is also becoming a popular platform for virtual events, such as concerts, festivals, and conferences, which provide a unique and interactive experience for attendees. Furthermore, consumers can use the Metaverse to network and connect with others, forming communities based on shared interests and experiences.

Figure 4. Metaverse fashion week
Source: Current study and Everyrealm (2023)

The Metaverse also provides new opportunities for digital marketing and advertising. Companies will be able to advertise their products and services to a larger audience while also providing valuable information to their customers. This will help increase brand loyalty and engagement with customers while providing a better overall experience. A survey (Morning Consult, 2022a, 2022b) performed in March 2022 in the United States (Figure 5) revealed that 36 per cent of internet adults were interested in accessing the Metaverse, with 12 per cent indicating they were highly interested. Men were more likely than women to be interested in using the Metaverse, with 7 per cent of women expressing strong interest and 50 per cent expressing no interest. Just over a third of males were not at all interested, while 18 per cent of men were very interested (Morning Consult, 2022a). Furthermore (see Figure 6), in a subsequent question about possessing a digital avatar as a representative in the Metaverse, Baby Boomers were by far the least interested in establishing an avatar to represent them in the Metaverse, while Gen Z and Millennials were the most likely to be interested in doing so (Morning Consult, 2022b). Additionally, a global poll (Dynata, 2022) conducted in February 2022 revealed that Generation Z and Millennials were most interested in metaverse activities. Thirty-seven per cent of Gen Z and 38 per cent of Millennial online users indicated that they were extremely or very interested in attending virtual concerts of their favourite musical artists (Dynata, 2022). Therefore, as Web 3.0 continues to evolve, tech-savvy (or -native) consumers will be better prepared to make informed decisions about their online lives (Mahmoud, Ball, et al., 2021; Mahmoud, Hack-Polay, et al., 2021).

As the Metaverse continues to evolve, its potential for providing new and exciting experiences will be fully realised. As technology continues to develop, the possibilities for the Metaverse will also continue to expand and become more integrated with everyday life. From virtual education to virtual shopping and entertainment, the Metaverse will likely provide unprecedented engagement and convenience to its users (Dwivedi et al., 2022).

Figure 5. March 2022, the percentage of internet users in the United States who are interested in accessing the Metaverse by gender
Source: (Morning Consult, 2022a)

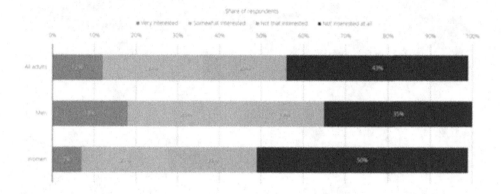

Figure 6. March 2022, the percentage of internet users in the United States who are interested in accessing the Metaverse by generation
Source: (Morning Consult, 2022b)

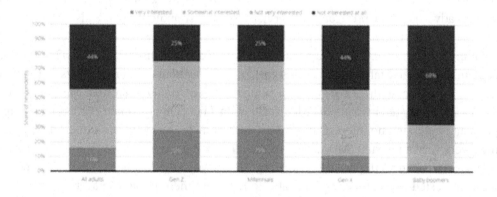

Figure 7. Share of adults worldwide who are interested in trying select types of metaverse experiences as of February 2022 by generation
Source: (Dynata, 2022)

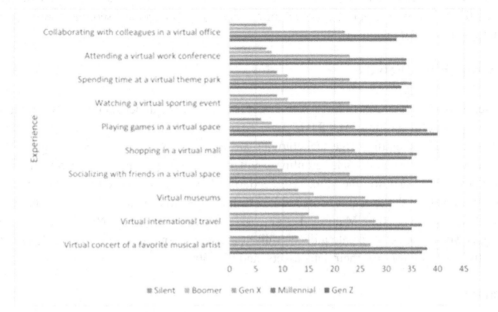

WEB 3.0 AND THE METAVERSE

The Metaverse is undergoing rapid transformation due to the introduction of Web 3.0. The availability of data and technology has enabled the creation of new experiences, platforms, and interactions (Joy et al., 2022) such that the Metaverse is becoming more connected, and internet users' interactions with it are changing. As a result, one of the most noticeable changes is the increased use of digital marketing and blockchain technology. The proliferation of available information has enabled marketers to target customers more precisely while making it easier to have conversations and exchange data in real-time (Haleem et al., 2022).

Additionally, the use of blockchain technology has enabled businesses to securely store information, access data more efficiently, and facilitate transactions between multiple parties (Peres et al., 2022). This is crucial for businesses in a world making its first steps into the fifth industrial revolution or Industry 5.0, which aims to create a smart, interconnected, and sustainable industrial ecosystem with a focus on human-centred values and experiences through the integration of advanced technologies, such as artificial intelligence (AI), the Internet of Things (IoT), and robotics, into various processes and systems, leading to greater efficiency and productivity (Keikhosrokiani & Pourya Asl, 2023).

Furthermore, the Metaverse is becoming more informative, entertaining, and interactive. As information and media become more accessible, the amount of content available to users is more varied and engaging. Announcements and events can be shared more quickly and with greater accuracy. Live streaming has become a growing form of entertainment and communication, allowing users to come together and express their thoughts and ideas more personally (Baía Reis & Ashmore, 2022). As a result, the Metaverse is becoming more personalised to individual users. As users continue to share their personal information, the Metaverse will be able to tailor content and services to the unique needs of each user (Plechatá et al., 2022). Rather than simply being a platform for communication, the Metaverse is set to become a tool for managing personal data and creating an individualised experience (Zallio & Clarkson, 2022). These developments are enabling a new era of decentralised and user-driven virtual experiences—a Web 3.0-enabled Metaverse.

Technologies for Web 3.0

When discussing consumer reactions to Web 3.0, it is important to understand the underlying technology that enables its functioning. Web 3.0 is powered by emerging technologies such as blockchain and smart contracts. These cutting-edge technologies are aimed at providing a secure infrastructure for users to carry out tasks such as making online payments and transferring data. Such technologies and features set to be used to power the Metaverse need to be highly secure, versatile, and user-friendly. As a decentralised web, Web 3.0 requires several key technologies to function (Garfatta et al., 2021; Goel et al., 2022; Lacity et al., 2022; Mahmoud et al., 2020; Murray et al., 2022; Nkosinkulu, 2023). These technologies work together to create a decentralised and secure online environment where users have substantially more control over their data, assets, and identities.

Blockchain

Blockchain is a secure, decentralised ledger that enables the development of decentralised applications and platforms. The decentralised and secure nature of the blockchain can contribute to the transparency, immutability, and security of digital data and transactions (Gad et al., 2022) and create decentralised autonomous organisations (DAOs) and decentralised applications (dApps), which can provide more equitable and transparent method of managing digital assets and services (Santana & Albareda, 2022). For instance, blockchain technology is used by dApps to secure transactions and maintain a tamper-proof ledger of all activity on the network. Also, decentralised infrastructure makes dApps less vulnerable to downtime, hacking, or censorship. Additionally, many dApps use tokens to incentivise users to contribute to the network, providing a means of distributing rewards and creating value. This resonates with the arguments suggesting that the landscape of marketing communication is adapting, and digital customers are presently more empowered (Mahmoud et al., 2022).

Decentralised Storage

Frameworks like InterPlanetary File Systems (IPFS) that enable decentralised data and file storage and retrieval (Muralidharan & Ko, 2019). These solutions eliminate the need for centralised data storage and lower the risk of data breaches and censorship by distributing and storing data through a peer-to-peer network (Garcia-Font, 2020). Decentralised storage options can also lower the price of conventional data storage while enhancing the scalability and dependability of digital data storage (Miyachi & Mackey, 2021). This may offer a more accessible and secure platform for digital data, enabling the creation of fresh and cutting-edge services and applications.

Unassailable Internet Connection

A secure and reliable internet connection is required to power the Metaverse successfully. The internet connection must be able to handle a large amount of traffic and must be able to support all the applications that will be used in the Metaverse. Additionally, an internet-protocol-based system needs to be in place for data transfer, data storage, and application access.

Decentralised Identity

Technologies like decentralised identity systems enable users to securely and decentrally control and manage their personal data and digital identities (Avellaneda et al., 2019). These systems give people more ownership and control over personal data by using decentralised technologies like blockchain to store and manage identity information (Stockburger et al., 2021). Decentralised identity systems can also lessen the chance of fraud and identity theft and increase the speed and convenience of identity verification procedures (Sung & Park, 2021).

Semantic Web

Semantic Web is a web where the data and information are organised in a meaningful and easily accessible way, allowing for more intuitive searches and data analysis (Patel & Jain, 2021). The semantic Web is a vision for the future of the Web, where information is not only accessible to humans but can also be understood and processed by computers. This is achieved by using common standards such as RDF (Resource Description Framework) and OWL (Web Ontology Language) to describe and represent the meaning of data on the Web (Houssein et al., 2022). The Semantic Web is intended to enable intelligent applications to process and integrate information from a variety of sources, provide new and innovative services, and make the Web more accessible and useful. By representing information in a machine-readable format, the Semantic Web aims to create a more connected, intelligent, and open web, where data can be linked and combined to provide a more comprehensive understanding of the world.

Smart Contracts

Smart contracts can automate and streamline numerous processes and transactions, such as property transfers, supply chain management, and financial transactions, resulting in a more efficient, transparent, and secure digital environment, as the functionality of such contracts can enforce agreement terms without needing go-betweens (E. Nwafor, 2021). In addition, smart contracts can reduce the costs associated with conventional agreements and improve contract accuracy and enactment speed (Peters & Panayi, 2016).

Decentralised Exchanges

Platforms that facilitate the decentralised exchange of cryptocurrencies and other digital assets without the need for mediators (e.g. 0x Protocol, Kyber Network).

Cryptography

Advanced cryptographic algorithms ensure the security and privacy of data and transactions in a decentralised network. Cryptographic algorithms are mathematical functions that are used to secure and protect data in Web 3.0. These algorithms provide essential security features, such as confidentiality, integrity, and authenticity, for digital transactions and communications (Xu et al., 2022).

AI and Machine Learning

AI and machine learning have the potential to greatly empower Web 3.0 as a decentralised and more intelligent version of the internet. With the use of machine learning algorithms, Web 3.0 can analyse vast amounts of data and make predictions or decisions based on that data. This can result in more personalised and relevant experiences for users, as well as enable new and innovative applications and services. AI can also enhance the security and privacy of the web by detecting and preventing malicious activities. Additionally, machine learning can help to make sense of unstructured data, such as text and images, and transform it into structured information that can be easily analysed and utilised. By combining AI and machine learning with the decentralised architecture of Web 3.0, the internet can become a more intelligent, secure, and empowering place for individuals and organisations alike.

Natural Language Processing (NLP)

The rising disruptive power of artificial intelligence technology has changed the phase of marketing (Anifa et al., 2022). Methods in artificial intelligence that facilitate the processing and understanding of human language, with applications in the development of intelligent and conversational user interfaces. Some applications of natural language processing in Web 3.0 include (Keikhosrokiani & Pourya Asl, 2023; Mahmoud, 2021; Solakis et al., 2022): a) conversational interfaces and chatbots: NLP can be used to create chatbots and conversational interfaces that understand and respond to users' natural language inputs. As a result, people will smoothly navigate and use digital services and applications, which can enhance their overall experience. NLP can be used to analyse and extract meaningful information from large amounts of text data, such as news articles, reports, and research papers, for the purposes of information retrieval and summarisation. Users may be able to save time and effort due to this. c) Sentiment analysis: Natural language processing can be used to analyse and classify the tone of large amounts of text data, such as social media posts and customer reviews (e.g. Mahmoud, Hack-Polay, et al., 2021). Information about public opinion and responses from customers can be gleaned from this. d) Text generation: Natural language processing can be used to generate new text based on preexisting patterns and associations in a given dataset. Summaries, reports, and other written materials can all benefit from this technique.

Extended Reality (XR)

The term *Extended Reality* (XR) encompasses all *forms of immersive technology, including but not limited to Augmented* Reality (AR), *Virtual Reality* (VR), *Mixed Reality* (MR), and their hybrids. Integrating XR technologies into the web can provide a more immersive and interactive experience for users, enabling them to engage with digital content more intuitively and naturally. Additionally, these technologies can be leveraged to create new and innovative applications and services, such as virtual marketplaces, training simulations, and collaborative workspaces. By incorporating XR into Web 3.0, users can gain access to a wider range of experiences and interact with digital content in a more intuitive and engaging manner. Furthermore, the decentralised architecture of Web 3.0 can provide a more secure and decentralised platform for XR applications, allowing for greater user control and privacy. In this way, XR variants have the potential to greatly enhance the capabilities of Web 3.0 and empower a more immersive and connected digital experience. Ultimately, XR technologies can help bring the Metaverse to life by providing immersive experiences that allow users to feel as if they are truly present in the virtual space. For example, VR headsets can be used to provide a fully immersive experience within the Metaverse, while AR technologies can overlay virtual objects onto the physical world, creating a mixed-reality experience that blends the real and virtual worlds.

The Internet of Things (IoT)

The interconnectedness of physical devices, vehicles, buildings, and other objects embedded with electronics, software, sensors, and connectivity which enables them to collect and exchange data. The Internet of Things (IoT) has the potential to greatly enhance and empower Web 3.0, a decentralised and more intelligent version of the internet. IoT involves connecting everyday devices, such as appliances, vehicles, and medical equipment, to the internet, allowing for the exchange of data and remote control. This can result in a more connected and efficient world, where devices can communicate and collaborate with one another to provide new and innovative services. By incorporating IoT into Web 3.0, users can gain access to a more connected and intelligent digital environment, where devices can work together to provide a more seamless and personalised experience. Additionally, the decentralised architecture of Web 3.0 can provide a more secure and decentralised platform for IoT devices, allowing for greater user control and privacy. In this way, IoT has the potential to greatly enhance the capabilities of Web 3.0 and empower a more connected and efficient digital world

DISCUSSION

The Metaverse and Web 3.0 are expected to create significant value in the future digital economy by emphasising decentralisation and the democratisation of data, allowing individuals more control over their data and leading to greater privacy and security regarding online interactions.

We are already starting to see this by introducing decentralised media platforms, such as voice and video streaming protocols like Steemit (see Figure 8). This shift towards a user-centric model is predicted to pave the way for the creation of novel business models like programmable economies and virtual real estate, both of which have the potential to open up fresh revenue channels and expansion possibilities. One example is the improved ease with which content creators can monetise their efforts, thereby realising financial rewards without onerous contractual commitments. Because of this, it is hoped that end users will exercise more discretion over their personal information.

One key aspect of Web 3.0 and the Metaverse is the use of blockchain technology. Blockchain technology will allow for the creation of transparent and secure decentralised systems less susceptible to intermediaries and single points of failure. This will lead to increased efficiency, lower costs for businesses and consumers and the development of new digital currency and assets. Additionally, blockchain technology will enable the creation of NFT marketplaces, where unique virtual items and purchases can be bought, sold, and traded, creating new forms of value and wealth. Besides, the Metaverse is designed to support smart contracts, allowing users to take advantage of seamless data exchange and automated processes. This will create a much smoother, more intuitive, and more efficient online experience.

Figure 8. Steemit is a blockchain-based blogging and social media website
Source: Current study and Steemit (2023)

In addition to the benefits to businesses, the development of Web 3.0 also offers unexpected advantages to consumers. The ability to purchase products, complete transactions and connect with friends and family has been revolutionised with the introduction of the Metaverse. This can help keep marketing functioning in extreme contexts like warzones or pandemic-hit territories with restricted movement and social isolation imposed (e.g. Ezimmuo & Keikhosrokiani, 2022; Mahmoud, Ball, et al., 2021; Mohr et al., 2022b; Xian et al., 2022). More than 92 per cent of responding businesses in a March 2022 survey of companies from selected countries that had already invested in the Metaverse felt that the global COVID-19 pandemic had spurred the development of metaverse technologies (Sortlist, 2022a). Online transactions are now more secure thanks to the addition of blockchain technology, which is proven to be more effective than traditional networks. Furthermore, many popular platforms, such as Facebook, Instagram and YouTube, are now available to users in a 3D format with enhanced user experience, allowing them to easily interact with their favourite content. For instance, Amazon launched a new service called 'Virtual Try-on' where customers can use AR via their phones to visualise how fashion products would like on the customer from different angles (see Figure 9).

Ultimately, a Web 3.0-enabled Metaverse brings new possibilities and value to the digital economy. This can be achieved by enabling new configurations of digital interaction and exchange as well as allowing for the development of decentralised applications, such as peer-to-peer marketplaces and decentralised finance (Minevich, 2022).

Figure 9. Amazon's Virtual Try-on
Source: Current study and Amazon.com (2023)

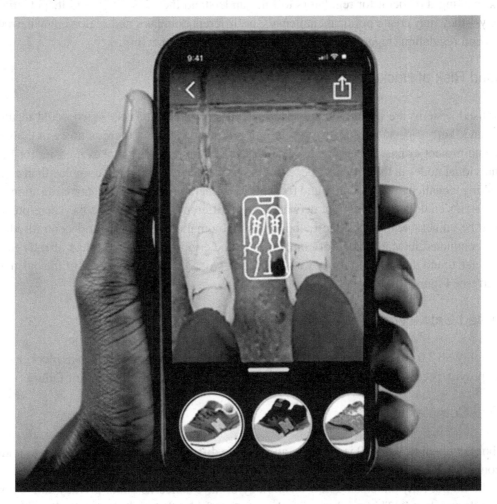

Web 3.0—A Double-Edged Sword

Web 3.0, like any new technology, has both potentially positive and negative aspects. Web 3.0 poses new difficulties in addition to promising a number of advantages, including increased security, privacy, and control for users. The following are some of the most important privacy issues that Web 3.0 may introduce (Ellul et al., 2020; Kim, 2021; Lesavre et al., 2019; Li et al., 2021; Rowland et al., 2020; Saqib et al., 2021).

Lack of Standardisation and Regulation

In societies where individuals mainly consider online communication instead of face-to-face interaction (Ashaye et al., 2023), Web 3.0 is an evolving technology, and there is currently a lack of clear regulatory frameworks for its use. This could create uncertainties for users and businesses and lead to privacy abuses. The decentralised nature of Web 3.0 makes it difficult to standardise and regulate, which could result in security vulnerabilities and a lack of privacy protection. Decentralised systems can be technically complex, making it difficult for regulators to fully understand the technology and its potential impact on society—they may create political challenges, as different countries and regions may have different priorities and regulations regarding privacy, security, and data ownership.

Increased Risk of Hacking and Cyber Attacks

Decentralised systems are more vulnerable to hacking and cyber attacks, which could result in data breaches and theft of personal information. In a decentralised system, there is no central authority to monitor and protect against cyber attacks. The lack of central authority makes it easier for hackers to target individual nodes in the network. Decentralised systems are often more complex than central systems, making it challenging to identify and fix security vulnerabilities. Lack of standardisation in decentralised systems could lead to different networks using different security protocols. Therefore, personal data could be vulnerable to hacks, theft, and exposure by malicious actors in a decentralised network. A survey conducted in March 2022 of companies from certain countries that had already invested in the Metaverse found that cyber security was the biggest worry for more than 38% of the businesses that responded (see Figure 10).

Centralised Gatekeepers

Even though Web 3.0 is designed to be decentralised, centralised gatekeepers such as blockchain miners or wallet providers could still have control over user data, creating a single point of failure.

Technical Complexity

The technology behind Web 3.0 is complex and may be difficult for the average person to understand, which could lead to confusion and mistrust, which can have a significant impact on technology adoption. People who do not fully understand new technology or have concerns about privacy and security may be less likely to adopt it. This can lead to a slower rate of adoption and potentially limit the potential benefits that the technology can bring.

Lack of Interoperability

Different Web 3.0 systems may not be compatible with each other, which could limit the growth and adoption of the technology. Therefore, one of the main challenges facing the growth and adoption of Web 3.0 is the lack of interoperability between different systems. Due to the decentralised and open-source nature of Web 3.0, different systems may use different technologies, protocols, and standards, making it difficult for them to communicate and exchange data seamlessly. This can lead to fragmentation in the Web 3.0 ecosystem, making it challenging for users to move their data and assets between different platforms and services. This lack of interoperability can limit the potential benefits of Web 3.0, as it can make it more difficult for users to take advantage of the full range of services and applications available on the decentralised Web. Addressing the interoperability challenge will be critical for the growth and adoption of Web 3.0, as it will enable users to fully realise the potential of the decentralised Web.

Financial Privacy

Transactions on a decentralised network can be traced, potentially revealing sensitive financial information. Financial privacy is an important aspect of Web 3.0, as decentralised financial systems offer the potential for greater privacy and security compared to traditional centralised systems. In a decentralised financial system, users can transact directly with each other without the need for intermediaries, reducing the risk of data breaches and the unauthorised use of personal information. Additionally, the use of cryptographic technologies, such as zero-knowledge proofs, can enable users to transact without revealing their identity, providing greater privacy and protection against financial fraud. However, ensuring financial privacy in Web 3.0 also presents its own set of challenges, including the potential for money laundering and other illegal activities and the difficulty in enforcing financial regulations in a decentralised system. Addressing these challenges will be important for ensuring the responsible use of financial privacy in Web 3.0 and for building trust in decentralised financial systems.

Pseudonymity

While Web 3.0 provides users with more control over their personal data, it may also make it easier for malicious actors to create pseudonyms to engage in illegal activities. Web 3.0 offers the potential for greater pseudonymity compared to the current centralised Web. In a decentralised system, users can create and use digital identities that are not tied to their real-world identity, providing greater privacy and protection against data breaches and other privacy risks. This can help to mitigate concerns about the collection and use of personal data by central authorities and intermediaries and enable users to have greater control over their personal information. However, pseudonymity in Web 3.0 also presents its own set of challenges, including the potential for misuse and abuse and the difficulty in enforcing laws and regulations in a decentralised system. Addressing these challenges will be important for ensuring the responsible use of pseudonymity in Web 3.0 and building trust in the decentralised Web.

Location Privacy

Decentralised networks may store metadata that could be used to track a user's location and online activities. This metadata may include information about the time and location of transactions, as well as other data that could be used to build a profile of the user's online behaviour. To address this challenge, it will be important for Web 3.0 systems to implement strong privacy and security measures that protect user data and ensure that users have control over their metadata and can choose what information is shared and with whom. This can help to build trust in decentralised networks and encourage wider adoption of Web 3.0.

CONCLUSION

This chapter has examined the potential for Web 3.0 to revolutionise how we interact with and utilise the Metaverse. This chapter has discussed the technical requirements for Web 3.0, as well as the opportunities, challenges, and potential privacy threats associated with this technology, as well as the reactions of consumers. Evidently, the development of Web 3.0 is set to have a significant impact on the Metaverse, bringing with it both opportunities and obstacles.

Figure 10. Main doubts regarding the metaverse
Source: (Sortlist, 2022b)

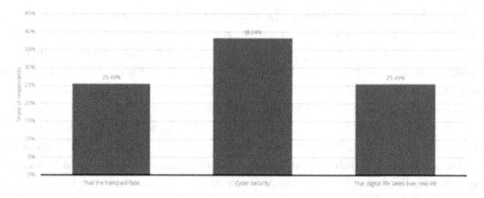

Web 3.0 will likely become a standard component powering the Metaverse in the coming years. This will give people more and better ways to access and interact with their digital environment. Consumers' reactions to Web 3.0 will improve as they learn more about it and its potential advantages, speeding up its adoption. The Metaverse is anticipated to expand in both accessibility and immersion over the next few years, enabling more significant user interaction and social connection. People can participate in immersive and interactive experiences in the Metaverse, such as video games, concerts, and sporting events. Despite expectations of leading to social patterns where humans are set to live in more and more isolation, the Metaverse can help people connect with others with similar interests and passions through these experiences, which can foster a stronger sense of community and social belonging. The Metaverse can significantly alter future consumer behaviour. People can access and buy goods and services in a virtual environment called the Metaverse without travelling long distances or dealing with traffic. This could make shopping more accessible and convenient because people can look at products and buy them from the comfort of their homes or even from inside a virtual world. The Metaverse is expected to have a bright future ahead of it as technology develops and advances. The Metaverse is also likely to give rise to new forms of commerce and entertainment, potentially creating entirely new industries and markets, meaning that the Metaverse is set to disrupt digital marketing practice. Therefore, businesses wanting to thrive in the inevitable *metaversal era* will need to assess their digital marketing workforce against the potential of Web 3.0 technologies for marketing practice and ensure the human arsenal of digital marketing is competitively equipped with relevant skills, knowledge and attitudes. However, with this increased integration into our lives, there will also be important considerations around privacy and security that must be addressed. Therefore, regulation of the Metaverse and Web 3.0 is necessary to ensure that these technologies are developed and used *responsibly and ethically* and to protect the rights and interests of users and consumers.

REFERENCES

Amazon.com. (2023). *Virtual Try On: Fashion - Amazon.co.uk*. Amazon.com, Inc. Retrieved 18 February from https://www.amazon.co.uk/b?ie=UTF8&node=29542815031

Anifa, M., P, M. J., Hack-Polay, D., Mahmoud, A. B., & Grigoriou, N. (2022). Segmenting the Retail Customers: A Multi-Model Approach of Clustering in Machine Learning. In P. Keikhosrokiani (Ed.), Handbook of Research on Consumer Behavior Change and Data Analytics in the Socio-Digital Era (pp. 25-50). IGI Global. doi:10.4018/978-1-6684-4168-8.ch002

Armstrong, P. (2023). *Disruptive Technologies: A Framework to Understand, Evaluate and Respond to Digital Disruption.* Kogan Page. https://books.google.co.uk/books?id=7oChEAAAQBAJ

Ashaye, O. R., Mahmoud, A. B., Munna, A. S., & Ali, N. (2023). The role of social media engagement and emotional intelligence in successful employment. *Higher Education, Skills and Work-Based Learning.* doi:10.1108/HESWBL-07-2022-0158

Avellaneda, O., Bachmann, A., Barbir, A., Brenan, J., Dingle, P., Duffy, K. H., Maler, E., Reed, D., & Sporny, M. (2019). Decentralized Identity: Where Did It Come From and Where Is It Going? *IEEE Communications Standards Magazine, 3*(4), 10–13. doi:10.1109/MCOMSTD.2019.9031542

Babu, M. U. A., & Mohan, P. (2022, June 22-24). Impact of the Metaverse on the Digital Future: People's Perspective. *2022 7th International Conference on Communication and Electronics Systems (ICCES).* doi:10.1080/14794713.2021.2024398

Baía Reis, A., & Ashmore, M. (2022). From video streaming to virtual reality worlds: an academic, reflective, and creative study on live theatre and performance in the metaverse. *International Journal of Performance Arts and Digital Media, 18*(1), 7–28. doi:10.1080/14794713.2021.2024398

Chen, Y. (2022). *Research on the Communication of Sports Events in the Context of Metaverse.* Academic Press.

Choudhary, V. V. (2022). *The metaverse: Gain insight into the exciting future of the internet* (Vol. 1). Vicky Choudhary.

Darbinyan, R. (2022). Council Post: Virtual Shopping In The Metaverse: What Is It And How Will AI Make It Work. *Forbes.* Retrieved 28 January from https://www.forbes.com/sites/forbestechcouncil/2022/03/16/virtual-shopping-in-the-metaverse-what-is-it-and-how-will-ai-make-it-work/

Decentraland. (2023). *Marketplace—land.* Decentraland. Retrieved 18 February from https://market.decentraland.org/lands

Dwivedi, Y. K., Hughes, L., Wang, Y., Alalwan, A. A., Ahn, S. J., Balakrishnan, J., Barta, S., Belk, R., Buhalis, D., Dutot, V., Felix, R., Filieri, R., Flavián, C., Gustafsson, A., Hinsch, C., Hollensen, S., Jain, V., Kim, J., Krishen, A. S., . . . Wirtz, J. (2022). Metaverse marketing: How the metaverse will shape the future of consumer research and practice. *Psychology & Marketing.* doi:10.1002/mar.21767

Dynata. (2022). *Share of adults worldwide who are interested in trying select types of metaverse experiences as of February 2022, by generation.* Statista. Retrieved 18 February from https://www-statista-com.jerome.stjohns.edu/statistics/1305147/interest-in-trying-metaverse-experiences-worldwide-generation/?locale=en

Ellul, J., Galea, J., Ganado, M., McCarthy, S., & Pace, G. J. (2020). Regulating Blockchain, DLT and Smart Contracts: a technology regulator's perspective. *ERA Forum, 21*(2), 209-220. 10.100712027-020-00617-7

Everyrealm, I. (2023). *Metaverse Fashion Week.* Everyrealm, Inc. Retrieved 18 February from https://everyrealm.com/mvfw

Ezimmuo, C. M., & Keikhosrokiani, P. (2022). Predicting Consumer Behavior Change Towards Using Online Shopping in Nigeria: The Impact of the COVID-19 Pandemic. In P. Keikhosrokiani (Ed.), *Handbook of Research on Consumer Behavior Change and Data Analytics in the Socio-Digital Era* (pp. 210–254). IGI Global. doi:10.4018/978-1-6684-4168-8.ch010

Falchuk, B., Loeb, S., & Neff, R. (2018). The Social Metaverse: Battle for Privacy. *IEEE Technology and Society Magazine, 37*(2), 52–61. doi:10.1109/MTS.2018.2826060

Ferrari, S. (2016). Marketing strategies in the age of web 3.0. In Mobile Computing and Wireless Networks: Concepts, Methodologies, Tools, and Applications (pp. 2132-2149). IGI Global.

Fleishman-Hillard, & Website (eleve.co). (2022). *Leading sectors in Web 3.0 landscape in India as of April 2022, by topic volume (in 1,000s)* [Graph]. Statista. Retrieved 03 February from https://www-statista-com.jerome.stjohns.edu/statistics/1353170/india-leading-sectors-in-web-30-in-by-topic-volume/

Gad, A. G., Mosa, D. T., Abualigah, L., & Abohany, A. A. (2022). Emerging Trends in Blockchain Technology and Applications: A Review and Outlook. *Journal of King Saud University - Computer and Information Sciences, 34*(9), 6719-6742.

Gadekallu, T. R., Huynh-The, T., Wang, W., Yenduri, G., Ranaweera, P., Pham, Q.-V., da Costa, D. B., & Liyanage, M. (2022). *Blockchain for the metaverse: A review.* arXiv preprint arXiv:2203.09738.

Garcia-Font, V. (2020). SocialBlock: An architecture for decentralized user-centric data management applications for communications in smart cities. *Journal of Parallel and Distributed Computing, 145*, 13–23. doi:10.1016/j.jpdc.2020.06.004

Garfatta, I., Klai, K., Gaaloul, W., & Graiet, M. (2021). A Survey on Formal Verification for Solidity Smart Contracts *2021 Australasian Computer Science Week Multiconference.* 10.1145/3437378.3437879

Goel, A. K., Bakshi, R., & Agrawal, K. K. (2022). Web 3.0 and Decentralized Applications. *Materials Proceedings, 10*(1).

Grand View Research. (2022). *Metaverse market revenue worldwide from 2021 to 2030 (in billion U.S. dollars)* [Graph]. Statista. Retrieved 18 February from https://www-statista-com.jerome.stjohns.edu/statistics/1295784/metaverse-market-size/?locale=en

Haleem, A., Javaid, M., Asim Qadri, M., Pratap Singh, R., & Suman, R. (2022). Artificial intelligence (AI) applications for marketing: A literature-based study. *International Journal of Intelligent Networks, 3*, 119–132. doi:10.1016/j.ijin.2022.08.005

Hazan, E., Kelly, G., Khan, H., Spillecke, D., & Yee, L. (2022). *Marketing in the metaverse: An opportunity for innovation and experimentation*. McKinsey & Company. Retrieved 28 January from https://www.mckinsey.com/capabilities/growth-marketing-and-sales/our-insights/marketing-in-the-metaverse-an-opportunity-for-innovation-and-experimentation

Hollensen, S., Kotler, P., & Opresnik, M. O. (2022). Metaverse – the new marketing universe. *Journal of Business Strategy*. doi:10.1108/JBS-01-2022-0014

Houssein, E. H., Ibrahem, N., Zaki, A. M., & Sayed, A. (2022). Semantic Protocol and Resource Description Framework Query Language: A Comprehensive Review. *Mathematics, 10*(17), 3203. doi:10.3390/math10173203

Jeon, H. J., Youn, H. C., Ko, S. M., & Kim, T. H. (2022). Blockchain and AI Meet in the Metaverse. *Advances in the Convergence of Blockchain and Artificial Intelligence, 73*.

Joy, A., Zhu, Y., Peña, C., & Brouard, M. (2022). Digital future of luxury brands: Metaverse, digital fashion, and non-fungible tokens. *Strategic Change, 31*(3), 337-343. doi:10.1002/jsc.2502

Keikhosrokiani, P. (Ed.). (2022). *Handbook of Research on Consumer Behavior Change and Data Analytics in the Socio-Digital Era*. IGI Global. doi:10.4018/978-1-6684-4168-8

Keikhosrokiani, P., & Pourya Asl, M. (Eds.). (2023). *Handbook of Research on Artificial Intelligence Applications in Literary Works and Social Media*. IGI Global. doi:10.4018/978-1-6684-6242-3

Kharjule, N. (2022). Metaverse gaming: The new-gen immersive gaming experiences. *Times of India*. Retrieved 07 February from https://timesofindia.indiatimes.com/readersblog/metaverseblockchain/metaverse-gaming-the-new-gen-immersive-gaming-experiences-48054/

Kim, G.-H. (2021). How Will Blockchain Technology Affect the Future of the Internet? Advances in Computer Science and Ubiquitous Computing.

Kumar, V. (2021). *Intelligent Marketing: Employing New-Age Technologies*. SAGE Publications Ltd. doi:10.4135/9789354792984

Lacity, M. C., Lupien, S. C., & Long, C. (2022). *Blockchain Fundamentals for Web 3.0*. Epic Books. https://books.google.co.uk/books?id=htmPEAAAQBAJ

Lesavre, L., Varin, P., Mell, P., Davidson, M., & Shook, J. (2019). *A taxonomic approach to understanding emerging blockchain identity management systems*. arXiv preprint arXiv:1908.00929.

Li, W., Yigitcanlar, T., Erol, I., & Liu, A. (2021). Motivations, barriers and risks of smart home adoption: From systematic literature review to conceptual framework. *Energy Research & Social Science, 80*, 102211. doi:10.1016/j.erss.2021.102211

Lim, W. Y. B., Xiong, Z., Niyato, D., Cao, X., Miao, C., Sun, S., & Yang, Q. (2022). Realizing the Metaverse with Edge Intelligence: A Match Made in Heaven. *IEEE Wireless Communications*, 1–9. doi:10.1109/MWC.018.2100716

Mahmoud, A. B. (2015). E-mail Advertising in Syria: Assessing Beliefs, Attitudes, and Behaviors. *Journal of Promotion Management, 21*(6), 649–665. doi:10.1080/10496491.2015.1055044

Mahmoud, A. B. (2021). Like a Cog in a Machine. In C. Machado & J. P. Davim (Eds.), *Advances in Intelligent, Flexible, and Lean Management and Engineering* (pp. 1–20). IGI Global. doi:10.4018/978-1-7998-5768-6.ch001

Mahmoud, A. B., Ball, J., Rubin, D., Fuxman, L., Mohr, I., Hack-Polay, D., Grigoriou, N., & Wakibi, A. (2021). Pandemic pains to Instagram gains! COVID-19 perceptions effects on behaviours towards fashion brands on Instagram in Sub-Saharan Africa: Tech-native vs non-native generations. *Journal of Marketing Communications*, 1–25. doi:10.1080/13527266.2021.1971282

Mahmoud, A. B., Berman, A., Tehseen, S., & Hack-Polay, D. (2022). Modelling Socio-Digital Customer Relationship Management in the Hospitality Sector During the Pandemic Time. In P. Keikhosrokiani (Ed.), *Handbook of Research on Consumer Behavior Change and Data Analytics in the Socio-Digital Era* (pp. 169–191). IGI Global. doi:10.4018/978-1-6684-4168-8.ch008

Mahmoud, A. B., Grigoriou, N., Fuxman, L., Hack-Polay, D., Mahmoud, F. B., Yafi, E., & Tehseen, S. (2019). Email is evil! *Journal of Research in Interactive Marketing*, *13*(2), 227–248. doi:10.1108/JRIM-09-2018-0112

Mahmoud, A. B., Hack-Polay, D., Grigoriou, N., Mohr, I., & Fuxman, L. (2021). A generational investigation and sentiment and emotion analyses of female fashion brand users on Instagram in Sub-Saharan Africa. *Journal of Brand Management*, *28*(5), 526–544. doi:10.105741262-021-00244-8

Mahmoud, A. B., Tehseen, S., & Fuxman, L. (2020). The Dark Side of Artificial Intelligence in Retail Innovation. In E. Pantano (Ed.), *Retail Futures* (pp. 165–180). Emerald Publishing Limited. doi:10.1108/978-1-83867-663-620201019

Minevich, M. (2022). The Metaverse And Web3 Creating Value In The Future Digital Economy. *Forbes*. Retrieved 25 February from https://www.forbes.com/sites/markminevich/2022/06/17/the-metaverse-and-web3-creating-value-in-the-future-digital-economy/

Miyachi, K., & Mackey, T. K. (2021). hOCBS: A privacy-preserving blockchain framework for healthcare data leveraging an on-chain and off-chain system design. *Information Processing & Management*, *58*(3), 102535. doi:10.1016/j.ipm.2021.102535

Mohr, I., Fuxman, L., & Mahmoud, A. B. (2022a). Fashion Resale Behaviours and Technology Disruption: An In-depth Review. In P. Keikhosrokiani (Ed.), *Consumer Behavior Change and Data Analytics in the Socio-Digital Era*. IGI Global. doi:10.4018/978-1-6684-4168-8.ch015

Mohr, I., Fuxman, L., & Mahmoud, A. B. (2022b). Fashion Resale Behaviours and Technology Disruption: An In-Depth Review. In P. Keikhosrokiani (Ed.), *Handbook of Research on Consumer Behavior Change and Data Analytics in the Socio-Digital Era* (pp. 351–373). IGI Global. doi:10.4018/978-1-6684-4168-8.ch015

Morning Consult. (2022a). *Share of internet users in the United States who are interested in using the metaverse as of March 2022, by gender* [Graph]. Statista. Retrieved 03 February from https://www-statista-com.jerome.stjohns.edu/statistics/1302575/us-adults-using-on-the-metaverse-by-gender/

Morning Consult. (2022b). *Share of internet users in the United States who would be interested in creating an avatar for the metaverse as of March 2022, by generation* [Graph]. Statista. Retrieved 03 February from https://www-statista-com.jerome.stjohns.edu/statistics/1302449/us-adults-creating-an-avatar-for-the-metaverse-generation/

Muralidharan, S., & Ko, H. (2019). An InterPlanetary File System (IPFS) based IoT framework. *2019 IEEE International Conference on Consumer Electronics (ICCE).*

Murray, A., Kim, D., & Combs, J. (2022). The promise of a better internet: What is web 3.0 and what are we building? *SSRN.*

Netcore Cloud. (2021). *Online shopping conversion rate in select verticals before and after offering personalized shopping experience in the United States in 2021* [Graph]. Statista. Retrieved 07 February from https://www-statista-com.jerome.stjohns.edu/statistics/1300238/conversion-rates-before-after-personalization-segment/

Nkosinkulu, Z. (2023). Humanities in the Age of Blockchain Technology and Web 3.0. In J. Tatlock (Ed.), *Shaping Online Spaces Through Online Humanities Curricula* (pp. 208–225). IGI Global. doi:10.4018/978-1-6684-4055-1.ch010

Nwafor, E. I. (2021). The Effectiveness of Blockchain Smart Contracts in Reshaping the Business Landscape in Nigeria. *Business Law Review*, 195-200. https://www.kluwerlawonline.com/api/Product/CitationPDFURL?file=Journals\BULA\BULA2021027.pdf

Patel, A., & Jain, S. (2021). Present and future of semantic web technologies: A research statement. *International Journal of Computers and Applications*, *43*(5), 413–422. doi:10.1080/1206212X.2019.1570666

Peres, R., Schreier, M., Schweidel, D. A., & Sorescu, A. (2022). Blockchain meets marketing: Opportunities, threats, and avenues for future research. *International Journal of Research in Marketing.*

Peters, G. W., & Panayi, E. (2016). Understanding Modern Banking Ledgers Through Blockchain Technologies: Future of Transaction Processing and Smart Contracts on the Internet of Money. In P. Tasca, T. Aste, L. Pelizzon, & N. Perony (Eds.), *Banking Beyond Banks and Money: A Guide to Banking Services in the Twenty-First Century* (pp. 239–278). Springer International Publishing. doi:10.1007/978-3-319-42448-4_13

Plechatá, A., Makransky, G., & Böhm, R. (2022). Can extended reality in the metaverse revolutionise health communication? *NPJ Digital Medicine*, *5*(1), 132. doi:10.103841746-022-00682-x PMID:36056245

Read, S. (2022). *How many consumers are shopping in virtual reality and what can it offer them?* World Economic Forum. Retrieved 07 Februrary from https://www.weforum.org/agenda/2022/08/virtual-reality-shopping-retail/

Rowland, A., Folmer, E., & Beek, W. (2020). Towards Self-Service GIS—Combining the Best of the Semantic Web and Web GIS. *ISPRS International Journal of Geo-Information*, *9*(12), 753. doi:10.3390/ijgi9120753

Salar, H. C., Başarmak, U., & Sezgin, M. E. (2023). Educational Integration of the Metaverse Environment in the Context of Web 3.0 Technologies: A Critical Overview of Planning, Implementation, and Evaluation. In G. Durak & S. Cankaya (Eds.), *Shaping the Future of Online Learning: Education in the Metaverse* (pp. 154–173). IGI Global. doi:10.4018/978-1-6684-6513-4.ch009

Santana, C., & Albareda, L. (2022). Blockchain and the emergence of Decentralized Autonomous Organizations (DAOs): An integrative model and research agenda. *Technological Forecasting and Social Change, 182,* 121806. doi:10.1016/j.techfore.2022.121806

Saqib, N. A., Salam, A. A., Atta Ur, R., & Dash, S. (2021). Reviewing risks and vulnerabilities in web 2.0 for matching security considerations in web 3.0. *Journal of Discrete Mathematical Sciences and Cryptography, 24*(3), 809–825. doi:10.1080/09720529.2020.1857903

Solakis, K., Katsoni, V., Mahmoud, A. B., & Grigoriou, N. (2022). Factors affecting value co-creation through artificial intelligence in tourism: A general literature review. *Journal of Tourism Futures.* doi:10.1108/JTF-06-2021-0157

Sortlist. (2022a). *Did the pandemic accelerate metaverse technology?* [Graph]. Statista. Retrieved 18 February from https://www-statista-com.jerome.stjohns.edu/statistics/1302264/metaverse-acceleration-due-to-covid-19/?locale=en

Sortlist. (2022b). *What are your main doubts regarding the metaverse?* [Graph]. Statista. Retrieved 18 February from https://www-statista-com.jerome.stjohns.edu/statistics/1302221/metaverse-project-doubt-businesses/?locale=en

Steemit. (2023). *Main page.* Steemit Inc. Retrieved 18 February from https://steemit.com/

Stockburger, L., Kokosioulis, G., Mukkamala, A., Mukkamala, R. R., & Avital, M. (2021). Blockchain-enabled decentralized identity management: The case of self-sovereign identity in public transportation. *Blockchain: Research and Applications, 2*(2), 100014.

Sung, C. S., & Park, J. Y. (2021). Understanding of blockchain-based identity management system adoption in the public sector. *Journal of Enterprise Information Management, 34*(5), 1481–1505. doi:10.1108/JEIM-12-2020-0532

Tan, T. F., Li, Y., Lim, J. S., Gunasekeran, D. V., Teo, Z. L., Ng, W. Y., & Ting, D. S. W. (2022). Metaverse and Virtual Health Care in Ophthalmology: Opportunities and Challenges. *Asia-Pacific Journal of Ophthalmology, 11*(3), 237–246. doi:10.1097/APO.0000000000000537 PMID:35772084

Templier, M., & Paré, G. (2015). A framework for guiding and evaluating literature reviews. *Communications of the Association for Information Systems, 37*(1), 6. doi:10.17705/1CAIS.03706

The Economist. (2022). From shared virtual experience to real value. *The Economist.* Retrieved 28 January from https://events.economist.com/metaverse/

Xian, Z., Keikhosrokiani, P., XinYing, C., & Li, Z. (2022). An RFM Model Using K-Means Clustering to Improve Customer Segmentation and Product Recommendation. In P. Keikhosrokiani (Ed.), Handbook of Research on Consumer Behavior Change and Data Analytics in the Socio-Digital Era (pp. 124-145). IGI Global. doi:10.4018/978-1-6684-4168-8.ch006

Xu, M., Ren, X., Niyato, D., Kang, J., Qiu, C., Xiong, Z., Wang, X., & Leung, V. (2022). *When Quantum Information Technologies Meet Blockchain in Web 3.0.* arXiv preprint arXiv:2211.15941.

Yli-Huumo, J., Ko, D., Choi, S., Park, S., & Smolander, K. (2016). Where is current research on blockchain technology?—A systematic review. *PLoS One, 11*(10), e0163477. doi:10.1371/journal.pone.0163477 PMID:27695049

Zallio, M., & Clarkson, P. J. (2022). Designing the metaverse: A study on inclusion, diversity, equity, accessibility and safety for digital immersive environments. *Telematics and Informatics, 75*, 101909. doi:10.1016/j.tele.2022.101909

Compilation of References

3D Metaverse. (2022). *2B3D Metaverse*. 2B3D Metaverse. https://2b3d.com/

Abadah, M. S. K., Keikhosrokiani, P., & Zhao, X. (2023). Analytics of Public Reactions to the COVID-19 Vaccine on Twitter Using Sentiment Analysis and Topic Modelling. In D. Valle-Cruz, N. Plata-Cesar, & J. L. González-Ruíz (Eds.), *Handbook of Research on Applied Artificial Intelligence and Robotics for Government Processes* (pp. 156–188). IGI Global. doi:10.4018/978-1-6684-5624-8.ch008

Abdul Aziz, M. N., Harun, S., Baharom, M., & Kamaruddin, N. (2020). The Evolution of The Technology Acceptance Model (TAM). 242.

Abdul Mutalib, N., & Mohd Nor, N. A. (2021). Teaching literature studies in universities and challenges Malaysian students face in IR4.0. *International Journal of Academic Research in Business & Social Sciences*, *11*(3), 76–88.

Abdullah, M. N., & Othman, N. (2017). Multi-culturalism and diversity in Malaysian education. In J. Zajda, S. Majhanovich, & V. Rust (Eds.), *Education and social transition: societal change, public policy and curriculum development* (pp. 327–342). Springer.

Abed, S. S. (2020). Social commerce adoption using TOE framework: An empirical investigation of Saudi Arabian SMEs. *International Journal of Information Management*, *53*(March), 102118. doi:10.1016/j.ijinfomgt.2020.102118

Abu Bakar, A. R., Ahmsad, S. Z., & Ahmad, N. (2019). SME social media use: A study of predictive factors in the United Arab Emirates. *Global Business and Organizational Excellence*, *38*(5), 53–68. doi:10.1002/joe.21951

Abu Madi, A., Ayoubi, R. M., & Alzbaidi, M. (2022). Spotting the Critical Success Factors of Enterprise Resource Planning Implementation in the Context of Public Higher Education Sector. *International Journal of Public Administration*, 1–17. Advance online publication. doi:10.1080/01900692.2022.2085300

Abubakre, M., Zhou, Y., & Zhou, Z. (2022). The impact of information technology culture and personal innovativeness in information technology on digital entrepreneurship success. *Information Technology & People*, *35*(1), 204–231. doi:10.1108/ITP-01-2020-0002

Aburbeian, A. M., Owda, A. Y., & Owda, M. (2022). A Technology Acceptance Model Survey of the Metaverse Prospects. *AI*, *3*(2), 285–302. doi:10.3390/ai3020018

Adner, R., & Kapoor, R. (2010). Value creation in innovation ecosystems: How the structure of technological interdependence affects firm performance in new technology generations. *Strategic Management Journal*, *31*(3), 306–333. doi:10.1002mj.821

Aebersold, M., Voepel-Lewis, T., Cherara, L., Weber, M., Khouri, C., Levine, R., & Tait, A. R. (2018). Interactive anatomy-augmented virtual simulation training. *Clinical Simulation in Nursing*, *15*, 34–41. doi: 10.1016/j.ecns.2017.09.008

Agarwal, R., & Karahanna, E. (2000). Time flies when you're having fun: Cognitive absorption and beliefs about information technology usage. *Management Information Systems Quarterly, 24*(4), 665–694. doi:10.2307/3250951

Aghion, P. J. (2018). Artificial intelligence and economic growth. In *The economics of artificial intelligence: An agenda* (pp. 237–282). University of Chicago Press.

Agnusdei, G. P., Elia, V., & Gnoni, M. G. (2021). A classification proposal of digital twin applications in the safety domain. *Computers & Industrial Engineering, 154*, 107137. doi:10.1016/j.cie.2021.107137

Ahmed, A., Moncey, A., Mohan, M., Cyriac, N. T., Ali, S. A., Mariam, S., Lyu, M., & Baskaran, K. (2020). Journey of education technology towards innovation. *2020 Advances in Science and Engineering Technology International Conferences (ASET)*. 10.1109/ASET48392.2020.9118334

Ahmed, A. L., & Kassem, M. (2018). A unified BIM adoption taxonomy: Conceptual development, empirical validation and application. *Automation in Construction, 96*, 103–127. doi:10.1016/j.autcon.2018.08.017

Ahn, S., Kim, J., & Kim, J. (2022). The Bifold Triadic Relationships Framework: A Theoretical Primer for Advertising Research in the Metaverse. *Journal of Advertising, 51*(5), 592–607. doi:10.1080/00913367.2022.2111729

Ahuja, A. S., Polascik, B. W., Doddapaneni, D., Byrnes, E. S., & Sridhar, J. (2023). The Digital Metaverse: Applications in Artificial Intelligence, Medical Education, and Integrative Health. In Integrative Medicine Research (Vol. 12, Issue 1). Korea Institute of Oriental Medicine. doi:10.1016/j.imr.2022.100917

Ahuja, R., Jain, M., Sawhney, A., & Arif, M. (2016). Adoption of BIM by architectural firms in India: Technology–organization–environment perspective. *Architectural Engineering and Design Management, 12*(4), 311–330. doi:10.1080/17452007.2016.1186589

Ajina, A. S. (2019). The perceived value of social media marketing: An empirical study of online word of mouth in Saudi Arabian context. *Entrepreneurship and Sustainability Issues, 6*(3), 1512–1527. doi:10.9770/jesi.2019.6.3(32)

Ajzen, I. (1991). The theory of planned behaviour. *Organizational Behavior and Human Decision Processes, 50*(2), 179–211. doi:10.1016/0749-5978(91)90020-T

Akalın, B. (2020). Sağlikta dijitalleşme ve yapay zekâ. *SDÜ Sağlık Yönetimi Dergisi, 2*(2), 128–137.

Akkus, H. T., Gursoy, S., Dogan, M., & Demir, A. B. Metaverse and Metaverse Cryptocurrencies (Meta Coins): Bubbles or Future?. *Journal of Economics Finance and Accounting, 9*(1), 22-29. doi:10.17261/Pressacademia.2022.1542

Akour, I. A., Al-Maroof, R. S., Alfaisal, R., & Salloum, S. A. (2022). A conceptual framework for determining metaverse adoption in higher institutions of gulf area: An empirical study using hybrid SEM-ANN approach. *Computers and Education: Artificial Intelligence, 3*, 100052.

Akour, I. A., Al-Maroof, R. S., Alfaisal, R., & Salloum, S. A. (2022). A conceptual framework for determining metaverse adoption in higher institutions of gulf area: An empirical study using hybrid SEM-ANN approach. *Computers and Education: Artificial Intelligence, 3*.

Akour, I. A., Al-Maroof, R. S., Alfaisal, R., & Salloum, S. A. (2022). A conceptual framework for determining metaverse adoption in higher institutions of gulf area: An empirical study using hybrid SEM-ANN approach. *Computers and Education: Artificial Intelligence, 3*, 100052. Advance online publication. doi:10.1016/j.caeai.2022.100052

Al Mamun, M. H., & Keikhosrokiani, P. (2022). Predicting onset (type-2) of diabetes from medical records using binary class classification. In P. Keikhosrokiani (Ed.), *Big Data Analytics for Healthcare* (pp. 301–312). Academic Press., https://doi.org/https://doi.org/10.1016/B978-0-323-91907-4.00012-1

al Mamun, M. H., Keikhosrokiani, P., Asl, M. P., Anuar, N. A. N., Hadi, N. H. A., & Humida, T. (2022). Sentiment Analysis of the Harry Potter Series Using a Lexicon-Based Approach. In P. Keikhosrokiani & M. Pourya Asl (Eds.), *Handbook of Research on Opinion Mining and Text Analytics on Literary Works and Social Media* (pp. 263–291). IGI Global. doi:10.4018/978-1-7998-9594-7.ch011

Alaba, O., Abass, O., & Igwe, E. (2022). Mobile Learning via Mobile Devices in Nigeria Higher Education: Usage Analysis Based on Utaut Model. *The Journal of the Southern Association for Information Systems*, *9*(1), 64–80. doi:10.17705/3JSIS.00022

Al-Alawi, A. I., & Al-Ali, F. M. (2015). Factors affecting e-commerce adoption in SMEs in the GCC: An empirical study of Kuwait. *Research Journal of Information Technology*, *7*(1), 1–21. doi:10.3923/rjit.2015.1.21

AlArabia News. (2022). *UAE sets up economy ministry in the metaverse.* Retrieved from: https://english.alarabiya.net/News/gulf/2022/10/03/UAE-sets-up-economy-ministry-in-the-metaverse

Alawadhi, M., Alhumaid, K., Almarzooqi, S. Sh. A., Aburayya, A., Salloum, S. A., & Almesmari, W. (2022). Factors Affecting Medical Students. *Acceptance of the Metaverse System in Medical Training in the United Arab Emirates*, *25.* Advance online publication. doi:10.11576eejph

Albanesius, C. (2012). Google 'project glass' replaces the smartphone with glasses. *PC Mag*, 4.

Alderete, M. V. (2019). Electronic commerce contribution to the SME performance in manufacturing firms: A structural equation model [Contribución del comercio electrónico al desempeño de las PyMEs industriales: Un modelo structural]. *Contaduría y Administración*, *64*(4), 1–24.

Alfaisal, R., Hashim, H., & Azizan, U. H. (2022). Metaverse system adoption in education: a systematic literature review. *Journal of Computers in Education.* doi:10.1007/s40692-022-00256-6

Al-Fraihat, D., Joy, M., Masa'deh, R., & Sinclair, J. (2020). Evaluating E-learning systems success: An empirical study. *Computers in Human Behavior*, *102*, 67–86. doi:10.1016/j.chb.2019.08.004

Al-Haj, H. (2018). Reading literature in a multicultural society: Cultural sensitivity and literary appreciation. *Intercultural Education*, *29*(3), 297–309.

Allam, Z., Sharifi, A., Bibri, S. E., Jones, D. S., & Krogstie, J. (2022). The Metaverse as a virtual form of smart cities: Opportunities and challenges for environmental, economic, and social sustainability in urban futures. *Smart Cities*, *5*(3), 771–801. doi:10.3390martcities5030040

Almaiah, M. A., Alhumaid, K., Aldhuhoori, A., Alnazzawi, N., Aburayya, A., Alfaisal, R., Salloum, S. A., Lutfi, A., Al Mulhem, A., Alkhdour, T., Awad, A. B., & Shehab, R. (2022). Factors Affecting the Adoption of Digital Information Technologies in Higher Education: An Empirical Study. *Electronics (Switzerland)*, *11*(21), 3572. Advance online publication. doi:10.3390/electronics11213572

Almarzouqi, A., Aburayya, A., & Salloum, S. A. (2022). Prediction of User's Intention to Use Metaverse System in Medical Education: A Hybrid SEM-ML Learning Approach. *IEEE Access: Practical Innovations, Open Solutions*, *10*, 43421–43434. doi:10.1109/ACCESS.2022.3169285

Alon, I. Q., Qi, M., & Sadowski, R. J. (2001). Forecasting aggregate retail sales: A comparison of artificial neural networks and traditional methods. *Journal of Retailing and Consumer Services*, *8*(3), 147–156. doi:10.1016/S0969-6989(00)00011-4

Alpala, L., Quiroga-Parra, D., Torres, J., & Peluffo-Ordóñez, D. (2022). Smart Factory Using Virtual Reality and Online Multi-User: Towards a Metaverse for Experimental Frameworks. *Applied Sciences (Basel, Switzerland)*, *12*(12), 6258. doi:10.3390/app12126258

Alqahtani, A. Y., & Rajkhan, A. A. (2020). E-learning critical success factors during the covid-19 pandemic: A comprehensive analysis of e-learning managerial perspectives. *Education Sciences*, *10*(9), 1–16. doi:10.3390/educsci10090216

Al-Rahmi, W. M., Yahaya, N., Aldraiweesh, A. A., Alamri, M. M., Aljarboa, N. A., Alturki, U., & Aljeraiwi, A. A. (2019). Integrating Technology Acceptance Model with Innovation Diffusion Theory: An Empirical Investigation on Students' Intention to Use E-Learning Systems. *IEEE Access: Practical Innovations, Open Solutions*, *7*, 26797–26809. doi:10.1109/ACCESS.2019.2899368

Al-rawashdeh, M., Keikhosrokiani, P., Belaton, B., Alawida, M., & Zwiri, A. (2022). IoT Adoption and Application for Smart Healthcare: A Systematic Review. *Sensors (Basel)*, *22*(14), 5377. Advance online publication. doi:10.339022145377 PMID:35891056

AlSharji, A., Ahmad, S. Z., & Abu Bakar, A. R. (2018). Understanding social media adoption in SMEs: Empirical evidence from the United Arab Emirates. *Journal of Entrepreneurship in Emerging Economies*, *10*(2), 302–328. doi:10.1108/JEEE-08-2017-0058

Alzahrani, A. I., Mahmud, I., Ramayah, T., Alfarraj, O., & Alalwan, N. (2017). Extending the theory of planned behavior (TPB) to explain online game playing among Malaysian undergraduate students. *Telematics and Informatics*, *34*(4), 239–251. doi:10.1016/j.tele.2016.07.001

Amazon.com. (2023). *Virtual Try On: Fashion - Amazon.co.uk*. Amazon.com, Inc. Retrieved 18 Februrary from https://www.amazon.co.uk/b?ie=UTF8&node=29542815031

American Marketing Association. (2017). Retrieved from https://www.ama.org/the-definition-of-marketing-what-is-marketing/

Amores, J., Hernandez, J., Dementyev, A., Wang, X., & Maes, P. (2018, July). Bioessence: a wearable olfactory display that monitors cardio-respiratory information to support mental wellbeing. In *2018 40th Annual International Conference of the IEEE Engineering in Medicine and Biology Society (EMBC)* (pp. 5131-5134). IEEE.

Anderson, J., & Rainie, L. (2022). *The metaverse in 2040*. Pew Research Center.

Anderson, K. (2016). Digital media in the literature classroom: A critical evaluation. *English Teaching*, *15*(1), 7–23. doi:10.1108/ETPC-10-2014-0081

Ando, Y., Thawonmas, R., & Rinaldo, F. (2013). Inference of Viewed Exhibits in a Metaverse Museum. *2013 International Conference on Culture and Computing*, 218–219. 10.1109/CultureComputing.2013.73

André, Q. C., Carmon, Z., Wertenbroch, K., Crum, A., Frank, D., Goldstein, W., Huber, J., van Boven, L., Weber, B., & Yang, H. (2018). Consumer choice and autonomy in the age of artificial intelligence and big data. *Customer Needs and Solutions*, *5*(1), 28–37. doi:10.100740547-017-0085-8

Anifa, M., P, M. J., Hack-Polay, D., Mahmoud, A. B., & Grigoriou, N. (2022). Segmenting the Retail Customers: A Multi-Model Approach of Clustering in Machine Learning. In P. Keikhosrokiani (Ed.), Handbook of Research on Consumer Behavior Change and Data Analytics in the Socio-Digital Era (pp. 25-50). IGI Global. doi:10.4018/978-1-6684-4168-8.ch002

Anıl, F., & Alankuş, Z. (2022). Metaverse Evreninde Pazarlama: 7P Pazarlama Karması Üzerinden Bir Değerlendirme. *Uluslararası Halkla İlişkiler ve Reklam Çalışmaları Dergisi*, *5*(1), 134–168.

Ante, L., Fischer, C., & Strehle, E. (2022). A bibliometric review of research on digital identity: Research streams, influential works and future research paths. *Journal of Manufacturing Systems*, *62*, 523–538. doi:10.1016/j.jmsy.2022.01.005

Ariffin, N. M., & Rahman, N. A. (2019). Challenges of English language teaching and learning in Malaysia. *English Language Teaching*, *12*(1), 55–63.

Ariff, M. S. M., Sylvester, M., Zakuan, N., Ismail, K., & Ali, K. M. (2014). Consumer perceived risk, attitude and online shopping behavior : Empirical evidence from Malaysia. *Proceedings of the 2014 International Conference on Manufacturing, Optimization, Industrial and Material Engineering*.

Armstrong, P. (2023). *Disruptive Technologies: A Framework to Understand, Evaluate and Respond to Digital Disruption*. Kogan Page. https://books.google.co.uk/books?id=7oChEAAAQBAJ

Arnold, G., Spence, C., & Auvray, M. (2017). A unity of the self or a multiplicity of locations? How the graphesthesia task sheds light on the role of spatial perspectives in bodily self-consciousness. *Consciousness and Cognition*, *56*, 100–114. doi:10.1016/j.concog.2017.06.012 PMID:28712507

Arpaci, I., Karatas, K., Kusci, I., & Al-Emran, M. (2022). Understanding the social sustainability of the Metaverse by integrating UTAUT2 and big five personality traits: A hybrid SEM-ANN approach. *Technology in Society*, *71*, 102120. Advance online publication. doi:10.1016/j.techsoc.2022.102120

Article, R., & Thomason, J. (n.d.). *Journal of Metaverse MetaHealth-How will the Metaverse Change Health Care?* https://www.influencive.com/flickplays-3d-social-media-platform-

Asemi, A., Ko, A., & Nowkarizi, M. (2021). Intelligent libraries: A review on expert systems, artificial intelligence, and robot. *Library Hi Tech*, *39*(2), 412–434. doi:10.1108/LHT-02-2020-0038

Ashaye, O. R., Mahmoud, A. B., Munna, A. S., & Ali, N. (2023). The role of social media engagement and emotional intelligence in successful employment. *Higher Education, Skills and Work-Based Learning*. doi:10.1108/HESWBL-07-2022-0158

Ashok, S., & Baskaran, K. (2022). The prominence of corporate governance in banking sector with reference to UAE. In *Pervasive Computing and Social Networking* (pp. 417–430). Springer Singapore. doi:10.1007/978-981-16-5640-8_33

Ashrafuzzaman, M., Mahmudul Haque Milu, M., Anjum, A., Khanam, F., & Asadur Rahman, M. (2022). Big data analytics techniques for healthcare. In P. Keikhosrokiani (Ed.), *Big Data Analytics for Healthcare* (pp. 49–62). Academic Press.

Ashworth, S. J. (2020). *The evolution of facility management (FM) in the building information modelling (BIM) process: An opportunity to use critical success factors (CSF) for optimising built assets*. Academic Press.

Asri, M. A. Z. B. M., Keikhosrokiani, P., & Asl, M. P. (2022). Opinion Mining Using Topic Modeling: A Case Study of Firoozeh Dumas's Funny in Farsi in Goodreads. In F. Saeed, F. Mohammed, & F. Ghaleb (Eds.), *Advances on Intelligent Informatics and Computing* (pp. 219–230). Springer International Publishing. doi:10.1007/978-3-030-98741-1_19

Atıcı, U., Adem, A., Şenol, M. B., & Dağdeviren, M. (2022). A comprehensive decision framework with interval valued type-2 fuzzy AHP for evaluating all critical success factors of e-learning platforms. *Education and Information Technologies*, *27*(5), 5989–6014. doi:10.100710639-021-10834-3 PMID:35095324

Avellaneda, O., Bachmann, A., Barbir, A., Brenan, J., Dingle, P., Duffy, K. H., Maler, E., Reed, D., & Sporny, M. (2019). Decentralized Identity: Where Did It Come From and Where Is It Going? *IEEE Communications Standards Magazine*, *3*(4), 10–13. doi:10.1109/MCOMSTD.2019.9031542

Avila, A. (2022). Prophetic Churches for the Metaverse: Communities who sing the melody of hope. *Indonesian Journal of Theology*, *10*(2), 209–230. doi:10.46567/ijt.v10i2.250

Awasthi, S., Ahuja, R., & Sharma, S. (2022). Leadership and Emotional Intelligence: A Comparative Study. In D. Bathla & A. Singh (Eds.), *Applying Metalytics to Measure Customer Experience in the Metaverse* (pp. 99–110). IGI Global. doi:10.4018/978-1-6684-6133-4.ch009

Azeem, M., Salfi, N. A., & Dogar, A. H. (2012). Usage of NVivo software for qualitative data analysis. *Academic Research International*, 2(1), 262–266. doi:10.4135/9781412957397.n71

Azuma, R. T. (1997). A survey of augmented reality. *Presence (Cambridge, Mass.)*, 6(4), 355–385. doi:10.1162/pres.1997.6.4.355

Babu, M. U. A., & Mohan, P. (2022, June 22-24). Impact of the Metaverse on the Digital Future: People's Perspective. *2022 7th International Conference on Communication and Electronics Systems (ICCES)*. doi:10.1080/14794713.2021.2024398

Baghalzadeh Shishehgarkhaneh, M., Keivani, A., Moehler, R. C., Jelodari, N., & Roshdi Laleh, S. (2022). Internet of Things (IoT), Building Information Modeling (BIM), and Digital Twin (DT) in Construction Industry: A Review, Bibliometric, and Network Analysis. In Buildings (Vol. 12, Issue 10). MDPI. doi:10.3390/buildings12101503

Baier, L. K., Kühl, N., Schüritz, R., & Satzger, G. (2020). Will the customers be happy? Identifying unsatisfied customers from service encounter data. *Journal of Service Management*, 32(2), 265–288. doi:10.1108/JOSM-06-2019-0173

Bal, F. (2022). Metaverse'de Duygusal ve İkili İlişkiler. A. Güven & M. S. Tam (Ed.), Alternatif Dijital Evren Metaverse-I Kavramsal Tartışmalar, Sosyoloji, Psikoloji, Sanat ve Etik (123-138). Necmettin Erbakan Üniversitesi Yayınları

Bale, A. S., Ghorpade, N., Hashim, M. F., Vaishnav, J., & Almaspoor, Z. (2022). A Comprehensive Study on Metaverse and Its Impacts on Humans. In *Advances in Human-Computer Interaction* (Vol. 2022). Hindawi Limited. doi:10.1155/2022/3247060

Ball, M. (2021). *Framework for the Metaverse*. Academic Press.

Ball, M. (2022). *The metaverse and how it will revolutionize everything*. Liveright Publishing.

Barbosa Escobar, F., Petit, O., & Velasco, C. (2021). Virtual terroir and the premium coffee experience. *Frontiers in Psychology*, 12, 586983. doi:10.3389/fpsyg.2021.586983 PMID:33815192

Barrera, K. G., & Shah, D. (2023). Marketing in the Metaverse: Conceptual understanding, framework, and research agenda. *Journal of Business Research*, 155, 113420. doi:10.1016/j.jbusres.2022.113420

Barwise, P., Elberse, A., & Hammond, K. (2002). *Marketing and the Internet: A research review*. London Business School. doi:10.4135/9781848608283.n22

Baskaran, K. (2019). An Interpretive Study of Customer Experience Management towards Online Shopping in UAE. *International Journal of Mechanical Engineering and Technology*, 10(02), 1071–1077. https://iaeme.com/MasterAdmin/Journal_uploads/IJMET/VOLUME_10_ISSUE_2/IJMET_10_02_112.pdf

Baskaran, K. (2019b). The impact of digital transformation in Singapore e-tail market. *International Journal of Innovative Technology and Exploring Engineering*, 8(11), 2320–2324. doi:10.35940/ijitee.I8046.0981119

Baskaran, K. (2022). E-Consumer Behavioral Analytics: Paradigm Shift in Online Purchase Decision Making. In P. Keikhosrokiani (Ed.), *Handbook of Research on Consumer Behavior Change and Data Analytics in the Socio-Digital Era* (pp. 192–209). IGI Global. doi:10.4018/978-1-6684-4168-8.ch009

Baskaran, K., & Rajavelu, S. (2020). Digital innovation in industry 4.0 era – rebooting UAE's retail. *2020 International Conference on Communication and Signal Processing (ICCSP)*. 10.1109/ICCSP48568.2020.9182301

Baskaran, K., & Vanithamani, M. R. (2014). E-Customers Attitude towards E-Store Information and Design Quality in India, Applied Research in Science, Engineering and Management. *Applied Research in Science, Engineering and Management. World Applied Sciences Journal*, 51–56. doi:10.5829/idosi.wasj.2014.31.arsem.555

Basu, T. (2021). *The metaverse has a groping problem already.* MIT Technology Review.

Batra, R., & Keller, K. L. (2016). Integrating Marketing Communications: New Findings, New Lessons, and New Ideas. *Journal of Marketing*, *80*(6), 122–145. doi:10.1509/jm.15.0419

Bec, A., Moyle, B., Schaffer, V., & Timms, K. (2021). Virtual reality and mixed reality for second chance tourism. *Tourism Management*, *83*, 104256. Advance online publication. doi:10.1016/j.tourman.2020.104256

Becker, V., Rauchenstein, F., & Sörös, G. (2020). Connecting and controlling appliances through wearable augmented reality. *Augment Hum Res*, *5*(1), 2. doi:10.100741133-019-0019-0

Belli, K., Akbaş, E., & Yazici, A. (2019). Activity learning from lifelogging images. *In International Conference on Artificial Intelligence and Soft Computing* (pp. 327-337). Springer, Cham.

Benmamoun, M., Singh, N., Lehnert, K., & Lee, S. B. (2018). Internationalization of e-commerce corporations (ECCs) Advanced vs emerging markets ECCs. *Multinational Business Review*. Retrieved from https://www.emeraldinsight.com/doi/abs/10.1108/MBR-02-2018-0010

Berg, C., Davidson, S., & Potts, J. (2019). Blockchain technology as economic infrastructure: Revisiting the electronic markets hypothesis. *Frontiers in Blockchain*, *2*, 22. doi:10.3389/fbloc.2019.00022

Berry, L. L., Carbone, L. P., & Haeckel, S. H. (2002). Managing the total customer experience. *MIT Sloan Management Review*, *43*(3), 85–89.

Berryman, D. R. (2012). Augmented reality: A review. *Medical Reference Services Quarterly*, *31*(2), 212–218. doi:10.1080/02763869.2012.670604 PMID:22559183

Bhat, J. R., AlQahtani, S. A., & Nekovee, M. (2023). FinTech enablers, use cases, and role of future internet of things. *Journal of King Saud University - Computer and Information Sciences*, *35*(1), 87–101. doi:10.1016/j.jksuci.2022.08.033

Bibri, S. (2022). The Social Shaping of the Metaverse as an Alternative to the Imaginaries of Data-Driven Smart Cities: A Study in Science, Technology, and Society. *Smart Cities*, *5*(3), 832–874. doi:10.3390martcities5030043

Bibri, S. E., & Allam, Z. (2022). The Metaverse as a virtual form of data-driven smart urbanism: On post-pandemic governance through the prism of the logic of surveillance capitalism. *Smart Cities*, *5*(2), 715–727. doi:10.3390martcities5020037

Bibri, S. E., Allam, Z., & Krogstie, J. (2022). The Metaverse as a virtual form of data-driven smart urbanism: Platformization and its underlying processes, institutional dimensions, and disruptive impacts. *Computers & Urban Society*, *2*(1), 1–22. doi:10.100743762-022-00051-0 PMID:35974838

Bilton, N. (2012). Behind the Google Goggles, virtual reality. *New York Times*, 22.

Bimber, O., & Raskar, R. (2005). *Spatial augmented reality: merging real and virtual worlds.* CRC press.

Bini, S. A. (2018). Artificial intelligence, machine learning, deep learning, and cognitive computing: What do these terms mean and how will they impact health care? *The Journal of Arthroplasty*, *33*(8), 2358–2361. doi:10.1016/j.arth.2018.02.067 PMID:29656964

Binti Rosli, N. H., & Keikhosrokiani, P. (2022). Big medical data mining system (BigMed) for the detection and classification of COVID-19 misinformation. In P. Keikhosrokiani (Ed.), *Big Data Analytics for Healthcare* (pp. 233–244). Academic Press. doi:10.1016/B978-0-323-91907-4.00014-5

Bi, S., Wang, C., Zhang, J., Huang, W., Wu, B., Gong, Y., & Ni, W. (2022). A Survey on Artificial Intelligence Aided Internet-of-Things Technologies in Emerging Smart Libraries. *Sensors (Basel)*, *22*(8), 2991. doi:10.339022082991 PMID:35458974

Blumler, J. G. (n.d.). *The role of theory in uses and gratifications studies*. Academic Press.

Bojic, L. (2022). Metaverse through the prism of power and addiction: what will happen when the virtual world becomes more attractive than reality? In European Journal of Futures Research (Vol. 10, Issue 1). Springer Science and Business Media Deutschland GmbH. doi:10.118640309-022-00208-4

Bolger, R. K. (2021). Finding wholes in the metaverse: Posthuman mystics as agents of evolutionary contextualization. *Religions*, *12*(9), 768. doi:10.3390/rel12090768

Bolluyt, J. (2015). *15 Ideas for Augmented Reality From Google-Backed Startup*. The Cheat Sheet.

Borr, M. L. (2015). Miller, M.D. (2014). Minds Online: Teaching Effectively with Technology. Cambridge, MA: Harvard University Press. ISBN: 978-0674368248. 279 pp. (hardcover). *Family and Consumer Sciences Research Journal*, *44*(2), 234–236. doi:10.1111/fcsr.12137

Boulos, M. N., Hetherington, L., & Wheeler, S. (2007). Second life: An overview of the potential of 3-D virtual worlds in medical and Health Education. *Health Information and Libraries Journal*, *24*(4), 233–245. doi:10.1111/j.1471-1842.2007.00733.x

Boursier, V., Gioia, F., & Griffiths, M. D. (2020). Objectified body consciousness, body image control in photos, and problematic social networking: The role of appearance control beliefs. *Frontiers in Psychology*, *11*, 147. doi:10.3389/fpsyg.2020.00147 PMID:32158409

Branca, G., Resciniti, R., & Loureiro, S.M.C. (2022). Virtual is so real! Consumers' evaluation of product packaging in virtual reality. *Psychology & Marketing*.

Branstetter, B. (2016). *Cardboard is everything Google Glass never was*. http://kernelmag. dailydot. com/issue-secti staff-editorials/13490/google-cardboard-review-plus

Braud, T., Zhou, P., Lee, L.-H., Wang, L., Xu, D., Lin, Z., Kumar, A., Bermejo, C., & Hui, P. (n.d.). *All One Needs to Know about Metaverse: A Complete Survey on Technological Singularity*. Virtual Ecosystem, and Research Agenda. doi:10.13140/RG.2.2.11200.05124/8

Brown, D. (2021, October 28). Big Tech wants to build the 'metaverse.' What on Earth does that mean? *The Seattle Times*. https://www.seattletimes.com/business/technology/big-tech-wants-to-build-the-metaverse-what-on-earth-does-that-mean/

Bryant, R., Katz, R. H., & Lazowska, E. D. (2008). *Big-data computing: creating revolutionary breakthroughs in commerce, science and society*. Academic Press.

Buabeng-Andoh, C. (2018). Predicting students' intention to adopt mobile learning. *Journal of Research in Innovative Teaching & Learning*, *11*(2), 178–191. doi:10.1108/JRIT-03-2017-0004

Buhalis, D., Lin, M., & Leung, D. (2022). Metaverse as a driver for customer experience and value co-creation: implications for hospitality and tourism management and marketing. *International Journal of Contemporary Hospitality Management*. doi:10.1108/IJCHM-05-2022-0631

Buhalis, D., Leung, D., & Lin, M. (2023). Metaverse as a disruptive technology revolutionising tourism management and marketing. *Tourism Management*, *97*(January), 104724. doi:10.1016/j.tourman.2023.104724

Built in. (2022). *Built in*. Built in.

Bullen, C. V., & Rockart, J. F. (1981). *A primer on critical success factors*. Academic Press.

Carayannis, E. G., & Morawska-Jancelewicz, J. (2022). The Futures of Europe: Society 5.0 and Industry 5.0 as Driving Forces of Future Universities. *Journal of the Knowledge Economy*, *13*(4), 3445–3471. doi:10.100713132-021-00854-2

Carr, A. R. (1999). *Predicting College of Agriculture professors' adoption of computers and distance education technologies for self-education and teaching at the University of Guadalajara*. Iowa State University.

Castro-Lopez, A., Cervero, A., Galve-González, C., Puente, J., & Bernardo, A. B. (2022). Evaluating critical success factors in the permanence in Higher Education using multi-criteria decision-making. *Higher Education Research & Development*, *41*(3), 628–646. doi:10.1080/07294360.2021.1877631

Caulfield, B. (2022, November 3). *What is the metaverse?* NVIDIA Blog. https://blogs.nvidia.com/blog/2021/08/10/what-is-the-metaverse/

Çelikkol, Ş. (2022). Metaverse Dünyasi'nin, Tüketici Satin Alma Davranişlari Açisindan Değerlendirilmesi. *İstanbul Kent Üniversitesi İnsan ve Toplum Bilimleri Dergisi*. 3 (1). 64-75.

Çelik, R. (2022). Metaverse Nedir? Kavramsal Değerlendirme ve Genel Bakış. *Balkan ve Yakın Doğu Sosyal Bilimler Dergisi*, *8*(1), 67–74.

Chaiya, C., & Ahmad, M. M. (2021). Success or failure of the thai higher education development—Critical factors in the policy process of quality assurance. *Sustainability (Switzerland)*, *13*(17), 9486. Advance online publication. doi:10.3390u13179486

Chalmers, D., Fisch, C., Matthews, R., Quinn, W., & Recker, J. (2022). Beyond the bubble: Will NFTs and digital proof of ownership empower creative industry entrepreneurs? *Journal of Business Venturing Insights*, *17*, e00309. doi:10.1016/j.jbvi.2022.e00309

Chang, E., Kim, H. T., & Yoo, B. (2020). Virtual Reality Sickness: A Review of Causes and Measurements. *International Journal of Human-Computer Interaction*, *36*(17), 1658–1682. doi:10.1080/10447318.2020.1778351

Chang, S., & Nam, K. (2021). Smart home adoption: The impact of user characteristics and differences in perception of benefits. *Buildings*, *11*(9), 393. doi:10.3390/buildings11090393

Chatterjee, S., Kar, A. K., & Gupta, M. P. (2018). Success of IoT in Smart Cities of India: An empirical analysis. *Government Information Quarterly*, *35*(3), 349–361. doi:10.1016/j.giq.2018.05.002

Chen, Y. (2022). *Research on the Communication of Sports Events in the Context of Metaverse*. Academic Press.

Chengoden, R. V.-T. (2022). *Cornell University*. Cornell University.

Chen, H. (2006). Flow on the net–detecting web users' positive effects and their flow states. *Computers in Human Behavior*, *22*(2), 221–233. doi:10.1016/j.chb.2004.07.001

Chen, H., Wigand, R. T., & Nilan, M. (2000). Exploring web users' optimal flow experiences. *Information Technology & People*, *13*(4), 263–281. doi:10.1108/09593840010359473

Chen, J. (2007). Flow in games (and everything else). *Communications of the ACM*, *50*(4), 31–34. doi:10.1145/1232743.1232769

Chen, X. (2020). Application of digital technology in literature teaching in the age of industry 4.0. In *2020 International Conference on Modern Educational Technology and Computer Science (METCS)* (pp. 248-252). IEEE.

Chen, Z. (2022). Exploring the application scenarios and issues facing Metaverse technology in education. *Interactive Learning Environments*, 1–13. Advance online publication. doi:10.1080/10494820.2022.2133148

Cheung, C. M. K., Risius, M., Lee, M. K. O., Wagner, C., Malik, O., Karhade, P., Kathuria, A., Jaiswal, A., & Yen, B. (n.d.). *Introduction to Adversarial Coordination in Collaboration and Social Media Systems Minitrack of the Collaboration Systems and Technologies Track.* https://hdl.handle.net/10125/79343

Chin, L. S., & Tan, C. Y. (2019). Multimodal pedagogy in the Malaysian ESL classroom: The role of digital technology in enhancing student literacy. *Malaysian Journal of Learning and Instruction*, *16*(1), 1–33.

Chinnamgari, S. K. (2019). *Machine Learning Projects: Implement supervised, unsupervised, and reinforcement learning techniques using R 3.5.* Packt Publishing Ltd.

Chittipaka, V., Kumar, S., Sivarajah, U., Bowden, J. L. H., & Baral, M. M. (2022). Blockchain Technology for Supply Chains operating in emerging markets: An empirical examination of technology-organization-environment (TOE) framework. *Annals of Operations Research*. Advance online publication. doi:10.100710479-022-04801-5

Choi, H. S., & Kim, S. (2017). A content service deployment plan for metaverse museum exhibitions—Centering on the combination of beacons and HMDs. *International Journal of Information Management*, *37*(1), 1519–1527. doi:10.1016/j.ijinfomgt.2016.04.017

Choi, R. Y., Coyner, A. S., Kalpathy-Cramer, J., Chiang, M. F., & Campbell, J. P. (2020). Introduction to Machine Learning, Neural Networks, and Deep Learning. *Translational Vision Science & Technology*, *9*(2), 14. doi:10.1167/tvst.9.2.14 PMID:32704420

Choudhary, V. V. (2022). *The metaverse: Gain insight into the exciting future of the internet* (Vol. 1). Vicky Choudhary.

Chua, R. Y. (2018). Diversity and inclusion in the classroom: A case study of cultural sensitivity in teaching literature. *Journal of Language, Identity, and Education*, *17*(5), 276–287.

Chu, K. E., Keikhosrokiani, P., & Asl, M. P. (2022). A Topic Modeling and Sentiment Analysis Model for Detection and Visualization of Themes in Literary Texts. *Pertanika Journal of Science & Technology*, *30*(4), 2535–2561. doi:10.47836/pjst.30.4.14

Chung, N., Tyan, I., & Chung, H. C. (2017). Social support and commitment within social networking site in tourism experience. *Sustainability*, *9*(11), 2102. doi:10.3390u9112102

Chu, S. C., & Choi, S. M. (2011). Electronic word-of-mouth in social networking sites: A cross-cultural study of the United States and China. *Journal of Global Marketing*, *24*(3), 263–281. doi:10.1080/08911762.2011.592461

Chylinski, M., Heller, J., Hilken, T., Keeling, D. I., Mahr, D., & de Ruyter, K. (2020). Augmented reality marketing: A technology-enabled approach to situated customer experience. [AMJ]. *Australasian Marketing Journal*, *28*(4), 374–384. doi:10.1016/j.ausmj.2020.04.004

Clark, J.-A., Liu, Y., & Isaias, P. (n.d.). Critical success factors for implementing learning analytics in higher education: A mixed-method inquiry. In Australasian Journal of Educational Technology (Vol. 2020, Issue 6). doi:10.14742/ajet.6164

Çöltekin, A., Lochhead, I., Madden, M., Christophe, S., Devaux, A., Pettit, C., Lock, O., Shukla, S., Herman, L., Stachoň, Z., Kubíček, P., Snopková, D., Bernardes, S., & Hedley, N. (2020). Extended reality in spatial sciences: A review of research challenges and future directions. *ISPRS International Journal of Geo-Information*, *9*(7), 439. doi:10.3390/ijgi9070439

Consultant, H. I. T. (2020). *HIT Consultant*. HIT Consultant.

Cordle, D., & Thompson, S. (2021). Teaching in the age of industry 4.0: Opportunities and challenges for literary studies. *College Literature*, *48*(2), 343–365.

Cortés, M. (2022). *Anàlisi i reflexions sobre el potencial impacte del metavers en el sector educatiu*. Academic Press.

Cowley, B., Charles, D., Black, M., & Hickey, R. (2008). Toward an understanding of flow in video games. *Computers in Entertainment*, *6*(2), 1–27. doi:10.1145/1371216.1371223

Criado, J. I., & Gil-Garcia, J. R. (2019). Creating public value through smart technologies and strategies: From digital services to artificial intelligence and beyond. *International Journal of Public Sector Management*, *32*(5), 438–450. doi:10.1108/IJPSM-07-2019-0178

Csikszentmihalyi, M. (2000). *Beyond boredom and anxiety*. Jossey-Bass. doi:10.2307/2065805

Cyriac, N. T., & Baskaran, K. (2020). A study on the effectiveness of non-monetary retention strategies in UAE. *2020 8ᵗʰ International Conference on Reliability, Infocom Technologies and Optimization (Trends and Future Directions) (ICRITO)*. 10.1109/ICRITO48877.2020.9197867

Cyriac, N. T., & Baskaran, K. (2021). Predictive Analytics in a Post Covid-19 World: India's Travel and Tourism Industry. *Proceedings of International Conference on Advances in Technology, Management & Education*. 10.1109/ICATME50232.2021.9732706

Dahan, N., Al-Razgan, M., Al-Laith, A., Alsoufi, M., Al-Asaly, M., & Alfakih, T. (2022). Metaverse Framework: A Case Study on E-Learning Environment (ELEM). *Electronics (Basel)*, *11*(10), 1616. doi:10.3390/electronics11101616

Darbinyan, R. (2022). Council Post: Virtual Shopping In The Metaverse: What Is It And How Will AI Make It Work. *Forbes*. Retrieved 28 January from https://www.forbes.com/sites/forbestechcouncil/2022/03/16/virtual-shopping-in-the-metaverse-what-is-it-and-how-will-ai-make-it-work/

Dastin, J., & Chmielewski, D. (2022, October 13). *Metaverse could accelerate manufacturing as well as social ills*. The Star. https://www.thestar.com.my/tech/tech-news/2022/10/13/metaverse-could-accelerate-manufacturing-as-well-as-social-ills

Davis, F. D., Bagozzi, R. P., & Warshaw, P. R. (1992). Extrinsic and intrinsic motivation to use computers in the workplace. *Journal of Applied Social Psychology*, *22*(14), 1111–1132. doi:10.1111/j.1559-1816.1992.tb00945.x

Decentraland. (2023). *Marketplace—land*. Decentraland. Retrieved 18 February from https://market.decentraland.org/lands

Deepak, R. K. (2009). *Marketing management*. Educreation Publishing.

De, F. (2023). Physical and digital worlds : On implications and opportunities of the 4th International Conference metaverse. *Procedia Computer Science*, *217*, 1744–1754. doi:10.1016/j.procs.2022.12.374

Delio, I. (2020). *Re-Enchanting the Earth: Why AI Needs Religion*. Orbis.

DeLone, W. H., & McLean, E. R. (2016). Information Systems Success Measurement. *Foundations and Trends® in Information Systems*, *2*(1), 1–116. doi:10.1561/2900000005

Delveinsight. (n.d.). *Delveinsight*. Delveinsight Website. https://delveinsight.com

Devi, M., Annamalai, M. A. R., & Veeramuthu, S. P. (2020). Literature education and industrial revolution 4.0. *Universal Journal of Educational Research*, *8*(3), 1027–1036. doi:10.13189/ujer.2020.080337

di Martino, B., Rak, M., Ficco, M., Esposito, A., Maisto, S. A., & Nacchia, S. (2018). Internet of things reference architectures, security and interoperability: A survey. In Internet of Things (Netherlands) (Vols. 1–2, pp. 99–112). Elsevier B.V. doi:10.1016/j.iot.2018.08.008

Di Martino, B., Rak, M., Ficco, M., Esposito, A., Maisto, S. A., & Nacchia, S. (2018). Internet of things reference architectures, security and interoperability: A survey. *Internet of Things, 1-2*, 99-112.

Díaz, J. E. M., Saldaña, C. A. D., & Avila, C. A. R. (2020). Virtual world as a resource for hybrid education. *International Journal of Emerging Technologies in Learning, 15*(15), 94–109. doi:10.3991/ijet.v15i15.13025

Dickey, M. D. (2005). Engaging by design: How engagement strategies in popular computer and video games can inform instructional design. *Educational Technology Research and Development, 53*(2), 67–83. doi:10.1007/BF02504866

Dietz, M., & Pernul, G. (2020). Digital twin: Empowering enterprises towards a system-of-systems approach. *Business & Information Systems Engineering, 62*(2), 179–184. doi:10.100712599-019-00624-0

Dionisio, J. D. N., III, W. G. B., & Gilbert, R. (2013). 3D virtual worlds and the metaverse: Current status and future possibilities. *ACM Computing Surveys (CSUR), 45*(3), 1-38. doi:10.1145/2480741.2480751

Dittenbach, M., Merkl, D., & Berger, H. (2003). A natural language query interface for tourism information. *ENTER 2003: 10th International Conference on Information Technologies in Tourism.* 10.1007/978-3-7091-6027-5_17

Divjak, B., Svetec, B., Horvat, D., & Kadoić, N. (2022). Assessment validity and learning analytics as prerequisites for ensuring student-centred learning design. *British Journal of Educational Technology.* Advance online publication. doi:10.1111/bjet.13290

Doko, E. (2021). Alternatif bir dünya arayışı: Metaverse. *Lacivert., 85*, 79–81.

Domina, T., Lee, S. E., & MacGillivray, M. (2012). Understanding factors affecting consumer intention to shop in a virtual world. *Journal of Retailing and Consumer Services, 19*(6), 613–620. doi:10.1016/j.jretconser.2012.08.001

Doolani, S., Owens, L., Wessels, C., & Makedon, F. (2020). Vis: An immersive virtual storytelling system for vocational training. *Applied Sciences (Basel, Switzerland), 10*(22), 8143. doi:10.3390/app10228143

D'Orazio, D., & Savov, V. (2015). Valve's VR Headset is Called the Vive and it's Made by HTC. *The Verge.*

Dozio, N., Marcolin, F., Scurati, G. W., Ulrich, L., Nonis, F., Vezzetti, E., Marsocci, G., la Rosa, A., & Ferrise, F. (2022). A design methodology for affective Virtual Reality. *International Journal of Human-Computer Studies, 162*, 102791. Advance online publication. doi:10.1016/j.ijhcs.2022.102791

Driscoll, T. (2022). *Making Sense of the Metaverse in Education.* EdTechTeacher. https://edtechteacher.org/making-sense-of-the-metaverse-in-education/

Du, H., Ma, B., Niyato, D., Kang, J., Xiong, Z., & Yang, Z. (2022). *Rethinking Quality of Experience for Metaverse Services: A Consumer-based Economics Perspective.* https://arxiv.org/abs/2208.01076

Duan, H. (2021). Metaverse for social good: A university campus prototype. *Proceedings of the 29th ACM International Conference on Multimedia*, 153–161. 10.1145/3474085.3479238

Dubai Metaverse Strategy. (2022). Retrieved from UAE Government Portal: https://u.ae/en/about-the-uae/strategies-initiatives-and-awards/local-governments-strategies-and-plans/dubai-metaverse-strategy

Duncan, A. (2021). Opportunities for academic smart libraries in the Caribbean. *Library Hi Tech News, 38*(5), 9–12. doi:10.1108/LHTN-06-2021-0035

Dwivedi, Y. K., Hughes, L., Baabdullah, A. M., Ribeiro-Navarrete, S., Giannakis, M., Al-Debei, M. M., Dennehy, D., Metri, B., Buhalis, D., Cheung, C. M. K., Conboy, K., Doyle, R., Dubey, R., Dutot, V., Felix, R., Goyal, D. P., Gustafsson, A., Hinsch, C., Jebabli, I., ... Wamba, S. F. (2022). Metaverse beyond the hype: Multidisciplinary perspectives on emerging challenges, opportunities, and agenda for research, practice and policy. *International Journal of Information Management*, *66*, 102542. doi:10.1016/j.ijinfomgt.2022.102542

Dwivedi, Y. K., Hughes, L., Wang, Y., Alalwan, A. A., Ahn, S. J., Balakrishnan, J., Barta, S., Belk, R., Buhalis, D., Dutot, V., Felix, R., Filieri, R., Flavián, C., Gustafsson, A., Hinsch, C., Hollensen, S., Jain, V., Kim, J., Krishen, A. S., ... Wirtz, J. (2022). Metaverse marketing: How the metaverse will shape the future of consumer research and practice. *Psychology and Marketing*. Advance online publication. doi:10.1002/mar.21767

Dynata. (2022). *Share of adults worldwide who are interested in trying select types of metaverse experiences as of February 2022, by generation*. Statista. Retrieved 18 February from https://www-statista-com.jerome.stjohns.edu/statistics/1305147/interest-in-trying-metaverse-experiences-worldwide-generation/?locale=en

Efendioglu, I. H. (2022). Metaverse Platformları, Metaverse Oyunları ve Metaverse'e Giriş Yapan İşletmeler. A. Güven & M. S. Tam (Ed.), Alternatif Dijital Evren Metaverse-I Kavramsal Tartışmalar, Sosyoloji, Psikoloji, Sanat ve Etik (101-126). Necmettin Erbakan Üniversitesi Yayınları

Efraim Turban, E. T., & King Jae Kyu Lee, D. K. J. K. (2015). *Electronic commerce a managerial and social networks perspective.* . doi:10.1007/978-3-319-10091-3

El Sawy, N. (2019). *Souq becomes Amazon.ae in the UAE*. Retrieved from https://www.thenational.ae/business/technology/souq-becomes-amazon-ae-in-the-uae-1.855759

Elciyar, K., & Simsek, A. (2021). An investigation of cyberloafing in a large-scale technology organization from the perspective of the theory of interpersonal behavior. *Online Journal of Communication and Media Technologies*, *11*(2), e202106. Advance online publication. doi:10.30935/ojcmt/10823

Elder, R. S., & Krishna, A. (2022). A review of sensory imagery for consumer psychology. *Journal of Consumer Psychology*, *32*(2), 293–315. doi:10.1002/jcpy.1242

Ellis, G. D., Voelkl, J. E., & Morris, C. (1994). Measurement and analysis issues with explanation of variance in daily experience using the flow model. *Journal of Leisure Research*, *26*(4), 337–356. doi:10.1080/00222216.1994.11969966

Ellul, J., Galea, J., Ganado, M., McCarthy, S., & Pace, G. J. (2020). Regulating Blockchain, DLT and Smart Contracts: a technology regulator's perspective. *ERA Forum, 21*(2), 209-220. 10.100712027-020-00617-7

Elmi, A. H., Keikhosrokiani, P., & Asl, M. P. (2023). A Machine Learning Approach to the Analytics of Representations of Violence in Khaled Hosseini's Novels. In P. Keikhosrokiani & M. Pourya Asl (Eds.), *Handbook of Research on Artificial Intelligence Applications in Literary Works and Social Media* (pp. 36–67). IGI Global. doi:10.4018/978-1-6684-6242-3.ch003

Emara, S. (2019). *UAE the fastest growing e-commerce market in the Middle East and North Africa*. Retrieved from tellerreport.com: https://www.tellerreport.com/business/2019-07-23---uae-the-fastest-growing-e-commerce-market-in-the-middle-east-and-north-africa-.B1L0BU-HfB.html

Eng, N. (2020). Impression Management After Image-Threatening Events. *The Journal of Public Interest Communications*, *4*(2), 32. doi:10.32473/jpic.v4.i2.p32

Eom, S. (2022). The Emerging Digital Twin Bureaucracy in the 21st Century. *Perspectives on Public Management and Governance*, *5*(2), 174–186. doi:10.1093/ppmgov/gvac005

Erdei, T., Krakó, R., & Husi, G. (2022). Design of a Digital Twin Training Centre for an Industrial Robot Arm. *Applied Sciences (Basel, Switzerland)*, *12*(17), 8862. doi:10.3390/app12178862

Erdmann, A., & Ponzoa, J.M. (2021). Digital inbound marketing: Measuring the economic performance of grocery e-commerce in Europe and the USA. *Technological Forecasting and Social Change, 162*. doi:10.1016/j.techfore.2020.120373

Estrada Villalba, É., San Martín Azócar, A. L., & Jacques-García, F. A. (2021). State of the art on immersive virtual reality and its use in developing meaningful empathy. *Computers & Electrical Engineering*, *93*, 107272. doi:10.1016/j.compeleceng.2021.107272

Everyrealm, I. (2023). *Metaverse Fashion Week*. Everyrealm, Inc. Retrieved 18 February from https://everyrealm.com/mvfw

Exarta. (2022, November 17). *The 7 layers of the Metaverse*. Exarta. https://exarta.com/blog/the-7-layers-of-the-metaverse/

Expert, E. (2022). *Briefings*. Emerald.

Ezimmuo, C. M., & Keikhosrokiani, P. (2022). Predicting Consumer Behavior Change Towards Using Online Shopping in Nigeria: The Impact of the COVID-19 Pandemic. In P. Keikhosrokiani (Ed.), *Handbook of Research on Consumer Behavior Change and Data Analytics in the Socio-Digital Era* (pp. 210–254). IGI Global. doi:10.4018/978-1-6684-4168-8.ch010

Falchuk, B., Loeb, S., & Neff, R. (2018). The Social Metaverse: Battle for Privacy. *IEEE Technology and Society Magazine*, *37*(2), 52–61. doi:10.1109/MTS.2018.2826060

Falomo Bernarduzzi, L., Bernardi, E. M., Ferrari, A., Garbarino, M. C., & Vai, A. (2021). Augmented Reality Application for Handheld Devices: How to Make It hAPPen at the Pavia University History Museum. *Science and Education*, *30*(3), 755–773. doi:10.100711191-021-00197-z PMID:33758467

Faraboschi, P., Frachtenberg, E., Laplante, P., Milojicic, D., & Saracco, R. (2022). Virtual Worlds (Metaverse): From Skepticism, to Fear, to Immersive Opportunities. *Computer*, *55*(10), 100–106. doi:10.1109/MC.2022.3192702

Farjami, S., Taguchi, R., Nakahira, K. T., Fukumura, Y., & Kanematsu, H. (2011). W-02 Problem Based Learning for Materials Science Education in Metaverse. *JSEE Annual Conference International Session Proceedings*, *2011*, 20–23. 10.20549/jseeen.2011.0_20

Far, S. B., & Rad, A. I. (2022). Applying Digital Twins in Metaverse: User Interface, Security and Privacy Challenges. *Journal of Metaverse*, *2*(1), 8–16.

Farshid, M., Paschen, J., Eriksson, T., & Kietzmann, J. (2018). Go boldly!: Explore augmented reality (AR), virtual reality (VR), and mixed reality (MR) for business. *Business Horizons, 61*(5), 657 663. doi:10.1016/j.bushor.2018.05.009

Fasha, E. F. B. K., Keikhosrokiani, P., & Asl, M. P. (2022). Opinion Mining Using Sentiment Analysis: A Case Study of Readers' Response on Long Litt Woon's The Way Through the Woods in Goodreads. In F. Saeed, F. Mohammed, & F. Ghaleb (Eds.), *Advances on Intelligent Informatics and Computing* (pp. 231–242). Springer International Publishing. doi:10.1007/978-3-030-98741-1_20

Fernandes, J., Machado, C., & Amaral, L. (2022). Identifying critical success factors for the General Data Protection Regulation implementation in higher education institutions. *Digital Policy, Regulation & Governance*, *24*(4), 355–379. doi:10.1108/DPRG-03-2021-0041

Ferrari, S. (2016). Marketing strategies in the age of web 3.0. In Mobile Computing and Wireless Networks: Concepts, Methodologies, Tools, and Applications (pp. 2132-2149). IGI Global.

Filimonau, V., Ashton, M., & Stankov, U. (2022). Virtual spaces as the future of consumption in tourism, hospitality and events. *Journal of Tourism Futures*.

Finneran, C. M., & Zhang, P. (2005). Flow in computer-mediated environments: Promises and challenges. *Communications of the Association for Information Systems*, *15*(1), 4. doi:10.17705/1CAIS.01504

Flavián, C., Ibáñez-Sánchez, S., & Orús, C. (2019). The impact of virtual, augmented and mixed reality technologies on the customer experience. *Journal of Business Research*, *100*, 547–560. doi:10.1016/j.jbusres.2018.10.050

Flavin, M. (2017). *Disruptive technology enhanced learning: The use and misuse of digital technologies in higher education.* Springer. doi:10.1057/978-1-137-57284-4

Fleishman-Hillard, & Website (eleve.co). (2022). *Leading sectors in Web 3.0 landscape in India as of April 2022, by topic volume (in 1,000s)* [Graph]. Statista. Retrieved 03 February from https://www-statista-com.jerome.stjohns.edu/statistics/1353170/india-leading-sectors-in-web-30-in-by-topic-volume/

Fong Yew, O., & Jambulingam, M. (2015). Critical Success Factors of E-learning Implementation at Educational Institutions. In Journal of Interdisciplinary Research in Education (Vol. 5, Issue 1).

Forbes India. (2022). *UAE's economy ministry to set up shop in the metaverse.* Retrieved from https://www.forbesindia.com/article/news/uaes-economy-ministry-to-set-up-shop-in-the-metaverse/80255/1

Fowler, J. W., & Mönch, L. (2018). A survey of semiconductor supply chain models Part II: Demand planning, inventory management, and capacity planning. *International Journal of Production Research*, *56*(13), 4546–4564. doi:10.1080/00207543.2018.1424363

Francescatto, M., Neuenfeldt Júnior, A., Kubota, F. I., Guimarães, G., & de Oliveira, B. (2023). Lean Six Sigma case studies literature overview: critical success factors and difficulties. In International Journal of Productivity and Performance Management (Vol. 72, Issue 1, pp. 1–23). Emerald Publishing. doi:10.1108/IJPPM-12-2021-0681

Fredrickson, B. L., Tugade, M. M., Waugh, C. E., & Larkin, G. R. (2003). What good are positive emotions in crisis? A prospective study of resilience and emotions following the terrorist attacks on the United States on September 11th, 2001. *Journal of Personality and Social Psychology*, *84*(2), 365–376. doi:10.1037/0022-3514.84.2.365 PMID:12585810

Fussell, S. G., & Truong, D. (2022). Using virtual reality for dynamic learning: An extended technology acceptance model. *Virtual Reality (Waltham Cross)*, *26*(1), 249–267. doi:10.100710055-021-00554-x PMID:34276237

Gad, A. G., Mosa, D. T., Abualigah, L., & Abohany, A. A. (2022). Emerging Trends in Blockchain Technology and Applications: A Review and Outlook. *Journal of King Saud University - Computer and Information Sciences, 34*(9), 6719-6742.

Gadekallu, T. R., Huynh-The, T., Wang, W., Yenduri, G., Ranaweera, P., Pham, Q. V., . . . Liyanage, M. (2022). *Blockchain for the Metaverse: A Review.* arXiv preprint arXiv:2203.09738. doi:10.48550/arXiv.2203.09738

Gadekallu, T. R., Huynh-The, T., Wang, W., Yenduri, G., Ranaweera, P., Pham, Q.-V., da Costa, D. B., & Liyanage, M. (2022). *Blockchain for the metaverse: A review.* arXiv preprint arXiv:2203.09738.

Gadekallu, T. R., Huynh-The, T., Wang, W., Yenduri, G., Ranaweera, P., Pham, Q.-V., da Costa, D. B., & Liyanage, M. (2022). *Blockchain for the metaverse: A review.* ArXiv Preprint ArXiv:2203.09738. doi:10.48550/arxiv.2203.09738

Garcia-Font, V. (2020). SocialBlock: An architecture for decentralized user-centric data management applications for communications in smart cities. *Journal of Parallel and Distributed Computing*, *145*, 13–23. doi:10.1016/j.jpdc.2020.06.004

Garduño, J. C. (2023). Deep Learning Implementation for Pattern and Incidences Identification of Gender Violence in Mexican Contexts. In *Handbook of Research on Applied Artificial Intelligence and Robotics for Government Processes* (pp. 345–371). IGI Global.

Garfatta, I., Klai, K., Gaaloul, W., & Graiet, M. (2021). A Survey on Formal Verification for Solidity Smart Contracts *2021 Australasian Computer Science Week Multiconference.* 10.1145/3437378.3437879

Gavilan, D., Avello, M., & Martinez-Navarro, G. (2018). The influence of online ratings and reviews on hotel booking consideration. *Tourism Management, 66,* 53–61. doi:10.1016/j.tourman.2017.10.018

Geaghan-Breiner, C., & Bach, A. (2018). Reading literature in the digital age: An exploration of e-readers and reading habits. *Journal of Adolescent & Adult Literacy, 62*(4), 395–404.

George, J., & Gnanayutham, P. (2010). Human computer interaction and theories. In M. Sarrafzadeh & P. Petratos (Eds.), *Strategic advantage of computing information systems in enterprise management* (pp. 255–272). Atiner.

Gerup, J., Soerensen, C. B., & Dieckmann, P. (2020). Augmented reality and mixed reality for healthcare education beyond surgery: An integrative review. *International Journal of Medical Education, 11,* 1. doi: 10.5116/ijme.5e01.eb1a

Ghani, J. A., & Deshpande, S. P. (1994). Task characteristics and the experience of optimal flow in human—Computer interaction. *The Journal of Psychology, 128*(4), 381–391. doi:10.1080/00223980.1994.9712742

Gil-Garcia, J. R., Helbig, N., & Ojo, A. (2014). Being smart: Emerging technologies and innovation in the public sector. *Government Information Quarterly, 31*(Supple), I1–I8. doi:10.1016/j.giq.2014.09.001

Gilmour, P. M. (2022). *Smart Contracts and the Metaverse.* The Company Lawyer.

Gim, G., Bae, H., & Kang, S. (2022). Metaverse learning: The relationship among quality of VR-based education, self-determination, and learner satisfaction. In *7th International Conference on Big Data, Cloud Computing, and Data Science (BCD), 2022* (pp. 279–284). IEEE Publications/Australasian Center for Italian Studies. 10.1109/BCD54882.2022.9900629

Glavish, M. (2022, March 17). *The dark side of the metaverse, Part I.* https://www.aei.org/technology-and-innovation/the-dark-side-of-the-metaverse-part-i/

Glover, J., & Linowes, J. (n.d.). *Complete Virtual Reality and Augmented Reality Development with Unity ... Complete Virtual Rea Complete Virtual Reality and Augmented Reality.* https://books.google.com.my/books?hl=en&lr=&id=xEuTDwAAQBAJ&oi=fnd&pg=PP1&dq=Complete+Virtual+Reality+and+Augmented+Reality++Dev...1/1

Godwin-Jones, R. (2019). In a world of SMART technology, why learn another language? *Journal of Educational Technology & Society, 22*(2), 4–13.

Godwin-Jones, R. (2023). Emerging spaces for language learning: AI bots, ambient intelligence, and the metaverse. *Language Learning & Technology, 27*(2). https://hdl.handle.net/10125/73501

Goel, A. K., Bakshi, R., & Agrawal, K. K. (2022). Web 3.0 and Decentralized Applications. *Materials Proceedings, 10*(1).

Gong, P., Zeng, N., Ye, K., & König, M. (2019). An Empirical Study on the Acceptance of 4D BIM in EPC Projects in China. *Sustainability (Switzerland), 11*(5). doi:10.3390/su11051316

Goodfellow, I., Bengio, Y., & Courville, A. I. B. (2016). Deep learning. MIT Press.

Goodman, J. (2019). *Strategic customer service: Managing the customer experience to increase positive word of mouth, build loyalty, and maximize profits.* AMACOM.

Google Trends. (2022). https://trends.google.com/trends/explore?q=metaverse Access Date: 11.12.2022

Grab, B., Gavril, R. M., & Bothe, J. (2018, May). Managing the challenges and opportunities of e-commerce platforms in the Gulf region. In *ICMLG 2018 6th International Conference on Management Leadership and Governance* (p. 368). Academic Conferences and Publishing Limited.

Grand View Research. (2022). *Metaverse market revenue worldwide from 2021 to 2030 (in billion U.S. dollars)* [Graph]. Statista. Retrieved 18 February from https://www-statista-com.jerome.stjohns.edu/statistics/1295784/metaverse-market-size/?locale=en

Gregor, S. (2006). The Nature of Theory in Information Systems The Nature of Theory in Information Systems. *Management Information Systems Quarterly, 30*(3).

Grieves, M., & Vickers, J. (2017). Digital twin: Mitigating unpredictable, undesirable emergent behavior in complex systems. In J. Kahlen, S. Flumerfelt, & A. Alves (Eds.), *Transdisciplinary perspectives on complex systems*. Springer. doi:10.1007/978-3-319-38756-7_4

Gulf Today. (2019). *UAE's e-commerce market is estimated to hit $27.1b by 2022*. Retrieved from https://www.gulftoday.ae/business/2019/06/18/uaes-e-commerce-market-is-estimated-to-hit-$27-1b-by-2022

Gümüş, B. (2022). Modadan Dijital Modaya – Modanin Teknolojik Dönüşümü. A. Güven & M. S. Tam (Ed.), Alternatif Dijital Evren Metaverse-I Kavramsal Tartışmalar, Sosyoloji, Psikoloji, Sanat ve Etik (269-286). Necmettin Erbakan Üniversitesi Yayınları

Guo, L., & Huang, Y. (2019). Application of big data analysis in Chinese literature research. *Journal of Digital Information Management, 17*(4), 255–260.

Gurcaglar, S. S. (2020). Integrating technology in the teaching of literature: A survey of undergraduate English language and literature programs in Turkey. *Journal of Language and Linguistic Studies, 16*(1), 1–14. doi:10.17263/jlls.717274

Gursoy, D., Malodia, S., & Dhir, A. (2022). The metaverse in the hospitality and tourism industry: An overview of current trends and future research directions. *Journal of Hospitality Marketing & Management,* 1–8.

Gutierrez-Bucheli, L., Kidman, G., & Reid, A. (2022). Sustainability in engineering education: A review of learning outcomes. In *Journal of Cleaner Production* (Vol. 330). Elsevier Ltd. doi:10.1016/j.jclepro.2021.129734

Hackl, C., Lueth, D., & Di Bartolo, T. (2022). *Navigating the metaverse: A guide to limitless possibilities in a Web 3.0 world*. John Wiley & Sons.

Haenlein, M., Kaplan, A., Tan, C. W., & Zhang, P. (2019). Artificial intelligence (AI) and management analytics. *Journal of Management Analytics, 6*(4), 341–343. doi:10.1080/23270012.2019.1699876

Haleem, A., Javaid, M., Asim Qadri, M., Pratap Singh, R., & Suman, R. (2022). Artificial intelligence (AI) applications for marketing: A literature-based study. *International Journal of Intelligent Networks, 3*, 119–132. doi:10.1016/j.ijin.2022.08.005

Hampton-Sosa, W., & Koufaris, M. (2005). The effect of web site perceptions on initial trust in the owner company. *International Journal of Electronic Commerce, 10*(1), 55–81. doi:10.1080/10864415.2005.11043965

Han, H.-C. (2020). From Visual Culture in the Immersive Metaverse to Visual Cognition in Education. In R. Z. Zheng (Ed.), *Cognitive and Affective Perspectives on Immersive Technology in Education* (pp. 67–84). IGI Global. doi:10.4018/978-1-7998-3250-8.ch004

Han, J., & Heo, J., ve You, E. (2021). *Analysis of metaverse platform as a new play culture: Focusing on roblox and zepeto*. In Proceedings of the 2nd International Conference on Human centered Artificial Intelligence (Computing 4 Human 2021). CEUR Workshop Proceedings, Da Nang, Vietnam

Han, S., & Noh, Y. (2021). Analyzing Higher Education Instructors' perception on Metaverse-based Education. *Journal of Digital Contents Society, 22*(11), 1793–1806. doi:10.9728/dcs.2021.22.11.1793

Haque, S., Eberhart, Z., Bansal, A., & McMillan, C. (2022). Semantic Similarity Metrics for Evaluating Source Code Summarization. *IEEE International Conference on Program Comprehension, 2022-March*, 36–47. 10.1145/3524610.3527909

Harisanty, D., Anna, N., Putri, T., Firdaus, A., & Noor Azizi, N. (2022). Leaders, practitioners and scientists' awareness of artificial intelligence in libraries: a pilot study. *Library Hi Tech*. doi:10.1108/LHT-10-2021-0356

Harrisson-Boudreau, J.-P., & Bellemare, J. (2021). Going Above and Beyond eCommerce in the Future Highly Virtualized World and Increasingly Digital Ecosystem. In *Towards Sustainable Customization: Bridging Smart Products and Manufacturing Systems* (pp. 789–797). Springer.

Haryana, M. R. A., Warsono, S., Achjari, D., & Nahartyo, E. (2022). Virtual reality learning media with innovative learning materials to enhance individual learning outcomes based on cognitive load theory. *International Journal of Management Education*, *20*(3), 100657. Advance online publication. doi:10.1016/j.ijme.2022.100657

Hassani, H., Huang, X., & MacFeely, S. (2022). Impactful Digital Twin in the Healthcare Revolution. *Big Data and Cognitive Computing*, *6*(3), 83. doi:10.3390/bdcc6030083

Hazan, E., Kelly, G., Khan, H., Spillecke, D., & Yee, L. (2022). *Marketing in the metaverse: An opportunity for innovation and experimentation*. McKinsey & Company. Retrieved 28 January from https://www.mckinsey.com/capabilities/growth-marketing-and-sales/our-insights/marketing-in-the-metaverse-an-opportunity-for-innovation-and-experimentation

Healthcare, G. E. (2022). *GE Healthcare*. GE Healthcare.

Hedrick, E., Harper, M., Oliver, E., & Hatch, D. (2022). Teaching & Learning in Virtual Reality: Metaverse Classroom Exploration. *2022 Intermountain Engineering Technology and Computing*, 1–5. Advance online publication. doi:10.1109/IETC54973.2022.9796765

Heller, J., Chylinski, M., de Ruyter, K., Mahr, D., & Keeling, D. I. (2019). Touching the untouchable: Exploring multi-sensory augmented reality in the context of online retailing. *Journal of Retailing*, *95*(4), 219–234. doi:10.1016/j.jretai.2019.10.008

Heller, J., Hilken, T., Chylinski, M., de Ruyter, K., Keeling, D. I., & Mahr, D. (2022). Embracing falsity through the Metaverse: The case of synthetic customer experiences. *Business Horizons*, *65*(6), 739–749. doi:10.1016/j.bushor.2022.07.007

Hempel, J. (2015). Project hololens: Our exclusive hands-on with Microsoft's holographic goggles. *Wired*. Wired. com. Conde Nast Digital, 21.

Hendaoui, A., Limayem, M., & Thompson, C. W. (2008). 3D social virtual worlds: Research issues and challenges. *IEEE Internet Computing*, *12*(1), 88–92. doi:10.1109/MIC.2008.1

Henderson, J. C., & Venkatraman, H. (1999). Strategic alignment: Leveraging information technology for transforming organizations. *IBM Systems Journal*, *38*(2.3), 472-484.

Hernández, P. R., Valle-Cruz, D., & Méndez, R. V. M. (2023). Review on the Application of Artificial Intelligence-Based Chatbots in Public Administration. In *Handbook of Research on Applied Artificial Intelligence and Robotics for Government Processes* (pp. 133–155). IGI Global.

Hill, C. A., & O'Hara, A. (2006). *A Cognitive Theory of Trust* (Vol. 84). Academic Press.

Hirsh, S. G. (2019). Technology in the literature classroom: Exploring new pedagogical approaches. *Journal of Interactive Technology and Pedagogy, 14*.

Hodgson, P., Lee, V. W. Y., Chan, J. C. S., Fong, A., Tang, C. S. Y., Chan, L., & Wong, C. (2019). Immersive Virtual Reality (IVR) in Higher Education: Development and Implementation. doi:10.1007/978-3-030-06246-0_12

Hoffman, D. L., & Novak, T. P. (1996). Marketing in hypermedia computer-mediated environments: Conceptual foundations. *Journal of Marketing*, *60*(3), 50–68. doi:10.1177/002224299606000304

Hoffman, J. (2017). Virtual reality and education: Opportunities and challenges. *Computers & Education*, *110*, 1–2. doi:10.1016/j.compedu.2017.03.013

Hollensen, S., Kotler, P., & Opresnik, M. O. (2022). Metaverse – the new marketing universe. *The Journal of Business Strategy*. Advance online publication. doi:10.1108/JBS-01-2022-0014

Houssein, E. H., Ibrahem, N., Zaki, A. M., & Sayed, A. (2022). Semantic Protocol and Resource Description Framework Query Language: A Comprehensive Review. *Mathematics*, *10*(17), 3203. doi:10.3390/math10173203

Hsu, C. L., & Lu, H. P. (2004). Why do people play on-line games? An extended TAM with social influences and flow experience. *Information & Management*, *41*(7), 853–868. doi:10.1016/j.im.2003.08.014

Huang, M. H., & Rust, R. T. (2021). A strategic framework for artificial intelligence in marketing. *Journal of the Academy of Marketing Science*, *49*(1), 30–50. doi:10.100711747-020-00749-9

Huang, Y. C., Backman, S. J., & Backman, K. F. (2012). Exploring the impacts of involvement and flow experiences in second life on people's travel intentions. *Journal of Hospitality and Tourism Technology*, *3*(1), 4–23. doi:10.1108/17579881211206507

Hu, J., Guo, Y., & Wang, Y. (2019). The impact of digital technology on teaching and learning in higher education. *Education Sciences*, *9*(2), 100. doi:10.3390/educsci9020100

Humida, T., Al Mamun, M. H., & Keikhosrokiani, P. (2021). Predicting behavioral intention to use e-learning system: A case-study in Begum Rokeya University, Rangpur, Bangladesh. *Education and Information Technologies*. doi:10.1007/s10639-021-10707-9

Huynh-The, T., Gadekallu, T. R., Wang, W., Yenduri, G., Ranaweera, P., Pham, Q.-V., da Costa, D. B., & Liyanage, M. (2023). Blockchain for the metaverse: A Review. *Future Generation Computer Systems*, *143*, 401–419. doi:10.1016/j.future.2023.02.008

Huynh-The, T., Pham, Q. V., Pham, X. Q., Nguyen, T. T., Han, Z., & Kim, D. S. (2023). Artificial intelligence for the metaverse: A survey. In *Engineering Applications of Artificial Intelligence* (Vol. 117). Elsevier Ltd. doi:10.1016/j.engappai.2022.105581

Hwang, G. J., & Chien, S. Y. (2022). Definition, roles, and potential research issues of the metaverse in education: An artificial intelligence perspective. *Computers and Education: Artificial Intelligence*, *3*, 100082. Advance online publication. doi:10.1016/j.caeai.2022.100082

Ibáñez, M. B., & Delgado-Kloos, C. (2018). Augmented reality for STEM learning: A systematic review. *Computers & Education*, *123*, 109–123. doi:10.1016/j.compedu.2018.05.002

Ibrahim, M. A. (2020). The Fourth Industrial Revolution (4IR) and the higher education landscape: A systematic review of the literature. *Education Sciences*, *10*(7), 173. doi:10.3390/educsci10070173

Insider Intelligence. (2022). *Insider Intelligence*. Insider Intelligence.

Insider Intelligence. (2023, January 25). *Here are the top health tech companies and startups developing wearable medical devices in 2023*. Insider Intelligence. https://www.insiderintelligence.com/insights/wearable-tech-companies-startups/

Islam, M., Zhou, L., & Li, F. (2009). *Application of artificial intelligence (artificial neural network) to assess credit risk: A predictive model for credit card scoring*. Academic Press.

Ismail, H. B., Yusoff, N. M., & Saad, N. F. M. (2019). Integrating digital technology into the teaching of literature: A case study of a Malaysian university. *International Journal of Emerging Technologies in Learning*, *14*(02), 157–170.

Israfilzade, K. (2022). Marketing in the Metaverse: A Sceptical Viewpoint of Opportunities and Future Research Directions. *The Eurasia Proceedings of Educational and Social Sciences*, *24*, 53–60. doi:10.55549/epess.1179349

Jafery, N. N., Keikhosrokiani, P., & Asl, M. P. (2022). Text Analytics Model to Identify the Connection Between Theme and Sentiment in Literary Works: A Case Study of Iraqi Life Writings. In P. Keikhosrokiani & M. Pourya Asl (Eds.), Handbook of Research on Opinion Mining and Text Analytics on Literary Works and Social Media (pp. 173–190). IGI Global. doi:10.4018/978-1-7998-9594-7.ch0088

Jafery, N. N., Keikhosrokiani, P., & Asl, M. P. (2023). An Artificial Intelligence Application of Theme and Space in Life Writings of Middle Eastern Women: A Topic Modelling and Sentiment Analysis Approach. In P. Keikhosrokiani & M. Pourya Asl (Eds.), Handbook of Research on Artificial Intelligence Applications in Literary Works and Social Media (pp. 19–35). IGI Global. doi: 10.4018/978-1-6684-6242-3.ch002

Jafery, N. N., Keikhosrokiani, P., & Asl, M. P. (2022). Text Analytics Model to Identify the Connection Between Theme and Sentiment in Literary Works: A Case Study of Iraqi Life Writings. In P. Keikhosrokiani & M. Pourya Asl (Eds.), *Handbook of Research on Opinion Mining and Text Analytics on Literary Works and Social Media* (pp. 173–190). IGI Global. doi:10.4018/978-1-7998-9594-7.ch008

Jafery, N. N., Keikhosrokiani, P., & Asl, M. P. (2023). An artificial intelligence application of theme and space in life writings of Middle Eastern women: A topic modelling and sentiment analysis approach. In P. Keikhosrokiani & M. P. Asl (Eds.), *Handbook of research on artificial intelligence applications in literary works and social media* (pp. 19–35). IGI Global. doi:10.4018/978-1-6684-6242-3.ch002

Jagatheesaperumal, S. K., Ahmad, K., Al-Fuqaha, A., & Qadir, J. (2022). *Advancing Education Through Extended Reality and Internet of Everything Enabled Metaverses: Applications, Challenges, and Open Issues*. https://arxiv.org/abs/2207.01512

Jamil, S., Rahman, M., & Fawad, M. (2022). A Comprehensive Survey of Digital Twins and Federated Learning for Industrial Internet of Things (IIoT), Internet of Vehicles (IoV) and Internet of Drones (IoD). *Applied System Innovation*, *5*(3), 56. doi:10.3390/asi5030056

Jason, J. (2016). *The VR book: Human centered design for virtual reality*. ACM Books.

Javornik, A., Marder, B., Pizzetti, M., & Warlop, L. (2021). Augmented self – The effects of virtual face augmentation on consumers' self-concept. *Journal of Business Research*, *130*, 170–187. doi:10.1016/j.jbusres.2021.03.026

Jeon, H. J., Youn, H. C., Ko, S. M., & Kim, T. H. (2022). Blockchain and AI Meet in the Metaverse. *Advances in the Convergence of Blockchain and Artificial Intelligence, 73*.

Jeong, M., Zo, H., Lee, C. H., & Ceran, Y. (2019). Feeling displeasure from online social media postings: A study using cognitive dissonance theory. *Computers in Human Behavior*, *97*, 231–240. doi: 10.1016/j.chb.2019.02.021

Jeyaraj, A. (2020). DeLone & McLean models of information system success: Critical meta-review and research directions. *International Journal of Information Management, 54*. doi:10.1016/j.ijinfomgt.2020.102139

Jin, J., Xu, H., & Leng, B. (2022). Adaptive Points Sampling for Implicit Field Reconstruction of Industrial Digital Twin. *Sensors (Basel)*, *22*(17), 6630. doi:10.339022176630 PMID:36081088

Jinjri, W. M., Keikhosrokiani, P., & Abdullah, N. L. (2021). Machine Learning Algorithms for The Classification of Cardiovascular Disease- A Comparative Study. *2021 International Conference on Information Technology (ICIT)*, 132–138. doi:10.1109/ICIT52682.2021.9491677

Jin, Q., Liu, Y., Yarosh, S., Han, B., & Qian, F. (2022). How Will VR Enter University Classrooms? Multi-stakeholders Investigation of VR in Higher Education. *Proceedings of the 2022 CHI Conference on Human Factors in Computing Systems*, 1–17. 10.1145/3491102.3517542

Johns Hopkins Medicine. (2021). *Johns Hopkins Medicine*. Johns Hopkins.

Johnson, B. (2014). *How the oculus rift works*. Academic Press.

Jordan, M. I., & Mitchell, T. M. (2015). Machine learning: Trends, perspectives, and prospects. *Science*, *349*(6245), 255–260. doi:10.1126cience.aaa8415 PMID:26185243

Joy, A., Zhu, Y., Peña, C., & Brouard, M. (2022). Digital future of luxury brands: Metaverse, digital fashion, and non-fungible tokens. *Strategic Change, 31*(3), 337-343. doi:10.1002/jsc.2502

Jung, S. Y., Kim, J. W., Hwang, H., Lee, K., Baek, R. M., Lee, H. Y., Yoo, S., Song, W., & Han, J. S. (2019). Development of comprehensive personal health records integrating patient-generated health data directly from samsung s-health and apple health apps: Retrospective cross-sectional observational study. *JMIR mHealth and uHealth*, *7*(5), e12691. Advance online publication. doi:10.2196/12691 PMID:31140446

Juntunen, M. (2019). Teaching literature in the digital age: The pros and cons of online courses. *Scandinavian Journal of Educational Research*, *63*(4), 601–614.

Kabilan, M. K., & Nambiar, R. M. K. (2019). The integration of digital literacy in English language curriculum in Malaysian universities. *English Teaching*, *48*(1), 1–17.

Kahraman, M. E. (2022). Blok zincir, Deepfake, Avatar, Kripto para, NFT ve Metaverse ile Yaygınlaşan Sanal Yaşam. [UKSAD]. *Uluslararası Kültürel ve Sosyal Araştırmalar Dergisi, 8*(1), 149–162. doi:10.46442/intjcss.1106228

Kalinkara, Y., & Talan, T. (2022). Rethinking Evaluating the Use of Distance Learning Systems in the Context of the Unified Theory of Acceptance and Use of Technology-2. *Journal of Learning for Development*, *9*(2), 229–252. doi:10.56059/jl4d.v9i2.617

Kanematsu, H., Kobayashi, T., Ogawa, N., Barry, D. M., Fukumura, Y., & Nagai, H. (2013). Eco Car Project for Japan Students as a Virtual PBL Class. *Procedia Computer Science*, *22*, 828–835. doi: 10.1016/j.procs.2013.09.165

Kang, M., & Jameson, N. J. (2018). Machine Learning: Fundamentals. Prognostics and Health Management of Electronics. *Fundamentals, Machine Learning, and the Internet of Things*, 85-109.

Kang, M., & Schuett, M. A. (2013). Determinants of sharing travel experiences in social media. *Journal of Travel & Tourism Marketing*, *30*(1-2), 93–107. doi:10.1080/10548408.2013.751237

Kang, Y., Choi, N., & Kim, S. (2021). Searching for New Model of Digital Informatics for Human-Computer Interaction: Testing the Institution-Based Technology Acceptance Model (ITAM). *International Journal of Environmental Research and Public Health*, *18*(11). doi: 10.3390/ijerph18115593

Kao, C. H., & Lee, H. J. (2020). Natural language processing and machine learning techniques for literary studies: A case study of Jane Austen's novels. *Journal of English for Academic Purposes*, *45*, 100873.

Kaplan, A. D., Cruit, J., Endsley, M., Beers, S. M., Sawyer, B. D., & Hancock, P. A. (2021). The effects of virtual reality, augmented reality, and mixed reality as training enhancement methods: A meta analysis. *Human Factors*, *63*(4), 706–726. doi:10.1177/0018720820904229 PMID:32091937

Kassem, M., & Succar, B. (2017). Macro BIM adoption: Comparative market analysis. *Automation in Construction*, *81*, 286–299. doi: 10.1016/j.autcon.2017.04.005

Kaya, O., & Schildbach, J., & Schneider, S. (2019). Artificial intelligence in banking. Artificial Intelligence.

Keikhosrokiani, P. (2020b). *Behavioral intention to use of Mobile Medical Information System (mMIS)*. Academic Press.

Keikhosrokiani, P. (2020c). *Success factors of mobile medical information system (mMIS)*. Academic Press.

Keikhosrokiani, P. (2021). IoT for enhanced decision-making in medical information systems: A systematic review. In G. Marques, A. Kumar Bhoi, I. de la Torre Díez, & B. Garcia-Zapirain (Eds.), Enhanced Telemedicine and e-Health: Advanced IoT Enabled Soft Computing Framework (Vol. 410, pp. 119–140). Springer International Publishing. doi:10.1007/978-3-030-70111-6_6

Keikhosrokiani, P. (2022a). Big Data Analytics for Healthcare: Datasets, Techniques, Life Cycles, Management, and Applications. Elsevier Science. doi:10.1016/C2021-0-00369-2

Keikhosrokiani, P. (2022a). *Big Data Analytics for Healthcare: Datasets, Techniques, Life Cycles, Management, and Applications*. Elsevier Science. https://books.google.com.my/books?id=WbJYEAAAQBAJ

Keikhosrokiani, P. (2022b). Handbook of Research on Consumer Behavior Change and Data Analytics in the Socio-Digital Era. IGI Global. doi: 10.4018/978-1-6684-4168-8

Keikhosrokiani, P., & Asl, M. P. (2022). Handbook of research on opinion mining and text analytics on literary works and social media. IGI Global. doi:10.4018/978-1-7998-9594-7

Keikhosrokiani, P., & Kamaruddin, N. S. A. B. (2022). IoT-Based In-Hospital-In-Home Heart Disease Remote Monitoring System with Machine Learning Features for Decision Making. In S. Mishra, A. González-Briones, A. K. Bhoi, P. K. Mallick, & J. M. Corchado (Eds.), Connected e-Health: Integrated IoT and Cloud Computing (pp. 349–369). Springer International Publishing. doi: 10.1007/978-3-030-97929-4_16

Keikhosrokiani, P., Mustaffa, N., Sarwar, M. I., Kianpisheh, A., Damanhoori, F., & Zakaria, N. (2011). A Study towards Proposing GPS-Based Mobile Advertisement Service. Informatics Engineering and Information Science.

Keikhosrokiani, P., Mustaffa, N., Zakaria, N., & Baharudin, A. S. (2019). User Behavioral Intention Toward Using Mobile Healthcare System. In Consumer-Driven Technologies in Healthcare: Breakthroughs in Research and Practice (pp. 429-444). IGI Global. doi:10.4018/978-1-5225-6198-9.ch022

Keikhosrokiani, P., Naidu, A. B., Iryanti Fadilah, S., Manickam, S., & Li, Z. (2023). Heartbeat sound classification using a hybrid adaptive neuro-fuzzy inferences system (ANFIS) and artificial bee colony. *Digital Health, 9*. doi:10.1177/20552076221150741

Keikhosrokiani, P. (2019). *Perspectives in the Development of Mobile Medical Information Systems: Life Cycle, Management, Methodological Approach and Application*. Academic Press.

Keikhosrokiani, P. (2019). Perspectives in the development of mobile medical information systems: Life cycle, management, methodological approach and application. In *Perspectives in the Development of Mobile Medical Information Systems*. Life Cycle, Management, Methodological Approach and Application. doi:10.1016/C2018-0-02485-8

Keikhosrokiani, P. (2020a). Introduction to Mobile Medical Information System (mMIS) development. In P. Keikhosrokiani (Ed.), *Perspectives in the Development of Mobile Medical Information Systems* (pp. 1–22). Academic Press. doi:10.1016/B978-0-12-817657-3.00001-8

Keikhosrokiani, P. (2020b). Behavioral intention to use of Mobile Medical Information System (mMIS). In P. Keikhosrokiani (Ed.), *Perspectives in the Development of Mobile Medical Information Systems* (pp. 57–73). Academic Press., doi:10.1016/B978-0-12-817657-3.00004-3

Keikhosrokiani, P. (2020c). Success factors of mobile medical information system (mMIS). In P. Keikhosrokiani (Ed.), *Perspectives in the Development of Mobile Medical Information Systems* (pp. 75–99). Academic Press., doi:10.1016/B978-0-12-817657-3.00005-5

Keikhosrokiani, P. (2021a). IoT for enhanced decision-making in medical information systems: A systematic review. In G. Marques, A. Kumar Bhoi, I. de la Torre Díez, & B. Garcia-Zapirain (Eds.), *Enhanced Telemedicine and e-Health: Advanced IoT Enabled Soft Computing Framework* (Vol. 410, pp. 119–140). Springer International Publishing. doi:10.1007/978-3-030-70111-6_6

Keikhosrokiani, P. (2021b). Predicating Smartphone Users' Behaviour Towards a Location-Aware IoMT-Based Information System: An Empirical Study. *International Journal of E-Adoption*, *13*(2), 52–77. doi:10.4018/IJEA.2021070104

Keikhosrokiani, P. (2022b). *Handbook of Research on Consumer Behavior Change and Data Analytics in the Socio-Digital Era*. IGI Global. doi:10.4018/978-1-6684-4168-8

Keikhosrokiani, P. (Ed.). (2022a). *Big Data Analytics for Healthcare: Datasets, Techniques, Life Cycles, Management, and Applications*. Elsevier Science., doi:10.1016/C2021-0-00369-2

Keikhosrokiani, P., & Asl, M. P. (2022). *Handbook of research on opinion mining and text analytics on literary works and social media*. IGI Global. doi:10.4018/978-1-7998-9594-7

Keikhosrokiani, P., & Asl, M. P. (2023b). Introduction to artificial intelligence for the analytics of literary works and social media: A review. In P. Keikhosrokiani & M. P. Asl (Eds.), *Handbook of research on artificial intelligence applications in literary works and social media* (pp. 1–17). IGI Global. doi:10.4018/978-1-6684-6242-3.ch001

Keikhosrokiani, P., & Asl, M. P. (Eds.). (2023). *Handbook of Research on Artificial Intelligence Applications in Literary Works and Social Media*. IGI Global. doi:10.4018/978-1-6684-6242-3

Keikhosrokiani, P., Asl, M. P., Chu, K. E., & Anuar, N. A. N. (2023). Artificial intelligence framework for opinion mining of netizen readers' reviews of Arundhati Roy's The God of Small Things. In P. Keikhosrokiani & M. P. Asl (Eds.), *Handbook of research on artificial intelligence applications in literary works and social media* (pp. 68–92). IGI Global. doi:10.4018/978-1-6684-6242-3.ch004

Keikhosrokiani, P., & Kamaruddin, N. S. A. B. (2022). IoT-Based In-Hospital-In-Home Heart Disease Remote Monitoring System with Machine Learning Features for Decision Making. In S. Mishra, A. González-Briones, A. K. Bhoi, P. K. Mallick, & J. M. Corchado (Eds.), *Connected e-Health: Integrated IoT and Cloud Computing* (pp. 349–369). Springer International Publishing. doi:10.1007/978-3-030-97929-4_16

Keikhosrokiani, P., Kianpisheh, A., Zakaria, N., Limtrairut, P., Mustaffa, N., & Sarwar, M. I. (2012). A Proposal to Measure Success Factors for Location-Based Mobile Cardiac Telemedicine System (LMCTS). *International Journal of Smart Home*, *6*(3).

Keikhosrokiani, P., Mustaffa, N., Sarwar, M. I., & Zakaria, N. (2013). E-Torch: A Mobile Commerce Location-Based Promotion System. *The International Technology Management Review*, *3*(3), 140–159. doi:10.2991/itmr.2013.3.3.1

Keikhosrokiani, P., Mustaffa, N., & Zakaria, N. (2018). Success factors in developing iHeart as a patient-centric healthcare system: A multi-group analysis. *Telematics and Informatics*, *35*(4). doi:10.1016/j.tele.2017.11.006

Keikhosrokiani, P., Mustaffa, N., Zakaria, N., & Abdullah, R. (2020). Assessment of a medical information system: The mediating role of use and user satisfaction on the success of human interaction with the mobile healthcare system (iHeart). *Cognition Technology and Work*, *22*(2), 281–305. doi:10.100710111-019-00565-4

Kesharwani, A. (2020). Do (how) digital natives adopt a new technology differently than digital immigrants? A longitudinal study. *Information & Management*, *57*(2). doi:10.1016/j.im.2019.103170

Keshmiri Neghab, H., Jamshidi, M., & Keshmiri Neghab, H. (2022). Digital Twin of a Magnetic Medical Microrobot with Stochastic Model Predictive Controller Boosted by Machine Learning in Cyber-Physical Healthcare Systems. *Information (Basel)*, *13*(7), 321. doi:10.3390/info13070321

Kesselman, M., & Esquivel, W. (2022). Technology on the move, Consumer Electronics Show 2022: The evolving metaverse and much more. *Library Hi Tech News*, *39*(5), 1–4. doi:10.1108/LHTN-03-2022-0038

Khan, L. U., Han, Z., Niyato, D., Hossain, E., & Hong, C. S. (2022). *Metaverse for Wireless Systems: Vision, Enablers, Architecture, and Future Directions*. https://arxiv.org/abs/2207.00413

Khan, M., Khusro, S., & Alam, I. (2022). Smart TV-based lifelogging systems: current trends, challenges, and the road ahead. *Information and Knowledge in Internet of Things*, 31-58. doi:10.1007/978-3-030-75123-4_2

Khan, S., Tomar, S., Fatima, M., & Khan, M. Z. (2022). Impact of artificial intelligent and industry 4.0 based products on consumer behaviour characteristics: A meta-analysis-based review. *Sustainable Operations and Computers*, *3*(January), 218–225. doi:10.1016/j.susoc.2022.01.009

Kharjule, N. (2022). Metaverse gaming: The new-gen immersive gaming experiences. *Times of India*. Retrieved 07 February from https://timesofindia.indiatimes.com/readersblog/metaverseblockchain/metaverse-gaming-the-new-gen-immersive-gaming-experiences-48054/

Kim, G.-H. (2021). How Will Blockchain Technology Affect the Future of the Internet? Advances in Computer Science and Ubiquitous Computing.

Kim, H. S., Kim, H. C., & Ji, Y. G. (2015). User requirement elicitation for U-city residential environment: Concentrated on smart home service. *Journal of Society for e-Business Studies*, *20*(1), 167–182. doi:10.7838/jsebs.2015.20.1.167

Kim, S.. 2021. The Metaverse: The Digital Earth—The World of Rising Trends. Kindle Edition. Paju: SPlanB Design.

Kim, J. (2021). Advertising in the Metaverse: Research agenda. *Journal of Interactive Advertising*, *21*(3), 141–144. doi:10.1080/15252019.2021.2001273

Kim, J.-H., Kim, M., Park, M., & Yoo, J. (2021). How interactivity and vividness influence consumer virtual reality shopping experience: The mediating role of telepresence. *Journal of Research in Interactive Marketing*, *15*(3), 502–525. doi:10.1108/JRIM-07-2020-0148

Kirkcaldy, B., & Furnham, A. (2016). The Changing Face of Education and Work: Attitudes toward Work and Its Impact on Economic Growth and the Wealth of Nations. In The Aging Workforce Handbook: Individual, Organizational, and Societal Challenges (pp. 135-157). Emerald Group Publishing Limited.

Klopfer, E. (2008). *Augmented learning: Research and design of mobile educational games*. MIT Press. doi:10.7551/mitpress/9780262113151.001.0001

Kng, C. K., Keikhosrokiani, P., & Asl, M. P. (2023). Artificial Intelligence and Human Rights Activism: A Case Study of Boochani's No Friend But the Mountains and His Tweets on Justice and Equality. In P. Keikhosrokiani & M. Pourya Asl (Eds.), Handbook of Research on Artificial Intelligence Applications in Literary Works and Social Media (pp. 114–141). IGI Global. doi:10.4018/978-1-6684-6242-3.ch006

Kng, C. K., Keikhosrokiani, P., & Asl, M. P. (2023). Artificial intelligence and human rights activism: A case study of Boochani's No Friend But the Mountains and his tweets on justice and equality. In P. Keikhosrokiani & M. P. Asl (Eds.), *Handbook of research on artificial intelligence applications in literary works and social media* (pp. 114–141). IGI Global. doi:10.4018/978-1-6684-6242-3.ch006

Kokkinou, A., & van Kollenburg, T. (2022). Critical success factors of Lean in Higher Education: an international perspective. *International Journal of Lean Six Sigma*. doi:10.1108/IJLSS-04-2022-0076

Kong, J. S. L., Kwok, R. C. W., & Fang, Y. (2012). The effects of peer intrinsic and extrinsic motivation on MMOG game-based collaborative learning. *Information & Management*, 49(1), 1–9. doi:10.1016/j.im.2011.10.004

König, C. M., Karrenbauer, C., & Breitner, M. H. (2022). Critical success factors and challenges for individual digital study assistants in higher education: A mixed methods analysis. *Education and Information Technologies*. doi:10.1007/s10639-022-11394-w

Kopp, T., Riekert, M., & Utz, S. (2018). When cognitive fit outweighs cognitive load: Redundant data labels in charts increase accuracy and speed of information extraction. *Computers in Human Behavior*, 86, 367–376. doi: 10.1016/j.chb.2018.04.037

Kor, M., Yitmen, I., & Alizadehsalehi, S. (2022). *An investigation for integration of deep learning and digital twins towards Construction 4.0*. Smart and Sustainable Built Environment. doi:10.1108/SASBE-08-2021-0148

Korzaan, M. L. (2003). Going with the flow: Predicting online purchase intentions. *Journal of Computer Information Systems*, 43(4), 25–31. doi:10.1057/palgrave.ejis.3000445

Kotler, P., & Keller, K. L. (2006). Marketing management (12th ed.). Academic Press.

Kotler, P. (2019). The market for transformation. *Journal of Marketing Management*, 35(5-6), 407–409. doi:10.1080/0267257X.2019.1585713

Kotler, P. A.-M. (2012). *Principles of marketing: An Asian perspective*. Pearson/Prentice-Hall.

Koufaris, M. (2002). Applying the technology acceptance model and flow theory to online consumer behavior. *Information Systems Research*, 13(2), 205–223. doi:10.1287/isre.13.2.205.83

Koufaris, M., Kambil, A., & LaBarbera, P. A. (2001). Consumer behavior in web-based commerce: An empirical study. *International Journal of Electronic Commerce*, 6(2), 115–138. doi:10.1080/10864415.2001.11044233

Kou, W. (Ed.). (2013). *Payment technologies for E-commerce*. Springer Science & Business Media.

Kovacova, M., Horak, J., & Higgins, M. (2022). Behavioral analytics, immersive technologies, and machine vision algorithms in the Web3-powered Metaverse world. *Linguistic and Philosophical Investigations*, 21(0), 57–72. doi:10.22381/lpi2120224

Kovács, P. T., Murray, N., Rozinaj, G., Sulema, Y., & Rybárová, R. (2015). Application of immersive technologies for education: State of the art. *2015 International Conference on Interactive Mobile Communication Technologies and Learning (IMCL)*. 10.1109/IMCTL.2015.7359604

Krüger, J. M., Buchholz, A., & Bodemer, D. (2019). *Human-centred AI in the chemical industry View project Learning with multiple external representations View project Characteristics from a User's Perspective.* https://www.researchgate.net/publication/337900854

Kumar, A., Nayyar, A., Upasani, S., & Arora, A. (2020). Empirical Study of Soft Clustering Technique for Determining Click Through Rate in Online Advertising. In N. Sharma, A. Chakrabarti, & V. Balas (Eds.), *Data Management, Analytics and Innovation. Advances in Intelligent Systems and Computing* (Vol. 1042). Springer. doi:10.1007/978-981-32-9949-8_1

Kumari, P., Mathew, L., & Syal, P. (2017). Increasing trend of wearables and multimodal interface for human activity monitoring: A review. In *Biosensors and Bioelectronics* (Vol. 90, pp. 298–307). Elsevier Ltd. doi:10.1016/j.bios.2016.12.001

Kumar, V. (2021). *Intelligent Marketing: Employing New-Age Technologies.* SAGE Publications Ltd. doi:10.4135/9789354792984

Kutlu, M. (2022). Metaverse Kapisini Aralayan Reklamlar. A. Güven & M. S. Tam (Ed.), Alternatif Dijital Evren Metaverse-II Reklam, Pazarlama, Marka ve İşletme Yönetimi (33-56). Necmettin Erbakan Üniversitesi Yayınları

Kwanya, T., Stilwell, C., & Underwood, P. (2012). Intelligent libraries and apomediators: Distinguishing between Library 3.0 and Library 2.0. *Journal of Librarianship and Information Science*, *45*(3), 187–197. doi:10.1177/0961000611435256

Kwasi, R. A., & Andrews, F. K. (2018). Integrating Information and Communication Technology in Education: Accessibility, Reliability and Convenience in Tertiary Institutions in the Upper West Region of Ghana. *International Journal of Recent Research in Mathematics Computer Science and Information Technology*, *4*(2), 46–54.

Kyaw, B. M., Saxena, N., Posadzki, P., Vseteckova, J., Nikolaou, C. K., George, P. P., Divakar, U., Masiello, I., Kononowicz, A. A., Zary, N., & Tudor Car, L. (2019). Virtual reality for health professions education: Systematic review and meta-analysis by the Digital Health Education Collaboration. *Journal of Medical Internet Research*, *21*(1). Advance online publication. doi:10.2196/12959

Kye, B., Han, N., Kim, E., Park, Y., & Jo, S. (2021). Educational applications of metaverse: Possibilities and limitations. In *Journal of Educational Evaluation for Health Professions* (Vol. 18). Korea Health Personnel Licensing Examination Institute. doi:10.3352/jeehp.2021.18.32

Lacity, M. C., Lupien, S. C., & Long, C. (2022). *Blockchain Fundamentals for Web 3.0.* Epic Books. https://books.google.co.uk/books?id=htmPEAAAQBAJ

Lapeer, R. J., Jeffrey, S. J., Dao, J. T., García, G. G., Chen, M., Shickell, S. M., ... Philpott, C. M. (2014). Using a passive coordinate measurement arm for motion tracking of a rigid endoscope for augmented-reality image-guided surgery. *International Journal of Medical Robotics and Computer Assisted Surgery*, *10*(1), 65–77. doi: 10.1002/rcs.1513

Lateef, M., & Keikhosrokiani, P. (2022). Predicting Critical Success Factors of Business Intelligence Implementation for Improving SMEs' Performances: A Case Study of Lagos State, Nigeria. *Journal of the Knowledge Economy.* Advance online publication. doi:10.100713132-022-00961-8

Laudon, K. C. (2016). *E-commerce: Business, technology.* Pearson India.

Lee, L. H., Braud, T., Zhou, P., Wang, L., Xu, D., Lin, Z., & Hui, P. (2021). *All one needs to know about metaverse: A complete survey on technological singularity, virtual ecosystem, and research agenda.* arXiv preprint arXiv:2110.05352. doi:10.48550/arXiv.2110.05352

Lee, L. H., Braud, T., Zhou, P., Wang, L., Xu, D., Lin, Z., ... Hui, P. (2021). *All one needs to know about metaverse: A complete survey on technological singularity, virtual ecosystem, and research agenda.* arXiv preprint arXiv:2110.05352.

Lee, L.-H. (2021). *All one needs to know about metaverse: A complete survey on technological singularity, virtual ecosystem, and research agenda.* arXiv preprint arXiv:2110.05352.

Lee, C. K. (2015). *Teaching literature to ESL students: A teacher's guide.* Pearson Malaysia.

Lee, J., & Kwon, K. H. (2022). Novel pathway regarding good cosmetics brands by NFT in the metaverse world. *Journal of Cosmetic Dermatology, 21*(12), 6584–6593. doi:10.1111/jocd.15277 PMID:35894837

Lee, L. S. (2019). E-learning in the teaching of literature: A case study of Malaysian tertiary students. *Arab World English Journal, 10*(2), 115–127.

Lee, S. M., & Chen, L. (2010). The impact of flow on online consumer behavior. *Journal of Computer Information Systems, 50*(4), 1–10. doi:10.1080/08874417.2013.11645645

Lee, S.-G., Trimi, S., Byun, W. K., & Kang, M. (2011). Innovation and imitation effects in Metaverse service adoption. *Service Business, 5*(2), 155–172. doi:10.100711628-011-0108-8

Lemenager, T., Neissner, M., Sabo, T., Mann, K., & Kiefer, F. (2020). "Who am i" and "how should I be": A systematic review on self-concept and avatar identification in gaming disorder. *Current Addiction Reports, 7*(2), 166–193. doi:10.100740429-020-00307-x

Lesavre, L., Varin, P., Mell, P., Davidson, M., & Shook, J. (2019). *A taxonomic approach to understanding emerging blockchain identity management systems.* arXiv preprint arXiv:1908.00929.

Levy, M. (2016). The impact of the digital age on editing and publishing. *Publishers Weekly, 263*(15), 20–21.

Li, K., Cui, Y., Li, W., Lv, T., Yuan, X., Li, S., Ni, W., Simsek, M., & Dressler, F. (2022). *When Internet of Things meets Metaverse: Convergence of Physical and Cyber Worlds.* https://arxiv.org/abs/2208.13501

Liang, R. H., Yu, B., Xue, M., Hu, J., & Feijs, L. M. (2018, April). BioFidget: Biofeedback for respiration training using an augmented fidget spinner. In *Proceedings of the 2018 CHI conference on human factors in computing systems* (pp. 1-12). ACM.

Liao, S. H., Widowati, R., & Hsieh, Y. C. (2021). Investigating online social media users' behaviors for social commerce recommendations. *Technology in Society, 66*(June), 101655. doi:10.1016/j.techsoc.2021.101655

Li, M., & Yost, R. S. (2000). Management-oriented modeling: Optimizing nitrogen management with artificial intelligence. *Agricultural Systems, 65*(1), 1–27. doi:10.1016/S0308-521X(00)00023-8

Lim, J. (2019). The impact of Industry 4.0 on education: What students need to succeed in Industry 4.0. *Journal of Education and Learning, 8*(1), 1–10. doi:10.5539/jel.v8n1p1

Lim, W. Y. B., Xiong, Z., Niyato, D., Cao, X., Miao, C., Sun, S., & Yang, Q. (2022). Realizing the Metaverse with Edge Intelligence: A Match Made in Heaven. *IEEE Wireless Communications*, 1–9. doi:10.1109/MWC.018.2100716

Ling, L. M., & Wah, L. L. (2019). Facing the challenges of the Fourth Industrial Revolution: A literature review. *International Journal of Academic Research in Business & Social Sciences, 9*(2), 400–417.

Lin, H., Wan, S., Gan, W., Chen, J., & Chao, H.-C. (2022). *Metaverse in Education: Vision.* Opportunities, and Challenges., doi:10.1109/BigData55660.2022.10021004

Liu, Y. (2018). Teaching literature in the digital age: A study of online discussion forums in a literature classroom. *Educational Media International, 55*(4), 301–315.

Li, W., Yigitcanlar, T., Erol, I., & Liu, A. (2021). Motivations, barriers and risks of smart home adoption: From systematic literature review to conceptual framework. *Energy Research & Social Science*, *80*, 102211. doi:10.1016/j.erss.2021.102211

Ljungholm, D. P. (2022). Metaverse-based 3D visual modeling, virtual reality training experiences, and wearable biological measuring devices in immersive workplaces. *Psychosociological Issues in Human Resource Management*, *10*(1), 64–77. doi:10.22381/pihrm10120225

López-Belmonte, J., Pozo-Sánchez, S., Lampropoulos, G., & Moreno-Guerrero, A.-J. (2022). Design and validation of a questionnaire for the evaluation of educational experiences in the metaverse in Spanish students (METAEDU). *Heliyon*, *8*(11), e11364. doi:10.1016/j.heliyon.2022.e11364 PMID:36387471

Lv, Z., Shang, W. L., & Guizani, M. (2022). Impact of Digital Twins and Metaverse on Cities: History, Current Situation, and Application Perspectives. *Applied Sciences (Basel, Switzerland)*, *12*(24), 12820. doi:10.3390/app122412820

MacCallum, K., & Parsons, D. (2019). Teacher perspectives on mobile augmented reality: The potential of metaverse for learning. In *World Conference on Mobile and Contextual Learning* (pp. 21-28). Academic Press.

MacDonald, K. (2022, January 25). I've seen the metaverse – And I don't want it. *The Guardian*. https://www.theguardian.com/games/2022/jan/25/ive-seen-the-metaverse-and-i-dont-want-it

MacIel-Monteon, M., Limon-Romero, J., Gastelum-Acosta, C., Tlapa, Di., Baez-Lopez, Y., & Solano-Lamphar, H. A. (2020). Measuring Critical Success Factors for Six Sigma in Higher Education Institutions: Development and Validation of a Surveying Instrument. *IEEE Access: Practical Innovations, Open Solutions*, *8*, 1813–1823. doi: 10.1109/ACCESS.2019.2962521

Maddahi, Y., & Chen, S. (2022). Applications of Digital Twins in the Healthcare Industry: Case Review of an IoT-Enabled Remote Technology in Dentistry. *Virtual Worlds*, *1*(1), 20–41. doi:10.3390/virtualworlds1010003

Madubuike, O. C., Anumba, C. J., & Khallaf, R. (2022). A review of digital twin applications in construction. *Journal of Information Technology in Construction*, *27*, 145–172. doi:10.36680/j.itcon.2022.008

Magalhães, L., Magalhães, L., Ramos, J., Moura, L., de Moraes, R., Gonçalves, J., Hisatugu, W. H., Souza, M. T., de Lacalle, L. N. L., & Ferreira, J. (2022). Conceiving a Digital Twin for a Flexible Manufacturing System. *Applied Sciences (Basel, Switzerland)*, *12*(19), 9864. doi:10.3390/app12199864

Mahfodz, N. A. (2019). Challenges and opportunities in teaching literature in the digital age: A Malaysian perspective. *Advances in Language and Literary Studies*, *10*(1), 26–35.

Mahmoud, A. B. (2015). E-mail Advertising in Syria: Assessing Beliefs, Attitudes, and Behaviors. *Journal of Promotion Management*, *21*(6), 649–665. doi:10.1080/10496491.2015.1055044

Mahmoud, A. B. (2021). Like a Cog in a Machine. In C. Machado & J. P. Davim (Eds.), *Advances in Intelligent, Flexible, and Lean Management and Engineering* (pp. 1–20). IGI Global. doi:10.4018/978-1-7998-5768-6.ch001

Mahmoud, A. B., Ball, J., Rubin, D., Fuxman, L., Mohr, I., Hack-Polay, D., Grigoriou, N., & Wakibi, A. (2021). Pandemic pains to Instagram gains! COVID-19 perceptions effects on behaviours towards fashion brands on Instagram in Sub-Saharan Africa: Tech-native vs non-native generations. *Journal of Marketing Communications*, 1–25. doi:10.1080/13527266.2021.1971282

Mahmoud, A. B., Berman, A., Tehseen, S., & Hack-Polay, D. (2022). Modelling Socio-Digital Customer Relationship Management in the Hospitality Sector During the Pandemic Time. In P. Keikhosrokiani (Ed.), *Handbook of Research on Consumer Behavior Change and Data Analytics in the Socio-Digital Era* (pp. 169–191). IGI Global. doi:10.4018/978-1-6684-4168-8.ch008

Mahmoud, A. B., Grigoriou, N., Fuxman, L., Hack-Polay, D., Mahmoud, F. B., Yafi, E., & Tehseen, S. (2019). Email is evil! *Journal of Research in Interactive Marketing, 13*(2), 227–248. doi:10.1108/JRIM-09-2018-0112

Mahmoud, A. B., Hack-Polay, D., Grigoriou, N., Mohr, I., & Fuxman, L. (2021). A generational investigation and sentiment and emotion analyses of female fashion brand users on Instagram in Sub-Saharan Africa. *Journal of Brand Management, 28*(5), 526–544. doi:10.105741262-021-00244-8

Mahmoud, A. B., Tehseen, S., & Fuxman, L. (2020). The Dark Side of Artificial Intelligence in Retail Innovation. In E. Pantano (Ed.), *Retail Futures* (pp. 165–180). Emerald Publishing Limited. doi:10.1108/978-1-83867-663-620201019

Mahmud, A., & Saka, K. A. (2020). *Application of ICT Facilities for Academic Activities among Engineering Lecturers in University Libraries.* Academic Press.

Majji, K. C., & Baskaran, K. (2021). Artificial intelligence analytics—virtual assistant in UAE automotive industry. In *Inventive Systems and Control* (pp. 309–322). Springer Singapore. doi:10.1007/978-981-16-1395-1_24

Makransky, G., & Petersen, G. B. (2021). The Cognitive Affective Model of Immersive Learning (CAMIL): A Theoretical Research-Based Model of Learning in Immersive Virtual Reality. *Educational Psychology Review, 33*(3), 937–958.

Maleki, A., & Shahbazinia, M. (2017). The role of e-books in developing reading habits among university students. *International Journal of Research in English Education, 2*(3), 1–7. doi:10.29252/ijree.2.3.1

Malik, E. F., Keikhosrokiani, P., & Asl, M. P. (2021). Text mining life cycle for a spatial reading of Viet Thanh Nguyen's The Refugees (2017). *2021 International Congress of Advanced Technology and Engineering (ICOTEN)*, 1-9. 10.1109/ICOTEN52080.2021.9493520

Mallem, M. (2010, July). Augmented Reality: Issues, trends and challenges. In *2010 2nd International Conference on Image Processing Theory, Tools and Applications* (pp. 8-8). IEEE.

Marinchak, C. M., Forrest, E., & Hoanca, B. (2018). Artificial intelligence: Redefining marketing management and the customer experience. *International Journal of E-Entrepreneurship and Innovation, 8*(2), 14–24. doi:10.4018/IJEEI.2018070102

Mark Zuckerberg is betting Facebook's future on the metaverse. (n.d.). *The Verge.* Retrieved November 6, 2022. https://www.theverge.com/22588022/mark-zuckerberg-facebook-ceo-metaverse-interview

Marketing in the metaverse: An opportunity for innovation and experimentation. (n.d.). Retrieved November 7, 2022. https://www.mckinsey.com/capabilities/growth-marketing-and-sales/our-insights/marketing-in-the-metaverse-an-opportunity-for-innovation-and-experimentation

Ma, S., Guo, J., & Zhang, H. (2019). Policy analysis and development evaluation of digital ttrade: An international comparison. *China & World Economy, 27*(3), 49–75. doi:10.1111/cwe.12280

Mayer, R. E., & Moreno, R. (n.d.). *Multimedia learning 1 A Cognitive Theory of Multimedia Learning: Implications for Design Principles.* Academic Press.

McLeod, A., & Dolezel, D. (2022). Information security policy non-compliance: Can capitulation theory explain user behaviors? *Computers and Security, 112.* doi:10.1016/j.cose.2021.102526

Medical Device Network. (2022). *Medical Device Network.* Medical Device Network.

Mehta, N. D. (2018). *Amazon changes prices on its products about every 10 minutes—here's how and why they do it.* Academic Press.

Metamandrill. (2022). *Amazon Metaverse; Amazon's Vision Entering the Metaverse.* Retrieved from: https://metamandrill.com/amazon-metaverse/

Meyer, C., & Schwager, A. (2007). Understanding customer experience. *Harvard Business Review, 85*(2), 116. PMID:17345685

Miah, M. R., Hossain, A., Shikder, R., Saha, T., & Neger, M. (2022). Evaluating the impact of social media on online shopping behavior during COVID-19 pandemic: A Bangladeshi consumers' perspectives. *Heliyon, 8*(9), e10600. doi:10.1016/j.heliyon.2022.e10600 PMID:36127921

Miikkulainen, R., Iscoe, N., Shagrin, A., Rapp, R., Nazari, S., McGrath, P., ... Lamba, G. (2018). Sentient ascend: AI-based massively multivariate conversion rate optimization. *Thirty-Second AAAI Conference on Artificial Intelligence.*

Milgram, P., Takemura, H., Utsumi, A., & Kishino, F. (1995). Augmented reality: A class of displays on the reality-virtuality continuum. *Telemanipulator and Telepresence Technologies, 2351*, 282-292. doi:10.1117/12.197321

Milgram, P., & Kishino, F. (1994). A taxonomy of mixed reality visual displays. *IEICE Transactions on Information and Systems, 77*(12), 1321–1329.

Milic, S., & Simeunovic, V. (2021). Exploring e-learning critical success factors in digitally underdeveloped countries during the first wave of the COVID-19. *Interactive Learning Environments.* doi:10.1080/10494820.2021.1990965

Miller, M. R., Herrera, F., Jun, H., Landay, J. A., & Bailenson, J. N. (2020). Personal identifiability of user tracking data during observation of 360-degree VR video. *Scientific Reports, 10*(1), 17404. Advance online publication. doi:10.103841598-020-74486-y PMID:33060713

Minevich, M. (2022). The Metaverse And Web3 Creating Value In The Future Digital Economy. *Forbes.* Retrieved 25 February from https://www.forbes.com/sites/markminevich/2022/06/17/the-metaverse-and-web3-creating-value-in-the-future-digital-economy/

Misirlis, N., & Bin Munawar, H. (n.d.). *An analysis of the technology acceptance model in understanding university students' behavioral intention to use metaverse technologies.* Academic Press.

Mistretta, S. (2022). The Metaverse—An Alternative Education Space. *AI. Computer Science and Robotics Technology, 2022*, 1–23. doi:10.5772/acrt.05

Mitra, A., Bera, B., Das, A. K., Jamal, S. S., & You, I. (2023). Impact on blockchain-based AI/ML enabled big data analytics for Cognitive Internet of Things environment. *Computer Communications, 197*, 173–185. doi:10.1016/j.comcom.2022.10.010

Miyachi, K., & Mackey, T. K. (2021). hOCBS: A privacy-preserving blockchain framework for healthcare data leveraging an on-chain and off-chain system design. *Information Processing & Management, 58*(3), 102535. doi:10.1016/j.ipm.2021.102535

Modgil, S., Dwivedi, Y. K., Rana, N. P., Gupta, S., & Kamble, S. (2022). Has Covid-19 accelerated opportunities for digital entrepreneurship? An Indian perspective. *Technological Forecasting and Social Change, 175*, 121415. Advance online publication. doi:10.1016/j.techfore.2021.121415 PMID:36536802

Mohammadi, N., & Taylor, J. (2017). Smart city digital twins. *IEEE Symposium Series on Computational Intelligence (SSCI).* 10.1109/SSCI.2017.8285439

Mohan, M., & Baskaran, K. (2021). Financial analytics: Investment behavior of middle income group in south India. *2021 11th International Conference on Cloud Computing, Data Science & Engineering (Confluence).* 10.1109/Confluence51648.2021.9377029

Mohr, I., Fuxman, L., & Mahmoud, A. B. (2022a). Fashion Resale Behaviours and Technology Disruption: An In-depth Review. In P. Keikhosrokiani (Ed.), *Consumer Behavior Change and Data Analytics in the Socio-Digital Era*. IGI Global. doi:10.4018/978-1-6684-4168-8.ch015

Moi, T., Cibicik, A., & Rølvåg, T. (2020). Digital twin based condition monitoring of a knuckle boom crane: An experimental study. *Engineering Failure Analysis*, *112*, 104517. doi:10.1016/j.engfailanal.2020.104517

Molinillo, S., Aguilar-Illescas, R., Anaya-Sánchez, R., & Liébana-Cabanillas, F. (2021). Social commerce website design, perceived value and loyalty behavior intentions: The moderating roles of gender, age and frequency of use. *Journal of Retailing and Consumer Services*, *63*(February), 102404. Advance online publication. doi:10.1016/j.jretconser.2020.102404

Momani, A. M., Jamous, M., & Jamous, M. M. (2017). The Evolution of Technology Acceptance Theories. In *International Journal of Contemporary Computer Research (IJCCR)* (Vol. 1, Issue 1). https://www.researchgate.net/publication/316644779

Moncey, A. A., & Baskaran, K. (2020). Digital marketing analytics: Building brand awareness and loyalty in UAE. *2020 IEEE International Conference on Technology Management, Operations and Decisions (ICTMOD)*. 10.1109/ICTMOD49425.2020.9380579

Moon, J.-W., An, Y., & Norman, W. (2022). Exploring the application of the uses and gratifications theory as a conceptual model for identifying the motivations for smartphone use by e-tourists. *Tourism Critiques: Practice and Theory, 3*(2), 102–119. doi:10.1108/trc-03-2022-0005

Moore, T., & Tschang, F. (2017). Reading and language learning with audio books: Raising the bar on reading strategies. *Reading in a Foreign Language*, *29*(2), 240–254.

Morabito, V. (2015). Managing change for big data driven innovation. In *Big Data and Analytics* (pp. 125–153). Springer. doi:10.1007/978-3-319-10665-6_7

Moraveji, N., Hagiwara, T., & Adiseshan, A. (2012). BreathTray: Influencing self-regulation without cognitive deficit. *Extended Abstracts of ACM CHI'12*.

Moreno, J. (2009). Trading strategies modeling in Colombian power market using artificial intelligence techniques. *Energy Policy*, *37*(3), 836–843. doi:10.1016/j.enpol.2008.10.033

Morning Consult. (2022a). *Share of internet users in the United States who are interested in using the metaverse as of March 2022, by gender* [Graph]. Statista. Retrieved 03 February from https://www-statista-com.jerome.stjohns.edu/statistics/1302575/us-adults-using-on-the-metaverse-by-gender/

Morning Consult. (2022b). *Share of internet users in the United States who would be interested in creating an avatar for the metaverse as of March 2022, by generation* [Graph]. Statista. Retrieved 03 February from https://www-statista-com.jerome.stjohns.edu/statistics/1302449/us-adults-creating-an-avatar-for-the-metaverse-generation/

Moro-Visconti, R. (2022). ESG-compliant Metaverse Ecosystems: Clues for Impact Investing. http://www.morovisconti.com/en Access date: 22.01.2022

Mostafa, L. (n.d.). *Measuring Technology Acceptance Model to use Metaverse Technology in Egypt*. https://jsst.journals.ekb.eg

Mosteanu, N. R. (2020). Artificial intelligence and cyber security–face to face with cyber attack–a maltese case of risk management approach. *Ecoforum Journal, 9*(2).

Mozumder, M. A. I., Sheeraz, M. M., Athar, A., Aich, S., & Kim, H. C. (2022). Overview: Technology roadmap of the future trend of metaverse based on IoT, blockchain, AI technique, and medical domain metaverse activity. In 2022 24th International Conference on Advanced Communication Technology (ICACT) (pp. 256-261). IEEE.

Multiple, A. I. (2020). *AI Multiple*. AI Multiple.

Mungwabi, H. N. (2018). Use of information and communication technologies (ICTs) in learning by undergraduate students at the University of Dar es Salaam library in Tanzania. *University of Dar Es Salaam Library Journal, 13*(2), 49–64.

Muñoz-Chávez, J. P., García-Contreras, R., & Valle-Cruz, D. (2022). Panic station: Consumer sentiment analysis of the evolving panic buying during the COVID-19 pandemic. Handbook of Research on Consumer Behavior Change and Data Analytics in the Socio-Digital Era, 51–73. doi:10.4018/978-1-6684-4168-8.ch003

Muñoz-Chávez, J. P., Hernández Rivera, A., & Bolaños-Rodríguez, E. (2021). Hacia la adopción del comercio social en micro y pequeñas empresas en México. *Economía Creativa*, (16), 189–211. doi:10.46840/ec.2021.16.07

Muralidharan, S., & Ko, H. (2019). An InterPlanetary File System (IPFS) based IoT framework. *2019 IEEE International Conference on Consumer Electronics (ICCE)*.

Murray, A., Kim, D., & Combs, J. (2022). The promise of a better internet: What is web 3.0 and what are we building? *SSRN*.

Murray, A., Kim, D., & Combs, J. (2022). The promise of a decentralized Internet: What is web 3.0 and HOW can firms prepare? *Business Horizons*. Advance online publication. doi:10.1016/j.bushor.2022.06.002

Mustaffa, R., & Nordin, N. M. (2017). The challenges of teaching literature in the era of the Fourth Industrial Revolution: The Malaysian context. *Advanced Science Letters, 23*(7), 6356–6358. doi:10.1166/asl.2017.9807

Mystakidis, S., Christopoulos, A., & Pellas, N. (2021). A systematic mapping review of augmented reality applications to support STEM learning in higher education. *Education and Information Technologies*, 1–45. doi:10.1080/014492 9X.2022.2079560

Nagaraj, S. (2021). Role of consumer health consciousness, food safety and attitude on organic food purchase in emerging market: A serial mediation model. *Journal of Retailing and Consumer Services, 59*, 102423. doi:10.1016/j.jretconser.2020.102423

Nair, K., & Gupta, R. (2021). Application of AI technology in modern digital marketing environment. *World Journal of Entrepreneurship, Management and Sustainable Development*. Advance online publication. doi:10.1108/WJEMSD-08-2020-0099

Nakamoto, S. (n.d.). *Bitcoin: A Peer-to-Peer Electronic Cash System*. www.bitcoin.org

Nashwa, A. (2019). The role of digital technologies in the teaching and learning of English literature. *International Journal of Education and Research, 7*(1), 219–228.

Nath, K. (2022). *Evolution of the Internet from Web 1.0 to Metaverse: The Good*. The Bad and The Ugly.

Nel, D., van Niekerk, R., Berthon, J. P., & Davies, T. (1999). Going with the flow: Web sites and customer involvement. *Internet Research, 9*(2), 109–116. doi:10.1108/10662249910264873

Nelson, K. M., Anggraini, E., & Schlüter, A. (2020). Virtual reality as a tool for environmental conservation and fundraising. *PLoS One, 15*(4), e0223631. doi:10.1371/journal.pone.0223631 PMID:32251442

Netcore Cloud. (2021). *Online shopping conversion rate in select verticals before and after offering personalized shopping experience in the United States in 2021* [Graph]. Statista. Retrieved 07 February from https://www-statista-com.jerome.stjohns.edu/statistics/1300238/conversion-rates-before-after-personalization-segment/

News, B. B. C. (2022). *BBC News*. BBC News.

Ng, C. S., & Lee, S. S. (2019). Teaching literature studies in universities and challenges Malaysian students face in IR4.0. *International Journal of Social Science and Humanity*, *9*(8), 215–219.

Ng, E. M. W., & Roslan, S. (2020). Challenges in teaching literature to Malaysian students in the era of IR 4.0. *Journal of Language and Communication*, *7*(1), 46–57.

Ng, S. H., & Tan, Y. S. (2019). Developing critical thinking skills in Malaysian ESL classrooms: An exploratory study. *English Language Teaching*, *12*(2), 68–79.

Nguyen, T. (2022). Toward Human Digital Twins for Cybersecurity Simulations on the Metaverse: Ontological and Network Science Approach. *JMIRx Med*, *3*(2), e33502. doi:10.2196/33502

Nicol, M. J. (2022). Uses, Applications, and Benefits of Virtual Reality Technologies in E-Business. In *Driving Transformative Change in E-Business Through Applied Intelligence and Emerging Technologies* (pp. 209–231). IGI Global. doi:10.4018/978-1-6684-5235-6.ch010

Ning, H., Wang, H., Lin, Y., Wang, W., Dhelim, S., Farha, F., . . . Daneshmand, M. (2021). *A Survey on Metaverse: the State-of-the-art, Technologies, Applications, and Challenges*. arXiv preprint arXiv:2111.09673. doi:10.48550/arXiv.2111.09673

Nita, K. (2014). Building Information Modelling Penetration Factors in Malaysia. *International Journal of Advances in Applied Sciences*, *3*(1), 47–56.

Njoku, J., Nwakanma, C., Amaizu, G., & Kim, D. (2022). Prospects and challenges of Metaverse application in data-driven intelligent transportation systems. *IET Intelligent Transport Systems*. doi:10.1049/itr2.12252

Nkosinkulu, Z. (2023). Humanities in the Age of Blockchain Technology and Web 3.0. In J. Tatlock (Ed.), *Shaping Online Spaces Through Online Humanities Curricula* (pp. 208–225). IGI Global. doi:10.4018/978-1-6684-4055-1.ch010

Nobanee, H., & Ellili, N. O. D. (2023). Non-fungible tokens (NFTs): A bibliometric and systematic review, current streams, developments, and directions for future research. *International Review of Economics & Finance*, *84*, 460–473. doi:10.1016/j.iref.2022.11.014

Noh, Y. (2022). A study on the discussion on Library 5.0 and the generation of Library 1.0 to Library 5.0. *Journal of Librarianship and Information Science*. Advance online publication. doi:10.1177/09610006221106183

Noorbakhsh-Sabet, N., Zand, R., Zhang, Y., & Abedi, V. (2019). Artificial intelligence transforms the future of health care. The American journal of medicine. *The American Journal of Medicine*, *132*(7), 795–801. doi:10.1016/j.amjmed.2019.01.017 PMID:30710543

Novak, T. P., Hoffman, D. L., & Duhachek, A. (2003). The influence of goal-directed and experiential activities on online flow experiences. *Journal of Consumer Psychology*, *13*(1-2), 3–16. doi:10.1207/S15327663JCP13-1&2_01

Novak, T. P., Hoffman, D. L., & Yung, Y. F. (2000). Measuring the customer experience in online environments: A structural modeling approach. *Marketing Science*, *19*(1), 22–42. doi:10.1287/mksc.19.1.22.15184

Nwafor, E. I. (2021). The Effectiveness of Blockchain Smart Contracts in Reshaping the Business Landscape in Nigeria. *Business Law Review*, 195-200. https://www.kluwerlawonline.com/api/Product/CitationPDFURL?file=Journals\BULA\BULA2021027.pdf

Oh, H. J., Kim, J., Chang, J. J. C., Park, N., & Lee, S. (2023). Social benefits of living in the metaverse: The relationships among social presence, supportive interaction, social self-efficacy, and feelings of loneliness. *Computers in Human Behavior*, *139*, 107498. Advance online publication. doi:10.1016/j.chb.2022.107498

Okasha, A. A. (2020). Entrepreneurship in the United Arab Emirates. In *Entrepreneurial Innovation and Economic Development in Dubai and Comparisons to Its Sister Cities* (pp. 158–182). IGI Global. doi:10.4018/978-1-5225-9377-5.ch008

Olaosebikan, J., & Osime, A. (2020). Challenges of teaching literature in the age of digital distraction: A case study of Nigerian undergraduate students. *International Journal of English Linguistics*, *10*(5), 267–277.

Oliver, R. L. (1980). A congitive model of the antecedents and consequences of satisfaction decisions. In Journal of Marketing Research (Vol. 17). Academic Press.

Omale, G. (2019). *Improve customer experience with artificial intelligence*. Academic Press.

Omonayajo, B., Al-Turjman, F., & Cavus, N. (2022). Interactive and innovative technologies for smart education. *Computer Science and Information Systems*, *00*(00), 27. doi:10.2298/CSIS210817027O

Ong, Y. S. (2019). AIR5: Five pillars of artificial intelligence research. *IEEE Transactions on Emerging Topics in Computational Intelligence*, *3*(5), 411–415. doi:10.1109/TETCI.2019.2928344

Oppenlaender, J. (2022). The Perception of Smart Contracts for Governance of the Metaverse. In *Proceedings of the 25th International Academic Mindtrek Conference* (pp. 1-8). 10.1145/3569219.3569300

Ovenden, R. (2015). The digital archive as a research tool: An overview of archival theory, practice and technology. In J. Drucker & P. D. Juhl (Eds.), *History of the digital humanities: A reader* (pp. 331–348). Routledge.

Overgoor, G., Chica, M., Rand, W., & Weishampel, A. (2019). Letting the Computers Take Over: Using AI to Solve Marketing Problems. *California Management Review*, *61*(4), 156–185. doi:10.1177/0008125619859318

Ovunc, S. S., Yolcu, M. B., Emre, S., Elicevik, M., & Celayir, S. (2021). Using Immersive Technologies to Develop Medical Education Materials. *Cureus*. Advance online publication. doi:10.7759/cureus.12647 PMID:33585133

Özel, N. G. (2022). *Metaverse ve Pazarlama Uygulamalarinin Değerlendirilmesi* (M. Saygılı, Ed.). Sürdürülebilirlik Güncel Konular ve Tartışmalar. Efe Akademi.

Ozkara, B. Y., & Bagozzi, R. (2021). The use of event related potentials brain methods in the study of conscious and unconscious consumer decision making processes. *Journal of Retailing and Consumer Services*, *58*, 102202. doi:10.1016/j.jretconser.2020.102202

Özkaynar, K. (2022). Marketing strategies of banks in the period of metaverse, blockchain, and cryptocurrency in the context of consumer behavior theories. *Sivas Soft Bilisim Proje Danismanlik Egitim Sanayi ve Ticaret Limited Sirketi*. doi:10.52898/ijif.2022.1

Page, M. J., McKenzie, J. E., Bossuyt, P. M., Boutron, I., Hoffmann, T. C., Mulrow, C. D., Shamseer, L., Tetzlaff, J. M., Akl, E. A., Brennan, S. E., Chou, R., Glanville, J., Grimshaw, J. M., Hróbjartsson, A., Lalu, M. M., Li, T., Loder, E. W., Mayo-Wilson, E., McDonald, S., ... Moher, D. (2021). The PRISMA 2020 statement: An updated guideline for reporting systematic reviews. *Systematic Reviews*, *10*(1), 1–11. doi:10.118613643-021-01626-4 PMID:33781348

Palaniappan, K., & Fraser, J. B. (n.d.). *Multiresolution tiling for interactive viewing of large datasets*. Academic Press.

Pamucar, D., Deveci, M., Gokasar, I., Tavana, M., & Köppen, M. (2022). A metaverse assessment model for sustainable transportation using ordinal priority approach and Aczel-Alsina norms. *Technological Forecasting and Social Change*, *182*, 121778. doi:10.1016/j.techfore.2022.121778

Panesar, S., Cagle, Y., Chander, D., Morey, J., Fernandez-Miranda, J., & Kliot, M. (2019). Artificial intelligence and the future of surgical robotics. *Annals of Surgery*, *270*(2), 223–226. doi:10.1097/SLA.0000000000003262 PMID:30907754

Papagiannidis, S., & Bourlakis, M. A. (2010). Staging the new retail drama: At a Metaverse near you! *Journal of Virtual Worlds Research*, *2*(5), 425–446. doi:10.4101/jvwr.v2i5.808

Papagiannidis, S., Bourlakis, M., & Li, F. (2008). Making real money in virtual worlds: MMORPGs and emerging business opportunities, challenges and ethical implications in metaverses. *Technological Forecasting and Social Change*, *75*(5), 610–622. doi:10.1016/j.techfore.2007.04.007

Papagiannidis, S., Pantano, E., See-To, E. W., & Bourlakis, M. (2013). Modelling the determinants of a simulated experience in a virtual retail store and users' product purchasing intentions. *Journal of Marketing Management*, *29*(13-14), 1462–1492. doi:10.1080/0267257X.2013.821150

Paremeswaran, P., Keikhosrokiani, P., & Asl, M. P. (2022). Opinion Mining of Readers' Responses to Literary Prize Nominees on Twitter: A Case Study of Public Reaction to the Booker Prize (2018–2020). In F. Saeed, F. Mohammed, & F. Ghaleb (Eds.), Advances on Intelligent Informatics and Computing (pp. 243–257). Springer International Publishing. doi:10.1007/978-3-030-98741-1_21

Park, E., Kim, S., Kim, Y., & Kwon, S. J. (2018). Smart home services as the next mainstream of the ICT industry: Determinants of the adoption of smart home services. *Universal Access in the Information Society*, *17*(1), 175–190. doi:10.100710209-017-0533-0

Park, S. M., & Kim, Y. G. (2022). A Metaverse: Taxonomy, Components, Applications, and Open Challenges. *IEEE Access: Practical Innovations, Open Solutions*, *10*, 4209–4251. doi:10.1109/ACCESS.2021.3140175

Park, S., & Kim, S. (2022). Identifying World Types to Deliver Gameful Experiences for Sustainable Learning in the Metaverse. *Sustainability*, *14*(3), 1361. doi:10.3390u14031361

Patel, A., & Jain, S. (2021). Present and future of semantic web technologies: A research statement. *International Journal of Computers and Applications*, *43*(5), 413–422. doi:10.1080/1206212X.2019.1570666

Patton, M. Q. (2002). Learning in the Field: An Introduction to Qualitative Research (G. B. Rossman & S. F. Rallis, Eds.). Sage.

Pellas, N., Dengel, A., & Christopoulos, A. (2020). A scoping review of immersive virtual reality in STEM education. *IEEE Transactions on Learning Technologies*, *13*(4), 748–761. doi:10.1109/TLT.2020.3019405

Pellas, N., Mystakidis, S., & Kazanidis, I. (2021). Immersive virtual reality in K-12 and higher education: A systematic review of the last decade scientific literature. *Virtual Reality (Waltham Cross)*, *25*(3), 835–861. doi:10.100710055-020-00489-9

Peltokorpi, V., & Hood, A. C. (2019). Communication in Theory and Research on Transactive Memory Systems: A Literature Review. *Topics in Cognitive Science*, *11*(4), 644–667. doi:10.1111/tops.12359

Pereira da Silva, N., Eloy, S., & Resende, R. (2022). Robotic construction analysis: Simulation with virtual reality. *Heliyon*, *8*(10), e11039. Advance online publication. doi:10.1016/j.heliyon.2022.e11039 PMID:36281420

Peres, R., Schreier, M., Schweidel, D. A., & Sorescu, A. (2022). Blockchain meets marketing: Opportunities, threats, and avenues for future research. *International Journal of Research in Marketing*.

Peres, R., Schreier, M., Schweidel, D. A., & Sorescu, A. (2022). Blockchain meets marketing: Opportunities, threats, and avenues for future research. *International Journal of Research in Marketing*. Advance online publication. doi:10.1016/j.ijresmar.2022.08.001

Perla, R., & Hebbalaguppe, R. (2017). *Google cardboard dates augmented reality: Issues, challenges and future opportunities.* arXiv preprint arXiv:1706.03851

Peters, G. W., & Panayi, E. (2016). Understanding Modern Banking Ledgers Through Blockchain Technologies: Future of Transaction Processing and Smart Contracts on the Internet of Money. In P. Tasca, T. Aste, L. Pelizzon, & N. Perony (Eds.), *Banking Beyond Banks and Money: A Guide to Banking Services in the Twenty-First Century* (pp. 239–278). Springer International Publishing. doi:10.1007/978-3-319-42448-4_13

Petit, O., Velasco, C., & Spence, C. (2019). Digital sensory marketing: Integrating new technologies into multisensory online experience. *Journal of Interactive Marketing*, *45*, 42–61. doi:10.1016/j.intmar.2018.07.004

Petit, O., Velasco, C., Wang, Q. J., & Spence, C. (2022). Consumer Consciousness in Multisensory Extended Reality. *Frontiers in Psychology*, *13*, 851753. Advance online publication. doi:10.3389/fpsyg.2022.851753 PMID:35529566

Petrigna, L., & Musumeci, G. (2022). The metaverse: A new challenge for the healthcare system: A scoping review. *Journal of Functional Morphology and Kinesiology*, *7*(3), 63. doi:10.3390/jfmk7030063

Petrilli, D., & Salomoni, P. (2019). Literature and digital literacy: New challenges and opportunities for teaching and learning. *Journal of Education and Training Studies*, *7*(3), 47–54.

Pettersson, A., & Berg, L.-O. (2020). Digital humanities and literary studies: Challenges and opportunities. *Journal of English Studies*, *18*, 65–85.

Pettersson, F. (2021). Understanding digitalization and educational change in school by means of activity theory and the levels of learning concept. *Education and Information Technologies*, *26*(1), 187–204. doi:10.1007/s10639-020-10239-8

Peukert, C., Pfeiffer, J., Meißner, M., Pfeiffer, T., & Weinhardt, C. (2019). Shopping in virtual reality stores: The influence of immersion on system adoption. *Journal of Management Information Systems*, *36*(3), 755–788. doi:10.1080/07421222.2019.1628889

Pierce, D. (2016). Inside Google's plan to make VR amazing for absolutely, positively everyone. *Wired Magazine*.

Plechatá, A., Makransky, G., & Böhm, R. (2022). Can extended reality in the metaverse revolutionise health communication? In NPJ Digital Medicine (Vol. 5, Issue 1). Nature Research. doi:10.103841746-022-00682-x

Polyviou, A., & Pappas, I. O. (2022). Chasing Metaverses: Reflecting on Existing Literature to Understand the Business Value of Metaverses. *Information Systems Frontiers*. Advance online publication. doi:10.100710796-022-10364-4 PMID:36589769

Popescu, D., Dragomir, M., Popescu, S., & Dragomir, D. (2022). Building Better Digital Twins for Production Systems by Incorporating Environmental Related Functions—Literature Analysis and Determining Alternatives. *Applied Sciences (Basel, Switzerland)*, *12*(17), 8657. doi:10.3390/app12178657

Poursoltan, M., Pinède, N., Traore, M. K., & Vallespir, B. (2021). A new descriptive, theoretical framework for cyber-physical and human systems based on activity theory. *IFAC-PapersOnLine*, *54*(1), 918–923. doi:10.1016/j.ifacol.2021.08.109

Priatna, T., Maylawati, D. S., Sugilar, H., & Ramdhani, M. A. (2020). Key success factors of e-learning implementation in higher education. *International Journal of Emerging Technologies in Learning*, *15*(17), 101–114. doi:10.3991/ijet.v15i17.14293

Prieto, J. de la F., Lacasa, P., & Martínez-Borda, R. (2022). *Approaching metaverses: Mixed reality interfaces in youth media platforms*. New Techno Humanities. doi:10.1016/j.techum.2022.04.004

Promwongsa, N., Ebrahimzadeh, A., Naboulsi, D., Kianpisheh, S., Belqasmi, F., Glitho, R., Crespi, N., & Alfandi, O. (2021). A Comprehensive Survey of the Tactile Internet: State-of-the-Art and Research Directions. *IEEE Communications Surveys and Tutorials*, *23*(1), 472–523. doi:10.1109/COMST.2020.3025995

Prova, O. S., Ahmed, F., Sultana, J., & Ashrafuzzaman, M. (2022). Big medical data analytics for diagnosis. In P. Keikhosrokiani (Ed.), *Big Data Analytics for Healthcare* (pp. 111–124). Academic Press., https://doi.org/https://doi.org/10.1016/B978-0-323-91907-4.00013-3

Puleng Modise, M., & Van Den Berg, G. (n.d.). *Covid-19 as an Accelerator for Training and Technology Adoption by Academics in Large-Scale Open and Distance Learning Institutions in Africa*. doi:10.25159/UnisaRxiv/000016.v1

Pu, Q., & Xiang, W. (2022). The metaverse and its influence and transformation on human society. *Metaverse*, *3*(1), 15. doi:10.54517/met.v3i1.1796

Qamar, S., Anwar, Z., & Afzal, M. (2023). A systematic threat analysis and defense strategies for the metaverse and extended reality systems. *Computers & Security*, *128*, 103127. doi:10.1016/j.cose.2023.103127

Qenaj, M., & Beqiri, G. (2022). Marketing in in Hospitality Industry and Its Effect on Consumer Behavior in Industry Behavior in Kosovo and Its Effect on Consumer Social Media Marketing in Hospitality Behavior in Kosovo. *IFAC-PapersOnLine*, *55*(39), 66–69. doi:10.1016/j.ifacol.2022.12.012

Qiu, S., Liu, Q., Zhou, S., & Wu, C. (2019). Review of artificial intelligence adversarial attack and defense technologies. *Applied Sciences (Basel, Switzerland)*, *9*(5), 909. doi:10.3390/app9050909

Rabaai, A. (2009). Identifying critical success factors of ERP Systems at the higher education sector. In *Proceedings of the Third International Symposium on Innovation in Information and Communication Technology* (pp. 133-147). British Computer Society.

Radianti, J., Majchrzak, T. A., Fromm, J., & Wohlgenannt, I. (2020). A systematic review of immersive virtual reality applications for higher education: Design elements, lessons learned, and research agenda. *Computers & Education*, *147*, 103778. Advance online publication. doi:10.1016/j.compedu.2019.103778

Radoff, J. (2021). Market map of the metaverse Medium, https://medium.com/ building-the metaverse/market-map -of-the-metaverse-8ae0cde89696 Access Date: 20.01.2022

Rahaman, T. (2022). Into the Metaverse – Perspectives on a New Reality. *Medical Reference Services Quarterly*, *41*(3), 330–337. doi:10.1080/02763869.2022.2096341 PMID:35980623

Rahill, K. M., & Sebrechts, M. M. (2021). Effects of Avatar player-similarity and player-construction on gaming performance. *Computers in Human Behavior Reports*, *4*, 100131. doi:10.1016/j.chbr.2021.100131

Rai, A. S., Rai, A. S., Mavrikakis, E., & Lam, W. C. (2017). Teaching binocular indirect ophthalmoscopy to novice residents using an augmented reality simulator. *Canadian Journal of Ophthalmology*, *52*(5), 430–434. doi: 10.1016/j.jcjo.2017.02.015

Rajagopal, A. (2019). *Managing startup enterprises in emerging markets: Leadership dynamics and marketing strategies*. Springer Nature. doi:10.1007/978-3-030-28155-7

Rana, S., Udunuwara, M., Dewasiri, N. J., Kashif, M., & Rathnasiri, M. S. H. (2022). Editorial: Is South Asia ready for the next universe – metaverse? Arguments and suggestions for further research. *South Asian Journal of Marketing*, *3*(2), 77–81. doi:10.1108/sajm-10-2022-141

Rauschnabel, P. A., Babin, B. J., tom Dieck, M. C., Krey, N., & Jung, T. (2022). What is augmented reality marketing? Its definition, complexity, and future. In *Journal of Business Research* (Vol. 142, pp. 1140–1150). Elsevier Inc. doi:10.1016/j.jbusres.2021.12.084

Rauschnabel, P. A., Felix, R., Hinsch, C., Shahab, H., & Alt, F. (2022). What is XR? Towards a Framework for Augmented and Virtual Reality. *Computers in Human Behavior, 133*, 107289. doi:10.1016/j.chb.2022.107289

Ravichandran, B. D., & Keikhosrokiani, P. (2022). Classification of Covid-19 misinformation on social media based on neuro-fuzzy and neural network: A systematic review. *Neural Computing & Applications*. Advance online publication. doi:10.100700521-022-07797-y PMID:36159189

Read, S. (2022). *How many consumers are shopping in virtual reality and what can it offer them?* World Economic Forum. Retrieved 07 Februrary from https://www.weforum.org/agenda/2022/08/virtual-reality-shopping-retail/

Riar, M., Xi, N., Korbel, J. J., Zarnekow, R., & Hamari, J. (2022). Using augmented reality for shopping: A framework for AR induced consumer behavior, literature review and future agenda. *Internet Research*. Advance online publication. doi:10.1108/INTR-08-2021-0611

Richards, L. (1999). *Using NVivo in qualitative research*. Sage Publication Ltd.

Rijmenam, V. M. (2022). *Step into the Metaverse: How the Immersive Internet Will Unlock a Trillion Dollar Social Economy*. John Wiley & Sons.

Rijsdijk, S. A., & Hultink, E. J. (2009). How today's consumers perceive tomorrow's smart products *. *Journal of Product Innovation Management, 26*(1), 24–42. doi:10.1111/j.1540-5885.2009.00332.x

Rimol, M. (2022, February 7). *Gartner predicts 25% of people will spend at least one hour per day in the metaverse by 2026*. Gartner. https://www.gartner.com/en/newsroom/press-releases/2022-02-07-gartner-predicts-25-percent-of-people-will-spend-at-least-one-hour-per-day-in-the-metaverse-by-2026

Robertson, H. (2021, December 25). *Wall street is pumped about the metaverse. but critics say it's massively overhyped and will be a regulatory minefield*. Business Insider. https://markets.businessinsider.com/news/stocks/metaverse-outlook-overhyped-regulations-facebook-meta-virtual-worlds-genz-2021-12

Robinson, A. R. III, Gravenstein, N., Cooper, L. A., Lizdas, D., Luria, I., & Lampotang, S. (2014). A mixed-reality part-task trainer for subclavian venous access. *Simulation in Healthcare, 9*(1), 56–64. doi: 10.1097/SIH.0b013e31829b3fb3

Rockart, J. F. (1982). *The changing role of the information systems executive: A critical success factors perspective*. Academic Press.

Rogers, E. M., & Singhal, A. (2003). Empowerment and Communication: Lessons Learned From Organizing for Social Change. *Annals of the International Communication Association, 27*(1), 67–85. doi:10.1080/23808985.2003.11679022

Rojas-Sánchez, M. A., Palos-Sánchez, P. R., & Folgado-Fernández, J. A. (2022). Systematic literature review and bibliometric analysis on virtual reality and education. *Education and Information Technologies*. Advance online publication. doi:10.100710639-022-11167-5 PMID:35789766

Rolland, J. P., & Fuchs, H. (2000). Optical versus video see-through head-mounted displays in medical visualization. *Presence, 9*(3), 287–309. doi:10.1162/105474600566808

Romao, M., Costa, J., & Costa, C. J. (2019). Robotic process automation: A case study in the banking industry. *2019 14th Iberian Conference on information systems and technologies*. 10.23919/CISTI.2019.8760733

Roo, J. S., Gervais, R., Frey, J., & Hachet, M. (2017, May). Inner garden: Connecting inner states to a mixed reality sandbox for mindfulness. In *Proceedings of the 2017 CHI conference on human factors in computing systems* (pp. 1459-1470). ACM.

Rostami, S., & Maier, M. (2022). The Metaverse and Beyond: Implementing Advanced Multiverse Realms With Smart Wearables. *IEEE Access: Practical Innovations, Open Solutions, 10*, 110796–110806. doi:10.1109/ACCESS.2022.3215736

Rowland, A., Folmer, E., & Beek, W. (2020). Towards Self-Service GIS—Combining the Best of the Semantic Web and Web GIS. *ISPRS International Journal of Geo-Information, 9*(12), 753. doi:10.3390/ijgi9120753

Roxin, I., & Bouchereau, A. (2017). Introduction to the Technologies of the Ecosystem of the Internet of Things. *Internet of Things: Evolutions and Innovations, 4*, 51–95. doi:10.1002/9781119427391.ch3

Ruiz Mejia, J., & Rawat, D. (2022). *Recent Advances in a Medical Domain Metaverse: Status, Challenges, and Perspective.* Paper presented at the 2022 Thirteenth International Conference on Ubiquitous and Future Networks (ICUFN). 10.1109/ICUFN55119.2022.9829645

Rusell, J. (2017). *Amazon completes its acquisition of Middle Eastern e-commerce firm Souq.* Retrieved from https://techcrunch.com/2017/07/03/amazon-souq-com-completed/

Ruwodo, V., Pinomaa, A., Vesisenaho, M., Ntinda, M., & Sutinen, E. (2022). Enhancing Software Engineering Education in Africa through a Metaversity. *2022 IEEE Frontiers in Education Conference (FIE)*, 1–8. 10.1109/FIE56618.2022.9962729

Sadovets, O., Martynyuk, O., Orlovska, O., Lysak, H., Korol, S., & Zembytska, M. (2022). Gamification in the Informal Learning Space of Higher Education (in the Context of the Digital Transformation of Education). *Postmodern Openings, 13*(1), 330–350. doi:10.18662/po/13.1/399

Sagnier, C., Loup-Escande, E., Lourdeaux, D., Thouvenin, I., & Valléry, G. (2020). User Acceptance of Virtual Reality: An Extended Technology Acceptance Model. *International Journal of Human-Computer Interaction, 36*(11), 993–1007. doi:10.1080/10447318.2019.1708612

Sahaf, M. A. (2019). *Strategic marketing: making decisions for strategic advantage.* PHI Learning Pvt. Ltd.

Şahin, D., & Mutlu, S. (2022). Meta Influencer: Dünyada Yer Alan Meta Influencer Örneklerinin Değerlendirilmesi. A. Güven & M. S. Tam (Ed.), Alternatif Dijital Evren Metaverse-II Reklam, Pazarlama, Marka ve İşletme Yönetimi (101-126). Necmettin Erbakan Üniversitesi Yayınları

Sahin, I. (2006). Detailed review of rogers' diffusion of innovations theory and educational technology-related studies based on rogers' theory. In The Turkish Online Journal of Educational Technology (Vol. 5). Academic Press.

Salar, H. C., Başarmak, U., & Sezgin, M. E. (2023). Educational Integration of the Metaverse Environment in the Context of Web 3.0 Technologies: A Critical Overview of Planning, Implementation, and Evaluation. In G. Durak & S. Cankaya (Eds.), *Shaping the Future of Online Learning: Education in the Metaverse* (pp. 154–173). IGI Global. doi:10.4018/978-1-6684-6513-4.ch009

Salem, T., & Dragomir, M. (2022). Options for and Challenges of Employing Digital Twins in Construction Management. *Applied Sciences (Basel, Switzerland), 12*(6), 2928. doi:10.3390/app12062928

Samara, D., Magnisalis, I., & Peristeras, V. (2020). Artificial intelligence and big data in tourism: A systematic literature review. *Journal of Hospitality and Tourism Technology, 11*(2), 343–367. doi:10.1108/JHTT-12-2018-0118

Samoilenko, S., & Osei-Bryson, K. M. (2019). Representation matters: An exploration of the socio-economic impacts of ICT-enabled public value in the context of sub-Saharan economies. *International Journal of Information Management, 49*, 69–85. doi:10.1016/j.ijinfomgt.2019.03.006

Sanji, M., Behzadi, H., & Gomroki, G. (2022). Chatbot: An intelligent tool for libraries. *Library Hi Tech News, 39*(3), 17–20. doi:10.1108/LHTN-01-2021-0002

Santana, C., & Albareda, L. (2022). Blockchain and the emergence of Decentralized Autonomous Organizations (DAOs): An integrative model and research agenda. *Technological Forecasting and Social Change, 182*, 121806. doi:10.1016/j.techfore.2022.121806

Saponaro, M., Le Gal, D., Gao, M., Guisiano, M., & Maniere, I. C. M. L. (2018). Challenges and opportunities of artificial intelligence in the fashion world. *International Conference on Intelligent and Innovative Computing Applications.*

Saqib, N. A., Salam, A. A., Atta Ur, R., & Dash, S. (2021). Reviewing risks and vulnerabilities in web 2.0 for matching security considerations in web 3.0. *Journal of Discrete Mathematical Sciences and Cryptography, 24*(3), 809–825. doi:10.1080/09720529.2020.1857903

Saykili, A. (2019). Higher Education in The Digital Age: The Impact of Digital Connective Technologies. *Journal of Educational Technology and Online Learning*, 1–15. doi:10.31681/jetol.516971

Scavarelli, A., Arya, A., & Teather, R. J. (2021). Virtual reality and augmented reality in social learning spaces: A literature review. *Virtual Reality (Waltham Cross), 25*(1), 257–277. doi:10.100710055-020-00444-8

Scherer, M. (2018). Technological advances and their impact on literature: Exploring ethical and societal implications. *Journal of Digital and Social Media Marketing, 6*(2), 173–181. doi:10.1080/24702405.2018.1480987

Schlosser, A. E. (2003). Computers as situational cues: Implications for consumers product cognitions and attitudes. *Journal of Consumer Psychology, 13*(1-2), 103–112. doi:10.1207/S15327663JCP13-1&2_09

Schmitt, B. (1999). Experiential marketing. *Journal of Marketing Management, 15*(1-3), 53–67. doi:10.1362/026725799784870496

Schreibman, S., & Siemens, R. (2016). A short history of digital humanities. In S. Schreibman, R. Siemens, & J. Unsworth (Eds.), *A new companion to digital humanities* (pp. 3–13). John Wiley & Sons.

Seetharaman, A., Niranjan, I., Saravanan, A. S., & Balaji, D. (2017). A Study of the Moderate Growth of Online Retailing (E-commerce) In the UAE. *Journal of Developing Areas, 51*(4), 397–412. doi:10.1353/jda.2017.0109

Segendorf, B. (2014). What is bitcoin. *Sveri ges Riksbank. Economic Review (Kansas City, Mo.), 2014*, 2–71.

Sela, E., & Sivan, Y. (2009). Enterprise e-learning success factors: An analysis of practitioners' perspective (with a downturn addendum). *Interdisciplinary Journal of E-Learning and Learning Objects, 5*(1), 335–343.

Senecal, S., Gharbi, J. E., & Nantel, J. (2002). *The influence of flow on hedonic and utilitarian shopping values.* ACR North American Advances.

Serin, H. (2020). Virtual reality in education from the perspective of teachers. Amazonia investiga, 9(26), 291-303. doi:10.34069/AI/2020.26.02.33

Shaari, N. N., & Kassim, N. A. (2019). Enhancing the teaching and learning of literature in ESL classroom: A study on the implementation of technology. *Journal of Nusantara Studies, 4*(2), 105–119.

Sharma, R. K., Kumar, D., & Kumar, P. (2007). Quality costing in process industries through QCAS: A practical case. *International Journal of Production Research, 45*(15), 3381–3403. doi:10.1080/00207540600774067

Shatat, A. S., & Shatat, A. S. (2021). Virtual migration of higher education institutions in times of crisis: Major challenges and critical success factors. *Human Systems Management, 40*(5), 653–667. doi:10.3233/HSM-201160

Shaw, J., Rudzicz, F., Jamieson, T., & Goldfarb, A. (2019, July 10). Artificial Intelligence and the Implementation Challenge. *Journal of Medical Internet Research*, *21*(7), e13659. doi:10.2196/13659 PMID:31293245

Shehzad, H. M. F., Ibrahim, R., Khaidzir, K. A. M., Alrefai, N., Chweya, R. K., Zrekat, M. M. Y., & Hassan, O. H. A. (2022). A Literature Review of Technology Adoption theories and Acceptance models for novelty in Building Information Modeling. *Journal of Information Technology Management*, *14*, 83–113.

Shen, B., Tan, W., Guo, J., Cai, H., Wang, B., & Zhuo, S. (2020). A study on design requirement development and satisfaction for future virtual world systems. *Future Internet*, *12*(7), 112. doi:10.3390/fi12070112

Shen, B., Tan, W., Guo, J., Zhao, L., & Qin, P. (2021). How to promote user purchase in metaverse? A systematic literature review on consumer behavior research and virtual commerce application design. *Applied Sciences (Basel, Switzerland)*, *11*(23), 11087. doi:10.3390/app112311087

Shen, L. (2019). The use of social media in teaching literature. *Journal of Language Teaching and Research*, *10*(2), 368–375.

Shen, X. L., Li, Y. J., & Sun, Y. (2018). Wearable health information systems intermittent discontinuance: A revised expectation-disconfirmation model. *Industrial Management & Data Systems*, *118*(3), 506–523. doi:10.1108/IMDS-05-2017-0222

Shen, Z., Tan, S., & Siau, K. (2018). Challenges in learning unified modeling language: From the perspective of diagrammatic representation and reasoning. *Communications of the Association for Information Systems*, *43*(1), 545–565. doi:10.17705/1CAIS.04330

Sherry, J. L. (2004). Flow and media enjoyment. *Communication Theory*, *14*(4), 328–347. doi:10.1111/j.1468-2885.2004.tb00318.x

Sholihin, M., Sari, R. C., Yuniarti, N., & Ilyana, S. (2020). A new way of teaching business ethics: The evaluation of virtual reality-based learning media. *International Journal of Management Education*, *18*(3), 100428. Advance online publication. doi:10.1016/j.ijme.2020.100428

Siegrist, M., Ung, C. Y., Zank, M., Marinello, M., Kunz, A., Hartmann, C., & Menozzi, M. (2019). Consumers' food selection behaviors in three-dimensional (3D) virtual reality. *Food Research International*, *117*, 50–59. doi:10.1016/j.foodres.2018.02.033 PMID:30736923

Siekpe, J. S. (2005). An examination of the multidimensionality of flow construct in a computer-mediated environment. *Journal of Electronic Commerce Research*, *6*(1), 31. doi:10.120715327744joce15024

Sila-Nowicka, K., & Thakuriah, P. (2019). Multi-sensor movement analysis for transport safety and health applications. *PLoS One*, *14*(1), e0210090. Advance online publication. doi:10.1371/journal.pone.0210090 PMID:30703128

Singh, A. K., Liu, J., Tirado Cortes, C. A., & Lin, C. T. (2021, May). *Virtual global landmark: An augmented reality technique to improve spatial navigation learning*. In *Extended Abstracts of the 2021 CHI Conference on Human Factors in Computing Systems* (pp. 1-6).

Size, D. I. M., & Growth, D. I. M. S. (2018). *Share & trends analysis report by product (Titanium Implants, Zirconium Implants), by region (North America, Europe, Asia Pacific, Latin America, MEA), and segment forecasts, 2018-2024*. Personalized Medicine Market Analysis by Product and Segment Forecasts to 2022.

Skadberg, Y. X., & Kimmel, J. R. (2004). Visitors' flow experience while browsing a Web site: Its measurement, contributing factors and consequences. *Computers in Human Behavior*, *20*(3), 403–422. doi:10.1016/S0747-5632(03)00050-5

Slater, M., & Sanchez-Vives, M. V. (2016). Enhancing our lives with immersive virtual reality. *Frontiers in Robotics and AI, 3*, 74. doi:10.3389/frobt.2016.00074

Sodhro, A. H., Pirbhulal, S., & Sangaiah, A. K. (2018). Convergence of IoT and product lifecycle management in medical health care. *Future Generation Computer Systems, 86*, 380–391. doi:10.1016/j.future.2018.03.052

Soegoto, E. S., Utami, R. D., & Hermawan, Y. A. (2019). Influence of artificial intelligence in automotive industry. *Journal of Physics: Conference Series, 1402*(6), 066081. doi:10.1088/1742-6596/1402/6/066081

Sofian, N. B., Keikhosrokiani, P., & Asl, M. P. (2022a). Opinion mining and text analytics of reader reviews of Yoko Ogawa's The Housekeeper and the Professor in Goodreads. In P. Keikhosrokiani & M. Pourya Asl (Eds.), Handbook of Research on Opinion Mining and Text Analytics on Literary Works and Social Media (pp. 240–262). IGI Global. doi:10.4018/978-1-7998-9594-7.ch010

Sofian, N. B., Keikhosrokiani, P., & Asl, M. P. (2022b). Opinion Mining and Text Analytics of Reader Reviews of Yoko Ogawa's The Housekeeper and the Professor in Goodreads. In P. Keikhosrokiani & M. Pourya Asl (Eds.), Handbook of Research on Opinion Mining and Text Analytics on Literary Works and Social Media (pp. 240–262). IGI Global. doi:10.4018/978-1-7998-9594-7.ch010

Sofian, N. B., Keikhosrokiani, P., & Asl, M. P. (2022). Opinion Mining and Text Analytics of Reader Reviews of Yoko Ogawa's The Housekeeper and the Professor in Goodreads. In P. Keikhosrokiani & M. Pourya Asl (Eds.), *Handbook of Research on Opinion Mining and Text Analytics on Literary Works and Social Media* (pp. 240–262). IGI Global. doi:10.4018/978-1-7998-9594-7.ch010

Sohaib, O., Hussain, W., Asif, M., Ahmad, M., & Mazzara, M. (2019). A PLS-SEM neural network approach for understanding cryptocurrency adoption. *IEEE Access: Practical Innovations, Open Solutions, 8*, 13138–13150. doi:10.1109/ACCESS.2019.2960083

Sohn, J. W., & Kim, J. K. (2020). Factors that influence purchase intentions in social commerce. *Technology in Society, 63*(August), 101365. doi:10.1016/j.techsoc.2020.101365

Solakis, K., Katsoni, V., Mahmoud, A. B., & Grigoriou, N. (2022). Factors affecting value co-creation through artificial intelligence in tourism: A general literature review. *Journal of Tourism Futures*. doi:10.1108/JTF-06-2021-0157

Soleimani, S. M., Jaeger, M., Faheiman, A., & Alaqqad, A. R. (2022). Success factors of recently implemented eLearning methods at higher education institutions in Kuwait. *Quality in Higher Education*. doi:10.1080/13538322.2022.2132702

Son, A. L. B., & Amparado, M. A. P. (2018). Integration of Information and Communications Technology (ICT) Tools in the Instructional Program of a University. *International Journal of Social Sciences & Educational Studies, 5*(1), 63.

Song, Y., Li, G., Li, T., & Li, Y. (2021). A purchase decision support model considering consumer personalization about aspirations and risk attitudes. *Journal of Retailing and Consumer Services, 63*(August), 102728. doi:10.1016/j.jretconser.2021.102728

Sony, M., & Naik, S. (2020). Industry 4.0 integration with socio-technical systems theory: A systematic review and proposed theoretical model. *Technology in Society, 61*. doi:10.1016/j.techsoc.2020.101248

Sortlist. (2022a). *Did the pandemic accelerate metaverse technology?* [Graph]. Statista. Retrieved 18 February from https://www-statista-com.jerome.stjohns.edu/statistics/1302264/metaverse-acceleration-due-to-covid-19/?locale=en

Sortlist. (2022b). *What are your main doubts regarding the metaverse?* [Graph]. Statista. Retrieved 18 February from https://www-statista-com.jerome.stjohns.edu/statistics/1302221/metaverse-project-doubt-businesses/?locale=en

Sparkes, M. (2021). What is a metaverse. *New Scientist, 251*(3348), 18. doi:10.1016/S0262-4079(21)01450-0

Srimadhaven, T., Chris Junni, A., Harshith, N., Jessenth Ebenezer, S., Shabari Girish, S., & Priyaadharshini, M. (2020). Learning analytics: Virtual reality for programming course in higher education. *Procedia Computer Science, 172,* 433–437. doi:10.1016/j.procs.2020.05.095

Stackpole, T. (2022, July 1). Exploring the metaverse. *Harvard Business Review.* https://hbr.org/2022/07/exploring-the-metaverse

Staff, A. (2017). *SOUQ.com and SAP to boost GCC e-commerce.* Retrieved from https://www.logisticsmiddleeast.com/article-12995-souqcom-and-sap-to-boost-gcc-e-commerce

Stair, R., & Reynolds, G. (2020). *Principles of information systems.* Cengage Learning.

Steemit. (2023). *Main page.* Steemit Inc. Retrieved 18 February from https://steemit.com/

Steffen, J. H., Gaskin, J. E., Meservy, T. O., Jenkins, J. L., & Wolman, I. (2019). Framework of affordances for virtual reality and augmented reality. *Journal of Management Information Systems, 36*(3), 683–729. doi:10.1080/07421222.2019.1628877

Step into the metaverse: How the immersive Internet will unlock a trillion-dollar social economy. (n.d.). Retrieved November 5, 2022. https://www.wiley.com/en-ie/Step+into+the+Metaverse%3A+How+the+Immersive+Internet+Will+Unlock+a+Trillion+Dollar+Social+Economy-p-9781119887591

Stephen, A. T. (2016). The role of digital and social media marketing in consumer behavior. *Current Opinion in Psychology, 10,* 17–21. doi:10.1016/j.copsyc.2015.10.016

Stephenson, N. (1992). *Snow Crash.* Del Rey.

Stockburger, L., Kokosioulis, G., Mukkamala, A., Mukkamala, R. R., & Avital, M. (2021). Blockchain-enabled decentralized identity management: The case of self-sovereign identity in public transportation. *Blockchain: Research and Applications, 2*(2), 100014.

Stone, M., Aravopoulou, E., Ekinci, Y., Evans, G., Hobbs, M., Labib, A., Laughlin, P., Machtynger, J., & Machtynger, L. (2020). Artificial intelligence (AI) in strategic marketing decision-making: A research agenda. *The Bottom Line (New York, N.Y.), 33*(2), 183–200. doi:10.1108/BL-03-2020-0022

Sugimoto, M., Yasuda, H., Koda, K., Suzuki, M., Yamazaki, M., Tezuka, T., ... Azuma, T. (2010). Image overlay navigation by markerless surface registration in gastrointestinal, hepatobiliary and pancreatic surgery. *Journal of Hepato-Biliary-Pancreatic Sciences, 17*(5), 629–636. doi: 10.1007/s00534-009-0199-y

Suh, A., & Prophet, J. (2018). The state of immersive technology research: A literature analysis. *Computers in Human Behavior, 86,* 77–90. doi:10.1016/j.chb.2018.04.019

Suhendra, N. H. B., Keikhosrokiani, P., Asl, M. P., & Zhao, X. (2022). Opinion Mining and Text Analytics of Literary Reader Responses: A Case Study of Reader Responses to KL Noir Volumes in Goodreads Using Sentiment Analysis and Topic. In P. Keikhosrokiani & M. Pourya Asl (Eds.), Handbook of Research on Opinion Mining and Text Analytics on Literary Works and Social Media (pp. 191–239). IGI Global. doi: 10.4018/978-1-7998-9594-7.ch009

Suhendra, N. H. B., Keikhosrokiani, P., Asl, M. P., & Zhao, X. (2022). Opinion Mining and Text Analytics of Literary Reader Responses: A Case Study of Reader Responses to KL Noir Volumes in Goodreads Using Sentiment Analysis and Topic. In P. Keikhosrokiani & M. Pourya Asl (Eds.), *Handbook of Research on Opinion Mining and Text Analytics on Literary Works and Social Media* (pp. 191–239). IGI Global. doi:10.4018/978-1-7998-9594-7.ch009

Sun, J., Gan, W., Chen, Z., Li, J., & Yu, P. S. (2022). *Big data meets metaverse: A survey.* arXiv preprint arXiv:2210.16282.

Sun, J., Gan, W., Chen, Z., Li, J., & Yu, P. S. (n.d.). *Big Data Meets Metaverse: A Survey.* https://www.roblox.com/

Sung, C. S., & Park, J. Y. (2021). Understanding of blockchain-based identity management system adoption in the public sector. *Journal of Enterprise Information Management, 34*(5), 1481–1505. doi:10.1108/JEIM-12-2020-0532

Sutherland, J., Belec, J., Sheikh, A., Chepelev, L., Althobaity, W., Chow, B. J., Mitsouras, D., Christensen, A., Rybicki, F. J., & La Russa, D. J. (2019). Applying modern virtual and augmented reality technologies to medical images and models. *Journal of Digital Imaging, 32*(1), 38–53. doi:10.100710278-018-0122-7

Syam, N., & Sharma, A. (2018). Waiting for a sales renaissance in the fourth industrial revolution: Machine learning and artificial intelligence in sales research and practice. *Industrial Marketing Management, 69*, 135–146. doi:10.1016/j.indmarman.2017.12.019

Szymkowiak, A., Melović, B., Dabić, M., Jeganathan, K., & Kundi, G. S. (2021). Information technology and Gen Z: The role of teachers, the internet, and technology in the education of young people. *Technology in Society, 65.* doi:10.1016/j.techsoc.2021.101565

Taherdoost, H. (2018). A review of technology acceptance and adoption models and theories. *Procedia Manufacturing, 22*, 960–967. doi:10.1016/j.promfg.2018.03.137

Tait, E., & Pierson, C. (2022). Artificial Intelligence and Robots in Libraries: Opportunities in LIS Curriculum for Preparing the Librarians of Tomorrow. *Journal of the Australian Library and Information Association, 71*(3), 256–274. doi:10.1080/24750158.2022.2081111

Takano, M., & Taka, F. (2022). Fancy avatar identification and behaviors in the virtual world: Preceding avatar customization and succeeding communication. *Computers in Human Behavior Reports, 6*, 100176. doi:10.1016/j.chbr.2022.100176

Tammi, M. M., Baki, R., & Siraj, S. (2021). Teaching literature studies in universities and challenges Malaysian students face in IR4.0. *Journal of Language and Cultural Education, 9*(2), 176–191.

Tammi, P. (2020). Industry 4.0 and the future of literature. *Journal of the Association for the Study of Australian Literature, 20*(2), 1–13.

Tammi, T., Käpylä, M., Vainio, L., & Sutinen, E. (2021). Promoting critical thinking in literature education: A systematic literature review. *Education Sciences, 11*(1), 36.

Tan, P. J. B. (2013). Applying the UTAUT to understand factors affecting the use of english e-learning websites in Taiwan. *SAGE Open, 3*(4). doi:10.1177/2158244013503837

Tan, T. F., Li, Y., Lim, J. S., Gunasekeran, D. V., Teo, Z. L., Ng, W. Y., & Ting, D. S. W. (2022). Metaverse and virtual health care in ophthalmology: Opportunities and challenges. *Asia-Pacific Journal of Ophthalmology, 11*(3), 237–246. doi:10.1097/apo.0000000000000537

Tan, T. F., Li, Y., Lim, J. S., Gunasekeran, D. V., Teo, Z. L., Ng, W. Y., & Ting, D. S. W. (2022). Metaverse and Virtual Health Care in Ophthalmology: Opportunities and Challenges. *Asia-Pacific Journal of Ophthalmology, 11*(3), 237–246. doi:10.1097/APO.0000000000000537 PMID:35772084

Tan, T. M., Makkonen, H., Kaur, P., & Salo, J. (2022). How do ethical consumers utilize sharing economy platforms as part of their sustainable resale behavior? The role of consumers' green consumption values. *Technological Forecasting and Social Change, 176*, 121432. doi:10.1016/j.techfore.2021.121432

Tan, Z. (2022). *Metaverse.* HCI, and Its Future.

Tarouco, L., Gorziza, B., Corrêa, Y., Amaral, É. M. H., & Müller, T. (2013). Virtual laboratory for teaching Calculus: An immersive experience. *2013 IEEE Global Engineering Education Conference (EDUCON)*, 774–781. 10.1109/EduCon.2013.6530195

Tayfun, A., Silik, C. E., Şimşek, E., & Dülger, A. S. (2022). Metaverse: Turizm İçin Bir Fırsat Mı? Yoksa Bir Tehdit Mi?(Metaverse: An Opportunity. *Journal of Tourism and Gastronomy Studies*, *10*(2), 818–836. doi:10.21325/jotags.2022.1017

Taylor, L. N. (2002). *Video games: Perspective, point-of-view, and immersion*. Academic Press.

Temesvári, Z. M., Maros, D., & Kádár, P. (2019). Review of Mobile Communication and the 5G in Manufacturing. *Procedia Manufacturing*, *32*, 600–612. doi:10.1016/j.promfg.2019.02.259

Templier, M., & Paré, G. (2015). A framework for guiding and evaluating literature reviews. *Communications of the Association for Information Systems*, *37*(1), 6. doi:10.17705/1CAIS.03706

Tengku Putri Norishah, T. M., & Abdullah, N. (2018). Issues and challenges in teaching English literature at Malaysian higher education institutions. *Journal of Nusantara Studies*, *3*(2), 47–64.

Teng, Z., Cai, Y., Gao, Y., Zhang, X., & Li, X. (2022). Factors affecting learners' adoption of an educational metaverse platform: An empirical study based on an extended UTAUT model. *Mobile Information Systems*, *2022*, 1–15. doi:10.1155/2022/4663740

Teng, Z., Cai, Y., Gao, Y., Zhang, X., & Li, X. (2022). Factors Affecting Learners' Adoption of an Educational Metaverse Platform: An Empirical Study Based on an Extended UTAUT Model. *Mobile Information Systems*, *2022*, 1–15. Advance online publication. doi:10.1155/2022/5479215

Teoh Yi Zhe, I., & Keikhosrokiani, P. (2020). Knowledge workers mental workload prediction using optimised ELANFIS. *Applied Intelligence*. Advance online publication. doi:10.100710489-020-01928-5

The acceptance of smart home technology—University of Twente Student Theses. (n.d.). Retrieved November 9, 2022. https://essay.utwente.nl/75338/ Value-creation-in-the-metaverse.pdf

The Economist. (2022). From shared virtual experience to real value. *The Economist*. Retrieved 28 January from https://events.economist.com/metaverse/

TheNational. (2019a). *UAE e-commerce transactions to reach $16bn in 2019, study says*. Retrieved from https://www.thenational.ae/business/technology/uae-e-commerce-transactions-to-reach-16bn-in-2019-study-says-1.889835

TheNational. (2019b). *Souq becomes Amazon.ae in the UAE*. Retrieved from https://www.thenational.ae/business/technology/souq-becomes-amazon-ae-in-the-uae-1.855759

Thomason, J. (2021). How will the Metaverse change health care? *Journal of Metaverse*, *1*(1), 13–16.

Thompson, R. L., Hlgglns, C. A., & Howell, J. M. (n.d.). *Utilization of Personal Computers Personal Computing: Toward a Conceptual Model of Utilization*. Academic Press.

Tichenor, M., & Sridhar, D. (2019). Metric partnerships: Global burden of disease estimates within the World Bank, the World Health Organisation and the Institute for Health Metrics and Evaluation. *Wellcome Open Research*, *4*. doi:10.12688/wellcomeopenres.15011.2

Tiggemann, M., & Anderberg, I. (2020). Social media is not real: The effect of 'Instagram vs reality' images on women's social comparison and body image. *New Media & Society*, *22*(12), 2183–2199. doi:10.1177/1461444819888720

Tlili, A., Huang, R., & Kinshuk. (2023). Metaverse for climbing the ladder toward 'Industry 5.0' and 'Society 5.0'? *Service Industries Journal*. doi:10.1080/02642069.2023.2178644

Tlili, A., Huang, R., Shehata, B., Liu, D., Zhao, J., Metwally, A. H. S., Wang, H., Denden, M., Bozkurt, A., Lee, L.-H., Beyoglu, D., Altinay, F., Sharma, R. C., Altinay, Z., Li, Z., Liu, J., Ahmad, F., Hu, Y., Salha, S., ... Burgos, D. (2022). Is Metaverse in education a blessing or a curse: A combined content and bibliometric analysis. *Smart Learning Environments*, *9*(1), 24. doi:10.118640561-022-00205-x

Toktay, Y. (2022). Metaverse Evrenlerinde Kripto Paralarin Rolü. A. Güven & M. S. Tam (Ed.), Alternatif Dijital Evren Metaverse-II Reklam, Pazarlama, Marka ve İşletme Yönetimi (59-78). Necmettin Erbakan Üniversitesi Yayınları

Topsümer, F., & Toktop, O. (2022). Metaverse Platformlarinda Pazarlama, Reklam ve Marka İletişimi. A. Güven & M. S. Tam (Ed.), Alternatif Dijital Evren Metaverse-II Reklam, Pazarlama, Marka ve İşletme Yönetimi (59-78). Necmettin Erbakan Üniversitesi Yayınları

Toraman, Y. (2018). *User Acceptance of Metaverse: Insights from Technology Acceptance Model (TAM) and Planned Behavior Theory (PBT)*, *7*(2). doi:10.5195/emaj.2018.134

Tor, S. F., Gora, R. C., & Ahmed, S. (2021). Identifying of ICT Tools to Improve Project Research by Graduating Undergraduates of a Nigerian Premier University. *Covenant Journal of Informatics & Tongxin Jishu*, *9*(2).

Triandis, H. C. (1978). 43 Cross-Cultural Social and Personality Psychologyl The paper will provide, first, definitions of ecology and the subsistence, cultural, social, individual, interindividual and projective systems. Second, the most plausible dimensions along which such systems. In *Triandis and Brislin*. Przeworski and Teune.

Trunfio, M., & Rossi, S. (2022). Advances in Metaverse Investigation: Streams of Research and Future Agenda. *Virtual Worlds*, *1*(2), 103–129. doi:10.3390/virtualworlds1020007

Tsai, J. T., Fang, J. C., & Chou, J. H. (2013). Optimized task scheduling and resource allocation on cloud computing environment using improved differential evolution algorithm. *Computers & Operations Research*, *40*(12), 3045–3055. doi:10.1016/j.cor.2013.06.012

Türk, G. D., Bayrakci, S., & Akçay, E. (2022). Metaverse ve Benlik Sunumu. *Turkish Online Journal of Design Art and Communication*, *12*(2), 316–333. doi:10.7456/11202100/008

Tuten, T. L., & Solomon, M. R. (2017). Social media marketing. *Sage (Atlanta, Ga.)*.

Unity. (n.d.). *Unity*. Unity Website.

Uppot, R. N., Laguna, B., McCarthy, C. J., De Novi, G., Phelps, A., Siegel, E., & Courtier, J. (2019). Implementing virtual and augmented reality tools for Radiology Education and training, communication, and clinical care. *Radiology*, *291*(3), 570–580. doi:10.1148/radiol.2019182210

Valaskova, K., Kramarova, K., & Bartosova, V. (2015). Multi criteria models used in Slovak consumer market for business decision making. *Procedia Economics and Finance*, *26*, 174–182. doi:10.1016/S2212-5671(15)00913-2

Valle-Cruz, D. (2019). Public value of e-government services through emerging technologies. *International Journal of Public Sector Management*, *32*(5), 530–545. Advance online publication. doi:10.1108/IJPSM-03-2018-0072

Valle-Cruz, D., Criado, J. I., Sandoval-Almazán, R., & Ruvalcaba-Gomez, E. A. (2020). Assessing the public policy-cycle framework in the age of artificial intelligence: From agenda-setting to policy evaluation. *Government Information Quarterly*, *37*(4), 101509. doi:10.1016/j.giq.2020.101509

Valle-Cruz, D., Fernandez-Cortez, V., & Gil-Garcia, J. R. (2022). From E-budgeting to smart budgeting: Exploring the potential of artificial intelligence in government decision-making for resource allocation. *Government Information Quarterly*, *39*(2), 101644. doi:10.1016/j.giq.2021.101644

Van Schaik, P., & Ling, J. (2011). An integrated model of interaction experience for information retrieval in a Web-based encyclopaedia. *Interacting with Computers*, *23*(1), 18–32. doi:10.1016/j.intcom.2010.07.002

VanDerSchaaf, H., & Daim, T. (2020). Critical Factors Related to Student Success Technology. *International Journal of Innovation and Technology Management*, *17*(06), 2050045. doi:10.1142/S0219877020500455

Varma, P., Nijjer, S., Kaur, B., & Sharma, S. (2022). Blockchain for transformation in digital marketing. In Handbook of Research on the Platform Economy and the Evolution of E-Commerce (pp. 274 298). IGI Global.

Vasarainen, M., Paavola, S., & Vetoshkina, L. (2021). A systematic literature review on extended reality: Virtual, augmented and mixed reality in working life. *The International Journal of Virtual Reality: a Multimedia Publication for Professionals*, *21*(2), 1–28. doi:10.20870/IJVR.2021.21.2.4620

Vasilevski, N., & Birt, J. (2020). Analysing construction student experiences of mobile mixed reality enhanced learning in virtual and augmented reality environments. *Research in Learning Technology*, *28*(0). Advance online publication. doi:10.25304/rlt.v28.2329

Vávra, P., Roman, J., Zonča, P., Ihnát, P., Němec, M., Kumar, J., ... El-Gendi, A. (2017). Recent development of augmented reality in surgery: A review. *Journal of Healthcare Engineering*, 2017, 4574172. doi: 10.1155/2017/4574172

Vázquez-Cano, E., & Sevillano-García, M. L. (2017). Lugares y espacios para el uso educativo y ubicuo de los dispositivos digitales móviles en la Educación Superior. *Edutec. Revista Electrónica de Tecnología Educativa*, (62), 48–61. doi:10.21556/edutec.2017.62.1007

Venkatesh, V. (2000). Determinants of perceived ease of use: Integrating control, intrinsic motivation, and emotion into the technology acceptance model. *Information Systems Research*, *11*(4), 342–365. doi:10.1287/isre.11.4.342.11872

Venkatesh, V., & Bala, H. (2008). Technology acceptance model 3 and a research agenda on interventions. *Decision Sciences*, *39*(2), 273–315. doi:10.1111/j.1540-5915.2008.00192.x

Venkatesh, V., & Davis, F. D. (2000). Theoretical extension of the Technology Acceptance Model: Four longitudinal field studies. *Management Science*, *46*(2), 186–204. doi:10.1287/mnsc.46.2.186.11926

VergneJ. P. (2021). The Future of Trust will be Dystopian or Decentralized: Escaping the Metaverse. *Available at* SSRN. doi:10.2139/ssrn.3925635

Verma, N., Malhotra, D., & Singh, J. (2020). Big data analytics for retail industry using MapReduce-Apriori framework. *Journal of Management Analytics*, *7*(3), 424–442. doi:10.1080/23270012.2020.1728403

Verma, S., Sharma, R., Deb, S., & Maitra, D. (2021). Artificial intelligence in marketing: Systematic review and future research direction. *International Journal of Information Management Data Insights*, *1*(1), 100002. doi:10.1016/j.jjimei.2020.100002

Vint, S. (2016). Science fiction and the Fourth Industrial Revolution. *The European Journal of Science Fiction Research*, 2, 2–10. doi:10.5281/zenodo.45537

Vishkaei, B. (2022). Metaverse: A New Platform for Circular Smart Cities. In P. De Giovanni (Ed.), *Cases on Circular Economy in Practice* (pp. 51–69). IGI Global. doi:10.4018/978-1-6684-5001-7.ch003

Vishnoi, S. K., Bagga, T., Sharma, A., & Wani, S. N. (2018). Artificial intelligence enabled marketing solutions: A review. *Indian Journal of Economics & Business*, *17*(4), 167–177.

Vlačić, B., Corbo, L., Silva, S. C., & Dabić, M. (2021). The evolving role of artificial intelligence in marketing: A review and research agenda. *Journal of Business Research*, *128*, 187–203. doi:10.1016/j.jbusres.2021.01.055

Volonté, F., Buchs, N. C., Pugin, F., Spaltenstein, J., Schiltz, B., Jung, M., ... Morel, P. (2013). Augmented reality to the rescue of the minimally invasive surgeon. The usefulness of the interposition of stereoscopic images in the Da Vinci™ robotic console. *International Journal of Medical Robotics and Computer Assisted Surgery*, *9*(3), e34–e38. doi: 10.1002/rcs.1471

Wan, C. S., & Chiou, W. B. (2006). Psychological motives and online games addiction: Atest of flow theory and humanistic needs theory for taiwanese adolescents. *Cyberpsychology & Behavior*, *9*(3), 317–324. doi:10.1089/cpb.2006.9.317 PMID:16780399

Wang, G., & Shin, C. (2022). Influencing Factors of Usage Intention of Metaverse Education Application Platform: Empirical Evidence Based on PPM and TAM Models. *Sustainability (Switzerland)*, *14*(24). doi:10.3390/su142417037

Wang, Q., Li, R., Wang, Q., & Chen, S. (2021). Non-fungible token (NFT): Overview, evaluation, opportunities and challenges. *arXiv preprint arXiv:2105.07447*.

Wang, G., Badal, A., Jia, X., Maltz, J. S., Mueller, K., Myers, K. J., Niu, C., Vannier, M., Yan, P., Yu, Z., & Zeng, R. (2022). Development of metaverse for Intelligent Healthcare. *Nature Machine Intelligence*, *4*(11), 922–929. doi:10.103842256-022-00549-6

Wang, H. N., Lin, Y., Wang, W., Dhelim, S., Farha, F., Ding, J., & Daneshmand, M. (n.d.). *A Survey on Metaverse: the State-of-the-art*. Technologies, Applications, and Challenges.

Wang, M., & Lau, N. (2023). NFT Digital Twins: A Digitalization Strategy to Preserve and Sustain Miao Silver Craftsmanship in the Metaverse Era. *Heritage*, *6*(2), 1921–1941. doi:10.3390/heritage6020103

Wang, M., Yu, H., Bell, Z., & Chu, X. (2022). Constructing an Edu-Metaverse Ecosystem: A New and Innovative Framework. *IEEE Transactions on Learning Technologies*, 1–13. doi:10.1109/TLT.2022.3226345

Wang, Q. J., Escobar, F. B., Da Mota, P. A., & Velasco, C. (2021). Getting started with virtual reality for sensory and consumer science: Current practices and future perspectives. *Food Research International*, *145*, 110410. doi:10.1016/j.foodres.2021.110410 PMID:34112413

Wang, Q., Chen, W., & Liang, Y. (2011). The effects of social media on college students. *Journal of Educational Technology Development and Exchange*, *4*(1), 1–14.

Wang, S., Parsons, M., Stone-McLean, J., Rogers, P., Boyd, S., Hoover, K., ... Smith, A. (2017). Augmented reality as a telemedicine platform for remote procedural training. *Sensors (Basel)*, *17*(10), 2294. doi:10.339017102294

Wang, Y., Kang, X., & Chen, Z. (2022). A survey of digital twin techniques in smart manufacturing and management of energy applications. *Green Energy and Intelligent Transportation*, *100014*(2), 100014. Advance online publication. doi:10.1016/j.geits.2022.100014

Wang, Y., Su, Z., Zhang, N., Xing, R., Liu, D., Luan, T. H., & Shen, X. (2023). A survey on Metaverse: Fundamentals, security, and privacy. *IEEE Communications Surveys and Tutorials*, *25*(1), 319–352. doi:10.1109/comst.2022.3202047

Wang, Y., Su, Z., Zhang, N., Xing, R., Liu, D., Luan, T., & Shen, X. (2022). A Survey on Metaverse: Fundamentals, Security, and Privacy. *IEEE Communications Surveys and Tutorials*, 1–1. doi:10.1109/COMST.2022.3202047

Wang, Y., & Zhao, J. (2022). *A Survey of Mobile Edge Computing for the Metaverse: Architectures.* Applications, and Challenges., doi:10.1109/CIC56439.2022.00011

Wankhede, C. (2022, August 1). *What is the metaverse and why is it so controversial?* Android Authority. https://www.androidauthority.com/what-is-the-metaverse-3107774/

Watanabe, E., Satoh, M., Konno, T., Hirai, M., & Yamaguchi, T. (2016). The trans-visible navigator: A see-through neuronavigation system using augmented reality. *World Neurosurgery, 87*, 399–405. doi:10.1016/j.wneu.2015.11.084

WatsonA. (2021, May 11). Retrieved from https://www.coinspeaker.com/blockchain-metaverses-vr-headset

Webster, J., Trevino, L. K., & Ryan, L. (1993). The dimensionality and correlates of flow in human-computer interactions. *Computers in Human Behavior, 9*(4), 411–426. doi:10.1016/0747-5632(93)90032-N

Weibel, D., Wissmath, B., Habegger, S., Steiner, Y., & Groner, R. (2008). Playing online games against computer-vs. human-controlled opponents: Effects on presence, flow, and enjoyment. *Computers in Human Behavior, 24*(5), 2274–2291. doi:10.1016/j.chb.2007.11.002

Weinberger, M. (2022). What Is Metaverse? A Definition Based on Qualitative Meta-Synthesis. *Future Internet, 14*(11), 310. doi:10.3390/fi14110310

Weking, J., Desouza, K. C., Fielt, E., & Kowalkiewicz, M. (2023). Metaverse-enabled entrepreneurship. *Journal of Business Venturing Insights, 19*, e00375. Advance online publication. doi:10.1016/j.jbvi.2023.e00375

Wesemann, A. (2022). Metaverse. *Tanz. Jahrbuch, 52–55*(1), 486–497. Advance online publication. doi:10.3390/encyclopedia2010031

Widerhold, B. K. (2019). The Fourth Industrial Revolution: Healthcare in the digital age. *Healthcare Technology Letters, 6*(6), 163–165.

Wiederhold, B. K. (2021). Ready (or Not) Player One: Initial Musings on the Metaverse. [editorial]. *Cyberpsychology, Behavior, and Social Networking, 25*(1), 1–2. doi:10.1089/cyber.2021.29234

Wisdom, J. P., Chor, K. H. B., Hoagwood, K. E., & Horwitz, S. M. (2014). Innovation adoption: A review of theories and constructs. *Administration and Policy in Mental Health, 41*(4), 480–502. doi:10.1007/s10488-013-0486-4

Wisnu Buana, I. M. (2023). Metaverse: Threat or Opportunity for Our Social World? In understanding Metaverse on sociological context. *Journal of Metaverse, 3*(1), 28–33. doi:10.57019/jmv.1144470

Wong, F. K., & Noor, N. M. (2019). Integrating digital technology in ESL classrooms: Opportunities and challenges. *Journal of Nusantara Studies, 4*(2), 91–102.

World Economic Forum. (2018). *The future of jobs report 2018.* World Economic Forum. https://www.weforum.org/reports/the-future-of-jobs-report-2018

Wright, M. (2008). Augmented duality: overlapping a metaverse with the real world. *Proceedings of the 2008 International Conference on Advances in Computer Entertainment Technology*, 263–266. 10.1145/1501750.1501812

WSJ. (2022). From Meatspace to Metaverse: Two Books on Virtual Reality. https://www.wsj.com/articles/from-meatspace-to-metaverse-review-books-on-virtual-reality 11663870672. Access Date: 20.12.2022

Wu, C., Huang, S., & Yuan, Q. (2022). Seven important theories in information system empirical research: A systematic review and future directions. *Data and Information Management, 6*(1). doi:10.1016/J.DIM.2022.100006

Wu, J., Sun, Y., Zhang, G., Zhou, Z., & Ren, Z. (2021). Virtual reality-assisted cognitive behavioral therapy for anxiety disorders: A systematic review and meta-analysis. *Frontiers in Psychiatry, 12*. Advance online publication. doi:10.3389/fpsyt.2021.575094

Wu, T. C., & Ho, C. T. B. (2022). A scoping review of metaverse in emergency medicine. In *Australasian Emergency Care*. Elsevier Australia. doi:10.37766/inplasy2022.5.0159

Wu, Y. C. J., Shen, J. P., & Chang, C. L. (2015). Electronic service quality of Facebook social commerce and collaborative learning. *Computers in Human Behavior, 51*, 1395–1402. doi:10.1016/j.chb.2014.10.001

Xian, Z., Keikhosrokiani, P., XinYing, C., & Li, Z. (2022). An RFM Model Using K-Means Clustering to Improve Customer Segmentation and Product Recommendation. In P. Keikhosrokiani (Ed.), Handbook of Research on Consumer Behavior Change and Data Analytics in the Socio-Digital Era (pp. 124-145). IGI Global. doi:10.4018/978-1-6684-4168-8.ch006

Xi, N., Chen, J., Gama, F., Riar, M., & Hamari, J. (2022). The challenges of entering the metaverse: An experiment on the effect of extended reality on workload. *Information Systems Frontiers*. Advance online publication. doi:10.100710796-022-10244-x PMID:35194390

Xu, M., Ren, X., Niyato, D., Kang, J., Qiu, C., Xiong, Z., Wang, X., & Leung, V. (2022). *When Quantum Information Technologies Meet Blockchain in Web 3.0*. arXiv preprint arXiv:2211.15941.

Xue, L., Parker, C. J., & McCormick, H. (2019). A virtual reality and retailing literature review: Current focus, underlying themes and future directions. In M. C. tom Dieck & T. Jung (Eds.), *Augmented Reality and Virtual Reality* (pp. 27–41). Springer. doi:10.1007/978-3-030-06246-0_3

Yadegari, M., Mohammadi, S., & Masoumi, A. H. (2022). Technology adoption: an analysis of the major models and theories. *Technology Analysis and Strategic Management*. doi:10.1080/09537325.2022.2071255

Yang, Y. &. (2018). A qualitative research on marketing and sales in the artificial intelligence age. *MWAIS 2018 Proceedings, 41*.

Yang, B., Yang, S., Lv, Z., Wang, F., & Olofsson, T. (2022). Application of Digital Twins and Metaverse in the Field of Fluid Machinery Pumps and Fans: A Review. *Sensors (Basel), 22*(23), 9294. doi:10.339022239294 PMID:36501994

Yang, C., Tu, X., Autiosalo, J., Ala-Laurinaho, R., Mattila, J., Salminen, P., & Tammi, K. (2022). Extended Reality Application Framework for a Digital-Twin-Based Smart Crane. *Applied Sciences (Basel, Switzerland), 12*(12), 6030. doi:10.3390/app12126030

Yang, Q., Zhao, Y., Huang, H., Xiong, Z., Kang, J., & Zheng, Z. (2022). Fusing blockchain and AI with metaverse: A survey. *IEEE Open Journal of the Computer Society, 3*, 122–136. doi:10.1109/ojcs.2022.3188249

Yap, C. H., & Zainol Abidin, N. A. (2021). Teaching literature studies in universities and challenges Malaysian students face in IR4.0. *The Journal of Asia TEFL, 18*(1), 192–206.

Yassin, A. K. (2022). The Metaverse Revolution and Its Impact on the Future of Advertising Industry. *Journal of Design Sciences and Applied Arts, 3*(2), 131–139. doi:10.21608/jdsaa.2022.129876.1171

Yazıcı, T. (2022). Dijital Pazarlamanin Yeni Evreni: Metaverse. A. Güven & M. S. Tam (Ed.), Alternatif Dijital Evren Metaverse-II Reklam, Pazarlama, Marka ve İşletme Yönetimi (79-98). Necmettin Erbakan Üniversitesi Yayınları

Yildiz, Y., & Sahin, M. (2020). Literature education in the digital age: Challenges and possibilities. *Journal of Language and Linguistic Studies, 16*(1), 238–248.

Yılmaz, A. (2022). Evren Ötesi Reklamcilik: Metavertising. A. Güven & M. S. Tam (Ed.), Alternatif Dijital Evren Metaverse-II Reklam, Pazarlama, Marka ve İşletme Yönetimi (3-29). Necmettin Erbakan Üniversitesi Yayınları

Ying, S. Y., Keikhosrokiani, P., & Asl, M. P. (2021). Comparison of data analytic techniques for a spatial opinion mining in literary works: A review paper. In F. Saeed, F. Mohammed, & A. Al-Nahari (Eds.), *Innovative Systems for Intelligent Health Informatics* (pp. 523–535). Springer International Publishing. doi:10.1007/978-3-030-70713-2_49

Yli-Huumo, J., Ko, D., Choi, S., Park, S., & Smolander, K. (2016). Where is current research on blockchain technology?—A systematic review. *PLoS One*, *11*(10), e0163477. doi:10.1371/journal.pone.0163477 PMID:27695049

Yu, C. W., Chao, C. M., Chang, C. F., Chen, R. J., Chen, P. C., & Liu, Y. X. (2021). Exploring Behavioral Intention to Use a Mobile Health Education Website: An Extension of the UTAUT 2 Model. *SAGE Open*, *11*(4). doi:10.1177/21582440211055721

Yu, H., Lee, H., & Jeon, H. (2017). What is 5G? Emerging 5G mobile services and network requirements. *Sustainability (Switzerland)*, *9*(10), 1848. Advance online publication. doi:10.3390u9101848

Yu, K.-H., Beam, A. L., & Kohane, I. S. (2018). Artificial Intelligence in healthcare. *Nature Biomedical Engineering*, *2*(10), 719–731. doi:10.103841551-018-0305-z

YükselY. (2021, November 12). *Webtekno*. Retrieved from https://www.webtekno.com/metaversete-varligini-gostermeye-baslamis-markalar-h117659.html

Yulianto, A., Mulyono, H., & Riyadi, R. (2020). Online discussion forum as a tool for developing critical thinking and social interaction among EFL students. *English Teaching & Learning*, *44*(3), 351–369.

Yu, Y., El Kamel, A., Gong, G., & Li, F. (2014). Multi-agent based modeling and simulation of microscopic traffic in virtual reality system. *Simulation Modelling Practice and Theory*, *45*, 62–79. doi:10.1016/j.simpat.2014.04.001

Zainol, A. F., Keikhosrokiani, P., Asl, M. P., & Anuar, N. A. N. (2023). Artificial intelligence applications in literary works: Emotion extraction and classification of Mohsin Hamid's Moth Smoke. In P. Keikhosrokiani & M. P. Asl (Eds.), *Handbook of research on artificial intelligence applications in literary works and social media* (pp. 93–113). IGI Global. doi:10.4018/978-1-6684-6242-3.ch005

Zainuddin, Z., & Attaran, M. (2016). Malaysian teachers' readiness for teaching with technology: Implications for further policy planning and curriculum development. *Journal of Educational Technology & Society*, *19*(3), 37–48.

Zainuddin, Z., & Mohamad, M. M. (2020). The impact of virtual reality on students' engagement and understanding in literature class. *International Journal of Emerging Technologies in Learning*, *15*(16), 140–153.

Zallio, M., & John Clarkson, P. (2022). Designing the Metaverse: A study on Inclusion, Diversity, Equity, Accessibility and Safety for digital immersive environments. *Telematics and Informatics*, *75*(October), 101909. doi:10.1016/j.tele.2022.101909

Zhang, C., Zhao, M., Cai, M., & Xiao, Q. (2020). Multi-stage multi-attribute decision making method based on online reviews for hotel selection considering the aspirations with different development speeds. *Computers & Industrial Engineering*, *143*(143), 106421. doi:10.1016/j.cie.2020.106421

Zhang, Y., Chen, J., Miao, D., & Zhang, C. (2018). Design and analysis of an interactive MOOC teaching system based on virtual reality. *International Journal of Emerging Technologies in Learning*, *13*(7), 111–123. doi:10.3991/ijet.v13i07.8790

Zhang, Z., Ning, H., Shi, F., Farha, F., Xu, Y., Xu, J., Zhang, F., & Choo, K.-K. R. (2022). Artificial intelligence in cyber security: Research advances, challenges, and opportunities. *Artificial Intelligence Review*, *55*(2), 1029–1053. doi:10.100710462-021-09976-0

Zhang, Z., Wen, F., Sun, Z., Guo, X., He, T., & Lee, C. (2022). Artificial Intelligence-Enabled Sensing Technologies in the 5G/Internet of Things Era: From Virtual Reality/Augmented Reality to the Digital Twin. *Advanced Intelligent Systems*, 4(7), 2100228. doi:10.1002/aisy.202100228

Zhan, T., Yin, K., Xiong, J., He, Z., & Wu, S. T. (2020). Augmented reality and virtual reality displays: Perspectives and challenges. *Iscience*, 23(8), 101397. doi:10.1016/j.isci.2020.101397

Zhao, Y., Jiang, J., Chen, Y., Liu, R., Yang, Y., Xue, X., & Chen, S. (2022). Metaverse: Perspectives from graphics, interactions and visualization. In Visual Informatics (Vol. 6, Issue 1, pp. 56–67). Elsevier B.V. doi:10.1016/j.visinf.2022.03.002

Zheng, Z., Xie, S., Dai, H. N., Chen, X., & Wang, H. (2018). Blockchain challenges and opportunities: A survey. *International Journal of Web and Grid Services*, 14(4), 352–375. doi:10.1504/IJWGS.2018.095647

Zhou, M. (2022). Editorial: Evolution from AI, IoT and Big Data Analytics to Metaverse. In IEEE/CAA Journal of Automatica Sinica (Vol. 9, Issue 12, pp. 2041–2042). Institute of Electrical and Electronics Engineers Inc. doi:10.1109/JAS.2022.106100

Zhu, X., & Liu, J. (2020). Education in and After Covid-19: Immediate Responses and Long-Term Visions. *Postdigital Science and Education*, 2(3), 695–699. doi:10.100742438-020-00126-3

Zhu, X., Tao, H., Wu, Z., Cao, J., Kalish, K., & Kayne, J. (2017). *Fraud Prevention in Online Digital Advertising*. Springer. doi:10.1007/978-3-319-56793-8

Zsarnoczky, M. (2017). *How does artificial intelligence affect the tourism industry?* Academic Press.

Zweifach, S. M., & Triola, M. M. (2019). Extended reality in medical education: Driving adoption through provider-centered design. *Digital Biomarkers*, 3(1), 14–21. doi:10.1159/000498923

About the Contributors

Pantea Keikhosrokiani received the Bachelor of Science degree in electrical and electronics engineering, the master's degree in information technology from the School of Computer Sciences, Universiti Sains Malaysia (USM), Malaysia, and the Ph.D. degree in service system engineering, information system. She was a Teaching Fellow with the National Advanced IPv6 Centre of Excellence (Nav6), USM, where she is currently a Senior Lecturer with the School of Computer Sciences. Her recent book was published entitled Perspectives in the Development of Mobile Medical Information Systems: Life Cycle, Management, Methodological Approach and Application, in 2019. Her articles have been published in distinguished edited books and journals, including Telematics and Informatics (Elsevier), Cognition, Technology, and Work (Springer), Taylors and Francis, and IGI Global. She was indexed by ISI, Scopus, and PubMed. Her research and teaching interests include information systems development, database systems, health and medical informatics, business informatics, location-based mobile applications, big data, and technopreneurship.

* * *

Nasuha Lee Abdullah is a senior lecturer at School of Computer Sciences, Universiti Sains Malaysia.

David Roland Andembubtob is a PhD student at School of Computer Sciences, Universiti Sains Malaysia.

Kamaladevi B. has over 18 years of international work experience in Industry, Applied Research & Academics. She is currently Programme Leader for MBA in Amity Business School, Dubai, UAE. She holds an Executive Education in Business Analytics from Wharton School at the University of Pennsylvania, USA. She is a certified Trainer to teach Innovation and Entrepreneurship from Stanford University Program Ambassadors. In the past, she worked as Director at Zelus Events, Dubai, UAE. Dr. Kamaladevi has vast skill & experience in creating, producing & executing large scale corporate & academic events. She has managed more than 120 large scale International professional events including business conferences & corporate incentive programs globally. Dr. Kamaladevi completed her Ph.D in Management at Bharathiar University, India and her graduate studies M.Phil & MBA at Dravidian University and Bharathidasan University respectively from India. Dr. Kamaladevi's research interests lie in the area of Business Analytics, Entrepreneurship, Business Research Methods and ecommerce ranging from theory to design to implementation. She has collaborated actively with researchers in several other disciplines of management & engineering in the areas of search engine optimization & digital transformational technologies in addressing real world problems at the process to root cause analysis level for the success of online stores. In her areas of research, Dr. Kamaladevi has written three management books as single author. She also presented and published in more than 30 peer-reviewed International conferences and journal research articles. She has served as a Keynote Speaker at various International conferences and Forums held in France, Spain, Thailand, UAE, India & Malaysia. Dr. Kamaladevi also has substantial influence in professional, community, and outreach activities that is demonstrated by the various roles she has undertaken.

Saurabh Bhattacharya is a Research Scholar at Chitkara Business School, Chitkara University-Punjab.

Rigoberto García-Contreras, Ph.D., is an assistant professor at the National Autonomous University of Mexico. National School of Higher Education, Leon Unit. His research interests are related to the Management of Intangibles and the Economics of Knowledge in Organizations. He holds a Ph.D. in Economic and Administrative Sciences, a Master's Degree in Administration with a specialization in Organizational Management, and a Bachelor's Degree in Administration. He has been a visiting researcher at the Laboratory of Personality Psychology, National University of Córdoba, Argentina. He has publications in several national and international journals and publishing houses. He is a member of the Mexican National System of Researchers.

Ibrahim Halil Efendioglu received a Bachelor of Science degree in computer engineering from Mersin University, Turkey. He graduated with a Master's degree in computer education from the Institute of Informatics, Gazi University, and a Ph.D. in business administration from Hasan Kalyoncu University. He is currently a Lecturer at Gaziantep University. His articles were published in distinguished journals, including the International Journal of Emerging Markets (SSCI), Transnational Marketing Journal (Scopus), and Review of Marketing Science (Scopus). His research and teaching interests include digital marketing and consumer behavior.

Princi Gupta is working as Assistant Professor in the department of Jaipur school of business in JECRC University, Jaipur, Rajasthan. she has ph.D in marketing her and area of specialisation are marketing, consumer behaviour and International business. she has written a book on Digital Marketing "An insight to fundamentals, strategies & implementations". she holds diploma in German Language, business communication & Behavioural Science. she has also actively participated & organised various departmental and university level workshops, conferences & events. To her credit there are research paper publications in various national, International, UGC, Scopus Indexed journlas.

Ali B. Mahmoud is a dual PhD holder in Digital Marketing and Organisational Behaviour. He also is a Higher Doctorate candidate at London South Bank University, United Kingdom. Dr Mahmoud is a Visiting Professor of Management in the Peter J. Tobin College of Business at St. John's University in New York City, a Senior Research Scholar at ResPeo, and a part-time Lecturer (Adjunct Assistant Professor) of International Business at Brunel Business School at Brunel University London, United Kingdom. Dr Mahmoud's current research interests include topics related to digital consumer behaviour, entrepreneurial marketing, familial marketing, work psychology, wartime perceptions effects, and research in higher education. He has published over 70 publications, including books, book chapters and journal articles featured in international journals like European Management Review, Technovation, Personnel Review, Journal of Brand Management, Journal of Strategic Marketing, Scandinavian Journal of Psychology, BMC Public Health, BMC Psychology, Higher Education Quarterly, Journal of Hospitality and Tourism Management and many others. He has presented his work at leading conferences like the Academy of Marketing Science (AMS), the British Academy of Management (BAM) and the British Educational Research Association (BERA).

Tasnuba Tabassum Mourin is a young researcher studying Biomedical Engineering at the Military Institute of Science and Technology (MIST). Her current research work focuses on biomaterials and bioinstrumentation. She is also extremely passionate about studying telehealth, epigenetics, and the various challenges faced by biomedical engineers. As a speaker at the 4th International Clinical Engineering and Health Technology Management Congress, Tasnuba won the Best Student Manuscript Award 2021 for her presentation on designing a platform for drug rehabilitation using telehealth. As a biomedical engineer, Tasnuba has completed her internship at the Evercare Hospital Bangladesh.

J. Patricia Muñoz-Chávez is a Ph.D. Associate Professor at the Technological University of the Metropolitan Area of the Valley of Mexico. Her research interests are related to Organizations, Higher Education, and Organizational Behavior. She holds a Ph.D. in Strategic Planning and Technology Management (Popular Autonomous University of the State of Puebla.), a Master's Degree in Management, and a Bachelor's Degree in Accountant (Autonomous University of the State of Hidalgo). She did a research stay at the University of Malaga, Spain. She has publications in several national and international journals and publishers.

Moussa Pourya Asl is a Senior Lecturer in literary studies at Universiti Sains Malaysia, where he also obtained his PhD (English Literature) from School of Humanities. His primary research area is in diasporic literature and gender and cultural studies, and he has published several articles in the above-mentioned areas in Women's Studies, Gender, Place & Culture, Asian Ethnicity, American Studies in Scandinavia, Cogent: Arts & Humanities, Gema Online, and 3L.

Mohamad Luthfi Bin Abdul Rahman is from Kedah. He received his Bachelor of Arts (Literature) and Master's Degree in Literature from Universiti Sains Malaysia. He obtained his PhD in 2008 at Universiti Kebangsaan Malaysia. He is currently a Senior Lecturer at the Department of Literature, School of Humanities, Universiti Sains Malaysia Penang. ORCID id: 0000-0002-6077-4302.

Krishnamurthy Rajeshwari is the Area- Chair(Marketing) and a Senior Associate Professor at Great Lakes Institute of Management. Winner of multiple awards in teaching and research, her areas of interest are- Metaverse, NPD, Brand communications in social media, and Omni channel sales. Spent 15 years at Unilever and Nippon Paint in brand building, media and advertisement.

Rayesa Haque Rupanti is a biomedical engineering student at Military Institute of Science and Technology (MIST). She received her HSC degree from Holy Cross College and her SSC degree from Shaheed Bir Uttam Lt Anwar Girls' College. She has great passion in the field of Biomaterials, Biochemistry and Bioinstrumentation. She has also keen interest in Tissue Engineering and Genetic Engineering. Besides, she would like to invest in the advancement of newer technology to enhance medical outcomes.

Babita Singla is an Associate Professor at Chitkara Business School, Chitkara University, Punjab, India. She spent a decade pursuing a career in academics, teaching, and research with passion and diligence. She worked as an Assistant Professor at the institute of national repute NIT Jalandhar. She completed an MBA program from RIMT-Mandi Gobindgarh, Punjab, India (2008-2010) in Finance & Marketing, and subsequently earned a doctoral degree from IKGPTU, Jalandhar, India. Her undergraduate studies in Mathematics and Economics from Government Rajindra College, Bathinda. She has cleared the National Eligibility Test (UGC NET) in 2011. She has over twenty research publications in international and national journals, over 11 publications/ presentations in international and national conferences, including 8 Keynote lectures/Invited Talks and ten books to her credit. Her current research interests are in business management, omnichannel retail, marketing management, and managerial economics. She loves to generate new ideas and devise feasible solutions to broadly relevant problems. She enjoys embracing the lessons learned from failure, stands up, and continues to grow.

Nawrin Tasnim is a biomedical engineering student at Military Institute of Science and Technology (MIST). She received her HSC degree from Adamjee Cantonment College and her SSC degree from Shaheed Bir Uttam Lt Anwar Girls' College. She has a keen interest in the field of bioinstrumentation and biomaterials. Moreover, she is quite interested in technical development, particularly in the sphere of biomedical field.

Shagun Trivedi did her graduation from University of Lucknow in Bachelor's of Commerce (Honours) in 2020. She has interned as Social Media Marketer for a student led organization on feminist called Lipstick Under Your Patriarchy. She initially worked as a content writer there and then took on the marketing portfolio. She has experience as a digital marketer as well and has done certification for the same from Udemy. Currently, she is currently pursuing PGDM at Great Lakes Institute of Management, Chennai and is aiming to major in Marketing with minors in Analytics and Operations.

David Valle-Cruz, Ph.D., MInf, BEng, is an Assistant Professor in the Unidad Académica Profesional Tianguistenco at the Universidad Autónoma del Estado de México and is a member of the Mexican National System of Researchers. David is a Computer Engineer, he holds a Master of Informatics, and a Ph.D. in Economics and Management. He has been a visiting researcher at the Center for Technology in Government (CTG), SUNY Albany, NY, and at the Computer Science and Multi-Agent Systems Laboratory of CINVESTAV, Guadalajara, Mexico. His articles have been published in leading journals, including Government Information Quarterly, Cognitive Computation, First Monday, Information Polity, and International Journal of Public Sector Management (among others). His research interests are related to Applied Artificial Intelligence, Social Media, and Emerging Technologies in the Public Sector.

Saravanan P. Veeramuthu is a Senior Lecturer in Malay Literature at the Literature Department, School of Humanities, Universiti Sains Malaysia, Penang, Malaysia. His research focuses on Modern Malay Literature, Environment and Literature, National Identity Studies in Malaysian Malay Literature with a special emphasis on non-Malay writers.

Index

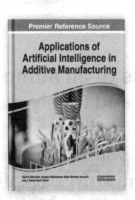
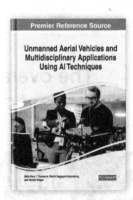

Ensure Quality Research is Introduced to the Academic Community

Become an Evaluator for IGI Global Authored Book Projects

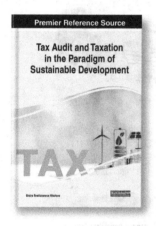

Premier Reference Source

Tax Audit and Taxation in the Paradigm of Sustainable Development

Premier Reference Source

Controlling Epidemics With Mathematical and Machine Learning Models

Premier Reference Source

School-Museum Relationships and Teaching Social Sciences in Formal Education

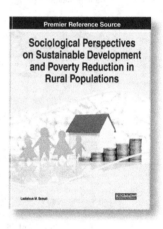

Premier Reference Source

Sociological Perspectives on Sustainable Development and Poverty Reduction in Rural Populations

The overall success of an authored book project is dependent on quality and timely manuscript evaluations.

Applications and Inquiries may be sent to:
development@igi-global.com

Applicants must have a doctorate (or equivalent degree) as well as publishing, research, and reviewing experience. Authored Book Evaluators are appointed for one-year terms and are expected to complete at least three evaluations per term. Upon successful completion of this term, evaluators can be considered for an additional term.

If you have a colleague that may be interested in this opportunity, we encourage you to share this information with them.

Printed in the United States
by Baker & Taylor Publisher Services